Canadian Good
ManufacturingPractices

Pharmaceutical, Biologics, and Medical Device
Regulations and Guidance

Concise Reference

I0131183

Canadian
Good Manufacturing Practices

*Pharmaceutical, Biologics, and Medical Device
Regulations and Guidance*

Concise Reference

Canadian Good Manufacturing Practices: Pharmaceutical, Biologics, and Medical Device Regulations and Guidance Concise Reference

PharmaLogika

PharmaLogika, Inc.
PO Box 461
Willow Springs, NC 27592

www.pharmalogika.com

Author / Editor: Mindy J. Allport-Settle

Published by PharmaLogika, Inc.

Printed in the United States of America. First Printing.

ISBN 0-9821476-4-3
ISBN-13 978-0-9821476-4-1

Contents

Part III

Annexes to the Current Edition of the Good Manufacturing Practices (GMP) Guidelines

Good Manufacturing Practices for Medical Gases - Questions and Answers 539

Importation and Exportation Questions and Answers 543

Part V

International Conference on Harmonisation (ICH) Guidance Documents 547

ICH Q1A(R2): Stability Testing of New Drug Substances and Products 549

Part VI

Compliance Policies 667

Drug Good Manufacturing Practices (GMP) and Establishment Licencing (EL) Enforcement Directive (POL-0004) 669

GMP Inspection Policy for Canadian Drug Establishments (POL-0011)

Inspection Strategy for Post-Market Surveillance (POL-0041)

Preface

About this Book

This book isdesigned to be a unified reference source for the Canadian Good Manufacturing Practices (GMPs) for human and veterinary pharmaceutical, biologics and medical device products. In addition to the regulations defining the GMPs, the Health Products and Food Branch (HPFB) procedures, guidance documents and forms related to GMPs have also been collected.

The included *Overview and Orientation* (Chapter 2 of this book) is designed to provide a foundation for understanding the background of Canada's regulations and its relationship with manufacturers and distributors.

This book is designed to be used both as a reference for experienced industry representatives and as a training resource for those new to the industry.

Included Documents and Features

Canadian Regulations and Associated HPFB Guidance:

- *Overview and Orientation*
- *Introduction*
- *Part I: Food and Drugs Act*
- *Part II: Guidance Documents*
- *Part III: Annexes to the Current Edition of the Good Manufacturing Practices (GMP) Guidelines*
- *Part IV: Questions and Answers*
- *Part V: International Conference on Harmonisation (ICH) Guidance Documents*

Health Products and Food Branch (HPFB) GMP Policies:

- *Part VI: Compliance Policies*

Health Products and Food Branch (HPFB) GMP Forms:

- *Part VII: Forms*

Reference Tools

- *Part VIII: Combined index for all Standards, Glossaries, Procedures, and Guidance Documents*

About the Reference Tools

Health Canada and HPFB Overview and Orientation

This overview provides the reader with a brief history of Health Canada's Health Protection and Food Branch and explains not only what good manufacturing practice is, but it exists and how it came to be.

Combined Index for all Regulations and Documents

The index is composed of a list of both words and terms specific to the good manufacturing practices. It is a tool that assists in cross-referencing the various regulations and guidance documents (rather than having to rely on reading and comparing each document individually).

Pharmaceutical, biotechnology, and medical device companies use terminology that combines scientific and technical jargon with legal phrases and concepts.

The index provides keywords and terminology as a tool to easily locate specific references across all documents rather than having to rely on memory or paging through the entire regulation.

Overview and Orientation

Health Canada and the Health Protection and Food Branch (HPFB)

Health Canada (French: Santé Canada) is the department of the government of Canada with responsibility for national public health.

Health Canada plays an active role in ensuring access to safe and effective drugs and health products. The Department strives to maintain a balance between the potential health benefits and risks posed by all drugs and health products by determining the balance of public safety.

Working together with other levels of government, health care professionals, patient and consumer interest groups, research communities and manufacturers, this department endeavours to minimize the health risk factors to consumers and maximize the safety provided by the regulatory system for these products.

Health Canada is not a manufacturer or distributor of drugs and health products. They are the federal regulator.[1]

Health Products and Food Branch (HPFB)

The Health Products and Food Branch (HPFB) is a division of Health Canada and manages the health-related risks and benefits of health products and food by minimizing risk factors while maximizing the safety provided by the regulatory system. HPFB has seven operational Directorates with direct regulatory responsibilities:

- Therapeutic Products Directorate
- Food Directorate
- Biologics and Genetic Therapies Directorate
- Natural Health Products Directorate
- Marketed Health Products Directorate (with responsibility for post-market surveillance)
- HPFB Inspectorate and the Veterinary Drugs Directorate.

Directorates and Offices

Health Products and Food Branch activities are carried out through offices in the National Capital Region and five regional offices: Atlantic, Quebec, Ontario, Manitoba-Saskatchewan and Western.[2]

- Biologics and Genetic Therapies Directorate

---

[1] Available on the Health Canada website at http://www.hc-sc.gc.ca/dhp-mps/index-eng.php

[2] Available on the Health Canada website at http://www.hc-sc.gc.ca/ahc-asc/branch-dirgen/hpfb-dgpsa/index-eng.php

- Food Directorate
- Health Products and Food Branch Inspectorate
- Marketed Health Products Directorate
- Natural Health Products Directorate
- Office of Consumer and Public Involvement
- Office of Management and Program Services
- Office of Nutrition Policy and Promotion
- Office of Paediatric Initiatives
- Departmental Biotechnology Office
- Office of the Assistant Deputy Minister
- Policy, Planning and International Affairs Directorate
- Regional Operations
- Therapeutic Products Directorate
- Veterinary Drugs Directorate

HPFB Newsletters

- TPD News - Quarterly Publication of the Therapeutics Products Directorate
- Profiles in Progress - the Health Products and Food Branch at Work
- Involving You - keeping stakeholders and interested Canadians in touch with HPFB activities and plans

The mandate of the Health Products and Food Branch (HPFB) is to promote good nutrition and informed use of drugs, food, medical devices and natural health products, and to maximize the safety and efficacy of drugs, food, natural health products, medical devices, biologics and related biotechnology products. The Branch plays a key role in managing the risks associated with the use of these products and in assuring the high quality of products used by Canadians. To this end, it is involved in the enforcement of federal legislation that sets standards for quality, conditions for sale and the prevention of fraud and diversion from legitimate uses.[3]

Health Products and Food Branch Inspectorate

The primary role of the HPFB Inspectorate is to deliver a national compliance and enforcement program for all products under the mandate of the Branch, with the exception of food products that are the responsibility of the Canadian Food Inspection Agency. This is done through industry inspection, product investigation, establishment licensing and related laboratory functions. In fulfilling these responsibilities, a risk management approach to decision-making is applied and senior management's vision of a comprehensive regulatory strategy across all product classes is supported.[4]

---

[3] Available on the Health Canada website at http://www.hc-sc.gc.ca/ahc-asc/branch-dirgen/hpfb-dgpsa/hpfi-ipsa/dgo-bdg-eng.php
[4] Available on the Health Canada website at http://www.hc-sc.gc.ca/ahc-asc/branch-dirgen/hpfb-dgpsa/hpfi-ipsa/dgo-bdg-eng.php

The Inspectorate is responsible for branch-wide compliance and enforcement activities, enabling consistency of approach across the spectrum of regulated products. The Inspectorate core functions are compliance monitoring, and compliance verification and investigation, supported by establishment licensing of drugs and medical devices, and laboratory analysis.[5]

The Inspectorate has 9 responsibility centres:

- Director General's Office (Longueuil).
- Inspectorate Ottawa (Ottawa): responsible for establishment licensing and for policy, planning and coordination activities.
- 2 Laboratory: Longueuil and Toronto: ensuring the support to inspection and investigation activities.
- 5 Operational Centres responsible for the conduct of inspections and investigations.
    - Atlantic Region (Halifax)
    - Quebec Region (Longueuil)
    - Ontario and Nunavut Region (Toronto)
    - Manitoba and Saskatchewan Region (Winnipeg)
    - Western Region (Burnaby)

Legislation and Regulatory Amendments

In carrying out its compliance and enforcement functions, the Health Products and Food Branch Inspectorate applies the Food and Drugs Act (FDA) and its associated regulations.

The Inspectorate may engage in the development of new regulations to support effective compliance and enforcement activities. To ensure that the regulatory process is open and transparent, the Inspectorate encourages industry, consumers and other stakeholders to participate in and provide input on legislative, regulatory and policy issues. This is achieved by consulting upon regulatory amendment proposals prior to pre-publication in the Canada Gazette Part I, as well as during the formal regulatory amendment process.[6]

Acts and Regulations

- Consultation: Regulations Amending the Food and Drug Regulations 1447 - Good Manufacturing Practices
- Publication of the Safety of Human Cells, Tissues and Organs Regulations
- Food and Drugs Act
- Food and Drugs Regulations
- Regulations Amending the Food and Drug Regulations (1024 - Clinical Trials)

---

[5] Available on the Health Canada website at http://www.hc-sc.gc.ca/ahc-asc/branch-dirgen/hpfb-dgpsa/hpfi-ipsa/index-eng.php
[6] Available on the Health Canada website at http://www.hc-sc.gc.ca/dhp-mps/compli-conform/legislation/index-eng.php

- Medical Devices Regulations

- Natural Health Products Regulations

- Letter to Stakeholders Regarding Proposed Amendments to the Medical Devices Regulations - Schedule 1426

- Food and Drugs Act, Regulations Amending the Medical Devices Regulations

- Processing and Distribution of Semen for Assisted Conception Regulations

- Controlled Drugs and Substances Act

Food and Drugs Act

Food and Drugs Act (R.S., 1985, c. F-27) Table of Contents:[7]

Short Title

Interpretation

Part I : Foods, Drugs, Cosmetics and Devices

- General

- Food

- Drugs

- Cosmetics

- Devices

Part II : Administration and Enforcement

- Inspection, Seizure and Forfeiture

- Analysis

- Regulations

- Interim Orders

- Interim Marketing Authorizations

- Offences and Punishment

- Exports

Parts III And IV

Schedule A

Schedule B

Schedule C

Schedule D

Schedule E

Schedule F

Schedules G and H

---

[7] http://laws.justice.gc.ca/en/F-27/index.html

Related Information

- Related Provis ons

Related Regulations

- Cosmetic Regulations
- Food and Drug Regulations
- Marihuana Exemption (Food and Drugs Act) Regulations
- Medical Devices Regulations
- Natural Health Products Regulations
- Processing and Distribution of Semen for Assisted Conception Regulations
- Safety of Human Cells, Tissues and Organs for Transplantation Regulations
- Food and Drugs Regulations
- Regulations Amending the Food and Drug Regulations (1024 - Clinical Trials)
- Medical Devices Regulations
- Natural Health Products Regulations
- Letter to Stakeholders Regarding Proposed Amendments to the Medical Devices Regulations - Schedule 1426
- Food and Drugs Act, Regulations Amending the Medical Devices Regulations
- Processing and Distribution of Semen for Assisted Conception Regulations
- Controlled Drugs and Substances Act

Compliance and Enforcement

Compliance and enforcement activities are a key element of safeguarding the drugs and health products to which Canadians have access.

As part of its regulatory responsibilities, Health Canada is responsible for compliance monitoring and enforcement activities related to health products in order to verify that regulatory requirements are being applied appropriately. The Health Products and Food Branch Inspectorate is the directorate primarily responsible for health product compliance monitoring activities such as industry inspection and product investigation. The Inspectorate develops and implements enforcement strategies in these areas. Establishment licensing and related laboratory functions support the Inspectorate's compliance and enforcement activities.

The Inspectorate's activities relate to:

- Blood and Donor Semen,
- Cells, Tissues and Organs,
- Drugs (Human and Veterinary),

- Medical Devices, and,
- Natural Health Products.

The Inspectorate is also developing monitoring and compliance activities in relation to Assisted Human Reproduction in collaboration with its partners within Health Canada.[8]

Organizational Structure

Branches, offices, and bureaus

- *Audit & Accountability Bureau*
- *Bureau of Veterinary Drugs*
- *Public Affairs, Consultation and Communications Branch*
- *Corporate Services Branch*
- *Departmental Secretariat*
- *First Nations & Inuit Health*
- *Strategic Policy Branch*
- *Health Products & Food Branch*
- *Healthy Environments & Consumer Safety Branch*
- *Information, Analysis & Connectivity Branch*
- *Legal Services*
- *Office of the Cameron Visiting Chair*
- *Office of the Chief Dental Officer*
- *Pest Management Regulatory Agency*
- *The National Office of the Workplace Hazardous Materials Information System*

Agencies

- *Assisted Human Reproduction Canada*
- *Canadian Institutes of Health Research*
- *Hazardous Materials Information Review Commission*
- *Patented Medicines Prices Review Board*
- *Public Health Agency of Canada*

Laboratories

- *Laboratory Centre for Disease Control*

---

[8] Available on the Health Canada website at http://www.hc-sc.gc.ca/dhp-mps/compli-conform/index-eng.php

- *Sir Frederick G Banting Research Centre*

Offices

- *Nurse Recruitment*

- *Public Services Health Medical Centre*

- *Chief Financial Officer*

Acts

An Act is a means by which laws are made. Generally, Acts begin in draft form ("bills") and can originate either in the House of Commons or in the Senate. For a bill to become law, it must be approved by both the House of Commons and the Senate and by the Governor General of Canada. Certain procedures must also be followed in the law-making process. Bills are discussed by members of both Houses during what is formally known as First Reading, Second Reading and Third Reading. As well, bills are submitted to a Parliamentary Committee for review. The Committee usually seeks out the views of interested parties, including the public. Finally, a bill becomes law (an Act) through a formal process known as proclamation. Proclamation is done by the Governor in Council (Cabinet, i.e., the Prime Minister and his or her Federal Ministers). [9]

The full text of many of the acts listed below can be accessed through the Consolidated Statutes Web page[10] of the Department of Justice of Canada.

Related Legislation

Acts for which Health Canada has Total or Partial Responsibility[11]

- *Assisted Human Reproduction Act*

- *Canada Health Act*

- *Canadian Centre on Substance Abuse Act*

- *Canadian Environmental Protection Act, 1999*

- *Canadian Institutes of Health Research Act*

- *Controlled Drugs and Substances Act*

- *Comprehensive Nuclear Test-Ban Treaty Implementation Act (Not in force)*

- *Department of Health Act*

- *Financial Administration Act*

- *Fitness and Amateur Sport Act*

- *Food and Drugs Act*

---

[9] Available on the Health Canada website at http://www.hc-sc.gc.ca/ahc-asc/legislation/acts-lois/index-eng.php

[10] Available on the Health Canada website at http://laws.justice.gc.ca/en/index.html

[11] Available on the Health Canada website at http://www.hc-sc.gc.ca/ahc-asc/legislation/acts-lois/index-eng.php

- *Hazardous Materials Information Review Act*
- *Hazardous Products Act*
- *Patent Act*
- *Pest Control Products Act*
- *Pesticide Residue Compensation Act*
- *Quarantine Act, 2005*
- *Radiation Emitting Devices Act*
- *Tobacco Act & Act to Amend the Tobacco Act (Sponsorship)*

Acts for which Health Canada is Involved or has a Special Interest

- *Broadcasting Act*
- *Canada Labour Code*
- *Canada Medical Act*
- *Canada Shipping Act*
- *Canadian Food Inspection Agency Act*
- *Emergency Preparedness Act*
- *Energy Supplies Emergency Act*
- *Excise Tax Act*
- *Federal-Provincial Fiscal Arrangements Act*
- *Feeds Act*
- *Immigration and Refugee Protection Act*
- *National Parks Act*
- *Nuclear Safety and Control Act*
- *Non-Smokers Health Act*
- *Queen Elizabeth II Canadian Research Fund Act*
- *Trade Marks Act*

Part I

Food and Drugs Act

Part A: Administration

Food and Drugs Act

Food and Drug Regulations

Regulations Respecting Food and Drugs (C.R.C., c. 870)

Enabling Statute: Food and Drugs Act

Regulation current to February 10th, 2010

Attention: See coming into force provision and notes, where applicable.

Part A
Administration[12]

General

A.01.001. These Regulations may be cited as the Food and Drug Regulations.

A.01.002. These Regulations, where applicable, prescribe the standards of composition, strength, potency, purity, quality or other property of the article of food or drug to which they refer.

A.01.003. [Repealed, SOR/94-289, s. 1]

Interpretation

A.01.010. In these Regulations,

"acceptable method" means a method of analysis or examination designated by the Director as acceptable for use in the administration of the Act and these Regulations; (méthode acceptable)

"Act" means the Food and Drugs Act, except in Parts G and J; (Loi)

"common-law partner", in relation to an individual, means a person who is cohabiting with the individual in a conjugal relationship, having so cohabited for a period of at least one year; (conjoint de fait)

"cubic centimetre" and its abbreviation "cc." shall be deemed to be interchangeable with the term "millilitre" and its abbreviation "ml."; (centimètre cube)

---

[12] Available on the Depratment of Justice website at http://laws.justice.gc.ca/eng/C.R.C.-C.870/FramesView.html

"Director" means the Assistant Deputy Minister, Health Products and Food Branch, of the Department of Health; (Directeur)

"inner label" means the label on or affixed to an immediate container of a food or drug; (étiquette intérieure)

"Lot number" means any combination of letters, figures, or both, by which any food or drug can be traced in manufacture and identified in distribution; (numéro de lot)

"manufacturer" [Repealed, SOR/97-12, s. 1]

"manufacturer" or "distributor" means a person, including an association or partnership, who under their own name, or under a trade-, design or word mark, trade name or other name, word or mark controlled by them, sells a food or drug; (fabricant) or (distributeur)

"official method" means a method of analysis or examination designated as such by the Director for use in the administration of the Act and these Regulations; (méthode officielle)

"outer label" means the label on or affixed to the outside of a package of a food or drug; (étiquette extérieure)

"principal display panel" has the same meaning as in the Consumer Packaging and Labelling Regulations; (espace principal)

"security package" means a package having a security feature that provides reasonable assurance to consumers that the package has not been opened prior to purchase. (emballage de sécurité)

SOR/84-300, s. 1(F); SOR/85-141, s. 1; SOR/89-455, s. 1; SOR/97-12, s. 1; SOR/2000-353, s. 1; SOR/2001-272, s. 5; SOR/2003-135, s. 1.

A.01.011. The Director shall, upon request, furnish copies of official methods.

A.01.012. The Director shall, upon request, indicate that a method is acceptable or otherwise upon its submission to him for a ruling.

A.01.013. Where a food, drug, vitamin or cosmetic has more than one name, whether proper or common, a reference in these Regulations to the food, drug, vitamin or cosmetic by any of its names is deemed to be a reference to the food, drug or vitamin by all of its names.

A.01.014. When a lot number is required by these Regulations to appear on any article, container, package or label it shall be preceded by one of the following designations:

(a) "Lot number";

(b) "Lot No.";

(c) "Lot"; or

(d) "(L)".

A.01.015. (1) Subject to subsection (2), any statement, information or declaration that is required by these Regulations to appear on the label of any drug shall be in either the French or the English language in addition to any other language.

(2) The adequate directions for use required to be shown on the inner and outer labels of a drug pursuant to subparagraph C.01.004(1)(c)(iii) shall be in both the French and English languages if the drug is available for sale without prescription in an open self-selection area.

SOR/85-140, s. 1.

A.01.016. All information required by these Regulations to appear on a label of a food or drug shall be

(a) clearly and prominently displayed on the label; and

(b) readily discernible to the purchaser or consumer under the customary conditions of purchase and use.

Analysts; Inspectors

A.01.020. and **A.01.021.** [Repealed, SOR/81-935, s. 1]

A.01.022. An inspector shall perform the functions and duties and carry out the responsibilities in respect of foods and drugs prescribed by the Act, and these Regulations.

A.01.023. The authority of an inspector extends to and includes the whole of Canada.

A.01.024. The certificate of designation required pursuant to subsection 22(2) of the Act shall

(a) certify that the person named therein is an inspector for the purpose of the Act; and

(b) be signed by

    (i) the Director and the person named in the certificate, in the case of an inspector on the staff of the Department, or

    (ii) [Repealed, SOR/2000-184, s. 60]

SOR/80-500, s. 1; SOR/92-626, s. 1; SOR/95-548, s. 5; SOR/2000-184, s. 60.

A.01.025. Where authorized by a regulation made pursuant to the Broadcasting Act, inspectors shall act as representatives of the Canadian Radio-television and Telecommunications Commission for the purpose of enforcing the provisions of regulations made by the Canadian Radio-Television and Telecommunications Commission concerning the advertising of any article to which the Proprietary or Patent Medicine Act or the Food and Drugs Act applies, or concerning recommendations for the prevention, treatment or cure of a disease or ailment.

A.01.026. An inspector may, for the proper administration of the Act or these Regulations, take photographs of

(a) any article that is referred to in subsection 23(2) of the Act;

(b) any place where, on reasonable grounds, he believes any article referred to in paragraph (a) is manufactured, prepared, preserved, packaged or stored; and

(c) anything that, on reasonable grounds, he believes is used or capable of being used for the manufacture, preparation, preservation, packaging or storing of any article referred to in paragraph (a).

SOR/90-814, s. 1.

Importations

A.01.040. Subject to section A.01.044, no person shall import into Canada for sale a food or drug the sale of which in Canada would constitute a violation of the Act or these Regulations.

SOR/92-626, s. 2(F).

A.01.041. An inspector may examine and take samples of any food or drug sought to be imported into Canada.

A.01.042. Where an inspector examines or takes a sample of a food or drug pursuant to section A.01.041, he may submit the food or drug or sample to an analyst for analysis or examination.

A.01.043. Where an inspector, upon examination of a food or drug or sample thereof or on receipt of a report of an analyst of the result of an analysis or examination of the food or drug or sample, is of the opinion that the sale of the food or drug in Canada would constitute a violation of the Act or these Regulations, the inspector shall so notify in writing the collector of customs concerned and the importer.

SOR/84-300, s. 2(E).

A.01.044. (1) Where a person seeks to import a food or drug into Canada for sale and the sale would constitute a violation of the Act or these Regulations, that person may, if the sale of the food or drug would be in conformity with the Act and these Regulations after its relabelling or modification, import it into Canada on condition that

(a) the person gives to an inspector notice of the proposed importation; and

(b) the food or drug will be relabelled or modified as may be necessary to enable its sale to be lawful in Canada.

(2) No person shall sell a food or drug that has been imported into Canada under subsection (1) unless the food or drug has been relabelled or modified within three months after the importation or within such longer period as may be specified by

(a) in the case of a drug, the Director; or

(b) in the case of food, the Director or the President of the Canadian Food Inspection Agency.

SOR/92-626, s. 3; SOR/95-548, s. 5; SOR/2000-184, s. 61; SOR/2000-317, s. 18.

Exports

A.01.045. A certificate referred to in section 37 of the Actshall be signed and issued by the exporter in the form set out in Appendix III.

SOR/80-318, s. 1; SOR/90-814, s. 2.

Sampling

A.01.050. When taking a sample of an article pursuant to paragraph 23(1)(a) of the Act, an inspector shall inform the owner thereof or the person from whom the sample is being obtained of the inspector's intention to submit the sample or a part thereof to an analyst for analysis or examination, and

(a) where, in the opinion of the inspector, division of the procured quantity would not interfere with analysis or examination

    (i) divide the quantity into three parts,

    (ii) identify the three parts as the owner's portion, the sample, and the duplicate sample and where only one part bears the label, that part shall be identified as the sample,

    (iii) seal each part in such a manner that it cannot be opened without breaking the seal, and

    (iv) deliver the part identified as the owner's portion to the owner or the person from whom the sample was obtained and forward the sample and the duplicate sample to an analyst for analysis or examination; or

(b) where, in the opinion of the inspector, division of the procured quantity would interfere with analysis or examination

    (i) identify the entire quantity as the sample,

    (ii) seal the sample in such a manner that it cannot be opened without breaking the seal, and

    (iii) forward the sample to an analyst for analysis or examination.

SOR/90-814, s. 3.

A.01.051. Where the owner or the person from whom the sample was obtained objects to the procedure followed by an inspector under section A.01.050 at the time the sample was obtained, the inspector shall follow both procedures set out in that section if the owner or the person from whom the sample was obtained supplies him with a sufficient quantity of the article.

Tariff of Fees

A.01.060. The cost of analysing a sample other than for the purpose of the Act, for a department of the Government of Canada for the purpose of legal action is $15.

Labelling of Food and Drugs in Pressurized Containers

A.01.060.1. In sections A.01.061 and A.01.062,

"flame projection" means the ability of the pressurized contents of an aerosol container to ignite and the length of that ignition, when tested in accordance with official method DO-30, Determination of Flame Projection, dated October 15, 1981; (projection de flamme)

"flashback" means that part of the flame projection that extends from its point of ignition back to the aerosol container when tested in accordance with official method DO-30, Determination of Flame Projection, dated October 15, 1981; (retour de flamme)

"principal display panel" [Repealed, SOR/2000-353, s. 2]

SOR/92-15, s. 1; SOR/2000-353, s. 2; SOR/2001-272, s. 6.

A.01.061. (1) Subject to section A.01.063, in the case of a food or a drug packaged in a disposable metal container designed to release pressurized contents by use of a manually operated valve that forms an integral part of the container, the principal display panel of the inner and outer labels of the food or drug shall display, in accordance with sections 15 to 18 of the Consumer Chemicals and Containers Regulations, as they read on September 30, 2001, the following information:

  (a) the hazard symbol set out in Column II of item 10 of Schedule II to those Regulations, accompanied by the signal word "CAUTION / ATTENTION"; and

  (b) the primary hazard statement "CONTAINER MAY EXPLODE IF HEATED. / CE CONTENANT PEUT EXPLOSER S'IL EST CHAUFFÉ.".

(2) Subject to section A.01.063, one panel of the inner and outer labels of a food or drug referred to in subsection (1) shall display, in the size required by paragraph 19(1)(b) of the Consumer Chemicals and Containers Regulations, as they read on September 30, 2001, the following additional hazard statement:

"Contents under pressure. Do not place in hot water or near radiators, stoves or other sources of heat. Do not puncture or incinerate container or store at temperatures over 50°C.

Contenu sous pression. Ne pas mettre dans l'eau chaude ni près des radiateurs, poêles ou autres sources de chaleur. Ne pas percer le contenant, ni le jeter au feu, ni le conserver à des températures dépassant 50 °C."

(3) The requirements of subsections (1) and (2) do not apply where

  (a) in relation to a drug or cosmetic, in the opinion of the Director, or

  (b) in relation to a food, in the opinion of the Minister of Consumer and Corporate Affairs, the design of the container, the materials used in its construction or the incorporation of a safety device eliminate the potential hazard therein.

SOR/81-616, s. 1; SOR/85-1023, s. 1; SOR/92-15, s. 2; SOR/2001-272, s. 7.

A.01.062. (1) Subject to section A.01.063, if a food or drug is packaged in a container described in subsection A.01.061(1) and has a flame projection of a length set out in column I of any of items 1 to 3 of the table to this subsection or a flashback as set out in column I of item 4 of that table, as determined by official method DO-30, Determination of Flame Projection, dated October 15, 1981, the principal display panel of the inner and outer labels of the food or drug shall display, in accordance with sections 15 to 18 of the Consumer Chemicals and Containers Regulations, as they read on September 30, 2001 the following information:

(a) the hazard symbol set out in Column II of the same item;

(b) in both official languages, the signal word set out in Column III of the same item; and

(c) in both official languages, the primary hazard statement set out in Column IV of the same item.

TABLE IS NOT DISPLAYED, SEE SOR/81-616, S. 2; SOR/92-15, S. 3.

(2) In addition to the requirements of subsection (1), one panel of the inner label and outer labels of a food or drug referred to in that subsection shall display, in the size required by paragraph 19(1)(b) of the Consumer Chemicals and Containers Regulations, as they read on September 30, 2001, the following additional hazard statement:

"Do not use in presence of open flame or spark.

Ne pas utiliser en présence d'une flamme nue ou d'étincelles."

SOR/81-616, s. 2; SOR/82-429, s. 1; SOR/85-1023, s. 2; SOR/92-15, s. 3; SOR/2001-272, s. 8.

A.01.063. (1) Where the labelled net contents of a container of a food or drug described in subsection A.01.061(1) or A.01.062(1) does not exceed 60 millilitres or 60 grams, the inner label may show only the information described in paragraph A.01.061(1)(a) or paragraphs A.01.062(1)(a) and (b), as the case may be.

(2) Where the labelled net contents of a container of a food or drug described in subsection A.01.061(1) or A.01.062(1) exceeds 60 millilitres or 60 grams but does not exceed 120 millilitres or 120 grams, the inner label may show only the information described in subsection A.01.061(1) or subsection A.01.062(1), as the case may be.

(3) Where the labelled net quantity, in a container, of a food or drug referred to in subsection A.01.061(1) or A.01.062(1) is less than 30 mL or 30 g, the hazard symbol shall be of such size as to be capable of being circumscribed by a circle with a diameter of at least 6 mm.

(4) Where a container of a food or drug, described in subsection (1) or (2) is sold in a package, the outer label may show only the information described in subsection A.01.061(2) and, where applicable, subsection A.01.062(2).

SOR/81-616, s. 2; SOR/92-15, s. 4.

A.01.064. [Repealed, SOR/93-243, s. 2]

Security Packaging

A.01.065. (1) In this section, "drug for human use" means a drug that is intended for human use, whether the drug is

(a) a mouthwash;

(b) to be inhaled, ingested or inserted into the body; or

(c) for ophthalmic use.

(2) Subject to subsection (3), no person shall sell or import a drug for human use that is packaged and available to the general public in a self-service display, unless the drug is contained in a security package.

(3) Subsection (2) does not apply to lozenges.

(4) Subject to subsection (5), a statement or illustration that draws attention to the security feature of the security package referred to in subsection (2) shall be carried

(a) on the inner label of the package; and

(b) if the security feature is a part of the outer package, on the outer label.

(5) Subsection (4) does not apply if the security feature of a security package is self-evident and is an integral part of the immediate product container.

SOR/85-141, s. 2; SOR/88-323, s. 1; SOR/92-664, s. 1.

Exemptions

Application

A.01.066. Sections A.01.067 and A.01.068 do not apply to

(a) a drug included in Schedule I, II, III, IV or V to the Controlled Drugs and Substances Act; or

(b) a drug that is listed or described in Schedule F, other than a drug that is listed or described in Part II of that Schedule and that is

(i) in a form not suitable for human use, or

(ii) labelled in the manner prescribed by paragraph C.01.046(b).

SOR/2007-288, s. 1.

Advertising

A.01.067. A drug is exempt from subsection 3(1) of the Act with respect to its advertisement to the general public as a preventative, but not as a treatment or cure, for any of the diseases, disorders or abnormal physical states referred to in Schedule A to the Act.

SOR/2007-288, s. 1.

Sale

A.01.068. A drug is exempt from subsection 3(2) of the Act with respect to its sale by a person where the drug is represented by label or is advertised by that person to the general public as a preventative, but not as a treatment or cure, for any of the diseases, disorders or abnormal physical states referred to in Schedule A to the Act.

SOR/2007-288, s. 1.

Part C: Drugs
Division 1

Regulations Respecting Food and Drugs (C.R.C., c. 870)

Enabling Statute: Food and Drugs Act

Regulation current to February 10th, 2010

Attention: See coming into force provision and notes, where applicable.

PART C
DRUGS
Division 1[13]

General

C.01.001. (1) In this Part

"acetaminophen product" has the same meaning as in Division 9; (produit d'acétaminophène)

"adult standard dosage unit" has, with reference to a drug, the same meaning as in Division 9; (dose normale pour adultes)

"adverse drug reaction" means a noxious and unintended response to a drug, which occurs at doses normally used or tested for the diagnosis, treatment or prevention of a disease or the modification of an organic function; (réaction indésirable à une drogue)

"antibiotic" means any drug or combination of drugs such as those named in C.01.410 to C.01 592 which is prepared from certain micro-organisms, or which formerly was prepared from micro-organisms but is now made synthetically and which possesses inhibitory action on the growth of other micro-organisms; (antibiotique)

"brand name" means, with reference to a drug, the name, whether or not including the name of any manufacturer, corporation, partnership or individual, in English or French,

   (a) that is assigned to the drug by its manufacturer,

   (b) under which the drug is sold or advertised, and

   (c) that is used to distinguish the drug; (marque nominative)

---

[13] Available on the Depratment of Justice website at http://laws.justice.gc.ca/eng/C.R.C.-C.870/FramesView.html

"case report" means a detailed record of all relevant data associated with the use of a drug in a subject; (fiche d'observation)

"children's standard dosage unit" has, with reference to a drug, the same meaning as in Division 9; (dose normale pour enfants)

"child resistant package" means a package that meets the requirements of subsection (2); (emballage protège-enfants)

"common name" means, with reference to a drug, the name in English or French by which the drug is

(a) commonly known, and

(b) designated in scientific or technical journals, other than the publications referred to in Schedule B to the Act; (nom usuel)

"expiration date" means the earlier of

(a) the date, expressed at minimum as a year and month, up to and including which a drug maintains its labelled potency, purity and physical characteristics, and

(b) the date, expressed at minimum as a year and month, after which the manufacturer recommends that the drug not be used; (date limite d'utilisation)

"immediate container" means the receptacle that is in direct contact with a drug; (récipient immédiat)

"internal use" means ingestion by mouth or application for systemic effect to any part of the body in which the drug comes into contact with mucous membrane; (usage interne)

"official drug" means any drug

(a) for which a standard is provided in these Regulations, or

(b) for which no standard is provided in these Regulations but for which a standard is provided in any of the publications mentioned in Schedule B to the Act; (drogue officielle)

"parenteral use" means administration of a drug by means of a hypodermic syringe, needle or other instrument through or into the skin or mucous membrane; (usage parentéral)

"per cent" means per cent by weight unless otherwise stated; (pour cent)

"practitioner" means a person authorized by the law of a province of Canada to treat patients with any drug listed or described in Schedule F to the Regulations; (praticien)

"prescription" means an order given by a practitioner directing that a stated amount of any drug or mixture of drugs specified therein be dispensed for the person named in the order; (ordonnance) "proper name" means, with reference to a drug, the name in English or French

    (a) assigned to the drug in section C.01.002,

    (b) that appears in bold-face type for the drug in these Regulations and, where the drug is dispensed in a form other than that described in this Part, the name of the dispensing form,

    (c) specified in the Canadian licence in the case of drugs included in Schedule C or Schedule D to the Act, or

    (d) assigned in any of the publications mentioned in Schedule B to the Act in the case of drugs not included in paragraph (a), (b) or (c); (nom propre)

"salicylate product" has the same meaning as in Division 9; (produit de salicylate)

"serious adverse drug reaction" means a noxious and unintended response to a drug that occurs at any dose and that requires in-patient hospitalization or prolongation of existing hospitalization, causes congenital malformation, results in persistent or significant disability or incapacity, is life-threatening or results in death; (réaction indésirable grave à une drogue)

"serious unexpected adverse drug reaction" means a serious adverse drug reaction that is not identified in nature, severity or frequency in the risk information set out on the label of the drug; (réaction indésirable grave et imprévue à une drogue)

"teaspoon" means, for the purpose of calculation of dosage, a volume of 5 cubic centimetres; (cuillerée à thé)

"test group" means a group that meets the requirements of subsection (3); (groupe d'essai)

"withdrawal period" means the length of time between the last administration of a drug to an animal and the time when tissues or products collected from the treated animal for consumption as food contain a level of residue of the drug that would not likely cause injury to human health. (délai d'attente)

    (2) A child resistant package is a package that

      (a) when tested in accordance with an acceptable method,

        (i) in the case of a test group comprising children, cannot be opened

        (A) by at least 85 per cent of those children prior to a demonstration to them of the proper means of opening the package, and

        (E) by at least 80 per cent of those children after the demonstration, and

(ii) in the case of a test group comprising adults

(A) can be opened by at least 90 per cent of those adults, and

(B) where the package is designed so that, once opened and reclosed, it continues to meet the requirements of subparagraph (i), can be so reclosed by at least 90 per cent of those adults; or

(b) complies with the requirements of one of the following standards, namely,

(i) Canadian Standards Association Standard CAN/CSA-Z76.1-M90, entitled Recloseable Child-Resistant Packages, published January 1990, as amended from time to time,

(ii) European Standard EN 28317:1992, entitled Child-resistant packaging—Requirements and testing procedures for reclosable packages, as adopted by the European Committee for Standardization on October 30, 1992, recognized by the British Standards Institution, and effective February 15, 1993 and by the Association française de normalisation, and effective December 20, 1992, and which reiterates fully the international standard ISO 8317:1989, as amended from time to time, and

(iii) Code of Federal Regulations (United States), Title 16, Section 1700.15, entitled Poison prevention packaging standards, as amended from time to time.

(3) For the purposes of this section, "test group" means

(a) in relation to children, a group of at least 200 children who

(i) are healthy and have no obvious physical or mental disability,

(ii) are between 42 and 51 months of age, and

(iii) represent evenly, within plus or minus 10 per cent, each monthly age between 42 and 51 months calculated to the nearest month; and

(b) in relation to adults, a group of at least 100 adults who

(i) are healthy and have no obvious physical or mental disability,

(ii) are between 18 and 45 years of age, and

(iii) represent evenly, within plus or minus 10 per cent, each yearly age between 18 and 45 years calculated to the nearest year.

(4) For the purpose of this section, an amendment from time to time to a standard referred to in paragraph (2)(b) becomes effective 18 months after the date designated by the competent authority as the effective date for the amendment.

SOR/80-543, s. 1; SOR/85-966, s. 1; SOR/86-93, s. 1; SOR/87-484, s. 1; SOR/92-654, s. 1; SOR/93-202, s. 1; SOR/95-411, s. 1; SOR/95-521, s. 1; SOR/96-399, s. 1; SOR/96-240, s. 1; SOR/97-543, s. 5.

C.01.001A. [Repealed, SOR/98-423, s. 1]

C.01.002. The Proper Name of a drug shown opposite an item number in the following Table in the column headed "Chemical Names and Synonyms" shall be the name shown opposite that item number in the column headed "Proper Names".

TABLE

Item No.	Proper Names	Chemical Names and Synonyms
A.1	Acepromazine	2-acetyl-10-(3-dimethylaminopropyl) iephenothiazine
A.2	Acetaminophen	*p*-Acetaminophenol, Paracetamol, *p*-Hydroxyacetanilide: N-acetyl-*p*-aminophenol
A.3	Acetanilide: Acetanilid	Acetylaminobenzene: Antifebrin: Phenylacetamide
A.4	Acetylsalicylic Acid	Acetylsalicylic acid
A.5	Allopurinol	1-H-Pyrazolo [3,4-*d*] pyrimidin-4-ol: 4-Hydroxypyrazolo (3,4-*d*) pyrimidine
A.6	Amantadine	1-Adamantanamine
A.7	Aminocaproic acid	6-Aminohexanoic acid
A.8	Aminopterin	N-[4-(2,4-diamino-6-pteridyl methyl) amino-benzoyl]-L- glumatic acid
A.9	Aminopyrine: Amidopyrine	1,5-dimethyl-2-phenyl-4-dimethylamino-3-pyrazolone: Dimethylaminophenazone
A.10	Amitriptyline	3-(3-Dimethylaminopropylidene)-1,2: 4,5-dibenzocyclohepta-1,4-diene
A.11	Azacyclonol	*a*,*a*-diphenyl-4-piperidinecarbinol
B.1	Bemegride	3-Ethyl-3-methylglutarimide
B.2	Benactyzine	Dimethylaminoethyl-1,1-diphenylglycolate
B.3	Bendroflumethiazide	3-benzyl-3,4-dihydro-6-(trifluoro- methyl)-2H-1,2,4-benzothiadiazine-7-sulfonamide-1,1-dioxide: Bendrofluazide (B.A.N.)
B.4	Betahistine	2-[2-(Methylamino)ethyl] pyridine
B.5	Bethanidine	N-Benzyl-N'N"-dimethylguanidine: 1-Benzyl-2,3-dimethylguanidine
B.6	Bretylium tosylate	N-2-Bromobenzyl-N-ethyl-N, N-dimethylammonium tosylate (Tosylic acid is trivial name for *p*-toluenesulphonic acid)
B.7	Bromisoval	2-monobromoisovalerylurea: Bromisovalum: Bromvalitone
C.1	Calcium Carbimide	Calcium cyanamide

Item No.	Proper Names	Chemical Names and Synonyms
C.2	Captodiamine	4-butylthio-*a*-phenylbenzyl-2-dimethylaminoethylsulfide
C.3	Carisoprodol	N-Isopropyl-2-methyl-2-propyl-1, 3-propanediol dicarbamate
C.4	Carphenazine	1-[10-(3[4-(2-Hydroxyethyl)-1-piperazinyl]propyl) phenothiazin-2yl]-1-propapone
C.5	Cephaloridine	7-[(2-Thienyl) acetamido]-3-(1-pyridylmethyl)-3-cephem-4-carboxylic acid betaine
C.6	Chlormezanone	2-(4-chlorophenyl)-3-methyl-4-methathiazanone-1,1-dioxide: Chlormethazone: Chlormethazanone
C.7	Chloromethapyrilene	N,N-dimethyl-N′-(2-pyridyl)-N′-(5-chloro-2-thenyl)-ethylenediamine: Chlorothen
C.8	Chlorphentermine	4-Chloro-*a*,*a*-dimethylphenethylamine
C.9	Cinchocaine	2-butoxy-N-(2-diethylaminoethyl) cinchoninamide: Dibucaine
C.10	Cinchophen	2-phenylquinoline-4-carboxylic acid: Quinophan
C.11	Clofibrate	Ethyl 2-(*p*-chlorophenoxy)-2-methylpropionate
C.12	Clomiphene	1-Chloro-2-[4-(2-diethylamino-ethoxy)phenyl]-1,2-diphenylethylene: 2-[*p*-(2-Chloro-1,2-diphenylvinyl)phenoxy] triethylamine
D.1	Desipramine	5-(3-Methylaminopropyl)-10,11-dihydro-5H-dibenz[b,f]azepine
D.2	Diazepam	7-Chloro-1,3-dihydro-1-methyl-5-phenyl-2H-1,4-benzodiazepin-2-one
D.3	Diethylpropion	1-phenyl-2-diethylaminopropanone-1
D.4	Diphenidol	1,1-Diphenyl-4-piperidinobutan-1-ol
D.5	Disulfiram	Tetraethylthiuram disulphide
E.1	Ectylurea	2-ethyl-*cis*-crotonylurea
E.2	Emylcamate	1-Ethyl-1-methylpropyl carbamate
E.3	Ethacrynic Acid	[2,3-Dichloro-4-(2-methylenebutyryl) phenoxy] acetic acid: 2,3-Dichloro-4-(2-ethylacryloyl) phenoxyacetic acid
E.4	Ethchlorvynol	3-(2-chlorovinyl)-1-pentyn-3-ol
E.5	Ethinamate	1-ethynylcyclohexyl carbamate
E.6	Ethionamide	2-Ethylisonicotinthioamide
E.7	Ethomoxane	2-*n*-Butylaminomethyl-8-ethoxy-benzo-1,4-dioxan
E.8	Ethyl Trichloramate	Ethyl *n*-[1-(2,2,2,-trichloro-1-hydroxyethyl)] carbamate

Item No.	Proper Names	Chemical Names and Synonyms
E.9	Etryptamine	3-(2-Aminobutyl) indole
E.10	Etymemazine	10-(3-Dimethylamino-2-methylpro-pyl)-2-ethylphenothiazine
F.1	Fluphenazine	10-{3-[4-(2-Hydroxyethyl) piperazin-1-yl] propyl}-2-tri-fluoromethylphenothiazine
F.2	Furosemide	4-Chloro-N-furfuryl-5-sulphamoylanthranilic acid: Frusemide (B.A.N.)
G.1	Glyburide	5-chloro-N-[2-[4-[[[(cyclohexylamino carbonyl]amino]sulfonyl]phenyl]ethyl]-2-methoxy benzamide: 1-4[4-[2-(5-chloro-2-methoxybenzamido)ethyl]phenyl- sulfonyl]-3-cyclohexylurea: Glibenclamide
H.1	Haloperidol	4-(4-Chlorophenyl)-1-[3-(4-fluorobenzoyl) propyl]-piperidin-4-ol: 4-[4-(p-Chlorophenyl)-4-hydro-xypiperidino]-4'-fluorobutyro-phenone
H.2	Hydroxychloroquine	7-Chloro-4[4-(N-ethyl-N-2-hydro-xyethylamino)-1-methylbutyl-amino] quinoline
H.3	Hydroxyzine	1-(p-chloro-a-phenylbenzyl)-4-(2-hydroxy ethoxyethyl) piperazine
I.1	Idoxuridine	5-Iodo-2'-deoxyuridine
I.2	Imipramine	5-(3-dimethylaminopropyl)-10,11-dihydro-5H-dibenz[b,f]azepine
I.3	Indomethacin	1-(p-Chlorobenzoyl)-5-methoxy-2-methyl-indole-3-acetic acid
I.4	Iproniazid	1-isonicotinoyl-2-isopropylhydrazine
I.5	Isocarboxazid	3-N-Benzylhydrazinocarbonyl-5-methylisoxazole
I.6	Isoproterenol	3,4-Dihydroxy-a-[isopropylamino) methyl] benzyl alcohol: Isoprenaline
L.1	Liothyronine	L-a-Amino-3-[(4-hydroxy-3-iodophenoxy)-3,5-di-iodo-phenyl] propionic acid
M.1	Mefenamic acid	N-(2,3-Xylyl)-anthranilic acid
M.2	Melphalan	4-Di-(2-chlorethyl)amino-L-phenylalanine
M.3	Mepazine	10-[(1-methyl-3-piperidyl) methyl] phenothiazine
M.4	Mephenesin	3-o-toloxy-1,2-propanediol
M.5	Mephenoxalone	5-(o-Methoxyphenoxymethyl)-2-oxazolidinone
M.6	Meprobamate	2,2-di(carbamoylmethyl) pentane
M.7	Methaqualone	2-Methyl-3-o-tolyquinazolin-4-one: 2-Methyl-3-o-tolyl-4-quinazolone
M.8	Methisazone	1-Methylindoline-2,3-dione-3-thiosemicarbazone: N-Methylisatin-β-thiosemicarbazone

Item No.	Proper Names	Chemical Names and Synonyms
M.9	Methotrimeprazine	10-[3-(2-Methyl)dimethylamino propyl]-2-methoxyphenothiazine: Levomepromazine
M.10	Methyldopa	1-3(3,4-Dihydroxyphenyl)-2-methylalanine
M.11	Methylparafynol	3-methyl-1-pentyn-3-ol: Methylpentynol
M.12	Methylphenidate	Methyl-1-phenyl-1-(2-piperidyl) acetate
M.13	Methyprylon	3,3-diethyl-5-methyl-2,4-piperidinedione
M.14	Methysergide	1-(Hydroxymethyl)propylamide of 1-methyl-*d*-lysergic acid
M.15	Metyrapone	2-Methyl-1,2-di(3-pyridyl)propan-1-one
N.1	Nalidixic Acid	1-Ethyl-7-methyl-4-oxo-1,8-naphthyridine-3-carboxylic acid
N.2	Nialamide	1-[2-(benzycarbamyl)ethyl]-2-isonicotinoyl-hydrazine
N.3	Nortriptyline	3-(3-Methylaminopropylidene)-1,2, 4,5-dibenzocyclohepta-1,4-diene
O.1	Oxanimide	2-ethyl-3-propyl-glycidamide
O.2	Oxazepam	7-Chloro-1,3-dihydro-3-hydroxy-5-phenyl-1,4-benzodiazepin-2-one
O.3	Oxyphenbutazone	4-*n*-Butyl-2-(4-hydroxyphenyl)-1-phenyl-pyrazolidine-3,5-dione
P.1	Paramethadione	3,5-dimethyl-5-ethyl-2,4-oxazolidinedione
P.2	Pargyline	N-Benzyl-N-methylprop-2-ynylamine
P.3	Pemoline	2-Imino-5-phenyloxazolidin-4-one
P.4	Pentazocine	1,2,3,4,5,6-Hexahydro-8-hydroxy-6,11-dimethyl-3-(3-methylbut-2-enyl)-2,6-methano-3-benzazocine: 1,2,3,4,5,6-Hexahydro-6,11-dimethyl-3-(3-methyl-2-butenyl)-2,6-methano-3-benzazocin-8-ol
P.5	Pentolinium Tartrate	NN'-Pentamethylenedi-(methylpryrrolidinium hydrogen, tartrate)
P.6	Perphenazine	2-chloro-10-{3-[1-(2-hydroxyethyl)-4-piperazinyl]propyl} phenothiazine
P.7	Phacetoperane	*l*-1-Phenyl-1(2'-piperidyl)-1-acetoxymethane
P.8	Phenacemide	(Phenylacetyl)urea
P.9	Phenacetin	*p*-acetphenetidin: Acetphenetidin: Acetophenetidin: *p*-ethoxyacetanilid
P.10	Phenaglycodol	2-*p*-chlorophenyl-3-methyl-2,3-butanediol
P.11	Phendimetrazine	3,4-Dimethyl-2 Phenylmorpholine
P.12	Phenelzine	2-phenylethylhydrazine

Item No.	Proper Names	Chemical Names and Synonyms
P.13	Phenformin	N'-β-phenethylformamidinyliminourea
P.14	Peniprazine	a-Methylphenethylhydrazine
P.15	Phenmetrazine	Tetrahydro-3-methyl-2-phenyl-1,4-oxazine: 3-methyl-2-phenylmorpholine
P.16	Phentermine	a, a-Dimethylphenethylamine: phenyl-*tert*-butylamine
P.17	Phenylindanedione	2-phenylindane-1,3-dione
P.18	Phenyltoloxamine	N,N-dimethyl-2-(a-phenyl-o-tolyloxy) ethylamine
P.19	Pholedrine	p-(4-hydroxyphenyl)-isopropylmethylamine
P.20	Piperliate	1-piperidine-ethanol benzilate
P.21	Pipradol	Diphenyl-2-piperidylmethanol
P.22	Prochlorperazine	2-Chloro-10-[3-(1-methyl-4-piperazinyl) propyl]phenothiazine
P.23	Prodilidine	1,2-Dimethyl-3-phenyl-3-pyrrolidinyl propionate
P.24	Propranolol	1-(Isopropylamino)-3-(1-naphthyloxy)-2-propanol
P.25	Prothipendyl	9-(3-Dimethylaminopropyl)-10-thia-1,9-diaza-anthracene
P.26	Protriptyline	7-(3-Methylaminopropyl)-1,2:5,6-dibenzocycloheptatrien: N-Methyl-5H-dibenzo [*a, d*] cycloheptene-5-propylamine
P.27	Pyrazinamide	Pyrazinoic acid amide
R.1	Rifampin	3-{[(4-methyl-1-piperazinyl)imino]methyl} rifamycin SV : Rifampicin (I.N.N.) (Rifamycin SV is an antibiotic produced by *Streptomyces mediterranei*)
S.01	Sodium Cromoglycate	4H-1-Benzopyran-2-carboxylic acid, 5,5'-[(2-hydroxy-1,3-propanediyl) bis(oxy)]bis[4-oxo-,disodium salt]:
		Disodium 5,5'-(2-hydroxytrimethylenedioxy) bis[4-oxo-4H-1-benzopyran-2- carboxylate]: Disodium 4,4'-dioxo-5,5'-(2-hydroxytrimethylenedioxy)di (chromene-2-carboxylate): Cromolyn Sodium (USP): Disodium Cromoglycate
S.1	Sulfameter	2-(4-Aminobenzenesulphonamido)-5-methoxypyrimidine: N'-(5-methoxy-2-pyrimidinyl) sulfanilamide: Sulfamethoxydiazine (B.A.N.)
S.2	Sulfamethazine	N'-(4,6-dimethyl-2- pyrimidyl)sulfanilamide: 2-(p-aminobenzenesulphonamide)-4,6-dimethylpyrimidine: sulphadimedine
S.3	Sulfinpyrazone	1,2-diphenyl-4-(2-phenylsulfinilethyl)-3,5-pyrazolidinedione

Item No.	Proper Names	Chemical Names and Synonyms
S.4	Sulfisoxazole	3,4-dimethyl-5-sulfanilamidoisoxazole: Sulphafurazole
T.1	Tetracaine	2-dimethylaminoethyl-*p-n-* butylaminobenzoate: Amethocaine
T.2	Thiethylperazine	2-Ethylthio-10-[3-(4- methylpiperazin-1-yl) propyl]phenothiazine
T.3	Thiopropazate	2-chloro-10-[3-[1-(2-acetoxyethyl)-4-piperazinyl] propyl]phenothiazine
T.4	Thioproperazine	2-Dimethylsulphamoyl-10-[3-(4-methylpiperazin-1-yl)- propyl]phenothiazine
T.5	Thioridazine	10-{2-[2-(1-methylpiperidyl)] ethyl *a*}-2-methylthiopheno- thiazine
T.6	Tranylcypromine	*Trans d*, 1-2-phenylcyclopropyl- amine
T.7	Triamterene	2,4,7-Triamino-6-phenylpteridine
T.8	Triflupromazine	10-(3-dimethylaminopropyl)-2-trifluoromethylphenothiazine: Fluopremazine
T.9	Trimeprazine	10-(3-dimethylamino-2-methylpropyl) phenothiazine
T.10	Trimethadione	3,5,5-trimethyl-2,4-oxazolidine- dione: Troxidone
T.11	Trimipramine	5-(3-Dimethylamino-2-methylpropyl)-10,11-dihydro-5H-dibenz[b,f]azepine: 5-(3'-Dimethylamino-2'-methylpropyl)iminodibenzyl
T.12	Tybamate	2-Methyl-2-propyltrimethylene butylcarbamate carbamate: 2-(Hydroxymethyl)-2-methyl-pentyl butylcarbamate carbamate
V.1	Vinblastine	An alkaloid derived from *Vinca rosea*
V.2	Vincristine	An alkaloid derived from *Vinca rosea*

SOR/87-565, s. 1; SOR/88-182, s. 1; SOR/88-482, s. 1(F); SOR/90-173, s. 1(F).

C.01.003. No person shall sell a drug that is not labelled as required by these Regulations.

SOR/80-544, s. 1.

C.01.004. (1) The inner and outer labels of a drug shall show

(a) on the principal display panel

    (i) the proper name, if any, of the drug which, if there is a brand name for the drug, shall immediately precede or follow the brand name in type not less than one-half the size of that of the brand name,

    (ii) if there is no proper name, the common name of the drug,

   (iii) where a standard for the drug is prescribed in Division 6 of this Part, a statement that the drug is a Canadian Standard Drug, for which the abbreviation C.S.D. may be used,

   (iv) where a standard for the drug is not prescribed in Division 6 of this Part but is contained in a publication mentioned in Schedule B to the Act, the name of the publication containing the standard used or its abbreviation as provided in Schedule B or, if a manufacturer's standard is used, a statement setting forth the fact that such a standard is used, and

   (v) in both official languages, the notation "sterile" stérile if the drug is required to be sterile by these Regulations;

 (b) on the upper left quarter of the principal display panel

   (i) the symbol Pr in the case of a drug required by this Part or Part D to be sold on prescription, but in no other case shall the symbol Pr appear on the label of a drug,

   (ii) the symbol *"C" in a clear manner and a conspicuous colour and size, in the case of a controlled drug, other than a controlled drug contained in an agricultural implant and set out in Part III of the schedule to Part G,

   (iii) the symbol "N" in a colour contrasting with the rest of the label or in type not less than half the size of any letters used thereon, in the case of a narcotic as defined in the Narcotic Control Regulations, and

   (iv) in the case of a targeted substance as defined in subsection 1(1) of the Benzodiazepines and Other Targeted Substances Regulations, the following symbol in a colour contrasting with the rest of the label and in type not less than half the size of any other letter used on the main panel, namely,

     GRAPHIC IS NOT DISPLAYED, SEE SOR/2000-219, S. 1

 (c) on any panel

   (i) the name and address of the manufacturer of the drug,

   (ii) the lot number of the drug,

   (iii) adequate directions for use of the drug,

   (iv) a quantitative list of the medicinal ingredients of the drug by their proper names or, if they have no proper names, by their common names, and

   (v) the expiration date of the drug.

(2) In addition to the requirements of subsection (1), the outer label of a drug shall show

 (a) the net amount of the drug in the container in terms of weight, measure or number;

 (b) in the case of a drug intended for parenteral use, a quantitative list of any preservatives present therein by their proper names or, if they have no proper names, by their common names; and

(c) in the case of a drug for human use that contains mercury or a salt or derivative thereof as a preservative, a quantitative list of all mercurial preservatives present therein by their proper names or, if they have no proper names, by their common names.

(3) Where the container of a drug is too small to accommodate an inner label that conforms to the requirements of these Regulations, the inner label requirements of these Regulations do not apply to the drug in that container if

(a) there is an outer label that complies with the labelling requirements of these Regulations; and

(b) the inner label shows

(i) the proper name of the drug, the common name of the drug if there is no proper name or, in the case of a drug with more than one medicinal ingredient, the brand name of the drug,

(ii) the potency of the drug except where, in the case of a drug with more than one medicinal ingredient, the name used pursuant to subparagraph (i) for that drug is unique for a particular potency of the drug,

(iii) the net contents of the drug if it is not in a discrete dosage form,

(iv) the route of administration of the drug if other than oral,

(v) the lot number of the drug,

(vi) the name of the manufacturer of the drug,

(vii) the expiration date of the drug, and

(viii) the identification of special characteristics of the dosage form if they are not evident from the name of the drug under subparagraphs (i) or (ii).

(4) [Repealed, SOR/92-654, s. 2]

(5) This section does not apply to

(a) a drug sold to a drug manufacturer; or

(b) a drug dispensed pursuant to a prescription, if its label carries suitable directions for use and complies with the requirements of section C.01.005.

SOR/80-543, s. 2; SOR/81-334, s. 1(E); SOR/85-715, s. 2; SOR/89-229, s. 1; SOR/90-216, s. 1; SOR/90-586, s. 1; SOR/92-654, s. 2; SOR/93-202, s. 2; SOR/97-228, s. 1; SOR/97-515, s. 1; SOR/2000-219, s. 1; SOR/2001-181, s. 4.

* Small graphic is not displayed.

C.01.004.1 (1) No person shall import a drug in dosage form into Canada for the purpose of sale unless they have in Canada a person who is responsible for the sale of the drug.

(2) No person who imports a drug in dosage form into Canada shall sell any lot or batch of the drug unless the name of the person who imports it, and the address of the principal place of business in Canada of the person responsible for its sale, appears on the inner and outer labels of the drug.

SOR/82-524, s. 1; SOR/93-475, s. 1; SOR/97-12, s. 2.

C.01.005. (1) The principal display panel of both the inner and outer label of a drug sold in dosage form shall show in a clear and legible manner the drug identification number assigned by the Director for that drug pursuant to subsection C.01.014.2(1), preceded by the words "Drug Identification Number" or Drogue : identification numérique or both, or the letters "DIN".

(2) Subsection (1) does not apply to a drug

   (a) compounded by a pharmacist pursuant to a prescription or by a practitioner; or

   (b) sold pursuant to a prescription, where the label of that drug indicates:

      (i) the proper name, the common name or the brand name of the drug,

      (ii) the potency of the drug, and

      (iii) the name of the manufacturer of the drug.

(3) For the purposes of this section and section C.01.014, "a drug in dosage form" means a drug in a form in which it is ready for use by the consumer without requiring any further manufacturing.

(4) and (5) [Repealed, SOR/81-248, s. 1]

SOR/81-248, s. 1; SOR/93-202, s. 3; SOR/98-423, s. 2; SOR/2001-181, s. 4.

C.01.006. Where a package of a drug has only one label, that label shall contain all the information required by these Regulations to be shown on both the inner and the outer labels.

C.01.007. No reference, direct or indirect, to the Act or to these Regulations shall be made upon any label of or in any advertisement for a drug unless such reference is a specific requirement of the Act or these Regulations.

C.01.008. [Repealed, SOR/80-544, s. 2]

C.01.009. Where by any statute of the Parliament of Canada or any regulation made thereunder a standard or grade is prescribed for a drug and that standard is given a name or designation by such statute or regulation, no person shall on a label of or in any advertisement for that drug use that name or designation unless the drug conforms with the standard or grade.

C.01.010. Where it is necessary to provide adequate directions for the safe use of a parenteral drug or Schedule F drug that is used in the treatment or prevention of any disease, disorder or abnormal physical state mentioned in Schedule A to the Act, such diseases, disorders or abnormal physical state may be mentioned on the labels and inserts accompanying that drug and to such extent, that drug is hereby exempted from the provisions of section 3 of the Act.

C.01.011. (1) A drug referred to in subsection 10(2) of the Act shall be exempt from the standard for any drug contained in any publication mentioned in Schedule B to the Act to the extent that such drug differs from that standard with respect to colour, flavour, shape and size, if such difference does not interfere with any method of assay prescribed in any such publication.

(2) [Repealed, SOR/93-243, s. 2]

(3) Where a manufacturer's standard is used for a drug, the manufacturer shall make available to the Director, on request, details of that standard and of a method of analysis for the drug acceptable to the Director.

(4) No person shall use a manufacturer's standard for a drug that provides

(a) a lesser degree of purity than the highest degree of purity, or

(b) a greater variation in potency than the least variation in potency, provided for that drug in any publication mentioned in Schedule B to the Act.

SOR/93-243, s. 2.

C.01.012. A manufacturer who makes representations on a label of a drug in oral dosage form, or in any advertisement, with respect to the site, rate or extent of release to the body of a medicinal ingredient of the drug, or the availability to the body of a medicinal ingredient of the drug, shall

(a) before making the representations, conduct such investigations, using an acceptable method, as may be necessary to demonstrate that the site, rate or extent of release to the body of the medicinal ingredient of the drug and the availability to the body of the medicinal ingredient of the drug, correspond to the representations; and

(b) on request submit the record of such investigations to the Director.

SOR/89-455, s. 2; SOR/94-36, s. 1.

C.01.013. (1) Where the manufacturer of a drug is requested in writing by the Director to submit on or before a specified day evidence with respect to a drug, the manufacturer shall make no further sales of that drug after that day unless he has submitted the evidence requested.

(2) Where the Director is of the opinion that the evidence submitted by a manufacturer, pursuant to subsection (1), is not sufficient, he shall notify the manufacturer in writing that the evidence is not sufficient.

(3) Where, pursuant to subsection (2), a manufacturer is notified that the evidence with respect to a drug is not sufficient, he shall make no further sales of that drug unless he submits further evidence and is notified in writing by the Director that that further evidence is sufficient.

(4) A reference in this section to evidence with respect to a drug means evidence to establish the safety of the drug under the conditions of use recommended and the effectiveness of the drug for the purposes recommended.

Assignment and Cancellation of Drug Identification Numbers

C.01.014. (1) No manufacturer shall sell a drug in dosage form unless a drug identification number has been assigned for that drug and the assignment of the number has not been cancelled pursuant to section C.01.014.6.

(2) Subsection (1) does not apply in respect of a drug listed in Schedule C to the Act, whole blood and its components, or a medicated feed as defined in section 2 of the Feeds Regulations, 1983.

SOR/81-248, s. 2; SOR/97-12, s. 3.

C.01.014.1. (1) A manufacturer of a drug, a person authorized by a manufacturer or, in the case of a drug to be imported into Canada, the importer of the drug may make an application for a drug identification number for that drug.

(2) An application under subsection (1) shall be made to the Director in writing and shall set out the following information:

(a) the name of the manufacturer of the drug as it will appear on the label;

(b) the pharmaceutical form in which the drug is to be sold;

(c) in the case of any drug other than a drug described in paragraph (d), the recommended route of administration;

(d) in the case of a drug for disinfection in premises, the types of premises for which its use is recommended;

(e) a quantitative list of the medicinal ingredients contained in the drug by their proper names or, if they have no proper names, by their common names;

(f) the brand name under which the drug is to be sold;

(g) whether the drug is for human use, veterinary use or disinfection in premises;

(h) the name and quantity of each colouring ingredient that is not a medicinal ingredient;

(i) the use or purpose for which the drug is recommended;

(j) the recommended dosage of the drug;

(k) the address of the manufacturer referred to in paragraph (a) and, where the address is outside the country, the name and address of the importer of the drug;

(l) the name and address of any individual, firm, partnership or corporation, other than the names and addresses referred to in paragraphs (a) and (k), that will appear on the label of the drug;

(m) the written text of all labels and package inserts to be used in connection with the drug and of any further prescribing information stated to be available on request; and

(n) the name and position of the person who signed the application and the date of signature.

(3) In the case of a new drug, a new drug submission or an abbreviated new drug submission filed pursuant to section C.08.002 or C.08.002.1 shall be regarded as an application for a drug identification number.

SOR/81-248, s. 2 SOR/93-202, s. 4; SOR/98-423, s. 3.

C.01.014.2. (1) Subject to subsection (2), if a manufacturer or importer has provided all the information described in subsection C.01.014.1(2) or section C.08.002 or C.08.002.1, as the case may be, in respect of a drug, the Director shall issue to the manufacturer or importer a document that

(a) sets out

   (i) the drug identification number assigned for the drug, preceded by the letters "DIN", or

   (ii) if there are two or more brand names for the drug, the drug identification numbers assigned by the Director for the drug, each of which pertains to one of the brand names and is preceded by the letters "DIN"; and

(b) contains the information referred to in paragraphs C.01.014.1(2)(a) to (f).

(2) Where the Director believes on reasonable grounds that a product in respect of which an application referred to in section C.01.014.1 has been made

(a) is not a drug, or

(b) is a drug but that its sale would cause injury to the health of the consumer or purchaser or would be a violation of the Act or these Regulations, he may refuse to issue the document referred to in subsection (1).

(3) Where the Director, pursuant to subsection (2), refuses to issue the document, the applicant may submit additional information and request the Director to reconsider his decision.

(4) On the basis of the additional information submitted pursuant to subsection (3), the Director shall reconsider the grounds on which the refusal to issue the document was made.

SOR/81-248, s. 2; SOR/92-230, s. 1; SOR/98-423, s. 4.

C.01.014.3. The manufacturer or importer or person authorized by the manufacturer or importer shall, within 30 days after commencing sale of a drug, date and sign the document issued pursuant to subsection C.01.014.2(1) in respect of the drug and return the document

(a) with a confirmation that the information recorded therein is correct;

(b) indicating the date on which the drug was first sold in Canada; and

(c) accompanied by samples or facsimiles of all labels and package inserts and any further prescribing information stated to be available on request.

SOR/81-248, s. 2; SOR/98-423, s. 5.

C.01.014.4. If the information referred to in subsection C.01.014.1(2) in respect of a drug is no longer correct owing to a change in the subject matter of the information,

(a) in the case of a change in the subject matter of any of the information referred to in paragraphs C.01.014.1(2)(a) to (f)

(i) that occurs prior to the sale of the drug, a new application shall be made, or

(ii) that occurs after the sale of the drug, no further sale of the drug shall be made until a new application for a drug identification number in respect of that drug is made and a number is assigned; and

(b) in the case of a change in the subject matter of any of the information referred to in paragraphs C.01.014.1(2)(g) to (k)

(i) that occurs prior to the sale of the drug, the particulars of the change shall be submitted with the return of the document referred to in section C.01.014.3, or

(ii) that occurs after the sale of the drug, the person to whom the drug identification number in respect of that drug was issued shall, within 30 days of the change, inform the Director of the change.

SOR/81-248, s. 2; SOR/92-230, s. 2; SOR/98-423, s. 6.

C.01.014.5. Every manufacturer of a drug shall, annually before the first day of October and in a form authorized by the Director, furnish the Director with a notification signed by the manufacturer or by a person authorized to sign on his behalf, confirming that all the information previously supplied by the manufacturer with respect to that drug is correct.

SOR/81-248, s. 2.

C.01.014.6. (1) The Director shall cancel the assignment of a drug identification number for a drug where

(a) the person to whom the number was assigned advises that the sale or import of the drug has been discontinued;

(b) the drug is a new drug in respect of which the notice of compliance has been suspended pursuant to section C.08.006; or

(c) it has been determined that the product in respect of which the number was assigned is not a drug.

(2) The Director may cancel the assignment of a drug identification number for a drug where

(a) the manufacturer of the drug has failed to comply with section C.01.014.5; or

(b) the manufacturer to whom the number was assigned has been notified pursuant to section C.01.013 that the evidence he submitted in respect of the drug is insufficient.

SOR/81-248, s. 2.

C.01.014.7. Where a person who has been assigned a drug identification number for a drug discontinues sale of the drug in Canada, he shall, within 30 days of such discontinuation, inform the Director that he is no longer selling the drug.

SOR/81-248, s. 2.

Tablet Disintegration Times

C.01.015. (1) Subject to subsection (2), no person shall sell for human use a drug in the form of a tablet that is intended to be swallowed whole unless, when tested by the official method DO-25, Determination of the Disintegration Time of Tablets, dated July 5, 1989,

(a) in the case of an uncoated tablet, the tablet disintegrates in not more than 45 minutes;

(b) in the case of a plain coated tablet, the tablet disintegrates in not more than 60 minutes; and

(c) in the case where the label of the drug indicates that the tablet carries an enteric coating or a coating designed to serve a purpose similar to that of an enteric coating, the tablet does not disintegrate when exposed for 60 minutes to simulated gastric fluid, but when it is subsequently exposed for a continuous period to simulated intestinal fluid, the tablet disintegrates in not more than 60 minutes.

(2) Subsection (1) does not apply in respect of a drug in the form of a tablet where

(a) a notice of compliance in respect of the drug in the form of a tablet has been issued pursuant to section C.08.004;

(b) [Repealed, SOR/98-423, s. 7]

(c) a dissolution or disintegration test for the drug in the form of a tablet is prescribed in Division 6 of this Part;

(d) the drug is labelled as complying with a standard contained in a publication referred to in Schedule B to the Act;

(e) the drug has been demonstrated by an acceptable method to be available to the body; or

(f) representations regarding the drug are made on its label, or in any advertisement, with respect to the site, rate or extent of release to the body of a medicinal ingredient of that drug, or the availability to the body of a medicinal ingredient of that drug.

SOR/89-429, s. 2; SOR/89-455, s. 3; SOR/94-36, s. 2; SOR/98-423, s. 7.

Adverse Drug Reaction Reporting

C.01.016. (1) No manufacturer shall sell a drug unless the manufacturer, with respect to any adverse drug reaction or any serious adverse drug reaction known to the manufacturer that occurs after this section comes into force, furnishes to the Director

(a) a report of all information in respect of any serious adverse drug reaction that has occurred in Canada with respect to the drug, within 15 days after receiving the information; and

(b) a report of all information in respect of any serious unexpected adverse drug reaction that has occurred outside Canada with respect to the drug, within 15 days after receiving the information.

(2) The manufacturer shall, on an annual basis and whenever requested to do so by the Director, conduct a concise, critical analysis of the adverse drug reactions and serious adverse drug reactions to a drug referred to in subsection (1) and prepare a summary report in respect of the reports received during the previous twelve months or received during such period of time as the Director may specify.

(3) Where, after reviewing any report furnished pursuant to subsection (1) and any available safety data relating to the drug, the Director considers that the drug may not be safe when used under the recommended conditions of use, the Director may, for the purpose of assessing the safety of the drug, request in writing, that the manufacturer submit

(a) case reports of all adverse drug reactions and serious adverse drug reactions to that drug that are known to the manufacturer; and

(b) a summary report prepared pursuant to subsection (2).

(4) The manufacturer shall submit the case reports and summary report referred to in subsection (3) within 30 days after receiving the request from the Director.

SOR/95-521, s. 2.

C.01.017. The manufacturer shall maintain records of the reports and case reports referred to in section C.01.016 for auditing purposes.

SOR/95-521, s. 2.

C.01.018. [Repealed, SOR/89-455, s. 3]

Limits of Drug Dosage

C.01.021. Except as provided in these Regulations, no person shall sell a drug for human use listed in the following table unless both the inner and the outer labels other than the inner label of a single dose container carry a statement of

(a) the quantitative content of the drug,

(b) the recommended single and daily adult dose designated as such, except for

    (i) preparations sole y for external use, or

    (ii) preparations sole y for children's use; and

(c) adequate directions for use when the drug is recommended for children which shall be either

    (i) the statement "CHILDREN: As directed by the physician", or

(ii) a suitable reduced maximum single and daily dose which shall not exceed the following:

Age in years	Proportion of adult dose
10 - 14	one-half
5 - 9	one-fourth
2 - 4	one-sixth
under 2 years	as directed by physician

TABLE

TABLE OF LIMITS OF DRUG DOSAGE FOR ADULTS

Item	External Use	Internal Use	
	—	—	
	Maximum Limit	Maximum Dosage Unless otherwise stated, doses are in milligrams	
	Per cent	Single	Daily
Acetaminophen	—	650	4.0 g
Acetanilide and derivatives (except N-Acetyl-*p*-amino phenol)	—	65	195
Acetylsalicylic Acid	—	650	4.0 g
Aconitine, its preparations and derivatives	0.2	0.1	0.1
Adonis vernalis	—	65	195
Amylocaine, its salts and derivatives when sold or recommended for opthalmic use	0.0	0.0	0.0
Amylocaine Hydrochloride, except when sold or recommended for ophthalmic use	1.0	0.0	0.0
Antimony, compounds of	—	3.3	13
Atropine, Methylatropine, and their salts	1.0	0.13	0.44
Belladonna and its preparations, on the basis of belladonna alkaloids	0.375	0.13	0.44
Benzene (Benzol)	—	—	—
Benzocaine	8.0	195	585
Beta-Naphthol	—	195	585

Item	External Use — Maximum Limit	Internal Use — Maximum Dosage Unless otherwise stated, doses are in milligrams	
	Per cent	Single	Daily
Butacaine, its salts and derivatives when sold or recommended for ophthalmic use	0.0	0.0	0.0
Butacaine Sulphate, except when sold or recommended for opthalmic use	1.0	0.0	0.0
Cadexomer Iodine	0.0	0.0	0.0
Cantharides, cantharidin, and their preparations, on the basis of cantharidin, except blisters	0.03	0.0	0.0
Cantharides, blisters only	0.2	0.0	0.0
Cedar Oil	25.0	0.0	0.0
Chlorbutol (not more often than every 4 hours)	—	325	975
Choline Salicylate	—	870	5.22 g
Cinchocaine Hydrochloride, except suppositories	1.0	0.0	0.0
Cinchocaine Hydrochloride, suppositories only	—	11	11
Colchicine and its salts	—	0.55	1.65
Colchicum and its preparations, on the basis of colchicine	—	0.27	0.81
Croton Oil	10.0	0.0	0.0
Cyproheptadine and its salts—when sold or recommended for the promotion of weight gain	—	0.0	0.0
Ephedrine and its salts	—	11	32.5
Ephedrine and its salts, sprays	1.0	—	—
Epinephrine and its salts, sprays	1.0	—	—
Gelseminine (Gelsemine) and its salts (not to be repeated within 4 hours)	—	0.55	1.65
Gelsemium and its preparations, on the basis of the crude drug	—	16.2	48.6
Hydrocyanic (Prussic) Acid as 2 per cent solution	—	0.062 ml	0.31 ml

Item	External Use	Internal Use	
	—	—	
	Maximum Limit	Maximum Dosage Unless otherwise stated, doses are in milligrams	
	Per cent	Single	Daily
Hydroquinone	2.0	—	—
Hyoscine (Scopolamine) and its salts	0.5	0.325	0.975
Hyoscine aminoxide hydrobromide	0.5	0.325	0.975
Hyoscyamine and its salts	—	0.325	0.975
Hyoscyamus and its preparations, on the basis of hyoscyamus alkaloids	—	0.073	0.22
Lobelia and its preparations, on the basis of the crude drug	—	130	390
Lobeline and its salts	—	2.0	6.0
Magnesium Salicylate	—	650	4.0 g
Methyl Salicylate	30	—	—
Methylene Blue	—	130	390
Phenacetin	—	650	1.95 g
Phenazone and compounds thereof	—	325	975
Phenol	2.0	32.5	260
Phenylpropanolamine when sold or recommended as an appetite depressent	—	0.0	0.0
Phosphorus	—	0.0	0.0
Podophyllin	0.0	0.0	0.0
Potassium Chlorate	—	325	975
Potassium Chlorate, gargle	2.5	—	—
Procaine and its salts	—	—	—
Proxymetacaine, its salts and derivatives when sold or recommended for ophthalmic use	0.0	0.0	0.0
Salicylamide	—	975	2.925 g
Santonin	—	65	130
Selenium and its compounds	2.5	0.0	0.0
Sodium Chlorate	—	325	975

Item	External Use	Internal Use	
	—	—	
	Maximum Limit	Maximum Dosage Unless otherwise stated, doses are in milligrams	
	Per cent	Single	Daily
Sodium Fluoride	—	0.1	0.1
Sodium Salicylate	—	650	4.0 g
Squill and its preparations, on the basis of crude drug	—	32.5	97.5
Stramonium and its preparations on the basis of stramonium alkaloids	—	0.16	0.65
Strychnine and its salts	—	0.0	0.0
Tannic Acid	—	150	1 000
Tetracaine, its salts and derivatives when sold or recommended for ophthalmic use	0.0	0.0	0.0
Thiocyanates	0.0	0.0	0.0
Urethane	0.0	0.0	0.0

Where drugs having similar physiological actions occur in combination, the dosage of each shall be proportionately reduced.

Accurate dosages may be expressed in either metric units or imperial units. If the dosage is expressed in both systems, then an approximation may be used for one expression, but such approximation must precede or follow the accurate statement by which the product will be judged and must be in brackets.

SOR/78-422, s. 1; SOR/80-544, s. 3; SOR/84-145, s. 1; SOR/85-715, s. 3; SOR/85-966, s. 2; SOR/88-94, s. 1; SOR/89-229, s. 2; SOR/89-548, s. 1.

C.01.022. Notwithstanding paragraph C.01.021(b), the recommended single and daily dosage of a drug

(a) intended to be burned and the smoke inhaled may be increased to 10 times the oral dose, and

(b) intended for use as suppositories may be increased to 33 1/3 per cent in excess of the oral dose.

C.01.024. (1) Sections C.01.021 and C.01.022 do not apply to

(a) a drug sold to a drug manufacturer; or

(b) a drug sold on prescription.

(2) Paragraph C.01.021(c) does not apply to

    (a) acetaminophen;

    (b) acetylsalicylic acid;

    (c) magnesium salicylate;

    (d) sodium salicylate; or

    (e) choline salicylate.

(3) Where a drug mentioned in any of paragraphs (2)(a) to (d) is recommended for children, no person shall sell the drug for human use unless both the inner and the outer labels carry a statement that it is recommended

    (a) that the drug be used as directed by a physician; or

    (b) that the maximum doses of the drug not exceed the amounts set out in the following table and that single doses not be administered more frequently than every four hours.

TABLE
MAXIMUM DOSE

Item	Age	Column I Maximum Children's Dose (80 mg units) Acetaminophen Drops	Column II Maximum Children's Dose (80 mg units)	Column III Maximum Children's Dose (160 mg units) Acetaminophen	Column IV Maximum Adult's Dose (325 mg units)	Column V Maximum Single Dose (mg)	Column VI Maximum Daily Dose (mg)
1.	11 to under 12 years	—	6	3	1.5	480	2 400
2.	9 to under 11 years	—	5	2.5	1.25	400	2 000
3.	6 to under 9 years	—	4	2	1	320	1 600
4.	4 to under 6 years	—	3	1.5	—	240	1 200
5.	2 to under 4 years	—	2	1	—	160	800
6.	1 to under 2 years	1.5 or as directed by a physician	—	—	—	120	600
7.	4 months to under 1 year	1 or as directed by a physician	—	—	—	80	400
8.	0 to under 4 months	0.5 or as directed by a physician	—	—	—	40	200

(4) Where choline salicylate is recommended for children, no person shall sell the drug for human use unless both the inner and the outer labels carry a statement that it is recommended

(a) that the drug be used as directed by physician; or

(b) that the maximum doses of the drug not exceed the amounts set out in the following table and that single doses not be administered more frequently than every four hours.

TABLE

MAXIMUM DOSE

Age (Years)	Adult Dosage Units (435 mg)	Single Dose (mg)	Maximum Daily Dose (mg)
11 to under 12	1 1/2	660	3 300
9 to under 11	1 1/4	550	2 750
6 to under 9	1	440	2 200
4 to under 6	3/4	330	1 650
2 to under 4	1/2	220	1 100
Under 2	As directed by physician		

SOR/84-145, s. 2; SOR/90-587, s. 1.

C.01.025. Both the inner and the outer labels of a drug that carry a recommended single or daily dosage or a statement of concentration in excess of the limits provided by section C.01.021 shall carry a caution that the product is to be used only on the advice of a physician.

C.01.026. The provisions of section C.01.025 do not apply to

(a) a drug sold on prescription, or

(b) the inner label of a single-dose container.

C.01.027. (1) Where a person advertises to the general public a drug for human use, the person shall not make any representation other than with respect to the brand name, proper name, common name, price and quantity of the drug if it

(a) contains a drug set out in the table to section C.01.021; and

(b) carries on its label

(i) a statement of the recommended single or daily adult dosage that results in a single or daily adult dosage of the drug referred to in paragraph (a) in excess of the maximum dosage set out in the table to section C.01.021 for that drug, or

(ii) a statement that shows a concentration of the drug referred to in paragraph (a) in excess of the maximum limit set out in the table to section C.01.021 for that drug.

(2) Subsection (1) does not apply to products containing

Part C:
Drugs, Division 1

(a) acetaminophen;

(b) acetylsalicylic acid;

(c) choline salicylate;

(d) magnesium salicylate; or

(e) sodium salicylate.

(3) [Repealed, SOR/94-409, s. 1]

(4) Where a person advertises to the general public a drug for human use that contains acetylsalicylic acid, the person shall not make any representation with respect to its administration to or use by children or teenagers.

SOR/81-358, s. 1; SOR/84-145, s. 3; SOR/85-715, s. 4(F); SOR/85-966, s. 3; SOR/93-202, s. 5; SOR/93-411, s. 1; SOR/94-409, s. 1.

Cautionary Statements and Child Resistant Packages

C.01.028. (1) Subject to subsection (2), the inner and outer labels of a drug that contains

(a) acetylsalicylic acid or any of its salts or derivatives, salicylic acid or a salt thereof, or salicylamide, where the drug is recommended for children, shall carry a cautionary statement to the effect that the drug should not be administered to a child under two years of age except on the advice of a physician;

(b) boric acid or sodium borate as a medicinal ingredient shall carry a cautionary statement to the effect that the drug should not be administered to a child under three years of age;

(c) hyoscine (scopolamine) or a salt thereof shall carry a cautionary statement to the effect that the drug should not be used by persons suffering from glaucoma or where it causes blurring of the vision or pressure pain within the eye;

(d) phenacetin, either singly or in combination with other drugs, shall carry the following cautionary statement:

«"CAUTION: May be injurious if taken in large doses or for a long time. Do not exceed the recommended dose without consulting a physician."; or»

(e) acetylsalicylic acid for internal use shall carry a cautionary statement to the effect that the drug should not be administered to or used by children or teenagers who have chicken pox or manifest flu symptoms before a physician or pharmacist is consulted about Reye's syndrome, which statement shall also refer to the fact that Reye's syndrome is a rare and serious illness.

(2) Subsection (1) does not apply to a drug that is

(a) intended for parenteral use only;

(b) dispensed pursuant to a prescription; or

(c) required to be sold on prescription pursuant to these Regulations or pursuant to the Narcotic Control Regulations.

SOR/86-93, s. 2; SOR/88-323, s. 2(F); SOR/93-411, s. 2.

C.01.029. (1) Subject to subsections C.01.031.2(1) and (2), the inner and outer labels of a drug

(a) that contains

  (i) salicylic acid, a salt thereof or salicylamide,

  (ii) acetylsalicylic acid, or any of its salts or derivatives,

  (iii) acetaminophen, or

  (iv) more than five per cent alkyl salicylates, or

(b) that is in a package that contains

  (i) more than the equivalent of 250 mg of elemental iron, or

  (ii) more than the equivalent of 120 mg of fluoride ion, unless the drug is intended solely for use in dentists' offices, shall carry a cautionary statement to the effect that the drug should be kept out of the reach of children.

(2) Subject to subsections C.01.031.2(1) and (2), the inner and outer labels of a drug that is in a package that contains

(a) more than 1.5 g of salicylic acid or the equivalent quantity of any of its salts or salicylamide,

(b) more than 2 g of acetylsalicylic acid or the equivalent quantity of any of its salts or derivatives,

(c) more than 3.2 g of acetaminophen,

(d) more than the equivalent of 250 mg of elemental iron, or

(e) more than the equivalent of 120 mg of fluoride ion, unless the drug is intended solely for use in dentists' offices, shall carry a cautionary statement to the effect that there is enough drug in the package to seriously harm a child.

(3) The cautionary statements required under subsections (1) and (2) shall be preceded by a prominently displayed symbol that is octagonal in shape, conspicuous in colour and on a background of a contrasting colour.

SOR/86-93, s. 2; SOR/87-484, s. 2; SOR/88-323, s. 3(F); SOR/90-587, s. 2; SOR/93-468, s. 1.

C.01.030. [Repealed, SOR/2003-196, s. 104]

C.01.031. (1) Subject to section C.01.031.2,

(a) no person shall sell a drug described in subsection C.01.029(1) unless

**Part C:
Drugs, Division 1**

     (i)   where the drug is recommended solely for children, it is packaged in a child resistant package, or

    (ii)   where the drug is not recommended solely for children, at least one of the sizes of packages available for sale is packaged in a child resistant package; and

(b) where a drug described in subsection C.01.029(1) is packaged in a package that is not a child resistant package, the outer label shall carry a statement that the drug is available in a child resistant package.

(2) [Repealed, SOR/93-468, s. 2]

SOR/86-93, s. 2; SOR/87-16, s. 1; SOR/93-468, s. 2.

C.01.031.1. [Repealed, SOR/87-484, s. 3]

C.01.031.2. (1) Sections C.01.029 to C.01.031 do not apply to a drug that is

(a) required by these Regulations or the Narcotic Control Regulations to be sold on prescription;

(b) intended for parenteral use only;

(c) in effervescent or powder form;

(d) in suppository form;

(e) intended for topical use, unless it is a liquid preparation containing more than five per cent alkyl salicylates;

(f) packaged in a non-reclosable package containing not more than two adult standard dosage units per package; or

(g) in toothpaste form.

(2) Sections C.01.029 to C.01.031 do not apply to a drug that is repackaged by a pharmacist or practitioner at the time of sale.

(3) Section C.01.031 does not apply to a drug that is

(a) sold only in containers that have roll-on or spray applicators or permanently installed wick applicators;

(b) sold for exclusive use in animals other than household pets; or

(c) intended solely for use in dentists' offices, or packaged for hospital use only.

SOR/86-93, s. 2; SOR/87-484, s. 4; SOR/88-323, s. 5(F); SOR/93-468, s. 3.

C.01.032. No person shall sell a corticosteroid drug for ophthalmic use unless

(a) the outer label or the package insert carries, as part of the directions for use, the following statements:

"Contraindications

«Viral diseases of the cornea and conjunctiva;»

«Tuberculosis of the eye;»

«Fungal diseases of the eye;»

«Acute purulent untreated infections of the eye, which, like other diseases caused by micro-organisms, may be masked or enhanced by the presence of the steroid.»

Side Effects

«Extended ophthalmic use of corticosteroid drugs may cause increased intraocular pressure in certain individuals and in those diseases causing thinning of the cornea, perforation has been known to occur.";»

and

(b) the inner label carries the statements required by paragraph (a) or instructions to see the outer label or package insert for information about contraindications and side effects.

C.01.033. Section C.01.032 does not apply to a corticosteroid drug that is dispensed by a registered pharmacist pursuant to a prescription.

C.01.034. No person shall disseminate to a practitioner promotional literature about corticosteroid drugs for ophthalmic use unless the statements required by paragraph C.01.032(a) are included in that literature.

C.01.035. Sections C.01.032 and C.01.034 do not apply to a drug sold solely for veterinary use.

Miscellaneous

C.01.036. (1) No manufacturer or importer shall sell

(a) a drug that contains phenacetin in combination with any salt or derivative of salicylic acid;

(b) a drug for human use that contains

   (i) oxyphenisatin,

   (ii) oxyphenisatin acetate, or

   (iii) phenisatin; or

(c) a drug for human use that contains mercury or a salt or derivative thereof, unless the drug is

   (i) a drug described in Schedule C or D to the Act, or

   (ii) one of the following drugs, namely,

      (A) an ophthalmic drug or other drug to be used in the area of the eye,

      (B) a drug for nasal administration,

(C) a drug for otic administration, or

(D) a drug for parenteral administration that is packaged in a multi-dose container, in which the mercury or the salt or derivative thereof is present as a preservative and the manufacturer or importer has submitted evidence to the Director demonstrating that the only satisfactory way to maintain the sterility or stability of the drug is to use that preservative.

(2) For the purpose of clause (1)(c)(ii)(A), "area of the eye" means the area bounded by the supraorbital and infraorbital ridges and includes the eyebrows, the skin underlying the eyebrows, the eyelids, the eyelashes, the conjunctival sac of the eye, the eyeball and the soft tissue that lies below the eye and within the infraorbital ridge.

SOR/78-423, s. 2; SOR/86-93, s. 3; SOR/89-229, s. 3.

C.01.036.1 No person shall sell, or advertise for sale, nitrous oxide to the general public.

SOR/78-875, s. 1.

C.01.037. (1) No person shall sell to the general public a drug that is recommended solely for children if the package in which the drug is sold contains

(a) more than 1.92 g of salicylamide or salicylic acid or the equivalent quantity of a salt of salicylic acid;

(b) more than 1.92 g of acetylsalicylic acid or the equivalent quantity of a salt or derivative thereof;

(c) more than 3.2 g of acetaminophen in 160 mg dosage units; or

(d) more than 1.92 g of acetaminophen in 80 mg dosage units.

(2) Subsection (1) does not apply to a drug dispensed pursuant to a prescription.

SOR/86-93, s. 4; SOR/87-484, s. 5; SOR/88-323, s. 6; SOR/90-587, s. 3.

C.01.038. A drug for human use is adulterated if it contains

(a) Strychnine or any of its salts;

(b) extracts or tinctures of

(i) Strychnos nux vomica,

(ii) Strychnos Ignatii, or

(iii) a Strychnos species containing strychnine, other than those species mentioned in subparagraphs (i) and (ii);

(c) Methapyrilene or any of its salts;

(d) Echimidine or any of its salts; or

(e) any of the following plant species or extracts or tinctures thereof:

(i) Symphytum asperum,

(ii) Symphytum x up andicum, or

(iii) any other plant species containing echimidine.

SOR/79-512, s. ˙; SOR/88-173, s. 1.

C.01.039. In vitro diagnostic products that are or contain drugs other than drugs listed in Schedule E to the Act, and drugs listed in Schedule D to the Act that are labelled for veterinary use only, are exempt from the application of this Part.

SOR/97-12, s. 4.

C.01.040. No manufacturer or importer shall sell a drug for human use that contains as an ingredient

(a) chloroform; or

(b) arsenic or any of its salts or derivatives.

SOR/89-229, s. 4.

C.01.040.1. No manufacturer shall use methyl salicylate as a medicinal ingredient in a drug for internal use in humans.

SOR/78-422, s. 2; SOR/78-801, s. 1; SOR/81-334, s. 2(F); SOR/89-176, s. 1; SOR/92-662, s. 1.

Colouring Agents

C.01.040.2 (1) No manufacturer shall use a colouring agent in a drug other than a colouring agent listed in subsections (3) and (4).

(2) No person shall import for sale a drug that contains a colouring agent other than a colouring agent listed in subsections (3) and (4).

(2.1) In subsections (3) and (4),

"C.I. (indication of the number)" means the designation used to identify a colouring agent in the Colour Index published by The Society of Dyers and Colourists, as amended from time to time; (C.I. (indication du numéro))

"D & C (indication of the colour and the number)" means the designation used to identify, in accordance with the Code of Federal Regulations of the United States, a colouring agent that can be used in the United States in drugs and cosmetics; (D&C (indication de la couleur et du numéro))

"FD & C (indication of the colour and the number)" means the designation used to identify, in accordance with the Code of Federal Regulations of the United States, a colouring agent that can be used in the United States in food, drugs and cosmetics. (FD&C (indication de la couleur et du numéro))

(3) The following colouring agents are permitted in drugs for internal and external use, namely,

(a) ACID FUCHSIN D (D & C Red No. 33; C.I. No. 17200),

ALIZARIN CYANINE GREEN F (D & C Green No. 5; C.I. No. 61570),

ALLURA RED AC (FD & C Red No. 40; C.I. No. 16035),

AMARANTH (Delisted FD & C Red No. 2; C.I. No. 16185),

ANTHOCYANIN DERIVED FROM JUICE EXPRESSED FROM FRESH EDIBLE FRUITS

OR VEGETABLES,

ß-APO-81-CAROTENAL (C.I. No. 40820),

BRILLIANT BLUE FCF SODIUM SALT (FD & C Blue No. 1; C.I. No. 42090),

BRILLIANT BLUE FCF AMMONIUM SALT (D & C Blue No. 4; C.I. No. 42090),

CANTHAXANTHIN (C.I. No. 40850),

CARAMEL,

CARBON BLACK (C.I. No. 77266),

CARMINE (C.I. No. 75470),

CARMOISINE (Delisted Ext. D & C Red No. 10; C.I. No. 14720),

ß-CAROTENE (C.I. No. 40800),

CHLOROPHYLL (C.I. No. 75810),

EOSIN YS ACID FORM (D & C Red No. 21; C.I. No. 45380:2),

EOSIN YS SODIUM SALT (D & C Red No. 22; C.I. No. 45380),

ERYTHROSINE (FD & C Red No. 3; C.I. No. 45430),

FAST GREEN FCF (FD & C Green No. 3; C.I. No. 42053),

FLAMING RED (D & C Red No. 36; C.I. No. 12085),

HELINDONE PINK CN (D & C Red No. 30; C.I. No. 73360),

INDIGO (D & C Blue No. 6; C.I. No. 73000),

INDIGOTINE (FD & C Blue No. 2; C.I. No. 73015),

IRON OXIDES (C.I. Nos. 77489, 77491, 77492, 77499),

LITHOL RUBIN B SODIUM SALT (D & C Red No. 6; C.I. No. 15850),

LITHOL RUBIN B CALCIUM SALT (D & C Red No. 7; C.I. No. 15850:1),

PHLOXINE B ACID FORM (D & C Red No. 27; C.I. No. 45410:1),

PHLOXINE B SODIUM SALT (D & C Red No. 28; C.I. No. 45410),

PONCEAU 4R (C.I. No. 16255),

PONCEAU SX (FD & C Red No. 4; C.I. No. 14700),

QUINOLINE YELLOW WS (D & C Yellow No. 10; C.I. No. 47005),

RIBOFLAVIN,

SUNSET YELLOW FCF (FD & C Yellow No. 6; C.I. No. 15985),

TARTRAZINE (FD & C Yellow No. 5; C.I. No. 19140),

TITANIUM DIOXIDE (C.I. No. 77891);

(b) preparations made by extending any of the colouring agents listed in paragraph (a) on a substratum of

    (i)   alumina,

    (ii) blanc fixe,

    (iii) gloss white,

    (iv) clay,

    (v) zinc oxide,

    (vi) talc,

    (vii) rosin,

    (viii) aluminum benzoate,

    (ix) calcium carbonate, or

    (x) any combination of the substances listed in subparagraphs (i) to (ix); and

(c) preparations made by extending any sodium, potassium, aluminum, barium, calcium, strontium or zirconium salt of any of the colouring agents listed in paragraph (a) on a substratum of

    (i)   alumina,

    (ii) blanc fixe,

    (iii) gloss white,

    (iv) clay,

    (v) zinc oxide,

    (vi) talc,

    (vii) rosin,

    (viii) aluminum benzoate,

(ix) calcium carbonate, or

(x) any combination of the substances listed in subparagraphs (i) to (ix).

(4) The following colouring agents are permitted in drugs for external use, namely,

(a) ACID VIOLET 43 (Ext. D & C Violet No. 2; C.I. No. 60730),

ALIZUROL PURPLE SS (D&C Violet No. 2; C.I. No. 60725),

ANNATTO (C.I. No. 75120),

BISMUTH OXYCHLORIDE (C.I. No. 77163),

CHROMIUM HYDROXIDE GREEN (PIGMENT GREEN 18 (C.I. No. 77289)),

DEEP MAROON (D&C Red No. 34; C.I. No. 15880:1),

DIBROMOFLUORESCEIN (SOLVENT RED 72 (C.I. No. 45370:1); ORANGE No. 5 (D & C Orange No. 5)),

FERRIC FERROCYANIDE (C.I. No. 77510),

GUANINE (C.I. No. 75170),

MANGANESE VIOLET (C.I. No. 77742),

MICA (C.I. No. 77019),

ORANGE II (D&C Orange No. 4; C.I. No. 15510),

PYRANINE CONCENTRATED (D&C Green No. 8; C.I. No. 59040),

QUINIZARIN GREEN SS (D&C Green No. 6; C.I. No. 61565),

TONEY RED (D&C Red No. 17; C.I. No. 26100),

URANINE ACID FORM (D&C Yellow No. 7; C.I. No. 45350:1),

URANINE SODIUM SALT (D&C Yellow No. 8; C.I. No. 45350);

ZINC OXIDE (C.I. No. 77947);

(b) preparations made by extending any of the colouring agents listed in paragraph (a) on a substratum of

(i) alumina,

(ii) blanc fixe,

(iii) gloss white,

(iv) clay,

(v) zinc oxide,

(vi) talc,

(vii) rosin,

(viii) aluminum benzoate,

(ix) calcium carbonate, or

(x) any combination of the substances listed in subparagraphs (i) to (ix); and

(c) preparations made by extending any sodium, potassium, aluminum, barium, calcium, strontium or zirconium salt of any of the colouring agents listed in paragraph (a) on a substratum of

(i) alumina,

(ii) blanc fixe,

(iii) gloss white,

(iv) clay,

(v) zinc oxide,

(vi) talc,

(vii) rosin,

(viii) aluminum benzoate,

(ix) calcium carbonate, or

(x) any combination of the substances listed in subparagraphs (i) to (ix).

(5) Subsections (1) and (2) do not apply in respect of a drug that is represented as being solely for use in the disinfection, for disease prevention, of

(a) medical devices;

(b) health care facilities; or

(c) premises in which food is manufactured, prepared or kept.

SOR/84-949, s. 1; SOR/86-590, s. 1(E); SOR/94-460, s. 1; SOR/95-431, s. 1; SOR/2002-369, s. 1; SOR/2005-95, s. 1.

Schedule F Drugs

C.01.041. (1) In this section and sections C.01.041.1 to C.01.046, "Schedule F Drug" means a drug listed or described in Schedule F to these Regulations.

(1.1) Subject to sections C.01.043 and C.01.046, no person shall sell a substance containing a Schedule F Drug unless

(a) the sale is made pursuant to a verbal or written prescription received by the seller; and

(b) where the prescription has been transferred to the seller under section C.01.041.1, the requirements of section C.01.041.2 have been complied with.

(2) Where the prescription for a Schedule F Drug is written, the person selling the drug shall retain the prescription for at least two years from the date of filling.

(3) Where the prescription for a Schedule F Drug is verbal, the person to whom the prescription is communicated by the practitioner shall forthwith reduce the prescription to writing and the person selling the drug shall retain that written prescription for a period of at least two years from the date of filling.

(4) The person reducing a verbal prescription to writing shall indicate on the written prescription

(a) the date and number of the prescription;

(b) the name and address of the person for whose benefit the prescription is given;

(c) the proper name, common name or brand name of the specified drug and the quantity thereof;

(d) his name and the name of the practitioner who issued the prescription; and

(e) the directions for use given with the prescription, including whether or not the practitioner authorized the refilling of the prescription and, if the prescription is to be refilled, the number of times it may be refilled.

(5) Subsections (1.1) to (4) do not apply to a substance containing

(a) chloral hydrate in preparations for external use, where it constitutes not more than one per cent of the substance, or

(b) hexachlorophene and its salts, where it constitutes not more than 0.75 per cent of the substance, calculated as hexachlorophene.

SOR/78-424, s. 2; SOR/80-543, s. 3; SOR/93-202, s. 6; SOR/93-407, s. 2.

C.01.041.1. A pharmacist may transfer to another pharmacist a prescription for a Schedule F Drug.

SOR/78-424, s. 3.

C.01.041.2. A pharmacist to whom a prescription has been transferred under section C.01.041.1 shall not sell a drug pursuant thereto until

(a) he has obtained from the pharmacist transferring the prescription his name and address, the number of authorized refills remaining and the date of the last refill; and

(b) he has

(i) received a copy of the prescription as written by the practitioner or as reduced to writing as required by subsections C.01.041(3) and (4), as the case may be, or

(ii) where the prescription has been transferred to him verbally, reduced the prescription to writing indicating therein the information specified in subsection C.01.041(4).

SOR/78-424, s. 3.

C.01.041.3. The pharmacist to whom a prescription for a Schedule F Drug is transferred under section C.01.041.1 shall retain in his files for a period of two years the information and documents referred to in section C.01.041.2.

SOR/78-424, s. 3.

C.01.041.4. A pharmacist who transfers a prescription under section C.01.041.1

(a) shall enter on the original of the prescription or in a suitable record of prescription kept under the name of each patient, the date of transfer; and

(b) shall not make any further sales under the prescription nor transfer it to another pharmacist.

SOR/78-424, s. 3.

C.01.042. (1) No person shall refill a prescription for a Schedule F Drug unless the practitioner so directs and no person shall refill such a prescription more times than the number of times prescribed by the practitioner.

(2) The person filling or refilling a prescription for a Schedule F Drug shall enter on the original of the prescription or in a suitable record of prescriptions kept under the name of each patient

(a) the date of filling;

(b) the date of each refill, if applicable;

(c) the quantity of drug dispensed at the original filling and each refill; and

(d) his name.

SOR/78-424, s. 4.

C.01.043. (1) A person may sell a Schedule F Drug, without having received a prescription therefor, to

(a) a drug manufacturer;

(b) a practitioner;

(c) a wholesale druggist;

(d) a registered pharmacist;

(e) a hospital certified by the Department of National Health and Welfare;

(f) a Department of the Government of Canada or of a province, upon receipt of a written order signed by the Minister thereof or his duly authorized representative; or

(g) any person upon receipt of a written order signed by the Director.

(2) Where a person makes a sale authorized by paragraph (1)(f) or (1)(g), he shall retain the written order for the drug for a period of at least two years from the date of filling the order.

C.01.044. (1) Where a person advertises to the general public a Schedule F Drug, the person shall not make any representation other than with respect to the brand name, proper name, common name, price and quantity of the drug.

(2) Subsection (1) does not apply where

(a) the drug is listed in Part II of Schedule F; and

(b) the drug is

(i)   in a form not suitable for human use, or

(ii) labelled in the manner prescribed by paragraph C.01.046(b).

SOR/78-424, s. 5; SOR/93-202, s. 7; SOR/93-407, s. 3.

C.01.045. (1) Subject to subsection (2), no person other than

(a) a practitioner,

(b) a drug manufacturer,

(c) a wholesale druggist,

(d) a registered pharmacist, or

(e) a resident of a foreign country while a visitor in Canada, shall import a Schedule F Drug.

(2) Any person may import a Schedule F Drug listed in Part II of Schedule F if the drug is imported in such form or so labelled that it could be sold by that person pursuant to section C.01.046.

SOR/93-407, s. 4.

C.01.046. A person may sell a drug listed or described in Part II of Schedule F to the Regulations, without having received a prescription therefor, if

(a) the drug is in a form not suitable for human use; or

(b) the principal display panel of both the inner label and the outer label carries, in both official languages, the statement "For Veterinary Use Only/Pour usage vétérinaire seulement" or "Veterinary Use Only/Usage vétérinaire seulement", immediately following or preceding the brand name, proper name or common name, in type size not less than one-half as large as the largest type on the label.

SOR/93-202, s. 8; SOR/93-407, s. 5; SOR/2001-181, s. 1(E).

C.01.047. [Repealed, SOR/80-543, s. 4]

C.01.048. (1) Where a person who is a physician, dentist, veterinary surgeon or pharmacist registered and entitled to practise that person's profession in a province has s gned an order specifying the brand name, proper name or common name and the quantity of a drug, other than

(a) a narcotic as defined in the Narcotic Control Regulations,

(b) a controlled drug as defined in subsection G.01.001(1), or

(c) a new drug in respect of which a notice of compliance has not been issued under section C.08.004, the person who receives the order may distribute the drug to the physician, dentist, veterinary surgeon or pharmacist as a sample if the drug is labelled in accordance with these Regulations.

(2) An order referred to in subsection (1) may provide that the order be repeated at specified intervals du ng any period not exceeding six months.

SOR/93-202, s. 9; SOR/97-228, s. 2.

C.01.049. A person who, under section C.01.048, distributes a drug as a sample shall

(a) maintain records showing

  (i) the name, address and description of each person to whom the drug is distributed,

  (ii) the brand name, quantity and form of the drug distributed, and

  (iii) the date upon which each such distribution was made; and

(b) keep those records and all orders received for drugs in accordance with section C.01.048 for a period of not less than two years from the date upon which the distribution referred to in the records was made.

SOR/93-202, s. 0.

Recalls

C.01.051. Where a manufacturer who sells a drug in dosage form or a person who imports into and sells in Canada a drug in dosage form commences a recall of the drug, the manufacturer or importer shall forthwith submit to the Director the following information:

(a) the proper name of the drug, the common name of the drug if there is no proper name, the brand name of the drug and the lot number;

(b) in the case of an imported drug, the names of the manufacturer and importer;

(c) the quantity of the drug manufactured or imported;

(d) the quantity of the drug distributed;

(e) the quantity of the drug remaining on the premises of the manufacturer or importer;

(f) the reasons for initiating the recall; and

(g) a description of any other action taken by the manufacturer or importer with respect to the recall.

SOR/82-524, s. 2; SOR/93-202, s. 11.

C.01.052. [Repealed, SOR/82-524, s. 2]

C.01.055. and **C.01.056.** [Repealed, SOR/82-524, s. 2]

Limits of Variability

C.01.061. (1) Where the net amount of a drug in a package is not expressed on the label in terms of number of dosage units, any 10 packages of the drug selected as provided by official method DO-31, Determination of Net Contents, dated December 7, 1988, shall contain an amount of the drug such that, when determined by that official method, the average of the net amounts of the drug in the 10 packages is not less than the net amount of the drug shown on the label.

(2) Where the net amount of a drug in a package is expressed on the label in terms of the number of dosage units, any 10 packages of the drug selected as provided by official method DO-31, Determination of Net Contents, dated December 7, 1988, shall contain a number of units such that, when determined by that official method,

(a) the average number of dosage units in the 10 packages is not less than the number of dosage units shown on the label;

(b) no package contains less than the number of dosage units shown on the label except as provided in the table; and

(c) where the drug is a controlled drug as defined in subsection G.01.001(1) or a narcotic as defined in the Narcotic Control Regulations, no package contains more than the number of dosage units shown on the label except as provided in the table to this section.

TABLE

Item	Column I Labelled Number of Dosage Units Per Package	Column II Permitted Variation from the Labelled Number
1.	50 or less	0
2.	More than 50, but less than 101	1
3.	101 or more	the greater of one unit or 0.75% of the labelled number, rounded up to the next whole number

SOR/82-429, s. 4; SOR/89-455, s. 4; SOR/97-228, s. 3.

C.01.062. (1) Subject to subsections (2) to (5), no manufacturer shall sell a drug in dosage form where the amount of any medicinal ingredient therein, determined using an acceptable method, is

(a) less than 90.0 per cent of the amount of the medicinal ingredient shown on the label; or

(b) more than 110.0 per cent of the amount of the medicinal ingredient shown on the label.

(2) Subject to subsection (5), where a drug in dosage form contains a medicinal ingredient that is a volatile substance of botanical origin or its synthetic equivalent, the amount of that ingredient, determined using an acceptable method, shall be

(a) not less than 85.0 per cent of the amount of the medicinal ingredient shown on the label; and

(b) not more than 120.0 per cent of the amount of the medicinal ingredient shown on the label.

(3) Subject to subsection (5), where a drug in capsule form contains a medicinal ingredient that is a vitamin in a fish-liver oil, no variation from the amount of the medicinal ingredient as shown on the label, determined using an acceptable method, is permitted other than that which is in accordance with the variation for that fish-liver oil as stated in any publication whose name is referred to in Schedule B to the Act.

(4) Subject to subsection (5), where a drug in dosage form contains a medicinal ingredient that is a vitamin, no variation from the amount of the medicinal ingredient shown on the label, determined using an acceptable method, is permitted other than the variation set out in column III or IV of an item of the table to this section opposite the vitamin set out in column I of that item for the amount of vitamin set out in column II of that item.

(5) Subsections (1) to (4) do not apply in respect of

(a) a drug for which a notice of compliance has been issued pursuant to section C.08.004;

(b) [Repealed, SOR/98-423, s. 8]

(c) a drug for which a standard is contained in any publication whose name is referred to in Schedule B to the Act;

(d) a drug described in Schedule C or D to the Act or Division 6 of Part C of these Regulations; or

(e) a drug for which a drug identification number has been assigned under subsection C.01.014.2(1) and in respect of which

(i) the conditions of pharmaceutical production and quality control are suitable for controlling the identity, quality, purity, stability, safety, strength and potency of the drug,

(ii) all labels, package inserts, product brochures and file cards to be used in connection with the drug make proper claims in respect of the drug,

(iii) the drug can, without undue foreseeable risk to humans, be used for the purposes and under the conditions of use recommended by the manufacturer, and

(iv) the drug is effective for the purposes and under the conditions of use recommended by the manufacturer.

TABLE

Item	Column I Vitamin	Column II Recommended daily dose	Column III Limits of variation when the recommended daily dose shown on label is equal to or less then amount set out in column II	Column IV Limits of variation when the recommended daily dose shown on label is greater than amount set out in column II
1.	vitamin A (or as B-carotene)	10 000 I.U.	90.0 - 165.0 %	90.0 - 115.0 %
2.	thiamine	4.5 mg	90.0 - 145.0 %	90.0 - 125.0 %
3.	riboflavin	7.5 mg	90.0 - 125.0 %	90.0 - 125.0 %
4.	niacin or niacinamide	45 mg	90.0 - 125.0 %	90.0 - 125.0 %
5.	pyridoxine	3 mg	90.0 - 125.0 %	90.0 - 125.0 %
6.	d-pantothenic acid	15 mg	90.0 - 135.0 %	90.0 - 125.0 %
7.	folic acid	0.4 mg	90.0 - 135.0 %	90.0 - 115.0 %
8.	vitamin B_{12}	14 µg	90.0 - 135.0 %	90.0 - 125.0 %
9.	vitamin C	150 I.U.	90.0 - 145.0 %	90.0 - 125.0 %
10.	vitamin D	400 I.U.	90.0 - 145.0 %	90.0 - 115.0 %
11.	vitamin E	25 I.U.	90.0 - 125.0 %	90.0 - 125.0 %
12.	vitamin K	0.0 mg		90.0 - 115.0 %
13.	biotin	0.0 mg		90.0 - 135.0 %

SOR/92-131, s. 1; SOR/92-591, s. 2; SOR/94-689, s. 2(E); SOR/95-530, s. 2; SOR/98-423, s. 8.

C.01.063. [Repealed, SOR/96-399, s. 2]

C.01.064. Where a drug is prepared for ophthalmic or parenteral use and contains a preservative ingredient, that ingredient

(a) shall be present only in an amount necessary to obtain the intended action and that does not pose undue risk to humans or animals; and

(b) shall not interfere with the therapeutic properties of the drug.

SOR/90-586, s. 2.

C.01.065. No person shall sell a drug that is prepared for ophthalmic or parenteral use unless a representative sample of each lot of the drug in its immediate container

(a) is tested by an acceptable method for identity, and the drug is found to be true to its proper name, or to its common name if there is no proper name;

(b) is tested by an acceptable method for sterility, except

   (i) for living vaccines, or

   (ii) where the manufacturer has submitted evidence, satisfactory to the Director to prove that processing controls ensure the sterility of the drug in its immediate container, and the drug is found to be sterile; and

(c) is subjected to such further tests satisfactory to the Director to ensure that the drug is safe to use according to directions.

SOR/86-552, s. 1; SOR/90-586, s. 3; SOR/93-202, s. 12; SOR/96-399, s. 3.

C.01.066. No person shall sell a drug in aqueous solution that is prepared for parenteral use unless it has been prepared with non-pyrogenic water produced by distillation or reverse osmosis.

C.01.067. (1) Subject to subsection (2), no person shall sell a drug that is prepared for parenteral use unless a representative sample of each lot of the drug in its immediate container

(a) is tested by an acceptable method for the presence of pyrogens; and

(b) when so tested, is found to be non-pyrogenic.

(2) Subsection (1) does not apply in respect of a drug that cannot be tested for the presence of pyrogens or that is inherently pyrogenic.

SOR/81-335, s. 1; SOR/96-399, s. 4.

C.01.068. Detailed records of the tests required by sections C.01.065 and C.01.067 shall be retained by the manufacturer for a period of at least one year after the expiration date on the label of the drug.

SOR/85-715, s. 5; SOR/92-654, s. 3.

C.01.069. The packaging of a drug that is prepared for parenteral use shall meet the following requirements:

(a) the immediate container shall be of such material and construction that

   (i) no deleterious substance is yielded to the drug,

   (ii) it is non-reactive with the drug,

   (iii) visual or electronic inspection of the drug is possible,

   (iv) protection against environmental factors that cause deterioration or contamination of the drug is provided or, where that protection cannot be provided by the immediate container, it is provided by the secondary packaging, and

   (v) a sufficient quantity of the drug is contained to allow withdrawal of the labelled amount of the drug; and

**Part C:
Drugs, Division 1**

(b) the immediate closures and any material coming into contact with the drug in its immediate container shall meet the requirements of subparagraphs (a)(i) and (ii).

SOR/96-399, s. 5.

C.01.070. No person shall sell a drug that is a hypodermic tablet that does not completely dissolve in and form a clear solution with water.

Mercuric Chloride Tablets

C.01.071. No person shall sell mercuric chloride tablets for household use that are packaged in lots of 200 or less, unless

(a) such tablets are

  (i) of an irregular or angular shape,

  (ii) coloured blue, and

  (iii) packed in an immediate container that is readily distinguishable by touch; and

(b) the principal display panel of both the inner and the outer labels carries in prominent type and in a colour contrasting to that of such labels

  (i) the design of a skull and cross-bones, and

  (ii) the word "Poison".

SOR/2001-181, s. 2.

C.01.081. [Repealed, SOR/80-544, s. 4]

C.01.085. [Repealed, SOR/80-544, s. 5]

Synthetic Sweeteners

C.01.101. (1) [Repealed, SOR/78-422, s. 3]

(2) [Repealed, SOR/78-800, s. 1]

(3) [Repealed, SOR/78-422, s. 3]

C.01.121. and **C.01.122.** [Repealed, SOR/80-544, s. 6]

Aminopyrine and Dipyrone

C.01.131. No person shall sell Aminopyrine or Dipyrone (a derivative of Aminopyrine) for oral or parenteral use, unless

(a) the inner label carries the statement:

  "WARNING: Fatal agranulocytosis may be associated with the use of Aminopyrine and Dipyrone. It is essential that adequate blood studies be made. (See enclosed warnings and precautions)"; and

(b) the outer label or the package insert carries the following statements:

"WARNING: Serious and even fatal agranulocytosis is known to occur after the administration of Aminopyrine or Dipyrone. Fatal agranulocytosis has occurred after short term, intermittent and prolonged therapy with the drugs. Therefore, the use of these drugs should be as brief as possible. Bearing in mind the possibility that such reactions may occur, Aminopyrine or Dipyrone should be used only when other less potentially dangerous agents are ineffective.

PRECAUTIONS: It is essential that frequent white blood cell counts and differential counts be made during treatment with these drugs. However, it is emphasized that agranulocytosis may occur suddenly without prior warning. The drug should be discontinued at the first evidence of any alteration of the blood count or sign of agranulocytosis, and the patient should be instructed to discontinue use of the drug at the first indication of sore throat or sign of other infection in the mouth or throat (pain, swelling, tenderness, ulceration)."

C.01.132. No person shall disseminate to a practitioner promotional literature about Aminopyrine or Dipyrone unless the statements set out in section C.01.131 are included in such literature.

C.01.133. The provisions of sections C.01.131 and C.01.132 do not apply to preparations containing Aminopyrine or Dipyrone that are

(a) dispensed by a pharmacist pursuant to a prescription; or

(b) sold for veterinary use only.

Coated Potassium Salts

C.01.134. No person shall sell coated tablets containing potassium salts, with or without thiazide diuretics unless the inner label thereof or the package insert carries the following statement:

"WARNING: A probable association exists between the use of coated tablets containing potassium salts, with or without thiazide diuretics, and the incidence of serious small bowel ulceration. Such preparations should be used only when adequate dietary supplementation is not practical, and should be discontinued if abdominal pain, distension, nausea, vomiting or gastro-intestinal bleeding occur."

C.01.135. No person shall disseminate to a practitioner promotional literature about coated tablets containing potassium salts, with or without thiazide diuretics, unless the statement set out in section C.01.134 is included in such literature.

C.01.136. The provisions of sections C.01.134 and C.01.135 do not apply to coated tablets containing potassium salts with or without thiazide diuretics that

(a) are sold for veterinary use only;

(b) are dispensed by a pharmacist pursuant to a prescription; or

(c) contain 100 milligrams or less of elemental potassium per tablet.

Antibiotics

C.01.401. Except as provided in these Regulations, an antibiotic for other than parenteral use shall, in addition to meeting the requirements of section C.01.004, carry on both the inner label and outer label the potency of the drug, expressed in terms of International Units where established or, if no International Unit has been established, in terms of units, milligrams, micrograms or fractions of a gram,

(a) per gram in the case of solids or viscous liquids;

(b) per millilitre in the case of other liquids; and

(c) per individual dosage or dispensing form in the case of antibiotic preparations put up in individual dosage or dispensing form.

SOR/80-544, s. 7; SOR/92-654, s. 4.

C.01.402. [Repealed, SOR/92-654, s. 4]

C.01.410. to **C.01.412.** [Repealed, SOR/80-544, s. 8]

C.01.420. to **C.01.422.** [Repealed, SOR/80-544, s. 8]

Chloramphenicol

C.01.430. to **C.01.432.** [Repealed, SOR/80-544, s. 8]

C.01.433. No person shall sell chloramphenicol and its salts and derivatives, for oral or parenteral use, unless

(a) the inner label carries a warning statement to the effect that

(i) bone marrow depression has been associated with the use of chloramphenicol, and

(ii) the enclosed warnings and precautions should be read carefully; and

(b) the outer label or the package insert carries the following:

(i) a warning statement to the effect that chloramphenicol should not be used in the treatment or prophylaxis of minor infections or where it is not indicated, as in cold, influenza, or infections of the upper respiratory tract; that there are two types of bone marrow depression associated with the use of chloramphenicol; that some degree of depression of the bone marrow is commonly seen during therapy, is dose-related and is potentially reversible; that blood studies may detect early changes and; that the other type of bone marrow depression, a sudden, delayed and usually fatal bone marrow hypoplasia that may occur without warning, is very rare, and

(ii) a statement of precautions to be taken to the effect that it is essential that appropriate blood studies be made during treatment with chloramphenicol and that while blood studies may detect early peripheral blood changes, such studies cannot be relied on to detect the rare and generally irreversible bone marrow depression prior to development of aplastic anemia.

C.01.434. The provisions of section C.01.433 do not apply to chloramphenicol and its salts or derivatives sold by a registered pharmacist.

C.01.435. No person shall disseminate to a practitioner promotional literature about chloramphenicol and its salts or derivatives for oral or parenteral use unless the statements set out in paragraph C.01.433(b) are included in such literature.

C.01.436. The provisions of sections C.01.433 and C.01.435 do not apply to a drug sold solely for veterinary use.

C.01.440. to **C.01.442.** [Repealed, SOR/80-544, s. 8]

C.01.450. to **C.01.452.** [Repealed, SOR/80-544, s. 8]

C.01.460. to **C.01.462.** [Repealed, SOR/80-544, s. 8]

C.01.470. to **C.01.472.** [Repealed, SOR/80-544, s. 8]

C.01.480. [Repealed, SOR/80-544, s. 8]

C.01.490. to **C.01.497.** [Repealed, SOR/80-544, s. 8]

C.01.510. to **C.01.513.** [Repealed, SOR/80-544, s. 8]

C.01.520. to **C.01.522.** [Repealed, SOR/80-544, s. 8]

C.01.530. to **C.01.532.** [Repealed, SOR/80-544, s. 8]

C.01.540. to **C.01.542.** [Repealed, SOR/80-544, s. 8]

C.01.550. to **C.01.552.** [Repealed, SOR/80-544, s. 8]

C.01.560. to **C.01.563.** [Repealed, SOR/80-544, s. 8]

C.01.570. to **C.01.572.** [Repealed, SOR/80-544, s. 8]

C.01.580. [Repealed, SOR/80-544, s. 8]

C.01.590. to **C.01.592.** [Repealed, SOR/80-544, s. 8]

Veterinary Drugs

C.01.600. No person shall sell for veterinary use a drug listed in the Table of Limits of Drug Dosage for Adults, other than a drug in a form not suitable for human use, unless both the inner and outer labels carry the statement "For Veterinary Use Only" or "Veterinary Use Only".

SOR/80-543, s. 5.

C.01.601. [Repealed, SOR/93-407, s. 6]

C.01.602. The provisions of sections C.01.401 and C.01.402 do not apply to an antibiotic in amounts less than 50 parts per million contained in an animal food.

C.01.603. The provisions of paragraphs C.01.401 (b) and (c) and section C.01.402 do not apply to an antibiotic in amounts greater than 50 parts per million contained in an animal food.

C.01.604. Both the inner and outer labels of a veterinary drug represented as containing a vitamin shall carry

(a) a statement of the amount of each vitamin present in the drug, expressed in terms of the proper name only of the vitamin in

   (i) International Units per gram or per millilitre for vitamin A, provitamin A, vitamin D, and vitamin E,

   (ii) milligrams per gram in the case of solids or viscous liquids, or per millilitre in the case of other liquids, for thiamine, riboflavin, niacin, niacinamide, pyridoxine, d-pantothenic acid, d-panthenol, folic acid, ascorbic acid, and vitamin K,

(iii) micrograms per gram in the case of solids or viscous liquids, or per millilitre in the case of other liquids, for biotin, and vitamin B12,

(iv) Oral Units for vitamin B12 with intrinsic factor concentrate, or

(v) for vitamin products put up in individual dosage or dispensing form, the specified units per individual dosage or dispensing form;

(b) except for drugs in a form not suitable for human use, the statement "For Veterinary Use Only" or "Veterinary Use Only".

SOR/80-543, s. 6.

C.01.605. An antibiotic for parenteral use that is recommended for veterinary use only shall carry on both the inner and outer labels

(a) the potency of the drug expressed in terms of International Units where established, or, if no International Unit has been established, in terms of units, milligrams or fractions of a gram, per gram in the case of solids or viscous liquids, per millilitre in the case of other liquids, or per individual dosage or dispensing form for antibiotic preparations put up in individual dosage or dispensing form; and

(b) [Repealed, SOR/92-654, s. 5]

(c) the statement "For Veterinary Use Only" or "Veterinary Use Only".

SOR/80-543, s. 7; SOR/92-654, s. 5.

C.01.606. No person shall sell an antibiotic preparation for the treatment of animals, other than an antibiotic preparation that is a new drug sold pursuant to section C.08.013, unless,

(a) where the preparation is not to be used for lactating animals providing milk to be consumed as food, the inner and outer labels of the preparation carry a statement to that effect; or

(b) where the preparation may be used for lactating animals providing milk to be consumed as food,

(i) there has been submitted, on request, to the Director, acceptable evidence to show the period of time, not exceeding 96 hours, that must elapse after the last treatment with the preparation in order that the milk from treated lactating animals will contain no residue of antibiotics that would cause injury to human health, and

(ii) the principal display panel of the outer label of the preparation, the inner label and the packaging insert, if any, describing the antibiotic preparation carry the warning "WARNING: MILK TAKEN FROM TREATED ANIMALS DURING TREATMENT AND WITHIN ... HOURS AFTER THE LATEST TREATMENT MUST NOT BE USED AS FOOD", where the number of hours to be inserted is determined according to evidence submitted pursuant to subparagraph (i).

SOR/88-378, s. 1; SOR/92-364, s. 2; SOR/93-467, s. 1.

C.01.606.1. No person shall sell a product intended for the prevention or treatment of foot rot of cattle if that product contains Ethylenediamine Dihydroiodide (EDDI).

SOR/90-327, s. 1.

C.01.607. Notwithstanding subparagraph C.01.004(1)(c)(ii), the declaration of a lot number is not required on the label of an animal feeding-stuff containing a drug.

SOR/80-543, s. 8.

C.01.608. The provisions of section C.01.604 do not apply to medicated feeds registered under the Feeds Act.

C.01.609. Notwithstanding the provisions of section C.01.401(a), the potency of an antibiotic in in amounts greater than 50 parts per million contained in a medicated feed registered under the Feeds Act may be declared in grams per ton.

C.01.610. No person shall sell any substance having oestrogenic activity for administration to poultry that may be consumed as food.

C.01.610.1 No person shall sell a drug for administration to animals that produce food or that are intended for consumption as food if that drug contains

(a) chloramphenicol or its salts or derivatives;

(b) a 5-nitrofuran compound;

(c) clenbuterol or its salts or derivatives;

(d) a 5-nitroimidazole compound; or

(e) diethylstilbestrol or other stilbene compounds.

SOR/85-539, s. 1; SOR/85-685, s. 2; SOR/91-546, s. 1; SOR/94-568, s. 2; SOR/97-510, s. 2; SOR/2003-292, s. 3.

C.01.610.2 No person shall sell an antibiotic preparation containing chloramphenicol, its salts or derivatives, for administration to animals that do not produce food and that are not intended for consumption as food unless

(a) both the inner label and outer label of the preparation carry the words

> "WARNING: FEDERAL LAW PROHIBITS THE ADMINISTRATION OF THIS PREPARATION TO ANIMALS THAT PRODUCE FOOD OR ANIMALS THAT ARE INTENDED FOR CONSUMPTION AS FOOD/MISE EN GARDE : EN VERTU DES LOIS FÉDÉRALES, IL EST INTERDIT D'ADMINISTRER CETTE PRÉPARATION AUX ANIMAUX QUI PRODUISENT DES ALIMENTS OU AUX ANIMAUX DESTINÉS À ÊTRE CONSOMMÉS COMME ALIMENTS";

**Part C:
Drugs, Division 1**

(b) where the preparation is for parenteral use, the preparation contains, in the form of chloramphenicol sodium succinate, not more than one gram of chloramphenicol per vial;

(c) where the preparation is for ophthalmic use, the preparation contains not more than one per cent chloramphenicol; and

(d) where the preparation is for oral use, the preparation

   (i) is in tablet or capsule form and contains not more than one gram of chloramphenicol per tablet or capsule, or

   (ii) is in the form of a chloramphenicol palmitate suspension and contains not more than three grams of chloramphenicol per container.

SOR/91-546, s. 1.

C.01.611. (1) The Director may, in writing, from time to time require the manufacturer of a drug recommended for administration to animals that may be consumed as food

(a) to file with him in respect of that drug a submission, in form and content satisfactory to the Director, describing in detail tests carried out to determine that no residues of the drug, except residues within the limits prescribed by these Regulations, remain in meat, meat by-products, eggs or milk; and

(b) to print on the principal display panel of the outer label, the inner label and the packaging insert, if any, that describes the drug, a warning that meat, meat by-products, eggs or milk from animals to which the drug has been administered cannot be sold for consumption as food unless there has elapsed since the administration of the drug a period of time specified by the Director, based on a review of the available data with respect to drug residue.

(2) No manufacturer shall sell a drug in respect of which the Director has required a warning to be printed pursuant to paragraph (1)(b) unless the manufacturer has complied with that request.

SOR/93-467, s. 2.

C.01.612. [Repealed, SOR/94-568, s. 3]

Contraceptive Drugs

C.01.625. Contraceptive drugs that are manufactured, sold or represented for use in the prevention of conception and that are not listed in Schedule F may be advertised to the general public.

Division 1A:
Establishment Licences

Regulations Respecting Food and Drugs (C.R.C., c. 870)

Enabling Statute: Food and Drugs Act

Regulation current to February 10th, 2010

Attention: See coming into force provision and notes, where applicable.

Division 1A
Establishment Licenses[14]

Interpretation

C.01A.001.   (1) The definitions in this subsection apply in this Division and in Divisions 2 to 4.

"antimicrobial agent" means a drug that is capable of destroying pathogenic micro-organisms and that is labelled as being for use in the disinfection of environmental surfaces or medical devices, as defined in the Medical Devices Regulations, that

(a) are not invasive devices as defined in those Regulations; and

(b) are intended to come into contact with intact skin only. (agent antimicrobien)

"batch certificate" means a certificate issued by the fabricator of a lot or batch of a drug that is exported within the framework of a mutual recognition agreement and in which the fabricator

(a) identifies the master production document for the drug and certifies that the lot or batch has been fabricated, packaged/labelled and tested in accordance with the procedures described in that document;

(b) provides a detailed description of the drug, including

(i)   a statement of all properties and qualities of the drug, including the identity, potency and purity of the drug, and

(ii) a statement of tolerances for the properties and qualities of the drug;

---

[14] Available on the Depratment of Justice website at http://laws.justice.gc.ca/eng/C.R.C.-C.870/FramesView.html

(c) identifies the analytical methods used in testing the lot or batch and provides details of the analytical results obtained;

(d) sets out the addresses of the buildings at which the lot or batch was fabricated, packaged/labelled and tested; and

(e) certifies that the lot or batch was fabricated, packaged/labelled and tested in accordance with the good manufacturing practices of the regulatory authority that has recognized those buildings as meeting its good manufacturing practices standards. (certificat de lot)

"class monograph" means a document prepared by the Department of Health that

(a) lists the types and strengths of medicinal ingredients that may be contained in drugs of a specified class; and

(b) sets out labelling and other requirements that apply to those drugs. (monographie de classe)

"dilute drug premix" means a drug for veterinary use that results from mixing a drug premix with a feed as defined in section 2 of the Feeds Act, to such a level that at least 10 kg of the resulting mixture is required to medicate one tonne of complete feed, as defined in section 2 of the Feeds Regulations, 1983, with the lowest approved dosage level of the drug. (prémélange médicamenteux dilué)

"dosage form class" means a parenteral, tablet, capsule, solution, suspension, aerosol, powder, suppository, medical gas or drug premix, or any other dosage form class designated by the Minister. (classe de forme posologique)

"drug premix" means a drug for veterinary use to which a drug identification number has been assigned, where the directions on its label specify that it is to be mixed with feed as defined in section 2 of the Feeds Act. (prémélange médicamenteux)

"fabricate" means to prepare and preserve a drug for the purposes of sale. (manufacturer)

"import" means to import into Canada a drug for the purpose of sale. (importer)

"MRA country" means a country that is a participant in a mutual recognition agreement with Canada. (pays participant)

"mutual recognition agreement" means an international agreement that provides for the mutual recognition of compliance certification for good manufacturing practices for drugs. (accord de reconnaisance mutuelle)

"package/label" means to put a drug in its immediate container or to affix the inner or outer label to the drug. (emballer-étiqueter) "pharmaceutical" means a drug other than a drug listed in Schedule C or D to the Act. (produit pharmaceutique)

"recognized building" means, in respect of the fabrication, packaging/labelling or testing of a drug, a building that a regulatory authority that is designated under subsection C.01A.019(1) in respect of that activity for that drug has recognized as meeting its good manufacturing practices standards in respect of that activity for that drug. (bâtiment reconnu)

"regulatory authority" means a government agency or other entity in an MRA country that has a legal right to control the use or sale of drugs within that country and that may take enforcement action to ensure that drugs marketed within its jurisdiction comply with legal requirements. (autorité réglementaire)

"site" [Repealed, SOR/2002-368, s. 1]

"wholesale" means to sell any of the following drugs, other than at retail sale, where the seller's name does not appear on the label of the drugs:

(a) a drug listed in Schedule C or D to the Act or in Schedule F to these Regulations or a controlled drug as defined in subsection G.01.001(1) or

(b) a narcotic as defined in the Narcotic Control Regulations. (vendre en gros)

(2) In this Division and in Division 2, "drug" means a drug in dosage form, or a drug that is a bulk process intermediate that can be used in the preparation of a drug listed in Schedule C to the Act or in Schedule D to the Act that is of biological origin. It does not include a dilute drug premix, a medicated feed as defined section 2 of the Feeds Regulations, 1983, a drug that is used only for the purposes of an experimental study in accordance with a certificate issued under section C.08.015 or a drug listed in Schedule H to the Act.

(3) Where the Minister designates additional dosage form classes, the Minister shall make a list of those classes available on request.

SOR/97-12, s. 5; SOR/98-7 s. 1; SOR/2000-120, s. 1; SOR/2002-368, s. 1; SOR/2004-282, S. 1.

Application

C.01A.002. (1) This Division does not apply to

(a) wholesaling a drug premix;

(b) importing or compounding, pursuant to a prescription, a drug that is not commercial y available in Canada by one of the following persons, namely,

(i) a pharmacist,

(ii) a practitioner, and

Division 1A:
Establishment Licenses

      (iii) a person who compounds a drug under the supervision of a practitioner;

(c) any activity with respect to a drug that is used only for the purposes of clinical testing in accordance with subsection C.05.006(1) or section C.08.005,

(d) fabricating, packaging/labelling, testing as required under Division 2, distributing as a distributer referred to in section C.01A.003, wholesaling or importing any of the following drugs for which prescriptions are not required and that are for human use in dosage form and not represented as a treatment, preventative or cure for any of the diseases, disorders or abnormal physical states set out in Schedule A to the Act, namely,

      (i) homeopathic drugs,

      (ii) drugs that meet the requirements of a class monograph entitled "Vitamin Supplements", "Mineral Supplements", "Dietary Vitamin Supplements" or "Dietary Mineral Supplements", as the case may be, and

      (iii) drugs that

            (A) contain a plant, mineral or animal substance in respect of which therapeutic activity or disease prevention activity is claimed, including traditional herbal medicines, traditional Chinese medicines, ayurvedic (East Indian) medicines and traditional aboriginal (North American) medicines, and

            (B) the medical use of which is based solely on historical and ethnological evidence from references relating to a medical system other than one based on conventional scientific standards; and

(e) fabricating, packaging/labelling, testing, distributing, and importing of antimicrobial agents.

(2) This Division and Divisions 2 to 4 do not apply to the affixing of a label to a previously labelled container.

SOR/97-12, s. 5; SOR/98-7, s. 2; SOR/2001/-203, s. 1; SOR/2004-282, s. 2.

C.01A.003. This Division and Divisions 2 to 4 apply to the following distributors:

(a) a distributor of a drug listed in Schedule C or D to the Act or in Schedule F to these Regulations, a controlled drug as defined in subsection G.01.001(1) or a narcotic as defined in the Narcotic Control Regulations, who does not hold the drug identification number for the drug or narcotic; and

(b) a distributor of a drug for which that distributor holds the drug identification number.

SOR/97-12, s. 5; SOR/2002-368, s. 2.

Prohibition

C.01A.004. (1) Subject to subsection (2), no person shall, except in accordance with an establishment licence,

(a) fabricate, package/label, distribute as set out in section C.01A.003, import or wholesale a drug; or

(b) perform the tests, including examinations, required under Division 2.

(2) A person does not require an establishment licence to perform tests under Division 2 if the person holds an establishment licence as a fabricator, a packager/labeller, a distributor referred to in paragraph C.01A.003(b) or an importer.

(3) No person shall carry on an activity referred to in subsection (1) in respect of a narcotic as defined in the Narcotic Control Regulations or a controlled drug as defined in subsection G.01.001(1) unless the person holds a licence for that narcotic or drug under the Narcotic Control Regulations or Part G of these Regulations, as the case may be.

SOR/97-12, s. 5; SOR/2002-368, s. 3.

Application for Establishment Licence

C.01A.005. Subject to section C.01A.006, a person who wishes to apply for an establishment licence shall submit an application to the Minister, in a form established by the Minister, that contains the following information:

(a) the applicant's name, address and telephone number, and their facsimile number and electronic mail address, if any;

(b) the name and telephone number, and the facsimile number and electronic mail address, if any, of a person to contact in case of an emergency;

(c) each activity set out in Table I to section C.01A.008 for which the licence is requested;

(d) each category of drugs set out in Table II to section C.01A.008 for which the licence is requested;

(e) each dosage form class in respect of which the applicant proposes to carry out a licensed activity, and whether it will be in a sterile dosage form;

(f) whether the applicant proposes to carry out a licensed activity in respect of a drug that is a bulk process intermediate;

(g) the address of each building in Canada in which the applicant proposes to fabricate, package/label, test as required under Division 2 or store drugs, specifying for each building which of those activities and for which category of drugs and, for each category,

(i) the dosage form classes, and whether any drugs will be in a sterile dosage form, and

(ii) whether any drugs will be bulk process intermediates;

(h) the address of each building in Canada at which records will be maintained;

(i) whether any building referred to in paragraphs (g) and (h) is a dwelling-house;

(j) the drug identification number, if any, or a name that clearly identifies the drug,

    (i) for each narcotic as defined in the Narcotic Control Regulations or each controlled drug as defined in subsection G.01.001(1) for which the licence is requested, and

    (ii) for each other drug within a category of drugs for which the licence is requested, unless the licence is to perform tests required under Division 2, distribute as set out in paragraph C.01A.003(a), or wholesale;

(k) if any of the buildings referred to in paragraph (g) have been inspected under the Act or these Regulations, the date of the last inspection;

(l) evidence that the applicant's buildings, equipment and proposed practices and procedures meet the applicable requirements of Divisions 2 to 4;

(m) in the case of an importer of a drug that is fabricated, packaged/labelled or tested in an MRA country at a recognized building,

    (i) the name and address of each fabricator, packager/labeller and tester of the drug and the address of each building at which the drug is fabricated, packaged/labelled or tested, specifying for each building the activities and the category of drug and

        (A) the dosage form class and whether the drug is in a sterile dosage form, and

        (B) whether the drug is a bulk process intermediate,

    (ii) in respect of each activity done in an MRA country at a recognized building, the name of the regulatory authority that is designated under subsection C.01A.019(1) in respect of that activity for that drug and that has recognized that building as meeting its good manufacturing practices standards in respect of that activity for that drug, and

    (iii) in respect of any other activities,

        (A) a certificate from a Canadian inspector indicating that the fabricator's, packager/labeller's or tester's buildings, equipment, practices and procedures meet the applicable requirements of Divisions 2 to 4, or

        (B) other evidence establishing that the fabricator's, packager/labeller's or tester's buildings, equipment, practices and procedures meet the applicable requirements of Divisions 2 to 4;

(n) in the case of any other importer, the name and address of each fabricator, packager/labeller and tester of the drugs proposed to be imported and the address of each building at which the drugs will be fabricated, packaged/ abelled and tested, specifying for each building which of those activities and for which category of drugs and, for each category,

(i) the dosage form classes and whether any drugs will be in a sterile dosage form, and

(ii) whether any drugs will be bulk process intermediates; and

(o) in the case of an importer referred to in paragraph (n),

(i) a certificate from a Canadian inspector indicating that the fabricator's, packager/labeller's and tester's buildings, equipment, practices and procedures meet the applicable requirements of Divisions 2 to 4, or

(ii) other evidence establishing that the fabricator's, packager/labeller's and tester's buildings, equipment, practices and procedures meet the applicable requirements of Divisions 2 to 4.

SOR/97-12, s. 5; SOR/2000-120, s. 2; SOR/2002-368, s. 4.

C.01A.006. (1) A person who wishes to amend an establishment licence shall submit an application to the Minister, in a form established by the Minister, that contains the applicable information specified in section C.01A.005.

(2) An establishment licence must be amended where the licensee proposes

(a) to add an activity or category of drugs, as set out in the tables to section C.01A.008

(b) in respect of a category of drugs and activity indicated in the licence, to authorize sterile dosage forms of the category;

(c) to add any building in Canada at which drugs are authorized to be fabricated, packaged/labelled, tested as required under Division 2 or stored, or to add, for an existing building, an authorization to fabricate, package/label, test or store a category of drugs, or sterile dosage forms of the category; and

(d) in addition to the matters set out in paragraphs (a) to (c), in the case of an importer,

(i) to add a fabricator, packager/labeller or tester of a drug,

(ii) to amend the name or address of a fabricator, packager/labeller or tester indicated in the licence, and

(iii) if the address of the buildings at which drugs are authorized to be fabricated, packaged/labelled or tested is indicated in the licence, to add additional buildings or, for an existing building, to add an authorization to fabricate, package/label or test a category of drugs, or sterile dosage forms of the category.

SOR/97-12, s. 5.

C.01A.007. (1) The Minister may, on receipt of an application for an establishment licence or an amended establishment licence, require the

Division 1A:
Establishment Licenses

submission of further details pertaining to the information contained in the application that are necessary to enable the Minister to process the application.

(2) When considering an application for an establishment licence or an amended establishment licence, the Minister may require that

(a) an inspection be made during normal business hours of any building referred to in paragraph C.01A.005(1)(g) or (h); and

(b) the applicant, if a fabricator, a packager/labeller, a person who performs tests required under Division 2, a distributor referred to in paragraph C.01A.003(b) or an importer, supply samples of any material to be used in the fabrication, packaging/labelling or testing of a drug.

SOR/97-12, s. 5.

Issuance

C.01A.008. (1) Subject to section C.01A.010, the Minister shall, on receipt of the information and material required by sections C.01A.005 to C.01A.007, issue or amend an establishment licence.

(2) The establishment licence shall indicate

(a) each activity that is authorized and the category of drugs for which each activity is authorized, as set out in the tables to this section, specifying for each activity and category whether sterile dosage forms are authorized;

(b) the address of each building in Canada at which a category of drugs is authorized to be fabricated, packaged/labelled, tested as required under Division 2 or stored, specifying for each building which of those activities and for which category of drugs, and whether sterile dosage forms of the category are authorized; and

(c) in addition to the matters referred to in paragraphs (a) and (b), in the case of an importer,

(i) the name and address of each fabricator, packager/labeller and tester from whom the importer is authorized to obtain the drug for import, and

(ii) the address of each building at which the drug is authorized to be fabricated, packaged/labelled or tested, specifying for each building the activities and the category of drugs that are authorized, and whether sterile dosage forms are authorized.

(d) [Repealed, SOR/2002-368, s. 5]

(3) The Minister may indicate in an establishment licence a period for which records shall be retained under Division 2 that, based on the safety profile of the drug or materials, is sufficient to ensure the health of the consumer.

(4) The Minister may, in addition to the requirements of subsection (2), set out in an establishment licence terms and conditions respecting

(a) the tests to be performed in respect of a drug, and the equipment to be used, to ensure that the drug is not unsafe for use; and

(b) any other matters necessary to prevent injury to the health of consumers, including conditions under which drugs are fabricated, packaged/labelled or tested.

TABLE I

Item	Activities
1.	Fabricate
2.	Package/label
3.	Perform the tests, including any examinations, required under Division 2
4.	Distribute as set out in paragraph C.01A.003(*a*)
5.	Distribute as set out in paragraph C.01A.003(*b*)
6.	Import
7.	Wholesale

TABLE II

Item	Categories of drugs
1.	Pharmaceuticals
2.	Vaccines
3.	Whole blood and its components
4.	Drugs listed in Schedule D to the Act, other than vaccines or whole blood and its components
5.	Drugs listed in Schedule C to the Act
6.	Drugs listed in Schedule F to these Regulations, controlled drugs as defined in subsection G.01.001(1) and narcotics as defined in the *Narcotic Control Regulations*

SOR/97-12, s. 5; SOR/2000-120, s. 3; SOR/2002-368, s. 5.

C.01A.009. An establishment licence expires on December 31 of each year.

SOR/97-12, s. 5; SOR/97-298, s. 1.

Refusal to Issue

C.01A.010. (1) The Minister may refuse to issue or amend an establishment licence in respect of any or all matters indicated in subsection C.01A.008(2) if

(a) the applicant has made a false or misleading statement in relation to the application for the licence; or

(b) the applicant has had an establishment licence suspended in respect of the matter.

Division 1A:
Establishment Licenses

(2) The Minister shall refuse to issue or amend an establishment licence in respect of any or all matters indicated in subsection C.01A.008(2) if the Minister has reasonable grounds to believe that issuing or amending an establishment licence in respect of the matter would constitute a risk to the health of the consumer.

(3) Where the Minister refuses to issue or amend an establishment licence, the Minister shall

(a) notify the applicant in writing of the reasons for the refusal; and

(b) give the applicant an opportunity to be heard.

SOR/97-12, s. 5.

Terms and Conditions

C.01A.011. (1) Every person who holds an establishment licence shall comply with

(a) the requirements and the terms and conditions of the establishment licence; and

(b) the applicable requirements of Divisions 2 to 4.

(2) [Repealed, SOR/2000-120, s. 4]

SOR/97-12, s. 5; SOR/2000-120, s. 4.

C.01A.012. (1) The Minister may amend the terms and conditions of an establishment licence if the Minister believes on reasonable grounds that an amendment is necessary to prevent injury to the health of the consumer.

(2) The Minister shall give at least 15 days notice in writing to the holder of the establishment licence of the proposed amendment, the reasons for the amendment and its effective date.

SOR/97-12, s. 5.

Notification

C.01A.013. Every person who holds an establishment licence shall notify the Minister in writing within 15 days after

(a) there is any change to the information referred to in any of paragraphs C.01A.005(a),(b),(e),(f),(h) and (i), and subparagraphs C.01A.005(g)(i) and (ii); or

(b) an event occurs that results in their being in contravention of any of the applicable requirements of Divisions 2 to 4, where it may affect the quality, safety or efficacy of a drug fabricated, packaged/labelled, tested as required under Division 2 or stored by them.

SOR/97-12, s. 5.

C.01A.014. (1) No licensee shall carry on a licensed activity in respect of any category of drugs if a change referred to in subsection (2) has occurred in respect of that category unless

(a) they have filed with the Minister a notice that contains sufficient information to enable the Minister to assess the safety of the drug, taking into account the change; and

(b) the Minister has issued to them a letter indicating that the information will be reviewed and has not, within 90 days after issuing the letter, sent them a notice indicating that the change is not acceptable.

(2) Notification is required in respect of the following changes where they may affect whether a drug can be fabricated, packaged/labelled, tested or stored in accordance with the applicable requirements of Divisions 2 to 4:

(a) changes to the plans and specifications of a building where a drug is fabricated, packaged/labelled, tested or stored;

(b) changes to the equipment that is used in the fabrication, packaging/labelling or testing of a drug;

(c) changes to the practices or procedures; and

(d) in the case of an importer, other than an importer of a drug that is fabricated, packaged/labelled or tested in an MRA country at a recognized building, any change referred to in paragraphs (a) to (c) that relates to the fabricator, packager/labeller or tester of the drug being imported.

SOR/97-12, s. 5; SOR/2000-120, s. 5; SOR/2002-368, s. 6.

C.01A.015. (1) An importer of a drug that is fabricated, packaged/labelled or tested in an MRA country at a recognized building shall immediately notify the Minister if the fabricator, packager/labeller or tester indicated in the importer's establishment licence no longer holds a valid permit, licence or other authorization issued by the regulatory authority that recognized that building.

(2) The Minister shall, on receiving a notification under subsection (1), amend the importer's establishment licence by removing the name and address of that fabricator, packager/labeller or tester.

SOR/97-12, s. 5; SOR/2000-120, s. 6; SOR/2002-368, s. 7.

Suspension

C.01A.016. (1) Subject to subsection (3), the Minister may suspend an establishment licence in respect of any or all matters indicated in subsection C.01A.008(2) if the Minister has reasonable grounds to believe that

(a) the licensee has contravened any provision of the Act or these Regulations; or

(b) the licensee has made a false or misleading statement in the application for the establishment licence.

(2) Before suspending an establishment licence, the Minister shall consider

(a) the licensee's history of compliance with the Act and these Regulations; and

(b) the risk that allowing the licence to continue in force would constitute for the health of the consumer.

(3) Subject to subsection C.01A.017(1), the Minister shall not suspend an establishment licence until

(a) an inspector has sent the licensee a written notice that sets out the reason for the proposed suspension, any corrective action required to be taken and the time within which it must be taken;

(b) if corrective action is required, the time set out in the notice has passed without the action having been taken; and

(c) the licensee has been given an opportunity to be heard in respect of the suspension.

SOR/97-12, s. 5.

C.01A.017. (1) The Minister may suspend an establishment licence without giving the licensee an opportunity to be heard if it is necessary to do so to prevent injury to the health of the consumer, by giving the licensee a notice in writing that states the reason for the suspension.

(2) A licensee may request of the Minister, in writing, that the suspension be reconsidered.

(3) The Minister shall, within 45 days after the date of receiving the request, provide the licensee with the opportunity to be heard.

SOR/97-12, s. 5.

C.01A.018. The Minister may reinstate an establishment licence after it has been suspended.

SOR/97-12, s. 5.

Designation

C.01A.019 (1) For the purposes of this Division and Divisions 2 to 4, a regulatory authority that is set out in column 1 of the table to this section is hereby designated in respect of the activities set out in column 3 for the drug or category of drugs set out in column 2.

(2) Whole blood and its components are excluded from the drugs and categories of drugs set out in column 2 of the table to this section.

(3) The lot release of drugs listed in Schedule D to the Act is excluded from the activity of testing set out in column 3 of the table to this section.

TABLE
DESIGNATED REGULATORY AUTHORITIES

	Column 1	Column 2	Column 3
Item	Regulatory authority	Drug or category of drugs	Activities
1.	Swissmedic, Swiss Agency for Therapeutic Products, Bern, Switzerland	Pharmaceuticals for human or veterinary use	Fabricating, packaging/labelling, testing
		Drugs listed in Schedules C and D to the Act	
2.	Regional Medicines Inspectorate of Northwestern Switzerland (RFS-NW), Basel, Switzerland	Pharmaceuticals for human or veterinary use	Fabricating, packaging/labelling, testing
		Drugs listed in Schedules C and D to the Act	
3.	Regional Medicines Inspectorate of Eastern and Central Switzerland (RFS-OZ), Zurich, Switzerland	Pharmaceuticals for human or veterinary use	Fabricating, packaging/labelling, testing
		Drugs listed in Schedules C and D to the Act	
4.	Regional Medicines Inspectorate of Southern Switzerland (RFS-S), Ticino, Switzerland	Pharmaceuticals for human or veterinary use	Fabricating, packaging/labelling, testing
		Drugs listed in Schedules C and D to the Act	
5.	Regional Medicines Inspectorate of Western Switzerland (RFS-W), Lausanne, Switzerland	Pharmaceuticals for human or veterinary use	Fabricating, packaging/labelling, testing
		Drugs listed in Schedules C and D to the Act	

SOR/97-12, s. 5; SOR/2000-120, s. 7; SOR/2002-368, s. 8.

Division 1A: Establishment Licenses

Division 2:
Good Manufacturing Practices

Regulations Respecting Food and Drugs (C.R.C., c. 870)

Enabling Statute: Food and Drugs Act

Regulation current to February 10th, 2010

Attention: See coming into force provision and notes, where applicable.

Division 2
Good Manufacturing Practices[15]

C.02.001. [Repealed, SOR/97-12, s. 5.1]

C.02.002. In this Division,

"drug" [Repealed, SOR/97-12, s. 6]

"importer" [Repealed, SOR/97-12, s. 6]

"medical gas" means any gas or mixture of gases manufactured, sold or represented for use as a drug; (gaz médical)

"packaging material" includes a label; (matériel d'emballage)

"produce" [Repealed, SOR/97-12, s. 6]

"quality control department" means a quality control department referred to in section C.02.013; (service du contrôle de la qualité)

"specifications" means a detailed description of a drug, the raw material used in a drug or the packaging material for a drug and includes

    (a) a statement of all properties and qualities of the drug, raw material or packaging material that are relevant to the manufacture, packaging and use of the drug, including the identity, potency and purity of the drug, raw material or packaging material,

    (b) a detailed description of the methods used for testing and examining the drug, raw material or packaging material, and

---

[15] Available on the Depratment of Justice website at http://laws.justice.gc.ca/eng/C.R.C.-C.870/FramesView.html

(c) a statement of tolerances for the properties and qualities of the drug, raw material or packaging material. (spécifications)

SOR/82-524, s. 3; SOR/85-754, s. 1; SOR/89-174, s. 1; SOR/97-12, s. 6.

C.02.002.1. This Division does not apply to fabricating, packaging/labelling, testing, storing and importing of antimicrobial agents.

SOR/2004-282, s. 3.

Sale

C.02.003. No distributor referred to in paragraph C.01A.003(b) and no importer shall sell a drug unless it has been fabricated, packaged/labelled, tested and stored in accordance with the requirements of this Division.

SOR/82-524, s. 3; SOR/97-12, s. 7; SOR/2000-120, s. 8.

Premises

C.02.004. The premises in which a lot or batch of a drug is fabricated or packaged/labelled shall be designed, constructed and maintained in a manner that

(a) permits the operations therein to be performed under clean, sanitary and orderly conditions;

(b) permits the effective cleaning of all surfaces therein; and

(c) prevents the contamination of the drug and the addition of extraneous material to the drug.

SOR/82-524, s. 3; SOR/97-12, s. 8.

Equipment

C.02.005. The equipment with which a lot or batch of a drug is fabricated, packaged/labelled or tested shall be designed, constructed, maintained, operated and arranged in a manner that

(a) permits the effective cleaning of its surfaces;

(b) prevents the contamination of the drug and the addition of extraneous material to the drug; and

(c) permits it to function in accordance with its intended use.

SOR/82-524, s. 3; SOR/97-12, s. 9.

Personnel

C.02.006. Every lot or batch of a drug shall be fabricated, packaged/labelled, tested and stored under the supervision of personnel who, having regard to the duties and responsibilities involved, have had such technical, academic and other training as the Director considers satisfactory in the interests of the health of the consumer or purchaser.

SOR/82-524, s. 3; SOR/85-754, s. 2; SOR/97-12, s. 52.

Sanitation

C.02.007. (1) Every person who fabricates or packages/labels a drug shall have a written sanitation program that shall be implemented under the supervision of qualified personnel.

(2) The sanitation program referred to in subsection (1) shall include

(a) cleaning procedures for the premises where the drug is fabricated or packaged/labelled and for the equipment used in the fabrication or packaging/labelling; and

(b) instructions on the sanitary fabrication and packaging/labelling of drugs and the handling of materials used in the fabrication and packaging/labelling of drugs.

SOR/82-524, s. 3; SOR/97-12, ss. 10, 53.

C.02.008. (1) Every person who fabricates or packages/labels a drug shall have, in writing, minimum requirements for the health and the hygienic behaviour and clothing of personnel to ensure the clean and sanitary fabrication and packaging/labelling of the drug.

(2) No person shall have access to any area where a drug is exposed during its fabrication or packaging/labelling if the person

(a) is affected with or is a carrier of a disease in a communicable form; or

(b) has an open lesion on any exposed surface of the body.

SOR/82-524, s. 3; SOR/97-12, s. 11.

Raw Material Testing

C.02.009. (1) Each lot or batch of raw material shall be tested against the specifications for that raw material prior to its use in the fabrication of a drug.

(2) No lot or batch of raw material shall be used in the fabrication of a drug unless that lot or batch of raw material complies with the specifications for that raw material.

(3) Notwithstanding subsection (1), water may, prior to the completion of its tests under that subsection, be used in the fabrication of a drug.

(4) Where any property of a raw material is subject to change on storage, no lot or batch of that raw material shall be used in the fabrication of a drug after its storage unless the raw material is retested after an appropriate interval and complies with its specifications for that property.

(5) Where the specifications referred to in subsections (1), (2) and (4) are not prescribed, they shall

(a) be in writing;

(b) be acceptable to the Director who shall take into account the specifications contained in any publication mentioned in Schedule B to the Act; and

(c) be approved by the person in charge of the quality control department.

SOR/82-524, s. 3; SOR/97-12, s. 59.

C.02.010. (1) The testing referred to in section C.02.009 shall be performed on a sample taken

(a) after receipt of each lot or batch of raw material on the premises of the fabricator; or

(b) subject to subsection (2), before receipt of each lot or batch of raw material on the premises of the fabricator, if

    (i) the fabricator

        (A) has evidence satisfactory to the Director to demonstrate that raw materials sold to him by the vendor of that lot or batch of raw material are consistently manufactured in accordance with and consistently comply with the specifications for those raw materials, and

        (B) undertakes periodic complete confirmatory testing with a frequency satisfactory to the Director, and

    (ii) the raw material has not been transported or stored under conditions that may affect its compliance with the specifications for that raw material.

(2) After a lot or batch of raw material is received on the premises of the fabricator, the lot or batch of raw material shall be tested for identity.

SOR/82-524, s. 3; SOR/97-12, ss. 12, 60.

Manufacturing Control

C.02.011. (1) Every fabricator, packager/labeller, distributor referred to in paragraph C.01A.003(b) and importer of a drug shall have written procedures prepared by qualified personnel in respect of the drug to ensure that the drug meets the specifications for that drug.

(2) Every person required to have written procedures referred to in subsection (1) shall ensure that each lot or batch of the drug is fabricated, packaged/labelled and tested in compliance with those procedures.

SOR/82-524, s. 3; SOR/97-12, s. 13.

C.02.012. (1) Every fabricator, packager/labeller, distributor referred to in section C.01A.003, importer and wholesaler of a drug shall maintain

(a) a system of control that permits complete and rapid recall of any lot or batch of the drug that is on the market; and

(b) a program of self-inspection.

(2) Every fabricator and packager/labeller and, subject to subsections (3) and (4), every distributor referred to in paragraph C.01A.003(b) and importer of a drug shall maintain a system designed to ensure that any lot or batch of the drug fabricated and packaged/labelled on premises other than their own is fabricated and packaged/labelled in accordance with the requirements of this Division.

(3) The distributor referred to in paragraph C.01A.003(b) of a drug that is fabricated, packaged/labelled and tested in Canada by a person who holds an establishment licence that authorizes those activities is not required to comply with the requirements of subsection (2) in respect of that drug.

(4) If a drug is fabricated or packaged/labelled in an MRA country at a recognized building, the distributor referred to in paragraph C.01A.003(b) or importer of the drug is not required to comply with the requirements of subsection (2) in respect of that activity for that drug if

(a) the address of the building is set out in that person's establishment licence; and

(b) that person retains a copy of the batch certificate for each lot or batch of the drug received by that person.

SOR/82-524, s. 3; SOR/97-12, s. 13; SOR/2000-120, s. 9; SOR/2002-368, s. 9.

Quality Control Department

C.02.013. (1) Every fabricator, packager/labeller, distributor referred to in paragraph C.01A.003(b) and importer shall have on their premises in Canada a quality control department that is supervised by personnel described in section C.02.006.

(2) The quality control department referred to in subsection (1) shall be a distinct organizational unit that functions and reports to management independently of any other functional unit, including the manufacturing, processing, packaging or sales unit.

SOR/82-524, s. 3; SOR/89-174, s. 8(F); SOR/97-12, s. 55; SOR/2000-120, s. 10.

C.02.014. (1) No lot or batch of drug shall be made available for sale unless the sale of that lot or batch is approved by the person in charge of the quality control department.

(2) A drug that is returned to the fabricator, packager/labeller, distributor referred to in paragraph C.01A.003(b) or importer thereof shall not be made available for further sale unless the sale of that drug is approved by the person in charge of the quality control department.

(3) No lot or batch of raw material or of packaging/labelling material shall be used in the fabrication or packaging/labelling of a drug unless the material is approved for that use by the person in charge of the quality control department.

(4) No lot or batch of a drug shall be reprocessed without the approval of the person in charge of the quality control department.

SOR/82-524, s. 3; SOR/89-174, s. 8(F); SOR/97-12, ss. 14, 55.

C.02.015. (1) All fabrication, packaging/labelling, testing, storage and transportation methods and procedures that may affect the quality of a drug shall

Division 2: GMPs

be examined and approved by the person in charge of the quality control department before their implementation.

(2) The person in charge of the control department shall cause to be investigated every complaint on quality that is received and cause corrective action to be taken where necessary.

(3) The person in charge of the quality control department shall cause all tests or examinations required pursuant to this Division to be performed by a competent laboratory.

SOR/82-524, s. 3; SOR/97-12, s. 15.

Packaging Material Testing

C.02.016. (1) Each lot or batch of packaging material shall, prior to its use in the packaging of a drug, be examined or tested against the specifications for that packaging material.

(2) No lot or batch of packaging material shall be used in the packaging of a drug unless the lot or batch of packaging material complies with the specifications for that packaging material.

(3) The specifications referred to in subsections (1) and (2) shall

(a) be in writing;

(b) be acceptable to the Director who shall take into account the specifications contained in any publication mentioned in Schedule B to the Act; and

(c) be approved by the person in charge of the quality control department.

SOR/82-524, s. 3; SOR/89-174, s. 8(F).

C.02.017. (1) The examination or testing referred to in section C.02.016 shall be performed on a sample taken

(a) after receipt of each lot or batch of packaging material on the premises of the person who packages a drug; or

(b) subject to subsection (2), before receipt of each lot or batch of packaging material on the premises of the person who packages a drug, if

    (i) that person

        (A) has evidence satisfactory to the Director to demonstrate that packaging materials sold to him by the vendor of that lot or batch of packaging material are consistently manufactured in accordance with and consistently comply with the specifications for those packaging materials, and

        (B) undertakes periodic complete confirmatory examination or testing with a frequency satisfactory to the Director,

    (ii) the packaging material has not been transported or stored under conditions that may affect its compliance with the specifications for that packaging material.

(2) After a lot or batch of packaging material is received on the premises of the person who packages a drug,

(a) the lot or batch of the packaging material shall be examined or tested for identity; and

(b) the labels shall be examined or tested in order to ensure that they comply with the specifications for those labels.

SOR/82-524, s. 3; SOR/89-174, ss. 2(F), 8(F); SOR/97-12, s. 56(F).

Finished Product Testing

C.02.018. (1) Each lot or batch of a drug shall, prior to its availability for sale, be tested against the specifications for that drug.

(2) No lot or batch of a drug shall be available for sale unless it complies with the specifications for that drug.

(3) The specifications referred to in subsections (1) and (2) shall

(a) be in writing;

(b) be approved by the person in charge of the quality control department; and

(c) comply with the Act and these Regulations.

SOR/82-524, s. 3.

C.02.019. (1) Subject to subsections (3) and (4), in the case of a packager/labeller, distributor referred to in paragraph C.01A.003(b) or importer, the testing referred to in section C.02.018 shall be performed on a sample taken

(a) after receipt of each lot or batch of the drug on the premises in Canada of the packager/labeller, distributor referred to in paragraph C.01A.003(b) or importer of the drug; or

(b) subject to subsection (2), before receipt of each lot or batch of the drug on the premises described in paragraph (a), if

(i)   the packager/labeller, distributor referred to in paragraph C.01A.003(b) or importer

(A) has evidence satisfactory to the Director to demonstrate that drugs sold to him by the vendor of that lot or batch of the drug are consistently manufactured in accordance with and consistently comply with the specifications for those drugs, and

(B) undertakes periodic complete confirmatory testing with a frequency satisfactory to the Director, and

(ii) the drug has not been transported or stored under conditions that may affect its compliance with the specifications for that drug.

(2) Where the packager/labeller, distributor referred to in paragraph C.01A.003(b) or importer of a drug receives a lot or batch of the drug on their premises in Canada, and the useful life of the drug is more than 30 days, the lot or batch

Division 2: GMPs

shall be tested for identity, and the packager/labeller shall confirm the identity after the lot or batch is packaged/labelled.

(3) The distributor referred to in paragraph C.01A.003(b) of a drug that is fabricated, packaged/labelled and tested in Canada by a person who holds an establishment licence that authorizes those activities is not required to comply with the requirements of subsections (1) and (2) in respect of that drug.

(4) If a drug is fabricated, packaged/labelled and tested in an MRA country at a recognized building, the distributor referred to in paragraph C.01A.003(b) or importer of that drug is not required to comply with the requirements of subsections (1) and (2) in respect of that drug if

(a) the address of the building is set out in that person's establishment licence; and

(b) that person retains a copy of the batch certificate for each lot or batch of the drug received by that person.

SOR/82-524, s. 3; SOR/89-174, s. 8(F); SOR/97-12, ss. 16, 57; SOR/2000-120, s. 11; SOR/2002-368, s. 10.

Records

C.02.020. (1) Every fabricator, packager/labeller, distributor referred to in paragraph C.01A.003(b) and importer shall maintain on their premises in Canada, for each drug sold,

(a) master production documents for the drug;

(b) evidence that each lot or batch of the drug has been fabricated, packaged/labelled, tested and stored in accordance with the procedures described in the master production documents;

(c) evidence that the conditions under which the drug was fabricated, packaged/labelled, tested and stored are in compliance with the requirements of this Division;

(d) evidence establishing the period of time during which the drug in the container in which it is sold will meet the specifications for that drug; and

(e) adequate evidence of the testing referred to in section C.02.018.

(2) Every distributor referred to in paragraph C.01A.003(b) and importer shall make available to the Director, on request, the results of testing performed on raw materials and packaging/labelling material for each lot or batch of a drug sold.

(3) Every fabricator shall maintain on his premises

(a) the written specifications for the raw material; and

(b) adequate evidence of the testing of the raw materials referred to in section C.02.009.

(4) Every person who packages a drug shall maintain on his premises

(a) the written specifications for the packaging material; and

(b) adequate evidence of the packaging material examination or testing referred to in section C.02.016.

(5) Every fabricator shall maintain on their premises in Canada

(a) detailed plans and specifications of each building in Canada at which they fabricate, package/label or test; and

(b) a description of the design and construction of those buildings.

(6) Every fabricator, packager/labeller and tester shall maintain on their premises in Canada details of the personnel employed to supervise the fabrication, packaging/labelling and testing, including each person's title, responsibilities, qualifications, experience and training.

SOR/82-524, s. 3; SOR/89-174, ss. 3(F), 8(F); SOR/97-12, ss. 17, 52, 60.

C.02.021. (1) Subject to subsection (2), all records and evidence on the fabrication, packaging/labelling, testing and storage of a drug that are required to be maintained under this Division shall be retained for a period of at least one year after the expiration date on the label of the drug, unless otherwise specified in the person's establishment licence.

(2) All records and evidence on the testing of raw materials and packaging/labelling materials that are required to be maintained under this Division shall be retained for a period of at least five years after the materials were last used in the fabrication or packaging/labelling of a drug, unless otherwise specified in the person's establishment licence.

SOR/82-524, s. 3; SOR/89-174, s. 8(F); SOR/92-654, s. 6; SOR/97-12, s. 18.

C.02.022. Every distributor referred to in section C.01A.003, wholesaler and importer of a drug shall retain records of the sale of each lot or batch of the drug, which enable them to recall the lot or batch from the market, for a period of at least one year after the expiration date of that lot or batch, unless otherwise specified in their establishment licence.

SOR/82-524, s. 3; SOR/92-654, s. 7; SOR/97-12, s. 18.

C.02.023. (1) On receipt of a complaint respecting the quality of a drug, every distributor referred to in paragraph C.01A.003(b) and importer of the drug shall make a record of the complaint and of its investigation and retain the record for a period of at least one year after the expiration date of the lot or batch of that drug, unless otherwise specified in their establishment licence.

(2) On receipt of any information respecting the quality or hazards of a drug, every distributor referred to in paragraph C.01A.003(b) and importer of the drug shall make a record of the information and retain it for a period of at least one year after the expiration date of the lot or batch of that drug, unless otherwise specified in their establishment licence.

SOR/82-524, s. 3; SOR/92-654, s. 7; SOR/97-12, s. 18.

C.02.024. (1) Every fabricator, packager/labeller, distributor referred to in section C.01A.003, importer and wholesaler shall

(a) maintain records of the results of the self-inspection program required by section C.02.012 and of any action taken in connection with that program; and

Division 2: GMPs

(b) retain those records for a period of at least three years.

(2) Every person who fabricates or packages/labels a drug shall

(a) maintain records on the operation of the sanitation program required to be implemented under section C.02.007; and

(b) retain those records for a period of at least three years.

SOR/82-524, s. 3; SOR/97-12, ss. 19, 53.

Samples

C.02.025. (1) Every distributor referred to in paragraph C.01A.003(b) and importer of a drug shall retain in Canada a sample of each lot or batch of the packaged/labelled drug for a period of at least one year after the expiration date on the label of the drug, unless otherwise specified in the distributor's or importer's establishment licence.

(2) The fabricator shall retain a sample of each lot or batch of raw materials used in the fabrication of a drug for a period of at least two years after the materials were last used in the fabrication of the drug, unless otherwise specified in the fabricator's establishment licence.

SOR/82-524, s. 3; SOR/89-174, s. 4(F); SOR/92-654, s. 8; SOR/97-12, s. 20.

C.02.026. The samples referred to in section C.02.025 shall be in an amount that is sufficient to determine whether the drug or raw material complies with the specifications for that drug or raw material.

SOR/82-524, s. 3.

Stability

C.02.027. Every distributor referred to in paragraph C.01A.003(b) and importer shall establish the period of time during which each drug in the package in which it is sold will comply with the specifications.

SOR/82-524, s. 3; SOR/97-12, s. 58.

C.02.028. Every distributor referred to in paragraph C.01A.003(b) and importer shall monitor, by means of a continuing program, the stability of the drug in the package in which it is sold.

SOR/82-524, s. 3; SOR/97-12, s. 58.

Sterile Products

C.02.029. In addition to the other requirements of this Division, a drug that is intended to be sterile shall be fabricated and packaged/labelled

(a) in separate and enclosed areas;

(b) under the supervision of personnel trained in microbiology; and

(c) by a method scientifically proven to ensure sterility.

SOR/82-524, s. 3; SOR/97-12, s. 21.

Medical Gases

C.02.030. The provisions of sections C.02.025, C.02.027 and C.02.028 do not apply to medical gases.

SOR/85-754, s. 3.

Division 2: GMPs

Part II

Guidance Documents

Good Manufacturing Practices (GMP) Guidelines - 2009 Edition (GUI-0001)

Health Products and Food Branch Inspectorate

Supersedes: 2002 Edition, Version 2

Date issued: May 8, 2009

Date of implementation: November 8, 2009

Good Manufacturing Practices (GMP) Guidelines - 2009 Edition (GUI-0001)[16]

Disclaimer

This document does not constitute part of the Food and Drugs Act (Act) or the Food and Drugs Regulations (Regulations) and in the event of any inconsistency or conflict between that Act or Regulations and this document, the Act or the Regulations take precedence. This document is an administrative document that is intended to facilitate compliance by the regulated party with the Act, the Regulations and the applicable administrative policies. This document is not intended to provide legal advice regarding the interpretation of the Act or Regulations. If a regulated party has questions about their legal obligations or responsibilities under the Act or Regulations, they should seek the advice of legal counsel.

1.0 Introduction

These guidelines on Good Manufacturing Practices (GMP) pertain to Division 2, Part C of the Food and Drug Regulations. The guidelines apply to pharmaceutical, radiopharmaceutical, biological, and veterinary drugs and were developed by Health Canada in consultation with stakeholders. These guidelines are designed to facilitate compliance by the regulated industry and to enhance consistency in the application of the regulatory requirements.

Division 1A, Part C of the Food and Drug Regulations defines activities for which GMP compliance is to be demonstrated prior to the issuance of a drug establishment licence. In addition to these guidelines, further guidance in specific areas is provided in Appendix C to this document or in separate documents. The guidance regarding the fabrication, packaging, labelling, testing, distribution, and importation of medical gases is described in the guideline "Good Manufacturing Practices for Medical Gases (GUI-0031)".

---

[16] Available on the Health Canada website at http://www.hc-sc.gc.ca/dhp-mps/compli-conform/gmp-bpf/docs/gui-0001-eng.php

The content of this document should not be regarded as the only interpretation of the GMP Regulations, nor does it intend to cover every conceivable case. Alternative means of complying with these Regulations can be considered with the appropriate scientific justification. Different approaches may be called for as new technologies emerge.

The guidance given in this document has been written with a view to harmonize with GMP standards from other countries and with those of the World Health Organization (WHO), the Pharmaceutical Inspection Cooperation/Scheme (PIC/S), and the International Conference on Harmonisation (ICH).

This document takes into account the implementation of the current Mutual Recognition Agreements (MRA). The MRA establish mutual recognition of GMP compliance certification between Regulatory Authorities that are designated as equivalent. Exemptions from requirements under C.02.012 (2) and C.02.019 (1) and (2) are provided for importers of drugs where all activities (fabrication, packaging/labelling and testing) are carried out in MRA countries. All other regulatory requirements described in the Food and Drug Regulations apply.

The present edition of this document includes modified and/or new terminology, the incorporation of most GMP questions and answers, additional requirements such as annual product quality review, additional interpretations, and an updated table of requirements.

2.0 Purpose

To provide interpretive guidance for Part C, Division 2, of the Food and Drug Regulations. These guidelines are designed to facilitate compliance by the regulated industry and to enhance consistency in the application of the regulatory requirements.

3.0 Scope

The guidelines apply to pharmaceutical, radiopharmaceutical, biological, and veterinary drugs and were developed by Health Canada in consultation with stakeholders.

Chart 1.0: GMP Regulations Applicable to Licensable Activities

Section	Regulation	Fabri cator	Packager/ Labeller	Importer (MRA and non-MRA)	Distributor	Wholes aler	Tester
1. Premises	C.02.004	X	X	X	X	X	
2. Equipment	C.02.005	X	X				X
3. Personnel	C.02.006	X	X	X	X	X	X
4. Sanitation	C.02.007	X	X				
	C.02.008	X	X				
5. Raw Material Testing	C.02.009	X					*
	C.02.010	X					*
6. Manufacturing Control	C.02.011	X	X	X	X		
	C.02.012	X	X	X	X	X	
7. Quality Control	C.02.013	X	X	X	X	X	
	C.02.014	X	X	X	X	X	
	C.02.015	X	X	X	X	X	X

Section	Regulation	Fabricator	Packager/ Labeller	Importer (MRA and non-MRA)	Distributor	Wholesaler	Tester
8. Packaging Material Testing	C.02.016	X	X				*
	C.02.017	X	X				*
9. Finished Product Testing	C.02.018	X	X	X	X		*
	C.02.019		X	X	X		*
10. Records	C.02.020	X	X	X	X		X
	C.02.021	X	X	X	X	X	X
	C.02.022			X	X	X	
	C.02.023	X	X	X	X	X	
	C.02.024	X	X	X	X	X	
11. Samples	C.02.025	X		X	X		
	C.02.026	X		X	X		
12. Stability	C.02.027			X	X		*
	C.02.028			X	X		*
13. Sterile Products	C.02.029	X	X				*

* - Where applicable depending on the nature of the activities

4.0 Quality Management

4.1 Guiding Principle

The holder of an establishment licence, or any operation to which the requirements of Division 2 Part C of the Food and Drug Regulations are applicable, must ensure that the fabrication, packaging, labelling, distribution, testing and wholesaling of drugs comply with these requirements and the marketing authorization, and do not place consumers at risk due to inadequate safety and quality.

The attainment of this quality objective is the responsibility of senior management and requires the participation and commitment of personnel in many different departments and at all levels within the establishment and its suppliers. To ensure compliance, there must be a comprehensively designed and correctly implemented quality management system that incorporates GMP and quality control. The system should be fully documented and its effectiveness monitored. All parts of the quality management system should be adequately resourced with qualified personnel, suitable premises, equipment, and facilities.

4.2 Relationship among Quality Elements

The basic concepts of quality assurance, GMP, and quality control are inter-related. They are described here in order to emphasize their relationships and their fundamental importance to the production and control of drugs.

4.2.1 Quality Assurance

Quality assurance is a wide-ranging concept that covers all matters that individually or collectively influence the quality of a drug. It is the total of the organized arrangements made with the objective of ensuring that drugs are of the quality required for their intended use. Quality assurance therefore incorporates GMP, along with other factors that are outside the scope of these guidelines.

A system of quality assurance appropriate for the fabrication, packaging, labelling, testing, distribution, importation, and wholesale of drugs should ensure that:

1. Drugs are designed and developed in a way that takes into account the GMP requirements;

2. Managerial responsibilities are clearly specified;

3. Systems, facilities and procedures are adequate and qualified;

4. Production and control operations are clearly specified;

5. Analytical methods and critical processes are validated;

6. Arrangements are made for the supply and use of the correct raw and packaging materials;

7. All necessary control on intermediates, and any other in-process monitoring is carried out;

8. Outsourced activities are subject to appropriate controls and meet GMP requirements;

9. Fabrication, packaging/labelling, testing, distribution, importation, and wholesaling are performed in accordance with established procedures;

10. Drugs are not sold or supplied before the quality control department has certified that each lot has been produced and controlled in accordance with the marketing authorization and of any other regulations relevant to the production, control and release of drugs;

11. Satisfactory arrangements exist for ensuring that the drugs are stored, distributed, and subsequently handled in such a way that quality is maintained throughout their shelf life;

12. The quality risk management system should ensure that:

    ♦ the evaluation of the risk to quality is based on scientific knowledge, experience with the process and ultimately links to the protection of the patient

    ♦ the level of effort, formality and documentation of the quality risk management process is commensurate with the level of risk.

13. The effectiveness, applicability, and continuous improvement of the quality management system is ensured through regular management review and self-inspection;

14. An annual product quality review of all drugs should be conducted with the objective of verifying the consistency of the existing process, the appropriateness of current specifications for both raw materials and finished

product to highlight any trends and to identify product and process improvements.

4.2.2 Good Manufacturing Practices (GMP) for Drugs

GMP are the part of quality assurance that ensures that drugs are consistently produced and controlled in such a way to meet the quality standards appropriate to their intended use, as required by the marketing authorization.

GMP basic requirements are as follows:

1. Manufacturing processes are clearly defined and controlled to ensure consistency and compliance with approved specifications;

2. Critical steps of manufacturing processes and significant changes to the process are validated;

3. All necessary key elements for GMP are provided, including the following:

    *   qualified and trained personnel,

    *   adequate premises and space,

    *   suitable equipment and services,

    *   correct materials, containers and labels,

    *   approved procedures and instructions,

    *   suitable storage and transport.

4. Instructions and procedures are written in clear and unambiguous language;

5. Operators are trained to carry out and document procedures;

6. Records are made during manufacture that demonstrate that all the steps required by the defined procedures and instructions were in fact taken and that the quantity and quality of the drug was as expected. Deviations are investigated and documented;

7. Records of fabrication, packaging, labelling, testing, distribution, importation, and wholesaling that enable the complete history of a lot to be traced are retained in a comprehensible and accessible form;

8. Control of storage, handling, and transportation of the drugs minimizes any risk to their quality;

9. A system is available for recalling of drugs from sale;

10. Complaints about drugs are examined, the causes of quality defects are investigated, and appropriate measures are taken with respect to the defective drugs and to prevent recurrence

4.2.3 Quality Control

Quality control is the part of GMP that is concerned with sampling, specifications, testing, documentation, and release procedures. Quality control ensures that the necessary and relevant tests are carried out and that raw materials, packaging materials, and products are released for use or sale, only if their quality is

---

satisfactory. Quality control is not confined to laboratory operations but must be incorporated into all activities and decisions concerning the quality of the product.

The basic requirements of quality control are as follows:

1. Adequate facilities, trained personnel, and approved procedures are available for sampling, inspecting and testing of raw materials, packaging materials, intermediate bulk and finished products, and, where appropriate monitoring environmental conditions for GMP purposes;

    1.1 Samples of raw materials, packaging materials, and intermediate, bulk, and finished products are taken according to procedures approved by the quality control department;

    1.2 Test methods are validated;

    1.3 Records demonstrate that all the required sampling, inspecting, and testing procedures were carried out, and any deviations are recorded and investigated;

    1.4 Records are made of the results of the self-inspection program;

    1.5 The procedures for product release include a review and evaluation of relevant production documentation and an assessment of deviations from specified procedures;

    1.6 No drug is released for sale or supply prior to approval by the quality control department;

    1.7 Sufficient samples of raw material and finished product are retained to permit future examination if necessary.

5.0 Regulation

C.02.002

In this Division,

"medical gas" means any gas or mixture of gases manufactured, sold, or represented for use as a drug; (gaz médical)

"packaging material" includes a label; (matériel d'emballage)

"quality control department" means a quality control department referred to in section C.02.013; (service du contrôle de la qualité)

"specifications" means a detailed description of a drug, the raw material used in a drug, or the packaging material for a drug and includes:

(a) statement of all properties and qualities of the drug, raw material or packaging material that are relevant to the manufacture, packaging, and use of the drug, including the identity, potency, and purity of the drug, raw material, or packaging material,

(b) a detailed description of the methods used for testing and examining the drug, raw material, or packaging material, and

(c) a statement of tolerances for the properties and qualities of the drug, raw material, or packaging material. (spécifications)

C.02.002.1

This Division does not apply to fabricating, packaging/labelling, testing, storing and importing of antimicrobial agents.

Sale

C.02.003

No distributor referred to in paragraph C.01A.003(b) and no importer shall sell a drug unless it has been fabricated, packaged/labelled, tested, and stored in accordance with the requirements of this Division.

Premises

Regulation

C.02.004

The premises in which a lot or batch of a drug is fabricated or packaged/labelled shall be designed, constructed and maintained in a manner that

(a) permits the operations therein to be performed under clean, sanitary and orderly conditions;

(b) permits the effective cleaning of all surfaces therein; and

(c) prevents the contamination of the drug and the addition of extraneous material to the drug.

Rationale

The pharmaceutical establishment should be designed and constructed in a manner that permits cleanliness and orderliness while preventing contamination. Regular maintenance is required to prevent deterioration of the premises. The ultimate objective of all endeavours is product quality.

Interpretation

1. Buildings in which drugs are fabricated or packaged are located in an environment that, when considered together with measures being taken to protect the manufacturing processes, presents a minimal risk of causing any contamination of materials or drugs.

2. The premises are designed, constructed, and maintained such that they prevent the entry of pests into the building and also prevent the migration of extraneous material from the outside into the building and from one area to another.

    2.1 Doors windows, walls, ceilings, and floors are such that no holes or cracks are evident (other than those intended by design).

2.2 Doors giving direct access to the exterior from manufacturing and packaging areas are used for emergency purposes only. These doors are adequately sealed. Receiving and shipping area(s) do not allow direct access to production areas.

2.3 Production areas are segregated from all non-production areas. Individual manufacturing, packaging, and testing areas are clearly defined and if necessary segregated. Areas where biological, microbiological or radioisotope testing is carried out require special design and containment considerations.

2.4 Laboratory animals' quarters are segregated.

2.5 Engineering, boiler rooms, generators, etc. are isolated from production areas.

3. In all areas where raw materials, primary packaging materials, in-process drugs, or drugs are exposed, the following considerations apply to the extent necessary to prevent contamination.

3.1 Floors, walls, and ceilings permit cleaning. Brick, cement blocks, and other porous materials are sealed. Surface materials that shed particles are avoided.

3.2 Floors, walls, ceilings, and other surfaces are hard, smooth and free of sharp corners where extraneous material can collect.

3.3 Joints between walls, ceilings and floors are sealed.

3.4 Pipes, light fittings, ventilation points and other services do not create surfaces that cannot be cleaned.

3.5 Floor drains are screened and trapped.

3.6 Air quality is maintained through dust control, monitoring of pressure differentials between production areas and periodic verification and replacement of air filters. The air handling system is well defined, taking into consideration airflow volume, direction, and velocity. Air handling systems are subject to periodic verification to ensure compliance with their design specifications. Records are kept.

4. Temperature and humidity are controlled to the extent necessary to safeguard materials.

5. Rest, change, wash-up, and toilet facilities are well separated from production areas and are sufficiently spacious, well ventilated, and of a type that permits good sanitary practices.

6. Premises layout is designed to avoid mix-ups and generally optimize the flow of personnel and materials.

6.1 There is sufficient space for receiving and all production activities.

6.2 Working spaces allow the orderly and logical placement of equipment (including parts and tools) and materials.

6.3 Where physical quarantine areas are used, they are well marked, with access restricted to designated personnel. Where electronic quarantine is used, electronic access is restricted to designated personnel.

6.4 A separate sampling area is provided for raw materials. If sampling is performed in the storage area, it is conducted in such a way as to prevent contamination or cross-contamination.

6.5 Working areas are well lit.

7. Utilities and support systems (e.g., HVAC, dust collection, and supplies of purified water, steam, compressed air, nitrogen, etc.) for buildings in which drugs are fabricated or packaged/labelled are qualified and are subject to periodic verification. Further guidance is provided in Health Canada's document entitled "Validation Guidelines for Pharmaceutical Dosage Forms (GUI-0029)".

8. Outlets for liquids and gases used in the production of drugs are clearly identified as to their content.

9. Premises are maintained in a good state of repair. Repair and maintenance operations do not affect drug quality.

10. Where necessary, separate rooms are provided and maintained to protect equipment and associated control systems sensitive to vibration, electrical interference, and contact with excessive moisture or other external factors.

11. Fabricators and packagers must demonstrate that the premises are designed in such a manner that the risk of cross-contamination between products is minimized.

11.1 Campaign production can be accepted where, on a product by product basis, proper justification is provided, validation is conducted and rigorous validated controls and monitoring are in place and demonstrate the minimization of any risk of cross-contamination.

11.2 Self-contained facilities are required for:

11.2.1 certain classes of highly sensitizing drugs such as penicillins and cephalosporins.

11.2.2 other classes of highly potent drugs such as potent steroids, cytotoxics, or potentially pathogenic drugs (e.g., live vaccines), for which validated cleaning or inactivation procedures cannot be established (e.g., the acceptable level of residue is below the limit of detection by the best available analytical methods).

11.3 For the types of products listed in interpretations 11.2.1 and 11.2.2, external contamination with drug product residues of the final container and primary packaging does not exceed established limits.

11.3.1 Storage in common areas is allowed once the products are enclosed in their immediate final containers and controls are in place to minimize risks of cross-contamination.

11.4 No production activities of highly toxic non-pharmaceutical materials, such as pesticides and herbicides, are conducted in premises used for the production of drugs.

Equipment

Regulation

C.02.005

The equipment with which a lot or batch of a drug is fabricated, packaged/labelled or tested shall be designed, constructed, maintained, operated, and arranged in a manner that

(a) permits the effective cleaning of its surfaces;

(b) prevents the contamination of the drug and the addition of extraneous material to the drug; and

(c) permits it to function in accordance with its intended use.

Rationale

The purpose of these requirements is to prevent the contamination of drugs by other drugs, by dust, and by foreign materials such as rust, lubricant and particles coming from the equipment. Contamination problems may arise from poor maintenance, the misuse of equipment, exceeding the capacity of the equipment and the use of worn-out equipment. Equipment arranged in an orderly manner permits cleaning of adjacent areas and does not interfere with other processing operations. It also minimizes the circulation of personnel and optimizes the flow of materials. The fabrication of drugs of consistent quality requires that equipment perform in accordance with its intended use.

Interpretation

1. The design, construction and location of equipment permit cleaning, sanitizing, and inspection of the equipment.

    1.1 Equipment parts that come in contact with raw materials, in-process intermediates or drugs are accessible to cleaning or are removable.

    1.2 Tanks used in processing liquids and ointments are equipped with fittings that can be dismantled and cleaned. Validated Clean-In-Place (CIP) equipment can be dismantled for periodic verification.

    1.3 Filter assemblies are designed for easy dismantling.

    1.4 Equipment is located at a sufficient distance from other equipment and walls to permit cleaning of the equipment and adjacent area.

    1.5 The base of immovable equipment is adequately sealed along points of contact with the floor.

    1.6 Equipment is kept clean, dry and protected from contamination when stored.

2. equipment does not add extraneous material to the drug.

    2.1 Surfaces that come in contact with raw materials, in-process intermediates or drugs are smooth and are made of material that is non-toxic, corrosion resistant, non-reactive to the drug being fabricated or packaged and capable of withstanding repeated cleaning or sanitizing.

2.2 The design is such that the possibility of a lubricant or other maintenance material contaminating the drug is minimized.

2.3 Equipment made of material that is prone to shed particles or to harbour microorganisms does not come in contact with or contaminate raw materials, in-process drugs or drugs.

2.4 Chain drives and transmission gears are enclosed or properly covered.

2.5 Tanks, hoppers and other similar fabricating equipment are equipped with covers.

3. Equipment is operated in a manner that prevents contamination.

3.1 Ovens, autoclaves and similar equipment contain only one raw material, in-process drug or drug at a time, unless precautions are taken to prevent contamination and mix-ups.

3.2 The location of equipment precludes contamination from extraneous materials.

3.3 The placement of equipment optimizes the flow of material and minimizes the movement of personnel.

3.4 Equipment is located so that production operations undertaken in a common area are compatible and cross-contamination between such operations is prevented.

3.5 Fixed pipework is clearly labelled to indicate the contents and, where applicable, the direction of flow.

3.6 Dedicated production equipment is provided where appropriate.

3.7 Water purification, storage, and distribution equipment is operated in a manner that will ensure a reliable source of water of the appropriate chemical and microbial purity.

4. Equipment is maintained in a good state of repair.

4.1 Where a potential for contamination during fabrication or packaging of a drug exists, surfaces are free from cracks, peeling paint and other defects.

4.2 Gaskets are functional.

4.3 The use of temporary devices (e.g., tape) is avoided.

4.4 Equipment parts that come in contact with drugs are maintained in such a manner that drugs are fabricated or packaged within specifications. Equipment used for significant processing or testing operations is maintained in accordance with a written preventative maintenance program.. Maintenance records are kept.

5. Equipment s designed, located, and maintained to serve its intended purpose.

5.1 Measuring devices are of an appropriate range, precision and accuracy. Such equipment is calibrated on a scheduled basis, and corresponding records are kept.

5.2 Equipment that is unsuitable for its intended use is removed from fabrication, packaging/labelling, and testing areas. When removal is not feasible unsuitable equipment is clearly labelled as such.

5.3 Equipment used during the critical steps of fabrication, packaging/labelling, and testing, including computerized systems, is subject to installation and operational qualification. Equipment qualification is documented. Further guidance is provided in Health Canada's document entitled "Validation Guidelines for Pharmaceutical Dosage Forms" and "Annex 11 to the Current Edition of the Good Manufacturing Practices Guidelines - Computerised Systems (GUI-0050)".

5.4 Equipment used for significant processing and testing operations is calibrated, inspected or checked in accordance with a written program. Records are kept.

5.5 For equipment used for significant processing or testing operations, usage logs are maintained. These logs should include identification of products, dates of operation, and downtime due to frequent or serious malfunctions or breakdowns. The information should be collected to facilitate the identification of negative performance trends.

Personnel

Regulation

C.02.006

Every lot or batch of a drug shall be fabricated, packaged/labelled, tested and stored under the supervision of personnel who, having regard to the duties and responsibilities involved, have had such technical, academic, and other training as the Director considers satisfactory in the interests of the health of the consumer or purchaser.

Rationale

People are the most important element in any pharmaceutical operation, without the proper personnel with the appropriate attitude and sufficient training, it is almost impossible to fabricate, package/label, test, or store good quality drugs.

It is essential that qualified personnel be employed to supervise the fabrication of drugs. The operations involved in the fabrication of drugs are highly technical in nature and require constant vigilance, attention to details and a high degree of competence on the part of employees. Inadequate training of personnel or the absence of an appreciation of the importance of production control, often accounts for the failure of a product to meet the required standards.

Interpretation

1. The individual in charge of the quality control department of a fabricator, packager/labeller, tester, importer, and distributor; and the individual in charge of the manufacturing department of a fabricator or packager/labeller;

   1.1 holds a Canadian university degree or a degree recognized as equivalent by a Canadian university or Canadian accreditation body in a science related to the work being carried out;

   1.2 has practical experience in their responsibility area;

   1.3 directly controls and personally supervises on site, each working shift during which activities under their control are being conducted; and

   1.4 may delegate duties and responsibility (e.g., to cover all shifts) to a person in possession of a diploma, certificate or other evidence of formal qualifications awarded on completion of a course of study at a university, college or technical institute in a science related to the work being carried out combined with at least two years of relevant practical experience, while remaining accountable for those duties and responsibility.

2. The individual in charge of the quality control department of a wholesaler;

   2.1 is qualified by pertinent academic training and experience; and

   2.2 may delegate duties and responsibility to a person who meets the requirements defined under interpretation 2.1.

3. The individual responsible for packaging operations, including control over printed packaging materials and withdrawal of bulk drugs;

   3.1 is qualified by training and experience; and

   3.2 is directly responsible to the person in charge of the manufacturing department or a person having the same qualifications.

4. For secondary labellers, individuals in charge of labelling operations and individuals in charge of the quality control department;

   4.1 are qualified by pertinent academic training and experience; and

   4.2 can delegate their duties and responsibilities to a person who meets the requirements defined under 4.1.

5. An adequate number of personnel with the necessary qualifications and practical experience appropriate to their responsibilities are available on site.

   5.1 The responsibilities placed on any one individual are not so extensive as to present any risk to quality.

   5.2 All responsible personnel have their specific duties recorded in a written description and have adequate authority to carry out their responsibilities.

   5.3 When key personnel are absent, qualified personnel are appointed to carry out their duties and functions.

6. All personnel are aware of the principles of GMP that affect them, and all personnel receive initial and continuing training relevant to their job responsibilities.

    6.1 Training is provided by qualified personnel having regard to the function and in accordance with a written program for all personnel involved in the fabrication of a drug, including technical, maintenance, and cleaning personnel.

    6.2 The effectiveness of continuing training is periodically assessed.

    6.3 Training is provided prior to implementation of new or revised SOPs.

    6.4 Records of training are maintained.

    6.5 Personnel working in areas where highly active, toxic, infectious, or sensitizing materials are handled are given specific training.

    6.6 The performance of all personnel is periodically reviewed.

7. Consultants and contractors have the necessary qualifications, training, and experience to advise on the subjects for which they are retained.

Sanitation

Regulation

C.02.007

(1) Every person who fabricates or packages/labels a drug shall have a written sanitation program that shall be implemented under the supervision of qualified personnel.

(2) The sanitation program referred to in subsection (1) shall include:

    (a) cleaning procedures for the premises where the drug is fabricated or packaged/labelled and for the equipment used in the fabrication or packaging/labelling of the drug; and

    (b) instructions on the sanitary fabrication and packaging/labelling of drugs and the handling of materials used in the fabrication and packaging/labelling of drugs.

Rationale

Sanitation in a pharmaceutical plant, as well as employee attitude, influences the quality of drug products. The quality requirement for drug products demand that such products be fabricated and packaged in areas that are free from environmental contamination and free from contamination by another drug.

A written sanitation program provides some assurance that levels of cleanliness in the plant are maintained and that the provisions of Sections 8 and 11 of the Food and Drugs Act are satisfied.

Interpretation

1. Every person who fabricates or packages/labels a drug shall have a written sanitation program available on the premises.

2. The sanitation program contains procedures that describe the following:

2.1 cleaning requirements applicable to all production areas of the plant with emphasis on manufacturing areas that require special attention;

2.2 cleaning requirements applicable to processing equipment;

2.3 cleaning intervals;

2.4 products for cleaning and disinfection, along with their dilution and the equipment to be used;

2.5 the responsibilities of any outside contractor;

2.6 disposal procedures for waste material and debris;

2.7 pest control measures;

2.8 precautions required to prevent contamination of a drug when rodenticides, insecticides, and fumigation agents are used;

2.9 microbial and environmental monitoring procedures with alert and action limits in areas where susceptible products are fabricated or packaged; and

2.10 the personnel responsible for carrying out cleaning procedures.

3. The sanitation program is implemented and is effective in preventing unsanitary conditions.

3.1 Cleaning procedures for manufacturing equipment are validated based on the Health Canada document entitled "Cleaning Validation Guidelines (GUI-0028)".

3.2 Residues from the cleaning process itself (e.g., detergents, solvents, etc.) are also removed from equipment.

3.3 Evidence is available demonstrating that routine cleaning and storage does not allow microbial proliferation; Where necessary, sanitisers and disinfectants are filtered to remove spores (e.g., isopropyl alcohol).

3.4 Analytical methods used to detect residues or contaminants are validated. Guidance on analytical method validation can be obtained from publications such as the International Conference on Harmonisation (ICH) document entitled "ICH Q2(R1): Validation of Analytical Procedures: Text and Methodology", or in any standard listed in Schedule B to the Food and Drugs Act .

3.5 A cleaning procedure requiring complete product removal may not be necessary between batches of the same drug provided it meets the requirements of interpretation 3.1.

4. Individuals who supervise the implementation of the sanitation program;

4.1 are qualified by training or experience; and

4.2 are directly responsible to a person who has the qualifications described under Regulation C.02.006, interpretation 1.

5. Dusty operations are contained. The use of unit or portable dust collectors is avoided in fabrication areas especially in dispensing, unless the

---

effectiveness of their exhaust filtration is demonstrated and the units are regularly maintained in accordance with written approved procedures.

Regulation

C.02.008

(1) Every person who fabricates or packages/labels a drug shall have, in writing, minimum requirements for the health and the hygienic behaviour and clothing of personnel to ensure the clean and sanitary fabrication and packaging/labelling of the drug.

(2) No person shall have access to any area where a drug is exposed during its fabrication or packaging/labelling if the person

    (a) is affected with or is a carrier of a disease in a communicable form, or

    (b) has an open lesion on any exposed surface of the body.

Rationale

Employee's health, behaviour, and clothing may contribute to the contamination of the product. Poor personal hygiene will nullify the best sanitation program and greatly increase the risk of product contamination.

Interpretation

1. Minimum health requirements are available in writing.

    1.1 Personnel who have access to any area where a drug is exposed during its fabrication or packaging/labelling must undergo health examinations prior to employment. Medical re-examinations, based on job requirements take place periodically.

    Note: A person who is a known carrier of a disease in a communicable form should not have access to any area where a drug is exposed. The likelihood of disease transmission by means of a drug product would depend on the nature of the disease and the type of work the person carries out. Certain diseases could be transmitted through a drug product if proper hygiene procedures are not followed by an infected person handling the product. However, a person may also be a carrier of a communicable disease and not be aware of it. Therefore, in addition to strict personal hygiene procedures, systems should be in place to provide an effective barrier that would preclude contamination of the product. These procedures must be followed at all times by all personnel.

    1.2 Employees are instructed to report to their supervisor any health conditions they have that could adversely affect drug products.

    1.3 Supervisory checks are conducted to prevent any person who has an apparent illness or open lesions that may adversely affect the quality of drugs from handling exposed raw materials, primary packaging materials, in-process drugs or drugs until the condition is no longer judged to be a risk.

1.4 When an employee has been absent from the workplace due to an illness that may adversely affect the quality of products, that employee's health is assessed before he or she is allowed to return to the workplace.

1.5 A procedure in place which describes the actions to be taken in the event that a person who has been handling exposed raw materials, primary packaging materials, in-process drugs or drugs is identified as having a communicable disease.

1.6 Periodic eye examinations and/or periodic requalification are required for personnel who conduct visual inspections.

2. The written hygiene program clearly defines clothing requirements and hygiene procedures for personnel and visitors.

2.1 Where a potential for the contamination of a raw material, in-process material or drug exists, individuals wear clean clothing and protective covering.

2.2 Direct skin contact is avoided between the operator and raw materials, primary packaging materials, in-process drugs or drugs.

2.3 Unsanitary practices such as smoking, eating, drinking, chewing, and keeping plants, food, drink, smoking material and personal medicines are not permitted in production areas or in any other areas where they might adversely affect product quality.

2.4 Requirements concerning personal hygiene, with an emphasis on hand hygiene are outlined and are followed by employees.

2.5 Requirements concerning cosmetics and jewellery worn by employees are outlined and are observed by employees.

2.6 Soiled protective garments, if reusable, are stored in separate containers until properly laundered and, if necessary, disinfected or sterilized. A formalized procedure for the washing of protective garments under the control of the company is in place. Washing garments in a domestic setting is unacceptable.

2.7 Personal hygiene procedures including the use of protective clothing, apply to all persons entering production areas.

Raw Material Testing

Regulation

C.02.009

(1) Each lot or batch of raw material shall be tested against the specifications for the raw material prior to its use in the fabrication of a drug.

(2) No lot or batch of raw material shall be used in the fabrication of a drug unless that lot or batch of raw material complies with the specifications for that raw material.

(3) Notwithstanding subsection (1), water may, prior to the completion of its tests under that subsection, be used in the fabrication of a drug.

(4) Where any property of a raw material is subject to change on storage, no lot or batch of that raw material shall be used in the fabrication of a drug after its storage unless the raw material is retested after an appropriate interval and complies with its specifications for that property.

(5) Where the specifications referred to in subsections (1), (2) and (4) are not prescribed, they shall

   (a) be in writing;

   (b) be acceptable to the Director who shall take into account the specifications contained in any publication mentioned in Schedule B to the Act; and

   (c) be approved by the person in charge of the quality control department.

Rationale

The testing of raw materials before their use has three objectives: to confirm the identity of the raw materials, to provide assurance that the quality of the drug in dosage form will not be altered by raw material defects, and to obtain assurance that the raw materials have the characteristics that will provide the desired quantity or yield in a given manufacturing process.

Interpretation

1. Each raw material used in the production of a drug is covered by specifications (see regulation C.02.002) that are approved and dated by the person in charge of the quality control department or by a designated alternate who meets the requirements described under Regulation C.02.006, interpretation 1.4.

2. Specifications are of pharmacopoeial or equivalent status and are in compliance with the current marketing authorization. Where appropriate, additional properties or qualities not addressed by the pharmacopoeia (e.g., particle size, etc.) are included in the specifications.

3. Where a recognized pharmacopoeia (Schedule B of the Food and Drugs Act) contains a specification for microbial content, that requirement is included.

4. Purified water that meets any standard listed in Schedule B of the Food and Drugs Act is used in the formulation of a non-sterile drug product, unless otherwise required in one of these standards or as stated in the marketing authorization.

   4.1 Specifications should include requirements for total microbial count, which should not exceed 100 colony forming units (cfu)/ml.

   4.2 Purified water should be monitored on a routine basis for the purpose intended to ensure the absence of objectionable microorganisms (e.g., Escherichia coli and Salmonella for water used for oral preparations, Staphylococcus aureus and Pseudomonas aeruginosa for water used for topical preparations).

5. Test methods are validated, and the results of such validation studies are documented. Full validation is not required for methods included in any standard listed in Schedule B to the Food and Drugs Act , but the user of such a method establishes its suitability under actual conditions of use. Method transfer studies are conducted when applicable.

Note: Guidance for the validation of particular types of methods can be obtained in publications such as the ICH document entitled "ICH Q2(R1): Validation of Analytical Procedures: Text and Methodology" or in any standard listed in Schedule B to the Food and Drugs Act .

6. A sample of each lot of raw material is fully tested against specifications. Sampling is conducted according to a suitable statistically valid plan.

6.1 In addition, each container of a lot of a raw material is tested for the identity of its contents using a specifically discriminating identity test.

6.2 In lieu of testing each container for identity, testing a composite sample derived from sampling each container is acceptable, as long as the following conditions are met:

6.2.1 the number of individual containers for each composite sample does not exceed 10; and

6.2.2 a potency test is performed on each composite sample to establish the mass balance of the composite sample.

6.3 In lieu of testing each container for identity, testing only a proportion of the containers is acceptable where a validated procedure has been established to ensure that no single container of raw material has been incorrectly labelled.

6.3.1 Interpretation 6.3 applies to raw material coming from a single product manufacturer or plant or coming directly from a manufacturer or in the manufacturer's sealed container where there is a history of reliability and regular audits of the manufacturer's Quality Assurance system are conducted by or on behalf of the purchaser (drug fabricator).

6.3.2 Interpretation 6.3 does not apply when the raw material is used in parenterals or supplied by intermediaries such as brokers where the source of manufacture is unknown or not audited.

6.3.3 The validation should take into account at least the following aspects;

6.3.3.1 the nature and status of the manufacturer and the supplier and their understanding of the GMP requirements of the pharmaceutical industry;

6.3.3.2 the Quality Assurance system of the manufacturer of the raw material; and

6.3.3.3 the manufacturing conditions under which the raw material is produced and controlled.

6.4 Where a batch of any raw material, after leaving the site of its fabrication is handled in any substantial way (e.g., repackaged by a third party) prior to its receipt on the premises of the person who formulates the raw material into dosage forms, each container in that batch is sampled and its contents positively identified.

7. Only raw materials that have been released by the quality control department and that are not past their established re-test date or expiry date are used in fabrication.

7.1 If any raw material is held in storage after the established re-test date, that raw material is quarantined, evaluated, and tested prior to use. The re-test date or expiry date is based on acceptable stability data developed under predefined storage conditions or on any other acceptable evidence. A batch of raw material can be re-tested and used immediately (i.e., within 30 days) after the re-test as long as it continues to comply with the specifications and has not exceeded its expiry date. A raw material held in storage after the established expiry date should not be used in fabrication.

Regulation

C.02.010

(1) The testing referred to in section C.02.009 shall be performed on a sample taken

(a) after receipt of each lot or batch of raw material on the premises of the fabricator; or

(b) subject to subsection (2), before receipt of each lot or batch of raw material on the premises of the fabricator, if

(i) the fabricator

(A)   has evidence satisfactory to the Director to demonstrate that raw materials sold to him by the vendor of that lot or batch of raw material are consistently manufactured in accordance with and consistently comply with the specifications for those raw materials, and

(B)   undertakes periodic complete confirmatory testing with a frequency satisfactory to the Director, and

(ii) the raw material has not been transported or stored under conditions that may affect its compliance with the specifications for that raw material.

(2) After a lot or batch of raw material is received on the premises of the fabricator, the lot or batch of raw material shall be tested for identity.

Rationale

Section C.02.010 outlines options as to when the testing prescribed by Section C.02.009 is carried out. The purchase of raw materials is an important operation that requires a particular and thorough knowledge of the raw materials and their fabricator. To maintain consistency in the fabrication of drug products, raw materials should originate from reliable fabricators.

Interpretation

Testing other than identity testing:

1. The testing is performed on a sample taken after receipt of the raw material on the premises of the person who formulates the raw material into dosage form, unless the vendor is certified. A raw material vendor certification program, if employed, is documented in a standard operating procedure. At a minimum, such a program includes the following:

   1.1 A written agreement outlining the specific responsibilities of each party involved. The agreement specifies:

      1.1.1 the content and the format of the certificate of analysis, which exhibits actual numerical results and makes reference to the raw material specifications and validated test methods used;

      1.1.2 that the raw material vendor must inform the drug fabricator of any changes in the processing or specifications of the raw material; and

      1.1.3 that the raw material vendor must inform the drug fabricator in case of any critical deviation during the manufacturing of a particular batch of a raw material.

   1.2 An audit report is available.

      1.2.1 For medicinal ingredients/active pharmaceutical ingredient (API), the audit report is issued by a qualified authority demonstrating that the API vendor complies with the ICH document entitled "ICH Q7: Good Manufacturing Practices Guide for Active Pharmaceutical Ingredients" or with any standard or system of equivalent quality. This report should be less than 3 years old, but is valid for 4 years from the date of the inspection. If such an audit report is unavailable or is more than 4 years old, an on-site audit of the API vendor, against the same standard or its equivalent, by a person who meets the requirements of interpretation 1 under Section C.02.006, is acceptable.

      1.2.2 For other raw materials, an audit report issued by a person who meets the requirements of interpretation 1 under section C.02.006 is acceptable.

   1.3 Complete confirmatory testing is performed on the first three lots of any each raw material received from a vendor and after significant change to the manufacturing process. A copy of the residual solvent profile is obtained. Additionally, for medicinal ingredients, a copy of the impurity profile is also obtained.

   1.4 Identification of how re-testing failures and any subsequent re-qualification of the vendor are to be addressed.

   1.5 The list of raw materials not subject to the reduced testing program (e.g., reprocessed lots).

   1.6 Complete confirmatory testing is conducted on a minimum of one lot per year of a raw material received from each vendor, with the raw material being selected on a rotational basis.

1.6.1 In addition, where multiple raw materials are received from the same vendor, confirmatory testing is carried out for each raw material at least once every five years.

1.7 A document is issued for each vendor verifying that the vendor meets the criteria for certification. The document is approved by the quality control department and is updated at an appropriate frequency.

1.8 Generally, due to the nature of its operations, a broker or wholesaler of raw materials cannot be directly certified. However, when a broker or wholesaler supplies materials received from the original vendor without changing the existing labels, packaging, certificate of analysis, and general information, then certification of the original source is still acceptable.

2. Identity testing:

Specific identity testing is conducted on all lots of any raw material received on the premises of the person who formulates the raw material into dosage forms. This identity testing is performed in accordance with Regulation C.02.009, interpretation 6.

3. Provided that the identity test referred to in interpretation 2 is performed, the lot of raw material selected for confirmatory testing may be used in fabrication prior to completion of all tests with the approval of the quality control department.

4. Conditions of transportation and storage are such that they prevent alterations to the potency, purity, or physical characteristics of the raw material. In order to demonstrate that these conditions have been met, standard operating procedures and records for shipping and receiving are available and contain:

4.1 the type of immediate packaging for the raw material;

4.2 the labelling requirements including storage conditions and special precautions or warnings, for the packaged raw material;

4.3 the mode(s) of transportation approved for shipping the packaged raw material;

4.4 a description of how the packaged raw material is sealed;

4.5 the verification required to ensure that each package has not been tampered with and that there are no damaged containers; and

4.6 evidence that special shipping requirements (e.g., refrigeration) have been met if required.

5. If a delivery or shipment of raw material is made up of different batches, each batch is considered as separate for the purposes of sampling, testing, and release.

6. If the same batch of raw material is subsequently received, this batch is also considered as separate for the purpose of sampling, testing, and release.

However, full testing to specifications may not be necessary on such a batch provided that all the following conditions are met:

6. 1 a specifically discriminating identity test is conducted;

6. 2 the raw material has not been repackaged or re-labelled;

6. 3 the raw material is within the re-test date assigned by its vendor; and

6. 4 evidence is available to demonstrate that all pre-established transportation and storage conditions have been maintained.

Manufacturing Control

Regulation

C.02.011

(1) Every fabricator, packager/labeller, distributor referred to in paragraph C.01A.003(b) and importer of a drug shall have written procedures prepared by qualified personnel in respect of the drug to ensure that the drug meets the specifications for that drug.

(2) Every person required to have written procedures referred to in subsection (1) shall ensure that each lot or batch of the drug is fabricated, packaged/labelled and tested in compliance with those procedures.

Rationale

This Regulation requires that measures be taken to maintain the integrity of a drug product from the moment the various raw materials enter the plant to the time the finished dosage form is released for sale and distributed. These measures ensure that all manufacturing processes are clearly defined, systematically reviewed in light of experience, and demonstrated to be capable of consistently manufacturing pharmaceutical products of the required quality that comply with their established specifications.

Interpretation

1. All handling of raw materials, products, and packaging materials such as receipt, quarantine, sampling, storage, tracking, labelling, dispensing, processing, packaging and distribution is done in accordance with pre-approved written procedures or instructions and recorded.

2. All critical production processes are validated. Detailed information is provided in various Health Canada validation guidelines.

3. Validation studies are conducted in accordance with predefined protocols. A written report summarizing recorded results and conclusions is prepared, evaluated, approved, and maintained.

4. Changes to production processes, systems, equipment, or materials that may affect product quality and/or process reproducibility are validated prior to implementation.

5. Any deviation from instructions or procedures is avoided. If deviations occur, qualified personnel investigate, and write a report that describes the deviation, the investigation, the rationale for disposition, and any follow-up activities required. The report is approved by the quality control department and records maintained.

6. Checks on yields and reconciliation of quantities are carried out at appropriate stages of the process to ensure that yields are within acceptable limits.

7. Deviations from the expected yield are recorded and investigated.

8. Access to production areas is restricted to designated personnel.

9. Provided that validated changeover procedures are implemented, non-medicinal products may be fabricated or packaged/labelled in areas or with equipment that is also used for the production of pharmaceutical products.

10. Before any processing operation is started, steps are taken and documented to ensure that the work area and equipment are clean and free from any raw materials, products, product residues, labels, or documents not required for the current operation.

    10.1 Operations on different products should not be carried out simultaneously or consecutively in the same room unless there is no risk of mix-up or cross-contamination.

    10.2 Checks should be carried out to ensure that transfer lines and other pieces of equipment used for the transfer of products from one area to another are correctly connected.

11. At every stage of processing, products and materials are appropriately protected from microbial and other contamination.

12. In-process control activities that are performed within the production areas do not pose any risk to the quality of the product.

13. Measuring devices are regularly checked for accuracy and precision, and records of such checks are maintained.

14. At all times during processing, all materials, bulk containers, major items of equipment and the rooms used are labelled or otherwise identified with an indication of the product or material being processed, its strength, and the batch number and, if appropriate, the stage of manufacturing.

15. Rejected materials and products are clearly marked as such and are either stored separately in restricted areas or controlled by a system that ensures that they are either returned to their vendors or, where appropriate, reprocessed or destroyed. Actions taken are recorded.

16. Upon receipt, raw materials, packaging materials, in-process (intermediate) drugs, and bulk drugs, are accounted for, documented, labelled and held in quarantine until released by the quality control department.

17. Procedures are in place to ensure the identity of the contents of each container. Containers from which samples have been drawn are identified.

18. For each consignment, all containers are checked for integrity of package and seal and to verify that the information on the order, the delivery note and the vendor's labels is in agreement.

19. Damage to containers, along with any other problem that might adversely affect the quality of a material, is recorded, reported to the quality control department, and investigated.

20. Upon receipt, containers are cleaned where necessary and labelled with the prescribed data.

21. Labels for bulk drugs, in-process drugs, raw materials, and packaging materials bear the following information:

    21.1   the designated name and, if applicable, the code or reference number of the material;

    21.2   the specific batch number(s) given by the vendor and on receipt by the fabricator or packager/labeller;

    21.3   the status of the contents (e.g., in quarantine, on test, released, rejected, to be returned or recalled) appears on the label when a manual system is used;

    21.4   an expiry date or a date beyond which re-testing is necessary; and

    21.5   the stage of manufacturing of in-process material, if applicable.

    Note: When fully computerized storage systems are used, backup systems are available in case of system failure to satisfy the requirements of interpretation 21.

22. Raw materials are dispensed and verified by qualified personnel, following a written procedure, to ensure that the correct materials are accurately weighed or measured into clean and properly labelled containers. Raw materials which are being staged are properly sealed and stored under conditions consistent with the accepted storage conditions for that material.

Manufacturing Master Formula

23. Processing operations are covered by master formula, that are prepared by, and are subject to independent checks by, persons who have the qualifications described under Regulation C.02.006 interpretation 1, including the quality control department.

24. Master formula are written to provide not less than 100% of label claim. Overages may be allowed to compensate for processing losses with documented justification and approval if appropriate. In exceptional instances, overages to compensate for losses due to degradation during manufacturing or shelf-life must be scientifically justified and in accordance with the marketing authorization. Master formula also include the following:

    24.1   the name of the product, with a reference code relating to its specifications;

24.2 a description of the dosage form, strength of the product, and batch size;

24.3 a list of all raw materials to be used, along with the amount of each, described using the designated name and a reference that is unique to that material (mention is made of any processing aids that may not be present in the final product);

24.4 a statement of the expected final yield, along with the acceptable limits, and of relevant intermediate yields, where applicable;

24.5 Identification of the principal equipment to be used, and if applicable internal codes;

24.6 the procedures, or reference to the procedures, to be used for preparing the critical equipment, (e.g., cleaning, assembling, calibrating, sterilizing, etc.);

24.7 detailed stepwise processing instructions (e.g., checks on materials, pretreatment, sequence for adding materials, mixing times or temperatures, etc.);

24.8 the instructions for any in-process controls, along with their limits; and

24.9 where necessary, the requirements for storage of the products and in-process materials, including the container-closure system, labelling storage conditions, maximum validated hold time, and any special precautions to be observed.

Packaging Master Formula

25. In the case of a packaged product, the master formula also includes for each product, package size and type, the following:

25.1 the package size, expressed in terms of the number, weight, or volume of the product in the final container;

25.2 a complete list of all the packaging materials required for a standard batch size, including quantities, sizes and types with the code or reference number relating to the specifications for each packaging material;

25.3 where appropriate, an example or reproduction of the relevant printed packaging materials and specimens, indicating where the batch number and expiry date of the product are to be positioned;

25.4 special precautions to be observed, including a careful examination of the packaging area and equipment in order to ascertain the line clearance before operations begin. These verifications are recorded;

25.5 a description of the packaging operations, including any significant subsidiary operations and the equipment to be used; and

25.6 details of in-process controls, with instructions for sampling and acceptance limits.

Manufacturing Operations

26. Each batch processed is effectively governed by an individually numbered manufacturing order prepared by qualified personnel from the master formula by such means as to prevent errors in copying or calculation and verified by qualified personnel

27. As it becomes available during the process, the following information is included on or with the manufacturing batch record:

   27.1   the name of the product;

   27.2   the number of the batch being manufactured;

   27.3   dates and times of commencement and completion of significant intermediate stages, such as blending, heating, etc., and of production;

   27.4   the batch number and/or analytical control number, as well as the quantity of each raw material actually weighed and dispensed (for active raw material, the quantity is to be adjusted if the assay value is less than 98% calculated on "as is" basis and on which the master formula was based);

   27.5   confirmation by qualified personnel of each ingredient added to a batch;

   27.6   the identification of personnel performing each step of the process; and of the person who checked each of these steps;

   27.7   the actual results of the in-process quality checks performed at appropriate stages of the process and the identification of the person carrying them out;

   27.8   the actual yield of the batch at appropriate stages of processing and the actual final yields, together with explanations for any deviations from the expected yield;

   27.9   detailed notes on special problems with written approval for any deviation from the master formula; and

   27.10   after completion, the signature of the person responsible for the processing operations.

28. Batches are combined only with the approval of the quality control department and according to pre-established written procedures.

   28.1 The introduction of part of a previous batch, conforming to the required quality, into the next batch of the same product at a defined stage of fabrication is approved beforehand. This recovery is carried out in accordance with a validated procedure and is recorded.

Packaging Operations

29. Packaging operations are performed according to comprehensive and detailed written operating procedures or specifications, which include the identification of equipment and packaging lines used to package the drug, the adequate separation and if necessary, the dedication of packaging lines that are packaging different drugs and disposal procedures for unused printed packaging materials. Packaging orders are individually numbered.

30. The method of preparing packaging orders is designed to avoid transcription errors.

31. Before any packaging operation begins, checks are made that the equipment and work station are clear of previous products, documents, and materials that are not required for the planned packaging operations and that equipment is clean and suitable for use. These checks are recorded.

32. All products and packaging materials to be used are checked on receipt by the packaging department for quantity, identity and conformity with the packaging instructions.

33. Precautions are taken to ensure that containers to be filled are free from contamination with extraneous material.

34. The name and batch number of the product being handled is displayed at each packaging station or line.

35. Packaging orders include the following information (recorded at the time each action is taken):

    35.1 the date(s) and time(s) of the packaging operations;

    35.2 the name of the product, the batch number, packaging line used, and the quantity of bulk product to be packaged, as well as the batch number and the planned quantity of finished product that will be obtained, the quantity actually obtained and the reconciliation;

    35.3 the identification of the personnel who are supervising packaging operations and the withdrawal of bulks;

    35.4 the identification of the operators of the different significant steps;

    35.5 the checks made for identity and conformity with the packaging instructions, including the results of in-process controls;

    35.6 the general appearance of the packages;

    35.7 whether the packages are complete;

    35.8 whether the correct products and packaging materials are used;

    35.9 whether any on-line printing is correct;

    35.10 the correct functioning of line monitors;

    35.11 handling precautions applied to a partly packaged product;

    35.12 notes on any special problems, including details of any deviation from the packaging instructions with written approval by qualified personnel;

    35.13 the quantity, lot number, and/or analytical control number of each packaging material and bulk drug issued for use; and

    35.14 a reconciliation of the quantity of printed packaging material and bulk drug used, destroyed or returned to stock.

36. To prevent mix-ups, samples taken away from the packaging line are not returned.

37. Whenever possible, samples of the printed packaging materials used, including specimens bearing the batch number, expiry date, and any additional overprinting, are attached to packaging orders.

38. Filling and sealing are followed as quickly as possible by labelling. If labelling is delayed, procedures are applied to ensure that no mix-ups or mislabelling can occur.

39. Upon completion of the packaging operation, any unused batch-coded packaging materials are destroyed, and their destruction is recorded. A procedure is followed if non-coded printed materials are returned to stock.

40. Outdated or obsolete packaging materials are destroyed and their disposal is recorded.

41. Products that have been involved in non-standard occurrences during packaging are subject to inspection and investigation by qualified personnel. A detailed record is kept of this operation.

42. Any significant or unusual discrepancy observed during reconciliation of the amount of bulk product and printed packaging materials and the number of units packaged is investigated and satisfactorily accounted for before release. Validated electronic verification of all printed packaging materials on the packaging line may obviate the need for their full reconciliation.

43. Printed packaging materials are:

    43.1   stored in an area to which access is restricted to designated personnel who are supervised by persons who have the qualifications outlined under Regulation C.02.006;

    43.2   withdrawn against a packaging order;

    43.3   issued and checked by persons who have the qualifications outlined under Regulation C.02.006 interpretation 3; and

    43.4   identified in such a way as to be distinguishable during the packaging operations.

44. To prevent mix-ups, roll-fed labels are preferred to cut labels. Gang printing (printing more than one item of labelling on a sheet of material) is avoided.

45. Cut labels, cartons, and other loose printed materials are stored and transported in separate closed containers.

46. Special care is taken when cut labels are used, when overprinting is carried out off-line and in hand-packaging operations. On line verification of all labels by automated electronic means can be helpful in preventing mix-ups. Checks are made to ensure that any electronic code readers, label counters or similar devices are operating correctly.

47. The correct performance of any printing (e.g., of code numbers or expiry dates) done separately or in the course of the packaging is checked and recorded.

48. Raw materials, packaging materials, intermediates, bulk drugs and finished products are (a) stored in locations that are separate and removed from immediate manufacturing areas, and (b) transported under conditions designated by the quality control department to preserve their quality and safety.

49. All intermediate and finished products are held in quarantine and are so identified in accordance with interpretation 21, until released by the quality control department.

50. Every package of a drug is identified by a lot number.

Annual Product Quality Review

51. Regular periodic or rolling quality reviews of all drugs, should be conducted with the objective of verifying the consistency of the existing process, the appropriateness of current specifications for both raw materials and finished product to highlight any trends and to identify product and process improvements. Such reviews should normally be conducted and documented annually, taking into account previous reviews, and should include at least:

    51.1 A review of critical in-process controls, finished product testing results and specifications.

    51.2 A review of all batches that failed to meet established specification(s) and their investigation.

    51.3 A review of all significant deviations or non-conformances, their related investigations, and the effectiveness of resultant corrective and preventative actions taken.

    51.4 A review of all changes carried out to the processes, analytical methods, raw materials, packaging materials, or critical suppliers.

    51.5 A review of the results of the continuing stability program and any adverse trends.

    51.6 A review of all quality-related returns, complaints and recalls and the investigations performed at the time.

    51.7 A review of adequacy of any other previous product process or equipment corrective actions.

    51.8 The qualification status of relevant equipment and systems (e.g., HVAC, water, compressed gases, etc.); and

    51.9 A review of agreements to ensure that they are up to date.

52. Quality reviews may be grouped by product type (e.g., solid dosage forms, liquid dosage forms, sterile products, etc. where scientifically justified).

53. The quality control department of the importer or distributor should ensure that the annual product quality review is performed in a timely manner.

54. Where required, there should be an agreement in place between the various parties involved (e.g., importer and fabricator) that defines their respective responsibilities in producing and assessing the quality review and taking any subsequent corrective and preventative actions.

55. The quality control department should evaluate the results of this review and an assessment should be made whether corrective and preventative action or any revalidation should be undertaken. Reasons for such corrective actions should be documented. Agreed corrective and preventative actions should be completed in a timely and effective manner. There should be procedures for the ongoing management and review of these actions and the effectiveness of these procedures verified during self-inspection.

Regulation

C.02.012

(1) Every fabricator, packager/labeller, distributor referred to in section C.01A.003, importer and wholesaler of a drug shall maintain

(a) a system of control that permits complete and rapid recall of any lot or batch of the drug that is on the market; and

(b) a program of self-inspection.

(2) Every fabricator and packager/labeller and subject to subsections (3) and (4), every distributor referred to in paragraph C.01A.003(b) and importer of a drug shall maintain a system designed to ensure that any lot or batch of the drug fabricated and packaged/labelled on premises other than their own is fabricated and packaged/labelled in accordance with the requirements of this Division.

(3) The distributor referred to in paragraph C.01A.003(b) of a drug that is fabricated, packaged/labelled, and tested in Canada by a person who holds an establishment licence that authorizes those activities is not required to comply with the requirements of subsection (2) in respect of that drug.

(4) If a drug is fabricated or packaged/labelled in an MRA country at a recognized building, the distributor referred to in paragraph C.01A.003(b) or importer of the drug is not required to comply with the requirements of subsection (2) in respect of that activity for that drug if

(a) the address of the building is set out in that person's establishment licence; and

(b) that person retains a copy of the batch certificate for each lot or batch of the drug received by that person.

Rationale

The purpose of a recall is to remove from the market, a drug that represents an undue health risk.

Drugs that have left the premises of a fabricator, packager/labeller, distributor, wholesaler and importer can be found in a variety of locations. Depending on the severity of the health risk, it may be necessary to recall a product to one level or another. Fabricators, packagers/labellers, distributors, wholesalers, and importers are expected to be able to recall to the consumer level if necessary. Additional guidance on recalls can be found in Health Canada's document entitled "Product Recall Procedures".

This Regulation also requires fabricators, packagers/labellers, distributors, wholesalers, and importers to maintain a program of self-inspection. The purpose of self-inspection is to evaluate the compliance with GMP in all aspects of production and quality control. The self-inspection program is designed to detect any shortcomings in the implementation of GMP and to recommend the necessary corrective actions.

Drugs offered for sale in Canada, regardless of whether they are domestically produced or imported, must meet the requirements of Part C, Division 2 of the Food and Drug Regulations. Contract production and analysis must be correctly defined, agreed on, and controlled in order to avoid misunderstandings that could result in a product, work, or analysis of unsatisfactory quality. Normally, a written agreement exists between the parties involved, and that document clearly establishes the duties of each party.

Interpretation

1. A written recall system is in place to ensure compliance with Section C.01.051 of the Food and Drug Regulations and requires the following:

    1.1 Health Canada is to be notified of the recall;

    1.2 Action that is taken to recall a product suspected or known to be in violation is prompt and in accordance with a pre-determined plan; the procedures to be followed are in writing and are known to all concerned;

    1.3 The person(s) responsible for initiating and co-ordinating all recall activities are identified;

    1.4 The recall procedure is capable of being put into operation at any time, during and outside normal working hours;

    1.5 The recall procedure outlines the means of notifying and implementing a recall and of deciding its extent;

    1.6 Distribution records enable tracing of each drug product, and account is taken of any products that are in transit, any samples that have been removed by the quality control department, and any professional samples that have been distributed;

    1.7 Wholesalers must obtain drug products from companies that hold an establishment licence as required in Part C, Division 1A of the Food and Drug Regulations in order to facilitate a system of control that permits complete and rapid recall;

    1.8 A written agreement clearly describes respective responsibilities when the importer or distributor assumes some or all of the wholesaler's responsibilities with respect to recalls;

    1.9 Recalled products are identified and are stored separately in a secure area until their disposition is determined;

    1.10 The progress and efficacy of the recall is assessed and recorded at intervals, and a final report is issued (including a final reconciliation); and

    1.11 All Canadian and foreign establishments involved in the fabrication, distribution, or importation of the recalled product are notified.

GUI-0001

2. A self-inspection program appropriate to the type of operations of the company, in respect to drugs, ensures compliance with Division 2, Part C of the Food and Drug Regulations.

2.1 A comprehensive written procedure that describes the functions of the self-inspection program is available.

2.2 The program of a fabricator engaged in processing a drug from raw material through to the drug in dosage form addresses itself to all aspects of the operation. For packagers/labellers, distributors, importers, and wholesalers engaged only in packaging and/or distributing drugs fabricated by another fabricator, the written program covers only those aspects of the operations over which they exercise control on their premises.

2.3 The self-inspection team includes personnel who are suitably trained and qualified in GMP.

2.4 Periodic self-inspections are carried out.

2.5 Reports on the findings of the inspections and on corrective actions are reviewed by appropriate senior company management. Corrective actions are implemented in a timely manner.

3. To ensure compliance of contractors performing fabrication and packaging/labelling:

3.1 All arrangements for contract fabrication or packaging/labelling are in accordance with the marketing authorization for the drug product concerned.

3.2 There is a written agreement covering the fabrication or packaging/labelling arranged among the parties involved. The agreement specifies their respective responsibilities relating to the fabrication or packaging/labelling and control of the product.

3.2.1 Technical aspects of the agreement are drawn up by qualified personnel suitably knowledgeable in pharmaceutical technology, and GMP.

3.2.2 The agreement permits the distributor or importer to audit the facilities of the contractor.

3.2.3 The agreement clearly describes as a minimum who is responsible for:

3.2.3 1 purchasing, sampling, testing, and releasing materials;

3.2.3 2 undertaking production, quality, and in-process controls; and

3.2.3 3 process validation.

3.2.4 No subcontracting of any work should occur without written authorization.

3.2.5 The agreement specifies the way in which the quality control department of the distributor or importer releasing the lot or batch for sale, ensures that each lot or batch has been fabricated and packaged/labelled in compliance with the requirements of the marketing authorization.

3.2.6 The agreement describes the handling of raw materials, packaging materials, in-process drug, bulk drug and finished products if they are rejected.

3.3 The contractor's complaint/recall procedures specify that any records relevant to assessing the quality of a drug product in the event of complaints or a suspected defect are accessible to the distributor or importer.

3.4 The fabricator, packager/labeller, distributor, or importer provides the contractor with all the information necessary to carry out the contracted operations correctly in accordance with the marketing authorization and any other legal requirements. The fabricator, packager/labeller, distributor, or importer ensures that the contractor is fully aware of any problems associated with the product, work or tests that might pose a hazard to premises, equipment, personnel, other materials or other products.

3.5 The fabricator, packager/labeller, distributor, or importer is responsible for assessing the contractor's continuing competence to carry out the work or tests required in accordance with the principles of GMP described in these guidelines.

3.5.1 Distributors of drugs fabricated, packaged/labelled and tested at Canadian sites are required only to have a copy of the relevant valid Canadian establishment licence held by the Canadian fabricator or packager/labeller or tester.

3.5.2 Importers of drugs fabricated, packaged/labelled, or tested at a foreign site must meet the requirements described in Health Canada's policy document entitled "Guidance on Evidence to Demonstrate Drug GMP Compliance of Foreign Sites (GUI-0080)".

Quality Control Department

Regulation

C.02.013

(1) Every fabricator, packager/labeller, distributor referred to in paragraph C.01A.003(b), and importer shall have on their premises in Canada a quality control department that is supervised by personnel described in section C.02.006.

(2) The quality control department shall be a distinct organizational unit that functions and reports to management independently of any other functional unit, including the manufacturing, processing, packaging or sales unit.

Rationale

Quality control is the part of GMP concerned with sampling, specifications, and testing and with the organization, documentation, and release procedures. This Regulation ensures that the necessary and relevant tests are actually carried out and that raw materials and packaging materials are not released for use, nor products released for sale, until their quality has been judged to be satisfactory. Quality control is not confined to laboratory operations but must be incorporated into all activities and decisions concerning the quality of the product.

Although manufacturing and quality control personnel share the common goal of assuring that high-quality drugs are fabricated, their interests may sometimes conflict in the short run as decisions are made that will affect a company's output. For this reason, an objective and accountable quality control process can be achieved most effectively by establishing an independent quality control department. The independence of quality control from manufacturing is considered fundamental. The rationale for the requirement that the quality control department be supervised by qualified personnel is outlined under Regulation C.02.006.

GUI-0001

Interpretation

1. A person responsible for making decisions concerning quality control requirements of the fabricator, packager/labeller, distributor, and importer is on site or fully accessible to the quality control department and has adequate knowledge of on-site operations to fulfill the responsibilities of the position.

2. The quality control department has access to adequate facilities, trained personnel, and equipment in order to fulfill its duties and responsibilities.

3. Approved written procedures are available for sampling, inspecting, and testing raw materials, packaging materials, in-process drugs, bulk drugs, and finished products.

4. Quality control personnel have access to production areas for sampling and investigations as appropriate.

Regulation

C.02.014

(1) No lot or batch of drug shall be made available for sale unless the sale of that lot or batch is approved by the person in charge of the quality control department.

(2) A drug that is returned to the fabricator, packager/labeller, distributor referred to in paragraph C.01A.003(b) or importer thereof shall not be made available for further sale unless the sale of that drug is approved by the person in charge of the quality control department.

(3) No lot or batch of raw material or of packaging/labelling material shall be used in the fabrication or packaging/labelling of a drug unless that material is approved for that use by the person in charge of the quality control department.

(4) No lot or batch of a drug shall be reprocessed without the approval of the person in charge of the quality control department.

Rationale

The responsibility for the approval of all raw materials, packaging materials and finished products is vested in the quality control department. It is very important that adequate controls be exercised by this department in order to guarantee the quality of the end product.

To maintain this level of quality, it is also important to examine all returned drugs and to give special attention to reprocessed drugs.

Interpretation

1. All decisions made by the quality control department pursuant to Regulation C.02.014 are signed and dated by the person in charge of the quality control department or by a designated alternate meeting the requirements described under Section C.02.006.

2. The assessment for the release of finished products embraces all relevant factors, including the production conditions, the results of in-process testing, the fabrication and packaging documentation, compliance with the finished product specifications, an examination of the finished package, and if applicable, a review of the storage and transportation conditions.

    2.1 Deviations and borderline conformances are evaluated in accordance with a written procedure. The decision and rationale are documented. Where appropriate, batch deviations are subject to trend analysis.

    2.2 Any non-conformances, malfunctions or errors including those pertaining to premises, equipment, sanitation, and testing, that may have an impact on the quality and safety of batches pending release or released, should be assessed and the rationale documented.

    2.3 The quality control department of the importer/distributor should assure compliance to the current master production documents and the marketing authorization.

3. The quality control department ensures that raw materials and packaging materials are quarantined, sampled, tested, and released prior to their use in the fabrication or packaging/labelling of a drug.

4. Finished products returned from the market are destroyed unless it has been ascertained that their quality is satisfactory. Returned goods may be considered for resale only after they have been assessed in accordance with a written procedure. The reason for the return, the nature of the product, the storage and transportation conditions, the product's condition and history, and the time elapsed since it was originally sold are to be taken into consideration in this assessment. Records of any action taken are maintained.

    4.1 Documentation is available to support the rationale to place returned goods into inventory for further resale. Wholesalers should obtain guidance from importers/distributors to make an informed decision pertaining to the restock of the product.

5. Rejected materials and products are identified as such and quarantined. They are either returned to the vendors, reprocessed, or destroyed. Actions taken are recorded.

6. The reworking of any lot or batch of drug is given prior approval by the quality control department. Approval of a reworked lot or batch of a drug by the quality control department is based on documented scientific data, which may include validation. The reworking of products that fail to meet their specifications is undertaken only in exceptional cases. Reworking is permitted only when the following conditions are met:

   6.1 The quality of the finished product is not affected;

   6.2 The reworked lot meets specifications;

   6.3 If it is done in accordance with a defined procedure approved by the quality control department;

   6.4 All risks have been evaluated;

   6.5 Complete records of the reworking are kept;

   6.6 A new batch number is assigned; and

   6.7 The reworked lot is included in the ongoing stability program.

7. The reprocessing of any lot or batch of drug is given prior approval by the quality control department. Approval of a reprocessed lot or batch of a drug by the quality control department is based on documented scientific data, which may include validation. The reprocessing of products that fail to meet their specifications is undertaken only in exceptional cases. Reprocessing is permitted only when the following conditions are met:

   7.1 The quality of the finished product is not affected;

   7.2 The reprocessed lot meets specifications;

   7.3 The reprocessing is done in accordance with a defined procedure approved by the quality control department;

   7.4 All risks have been evaluated;

   7.5 Complete records of the reprocessing are kept;

   7.6 A new batch number is assigned; and

   7.7 Validation demonstrates that the quality of the finished product is not affected.

8. Recovery is not considered to be either a reprocessing or a reworking operation. Guidance regarding recovery is found under Regulation C.02.011, interpretation 28.1.

9. The need for additional testing of any finished product that has been reprocessed, or reworked, or into which a recovered product has been incorporated, is evaluated and acted on by the quality control department. A record is maintained.

Regulation

C.02.015

(1) All fabrication, packaging/labelling, testing, storage, and transportation methods and procedures that may affect the quality of a drug shall be

examined and approved by the person in charge of the quality control department before their implementation.

(2) The person in charge of the control department shall cause to be investigated every complaint on quality that is received respecting and cause corrective action to be taken where necessary.

(3) The person in charge of the quality control department shall cause all tests or examinations required pursuant to this Division to be performed by a competent laboratory.

Rationale

Pharmaceutical processes and products must be designed and developed taking GMP requirements into account. Production procedures and other control operations are independently examined by the quality control department. Proper storage, transportation, and distribution of materials and products minimize any risk to their quality. Complaints may indicate problems related to quality. By tracing their causes, one can determine which corrective measures should be taken to prevent recurrence. Having tests carried out by a competent laboratory provides assurance that test results are genuine and accurate.

Written agreements for consultants and contract laboratories describe the education, training, and experience of their personnel and the type of services provided and are available for examination and inspection. Records of the activities contracted are maintained.

Interpretation

The quality control department is responsible for the following:

1. All decisions made pursuant to Regulation C.02.015 are signed and dated by the person in charge of the quality control department or by a designated alternate who meets the requirements described under Regulation C.02.006 as applicable to the activity.

2. Ensuring that guidelines and procedures are in place and implemented for storage and transportation conditions, such as: temperature, humidity, lighting controls, stock rotation, sanitation, and any other precautions necessary to maintain the quality and safe distribution of the drug. Further guidance relating to storage and transportation are detailed in Health Canada's document entitled "Guidelines for Temperature Control of Drug Products during Storage and Transportation (GUI-0069)". Standard operating procedures and records for shipping and receiving are available and contain the following:

    2.1 a description of the shipping configuration and the type of packaging to be employed for shipping the finished product;

    2.2 the labelling requirements, including storage conditions and special precautions or warnings, for shipments of the finished product;

    2.3 mode(s) of transportation approved for shipping the finished product;

    2.4 the verifications required to ensure that no finished product in the shipment has been tampered with and that there are no damaged containers;

2.5 evidence that shipping requirements (e.g., temperature control) have been met if required; and

2.6 a written agreement clearly describes the respective responsibilities between the fabricator, the packager/labeller, the distributor, the importer, the wholesaler and the transportation provider relative to the storage and transportation of the drug.

3. The sampling of raw materials, packaging materials, in-process drugs, bulk drugs, and finished products is carried out in accordance with detailed written procedures. Samples are representative of the batches of material from which they are taken.

4. All complaints and other information concerning potentially defective products are reviewed according to written procedures. The complaint is recorded with all the original details and thoroughly investigated. Appropriate follow-up action is taken after investigation and evaluation of the complaint. All decisions and measures taken as a result of a complaint are recorded and referenced to the corresponding batch records. Complaint records are regularly reviewed for any indication of specific or recurring problems that require attention.

5. Establishing a change control system to provide the mechanisms for ongoing process optimization and for assuring a continuing state of control. All changes are properly documented, evaluated, and approved by the quality control department and are identified with the appropriate effective date. Any significant change may necessitate re-validation.

6. The tests are performed by a laboratory that meets all relevant GMP requirements.

   6.1 Laboratory facilities are designed, equipped, and maintained to conduct the required testing.

      6.1.1 In the microbiology laboratory, environmental monitoring is performed periodically. Microbiological cultures and sample testing are handled in an environment that minimizes contamination.

      6.1.2 The facility used to perform the sterility testing should comply with the microbial limits of an aseptic production facility which should conform to a Grade A within a Grade B background or in an isolator of a Grade A within an appropriate background and limited access to non-essential personnel.

   6.2 The individual in charge of the laboratory either (a) is an experienced university graduate who holds a degree in a science related to the work being carried out and has practical experience in his or her responsibility area or (b) reports to a person who has these qualifications C.02.006, interpretation 1).

   6.3 Laboratory personnel are sufficient in number and are qualified to carry out the work they undertake.

   6.4 Laboratory control equipment and instruments are suited to the testing procedures undertaken. Equipment and records are maintained as per the interpretations under C.02.005.

GUI-0001

6.5 Computerized systems are validated, and spreadsheets are qualified.

6.6 Water used for microbial and analytical tests meets the requirements of the test or assay in which it is used.

6.7 All reagents and culture media are recorded upon receipt or preparation. Reagents made up in the laboratory are prepared according to written procedures and are properly labelled.

6.7.1 Prepared media are sterilized using validated procedures and stored under controlled temperatures.

6.7.2 Prepared media are properly labelled with the lot numbers, expiration date and media identification. The expiration date of media is supported by growth-promotion testing results that show the performance of the media still meets acceptance criteria up to the expiration date.

6.7.3 Sterility and growth-promotion testing are performed to verify the suitability of culture media.

6.7.4 All purchased ready to use media received are accompanied by a certificate of analysis with expiry date and recommended storage conditions as well as the quality control organisms used in growth-promotion and selectivity testing of that media.

6.7.4.1 Procedures are in place to ensure that media are transported under conditions that minimize the loss of moisture and control the temperature.

6.7.4.2 Media are stored according to the vendor's instructions.

6.7.4.3 Sterility and growth-promotion testing are performed on lots received, unless the vendor is certified. Periodic confirmatory testing is performed for ready to use media received from each certified vendor.

6.7.4.4 Records are maintained.

6.8 Reference standards are available in the form of the current reference standards listed in Schedule B to the Food and Drugs Act . When such standards have not been established or are unavailable, primary standards can be used. Secondary standards are verified against a Schedule B reference standard or against the primary standard and are subject to complete confirmatory testing at predetermined intervals. All reference standards are stored and used in a manner that will not adversely affect their quality. Records relating to their testing, storage, and use are maintained.

6.9 Out of Specification (OOS) test results are investigated to determine the cause of the OOS.

6.9.1 Procedures are in place to describe the steps to be taken as part of the investigation.

6.9.2 In the case of a clearly identified laboratory or statistical error, the original results may be invalidated, and the test repeated. The original results should be retained and an explanation recorded.

6.9.3 When there is no clearly identified laboratory or statistical error and retesting is performed, the number of retests to be performed on the original sample and/or a new sample, and the statistical treatment of the resultant data, are specified in advance in the procedure.

6.9.4 All valid test results, both passing and suspect, should be reported and considered in batch release decisions.

6.9.5 If the original OOS result is found to be valid, a deviation is raised against the batch and a complete investigation is conducted. The investigation is performed in accordance to written procedures and should include an assessment of root cause, description of corrective actions and preventive actions carried out and conclusions.

6.10 To ensure compliance of contractors conducting testing required under Part C, Division 2 of the Food and Drug Regulations:

6.10.1 A Canadian contract laboratory must have a relevant valid current establishment licence. A foreign testing site must be listed on a Canadian establishment licence, as described in Health Canada's policy document entitled "Guidance on Evidence to Demonstrate Drug GMP Compliance of Foreign Sites (GUI-0080)";

6.10.2 All arrangements for external testing are in accordance with the marketing authorization for the drug product concerned, including the testing of in-process drugs, intermediates, raw materials, packaging materials and all other necessary testing required by Part C, Division 2 of the Food and Drug Regulations;

6.10.3 There is a written agreement covering all activities of testing between the contract laboratory and the parties involved. The agreement specifies their respective responsibilities relating to all aspects of testing;

6.10.3.1 Technical aspects of the agreement are drawn up by qualified personnel suitably knowledgeable in analysis and GMP;

6.10.3.2 The agreement permits audit of the facilities and operations of the external laboratory;

6.10.3.3 The agreement clearly describes as a minimum who is responsible for:

6.10.3.3.1 collection, transportation and storage conditions of samples before testing;

6.10.3.3.2 keeping stability samples at predetermined temperatures and humidity, if applicable;

6.10.3.3.3 testing methods to be used, limits and test method validation; and

6.10.3.3.4 retention of analytical results and supporting documentation (additional guidance under interpretations of C.02.021).

6.10.3.4 No subcontracting of any work should occur without written authorization.

Packaging Material Testing

Regulation

C.02.016

(1) Each lot or batch of packaging material shall, prior to its use in the packaging of a drug, be examined or tested against the specifications for that packaging material.

(2) No lot or batch of packaging material shall be used in the packaging of a drug unless the lot or batch of packaging material complies with the specifications for that packaging material.

(3) The specifications referred to in subsections (1) and (2) shall

(a) be in writing;

(b) be acceptable to the Director who shall take into account the specifications contained in any publication mentioned in Schedule B to the Act; and

(c) be approved by the person in charge of the quality control department.

Rationale

Where a drug product is presented in an inadequate package, the entire effort put into the initial research, product development and manufacturing control is wasted. Drug quality is directly dependent on packaging quality. In many cases (e.g., metered-dose aerosols), packaging quality is critical to the overall performance and effectiveness of the drug product. Faults in the packaging and labelling of a drug product continue to be a cause of drug recalls. Packaging materials are required to be tested or examined prior to their use in a packaging operation to ensure that materials of acceptable quality are used in the packaging of drugs.

Interpretation

1. Each packaging material used in the packaging/labelling of a drug is covered by specifications (as defined under C.02.002) that are approved and dated by the person in charge of the quality control department or by a designated alternate who meets the requirements described under Regulation C.02.006, interpretation 1.4. The use of recycled or reprocessed primary packaging components is permitted only after a full evaluation of the risks involved,

including any possible deleterious effects on product integrity. Specific provision is made for such a situation in the specifications.

2. Where applicable, specifications are of pharmacopeial or equivalent status and are in compliance with the marketing authorization.

3. The adequacy of test or examination methods that are not of pharmacopeial or equivalent status is established and documented.

4. Only packaging materials released by the quality control department are used in packaging/labelling.

5. Outdated or obsolete packaging material is adequately segregated until its disposition.

6. The sampling plan for packaging materials should take into account: the quantity received, the level of quality required, the nature of the material (e.g., primary packaging materials and/or printed packaging materials), the production methods, and knowledge of the Quality Assurance system of the packaging materials manufacturer. The number of samples taken should be determined statistically and specified in a sampling plan.

   6.1 Because of the higher risk of using cut labels, these labels are inspected upon receipt for absence of foreign labels using appropriate methods.

7. Sampling should take place in an appropriate environment and with precautions to prevent contamination where necessary.

Regulation

C.02.017

(1) The examination or testing referred to in section C.02.016 shall be performed on a sample taken

(a) after receipt of each lot or batch of packaging material on the premises of the person who packages a drug; or

(b) subject to subsection (2), before receipt of each lot or batch of packaging material on the premises of the person who packages a drug, if

   (i) that person

   (A) has evidence satisfactory to the Director to demonstrate that packaging materials sold to him by the vendor of that lot or batch of packaging material are consistently manufactured in accordance with and consistently comply with the specifications for those packaging materials; and

   (B) undertakes periodic complete confirmatory examination or testing with a frequency satisfactory to the Director,

(ii) the packaging material has not been transported or stored under conditions that may affect its compliance with the specifications for that packaging material.

(2) After a lot or batch of packaging material is received on the premises of the person who packages a drug,

(a) the lot or batch of the packaging material shall be examined or tested for identity; and

(b) the labels shall be examined or tested in order to ensure that they comply with the specifications for those labels.

Rationale

Regulation C.02.017 outlines options as to when the testing or examination prescribed by Regulation C.02.016 is carried out. As with raw materials, the purchase of packaging materials is an important operation that involves personnel who have thorough knowledge of the packaging materials and vendor.

Packaging materials originate only from vendors named in the relevant specifications. It is of benefit that all aspects of the production and control of packaging materials be discussed between the manufacturer and the vendor. Particular attention is paid to printed packaging materials; labels are examined or tested after receipt on the premises of the person who packages a drug.

Interpretation

1. The testing or examination of the packaging material is performed on a sample taken after their receipt on the premises of the person that packages the drug unless the vendor is certified. A packaging material vendor certification program, if employed, is documented in a standard operating procedure. At a minimum, such a program includes the following:

1.1 A written agreement outlines the specific responsibilities of each party involved. The agreement specifies:

1.1.1 all the tests to be performed by the vendor, along with the content and format of the certificate of analysis, which exhibits actual numerical results, if applicable, and makes reference to product specifications;

1.1.2 that the vendor must inform the drug packager/labeller of any changes in the processing or specifications of the packaging material; and

1.1.3 that the vendor must inform the drug packager/labeller of any critical deviations during the manufacturing of a particular batch of a packaging material.

1.2 In lieu of a written agreement, an on-site audit of the vendor's facilities and controls by qualified personnel is acceptable. The audit ensures that all criteria described under interpretation 1.1 are verified. These audits are performed at an appropriate frequency, and the results are documented;

1.3 The certification procedure also outlines how re-testing failures and any subsequent re-qualification is to be addressed;

1.4 A document is issued for each vendor verifying that the certification criteria have been met. The document is approved by the quality control department and is updated at an appropriate frequency;

1.5 When a certification program is implemented, complete confirmatory examination or testing of a minimum of one lot per year per vendor is required for non-printed packaging material; and

1.6 Generally, due to the nature of its operations, a broker or wholesaler of packaging materials cannot be directly certified. However, when a broker or wholesaler supplies materials received from the original vendor without changing the existing labels, packaging, certificate of analysis, and general information, then certification of the original source is still acceptable.

2. Provided that the material is properly identified, the lot of packaging material selected for confirmatory testing may, with the approval of the quality control department, be used in packaging prior to completion of that testing.

3. Conditions of transportation and storage are such that they prevent alterations of the characteristics of the packaging material. In order to demonstrate that these conditions have been met, standard operating procedures and records are available and contain the following:

3.1 the type of packaging to be employed;

3.2 labelling requirements;

3.3 mode of transportation;

3.4 the type of seal used on the package; and

3.5 the verification required to ensure that the package has not been tampered with and that there are no damaged containers.

4. Positive identification of all packaging materials, along with examination of all labels and other printed packaging materials, is conducted following their receipt on the premises of the person who packages the drug.

5. If a delivery or shipment of packaging material is made up of different batches, each batch is considered as separate for the purposes of sampling, testing, and release.

Finished Product Testing

Regulation

C.02.018

(1) Each lot or batch of a drug shall, prior to its availability for sale, be tested against the specifications for that drug.

(2) No lot or batch of a drug shall be available for sale unless it complies with the specifications for that drug.

(3) The specifications referred to in subsections (1) and (2) shall

(a) be in writing;

(b) be approved by the person in charge of the quality control department; and

(c) comply with the Act and these Regulations.

Rationale

Finished product tests complement the controls employed during the manufacturing process. It is the responsibility of each fabricator, packager/labeller, distributor, and importer to have adequate specifications and test methods that will help ensure that each drug sold is safe and meets the standard under which it is represented.

Interpretation

1. Written specifications are approved by the person in charge of the quality control department or by a designated alternate who meets the requirements described under Regulation C.02.006 as applicable to the activity.

   1.1. The written specifications contain a description of the drug in dosage form. This description includes all properties and qualities, including physical characteristics, identity, purity, and potency. The specifications also include tolerances and a description of all tests used to measure compliance with the established tolerances, in sufficient detail to permit performance by qualified personnel. When a unique identifier is used for identity testing, it is described in the specifications.

   1.2 Specifications are equal to or exceed a recognized standard as listed in Schedule B to the Food and Drugs Act and are in compliance with the marketing authorization.

   1.3 Where a recognized pharmacopoeia (Schedule B to the Food and Drugs Act) contains a specification for microbial content, that requirement is included.

2. Test methods are validated, and the results of such validation studies are documented. Method transfer studies are conducted when applicable.

   Note: Guidance for the validation of particular types of methods can be obtained in publications such as the ICH document entitled "ICH Q2(R1): Validation of Analytical procedures: Text and Methodology" or any standard listed in Schedule B to the Food and Drugs Act.

3. All tests are performed according to the approved specifications. These tests may be carried out by the distributor or by their contracted testing laboratory when a written agreement specifically excludes the fabricator from this obligation.

4. Any lot or batch of a drug that does not comply with specifications is quarantined pending final disposition and is not made available for sale.

Regulation

C.02.019

(1) Subject to subsections (3) and (4), in the case of a packager/labeller, distributor referred to in paragraph C.01A.003(b) or importer, the testing referred to in section C.02.018 shall be performed on a sample taken

  (a) after receipt of each lot or batch of the drug on the premises in Canada of the packager/labeller, distributor referred to in paragraph C.01A.003(b) or importer of the drug; or

  (b) subject to subsection (2), before receipt of each lot or batch of the drug on the premises described in paragraph (a), if;

    (i) the packager/labeller, distributor referred to in paragraph C.01A.003(b) or importer

      (A) has evidence satisfactory to the Director to demonstrate that drugs sold to him by the vendor of that lot or batch of the drug are consistent y manufactured in accordance with and consistently comply with the specifications for those drugs, and

      (B) undertakes periodic complete confirmatory testing with a frequency satisfactory to the Director, and

    (ii) the drug has not been transported or stored under conditions that may affect its compliance with the specifications for that drug.

(2) Where the packager/labeller, distributor referred to in paragraph C.01A.003(b) or importer of a drug receives a lot or batch of a drug on the premises in Canada, and the useful life of the drug is more than 30 days, the lot or batch of the drug shall be tested for identity, and the packager/labeller shall confirm the identity after the lot or batch is packaged/labelled.

(3) The distributor referred to in paragraph C.01A.003(b) of a drug that is fabricated, packaged/labelled and tested in Canada by a person who holds an establishment licence that authorizes those activities is not required to comply with the requirements of subsections (1) and (2) in respect of that drug.

(4) If a drug is fabricated, packaged/labelled and tested in an MRA country at a recognized building, the distributor referred to in paragraph C.01A.003(b) or importer of that drug is not required to comply with the requirements of subsections (1) and (2) in respect of that drug if

  (a) the address of the building is set out in that person's establishment licence; and

  (b) that person retains a copy of the batch certificate for each lot or batch of the drug received by that person.

Rationale

C.02.019 outlines conditions and exemptions as to when finished product testing is to be performed. Paragraph C.02.019(1) (b) outlines requirements that are to be met if the finished product testing is done before receipt on the premises of the packager/labeller, distributor, or importer of the drug. Paragraphs C.02.019(3) and C.02.019(4) outline exemptions to finished product testing.

Interpretation

1. Identity is confirmed by the packager/labeller after the lot or batch is packaged.

Sites Holding a Canadian Establishment Licence

2. To demonstrate compliance with finished product specifications, distributors of drugs fabricated, packaged/labelled and tested at Canadian sites are required only to have a copy of the authentic certificate of analysis from the licensed Canadian fabricator. This certificate shows actual numerical results and refers to the product specifications and validated test methods used. Re-testing, including identity testing, is not required.

Recognized Buildings by a Regulatory Authority in a MRA Country

3. To demonstrate compliance with finished product specifications, importers of drugs fabricated, packaged/labelled, and tested at recognized buildings authorized by a Regulatory Authority as listed by virtue of Regulation C.01A.019 and identified on their establishment licence are required only to have a batch certificate in the format agreed on by the MRA partners for each lot or batch of the drug received. Re-testing, including identity testing, is not required when the drug is fabricated, packaged/labelled, and tested in an MRA country.

Sites in Non-MRA Countries

4. For testing other than identity testing, the following conditions are to be met if the packager/labeller or importer chooses to rely on the test results provided by an establishment located in a non-MRA country:

   4.1 Evidence of ongoing GMP compliance is provided according to a system described in the interpretation of Regulation C.02.012 as demonstrated by listing on the packager/labeller's or importer's establishment licence;

   4.2 Each lot is accompanied by an authentic certificate of analysis or by a copy thereof (an electronic copy with an electronic signature is acceptable). The certificate of analysis exhibits actual numerical results and makes reference to the product specifications and validated test methods used;

       4.2.1 For terminally sterilized products, documented evidence is available from the fabricator to demonstrate that each sterilizer load was individually tested; and

       4.2.2 For aseptically filled products, evidence demonstrates that samples tested for sterility included the first container filled, the last container filled, and those filled after any significant interruption of work.

   4.3 Evidence is available to demonstrate that each lot or batch received has been transported and stored in a manner that maintains the quality of the drug. Further requirements are described in interpretation 2 of section C.02.C15;

4.4 Periodic complete confirmatory testing is performed on at least one lot per year per dosage form per fabricator. For each dosage form, products are selected on a rotational basis;

    4.4.1   In addition, where multiple drugs are received from the same fabricator, confirmatory testing is carried out for each drug at least once every five years;

    4.4.2   Confirmatory testing should be performed by an alternate laboratory. In exceptional circumstances (e.g., biologic) the original laboratory may perform confirmatory testing when justified; and

    4.4.3   No confirmatory testing for sterility, pyrogen, bacterial endotoxin, particulate matter, or general safety is required.

4.5 Provided that a specific identity test is performed, a lot or batch of the finished product selected for periodic confirmatory testing may, with the approval of the quality control department, be released for sale prior to completion of all tests.

5.   Should any failure to conform to finished product testing requirements be identified, an investigation of the extent of the non-compliance is to be conducted. This investigation may lead to reassessment and re-testing of all dosage forms from the fabricator. This procedure may include:

5.1 re-evaluation of GMP compliance; and

5.2 additional complete confirmatory testing, based on the risk associated with the non-compliance.

6.   Positive identification of each lot or batch in a shipment of a drug is carried out on a sample taken after receipt on the premises of the packager/labeller or the importer. This identity testing requirement applies to lots received from any non-MRA site. Laboratory chemical/biological testing is required unless the dosage form has unique physical characteristics. Acceptable identity testing methods include the following:

6.1 chemical testing;

6.2 biological testing; and

6.3 physical verification in cases where the product has unique identifiers.

    6.3.1   The unique identifier principle must be applied before the final chemical or biological identity testing is performed by the fabricator. Where only a portion of a lot is packaged/labelled for Canada, the identity testing must be performed after the unique identifier is applied on the Canadian labelled product.

    6.3.2   For each product and each strength, uniqueness must be confirmed in writing by the fabricator to the importer at least once a year, as well as whenever a change occurs. When no such confirmation can be obtained, chemical or biological identity testing will be required from the importer.

6.3.3   The unique identifier must be confirmed on the certificate of analysis for each lot received from the fabricator.

Note: Label review or examination of the shape and size of the container is not generally considered adequate identity testing.

6.3.4   The following unique identifiers are considered acceptable:

6.3.4.1   Tablets and capsules that are engraved, embossed, or printed with a unique logo;

6.3.4.2   Permanent identification on the drug's closure system that indicates the name and strength of the contents. This marking must be applied as part of a continuous filling process and only where the closure cannot be removed without being destroyed;

6.3.4.3   Colour closure systems as part of a continuous filling process when the fabricator uses a uniquely coloured cap or closure for only one product and strength;

6.3.4.4   A coloured vial, sometimes used for light-sensitive drugs, if it is unique to one product, strength, and fabricator;

6.3.4.5   A dedicated facility fabricating only one product;

6.3.4.6   Labelling, where preprinted containers are issued to the filling line and where the lot number either is pre-printed or is printed or crimped onto the package in a continuous process; and

6.3.4.7   Group 2 products subject to Health Canada's lot release program.

Records

Regulation

C.02.020

(1) Every fabricator, packager/labeller, distributor referred to in paragraph C.01A.003(b) and importer shall maintain on their premises in Canada, for each drug sold

(a) master production documents for the drug;

(b) evidence that each lot or batch of the drug has been fabricated, packaged/labelled, tested and stored in accordance with the procedures described in the master production documents;

(c) evidence that the conditions under which the drug was fabricated, packaged/labelled, tested and stored are in compliance with the requirements of this Division;

(d) evidence establishing the period of time during which the drug in the container in which it is sold will meet the specifications for that drug; and

(e) adequate evidence of the testing referred to in section C.02.018.

(2) Every distributor referred to in paragraph C.01A.003(b) and importer shall make available to the Director, on request, the results of testing performed on raw materials and packaging/labelling materials for each lot or batch of a drug sold.

(3) Every fabricator shall maintain on his premises

(a) the written specifications for the raw material; and

(b) adequate evidence of the raw materials testing referred to in section C.02.009.

(4) Every person who packages a drug shall maintain on his premises

(a) the written specifications for the packaging materials; and

(b) adequate evidence of the packaging material examination or testing referred to in section C.02.016.

(5) Every fabricator shall maintain on their premises in Canada

(a) detailed plans and specifications of each building in Canada at which they fabricate, package/label or test; and

(b) a description of the design and construction of those buildings.

(6) Every fabricator, packager/labeller and tester shall maintain on their premises in Canada details of the personnel employed to supervise the fabrication, packaging/labelling and testing, including each person's title, responsibilities, qualifications, experience and training.

C.02.021

(1) Subject to subsection (2), all records and evidence on the fabrication, packaging/labelling, testing and storage of a drug that are required to be maintained under this Division shall be retained for a period of at least one year after the expiration date on the label of the drug, unless otherwise specified in the person's establishment licence.

(2) All records and evidence on the testing of raw materials and packaging/labelling materials that are required to be maintained under this Division shall be retained for a period of at least five years after the materials were last used in the fabrication or packaging/labelling of a drug unless otherwise specified in the person's establishment licence.

C.02.022

Every distributor referred to in section C.01A.003, wholesaler and importer of a drug shall retain records of the sale of each lot or batch of the drug, which enable them to recall the lot or batch from the market for a period of at least one year after the expiration date of the lot or batch, unless otherwise specified in their establishment licence.

C.02.023

(1) On receipt of a complaint respecting the quality of a drug, every distributor referred to in paragraph C.01A.003(b), and importer of the drug shall make a record of the complaint and of its investigation and retain the record for a period of at least one year after the expiration date of the lot or batch of the drug, unless otherwise specified in their establishment licence.

(2) On receipt of any information respecting the quality or hazards of a drug, every distributor referred to in paragraph C.01A.003(b) and importer of the drug shall make a record of the information and retain it for a period of at least one year after the expiration date of the lot or batch of the drug unless otherwise specified in their establishment licence.

C.02.024

(1) Every fabricator, packager/labeller, distributor referred to in section C.01A.003 importer and wholesaler shall

   (a) maintain records of the results of the self-inspection program required by section C.02.012 and of any action taken in connection with that program; and

   (b) retain those records for a period of at least three years.

(2) Every person who fabricates or packages/labels a drug shall

   (a) maintain records on the operation of the sanitation program required to be implemented under section C.02.007; and

   (b) retain those records for a period of at least three years.

Rationale

Good documentation is an essential part of the quality assurance system and should therefore be related to all aspects of GMP. Its aims are to define the specifications for all materials and methods of fabrication, packaging/labelling, and control; to ensure that the quality control department has all the information necessary to decide whether or not to release a batch of a drug for sale; and to provide an audit trail that will permit investigation of the history of any batch that is suspected to be defective.

Evidence that drugs have been fabricated and packaged/labelled under prescribed conditions can be maintained only after developing adequate record systems. The information and evidence should provide assurance that imported drugs are fabricated and packaged/labelled in a like manner to those produced in Canada.

Interpretation

For all sections of Good Manufacturing Practices guidelines, standard operating procedures (SOPs) are retained for reference and inspection. These SOPs are regularly reviewed and kept up to date by qualified personnel. The reasons for any revisions are documented. A system is in place to ensure that only current SOPs are in use. Records of SOPs for all computer and automated systems are retained where appropriate.

All relevant GMP documents (such as associated records of actions taken or conclusions reached) and SOPs are approved, signed, and dated by the quality control department. Documents are not altered without the approval of the quality control department. Any alteration made to a document is signed and dated; the alteration permits the reading of the original information. Where appropriate, the reason for the change is recorded.

Records may be maintained in electronic format provided that backup copies are also maintained. Electronic data must be readily retrievable in a printed format. During the retention period, such records must be secured and accessible within 48 hours to the fabricator, packager/labeller, distributor, or importer.

An electronic signature is an acceptable alternative to a handwritten signature. When used, such a system must be evaluated and tested for security, validity, and reliability, and records of those evaluations and tests must be maintained. The validation of electronic signature identification systems is documented.

Any documentation requested for evaluation by Health Canada is provided in one of the official languages.

1. The following documents are maintained by the fabricator, packager/labeller, distributor referred to in paragraph C.01A.003(b) and importer of a drug.

    1.1 Master production documents as defined in the Glossary of Terms.

    1.1.1 When the fabricator is located in Canada, specific parts of a master production document considered to be a trade secret or confidential may be held by the fabricator rather than the distributor. When the fabricator is located outside Canada, specific parts of a master production document considered to be a trade secret or confidential may be held on behalf of the distributor or importer by an independent party in Canada. In either case, the distributor or importer must ensure that Health Canada has access to the data in a timely manner.

    1.1.2 Regardless of whether the fabricator is Canadian or foreign, the master production documents retained by the distributor or importer describe in general terms whatever information has been deleted as a trade secret or confidential.

    1.2 Evidence that each lot or batch of the drug has been fabricated, packaged/labelled, tested and stored in accordance with the procedures described in the master production documents.

    1.2.1 This evidence includes manufacturing orders, packaging orders, and test results for raw materials, packaging materials, and drugs in dosage form. However, when the drug is fabricated or packaged outside the premises of the distributor or importer, test results for raw materials and packaging materials need only be made available on request in a timely manner.

1.2.2   A certificate of manufacture is considered an acceptable alternative to complete batch documentation, provided that complete documentation is made available on request in a timely manner.

1.2.3   Where an importer of drugs from non-MRA countries employs a system involving a "certificate of manufacture", complete batch documentation is obtained at least once per year per drug.

1.2.4   A certificate of manufacture alone cannot be employed where reworking has taken place. Should there be changes to the production documents, the complete documentation is provided to the importer or distributor, and any changes that have been made are indicated.

1.3 Evidence that the conditions under which the drug was fabricated, packaged/labelled, tested, and stored are in compliance with the requirements of Part C, Division 2 of the Food and Drug Regulations.

1.3.1   This evidence includes records generated under subsection C.02.012(2) and evidence of validation. For additional guidance, refer to Health Canada's document entitled "Validation Documentation Requirements and Responsibilities for Drug Fabricators, Packagers/Labellers, Testers, Distributors and Importers (GUI-0042)".

1.3.2   Records are maintained detailing the qualifications/experience of any consultant employed for GMP purposes, along with the services that each consultant provides.

1.4 Evidence establishing the period of time during which the drug in the container in which it is sold will meet the specifications for that drug.

1.4.1   The documentation to be maintained includes the written stability program, the data generated in accordance with that program, and the conclusions leading to the establishment of the period of time during which each drug in the package in which it is sold complies with the specifications for that drug. Also included are data generated as part of the continuing stability program.

1.5 For each lot of drug in dosage form, there is adequate evidence of compliance with finished product specifications.

2.   The following documents are maintained by the fabricator, packager/labeller, distributor, wholesaler, and importer of a drug as they relate to all operations in Canada.

2.1 Distribution records of all sales of drugs, including those of professional samples.

2.1.1 Records of all sales are retained or are kept readily accessible in a manner that will permit a complete and rapid recall of any lot or batch of a drug. This requirement need not necessarily involve tracking by lot number.

2.1.2 Records to indicate that all customers who have received a recalled drug have been notified.

2.2 Records of the results of the self-inspection program, evaluation, and conclusions, and corrective measures implemented.

3. The following documents are maintained by every fabricator, packager/labeller, distributor, and importer of a drug:

3.1 Records of complaints relating to quality and of subsequent investigations of complaints, including corrective actions taken.

3.2 Records concerning information received respecting the quality or hazards of a drug.

4. The following documents are maintained by the fabricator:

4.1 the written specifications for the raw materials;

4.2 the results of the raw material testing;

4.3 the sources of the raw materials supplied;

4.4 records on the operation of the sanitation program required by Regulation C.02.007; and

4.5 detailed plans and specifications of each building where fabrication occurs, including a description of the design and construction.

5. The following documents are maintained by the person who packages or labels a drug:

5.1 the written specifications for the packaging materials;

5.2 the results of the packaging material examinations or testing;

5.3 the sources of the packaging materials supplied; and

5.4 records on the operation of the sanitation program required by Regulation C.02.007.

6. Every fabricator, packager/labeller, and tester maintains:

6.1 Details of the personnel employed to supervise the fabrication, packaging/labelling, and testing, including organization charts; each person's title, job description, responsibilities, qualifications, experience, and training; and the name(s) of each person's designated alternate(s).

7. Records required under Regulations C.02.021(1), C.02.022, and C.02.023 are retained for a period of at least one year past the expiration date of the drug to which the records apply.

Samples

Regulation

C.02.025

(1) Every distributor referred to in paragraph C.01A.003(b) and importer of a drug shall retain in Canada a sample of each lot or batch of the packaged/labelled drug for a period of at least one year after the expiration date on the label of the drug, unless otherwise specified in the distributor's or importer's establishment licence.

(2) The fabricator shall retain a sample of each lot or batch of raw materials used in the fabrication of a drug for a period of at least two years after the materials were last used in the fabrication of the drug, unless otherwise specified in the fabricator's establishment licence.

C.02.026

The samples referred to in section C.02.025 shall be in an amount that is sufficient to determine whether the drug or raw material complies with the specifications for that drug or raw material.

Rationale

These requirements help ensure that responsible officials at the establishment and Health Canada have ready access to those samples that are essential for re-examination should a product quality concern arise.

Interpretation

1. A sample of each lot or batch of a finished product is retained in Canada by the distributor referred to in paragraph C.01A.003(b) and by the importer of the drug.

   1.1 Retention samples are kept in their trade package, or in a container that is equivalent with respect to stability. In the case of large containers of finished products, a smaller representative sample may be retained, as supported by stability data. This allowance does not apply to sterile products.

   1.2 Retention samples are stored under the conditions indicated on the label.

   1.3 Retention samples are maintained in accordance with a written procedure.

   1.4 Retention samples may be stored at another site holding a Canadian Drug Establishment Licence pursuant to a written agreement clearly describing the respective responsibilities of each party.

2. A sample of each lot or batch of a raw material (including both active and inactive ingredients), is retained by the fabricator of the drug.

2.1 The sample is stored in the same packaging system in which the raw material is stored or in one that is equivalent to or more protective than the vendor's packaging system of the raw material.

2.2 The sample is stored under the conditions recommended by the vendor.

2.3 Retention samples are maintained in accordance with a written procedure.

3. In determining the size of sample to be maintained, it is to be kept in mind that Health Canada needs at least enough of the material to carry out tests to determine whether the drug or the raw material complies with its specifications. The fabricator, distributor, or importer may also wish to test the material in the event of a complaint; the sample should therefore be at least double the amount needed to complete all required tests.

4. This requirement is not considered to be applicable to the number of units normally required for sterility and pyrogen testing, or to water, solvents, and medical gases.

5. Health Canada will consider alternate sample retention sites outside of Canada for distributors and importers of pharmaceutical, radiopharmaceutical, biological, and veterinary drugs, as referred to in sub-section C.02.025(1) if a product specific request is submitted. Further guidance is available in "Alternate Sample Retention Site Guidelines (GUI-0014)".

Stability

Regulation

C.02.027

Every distributor referred to in paragraph C.01A.003(b) and importer shall establish the period of time during which each drug in the package in which it is sold will comply with the specifications.

Rationale

The purpose of the written stability program is to ascertain the normal shelf life of the products that is to determine how long the products can be expected to remain within specifications under recommended storage conditions. The requirements for the stability studies (primary and commitment batches) are outlined in the various Health Canada, ICH, and Veterinary International Conference on Harmonisation (VICH) Guidelines. Each packaged dosage form must be covered by a sufficient amount of data to support its shelf life in its trade package.

Interpretation

1. The stability of the drug is determined prior to marketing and prior to adoption of significant changes in formulation, fabrication procedures, or packaging materials that may affect the shelf life of the drug. This determination is made in accordance with Health Canada and ICH guidelines, which include conditions for storage of stability samples.

1.1 Accelerated stability data are considered to be preliminary information only. The accelerated data are supported by long term testing. When the shelf-life is assigned based on accelerated data and extrapolated long-term data, it should be verified by additional long term stability data as these data become available.

1.2 Stability studies are carried out on the drug in each package type in which it is to be sold in Canada.

1.3 For new chemical entities, at least three commercial-scale batches of each strength are sampled to verify or confirm shelf life post-approval, unless such data are submitted as a part of the application for marketing approval. For existing chemical entities (e.g., generic drugs), two commercial-scale batches of each strength are sampled. The principle of bracketing and matrixing designs may be applied if justified.

1.4 For imported products, stability studies originating from foreign sites are acceptable provided that the data meet the requirements of the various Health Canada and ICH guidelines regarding stability and that the site can demonstrate GMP compliance.

1.5 The shelf life is established based on the date of fabrication.

1.6 Stability data are available for drugs before and after constitution, reconstitution or dilution, if applicable.

1.7 Analytical test procedures used in stability evaluation are validated in accordance with the ICH document entitled "ICH Q2(R1): Validation of Analytical Procedures: Text and Methodology". Assays are to be stability-indicating, (e.g., sufficiently specific to detect and quantify degradation products and to distinguish between degraded and non-degraded materials). Limits for individual specified, unspecified, and total degradation products are included.

Regulation

C.02.028

Every distributor referred to in paragraph C.01A.003(b) and importer shall monitor, by means of a continuing program, the stability of the drug in the package in which it is sold.

Rationale

The purpose of the written continuing stability program is to monitor the validity of the product shelf life on an on-going basis. It also serves to determine how long the product can be expected to remain within specifications under recommended storage conditions. Each packaged dosage form must be covered by a sufficient amount of data to support its labelled expiry date in its trade package.

Interpretation

1. A continuing stability program is implemented to ensure compliance with the approved shelf life specifications. A protocol is available and is implemented for each drug marketed in Canada. A summary of all the data generated, including the evaluation and the conclusions of the study, is prepared. This program includes but is not limited to the following parameters:

- number of batch(es) per strength, packaging, and batch sizes,

- relevant physical, chemical, microbiological or biological test methods,

- acceptance criteria,

- container closure system(s),

- testing frequency,

- storage conditions (and tolerances) of samples, and

- other applicable parameters specific to the drug.

1.1 Any differences in the protocol for the continuing stability program and the protocol for the formal stability studies are scientifically justified.

1.2 A minimum of one batch of every strength and container closure system of the drug is enrolled into the continuing stability program each year the drug is produced. The principle of bracketing and matrixing designs may be applied if justified in accordance with the ICH document entitled "ICH Q1A (R): Stability Testing of New Drug Substances and Products".

1.3 Worst case situations should be addressed by the continuing stability program (e.g., inclusion of reworked or reprocessed lots).

1.4 Any confirmed out of specification result, or significant negative trend that may have an impact on the quality of the product should be assessed and may require further stability studies.

1.5 For imported products, stability studies originating from foreign sites are acceptable, provided that the data meet the requirements of the various Health Canada and ICH guidelines regarding stability and that the site can demonstrate GMP compliance. It is the importer's responsibility to obtain and maintain up to date records associated with the ongoing stability program.

Note: Chart 2.0 Stability is a guide for selecting parameters to be studied in the stability program. Each product must be examined separately.

a. The inclusion of a sterility test in the stability study of a sterile drug may not be necessary if the container closure system has been proven to be hermetic.

b. In addition to preservative content testing, a single regular production batch of the drug is to be tested for antimicrobial preservative effectiveness at the end of the proposed shelf life.

Chart 2.0: Stability

(Information to be used as guide only for selecting parameters to be studied in the stability program. Each product must be examined separately.)

Potency

- *Tablets:* Assay all active ingredients.

- *Capsules:* Assay all active ingredients.

- *Liquids and gels:* Assay all active ingredients, plus preservatives, antioxidants, and bacteriostats if effectiveness not checked under Purity section.

- *Ointments and creams:* Assay all active ingredients, plus preservatives, antioxidants, and bacteriostats if effectiveness not checked under Purity section.

- *Powders:* Assay all active ingredients, plus complete testing data on reconstituted forms.

- *Injectables:* Assay all active ingredients, plus preservatives, antioxidants, and bacteriostats if effectiveness not checked under Purity section.

- *Suppositories:* Assay all active ingredients,

- *Aerosols:* Assay all active ingredients, plus quantity delivered per spray for metered dose products.

Physical Characteristics

Containers (applicable to all listed dosage forms): (1) Appearance of inner walls and cap interiors colour (2) Integrity of seals (3) Appearance and adhesion of label.

- *Tablets:* Dissolution, disintegration, odour, hardness, color, appearance.

- *Capsules:* Dissolution, disintegration, condition of shells, color, appearance

- *Liquids and gels:* Odour, viscosity, specific gravity, pH, clarity of solution, precipitation of ingredients, non-homogeneity of suspensions, homogeneity (gels)

- *Ointments and Creams:* Odour, texture, pH, homogeneity, precipitation of ingredients

- *Powders:* Odour, texture, clarity of solution, homogeneity, pH (after reconstitution), particle size, flow characteristics (inhalation powders)

- *Injectables:* Clarity, particulate matter, pH, precipitation of ingredients, optical rotation, multiple dose vials: product integrity after initial use

- *Suppositories:* melting point, homogeneity

- *Aerosols:* net weight, delivery weight, delivery pressure, pH, delivery effectiveness (e.g. spray pattern and droplet size), number of doses or sprays per package

Purity

Containers (applicable to all listed dosage forms): (1) Migration of drug into plastic (2) Migration of plasticisers into drug (3) Corrosion

- *Tablets:* moisture content, microbial test, degradation products

- *Capsules:* moisture content, microbial test, degradation products

- *Liquids and gels:* sterility for ophthalmics, particulate matter for ophthalmics, microbial test, degradation products

GUI-0001

- *Ointments and Creams:* sterility for ophthalmics, particulate matter for ophthalmics, microbial test, degradation products

- *Powders.* moisture content, microbial test, degradation products

- *Injectables:* sterility, microbial test, degradation products

- *Suppositories:* microbial test, degradation products

- *Aerosols:* microbial test, degradation products

Image of "Chart 2.0 Stability"

STABILITY (Chart to be used as a guide only)								
	TABLETS	CAPSULES	LIQUIDS AND GELS	OINTMENTS AND CREAMS	POWDERS	INJECTABLES	SUPPOSITORIES	AEROSOLS
POTENCY	Assay all active ingredients as well as other "elements" outlined below							
			Plus: preservatives, antioxidants, and bacteriostats if effectiveness not checked under Purity section	Plus: preservatives, antioxidants, and bacteriostats if effectiveness not checked under Purity section	Plus: complete testing data on reconstituted forms	Plus: preservatives, antioxidants, and bacteriostats if effectiveness not checked under Purity section		Quantity delivered per spray for metered dose products
Physical Characteristics	Containers: (1) Appearance of inner walls and cap interiors colour (2) Integrity of seals (3) Appearance and adhesion of label							
	-dissolution -disintegration -odour -hardness -color -appearance	-dissolution -disintegration -condition of shells -color -appearance	-odour -viscosity -specific gravity -pH -clarity of solution -precipitation of ingredients -non-homogeneity of suspensions -homogeneity (gels)	-odour -texture -pH -homogeneity -precipitation of ingredients	-odour -texture -clarity of solution -homogeneity -pH (after reconstitution) -particle size -flow characteristics (inhalation powders)	-clarity -particulate matter -pH -precipitation of ingredients -optical rotation -multiple dose vials: product integrity after initial use	-melting point -homogeneity	-net weight -delivery weight -delivery pressure -pH -delivery effectiveness (e.g. spray pattern and droplet size) -number of doses or sprays per package
PURITY	Containers: (1) Migration of drug into plastic (2) Migration of plasticisers into drug (3) Corrosion							
	-moisture content	-moisture content	-sterility for ophthalmics -particulate matter for ophthalmics	-sterility for ophthalmics -particulate matter for ophthalmics	-moisture content	-sterility		
	Microbial Test							
	Degradation products							

Sterile Products

Regulation

C.02.029

In addition to the other requirements of this Division, a drug that is intended to be sterile shall be fabricated and packaged/labelled

(a) in separate and enclosed areas;

(b) under the supervision of personnel trained in microbiology; and

(c) by a method scientifically proven to ensure sterility.

Rationale

Sterile drugs are susceptible to particulate, pyrogenic and microbiological contamination. Due to the health hazard associated with the use of contaminated sterile products, special precautions are required in the production of these products. The skill, training, and competency of all personnel involved are critical.

Quality assurance is important and the production must follow carefully established and validated methods of preparation and sterilization.

Interpretation

General

1. Separate packaging and labelling operations of hermetically sealed containers are not subject to Regulation C.02.029 but are covered under Regulation C.02.011.

2. When designing procedures for achieving sterility, a number of factors must be considered, particularly airborne microorganisms, particulate matter, the size of the opening of the container, the length of time contents are exposed, and assurance that all the material is exposed to the sterilization condition or process.

3. All aqueous-based sterile products must be subjected to terminal steam sterilization, with the following exceptions:

    3.1 Instances where terminal steam sterilization is not practicable (e.g., where the sterilization process would cause product or packaging degradation). The rationale for the departure from the standard is fully evaluated and documented; and

    3.2 Aseptic processes that exclude human intervention (e.g., robotics, form-fill-seal, and barrier systems) may be employed in lieu of terminal sterilization, provided that the data developed demonstrate an acceptable level of sterility assurance. Any such methods introduced are fully validated, taking into account all critical factors of the technology used as well as the routine monitoring to be carried out.

4. Environmental Grade requirements and monitoring:

Drugs subject to terminal sterilization

    4.1 Formulation takes place in an environment with a minimum classification of Grade C, provided that the formulated bulk is immediately subjected to its subsequent processing step, (e.g., filtration, sterilization), in order to minimize bio-burden and particulates.

    4.2 Formulation may take place in a Grade D environment if additional measures (e.g., the use of closed systems of manufacture) are taken to minimize contamination.

    4.3 Parenterals are filled in an aseptic area with at least a Grade B environment or in a Grade A zone with at least a Grade C background, before terminal sterilization.

        4.3.1 Parenterals that are to be terminally sterilized may be filled in a Grade C area if the process or product does not pose a high-risk of microbial contamination. Examples of high-risk situations include slow filling operations, the use of wide-necked containers, or the exposure of filled containers to the environment for more than a few seconds before sealing.

GUI-0001

4.4 Non-parenterals may be filled in a Grade C environment before terminal sterilization.

Drugs not subject to terminal sterilization

4.5 Parenterals sterilized by filtration, are formulated in an environment with a minimum classification of a Grade C.

4.6 Non-parenteral products may be formulated in a Grade D environment if additional measures are taken to minimize contamination such as the use of closed systems.

4.7 Sterile filtration requires a minimum filter rating of 0.2 µm. The integrity of the filter is verified before and after use by an appropriate method such as a bubble point, diffusion or pressure hold tests.

4.8 Filling operations are performed under local Grade A conditions within a Grade B background environment. However a lower-grade background environment may be acceptable if specialized automated or barrier techniques are employed and if those techniques are validated to demonstrate that their use has no negative impact on the quality of the drug.

Drugs not subject to filtration or terminal sterilization

4.9 Sterile products subject to neither filtration nor terminal sterilization, are produced from sterile raw materials and packaging components in an aseptic area under local Grade A conditions with a Grade B background. Additional information pertaining to blow-fill-seal and isolator technology is provided in interpretations 82 and 83 under the Sterile Products section.

5. The air standards described in the following tables are to be achieved throughout the area when it is occupied and in operation. In the operational condition for Grade A zone, the air standards apply in the zone immediately surrounding the drug whenever it is exposed, and with at least a Grade B background. It may not always be possible to demonstrate conformity with air standards for non-viable particulates at the point of fill when filling is in progress, owing to the generation of particles or droplets by the product itself.

5.1 The "at rest" state is the condition where the installation is complete, including fabrication equipment installed and present in an operational condition but not in use and with operating personnel absent. The "in operation" state should not commence until all the predefined criteria have been met with the equipment and personnel in place.

6. The classification of aseptic and clean areas is based on environmental results obtained using acceptable standardized air sampling methods. Such methods take into account the volume and number of samples taken at each location and the total number of sampling locations. The number of sampling locations is based on room volume and on the nature of the operations being undertaken. Sampling methods used during the operational state do not interfere with zone protection.

7. Radiation sterilization is used mainly for heat-sensitive materials. Since drugs and packaging materials are radiation-sensitive, this method is

permissible only when, prior to use, evidence has confirmed the absence of any damaging effects on the material.

8. Ethylene Oxide sterilization is used only when other methods are not practicable. Evidence must be available to show the absence of any damaging effect on the drug when this method is used. The conditions and time allowed for degassing the drug are such that residual gas and reaction products are reduced to clearly defined acceptable limits.

9. Ultraviolet irradiation is not an acceptable method of sterilization.

Basic Environmental Standards for the Manufacture of Sterile Products

Chart 3.0: Airborne Particulate Classification for the Manufacture of Sterile Products

Grade	at rest (Note 5)		in operation	
	Maximum permitted number of particles / m³ equal to or above (Note 3)			
	0.5 µm	5 µm	0.5µm	5 µm
A (Note 1)	3,520	20	3,520	20
B (Note 2)	3,520	29	352,000	2,900
C (Note 2)	352,000	2,900	3,520,000	29,000
D (Note 2)	3,520,000	29,000	not defined (Note 4)	not defined (Note 4)

Notes :

1. Unidirectional airflow systems provide a homogeneous air speed of 0.45 meters/ second +/- 20% (guidance value) at the working position in open clean room applications. The maintenance of unidirectional air flow should be demonstrated and validated. A unidirectional air flow and lower velocities may be used in closed isolators and glove boxes.

2. In order to attain air Grades B, C, and D, the number of air changes will be related to the size of the area and to the equipment and personnel present in the area.

3. Low values for contaminants are reliable only when a large number of air samples are taken. Adequate data is available to generate confidence that the required conditions are met throughout the duration of the operations.

4. The requirement and limits for this area will depend on the nature of the operations carried out.

5. The particulate conditions given in the "at rest" column are to be achieved after a short clean-up period (15 to 20 minutes) in an unmanned state after completion of operations.

Chart 4.0: Recommended Limits for Microbial Contamination

GRADE	air sample cfu/m³	settle plates (diameter 90mm), colony-forming units (cfu)/4 hours (refer to Note b)	contact plates (diameter 55mm), colony-forming units (cfu)/plate (refer to Note c)	glove print (5 fingers) colony-forming units (cfu)/glove (refer to Note d)
Recommended limits for microbial contamination (refer to Note a and e)				
A	< 1	< 1	< 1	< 1
B	10	5	5	5

GUI-0001

Recommended limits for microbial contamination (refer to Note a and e)

GRADE	air sample cfu/m³	settle plates (diameter 90mm), colony-forming units (cfu)/4 hours (refer to Note b)	contact plates (diameter 55mm), colony-forming units (cfu)/plate (refer to Note c)	glove print (5 fingers) colony-forming units (cfu)/glove (refer to Note d)
C	100	50	25	-
D	200	100	50	-

Notes :

(a)   These are average values; however, averaging of results can mask unacceptable localized conditions, therefore individual excursions should be treated with caution. Appropriate alert and action limits should be set for microbial monitoring. If the limits are exceeded, operating procedures should prescribe investigation and corrective action. Samples from Grade A critical area environments should normally yield no microbial contaminants.

(b)   Individual settle plates may be exposed for less than 4 hours.

(c)   The surface sampled with a contact plate is subject to appropriate cleaning immediately after use.

(d)   Monitoring is conducted after critical operations are complete.

(e)   All indicated sampling methods are required unless alternative methods demonstrate equivalency.

Premises

10. To the extent possible, premises are designed to avoid the unnecessary entry of supervisory or control personnel. Grade B areas are designed so that all critical operations can be observed from outside.

11. To prevent the shedding or accumulation of dust and other particulate matter, ceilings, floors, and walls in aseptic areas, and floors and walls in clean areas, have smooth impervious surfaces that permit the repeated application of cleaning and disinfecting agents.

12. To reduce the accumulation of dust and to facilitate cleaning, projecting ledges or shelves and electrical and mechanical equipment are kept to a minimum. Covings are required where walls meet floors or ceilings. Walls, floors, and ceilings form an effective seal around any traversing pipe or duct.

13. False ceilings are sealed to prevent contamination from the space above them.

14. Uncleanable devices, such as certain sliding-door rails, are avoided.

15. Where required, sinks and drains are designed, located, and maintained so as to minimize risks of microbial contamination. Sinks and drains are excluded from areas where aseptic operations are carried out.

16. Hand-washing facilities are provided only in changing rooms.

17. Changing rooms are designed as airlocks and are used to separate the different stages of changing, thus minimizing microbial and particulate

contamination of protective clothing. They are effectively flushed with filtered air. In the final stage, they are, at rest, the same grade as the area into which they lead.

18. Access to clean and aseptic areas is provided only through air-locks. Doors to airlocks are arranged so that, either by design or by procedure, only one side or door may be opened at one time (except for emergencies).

19. The air for clean and aseptic areas is supplied through filters of suitable efficiency. Unidirectional air flow systems are of appropriate design.

20. The filtered air supply for clean and aseptic areas is designed to provide a fabrication environment that meets the required grade classifications. Under all operational conditions, a positive pressure of filtered airflow is maintained in relation to surrounding areas of a lower grade. Particular attention is paid to protecting critical areas, that is, the immediate environment in which the sterilized drug product, containers, and closures are exposed.

    20.1 The air system should be provided with appropriate terminal filters such as HEPA for Grades A, B and C. An intact HEPA filter should be capable of retaining at least 99.97% of particulates greater than 0.3 μm in diameter.

    20.2 In Grade A areas the air velocity should be sufficient to protect exposed product, product contact components and product contact surfaces from environmental contamination, by sweeping particles away from the filling/closing area and maintain a unidirectional airflow during operations. Air velocity measurements should be taken at locations where meaningful and reproducible results can be obtained. Such locations should normally be not more than 30 cm away from the work site, within the air flow.

    20.3 In "critical areas" HEPA filters should be leak tested at least twice a year. The purpose of performing regularly scheduled leak tests is to detect leaks from the filter media, filter frame or seal. The aerosol selected for HEPA leak testing should not support microbial growth and should be composed of a sufficient number of particles at approximately 0.3 μm.

    20.4 HEPA filtered air should be supplied in critical areas at a velocity sufficient to sweep particles away from the filling/ closing area and maintaining a unidirectional airflow. In situ air pattern analysis should be conducted at the critical area to demonstrate unidirectional air flow, sweeping action over and away from the product, and the absence of turbulence or eddy currents.

    20.5 For aseptically filled products, the transportation and loading of partially sealed containers, such as between filling and lyophilization, should be under Grade A conditions.

21. Warning systems alert personnel when air pressure or airflow falls below established limits. Pressure differentials between areas are monitored and recorded where such differences are of importance.

    21.1 Pressure differentials between 10 and 15 Pa (0.10 cm and 0.15 cm or 0.04" and 0.06" of water) are considered effective between zones of different environmental classifications.

21.2 Pressure differentials between aseptic areas and adjacent areas should be monitored continuously and documented. All alarms should be documented and deviations from established limits should be investigated. When doors are open, outward air flow should be sufficient to minimize ingress of contamination. It is critical that the time the door can remain ajar be strictly controlled.

22. Airflow patterns do not present a contamination risk. For example, care is taken to ensure that airflows do not distribute particles from a particle-generating person, operation, or machine to a zone of higher product risk.

23. All work with microorganisms and other infectious agents known to require special precautions in manipulation is safely segregated.

Equipment

24. Equipment is designed in such a way as to facilitate cleaning, disinfection, or sterilization. Electronic accessories and those parts of large equipment that are not readily amenable to such treatment are appropriately and adequately sealed or effectively isolated.

25. To the extent possible, equipment fittings and services are designed and installed so that operations, maintenance, and repairs can take place outside clean or aseptic areas.

26. When equipment maintenance is carried out within aseptic areas during operations, sterilized instruments and tools are used. If the required standards of cleanliness and/or asepsis are not maintained during the maintenance work, the area is cleaned and disinfected before processing recommences.

27. All equipment, including sterilizers, air-filtration systems, and water-treatment systems, are subject to planned maintenance, validation, and monitoring. Following maintenance/validation, the approval for use of the equipment is documented.

28. For aseptically filled products, conveyor belts do not pass through a partition from a Grade A or Grade B area to an area of lower cleanliness unless the belts are continuously sterilized (e.g., they pass through a sterilizing tunnel).

29. Vent filters used on equipment directly involved in aseptic filling such as receiving tanks, transfer lines, and surge vessels should be integrity tested upon installation where practical or prior to installation and after batch completion

30. Vent filters used on stationary equipment such as Water for Injection (WFI) storage tanks and sterilizers, and membrane filters used to filter compressed gases, should be integrity tested prior to installation and periodically there after.

31. Filter integrity test failures should be investigated. Filters should be replaced according to written criteria at appropriate, predefined intervals, and documented.

32. All critical surfaces that come in direct contact with sterile materials should be sterile.

Water Treatment Systems

33. Water treatment facilities are designed, constructed, and maintained so as to ensure the reliable production of water of an appropriate quality. They are not operated beyond their designed capacity. Water is produced, stored, and distributed in a manner that minimizes microbial growth and prevents other types of contamination.

34. The quality of the raw feed water is established by specification and is periodically monitored for compliance. The sampling plan takes seasonal variations into account. Records are maintained.

35. Purified water is used as feed water for WFI systems and for clean steam generators. WFI is produced either by distillation or by reverse osmosis.

36. WFI is used in the formulation of parenteral, irrigation, and intra-ocular products. Purified water may be used in the formulation of ophthalmic products.

37. Purified water and WFI systems are validated that is, the ability of the systems and its procedures to maintain the appropriate level of chemical and microbial control, taking seasonal variations into account, is demonstrated and documented.

38. Alert and action limits should be established for bacterial endotoxins and microbial load. These limits should meet any standard listed under Schedule B to the Food and Drugs Act .

39. WFI storage tanks are equipped with hydrophobic bacterial-retentive vent filters.

40. Sanitization or regeneration of water systems is carried out according to a predetermined schedule and also whenever established microbial counts are exceeded within any of the system's components. Consideration is given to controlling biofilm formation.

41. The WFI system is maintained at an elevated temperature and kept in continuous movement. Water velocity through pipes is sufficient to prevent microbial attachment.

42. Piping is sloped to provide for complete drainage of the system. The system is free of dead legs.

43. All metal surfaces in contact with WFI should be, as a minimum, 316 stainless steel, and should be passivated upon or prior to installation and after changes.

44. While in use during processing, WFI is sampled daily from at least two points on a rotating basis so as to cover all outlets.

45. Revalidation of water systems is required if any of the following situations arise:

    45.1 Unscheduled or extensive maintenance is performed on the system;

45.2   New or revised sections or components are added to or removed from the system; and

45.3   The system exhibits an out-of-control trend in either chemical or microbiological parameters.

46. The extent of the re-validation work necessary is determined jointly by the personnel from the quality control, engineering, production, and any other appropriate departments. A pre-approved protocol is signed and dated by the parties involved.

Note: Refer to interpretations 74 and 75 in the "Sterile Products" section for further requirements regarding water to be used in fabrication.

Personnel

47. In addition to the requirements outlined under Regulation C.02.006, the personnel responsible for the fabrication and testing of sterile products have had training in microbiology.

48. High standards of personal hygiene and cleanliness are maintained. Personnel involved in the fabrication of sterile preparations are instructed to report any condition that may cause the shedding of abnormal numbers or types of contaminants. Periodic health checks for such conditions are conducted, and appropriate action (e.g., deciding whether to allow an individual to be involved in a particular operation) is taken by designated qualified personnel when necessary.

49. All personnel (including those whose duties involve cleaning and maintenance) employed in such areas receive regular training in disciplines relevant to the correct fabrication of sterile products, including reference to hygiene and to the basic elements of microbiology. When outside personnel who have not received such training (e.g., building or maintenance contractors) need to be brought in, particular care is taken with regard to their supervision.

50. Personnel who have been engaged in the processing of animal-tissue materials or of cultures of microorganisms other than those used in the current fabrication process do not enter areas where sterile products are fabricated unless rigorous and clearly defined decontamination procedures have been followed.

51. Only the minimum number of personnel required are present in areas where sterile products are fabricated; this is particularly important during aseptic processes. Inspections and controls are conducted from outside such areas to the extent that such an approach is possible.

52. Outdoor clothing is not brought into these areas. Personnel entering the changing rooms are already clad in standard protective garments designed for factory facilities. Changing and washing follow written procedures.

53. The clothing worn by personnel and its quality are adapted to the particular process and workplace, and the clothing is worn in such a way as to protect the product from contamination.

54. Clothing is appropriate to the environmental grade of the area where the personnel will be working. Written gowning procedures must be established for each environmental grade. Personnel must be trained according to these procedures prior to entry. Such training must be documented. Descriptions of the clothing required for each grade are given below.

For Grades A and B areas: Headgear totally encloses the person's hair, as well as any beard or mustache, the headgear is tucked into the neck of the suit; a face mask is worn to prevent the shedding of droplets; sterilized non-powdered rubber or plastic gloves and sterilized or disinfected footwear are worn; trouser-bottoms are tucked inside the footwear and garment sleeves are tucked into the gloves. The protective clothing sheds virtually no fibres or particulate matter and retains particles shed by the body.

For Grade C areas: The person's hair, as well as any beard or mustache, is covered. A one- or two-piece trouser suit, gathered at the wrists and with a high neck, and appropriate shoes or overshoes are worn. The protective clothing sheds virtually no fibres or particulate matter.

For Grade D areas: The person's hair, as well as any beard or mustache, is covered. Protective clothing and appropriate shoes or overshoes are worn.

55. For every worker in an aseptic (Grades A and B) area, clean sterilized protective garments are provided at each re-entry. Gloves are regularly disinfected during operations. Masks and gloves are changed prior to every new working session.

56. Clothing used in clean and aseptic areas is laundered or cleaned in such a way that it does not gather additional particulate contaminants that can later be shed. Separate laundry facilities for such clothing are desirable. If fibres are damaged by inappropriate cleaning or sterilization, there may be an increased risk of shedding particles. Washing and sterilization operations follow standard operating procedures. Repair of clothing is carried out using appropriate materials (e.g., non-shedding thread).

57. Behavioural techniques aimed at maintaining sterility should be employed by personnel working in aseptic areas. These include:

57.1 moving slowly and deliberately;

57.2 keeping the entire body out of the path of unidirectional airflow;

57.3 approaching any manipulation in a manner that does not compromise sterility of the product; and

57.4 maintaining proper gown control.

Sanitation

58. Walls, floors, ceilings, and equipment in clean areas are cleaned and, when required, disinfected in accordance with a written procedure. This procedure differentiates between procedures that are followed daily and those that are undertaken whenever fabrication of a different drug is about to begin.

59. Walls, floors, ceilings, and equipment in aseptic areas are cleaned and, when required disinfected in accordance with a written procedure. This procedure differentiates between the cleaning and disinfection procedures that are followed daily and those that are undertaken whenever fabrication of a different drug is about to begin.

60. Disinfectants and cleaning agents to be used in aseptic processing areas should be sterile.

   60.1 A disinfectant program should also include a sporicidal agent since many common disinfectants are ineffective against spores.

61. Disinfectants and cleaning agents are monitored for microbial contamination and are sterile when used in Grades A or Grade B areas. Dilutions are kept in previously cleaned and sterilized containers and are not stored for long periods unless sterilized. Partly emptied containers are not topped up.

62. Fumigation of clean and aseptic areas may be useful for reducing microbiological contamination in inaccessible places.

63. The cleaning procedures are validated, and the disinfection procedures are monitored.

   63.1 The suitability, efficacy and limitations of disinfecting agents and procedures should be assessed including their ability to adequately remove potential contaminants from surfaces.

Manufacturing Control

64. During all processing stages, precautions are taken to minimize contamination.

65. Preparations containing live microorganisms are neither made nor transferred into containers in areas used for the processing of other pharmaceutical products. Preparations containing only dead organisms or bacterial extracts may be dispensed into containers, in the same premises as other sterile pharmaceutical products, provided that validated inactivation procedures and validated cleaning procedures are followed.

66. Activities in these areas are kept to a minimum, especially when aseptic operations are performed. The movement of personnel is controlled and methodical in order to avoid excessive shedding of particles and organisms. The ambient temperature and humidity are controlled and monitored to ensure the comfort of personnel.

67. Prior to sterilization, possibilities for microbiological contamination of raw materials and packaging materials are kept to a minimum. Specifications include requirements for microbiological quality when monitoring has indicated the need for such requirements.

68. Articles are sterilized and passed into the aseptic areas by the use of doubled-ended sterilizers equipped with interlocking doors or by another validated method.

69. Written standards are available specifying the air quality, including viable and non viable counts, to be maintained in clean and aseptic areas. Viable and non viable counts are taken at least once per shift in aseptic areas, while aseptic filling and aseptic fabrication operations are carried out, and at appropriate intervals in areas where other fabrication takes place.

   69.1   Air monitoring of "critical areas", Grade A environments should normally yield no microbiological contaminants. Contamination in a critical area should be investigated and corrective actions implemented.

   69.2   In Grades A and B areas regular monitoring for particulates and viables should be performed during each operating shift. The total sample volume should not be less than 1 cubic meter per sample for Grades A and B areas and preferably also in Grade C. For Grade C areas, monitoring frequency is justified based on the criticality of the operations and historical data for the specified area. Where product is exposed in a Grade C area, monitoring should be conducted at least once per week. Sampling locations should be based on a formal risk analysis study considering historical results and those obtained during the classification of rooms.

   69.3   Personnel working in aseptic processing areas should be microbiologically monitored once per shift. Typical monitoring sites should include operator's gloves and one gown site. Manual aseptic production processes require more aggressive personnel monitoring than automated aseptic production processes.

70. The presence of containers and materials liable to generate fibres is minimized in clean and aseptic areas.

71. Following cleaning and sterilization, components, bulk-product containers, and equipment are handled in such a way that they are not re-contaminated. The stage of processing of components, bulk-product containers, and equipment is properly identified.

72. The interval between cleaning and sterilization of components, bulk-product containers, and equipment, as well as between their sterilization and use, is as short as possible and subject to a time-limit appropriate to the validated storage conditions.

73. The time between the start of the preparation of a solution and its sterilization or filtration through a bacteria-retentive filter is as short as possible. A maximum permissible time is validated for each product, taking into account its composition and the prescribed method of storage.

74. Water used in the preparation of parenterals is tested for endotoxins and complies with its approved specifications.

75. Water used for the final rinsing of container components that are used for parenteral drugs is tested for endotoxins unless such components are depyrogenated subsequently.

76. Compressed air and gases that come in direct contact with the product/container primary surfaces must be of appropriate chemical,

GUI-0001

particulate and microbiological purity, free from oil, and must be filtered through a sterilizing filter at the point of use.

77. The microbial contamination of products (bioburden) is minimal prior to sterilization. The maximum acceptable bioburden is established on a product by product basis, and should be founded on adequate product/process design and control. Acceptable bioburden levels are further demonstrated through the execution of validation studies. This limit is related to the efficiency of the method to be used and to the risk of pyrogens and bacterial endotoxins, which are not removed by sterilization. The bioburden should be monitored before sterilization. All solutions, particularly large-volume parenterals, are passed through a bacteria-retentive filter; if possible, this filtering occurs immediately before the filling process. Where aqueous solutions are held in sealed vessels, any pressure-release outlets are protected (e.g., by hydrophobic microbial air filters).

78. Water, gas, or any heating or cooling fluid in contact with filled drug product containers (e.g., for the cool down cycle of sterilization loads) should present a low risk of microbial contamination.

79. Documented evidence that establishes the validation and validity of each sterilization process is available. The validation and validity of the sterilization process are verified at scheduled intervals, at least annually, and also whenever significant modifications or changes are made to the equipment. Loading patterns for all sterilization processes are established and validated.

79.1 Sterilization by heat

Chemical or biological indicators may also be used, but should not take the place of physical measurements.

79.1.1 Sufficient time is allowed for the whole load to reach the required temperature before measurement of the sterilizing time-period begins. This time is determined for each type of load to be processed.

79.1.2 After the high-temperature phase of a heat sterilization cycle, precautions are taken to prevent contamination of a sterilized load during cooling.

79.2 Sterilization by moist heat

79.2.1 Both temperature and pressure controls are used to monitor the process. Control instrumentation is independent from both monitoring instrumentation and recording charts. Where automated controls and monitoring systems are used for these applications, they are fully validated to ensure that the critical process requirements are met. System and cycle faults are registered by the system and observed by the operator. The reading of the independent temperature indicator is periodically monitored. For sterilizers fitted with a drain at the bottom of the chamber, it may also be necessary to record the temperature at this position throughout the sterilization period. There are frequent leak tests on the chamber when a vacuum phase is part of the cycle.

79.2.2   The items to be sterilized, other than products in sealed containers, are wrapped, if necessary, in a material that allows the removal of air and the penetration of steam but that prevents re-contamination after sterilization. All parts of the load are in contact with the sterilizing agent at the required temperature and pressure for the required time.

79.2.3   Clean steam is used for sterilization and does not contain additives at a level that could cause contamination of product or equipment.

79.3   Sterilization by dry heat

79.3.1   The process used includes air circulation within the chamber and the maintenance of a positive pressure to prevent the entry of non-sterile air. Any air admitted passes through a HEPA filter.

79.4   Sterilization by radiation

79.4.1   The radiation dose is measured during the sterilization procedure. For this purpose, dosimetry indicators that are independent of dose rate are to be used, giving a quantitative measurement of the dose received by the product itself. Dosimeters are inserted into the load in sufficient number and close enough together to ensure that there is always a dosimeter in the irradiator. Where plastic dosimeters are used, they are within the time limit of their calibration. Dosimeter absorbencies are read within a specified time period after exposure to radiation.

79.4.2   Biological indicators may be used as an additional control.

79.4.3   Materials handling procedures are designed so as to prevent mix-up between irradiated and non-irradiated materials. Radiation-sensitive colour disks are used on each package to differentiate between packages that have been subjected to irradiation and those that have not.

79.4.4   The total radiation dose is administered within a predetermined time span.

79.5   Sterilization with Ethylene Oxide (EtO)

79.5.1   Direct contact between gas and microbial cells is essential; precautions are taken to avoid the presence of organisms likely to be enclosed in such material as crystals or dried protein. The nature and quality of packaging materials can significantly affect the process.

79.5.2   Before exposure to gas, materials are brought into equilibrium with the humidity and temperature required by the process. The time required for this is balanced against the opposing need to minimize the time before sterilization.

79.5.3   Each sterilization cycle is monitored with suitable biological indicators, using the appropriate number of test pieces distributed throughout the load. The information so obtained is part of the batch record.

79.5.4   For each sterilization cycle, records are made of the time taken to complete the cycle, the pressure, the temperature and the humidity within the chamber during the process, the gas concentration, and total amount of gas used. The pressure and temperature are recorded throughout the cycle on a chart. The readings are part of the batch record.

79.5.5 After sterilization, the load is stored in a controlled manner under ventilated conditions to allow residual gas and reaction products to reduce to the defined level. This process is validated.

79.6 Biological indicators are considered only as an additional method for monitoring the sterilization, except in the case of ethylene oxide sterilization, where they are a normal part of the monitoring criteria. If they are used, strict precautions are taken to avoid transferring microbial contamination from them.

79.7 Records are available indicating that the requirements for each sterilization cycle have been met. These records include all recording charts (e.g., time/temperature).

79.8 A clear visual means is used for differentiating products that have not been sterilized from those that have been sterilized. Each basket, tray, or other carrier of products or components should be clearly labelled with the name of the material, its batch number, and an indication of whether or not it has been sterilized. Such indicators as autoclave tape or radiation sensitive colour disks may be used, where appropriate, to indicate whether or not a batch (or sub-batch) has passed through a sterilization process. These visual means are not intended to give an indication that the lot is sterile.

Note: Refer to Health Canada process validation guidelines for further guidance on these processes.

80. Aseptic Filling Operations

A written standard designed to test the efficiency of the overall aseptic filling operation is maintained. This standard includes a requirement to perform normal aseptic filling operations using sterile media.

80.1 The use of nutrient media that support microbial growth in trials to simulate aseptic operations (i.e., sterile media fills, "broth fills") is a valuable part of the overall validation of an aseptic process. Such trials have the following characteristics:

80.1.1 The trials simulate actual operations as closely as possible and also take into consideration worst case conditions;

80.1.2 The medium or media selected are capable of growing a wide spectrum of microorganisms, including those that would be expected to be found in the filling environment. Each batch of media used for process simulation must be tested for its growth promotion capabilities; and

80.1.3 The trials include a sufficient number of units of production to give a high degree of assurance that low levels of contamination, if present, would be detected.

80.2 The number of containers used for a media fill should be sufficient to allow a valid evaluation. If batches smaller than 5,000 units are filled, the minimum number of containers used for process simulation with sterile nutrient media should be equal to the maximum commercial batch size. The target is zero positives. Any positive unit indicates a potential problem regardless of the run size. All positives should be identified, and should result in a thorough, documented investigation and any identified corrective action implemented.

80.2.1 Recommended criteria for assessing state of aseptic line control are as follows:

80.2.1.1 When filling fewer than 5000 units, no contaminated units should be detected. One (1) contaminated unit is considered cause for re-validation, following an investigation.

80.2.1.2 When filling from 5,000 to 10,000 units, one (1) contaminated unit should result in an investigation, including consideration of a repeat media fill. Two (2) contaminated units are considered cause for re-validation, following investigation.

80.2.1.3 When filling more than 10,000 units, one (1) contaminated unit should result in an investigation. Two (2) contaminated units are considered cause for re-validation, following investigation.

80.2.2 Investigations of gross media fill failures should include an assessment of the potential impact on sterility assurance of batches filled since the last successful media fill.

80.3 A matrix approach to process simulation may be developed for each filling line, and should include elements such as the type of products filled, size of lots, container and closure configuration, fill volume, line speed, filling line configuration and components, and sterile hold times.

80.4 A process simulation run should be performed of sufficient duration to cover all routine manipulations and operations, various interventions known to occur during normal production, as well as worst case situations.

80.5 The process simulation test should simulate all the specific manufacturing steps, such as product transfer, sterile filtration, filling, transfer of semi-stoppered vials to the lyophilizer, the lyophilization process, and stoppering and crimping of vials.

80.6 The process simulation test program incorporates a representative number, type, and complexity of normal interventions that occur with each run, as well as non-routine interventions, and events (e.g., maintenance, stoppages, equipment, adjustments). A pre-defined list of all permitted interventions should be documented and incorporated into process simulation on a periodic basis.

80.7 The fill volume should be sufficient to assess potential microbial contamination, and to ensure the complete contact with all sterile surfaces inside the container when the container is inverted and swirled. Consideration should be given to incubation of filled vials with media contacting the closure system (e.g., inverted storage).

80.8 Incubation conditions should be suitable for recovery of bioburden and environmental isolates. Following the aseptic processing of the medium, the filled containers are incubated at 22.5 °C ± 2.5 °C or at 32.5 °C ± 2.5 °C. All media filled containers should be incubated for a minimum of 14 consecutive days. If two temperatures are used for incubation of media filled samples, then these filled containers should be incubated for at least 7 consecutive days at each temperature starting with the lower temperature.

80.9   Initial validation or re-validation requires three successful process simulation tests. In the absence of observed issues with respect to environmental monitoring or sterility testing, re-validation should take place at least semi-annually with a minimum of a single process simulation. Whenever a significant alteration in the product, premises, equipment, or process occurs or failure of process simulation occurs, re-validation is required.

80.10   Every person who is normally allowed to be in the filling room during aseptic filling operations must participate in the process simulation test, during which they must perform their normal assigned duties. Only trained and qualified personnel who have successfully participated in a process simulation test should be permitted to participate in aseptic processing. Records should be maintained.

81. Sterilization by Filtration

81.1   The sterilizing filtration should be validated to reproducibly remove viable microorganisms from the process stream, producing a sterile effluent. Validation studies should consider factors that can affect filter performance, which generally include viscosity and surface tension of the solution to be filtered, pH, compatibility of the material or formulation components with the filter, pressures, flow rates, batch volume maximum use time, temperature, osmolality, and the effects of hydraulic shock.

81.2   The microorganism Brevundimonas diminuta (ATCC 19146) when properly harvested, grown and used, is a common challenge microorganism for sterilizing filters because of its size (0.3 µm mean diameter). A challenge concentration of at least 107 organisms per cm2 of effective filtration area should generally be used, and should result in no passage of the challenge microorganism. Direct inoculation into the drug formulation is the preferred method because it provides an assessment of the effect of the drug product on the filter matrix and on the challenge organism (except for products with inherent bactericidal activity against this microbe, or oil-based formulations).

81.3   Use of redundant sterilizing filters should be considered. This second filtration via a further sterilized micro-organism retaining filter, immediately prior to filling, should be carried out as close as possible to the filling point.

81.4   When the use of one sterilizing filter has been validated to achieve sterilization of a specific product, then the sterilizing filter must satisfactorily pass integrity testing before and after use.

When more than one sterilizing filters are used in the filter train, all filters must be tested before use. The secondary sterilizing filter does not require post-use integrity testing unless the primary sterilizing filter fails. In that case, the secondary sterilizing filter must satisfactorily pass integrity testing before and after use. If there are documented reasons for not being able to perform pre-filtration filter integrity testing of either filter in a series after sterilization, (e.g., if sterility downstream of the first filter may be compromised), the filters should be tested both prior to sterilization and after use.

82. **Blow/fill/ seal**

82.1   Blow/ fill/ seal equipment used for aseptic production is fitted with an effective Grade A air shower and operated in at least a Grade C background environment. The background environment should comply with the viable and non viable limits at rest and viable limit when in operation.

82.2   Blow/ fill/ seal equipment used for the production of products that are terminally sterilized should be installed in at least a Grade D background environment.

83. **Isolator technology**

83.1   The environmental cleanliness within an isolator is a Grade A located in at least a Grade D background environment.

83.2   Decontamination procedures should ensure full exposure of all isolator surfaces to the chemical agent. Decontamination methods that render the inner surfaces of barrier and isolator systems free of viable microorganisms should be developed and validated. Residues from the decontamination process should not negatively impact product or primary contact surfaces.

83.3   For sterilization of the filling line, where decontamination methods are used to render certain product contact surfaces free of viable organisms, a minimum of a six-log reduction should be demonstrated using a suitable biological indicator.

83.4   When using Aseptic processing in isolators the integrity and seams of gloves and half suits should receive daily attention when in use and be addressed by a comprehensive preventative maintenance program. Replacement frequencies should be established in written standard operating procedures that will ensure that parts will be changed before they breakdown or degrade. Transfer systems, gaskets, and seals should be covered by a written maintenance program.

83.5   Protection against potential ingress of any airborne particles from the environment surrounding the isolator must be a design feature. A breach of isolator integrity should normally lead to a decontamination cycle. Integrity can be affected by power failures, valve failure, inadequate overpressure, holes in gloves and seams, or other leaks.

83.6   Air quality within the isolator should be monitored for microbiological quality and particulates during each shift.

Quality Control

84. Filled containers of parenteral products are inspected individually for the presence of particulates and other defects. When inspection is done visually, it takes place under suitable and controlled conditions of illumination, and background, and line speed. Operators doing the inspection pass regular eyesight checks, while wearing corrective lenses if such lenses are normally worn, and are allowed frequent breaks from inspection. Operators are subjected to routine checks for their efficiency in detecting defective units. Where other methods of inspection are used, the process is validated and the performance of the equipment is checked at intervals.

85. Filled ampules are subjected to a leaker test (e.g., dye immersion test). Samples of other containers closed by appropriately validated methods are checked for integrity of seal and/or maintenance of vacuum where applicable after an appropriate predetermined period.

86. Samples taken for sterility testing are representative of the whole of the batch, but in particular include samples taken from parts of the batch considered to be most at risk of contamination, for example:

    86.1 For products that have been filled aseptically, samples include the first and last containers filled, and those filled after any significant interruption.

    86.2 For products that have been heat-sterilized in their final containers, consideration is given to taking samples from the potentially coolest part of the load. Each sterilizer load is treated as a separate batch for sterility testing purposes.

    86.3 The validated sterility test applied to the finished product is only one measure taken to assure sterility. It is to be interpreted in conjunction with the environmental and batch processing records.

    86.4 Batches failing an initial sterility test are rejected unless a thorough investigation is carried out and the initial test is invalidated. The procedure for handling sterility test failures takes into account the guidance provided in official pharmacopeias (Schedule B to the Food and Drugs Act).

87. Where authorization for parametric release has been issued, after review of the submission which includes validation and monitoring of the process data pursuant to paragraph C.01.065(b)(ii), end product sterility testing is not required.

88. Biological indicators used for routine monitoring of a sterilization process and when used in validation/ re-validation studies should be tested to verify the accuracy of the population count stated by the vendor.

89. Media used for environmental monitoring should be tested for its growth promotion capability, in accordance with a formal written program.

90. Microbial quantification must be based on scientifically sound methods. Because devices (e.g., air sampler) vary, the user should assess the suitability of their selected monitoring devices before they are placed into service. Such devices should be calibrated and used according to appropriate procedures.

91. Environmental monitoring data generated in Grade A areas should be reviewed as part of product batch release. A written plan should be available that describes the actions to be taken when an environmental excursion occurs.

Medical Gases

Regulation

C.02.030

The provisions of C.02.025, C.02.027, and C.02.028 do not apply to medical gases.

Appendix A

Internationally Harmonized Requirements for Batch Certification

Content of the Fabricator's/Manufacturer's Batch Certificate

for Drug/Medicinal Products Exported to Countries

under the Scope of a Mutual Recognition Agreement (MRA)

Explanatory Note

In the framework of Mutual Recognition Agreements, the Sectoral Annex on Good Manufacturing Practices (GMP) requires a batch certification scheme for drug/medicinal products covered by the pharmaceutical Annex. The internationally harmonized requirements for the content of the batch certificate of a drug/medicinal product are attached. The importer of the batch is to receive and maintain the batch certificate issued by the fabricator/manufacturer. Upon request, the batch certificate has to be readily available to the regulatory authority of the importing country. This certification by the manufacturer regarding the conformity of each batch is essential to exempt the importer from re-control (re-analysis).

Each batch shipped between countries having an MRA in force must be accompanied by a batch certificate issued by the fabricator/manufacturer in the exporting country. This certificate will be issued after a full qualitative and quantitative analysis of all active and other relevant constituents to ensure that the quality of the products complies with the requirements of the marketing authorization of the importing country. The certificate will attest that the batch meets the specifications and has been manufactured in accordance with the marketing authorization of the importing country; will detail the specifications of the product, the analytical methods referenced, and the analytical results obtained; and will contain a statement that the batch processing and packaging quality control records were reviewed and found in conformity with GMP. The batch certificate will be signed by the person responsible for releasing the batch for sale or supply/export at the fabrication/manufacturing recognized building.

These harmonized requirements have been agreed on by the regulatory authorities of the following parties/countries: Australia, Canada, European Community, New Zealand, and Switzerland.

Appendix A1

Content of the Fabricator's/Manufacturer's Batch Certificate for Drug/Medicinal Products Exported to Countries under the Scope of a Mutual Recognition Agreement (MRA)

[Letterhead of Exporting Manufacturer]

1. **Name of product.**

   Proprietary, brand, or trade name in the importing country.

2. **Importing country.**

3. **Marketing authorization number.**

   The marketing authorization number of the product in the importing country should be provided

4. **Strength/Potency.**

   Identity (name) and amount per unit dose are required for all active ingredients/constituents.

5. **Dosage form** (pharmaceutical form).

6. **Package size** (contents of container) and type (e.g., vials, bottles, blisters).

7. **Lot/batch number.**

   As related to the product.

8. **Date of fabrication/manufacture.**

   In accordance with national (local) requirements.

9. **Expiry date.**

10. **Name and address of fabricator(s)/manufacturer(s) - manufacturing recognized building(s).**

    All recognized buildings involved in the manufacture of the batch including packaging and quality control of the batch, should be listed. The name(s) and address(es) given must correspond to the information provided on the manufacturing authorization/establishment licence.

11. **Number(s) of manufacturing authorization(s)/licence(s) or certificate(s) of GMP compliance held by fabricator(s)/manufacturer(s).**

    A number should be given for each recognized building listed under Item 10.

12. **Results of analysis.**

Should include the approved specifications, describe all results obtained, and refer to the analytical methods used (May refer to a separate certificate of analysis, which must be dated, signed, and attached).

13. **Comments/remarks.**

Any additional information that might be of value to the importer and/or inspector who must verify the compliance of the batch certificate (e.g., specific storage or transportation conditions).

14. **Certification statement.**

Should cover the fabrication/manufacturing, including packaging and quality control. The following text should be used: "I hereby certify that the above information is authentic and accurate. This batch of product has been fabricated/manufactured, including packaging and quality control, at the above-mentioned recognized building(s) in full compliance with the GMP requirements of the local regulatory authority and with the specifications in the marketing authorization of the importing country. The batch processing, packaging, and analysis records were reviewed and found to be in compliance with GMP".

15. **Name and position/title of person approving the batch release.**

Must include the person's company/recognized building name and address, if more than one company is mentioned under Item 10.

16. **Signature of person approving the batch release.**

17. **Date of signature.**

Appendix B

Acronyms

API:	Active Pharmaceutical Ingredient
CoC:	Certificate of Compliance
DIN:	Drug Identification Number
GMP:	Good Manufacturing Practices
HPFB:	Health Products and Food Branch
ICH:	International Conference on Harmonisation
MPD:	Master Production Documents
MRA:	Mutual Recognition Agreement
NOC:	Notice of Compliance
OOS:	Out of specification
PIC/S:	Pharmaceutical Inspection Cooperation/Scheme

VICH: Veterinary International Conference on Harmonisation

WFI: Water for Injection

WHO: World Health Organization

Glossary of Terms

The definitions given below apply to the terms used in these guidelines, they also apply to the terms used in the annexes unless otherwise specified therein. Definitions quoted from other documents are identified in brackets at the end of the definition.

Active Pharmaceutical Ingredient - "Any substance or mixture of substances that is intended to be used in the manufacture of a drug (medicinal) product and that, when used in the production of a drug, becomes an active ingredient of the drug product. Such substances are intended to furnish pharmacological activity or other direct effect in the diagnosis, cure, mitigation, treatment, or prevention of disease or to affect the structure and function of the body." (ICH, Q7)

Airlock - An enclosed space with two or more doors, that is interposed between two or more rooms, usually of differing classes of cleanliness, for the purpose of controlling the airflow between those rooms when either people or goods need to enter or leave them.

Alternate Sample Retention (ASR) Site - An alternate site specified on a Drug Establishment Licence for the storage of samples pursuant to section C.02.025 (1) of the Food and Drug Regulations.

Aseptic Area - A zone or zones within a clean area where Grade A or B (see table in Section C.02.029 of these guidelines) conditions are maintained.

Aseptic Process - A method of producing a sterile product in which sterile bulk drug or sterile raw materials are compounded and assembled with sterile packaging components under Grade A or B conditions (see table in Section C.02.029 of these guidelines).

Batch - A quantity of drug in dosage form, a raw material, or a packaging material, homogeneous within specified limits, produced according to a single production order and as attested by the signatories to the order. In the case of continuous manufacture, a batch corresponds to a defined fraction of the production, that is characterized by its intended homogeneity. It may sometimes be necessary to divide a batch into a number of sub-batches, which are later brought together to form a final homogeneous batch.

Batch Certificate - "A certificate issued by the fabricator of a lot or batch of a drug that is exported within the framework of a mutual recognition agreement and in which the fabricator

    a.   identifies the master production document for the drug and certifies that the lot or batch has been fabricated, packaged/labelled and tested in accordance with the procedures described in that document;

b.   provides a detailed description of the drug, including

   i.   a statement of all properties and qualities of the drug, including the identity, potency and purity of the drug, and

   ii.   a statement of tolerances for the properties and qualities of the drug;

c.   identifies the analytical methods used in testing the lot or batch and provides details of the analytical results obtained;

d.   sets out the addresses of the buildings at which the lot or batch was fabricated, packaged/labelled and tested; and

e.   certifies that the lot or batch was fabricated, packaged/labelled and tested in accordance with the good manufacturing practices of the regulatory authority that has recognized those buildings as meeting its good manufacturing practices standard." (C.01A.001)

(The certificate's content is also described in Appendix A).

Batch Number - A distinctive combination of numbers and/or letters that specifically identifies a batch. The batch number appears on the batch records, certificates of analysis, etc.

Biological Drug - A drug that is listed in Schedule D to the Food and Drugs Act.

Bracketing - "The design of a stability schedule such that only samples on the extremes of certain design factors (e.g., strength, package size) are tested at all time points as in a full design. The design assumes that the stability of any intermediate levels is represented by the stability of the extremes tested. Where a range of strengths is to be tested, bracketing is applicable if the strengths are identical or very closely related in composition (e.g., for a tablet range made with different compression weights of a similar basic granulation, or a capsule range made by filling different plug fill weights of the same basic composition into different sized capsule shells). Bracketing can be applied to different container sizes or to different fills in the same container closure system." (ICH, Q1AR)

Bulk Drug - A drug in dosage form that is not in its final packaging, usually in quantities larger than the largest commercially available package size.

Bulk Process Intermediate - Any intermediate form of a Schedule C or D drug (e.g., final bulk intermediate, bulk material, bulk concentrate, drug substance) which must undergo further processing before it becomes a final product. They are usually characterized by a holding time, storage conditions and the application of in-process tests.

Campaign Production - Sequential processing of material, either more than one product in a multi-product facility or more than one lot of the same product in a dedicated facility, over a defined period of time. Campaign production could occur at any point in a production process where common rooms/suites and/or equipment are reused for multiple products/lots.

Certificate of Analysis (COA) - A document containing the name and address of the laboratory performing the test(s), name and specifications of the material(s), test(s) performed, test method(s) used, actual numerical results, approval date(s), signature of approver, and any other technical information deemed necessary for its proper use.

Certificate of Compliance (CoC) - A certificate issued by a Regulatory Authority attesting to the GMP compliance of a recognized building in that country. In Canada, the CoC is issued by the HPFB Inspectorate.

Certificate of Manufacture - A document issued by a vendor to a distributor or importer that attests that a specific lot or batch of drug has been produced in accordance with its master production documents. Such certificates include a detailed summary of current batch documentation, with reference to respective dates of revision, manufacture, and packaging, and are signed and dated by the vendor's quality control department. For drugs that are fabricated, packaged/labelled and tested in MRA countries, the batch certificate is considered to be equivalent.

Certificate of Pharmaceutical Product (CPP) - A certificate issued by the Inspectorate establishing the regulatory status of the pharmaceutical, biological, radiopharmaceutical or veterinary product listed and the GMP status of the fabricator of the product. This certificate is in the format recommended by the WHO.

Change Control - A written procedure that describes the action to be taken if a change is proposed (a) to facilities, materials, equipment, and/or processes used in the fabrication, packaging, and testing of drugs, or (b) that may affect the operation of the quality or support system.

Changeover Procedure - A logical series of validated steps that ensures the proper cleaning of suites and equipment before the processing of a different product begins.

Clean Area - A room or suite of rooms where Grade C or D conditions (see table in Section C.02.029 of these guidelines) are required. The rooms have a defined environmental control of particulate and microbial contamination and are constructed, maintained, and used in such a way as to minimize the introduction, generation, and retention of contaminants.

Commitment Batches - "Production batches of a drug product for which the stability studies are initiated or completed post approval through a commitment made in the registration application." (ICH Q1A (R2))

Computerized Systems - Consists of all components, including but not limited to hardware, software, personnel, and documentation, necessary to capture, process, transfer, store, display, and manage information.

Containment - Total isolation of one or more steps of a manufacturing process to prevent cross-contamination of the product, or staff, from all other steps of the process.

Contractor - Legal entity carrying out activities on behalf of a company pursuant to a written agreement. This includes other sites within the same corporate structure.

Critical Area - Area in which the sterilized drug product, containers, and closures are exposed to environmental conditions that must be designed to maintain product sterility. Activities conducted in this area include manipulations, such as aseptic connections, sterile ingredient additions, filling and closing operations.

Critical Process - A process that if not properly controlled may cause significant variation in the quality of the finished product.

Date of Fabrication - Unless otherwise defined in the Food and Drug Regulations, this is the date when any active ingredient, excipient, anti-oxidant, preservative, or air/oxygen scavenger is first added to the lot being processed.

Dilute Drug Premix - "A drug for veterinary use that results from mixing a drug premix with a feed as defined in section 2 of the Feed Regulations, 1983, with the lowest approved dosage level of the drug." (C.01.A.001)

Director - "The Assistant Deputy Minister, Health Products and Food Branch, of the Department of Health." (A.01.010)

Distributor or Manufacturer - "A person, including an association or partnership, who under their own name, or under a trade, design or word mark, trade name or other name, word, or mark controlled by them, sells a food or drug." (A.01.010)

Divisions 1A and 2 to 4 apply to the following distributors (C.01A.003):

a. a distributor of a drug listed in Schedule C or D to the Act or in Schedule F to these Regulations, a controlled drug as defined in subsection G.01.001 (1) or a narcotic as defined in the Narcotic Control Regulations who does not hold the drug identification number for the drug or narcotic; and

b. a distributor of a drug for which that distributor holds the drug identification number.

Dosage Form - A drug product that has been processed to the point where it is now in a form in which it may be administered in individual doses.

Drug - "Any substance or mixture of substances manufactured, sold, or represented for use in (a) the diagnosis, treatment, mitigation, or prevention of a disease, a disorder, an abnormal physical state, or the symptoms thereof, in humans or animals, (b) restoring, correcting, or modifying organic functions in humans or animals, or (c) "disinfection"

in premises in which food is manufactured, prepared, or kept."
(Section 2 of the Food and Drugs Act)

In Division 1A and Division 2 of the Food and Drug Regulations, "drug" means a drug in dosage form, or a drug that is a bulk process intermediate that can be used in the preparation of a drug listed in Schedule C to the Act or in Schedule D to the Act that is of biological origin. It does not include a dilute drug premix, a medicated feed as defined in Section 2 of the Feeds Regulations, 1983, a drug that is used only for the purposes of an experimental study in accordance with a certificate issued under Section C.08.015 or a drug listed in Schedule H to the Act. (C.01A.001(2))

Drug Establishment Licence - A licence issued to a drug establishment in Canada which has been inspected and assessed as being in compliance with the applicable requirements of Divisions 2 to 4 of the Food and Drug Regulations.

Drug Identification Number - A number assigned to each drug in dosage form under the Food and Drug Regulations with the exception of blood and blood components and radiopharmaceuticals.

Drug Premix - "A drug for veterinary use to which a drug identification number has been assigned, where the directions on its label specify that it is to be mixed with feed as defined in Section 2 of the Feeds Act." (C.01A.001)

Expiry Date - "Means the earlier of (a) the date, expressed at minimum as a year and month, up to and including which a drug maintains its labelled potency, purity and physical characteristics, and (b) the date, expressed at minimum as a year and month, after which the manufacturer recommends that the drug not be used." C.01.001)

Export Certificate (under Section 37 of the Food and Drugs Act) - A certificate signed by the fabricator and a Commissioner for Taking Oaths to attest that the drug for which the certificate is prepared is not manufactured or sold for consumption in Canada and that its package and the contents do not contravene any known requirement of the law of the country to which it is or is about to be consigned.

Fabricate - "To prepare and preserve a drug for the purpose of sale." (C.01A.001)

Filling - Transferring a bulk drug into its final container and enclosing it in the container.

Finished Product - A product that has undergone all stages of production, including packaging in its final container and labelling.

Formulating - Preparing components and combining raw materials into a bulk drug.

Group 2 Products - Drugs listed in Schedule D to the Act and subject to Health Canada's lot release programme which require the highest level assessment after the notice of compliance (NOC) has been issued. This assessment includes targeted testing, protocol review, and written approval for sale of each lot in Canada in the form of a release letter.

Growth Promotion - A test in which prepared media is challenged with pre-selected organisms to assure that the media is capable of supporting growth.

Import - "To import into Canada a drug for the purpose of sale" (C.01A.001)

In-process Control - Checks performed during production in order to monitor and, if necessary, to adjust the process to ensure that the finished product conforms to its specifications. The control of the production environment or equipment may also be regarded as a part of in-process control.

In-process Drug - Any material or mixture of materials that must, to become a drug in dosage form, undergo further processing.

In-process Testing - The examination or testing of any material or mixture of materials during the manufacturing process.

Installation Qualification - The documented act of demonstrating that process equipment and ancillary systems are appropriately selected and correctly installed.

Label - "Includes any legend, word, or mark attached to, included in, belonging to, or accompanying any food, drug, cosmetic, device, or package (Section 2 of the Act). As described in package/label, the action of labelling refers to affixing the inner or outer label to the drug." (C.01A.001)

Long Term Testing - "Stability studies under the recommended storage condition, for the re-test period or shelf life proposed (or approved) for labelling." (ICH, Q1AR)

Lot - A quantity of any drug in dosage form, a raw material, or a packaging material, homogeneous within specified limits, constituting all or part of a single batch and identified by a distinctive lot number that appears on the label of the finished product.

Lot Number - "Any combination of letters, figures, or both, by which any food or drug can be traced in manufacture and identified in distribution." (A.01.010)

Manufacturer or Distributor - See definition under distributor.

Manufacturing Batch Record - Records demonstrating that the batch of a drug was fabricated in accordance with the approved master production documents.

Marketing Authorization - A legal document issued by Health Canada, authorizing the sale of a drug or a device based on the health and safety requirements of the Food and Drug Act and its associated Regulations. The marketing authorization may be in the form of a Notice of Compliance (NOC), Drug Identification Number (DIN), a device licence for classes II, III and IV medical devices, or a natural product number (NPN) or homeopathic DIN (DIN-HM).

Mass Balance - "The process of adding together the assay value and levels of degradation products to see how closely these add up to 100% of the initial value, with due consideration of the margin of analytical error." (ICH, Q1AR)

Master Formula - A document or set of documents specifying the raw materials with their quantities and the packaging materials, together with a detailed description of the procedures and precautions required to produce a specified quantity of a finished product as well as the processing instructions, including the in-process controls.

Master Production Documents (MPD) - Documents that includes specifications for raw material, for packaging material and for packaged dosage form; master formula (including composition and instructions as described in the definition above), sampling procedures, and critical processing related SOPs, whether or not these SOPs are specifically referenced in the master formula.

Matrixing - "The design of a stability schedule such that a selected subset of the total number of possible samples for all factor combinations is tested at a specified time point. At a subsequent time point, another subset of samples for all factor combinations is tested. The design assumes that the stability of each subset of samples tested represents the stability of all samples at a given time point. The differences in the samples for the same drug product should be identified as, for example, covering different batches, different strengths, different sizes of the same container closure system, and possibly in some cases, different container closure systems." (ICH, Q1A(R)) The concept of matrixing may also apply in other areas such as validation.

Medical Gas - "Any gas or mixture of gases manufactured, sold or represented for use as a drug" (C.02.002)

Medicinal Ingredient - Refer to the definition of active pharmaceutical ingredient.

MRA Country - A country that is a participant to a mutual recognition agreement with Canada. (C.01A.001).

Mutual Recognition Agreement (MRA) – "An international agreement that provides for the mutual recognition of compliance certification for Good Manufacturing Practices for drugs." (C.01A.001)

GUI-0001

Operational Qualification - The documented action of demonstrating that process equipment and ancillary systems work correctly and operate consistently in accordance with established specifications.

Package - "As described in package/label, the action of packaging refers to putting a drug in its immediate container." (C.01A.001)

Package/label - "To put a drug in its immediate container or to affix the inner or outer label to the drug." (C.01A.001)

Packaging Batch Record - Records demonstrating that the batch of a drug was packaged in accordance with the approved master production documents.

Packaging Material - Labels, printed packaging materials and those components in direct contact with the dosage form. (refer to C.02.002)

Parenteral Use - "Administration of a drug by means of hypodermic syringe, needle or other instrument through or into the skin or mucous membrane." C.01.001)

Pharmaceutical - "A drug other than a drug listed in Schedule C or D to the Act." (C.01A.001).

Potency - The activity or amount of active moiety, or any form thereof, indicated by label claim to be present.

Process Validation - Establishing documented evidence with a high degree of assurance, that a specific process will consistently produce a product meeting its predetermined specifications and quality characteristics. Process validation may take the form of Prospective, Concurrent or Retrospective Validation and Process Qualification or Re-validation.

Production - All operations involved in the preparation of a finished product, from receipt of materials, through processing and packaging, to completion of the finished product, including storage.

Purified Water - As defined in any standard listed in Schedule B to the Food and Drugs Act.

Purity - The extent to which a raw material or a drug in dosage form is free from undesirable or adulterating chemical, biological, or physical entities as defined by specifications.

Qualified Authority - A member of the Pharmaceutical Inspection Cooperation/Scheme (PIC/S) or the United States Food and Drug Administration (USFDA).

Quality Risk Management - A systematic process for the assessment, control, communication and review of risks to the quality of the medicinal product. It can be applied both proactively and retrospectively (ICH, Q9).

Quarantine - Effective restriction of the availability of material or product for use (physically or by system), until released by the quality control department.

Radiopharmaceutical - "A drug that exhibits spontaneous disintegration of unstable nuclei with the emission of nuclear particles or photons." C.03.201)

Raw Material - Any substance, other than in-process drug or packaging material, intended to be used in the manufacture of drugs, including those that appear in the master formula but that do not appear in the drug such as solvents and processing aids.

Recognized Building - "In respect of the fabrication, packaging/labelling or testing of a drug a building that a regulatory authority that is designated under subsection C.01A.019(1) in respect of that activity has recognized as meeting its Good Manufacturing Practices standards in respect of that activity for that drug." (C.01A.001)

Reconciliation - A comparison, making due allowance for normal variation, between the amount of product or materials theoretically produced or used and the amount actually produced or used.

Recovery - The introduction of all or part of previous batches of the required quality into another batch at a defined stage of manufacture.

Regulatory Authority - A government agency or other entity in an MRA country that has a legal right to control the use or sale of drugs within that country and that may take enforcement action to ensure that drugs marketed within its jurisdiction comply with legal requirements (C.01A.001)

Re-packaging / Re-labelling - Replacement of packaging or labelling of previously packaged and labelled products.

Reprocessing - Subjecting all or part of a batch or lot of an in-process drug a bulk process intermediate (final biological bulk intermediate) or a bulk drug of a single batch/lot to a previous step in the validated manufacturing process due to failure to meet predetermined specifications. Reprocessing procedures are foreseen as occasionally necessary and are validated and pre-approved by the quality control department or as part of the marketing authorization.

Re-test Date - "The date when a material should be re-examined to ensure that it is still suitable for use." (ICH Q7)

Re-test Period - "The period of time during which a drug substance can be considered to remain within the specifications and therefore acceptable for use in the fabrication of a given drug product, provided that it has been stored under defined conditions; after this period, the batch is re-tested for compliance with specifications and then used immediately." (ICH, Q1AR)

GUI-0001

Reworking - "Subjecting an in-process drug, a bulk process intermediate (final biological bulk intermediate), or final product of a single batch/lot to an alternate manufacturing process due to a failure to meet predetermined specifications. Reworking is an unexpected occurrence and is not pre-approved as part of the marketing authorization." (WHO GMP)

Secondary Labelling - The operation of affixing an inner or outer label to a previously labelled container to fulfill the regulatory requirements of Part C of the Food and Drug Regulations.

Self-contained Facility - Means a premise that provides complete and total separation of all aspects of the operation, including personnel and equipment movement, with well established procedures, controls and monitoring. This includes physical barriers and separate utilities such as air handling systems. A self-contained facility does not necessarily imply a distinct and separate building.

Sell - "Offer for sale, expose for sale, have in possession for sale, and distribute, regardless of whether the distribution is made for consideration." (Section 2 of the Food and Drugs Act)

Shelf Life - The time interval during which a drug product is expected to remain within the approved specification provided that it is stored under the conditions defined on the label and in the proposed containers and closure.

Specifications - "Means a detailed description of a drug, the raw material used in a drug, or the packaging material for a drug and includes:

    a. a statement of all properties and qualities of the drug, raw material or packaging material that are relevant to the manufacture, packaging, and use of the drug, including the identity, potency, and purity of the drug, raw material, or packaging material,

    b. a detailed description of the methods used for testing and examining the drug, raw material, or packaging material, and

    c. a statement of tolerances for the properties and qualities of the drug, raw material, or packaging material." C.02.002.)

Standard Operating Procedure (SOP) - A written procedure giving instructions for performing operations not necessarily specific to a given product or material but of a more general nature (e.g., equipment operation, maintenance and cleaning; validation; cleaning of premises and environmental control; sampling and inspection). Certain SOPs may be used to supplement product-specific master and batch production documents.

Sterile - Free from viable microorganisms.

Sterilizing Filter - A filter used to render a material sterile. Sterilizing filters have a rated pore size of 0.2 µm or less.

System - A regulated pattern of interacting activities and techniques that are united to form an organized whole.

Terminal Sterilization - Sterilizing a drug in its final closed container.

Test - To perform the tests, including any examinations, evaluations, and assessments, as specified in the Division 2 of the Food and Drug Regulations.

Validation - The documented act of demonstrating that any procedure, process, and activity will consistently lead to the expected results. Includes the qualification of systems and equipment.

Vendor - Person who is the fabricator of the item (raw material, packaging material, medicinal ingredients, reagents).

Veterinary Drugs - Drugs that are administered to food-producing and companion animals.

Wholesale - "To sell any of the following drugs, other than at retail sale, where the seller s name does not appear on the label of the drugs:

    i.   a drug listed in Schedule C or D to the Act or in Schedule F to these Regulations or a controlled drug as defined in subsection G.C1.001 (1); or

    ii.   a narcotic as defined in the Narcotic Control Regulations." (C.01A.001)

Appendix C

Annexes to the Current Edition of the Good Manufacturing Practices (GMP) Guidelines

The list of references in this Appendix has been updated. Annex numbers and document titles have been changed to correspond to those used by the European Union (EU) and PIC/S. This is done in order to work towards the global harmonization of technical standards and procedures related to GMP, and in preparation for Health Canada's revisions on these documents, which is anticipated to start in the near future. URLs to the documents, active at the time of this GUI-0001 posting, have been provided.

Annexes are available on Health Canada's Web site in the Compliance and Enforcement section.

1.   Annex 1 to the Current Edition of the Good Manufacturing Practices Guidelines - Selected Category IV Monograph Drugs (GUI-0066)

2.   Annex 2 to the Current Edition of the Good Manufacturing Practices Guidelines - Schedule D Drugs, Biological Drugs Including Fractionated Blood Products (GUI-0027)

3.   Annex 3 to the Current Edition of the Good Manufacturing Practices Guidelines - Schedule C Drugs (GUI-0026)

4. Annex 4 to the Current Edition of the Good Manufacturing Practices Guidelines - Veterinary Drugs (GUI-0012)

5. Annex 5 to the Current Edition of the Good Manufacturing Practices Guidelines - Positron Emitting Radiopharmaceuticals (PER's) (GUI-0071)

6. Annex 11 to the Current Edition of the Good Manufacturing Practices Guidelines - Computerised Systems (GUI-0050)

7. Annex 13 to the Current Edition of the Good Manufacturing Practices Guidelines - Drugs Used in Clinical Trials (GUI-0036)

8. Annex 14 to the Current Edition of the Good Manufacturing Practices Guidelines - Schedule D Drugs, Human Blood and Blood Components (GUI-0032)

9. Annex 17 to the Current Edition of the Good Manufacturing Practices Guidelines - Guidance on Parametric Release (GUI-0046)

References

Justice Canada

Acts and regulations of Canada are available on Justice Laws Web Site.

1. **Food and Drugs Act:**
   http://laws.justice.gc.ca/en/F-27

2. **Food and Drug Regulations:**
   http://laws.justice.gc.ca/en/F-27/C.R.C.-C.870

3. **Controlled Drugs and Substances Act:**
   http://laws.justice.gc.ca/en/C-38.8

Health Canada

Guides (GUI) and Questions and Answers (Q&As) that relate to GMPs are available on Health Canada's Web Site in the Compliance and Enforcement section under Good Manufacturing Practices.

4. Alternate Sample Retention Site Guidelines (GUI-0014)

5. Cleaning Validation Guidelines (GUI-0028)

6. Good Manufacturing Practices - Questions and Answers

7. Good Manufacturing Practices Guidelines for Medical Gases (GUI-0031)

8. Good Manufacturing Practices for Medical Gases - Questions and Answers

9. Guidance on Evidence to Demonstrate Drug Good Manufacturing Practices Compliance of Foreign Sites (GUI-0080)

10. Guidelines for Temperature Control of Drug Products during Storage and Transportation (GUI-0069)

11. Importation and Exportation Questions and Answers

12. Process Validation Guidelines:

- Aseptic Processes for Pharmaceuticals (GUI-0006)

- Form-Fill-Seal for Drugs (GUI-0008)

- Gaseous Sterilization for Pharmaceuticals (GUI-0007)

- Irradiation Sterilization for Pharmaceuticals (GUI-0009)

- Moist Heat Sterilization for Pharmaceuticals (GUI-0010)

13. Recall Procedures

- Product Recall Procedures

- Recall Policy (POL-0016)

- HPFBI Guidelines for Recall of Drug and Natural Health Products (GUI-0039)

14. Risk Classification of Good Manufacturing Practices Observations (GUI–0023)

15. Validation Documentation Requirements and Responsibilities for Drug Fabricators, Packagers/Labellers, Distributors and Importers (GUI-0042)

16. Validation Guidelines for Pharmaceutical Dosage Forms (GUI-0029)

Documents that relate to stability are available on Health Canada's Web site in the Drug Products secton under Application and Submissions

17. Stability Requirements for Changes to Marketed New Drugs

18. Stability Testing of Existing Drug Substances and Products

Guidance documents developed by the International Conference on Harmonisation (ICH) and adopted by Health Canada's Web site in the Drug Products section under CH (International Conference on Harmonisation)

19. ICH Q1A(R2): Stability Testing of New Drug Substances and Products

20. ICH Q1B: Stability Testing: Photostability Testing of New Drug Substances and Products

21. ICH Q1C: Stability Testing for New Dosage Forms

22. Validation of Analytical Procedures: Text and Methodology

ICH Q2(R1): Validation of Analytical Procedures: Text and Methodology

23. ICH Q7A: Good Manufacturing Practice Guide for Active Pharmaceutical Ingredients

24. ICH Q9: Quality Risk Management

Health Products and Food Branch Inspectorate - Operational Centres

Atlantic Operational Centre

Health Products and Food Branch Inspectorate
16th floor, suite 1625
1505 Barrington Street
Halifax, Nova Scotia
B3J 3Y6

Tel: 902-426-2160
Fax: 902-426-6676
E-mail: insp_aoc-coa@hc-sc.gc.ca

Inspectorate Ottawa

Health Products and Food Branch Inspectorate
Graham Spry Building, 2nd Floor
250 Lanark Avenue
Address Locator #2002B
Ottawa, Ontario
K1A 0K9

Tel: 613-957-1492
Fax: 613-957-6709
E-mail: GMP_questions_BPF@hc-sc.gc.ca

Ontario Operational Centre

Health Products and Food Branch Inspectorate
2301 Midland Avenue
Scarborough, Ontario
M1P 4R7

Tel: 416-973-1600
Fax: 416-973-1954
E-mail: insp_onoc-coon@hc-sc.gc.ca

Manitoba and Saskatchewan Operational Centre

Health Products and Food Branch Inspectorate
510 Lagimodière Blvd
Winnipeg, Manitoba
R2J 3Y1

Tel: 204-984-1341
Fax: 204-984-2155
E-mail: Insp_MSOC_COMS@hc-sc.gc.ca

Quebec Operational Centre

Health Products and Food Branch Inspectorate
1001 St-Laurent Street West
Longueuil, Quebec
J4K 1C7

Tel: 450-646-1353
Fax: 450-928-4455
E-mail: QOC-COQ@hc-sc.gc.ca

Western Operational Centre

Health Products and Food Branch Inspectorate
4th Floor
4595 Canada Way
Burnaby, British-Colombia
V5G 1J9

Tel: 604-666-3704
Fax: 604-666-3149
E-mail: insp_woc-coo@hc-sc.gc.ca

GUI-0001

Good Manufacturing Practices for Schedule D Drugs - Part 1 - Biological Drugs

Health Products and Food Branch Inspectorate

Annex to the GMP Guidelines

Supersedes: First Draft, March 24, 1998

Date issued: June 30th, 1999

Date of implementation: June 30th, 1999

Good Manufacturing Practices for Schedule D Drugs[17]

Part 1

Biological Drugs

including fractionated blood products

*Revisions were made to this document on 2002-02-25 to reflect changes to the Health Products and Food Branch organizational structure. There were no other changes made to the content of the document.

Preface

Biological Drugs are listed in Schedule D to the Food and Drugs Act and are regulated under the Food and Drugs Regulations. The Regulations which pertain to biological drugs are, for the most part, found within Divisions 1, 1A, 2, 4 and 8. With the advent of Establishment Licensing, the requirements of Division 1A and Division 2, apply to biological drugs, both as bulk process intermediates and in dosage form. Section 12 of The Food and Drugs Act prohibits the sale of Schedule D drugs unless the premises in which the drug was manufactured and the process and conditions of manufacture therein are suitable to ensure that the drug will not be unsafe for use.

The approach to the regulatory control of biological drugs is largely determined by the source of biological starting materials and the method of manufacture. Since the biological processes employed are inherently variable, there is a consequential effect on the end products and by-products. These processes also

---

[17] Available on the Health Canada website at http://www.hc-sc.gc.ca/dhp-mps/compli-conform/gmp-bpf/docs/sched_d_part1-annexe_d_part1_tc-tm-eng.php

have great potential for the introduction and/or proliferation of microbial contaminants.

This Annex to the GMP guidelines is intended to address special considerations and issues pertinent to the manufacture and control of biological drugs and is divided into 2 distinct parts. Part 1 addresses GMP requirements for biological drugs including fractionated blood products (animal and human) and Part 2, published separately, addresses the GMP requirements for human blood and blood components. The emerging issue of multi-product facilities (including a suite within a facility and a multi-suite complex) has also been given general consideration in developing this document.

Biological drugs include but are not limited to:

vaccines; human blood and blood components; fractionated blood products (human, animal); antigens; allergens; hormones; cytokines; enzymes and products of fermentation (including monoclonal antibodies and products derived from rDNA technology).

Biological drugs whose manufacture involves the following methods fall within the scope of the Annex Part 1:

a. Growth of microbial agents and eukaryotic cells,

b. Extraction and/or use of biological tissues, fluids or organs from human, animal or plant,

c. Recombinant DNA (rDNA) technology,

d. Hybridoma technology,

Other regulations including the Transportation of Dangerous Goods Act and Regulations, and Regulations governing the Importation of Pathogens or Semen, should be consulted for references to specific controls required for microorganisms. The Health Canada Laboratory Biosafety Guidelines should also be consulted for classification of facilities involved in the large-scale production of microorganisms.

This Annex Part 1 should be used, in context, with the Inspectorate Guidelines for Good Manufacturing Practices (GMP) to facilitate compliance with Division 2 of the Food and Drugs Regulations by fabricators, importers, testers and distributors of biological drugs. Fabricators are invited to refer to Division 4 of the Regulations for specific product requirements. Alternate means of complying with regulatory requirements must be justified and be consistent with the market authorization for the product.

Principles incorporated in international guidance (e.g., WHO, USA, and EU guidance documents for GMP for biological medicinal products) have been taken into account in the preparation of this Annex Part 1.

Glossary Of Terms

As used in Part 1, the following additional definitions supplement the definitions provided under the Glossary of Terms in the main GMP Guidelines and should be useful to fabricators, importers, testers and distributors of biological drugs.

Adventitious Virus (virus fortuit)

Unintentionally introduced contaminant virus.

Bio-Hazard (risque biologique)

>   Biological material considered to be hazardous to personnel and/or environment.

Biological Auxiliary Material (matériel biologique accessoire)

>   Raw material from a biological source which is intended to be used as a processing aid in the fabrication of the drug. It may be absent from the drug or may remain as an impurity in the drug at the end of the manufacturing process (e.g., biological additives used to supplement cell culture medium in production fermenter; human antithrombin III used to complex and remove human thrombin).

Biological Starting Material (matériel biologique de départ)

>   Raw material from a biological source which is intended to be used in the fabrication of a drug and from which the active ingredient is derived either directly (eg., plasma derivatives, ascitic fluid, bovine lung, etc.) or indirectly (eg., cell substrates, host/vector production cells, eggs, viral strains etc.).

By-Product (sous-produit)

>   A product arising incidentally in the fabrication of a specific biological drug.

Bulk Process Intermediate (produit intermédiaire en vrac)

>   Any intermediate form of a Schedule D drug (e.g., final bulk intermediate, bulk material, bulk concentrate, drug substance) which must undergo further processing before it becomes a final product. They are usually characterized by a holding time, storage conditions and the application of in-process tests.

Campaign Production (production consécutive)

>   Sequential processing of material, either more than one product in a multi-product facility or more than one lot of the same product in a dedicated facility, over a defined period of time. Campaign production could occur at any point in a production process where common rooms/suites and/or equipment are reused for multiple products/lots

Cell Bank (banque de cellules)

>   Collection of appropriate containers, whose contents are of uniform composition, stored under defined conditions. Each container represents an aliquot of a single pool of cells.

Cell Culture (culture cellulaire)

>   Maintenance or propagation of cells in vitro. Cell culture is performed according to good aseptic/sterile techniques to ensure the absence of microbial contamination.

Changeover Procedures (procédures de conversion)

> Logical series of validated steps ensuring a proper cleaning of suites and equipment before processing of a different product.

Cleaning Procedures Validation (validation des procédures de nettoyage)

> Testing of methods used to clean equipment/surfaces in a processing suite/facility with assays to validate the effectiveness of the cleaning. The use of "worst-case" cleaning challenges and the addition of a safety factor in the standard operating procedure, can provide further assurance of acceptability. Such challenge might be created by artificially soiling a piece of equipment or by using reduced cleaning parameters (rinse time or volume).

Closed System (système fermé)

> Process equipment (fermenter, transfer lines, harvest apparatus etc.) or process step in which the product is not exposed to the external environment. A closed system requires that the quality of materials entering or leaving the system and the manner in which these materials are added/removed from the system is carefully controlled.

Cold Chain (chaîne du froid)

> Maintenance of a designated temperature throughout the manufacturing process and during storage, until the product is used.

Concurrent Production (confinement)

> Total isolation of one or more steps of a manufacturing process to prevent cross-contamination of the product, or staff, from all other steps of the process.

Containment (médecin)

> A person registered and licensed under the laws of a province to practice the profession of medicine.

Continuous Culture (culture en continu)

> Process by which growth of cells is maintained by periodically replacing a portion of the cells and medium such that there is no lag or saturation phase.

Cross-Contamination (contamination croisée)

> Contamination of a drug or biological starting material or in-process intermediate with another drug or biological starting material or in-process intermediate. In multi-products facilities, cross-contamination can occur throughout the manufacturing process, from generation of the MCB and WCB through finishing.

Dedicated (dédié)

> Facility of piece of equipment used only in the fabrication of a particular product.

Detoxification (détoxification)

> Conversion of bacterial toxins to toxoids (non-toxic but immunogenic derivatives of toxins) by chemical treatment.

Drug Product (produit médicamenteux) - (dosage form, finished product, final container product)

> A pharmaceutical product type that contains a biological drug substance, generally in association with excipients. It corresponds to the dosage form in the immediate packaging intended for marketing.

Drug Substance (substance médicamenteuse)

> A defined process intermediate containing the active ingredient, which is subsequently formulated with excipients to produce the drug product.

Fermentation (fermentation)

> A process in which cells or microorganisms are cultured in a container (bioreactor or fermenter), in liquid or solid medium, for experimental or commercial processes.

Harvesting (récolte)

> Procedure by which the cells, inclusion bodies or crude supernatants containing the unpurified active ingredient are recovered.

Inactivation (inactivation)

> Removal of infectivity of microorganisms by chemical or physical modification.

In Vitro Cell Age (for production) (âge cellulaire In vitro)

> Measure of time between thaw of the MCB or WCB vial(s) to harvest of the production vessel measured by elapsed chronological time, by population doubling level of the cells, or by passage level of the cells when subcultivated, by a defined procedure for dilution of the culture.

Master Cell Bank (MCB) (banque de cellules primaires)

> An aliquot of a single pool of cells which generally has been prepared from the selected cell clone under defined conditions, dispensed into multiple containers and stored under defined conditions. The MCB is used to derive all working cell bank (WCB). The testing performed on a new MCB (from a previous initial clone, MCB or WCB) should be the same as for the MCB unless justified.

Multi-Suite Complex (complexe multi-suites)

> Facility where each suite is dedicated to the fabrication of a biological drug. Suites are located within the same building and are independent from one another.

Multi-Product Facility (établissement multi-produits)

> Facility where more than one product of the same type or products from different classes are fabricated (e.g., pharmaceutical and biological drugs).

Multi-Use Area (aire polyvalente)

> Area where more than one biological drug substance or drug product is manufactured. Manufacturing is either concurrent or on a campaign basis.

Product-Specific Cleaning (nettoyage adapté au produit)

> Cleaning procedure performed to ensure removal of product residuals from non-dedicated product-contact equipment/ containers which includes appropriate assays to validate the effectiveness of the cleaning.

Production Cells (cellules de production)

> Cell substrate used to fabricate the product.

Pure Culture (culture pure)

> A culture broth/ medium containing a single type of microorganism.

Reprocessing (retraitement)

> Subjecting of an in-process or a bulk process intermediate (final biological bulk intermediate) or final product of a single batch/lot to a previous step in the validated manufacturing process due to a failure to meet pre-determined specifications. Reprocessing procedures are foreseen as occasionally necessary for biological drugs and are validated and pre-approved as part of the market authorization.

Reworking (reprise)

> Subjecting of an in-process or bulk process intermediate (final biological bulk intermediate) or final product of a single batch/lot to an alternate manufacturing process due to a failure to meet predetermined specifications. Reworking is an unexpected occurrence and is not pre-approved as part of the market authorization.

Scale Up (1) (mise à l'échelle(1))

> Steps in the fermentation process whereby the production cell line/seed line is expanded until it reaches a sufficient concentration for seeding the seed and/or production bioreactors.

Scale Up (2) (mise à l'échelle(2))

> Increase in the production scale, for example, from pilot plant to production plant.

Seed Lot (lot de semences)

Collect on of appropriate containers, whose contents are of uniform composition, stored under defined conditions. In contrast to cell bank, seed lot may describe collections of plasmids, viruses etc. For master and working seed lots, refer to definitions provided for MCB and WCB.

Separated Facility (établissement séparé)

Facility which is physically separated from one another.

Subculture (repiquage)

Splitting of a cell population by a defined procedure to reduce the cell concentration or density and make possible cell expansion.

Suite (suite)

Functional manufacturing area consisting of one or more rooms with shared air handling and personnel access and which is segregated from the rest of the facility. It contains a separate air supply and exhaust, separate personnel access/egress and separate process equipment. It does not necessarily include a separate supply of water, compressed air/gas or steam, provided that suitable engineering controls are in place to prevent product contamination of these systems. A suite is referred to as a facility within a facility.

Working Cell Bank (WCB) (banque de cellules de travail)

Cell bank prepared from aliquots of a homogenous suspension of cells obtained from culturing the fully characterized MB under defined culture conditions.

Regulation

Premises

C.02.004

1. Air filtration units are dedicated to specific processing areas and air from areas handling pathogens is not recirculated but exhausted through H.E.P.A. filters which have regular, documented performance checks. Air from live areas may not be recirculated into non-live areas or into other live areas with different organisms.

    1.1 Air filtration units that supply, but are not dedicated to, specific areas handling risk group 1 or 2 pathogens may not be recirculated but must be exhausted whereby the use of H.E.P.A. filters for exhaust air is optional.

    1.2 Air filtration units are dedicated to specific processing areas and air from areas handling risk group 3 or 4 pathogens is not recirculated but exhausted through H.E.P.A. filters. In all instances where H.E.P.A. filters are used, they must have regular, documented performance checks.

2. Positive pressure areas are used to process sterile products but negative pressure used in specific areas at point of exposure of pathogens. This is necessary for containment purposes.

3. Where negative pressure areas or safety cabinets are used for aseptic processing of pathogens, the areas are surrounded by a positive pressure zone.

    3.1 Where negative pressure areas are used for the aseptic processing of risk group 1 or 2 pathogens, the adjoining rooms surrounding the negative pressure area must be at a higher (less negative or positive) differential pressure. Where negative pressure areas are used for the aseptic processing of risk group 3 pathogens, the adjoining rooms, ceiling space, service spaces, and floor space (if hollow or the negative pressure area is not on the lowest level of a multi-level building), surrounding the negative pressure area must be at a higher controlled (less negative or positive) differential pressure.

    3.2 Where negative pressure areas are used for the aseptic processing of risk group 4 pathogens, the negative pressure area must be completely surrounded by a controlled positive pressure zone on all faces, including adjoining rooms, service spaces, the ceiling space, and floor space (if hollow).

4. Pipework systems, including valves, pumps, vent filters and housings, that come into contact with final product, or with material used in final product, or with material that contacts surfaces which contact final product, must be designed to facilitate cleaning and sterilization, where other means to ensure sterility or monitoring of contact surfaces are not used. Where possible, 'clean-in-place' (CIP) and 'sterilize-in-place' (SIP) systems should be used. Other systems are also acceptable if validation is performed and approved.

5. Facilities are designed to be effectively decontaminated and prevent cross-contamination during movement of personnel and materials between different areas. The layout and design of production areas and equipment permits effective cleaning and decontamination.

6. If different biological products are fabricated, packaged and tested, or diagnostic work done in the same premises, precautions are taken to prevent the risk of cross-contamination (e.g., location of inlet/exhaust, separation of air supply). This is dictated by the products and equipment used.

7. Spore-forming microorganisms such as Bacillus anthracis, Clostridium botulinum, Clostridium tetani, as well as BCG vaccine (attenuated Mycobacterium tuberculosis Bacillus Calmette-Guerin strain) and live organisms used in the production of tuberculin products, are handled in dedicated facilities with dedicated equipment. Procedures describing plans for entry of personnel into restricted storage and handling areas are strictly enforced.

8. Once inactivated, certain spore forming microorganisms such as Clostridium tetani may be handled in non-dedicated facilities.

9. Concurrent production in the same area using closed systems or fermenters, may be acceptable for products which pose lower safety risks such as monoclonal antibodies and products prepared by rDNA technologies.

10. Separate, specially designed rooms with appropriate environmental and physical containment controls are provided for preparing, handling and storing microorganisms. Reference should be made to the Health Canada Laboratory Biosafety Guidelines, in designing facilities involved in the large-scale production of microorganisms.

11. Animal Facilities

    11.1 Animals are used for the manufacture of a number of biological drugs, for example polio vaccine (monkeys), snake antivenom (horses), rabies vaccine (rabbits, mice and hamsters) and serum gonadotropin (horses). In addition, animals may also be used in the quality control of most sera and vaccines, e.g. pertussis vaccine (mice), BCG vaccine (guinea-pigs), as well as for pyrogenicity (rabbits). Special considerations are required when animal facilities are present at a fabrication site.

    11.2 Procedures for animal quarantine and husbandry are required and must conform to GLP regulations (WHO) or to the Canadian Committee on Animal Care Guidelines.

    11.3 International guidelines (e.g., EC Directive 86/609/EEC) are consulted for general requirements for animal quarters, care and quarantine.

    11.4 Quarters for animals used in production and control of biological products are separate from all other manufacturing areas. The health status of animals from which some biological starting materials are derived and of those used for quality control and safety testing are monitored, recorded and reported as appropriate (e.g., certification of origin and certification of fitness for use).

    11.5 Separate staff are on site for animal care. Staff employed for work in animal facilities are provided with special clothing and separate changing facilities within the animal facility.

    11.6 Where monkeys are used for the production or quality control of biologicals, special consideration is required. International guidance documents should be consulted (e.g., current WHO requirements for Biological Substances No. 7).

Equipment

C.02.005

1. Equipment used for handling live organisms is designed, operated and maintained in a state to ensure that pure cultures are uncontaminated by external sources during all processing and storage operations.

2. Air vent filters on fermenters have hydrophobic media, are tested for integrity prior to use and have a validated scheduled life span.

3. Facilities are designed to be effectively decontaminated and prevent cross-contamination during movement of personnel and materials between different areas. The layout and design of production areas and equipment permits effective cleaning and decontamination.

Personnel

C.02.006

1. All personnel engaged in the fabrication of biologicals receive training, specific to their duties and to the products being manufactured. Training in hygiene and microbiology is particularly relevant to biological production, owing to the susceptibility to microbial contamination.

2. Persons responsible for fabrication and quality control have an adequate background in relevant scientific disciplines such as bacteriology, biology, biometry, chemistry, medicine, pharmacy, pharmacology, virology, immunology and veterinary medicine, together with sufficient practical experience to enable them to perform their duties.

3. For fabrication involving pathogenic microorganisms (as defined by the Transportation of Dangerous Goods Act and Regulations), it may be appropriate to have a designated Biosafety Officer who is experienced and knowledgeable in handling pathogenic microorganisms and eukaryotic cells, with expertise in large scale manufacturing.

4. In the course of a working day, personnel working with live organisms or animals do not pass from one area to another area where other products or different organisms are handled.

5. Adequate numbers of qualified/ trained personnel are available to preclude having the same personnel working in different areas on the same day. Where this is unavoidable, clearly defined decontamination measures, including change of clothing and shoes and, where necessary, showering is followed by staff involved in any such fabrication.

6. Since many of the vaccine product intermediates are infectious, the hazard to employees must be considered in these types of operations and reflected in the environmental and personal protective controls.

7. The health status of personnel should be considered for their own as well as for product safety. All personnel engaged in fabrication, maintenance, testing and animal care (including any outside persons entering the areas) are vaccinated with appropriate specific vaccines and have regular health checks. Apart from the obvious problem of exposure of staff to infectious agents, potent toxins or allergens, adverse health conditions of staff may present microbiological hazards to products and may compromise product safety or quality. Persons whose presence could adversely affect the safety and quality of the product (such as a person with known infectious diseases, serious infections or exposed skin lesions) are excluded from the fabrication area.

Sanitation

C.02.007 and C.02.008

1. The disposition of unsatisfactory biological products or infectious materials not used in fabrication follow approved procedures, designed to eliminate risks to products and personnel.

2. Effluent which may contain pathogenic microorganisms is effectively decontaminated. Appropriate decontamination procedures must also be used when handling animal tissue or cultures of microorganisms, particularly when these pose a potential risk for cross-contamination.

3. Pipework systems, valves and vent filters are designed to facilitate cleaning and sterilization. Where possible CIP and SIP systems are used. Valves on fermentation vessels are of sanitary design and steam sterilizable.

4. Equipment cleaning processes are designed to remove endotoxins, bacteria, toxic elements and residual contaminating proteins and/or other identified contaminants.

5. Cleaning validation of equipment is critical for a multi-product facility involved in campaign or concurrent production of biological drugs. Validated product-specific cleaning procedures are available for non-dedicated equipment.

6. Killed vaccines (including rDNA-derived vaccines), toxoids and bacterial extracts filled in the same premises as other sterile products, following inactivation or detoxification, require validated product-specific facility and equipment cleaning and/or decontamination procedures.

Raw Material Testing

C.02.009 and C.02.010

1. Specifications for biological materials (e.g., starting material, auxiliary material or excipient) includes details of their source, origin, method of fabrication and the (biological and microbiological) controls applied to ensure their suitability for use. All bovine materials are sourced from a country that is considered at low risk of bovine spongiform encephalomyelitis (BSE) as designated by Agriculture and Agri-food Canada. Human derived products such as albumin are sourced from donors known to be free of adventitious agents as outlined in accepted criteria for blood donors and are approvable when used as an excipient. Clinical evidence of safety may also be required. If such product is used as an auxiliary material, the requirements may be less stringent, to be assessed on case by case basis.

2. Biological starting materials are evaluated against appropriate specifications prior to use in the fabrication of the drug.

3. Where the time required to perform a test is lengthy, it may be permissible to process biological starting materials before the result of the test is available. In such cases, release of a finished product is conditional on satisfactory results being obtained for those tests. This requirement is usually a part of the premarket authorization.

4. Provisions for reduced testing in the GMP Guidelines may not be applicable to some biological products because of the inherent variability in range and nature of biological starting materials and their by-products.

5. Seed lot and Cell Bank System In addition to the principles stated in other Guidelines, the following should be noted:

    5.1 To prevent a drift of properties which might ensue from repeated subcultures and to ensure consistency of the biological starting material, the fabrication of biological drugs obtained by microbial culture, cell culture or propagation in embryos and animals is based on a system of master and working seed lots and cell banks.

    5.2 Scale up of the process do not result in a maximum in vitro cell age for production which is greater than that provided in the market authorization.

    5.3 Establishment of the seed lot and cell bank is performed in a suitably controlled environment to protect the seed lot and the cell bank and, if applicable, the personnel handling it. During the establishment of the seed lot and cell bank, no other living or infectious material (e.g., cell lines or microbial strains) is handled simultaneously in the same area or by the same persons.

    5.4 Seed lots and cell banks are adequately characterized and tested for the absence of contaminants. Their suitability for use is further demonstrated by the consistency of the characteristics and quality of the successive batches of product. Seed lots and cell banks are established, stored and used in such a way as to minimize the risks of contamination or alteration.

    5.5 Evidence of the stability and recovery of the seed lot and cell bank are documented. Storage containers are hermetically sealed, clearly labelled and kept at a suitable temperature. An inventory is meticulously kept. Storage temperatures are continuously recorded for freezers and properly monitored for liquid nitrogen. Any deviation from set limits and any corrective action taken are evaluated and documented.

    5.6 Any material is handled by authorized personnel only, under the supervision of a responsible person. A system is in place to ensure security of inventory of seed lots or cell banks and retrievability of seed lots or cell banks vials. Different seed lots or cell banks are stored to avoid confusion or cross-contamination between them. It is desirable to split the seed lots and cell banks and to store the parts at different locations so as to minimize the risks of total loss.

    5.7 All vials of master or working cell banks and seed lots are treated identically during storage. Once removed from storage, the vials are not returned to stock.

Manufacturing Control

C.02.011 and C.02.012

1. Campaign operations for different products require validated changeover procedures which include product-specific cleaning procedures for non-dedicated equipment.

2. Concurrent production of different products requires validated closed systems with effective barriers which preclude cross-contamination from other processes (e.g., adventitious agents from different host/ vector production cells). Concurrent purification not performed in closed systems requires dedicated areas.

3. Addition of media, materials or cultures to fermenters and other vessels and sampling is carried out using validated procedures to ensure that contamination and/or cross-contamination is avoided. Care is taken to avoid incorrect connections to ports during sampling and addition.

4. Additives or ingredients that must be measured or weighed during the production process (e.g., buffers) may be stored in small quantities in the production area.

5. Centrifugation and blending of products can lead to aerosol formation. Such operations must be contained to prevent transfer of live microorganisms.

6. Where possible, in-line sterilizing filters are used for routine addition of gases, media, acids, alkalis or defoaming agents to fermenters, and their usage is validated.

7. Virus removal and/or viral inactivation methods are validated using specific viruses or appropriate model viruses, and do not adversely affect the product.

8. Pure cultures are handled using appropriate controls to prevent adventitious contamination during production.

9. The storage and processing of inactivated and non-inactivated products is done in segregated areas, to avoid the potential for cross-contamination.

10. Chromatography equipment is dedicated to the purification of a single drug and the use of the same equipment at different processing steps is not recommended. The life span of columns and the acceptance criteria are defined in the sanitization / regeneration methods.

11. Batch records must document all biological starting materials and in-process materials used, in addition to all relevant test results.

12. Packaging of some biological drugs require strict control, monitoring and documenting of conditions such as temperature (e.g. maintenance of the cold-chain), humidity or light exposure.

13. If filling and sealing is not carried out immediately following fabrication of the drug, due to the need for specific assay results, a validated holding and/or shipping period in accordance with the market authorization may be allowed.

14. Special, appropriately documented precautions must be exercised in the storage and handling of microorganisms, in particular spore forming organisms.

15. The handling and destruction of rejected biological materials takes into consideration designation of the material (e.g., infectious, bio-hazard), and environmental protection requirements for their disposal.

Quality Control Department

C.02.013 to C.02.015

1. Biological analytical techniques are essential for control of most biologicals. Because of the inherent variability of biological processes, and the inability to fully characterise most biologicals, in-process controls during fabrication, packaging and labelling take on great importance in ensuring consistency in quality, safety and efficacy of the end product. Those controls which are crucial for quality (e.g., virus removal) but which cannot be carried out on the finished product, are performed at an appropriate stage of production.

2. Storage, transportation methods and procedures used (including distribution) may have major impacts on biological drugs. In some cases, transit time, transit method, temperature, humidity, light and/or vibration may be critical factors that could adversely affect the quality and effectiveness of the product. Biological drugs are stored, transported and handled in strict compliance with the market authorization.

3. Production methods utilizing continuous culture have specific requirements for in-process quality control. For example, continuous monitoring of critical parameters is required during fermentation. Such data should form part of the batch record.

4. For imported biological drugs that have been subjected to reprocessing, the quality control department is responsible for ensuring that the (documented) reprocessing carried out by the fabricator complies with the marketing authorization.

5. Reworking of an in-process or bulk process intermediate (final biological bulk intermediate) or final product of a single batch/lot is an unexpected occurrence and as such, the release of the final product is subjected to approval of both the procedure and the results by the marketing authorization review bureau within Biologics and Genetic Therapies Directorate.

Packaging Material Testing

C.02.016 and C.02.017

1. Many biological drugs are extremely susceptible to deleterious effects from container/ closure systems, and it is imperative to maintain strict control on the identity and quality of the immediate container and components in contact with the drug, in accordance with approved specifications.

2. For imported biological drugs, the quality control department is responsible for ensuring that the (documented) packaging materials used, comply with approved specifications.

Finished Product Testing

C.02.018 and C.02.019

1. The release of some finished biological drugs may be conditional on the satisfactory results of tests on biological starting materials or in-process materials.

2. For imported biological drugs, the quality control department is responsible for ensuring that finished product specifications and the testing done, comply with the marketing authorization.

Records

C.02.020 to C.02.024

1. For imported biological drugs, detailed summaries (e.g., Certified Product Information Document) of the current fabrication, packaging, labelling and testing procedures are maintained by the legal agent in Canada and master production documents are available on site at the fabricator.

2. Records are retained indefinitely on site at the fabricator, for biological drugs containing human blood-derived excipients (e.g., human albumin).

Samples

C.02.025 and C.02.026

See main GMP Guidelines

Stability

C.02.027 and C.02.028

1. For biological drugs stability assessment is also linked to retaining biologic activity within the label claim and is subjected to premarket authorization.

2. The stability assessment includes analysis of both the lyophilized and reconstituted single and multi-dose dosage forms of the drug product.

Sterile Products

C.02.029

1. Due to their labile nature, most sterile biological drugs are produced by sterile filtration / aseptic compounding, followed by aseptic filling rather than by terminal sterilization. Direct-contact packaging materials (i.e., vials, syringes, stoppers etc.) are subjected to processing which ensures and maintains sterility prior to filling.

2. In addition to environmental standards for particulates and viable microorganisms, biological drugs are produced in an environment where temperature and humidity are controlled within specified limits, since these can have a deleterious effect on the product.

Biological Drugs GMPs

Good Manufacturing Practices for Schedule D Drugs - Part 2 - Human Blood and Blood Components

Health Products and Food Branch Inspectorate

Annex to the GMP Guidelines

Supersedes: First draft, March 24, 1998

Date issued: December 1, 1999

Date of implementation: December 1, 1999

Good Manufacturing Practices for Schedule D Drugs

Part 2

Human Blood and Blood Components[18]

*Revisions were made to this document on 2002-02-25 to reflect changes to the Health Products and Food Branch organizational structure. There were no other changes made to the content of the document.

Preface

The purpose to this document is to provide specific guidance for the application of good manufacturing practices to blood establishments.

Glossary of Terms

Autologous Donation (don autologue)

Blood collected from an individual for the purpose of transfusion back to the same individual.

Allogeneic Donation (don allogénique)

Blood collected from an individual and placed in the general blood supply for the purpose of transfusion to another person.

---

[18] Available on the Health Canada website at http://www.hc-sc.gc.ca/dhp-mps/compli-conform/info-prod/don/sched_d_part2-annexe_d_part2-eng.php

Antibody Screen (dépistage des anticorps)

> Serological test by which donor serum/plasma is tested with reagent red cells of known antigenic profile to determine if unexpected clinically significant antibodies are present. "Clinically significant" refers to antibodies that may cause adverse reactions in the recipient due to incompatibility.

Blood (sang)

> Whole blood collected from a single donor and processed either for transfusion or further manufacturing. The term is often used to describe blood components in general.

Blood Component (composant du sang)

> A therapeutic agent produced by physical or mechanical separation of the constituents of whole blood. Components include, but are not limited to, red blood cells, platelets, plasma and cryoprecipitated Anti-Haemophiliac Factor (AHF).

Closed System (circuit fermé)

> A system for collecting and/or processing blood in containers that have been connected together before sterilization, so that there is no possibility of microbial contamination from outside after collection of blood from the donor.

Confidential Unit Exclusion (CUE) (demande d'exclusion confidentielle)

> A system that allows the donor, in private, to indicate that his/her collected blood should, or should not, be used for transfusion to another individual.

Contract Facility (établissement externe)

> Organisation performing work associated with the manufacturing process for the manufacturer.

Critical Labelling (étiquetage critique)

> Labelling which identifies a product or status, such as a quarantine label or blood group label, if it is used to control release for inventory.

Directed Donation (don dirigé)

> Blood collected from an individual for the purpose of transfusion to a different individual, named by the donor, who has been identified in advance to be compatible.

Facilities (installations)

> Any area, including mobile clinic sites, used for the collection, testing, component production, storage (including records) or distribution of blood and blood components.

Leukapheresis (leucophérèse)

> Separation of leukocytes by removing whole blood from the donor, separating the leukocytes, and returning the formed elements and plasma back to the donor.

Leuko Reduced Components (composants à teneur réduite en leucocytes)

> Component units that have been treated by centrifugation, filtration or other methods to reduce the amount of leukocytes per unit to a level below a standard acceptable value.

Lookback (étude des dons antérieurs)

> The process of identifying current or previous donations from a donor subsequently confirmed positive for a transfusion-transmitted agent in order to identify and notify consignees and recipients of suspect blood components from that donor, and retrieve available components. A lookback may be initiated through a traceback investigation or by a report of seroconversion or infection in a donor.

Medical Officer (médecin)

> A person registered and licensed under the laws of a province to practice the profession of medicine.

Mobile Clinic Site (centre de collecte itinérant)

> Blood collection location, not under the control of the fabricator, to which equipment and supplies must be brought prior to the donor clinic and from which they are removed at the conclusion of the clinic.

Open System (système ouvert)

> A blood collection and/or processing system which has been breached but where every effort is made to prevent external contamination by using sterilised materials and aseptic handling techniques in a clean environment.

Plasma

> The fluid portion of whole blood collected, stabilized against clotting and separated from the red blood cells.

Plasmapheresis (plasmaphérèse)

> Separation of plasma from whole blood and the continuous or intermittent return of red blood cells and formed elements to the donor. Plasma collected by plasmapheresis may be used either as source plasma for further manufacturing or fresh frozen plasma for transfusion.

Plateletpheresis (thrombocytaphérèse)

> Separation of platelets from whole blood and the continuous or intermittent return of red blood cells, with or without platelet-reduced

Blood and Components GMPs

plasma, to the donor. If plasma is collected as a final product during plateletpheresis, the regulations for plasmapheresis apply.

Post Donation Information (PDI) (renseignements obtenus après le don)

Information related to a donor or a donation made available to the collection facility following a donation. The information can be provided by the donor or other source. It may adversely affect the safety and/or quality of the donated blood/component. PDI does not include errors, accidents or anomalies that occur during screening or later during collection, processing or testing but are discovered at some point after the donation is made.

Processing (traitement)

Any fabricating step performed between the collection of blood and the issuing of a component.

Quality Assurance (QA) (assurance de la qualité)

The actions, planned and performed, to provide confidence that all systems and elements that influence the quality of the product are working as expected individually and collectively.

Quality Assurance Program (programme d'assurance qualité)

Comprehensive system of an establishment for manufacturing safe, effective, and quality products according to regulatory requirements. This program includes preventing, detecting, and correcting deficiencies that may compromise product quality.

Quality Control (QC) (contrôle de la qualité)

A component of a QA program that includes the activities and controls used to determine the accuracy and reliability of the establishment's personnel, equipment, reagents, and operations in the fabricating of blood components including testing and product release.

Quality Control/Assurance Unit (unité de contrôle/d'assurance de la qualité)

One or more individuals designated by, and reporting directly to, management with defined authority and responsibility to assure that all quality assurance policies are carried out in the organization.

Recovered Plasma (plasma récupéré)

The liquid portion of a single donation of whole blood separated from cellular components and intended for further manufacture.

Serum (sérum)

The liquid portion of clotted blood.

Source Plasma (plasma par aphérèse)

Plasma collected by plasmapheresis and used for further manufacture.

Sub-Centre (centre secondaire)

> Permanent site under the control of a Blood Centre, which is licensed for limited fabrication activities.

Traceback (enquête sur les produits sanguins transfusés)

> The process of investigating a report of a suspected transfusion-associated infection in order to identify a potential implicated donor. The purpose of the investigation is to determine whether any donor who contributed to the transfusion is infected with, or positive for, serologic markers of the same infectious agent, and to retrieve available blood components from that donor, and to notify consignees and recipients of components collected from the same donor.

Unit (unité)

> A specific volume of blood or one of its components obtained from a single collection of blood from one donor.

Regulation

Premises

C.02.004

1. See section C.02.007 (Sanitation) for additional explanation on premises.

2. Premises must be located, designed, constructed and adapted to suit the operations to be carried out. Their design and furnishing must be chosen to minimise the risk of errors. Premises should, if possible, be designed so that operations can proceed in an orderly manner. Buildings should be maintained so as to protect against the effects of weather or ground seepage and the entry of vermin, pests and birds.

3. The facility should be designed to align with the process flow but shall include:

   3.1 An area set aside for donor screening which maintains confidentiality for questioning and examination of individuals to determine their suitability as blood donors. If the Confidential Unit Exclusion (CUE) is used, a private area must be provided.

   3.2 An area set aside for the safe withdrawal of blood from donors and equipped with appropriate supplies for the treatment of donors experiencing adverse reactions or injuries from events associated with blood donation.

   3.3 A means of communication (e.g. telephone, cellular phone) whenever donors are being bled to ensure that emergency help is available, if required.

   3.4 A separate controlled area for the quarantine storage of blood or blood components prior to completion of processing, and for reagents and test kits prior to acceptance testing and approval at the processing facility.

Blood and Components GMPs

3.5 A separate secure area for the quarantine storage, handling and disposition of blood components and reagents not suitable for use or recalled.

3.6 A secure area in both quarantine and released storage for units collected under special criteria (e.g., Autologous/Directed Donation)

3.7 Separate dedicated areas for component preparation and laboratory testing. Entry to these areas shall be restricted to authorized personnel.

3.8 Separate controlled storage areas for released components available for distribution.

3.9 A designated area for safe storage of waste and items used during the collection, processing and testing of blood and blood components, or rejected blood or blood components, prior to disposal.

3.10 A dedicated area for the labelling and release of components into inventory.

3.11 A designated alternate storage site for blood components in the event of equipment or power failure in the main storage facility.

3.12 Adequate storage space for the dry, clean and orderly placement of stored material under monitored temperature conditions compatible with conditions specified on label. Storage areas shall provide for suitable and effective separation of quarantined and released material.

4. When blood collection clinics are conducted by mobile teams, a realistic attitude towards environmental standards is necessary. The premises should satisfy common sense requirements for the health and safety of both the mobile teams, and the donors concerned, with due regard for relevant legislation or regulation. Points to check should include adequate heating, lighting and ventilation, general cleanliness, provision of a secure supply of water and electricity, adequate sanitation, compliance with fire regulations, satisfactory access for unloading and loading of equipment, adequate space to allow free access to the bleed and rest beds. An area shall be provided for a confidential interview with a donor.

Equipment

C.02.005

1. See section C.02.015 (Quality Control Department) for Laboratory Testing Equipment information and water purification systems.

2. Schedules and procedures for equipment validation, maintenance and calibration must be maintained and followed. This requirement applies to all instruments, equipment and measuring devices critical to ensure that the provision of blood and blood components conform to applicable regulations, requirements and standards.

3. Manufacturing equipment used, or intended to be used, in whole blood collection, apheresis procedures, and component production should be designed and maintained to suit its intended purpose and shall not present

any hazard to donors, components or operators. All equipment shall be maintained, standardized and calibrated on a regularly scheduled basis according to established procedures described in operating procedures (OPs) and/or the equipment manual. If the instrument has been disturbed or is suspected of malfunctioning, these tests shall be carried out before further use.

4. Computers, which maintain data used to identify donors, to make decisions regarding the suitability of blood components for transfusion or further manufacture, and/or to maintain data used to trace a unit of blood or a blood component from collection to its final disposition, must be validated in accordance with current Health Canada guidelines (Validation of Computerised Systems in Blood Establishments) prior to implementation and must be maintained in a validated state.

Personnel

C.02.006

1. There shall be an organization chart showing the hierarchical structure with clear delineation of lines of responsibility and the relationship of individuals responsible for key functions.

2. A blood establishment shall be under the direction of designated, qualified personnel who shall exercise control of the establishment in all matters relating to good manufacturing practices (GMP) for blood component manufacturing. Designated staff shall have an understanding of the scientific principles and techniques involved in the manufacture of blood components. Training and competency evaluations must be documented.

3. The fabricator shall ensure the employment of adequate personnel qualified by education and/or experience, as specified in their job descriptions. The tasks and responsibilities of all individuals must be clearly understood and documented. All personnel shall be trained in the principles of GMP relevant to their work. Records of the qualifications, training, and continuing competence of individuals shall be maintained.

4. Personnel shall receive initial and continued training appropriate to their duties. Training programs shall be available for this purpose; the effectiveness of the programs shall be assessed by regular competency evaluation.

5. Key personnel shall include at least a Production Manager, a Quality Assurance (QC/QA) Manager and a Medical Officer. An individual may have more than one function but the Production Manager and Quality Assurance Manager must be independent of each other.

6. The Medical Officer, who is a licensed physician and qualified by training or experience, shall have responsibility and authority for all medical and technical procedures, including those that affect laboratory personnel and test performance, and for the consultative and support services that relate to the care and safety of donors. The acceptability of donors must be determined by trained qualified staff under the supervision of a qualified licensed physician.

7. Individuals in charge of production should hold a post secondary qualification (e.g., in management, medical laboratory science, general science or nursing) and have had practical experience under professional guidance in the manufacture and control of therapeutic products made under GMP. Individuals with equivalent combination of education, training and experience may be qualified.

8. QC/QA staff must hold a university degree in science or equivalent experience/knowledge directly related to Immunohematology or nursing.

Sanitation

C.02.007

1. Blood establishments routinely fabricate blood components in a closed system so that there is no possibility of microbial contamination from outside after collection of blood from the donor.

2. The blood establishment should be maintained in a clean and sanitary condition. A written sanitation program should be available that addresses good housekeeping issues. An accidental spill clean up procedure must be available and include instructions to dispose of blood spills as biohazardous material.

3. Blood and its components must be handled and discarded with precautions that recognize the potential for exposure to infectious agents.

4. There must be procedures for biological, chemical and radiation safety, where applicable.

5. Adequate hand washing facilities must be available for staff collecting and handling blood units. At mobile sites where hand washing facilities are not available, an alternate method to clean hands, i.e. bactericidal hand wipes, is acceptable.

C.02.008

1. Persons whose presence can adversely affect the safety or quality of the product shall be excluded from areas where the collection, processing, testing, storage or distribution of blood or blood components is conducted.

2. Personnel shall be aware that microbial contamination of themselves, the donors, the blood components and the environment must be prevented.

3. Hygiene instructions, including clothing and behaviour requirements, must be present in each department. These instructions should be understood and followed by all personnel.

Raw Material Testing

C.02.009

1. Because whole blood is the source material for blood components, special considerations are given to the procedures for donor screening and vendor audit (C.02.010).

2. Donor Screening

2.1 All blood donors must be found acceptable each time they donate based on the approved health screening criteria. A document shall be available at each blood collection site that details the approved health screening criteria for acceptance/deferral of donors.

2.2 Potential donors who do not meet all the applicable acceptance criteria for donating must be informed of the reason they cannot donate and the circumstances under which they have been deferred.

2.3 A comprehensive list of donors who are temporarily or permanently deferred must be maintained. If a blood manufacturer has multiple collection and processing facilities, a composite donor deferral registry, including the names and/or unique identifiers of all donors deferred at each facility, must be made available to each site and updated on a regular basis.

3. The collection bags, which are approved Medical Devices, do not require further testing. The certificate of analysis for each lot of collection bags must be reviewed and approved prior releasing for clinic use. Each collection bag must be visually examined prior to its use for blood collection, again at the time of product release into available inventory, and finally before the released product is distributed.

C.02.010

1. Vendor Audits

1.1 All vendors which supply critical materials that are used in blood collection (eg. blood collection bags, apheresis harness sets and apheresis collection bags) should be audited periodically by the manufacturer of blood/components to ensure that the vendor operates in compliance with GMPs and that the products they supply consistently meet pre established specifications.

1.2 There must be a system in place to ensure the timely reporting of complaints or product defects to the vendor and prompt effective remedial action by the vendor.

Manufacturing Control

C.02.011

1. Written Operating Procedures (OPs)

1.1 Every manufacturer shall maintain and control all documents (policies, processes, procedures and forms) relating to the requirements for each activity in the manufacturing process.

1.2 OPs must be clear, concise, current and approved, and be available in the area where the activity is performed.

Blood and Components GMPs

1.3 The issue of OPs and any changes made shall be controlled by a documented system which ensures that all OPs in use are current and authorised, and that obsolete documents are archived and protected.

1.4 The OPs must describe the significant steps of the operation:

    1.4.1 The determination of donor acceptability and deferral status, including the process for donor identification.

    1.4.2 Method of accurately and uniquely relating the blood components or product(s) to the donor, donor samples, and all associated records, for each donation.

    1.4.3 The procedure(s) used for blood collection, including methods used to prepare the site of phlebotomy, and to link critical materials (e.g., the collection pack lot number) to the clinic and donor.

    1.4.4 Specific manufacturing procedure(s) for the preparation of all components, including labelling steps (i.e., type of labels and method of labelling).

    1.4.5 All tests and repeat tests performed on blood and blood components including testing for infectious disease markers. Procedure(s) shall address the shipment of samples to off-site and contract facilities, as required.

    1.4.6 Procedure(s) for the capturing, assessing, investigating and monitoring of adverse donor and recipient reactions.

    1.4.7 Procedure(s) for determining the suitability of blood components for transfer to available inventory, i.e., formally approving the blood component for release. There must be a suitable means of identification to ensure that blood components which cannot be released for issue can be distinguished from those which conform to specification and are ready for release.

    1.4.8 Procedure(s) for the voluntary return of issued blood and blood components, specifying the conditions under which the returned blood may be suitable for re issue.

    1.4.9 Procedure(s) used for tracking a unit of blood or any blood component from the donor to its final disposition.

    1.4.10 Procedure(s) for the quality control of blood components, processing methods and laboratory testing.

    1.4.11 Procedure(s) for plasmapheresis, plateletpheresis and leukapheresis, including precautions to be taken to ensure reinfusion of a donor's own cells, if applicable.

    1.4.12 Procedure(s) for the operation, maintenance and validation of all computerized systems that contribute to decisions regarding the suitability and/or traceability of blood and blood components.

1.4.13 Procedure(s) for capturing, assessing, investigating, and monitoring errors and accidents (i.e., manufacturing discrepancies). Defined methods for identification, data collection, analysis, and follow-up of corrective and preventive action shall be used for process improvement.

1.4.14 Procedure(s) and criteria for performance of lookback and traceback investigations.

1.4.15 Procedure(s) which detail the requirements for units collected under special criteria (such as Autologous and Directed Donations).

1.4.16 Procedure(s) which details recall procedures including the identification of the person or persons responsible for initiating and co-ordinating the recall activities as well as the process for notifying the regulatory authorities.

1.4.17 Procedure(s) to detail the receipt, inspection, and storage of material and products within the premises.

1.4.18 Procedure(s) to describe the calibration of equipment. It shall include the method to be used, frequency of calibration and action to be taken when results deviate from defined acceptance limits. Parameters being tested should approximate operating conditions for that equipment.

1.4.19 Procedure(s) for the packaging and transport of blood components, to ensure they remain within specifications.

2. A system shall be established and maintained to identify, document, review, approve and control all process and product changes.

3. Supplies and Reagents

3.1 Each blood collecting container and its satellite container(s), if present, must be examined visually for damage or evidence of contamination prior to its use (before blood collection) and before the product is distributed. Where any defect, improper labelling or abnormal appearance is observed, the container shall not be used, or, if detected after filling, the component shall be properly discarded.

3.2 Representative samples of each lot of reagents or solutions shall be inspected and/or tested on each day of use as described in the Operating Procedure(s) to determine their suitability for use.

4. Labelling of blood components

4.1 See labelling requirements described in Division 4 of the Regulations.

4.2 Blood component labelling occurs at various stages in the manufacturing process. Each critical labelling procedure must include

Blood and Components GMPs

effective in process controls, appropriate to the system and equipment, to ensure correct labels have been applied. Component labelling must be reviewed prior to final product release

4.3 Each donation shall be identified in a unique manner and shall allow for the traceability of each blood component back to the donor and forward to final disposition.

4.4 If coloured labels are used to identify products for transfusion, the colours must follow the conventions outlined in the Guidelines for Blood Collection and Component Manufacturing (Part IV section 2.4.2) .

4.5 Each successful donation must be classified as to ABO and Rh group. Whole blood (WB), red cell concentrate (RCC), platelets (PLT), and granulocytes (GRAN) must be labelled with both ABO and Rh (D) groups, based on test of record. The label shall specify: "Rh positive" if D or weak D positive, or "Rh negative" if D and weak D negative.

4.6 The label shall state the composition and volume of anticoagulant/additive, the Establishment Licence Number and address of the component fabricator, and date of expiry. Expiry labels for products with a shelf-life of 72 hours or less must include the time of expiry.

4.7 Information and cautionary statements specific to blood component fabricating are outlined in the Guidelines for Blood Collection and Component manufacturing (Part IV).

5. Circular of Information

5.1 An information circular (package insert) is an extension of the blood component labelling and shall be available for distribution if the component or blood product is intended for transfusion. The information circular shall provide adequate directions for storage and use, including information on the composition and properties of the product, the indications for use, contraindications, and possible adverse events.

5.2 Packaging differs from pharmaceutical manufacturing, in that, the initial whole blood container with satellites is also the final packaging material.

C.02.012

1. Whole Blood and Blood Component Recall

1.1 All complaints and other information that may suggest that defective blood components have been issued must be carefully investigated. Written procedures must exist for recalling defective blood components or blood components suspected of being defective. All complaints about delivered blood components shall be dealt with and investigated as quickly as possible.

1.2 Blood establishments shall maintain a system of control that permits complete and rapid recall of any component to the consignee level (e.g., hospitals or fractionator). Distribution records shall be readily available and easy to follow so as to expedite the recall of any blood component or material whenever necessary.

1.3 Post Donation Information reports may lead to recall of all in date components.

1.4 The guidance on recalls in the document entitled "Product Recall Procedures" published by the Health Protection Branch does not apply in its entirety to Blood Components.

2. Internal audit

2.1 Internal audits are required to ensure that all procedures and the associated quality control are performed according to GMP, and applicable regulations and legislation. Internal audits should be comprehensive and performed according to an established program. The findings shall be documented.

2.2 The internal audit personnel shall be knowledgeable in the subject matter and process being audited, and shall have defined responsibilities and authority.

Quality Control Department

C.02.013

1. Quality Control/Quality Assurance department shall be a distinct organizational unit that is not linked to fabricating of blood components.

2. For sub-centres and mobile clinic sites, which are technically multiple sites of a single licence, it must be demonstrated that the overall supervision of quality and production is adequately controlled by the blood centre.

C.02.014

1. Sections C.02.014 (1), (3), and (4) do not apply to blood fabricators due to their nature, the fact that each component is a separate lot and that they are not reprocessed (as per definition of reprocessing for pharmaceuticals).

2. Within a blood component fabricating operation, the requirements of this section may be fulfilled by positions or departments other than the Quality Control Department as specified in the operating procedures.

3. Because of their intended use, good quality is crucial to blood components. Therefore, the collection of blood and the processing, storage and distribution of blood components must be organised in a way to ensure a high component quality. This can only be achieved if the fabricator has a system of quality management. Quality management is an integrated system of quality assurance covering all matters which individually or collectively influence the components in order to guarantee their quality.

4. The person or group of persons who coordinate, monitor and facilitate all QA activities is the QC/QA unit.

5. The quality requirements involve the following topics:

Blood and Components GMPs

- premises, equipment and materials
- personnel and organisation
- donor screening and blood collection
- blood processing
- documentation
- quality control and proficiency testing
- complaints and component recall
- internal and external audits

6. In the case of C.02.014 (2), if blood components are returned to the manufacturer they are only acceptable for re-issue if the manufacturer can document that the product, while out of their hands, was continuously stored under the appropriate storage conditions.

C.02.015

1. The donor screening criteria (see Raw Material Testing) and donor sample testing (Quality Control Department) are factors in determining the acceptable quality and safety of blood and blood components. In process controls, as specified in approved OPs, provide specific GMP for Blood Component fabrication.

2. A quality control program for assessing the quality and performance of all reagents and test kits used in the processing of blood components, must be in place.

3. Test kit procedures, acceptable to Health Canada, must follow the strict protocol of their applicable package inserts.

4. Detailed specifications for purchase of critical reagents and materials are required. Only reagents and materials that meet the documented requirements shall be used. Manufacturers shall provide a certificate of compliance for these reagents and materials.

5. Serological and Transmissible Disease Testing

    5.1 Testing is performed on blood samples (pilot samples) collected at the time of donation. The samples are marked with an identifier which links the sample to the donor and the corresponding unit of blood. Pilot samples must be collected by a technique that prevents external contamination of the blood product.

    5.2 Responsibilities between contract laboratories and the blood establishment shall be defined by written agreement.

    5.3 All donors of whole blood must be tested for the following serological tests at the time of each donation:

    - ABO group, including forward and reverse grouping
    - Rh group (D and weak D testing)
    - Antibody screen

5.4 All donors must be screened for the following transmissible disease markers at the time of each donation:

- Syphilis

- Hepatitis B surface antigen (HBsAg)

- Antibody to Hepatitis C virus (HCV)

- Antibody to HIV type 1 and 2

- Antibody to HTLV-I/II (except plasma for further manufacturing use only)

- HIV-1 p24 Ag

- Any disease marker(s) specifically required by the Minister

5.5 Units that are repeat reactive for a transmissible disease marker listed above must not be issued for allogeneic transfusion.

5.6 All donors that are found repeat reactive for a transmissible disease marker listed above must be deferred.

6. A quality control program which assesses the quality of all manufactured blood components must be followed by every fabricator. The frequency of quality control testing, expressed as a percent of overall production, as well as the minimum number specified over a period of time, and the acceptable criteria for quality control testing of each type of component must be established by each fabricator.

7. The results of quality control testing must be analysed on an ongoing basis and appropriate corrective action taken when values fall outside the acceptable limits.

8. Although blood is not a sterile drug, sterility testing should be performed as part of Quality Control testing. Sterility testing must be done with a methodology specific to aerobic and anaerobic pathogens in blood. Sterility testing serves as a monitor of the effectiveness of the protocol for phlebotomy site preparation.

9. Blood establishments must participate in a proficiency testing program. Proficiency testing is an aspect of Quality Assurance which monitors the ability to perform laboratory procedures within acceptable limits of accuracy through the analysis of unknown specimens.

Packaging Material Testing

C.02.016 and C.02.017

1. Packaging Material testing does not apply to blood component manufacturing as original collection bags and satellite bags must be approved Medical Devices. Additional routine testing is not required for use of approved collection bags. However, testing may be required during the investigation of a complaint or an adverse reaction.

Finished Product Testing

C.02.018 and C.02.019

1. The requirements for finished product testing cannot be applied to the manufacture of blood components since each unit of blood collected represents a separate lot. The safety of each component depends on the selection of donors, blood collection, and serological and transmissible disease testing. The quality of components is established by quality control testing as a method of the fabricating process eg. Factor VIII level in cryoprecipitate.

Records

C.02.020

1. Records shall be maintained concurrently with the performance of each significant step in the collection, processing, testing, storage and distribution of each unit of blood and blood components so that all steps can be clearly traced.

2. All records shall be legible and indelible, and shall identify the person performing the work, include dates of the various entries, show test results, the interpretation of the results, any retests or invalidation of test results.

3. All manual transcription of test results shall be independently verified.

C.02.021

1. Section C.02.021 does not apply to blood establishments as blood component records must be kept indefinitely. Blood establishments may decide to use microfiche, microfilm or other means of retaining permanent records. Records must be accessible at all times.

2. Records that substantiate the safety of blood and blood components and the traceability of the components from donor to final disposition shall be retained indefinitely. The records must enable the fabricator to trace blood or blood components to donors in the case of a traceback investigation, and to the point of end use in case of lookbacks.

C.02.022

1. Section C.02.022 applies directly to blood establishments in that procedures must clearly determine the distribution of all whole blood and blood components which will ensure an effective recall, if necessary. Records shall demonstrate that a blood component can be readily located during transportation to another site.

C.02.023

1. Records of complaints regarding blood components issued to consignees must be completely investigated.

2. Records of adverse transfusion reaction reports must be maintained.

3. Section C 02.023 (2) does not apply in that records are maintained indefinitely.

C.02.024

1. Records of self audits performed within the blood establishment must be available for review. C.02.024 (1)(b) does not apply as records are maintained indefinitely.

2. Records of sanitation need not to be retained.

Samples

C.02.025 and C.02.026

1. The provisions of this section do not apply to blood component manufacturing due to the fact that each unit is a lot. When a transfused blood component is associated with a post transfusion infection or serious adverse reaction, a thorough investigation is undertaken.

2. Blood components intended for transfusion which are stored long term in a frozen state (eg. frozen red cell units) must have a serum or plasma sample kept for future testing purposes.

Stability

C.02.027 and C.02.028

1. Blood components must be stored at all times under appropriate monitored storage conditions.

2. During shipment, blood components must be placed in appropriate shipping containers that ensure the maintenance of appropriate storage temperature during shipment as well as the security of the contents.

3. Shipment documentation must specify the shipping conditions of the blood components.

Sterile Products

C.02.029

1. Blood components are injectable but are generally not considered to be sterile products.

2. Using an appropriate sampling plan, blood components should periodically have sterility testing performed as part of routine quality control testing to evaluate the overall effectiveness of the arm scrub.

3. If a sterile connecting device is used to produce sterile welds (i.e. maintaining closed system) it must be an approved medical device. The weld made must be inspected for completeness.

4. A sample taken from every final product processed in an open system (e.g., red blood cells, deglycerolized) shall be tested retrospectively for sterility.

GMP requirements for blood manufacturing activities

Section	Regulation	Applies Directly	*Applies in part	**Does Not Apply
Premises	C.02.004		X	
Equipment	C.02.005		X	
Personnel	C.02.006		X	
Sanitation	C.02.007			X
	C.02.008			X
Raw Material Testing	C.02.009			X
	C.02.010			X
Manufacturing Control	C.02.011		X	
	C.02.012	X		
Quality Control	C.02.013		X	
	C.02.014			X
	C.02.015		X	
Packaging Material Testing	C.02.016			X
	C.02.017			X
Finished Product Testing	C.02.018			X
	C.02.019			X
Records	C.02.020		X	
	C.02.021			X
	C.02.022	X		
	C.02.023		X	
	C.02.024		X	
Samples	C.02.025			X
	C.02.026			X
Stability	C.02.027			X
	C.02.028			X
Sterile Products	C.02.029			X

*applies in part = applies as described in annex

**does not apply = does not apply as described in the guidelines, only applies as described in the annex

Blood and Components GMPs

Good Manufacturing Practices (GMP) for Medical Gases

Health Products and Food Branch Inspectorate

Supersedes: July 1st, 2000

Date issued: December 2006

Date of implementation: December 2006

Good Manufacturing Practices (GMP)

for Medical Gases[19]

(GUIDE-0031)

1. Introduction

These guidelines state generally applicable principles and practices that are acceptable to the Inspectorate and that should facilitate compliance of fabricators, packagers/labellers, distributors, importers, and home care providers of medical gases with Division 2, Part C of the Food and Drug Regulations on Good Manufacturing Practices (GMP). Commercial operations involving sales are subject to GMPs. The Inspectorate does not consider transfilling operations performed within services such as fire departments, ambulance services, hospitals, or health care facilities, to be subject to Establishment Licensing and GMPs when the medical gases are for their own use or administration to a patient.

Interpretations provided in the main GMP Guidelines are replaced by those given in this document for medical gases. During establishment inspections carried out under the authority of section 23 of the Foods and Drugs Act, this document will be used as a guide in judging compliance with the GMP Regulations. However, the content of these guidelines should not be regarded as the only interpretation of the GMP Regulations and are not intended to cover every conceivable case. Alternative means of complying with the GMP Regulations will be considered with the appropriate scientific justification. Furthermore, as new technologies emerge, different approaches may be called for. Establishments may use this guideline as a basis for the development of specific requirements appropriate to their individual needs.

Due to their unique production and handling characteristics, the application of the GMP Regulations to medical gases may be different from their application to other pharmaceuticals. For example, the synthesis or manufacture of a medical gas constitutes a special situation in that the resulting gas may be used as a raw material or it may be sold as a bulk drug or as a finished packaged product.

---

[19] Available on the Health Canada website at http://www.hc-sc.gc.ca/dhp-mps/compli-conform/gmp-bpf/docs/gui_0031_tc-tm-eng.php

These guidelines do not apply to aerosol preparations or to mixtures of solids that are used to generate gases.

The GMP guidelines are available on Health Canada's Compliance and Enforcement website at:

http://hc-sc.gc.ca/dhp-mps/compli-conform/index-eng.php

2. Purpose

The purpose of this guideline is to facilitate compliance with and enhance consistency in the application of Division 2 of the Food and Drug Regulations for fabricators, packagers/labellers, testers, distributors, and importers of medical gas establishments.

3. Scope

The guidelines apply to medical gases and were developed by Health Canada in consultation with stakeholders.

4. Quality Management

4.1 Guiding Principle

The holder of an establishment licence, or any operation to which the requirements of Part C, Division 2 of the Food and Drug Regulations are applicable, must ensure that the fabrication, packaging, labelling, distribution, testing and wholesaling of drugs comply with these requirements and the marketing authorization, and do not place consumers at risk due to inadequate safety and quality.

The attainment of this quality objective is the responsibility of senior management and requires the participation and commitment of personnel in many different departments and at all levels within the establishment and its suppliers. To ensure compliance, there must be a comprehensively designed and correctly implemented quality management system that incorporates GMP and quality control. The system should be fully documented and its effectiveness monitored. All parts of the quality management system should be adequately resourced with qualified personnel, suitable premises, equipment, and facilities.

4.2 Relationship Among Quality Elements

The basic concepts of quality assurance, Good Manufacturing Practices, and quality control are inter-related. They are described here in order to emphasize their relationships and their fundamental importance to the production and control of drugs.

4.2.1 Quality Assurance

Quality assurance is a wide-ranging concept that covers all matters that individually or collectively influence the quality of a drug. It is the total of the organized arrangements made with the objective of ensuring that drugs are of the quality required for their intended use. Quality assurance therefore incorporates Good Manufacturing Practices, along with other factors that are outside the scope of these guidelines.

A system of quality assurance appropriate for the fabrication, packaging, labelling, testing, distribution, importation, and wholesale of drugs should ensure that:

1. Drugs are designed and developed in a way that takes into account the GMP requirements;

2. Managerial responsibilities are clearly specified;

3. Systems, facilities, and procedures are adequate;

4. Production and control operations are clearly specified and validated;

5. Arrangements are made for the supply and use of the correct raw and packaging materials;

6. All necessary control on intermediates, and any other in-process monitoring is carried out;

7. Outsourced activities are subject to appropriate controls and meet GMP requirements;

8. Fabrication, packaging/labelling, testing, distribution, importation, and wholesaling are performed in accordance with established procedures;

9. Drugs are not sold or supplied before the quality control department has certified that each lot has been produced and controlled in accordance with the marketing authorization, and of any other regulations relevant to the production, control, and release of drugs;

10. Satisfactory arrangements exist for ensuring that the drugs are stored, distributed, and subsequently handled in such a way that quality is maintained throughout their shelf life;

11. The effectiveness and applicability of the quality management system is ensured through regular self-inspection and management review;

12. An annual product quality review of all drugs should be conducted with the objective of verifying the consistency of the existing process, the appropriateness of current specifications for both raw materials and finished product to highlight any trends and to identify product and process improvements.

4.2.2 Good Manufacturing Practices (GMP) for Drugs

Good Manufacturing Practices (GMP) are the part of quality assurance that ensures that drugs are consistently produced and controlled in such a way to meet the quality standards appropriate to their intended use, as required by the marketing authorization.

GMP basic requirements are as follows:

1. Manufacturing processes are clearly defined and controlled to ensure consistency and compliance with approved specifications;

2. Critical steps of manufacturing processes and significant changes to the process are validated;

Medical Gases GMPs

3. All necessary key elements for GMPs are provided, including the following:

   - qualified and trained personnel;
   - adequate premises and space;
   - suitable equipment and services;
   - correct materials, containers, and labels;
   - approved procedures and instructions;
   - suitable storage and transport;

4. Instructions and procedures are written in clear and unambiguous language;

5. Operators are trained to carry out and document procedures;

6. Records are made during manufacture that demonstrate that all the steps required by the defined procedures and instructions were in fact taken and that the quantity and quality of the drug was as expected. Deviations are investigated and documented;

7. Records of fabrication, packaging, labelling, testing, distribution, importation, and wholesaling that enable the complete history of a lot to be traced are retained in a comprehensible and accessible form;

8. Control of storage, handling, and transportation of the drugs minimizes any risk to their quality;

9. A system is available for recalling drugs from sale;

10. Complaints about drugs are examined, the causes of quality defects are investigated, and appropriate measures are taken with respect to the defective drugs and to prevent recurrence.

4.2.3 Quality Control

Quality control is the part of GMP that is concerned with sampling, specifications, testing, documentation, and release procedures. Quality control ensures that the necessary and relevant tests are carried out and that raw materials, packaging materials, and products are released for use, sale or supply, only if their quality is satisfactory. Quality control is not confined to laboratory operations but must be incorporated into all activities and decisions concerning the quality of the product.

The basic requirements of quality control are as follows:

1. Adequate facilities, trained personnel, and approved procedures are available for sampling, inspecting, and testing of raw materials, packaging materials, intermediate bulk and finished products, and, where appropriate monitoring environmental conditions for GMP purposes;

   1.1 Samples of raw materials, packaging materials, and intermediate, bulk, and finished products are taken according to procedures approved by the quality control department;

   1.2 Test methods are validated;

1.3 Records demonstrate that all the required sampling, inspecting, and testing procedures were carried out, and any deviations are recorded and investigated;

1.4 Records are made of the results of self-inspection and management reviews;

1.5 The procedures for product release include a review and evaluation of relevant production documentation and an assessment of deviations from specified procedures;

1.6 No drug is released for sale or supply prior to approval by the quality control department;

1.7 Sufficient samples of medicinal ingredients and drugs are retained to permit future examination if necessary, and the drug is retained in its final package unless exceptionally large packages are produced.

5. Regulation

C.02.002

In this Division,

"medical gas" means any gas or mixture of gases manufactured, sold, or represented for use as a drug; (gaz médical)

"packaging material" includes a label; (matériel d'emballage)

"quality control department" means a quality control department referred to in section C.02.013; (service du contrôle de la qualité)

"specifications" means a detailed description of a drug, the raw material used in a drug, or the packaging material for a drug and includes:

    a.   a statement of all properties and qualities of the drug, raw material or packaging material that are relevant to the manufacture, packaging, and use of the drug, including the identity, potency, and purity of the drug, raw material, or packaging material,

    b.   a detailed description of the methods used for testing and examining the drug, raw material, or packaging material, and

    c.   a statement of tolerances for the properties and qualities of the drug, raw material, or packaging material. (spécifications)

Sale

C.02.003

No distributor referred to in paragraph C.01A.003(b) and no importer shall sell a drug unless it has been fabricated, packaged/labelled, tested, and stored in accordance with the requirements of this Division.

Medical Gases GMPs

Premises

C.02.004

The premises in which a lot or batch of a drug is fabricated or packaged/labelled shall be designed, constructed and maintained in a manner that:

a. permits the operations therein to be performed under clean, sanitary and orderly conditions;

b. permits the effective cleaning of all surfaces therein; and

c. prevents the contamination of the drug and the addition of extraneous material to the drug.

Rationale

In a medical gas fabricating or packaging establishment appropriate cleanliness of work areas permits the achievement of sanitary conditions; orderliness helps to prevent mix-up; control of airborne and other contaminants safeguard product integrity. Cleanliness, orderliness, and prevention of contamination call for initial good design and continuing maintenance. Regular maintenance is also required to prevent deterioration of premises. The ultimate objective of all endeavours is product quality.

Interpretation

1. Buildings are located in an environment that, when considered together with measures being taken to protect the manufacturing processes, presents a minimum risk of causing any contamination of materials or drugs.

2. The premises are adequate for the operation performed therein and are designed to avoid mix-ups and prevent contamination.

    2.1 There is sufficient space for receiving and all production activities.

    2.2 Working spaces allow the orderly and logical placement of equipment (including parts and tools) and materials.

    2.3 Where physical quarantine areas are used, they are well marked, with access restricted to designated personnel. Where electronic quarantine is used, electronic access is restricted to designated personnel.

    2.4 Working areas are well lit.

3. Adequate segregation and area designation should be provided to distinguish:

    3.1 containers set aside for cleaning, testing or maintenance from containers that have been released for filling;

    3.2 different gases;

    3.3 medical gases from non-medical gases including their respective empty containers;

3.4 empty from full containers; and

3.5 quarantined finished products from those available for distribution.

4. Outlets are clearly identified as to their content.

5. Dead legs in which circulation may be restricted should be minimized.

6. Pipelines carrying medical gases between areas should be identified by colour or by standard markings at suitable intervals and direction of flow shown.

7. Intakes of air to be used in the production of medical gas are located such that contamination with waste gases and other pollutants is avoided. Filters, especially the ones to trap desiccants after driers, are of suitable construction, examined and changed as necessary.

8. Rest, change, wash-up, and toilet facilities are well separated from production areas and are sufficiently spacious, well ventilated, and of a type that permits good sanitary practices.

9. Fabrication and filling areas are adequately lighted.

10. Premises are maintained in a good state of repair.

11. Premises and vehicles used to store medical gases are secured from unauthorized entry.

Equipment

C.02.005

The equipment with which a lot or batch of a drug is fabricated, packaged/labelled or tested shall be designed, constructed, maintained, operated and arranged in a manner that:

a. permits the effective cleaning of its surfaces;

b. prevents the contamination of the drug and the addition of extraneous materials to the drug; and

c. permits it to function in accordance with its intended use.

Rationale

The purpose of these requirements is to prevent the contamination of medical gases by other gases, by dust, and by foreign materials such as rust, lubricant, and particles coming from the equipment. Contamination problems may arise from poor maintenance, misuse of equipment, exceeding the capacity of the equipment, and use of worn-out equipment. Equipment arranged in an orderly manner permits cleaning of adjacent areas and does not interfere with other processing operations. It also minimizes circulation of personnel and optimizes flow of material. The fabrication of medical gases of consistent quality requires that equipment perform in accordance with its intended use.

Interpretation

1. Parts that are in contact with medical gases are designed, constructed, and located so as to permit cleaning and to avoid contamination. Where required, fittings and accessory assemblies are designed for easy dismantling.

2. Tankers and trailers and their ancillary equipment (hoses, valves, pumps, etc.) are of suitable construction and maintained in a good state of repair. Special attention is given to the tankers and trailers owned by a contracting firm.

3. Filling and storage equipment are appropriate to medical gases. Materials used are non-toxic, and non-reactive to medical gases, and are corrosion-resistant. Medical gas filling equipment is designed to prevent wrong connections. It should be impossible to fill a container with the wrong gas. Containers may be connected either to different valves through an adapter or to a manifold that is itself connected to different medical gas outlets, provided the procedure is fully validated and documented to ensure no cross contamination. Either procedure precludes the possibility of connecting a container to the wrong line.

4. Equipment used during the critical steps of fabrication, packaging and testing, including computerized systems, is subject to installational and operational qualification. Equipment qualification is documented. Further guidance is provided in the Health Canada documents entitled "Validation Guidelines for Pharmaceutical Dosage Forms (GUI-0029)" and "PIC/S Annex 11: Computerized Systems."

5. Equipment used in the fabrication, packaging/labelling and testing of medical gases, including computerized equipment, is routinely checked and maintained and measuring devices are calibrated in accordance with a written program. Temporary devices for repairs are avoided. Records of maintenance and calibration are kept.

6. Openings for connections on lines supplying medical gases are adequately protected from contamination.

7. Check valves used to prevent contamination are verified on a scheduled frequency to ensure functionality.

Personnel

C.02.006

Every lot or batch of a drug shall be fabricated, packaged/labelled, tested and stored under the supervision of personnel who, having regard to the duties and responsibilities involved, have had such technical, academic and other training as the Director considers satisfactory in the interests of the health of the consumer or purchaser.

Rationale

People are the most important element in any medical gases operation, for without the proper staff with the right attitude and the right training, it is almost impossible to fabricate, package/label, test or store good quality drugs. It is essential that qualified personnel be employed to supervise the fabrication and packaging of medical gases. The operations involved in the fabrication of medical gases can be highly technical in nature and require constant vigilance, attention to details, and a high degree of competence on the part of employees. Inadequate training of personnel, or the absence of an appreciation of the importance of production control, often accounts for the failure of a product to meet the required standards.

Interpretation

1. Individuals in charge of the manufacturing and the quality control departments:

   1.1 have the managerial and professional or technical qualifications; and

   1.2 have practical experience in their responsibility area.

   1.3 can delegate their duties and responsibilities to an individual on site trained and certified with respect to the specific job function.

2. Individuals responsible for filling/packaging operations, including control over printed packaging materials and withdrawal of bulk gases:

   2.1 are persons qualified by training and experience; and

   2.2 are directly responsible to the person in charge of the manufacturing department or a person having the same qualifications.

   Note: At medical gas filling stations, personnel performing simple analytical tests and quality control functions in accordance with standard company procedures may be individuals with practical experience only.

3. Individuals in charge of the packaging operations and associated quality control for the medical gases used in respiratory therapy:

   3.1 may be persons registered as a respiratory therapist under applicable provincial legislation governing health professionals; or qualified by pertinent training; and

   3.2 have practical experience in their responsibility area.

4. An adequate number of personnel with the necessary qualifications and practical experience appropriate to their responsibilities are available on site.

   4.1 The responsibilities placed on any one individual are not so extensive as to present any risk to quality.

   4.2 All responsible personnel have their specific duties relating to medical gases recorded in a written description and have adequate authority to carry out their responsibilities.

   4.3 When key personnel are absent, qualified personnel are appointed to carry out their duties and functions.

5. All personnel are aware of the principles of GMP that affect them and receive initial and continuing training relevant to their job responsibilities.

Medical Gases GMPs

5.1 Training is provided by qualified personnel having regard to the function and in accordance with a written program for all personnel involved in the fabrication of a medical gas, including technical, maintenance and cleaning staff.

5.2 The effectiveness of continuing training is periodically assessed.

5.3 Training is provided prior to implementation of new or revised SOPs.

5.4 Records of training are maintained.

5.5 Personnel working in areas where highly active, toxic, infectious or sensitizing materials are handled, are given specific training.

5.6 Performance of personnel is periodically reviewed.

6. Consultants and contractors have the necessary qualifications, training, and experience to advise on the subjects for which they are retained.

Sanitation

C.02.007

1. Every person who fabricates or packages/labels a drug shall have a written sanitation program that shall be implemented under the supervision of qualified personnel.

2. The sanitation program referred to in subsection (1) shall include:

   a. cleaning procedures for the premises where the drug is fabricated or packaged/labelled and for the equipment used in the fabrication or packaging/labelling of the drug; and

   b. instructions on the sanitary fabrication and packaging/labelling of drugs and the handling of materials used in the fabrication and packaging/labelling of drugs.

Rationale

Sanitation in a medical gas fabricating and packaging facility influences the quality of medical gas products as well as employee attitude. The quality of a medical gas demands that it be fabricated and packaged in an area that is free from environmental contamination and free from contamination with another gas.

A written sanitation program provides some assurance that levels of cleanliness in the facility are maintained and that the provisions of Sections 8 and 11 of the Food and Drugs Act are satisfied.

Interpretation

1. Even though medical gases are handled in closed systems, areas where medical gases are filled are kept reasonably clean and tidy.

   1.1 A written sanitation or housekeeping program is available on the premises where medical gases are fabricated or packaged/labelled.

2. The sanitation or housekeeping program contains procedures that outline:

   2.1 clearing requirements applicable to the facility;

   2.2 clearing requirements applicable to processing equipment.

3. Cleaning of critical equipment used in fabrication, transportation, storage, and filling of medical gases, and cleaning and purging of pipelines that carry medical gases follow written procedures, including checks for the absence of cleaning agents or other contaminants. All of these procedures are validated and documented. Special attention is given to the tankers and trailers owned by a contracting firm. Further guidance is provided in the Health Canada document entitled "Cleaning Validation Guidelines (GUI-0028)".

C.02.008

1. Every person who fabricates or packages/labels a drug shall have, in writing, minimum requirements for the health, and the hygienic behaviour and clothing of personnel to ensure the clean and sanitary fabrication and packaging/labelling of the drug.

2. No person shall have access to any area where a drug is exposed during its fabrication or packaging/labelling if the person:

   a. is affected with or is a carrier of a disease in a communicable form; or

   b. has an open lesion on any exposed surface of the body.

Rationale

Employees' health, their behaviour, and their clothing may contribute to the contamination of the product. The manufacture of medical gases is generally carried out in closed equipment. Potential for environmental contamination of the product is minimal. The requirements for hygiene of personnel engaged in the production of medical gases are similar to those that are applicable to personnel involved with other dosage forms, although the extent to which they are applicable will greatly depend on the operation and the procedures used.

Interpretation

1. Requirements of health are available in writing and may include:

   1.1 pre-employment medical examination;

   1.2 assurance as far as is practicable that no person affected by an infectious disease or having open lesions on the exposed surface of the body is engaged in the manufacture and packaging of medical gases;

   1.3 assurances that individuals responsible for performing odour tests do not have ailments that can adversely affect test results;

   1.4 assurances that employees responsible for performing inspections involving distinguishing colours can distinguish colours appropriately.

Medical Gases GMPs

2. The hygiene program clearly defines clothing requirements and hygiene procedures for company personnel and visitors.

    2.1 Where a potential for contamination of a medical gas exists, individuals wear clean clothing and protective covering.

    2.2 Direct contact is avoided between the operator's hands and any parts of equipment that come in direct contact with the medical gas.

    2.3 Unsanitary practices are not permitted in processing areas.

    2.4 Requirements concerning personal hygiene are outlined when significant to the quality of the product.

Raw Material Testing

Note: Sections C.02.009 and C.02.010 are applicable only to batches of gases that are used in the fabrication of medical gas mixtures. For testing of bulk gases that are not used to produce gas mixtures, see sections C.02.011, C.02.018, and C.02.019.

C.02.009

1. Each lot or batch of raw material shall be tested against the specification of the raw material prior to its use in the fabrication of a drug.

2. No lot or batch of raw material shall be used in the fabrication of a drug unless that lot or batch of raw material complies with the specifications for that raw material.

3. Notwithstanding subsection (1), water may, prior to the completion of its tests under that subsection, be used in the production of a drug.

4. Where any property of a raw material is subject to change on storage, no lot or batch of that raw material shall be used in the fabrication of a drug after its storage unless the raw material is retested after an appropriate interval and complies with its specifications for that property.

5. Where the specifications referred to in subsections (1), (2) and (4) are not prescribed, they shall:

    a. be in writing;

    b. acceptable to the Director, who shall take into account the specifications contained in any publication mentioned in Scheduled B to the Act; and

    c. be approved by the person in charge of the quality control department.

Rationale

The testing of raw materials before their use has three objectives: confirm the identity of the raw materials, provide assurance that the quality of the medical gas in dosage form will not be altered by raw material defects, and obtain assurance that the raw materials have the characteristics that will provide the desired quantity or yield in a given manufacturing process.

Interpretation

1. Raw materials are tested to specification on receipt at the fabricating facility.

2. Specifications are in compliance with the marketing authorization. When a monograph exists in a pharmacopeia listed in Schedule B to the Food and Drugs Act, specifications meet the monograph.

3. Test methods used to test a raw material for which there is a pharmacopeial standard are equivalent to compendial methods. Non-pharmacopeial test methods are fully validated. Guidance on analytical method validation can be obtained in publications such as the ICH document entitled "ICH Q2(R1): Validation of Analytical Procedures: Text and Methodology" or any standard listed in Schedule B to the Food and Drugs Act.

4. Deliveries of raw material may be added to a bulk storage tank containing the same gas from previous deliveries. In this case:

    4.1 a sample of the delivered raw material is tested and found to be satisfactory; or

    4.2 when the raw material is a single gas accompanied by a Certificate of Analysis, the sample may be taken and tested after allowing for sufficient mixing of the delivery in the bulk storage tank after the sampling line has been adequately purged;

    4.3 when the raw material is a mixture, the testing verifies each component.

C.02.010

1. The testing referred to in section C.02.009 shall be performed on a sample taken

    a. after receipt of each lot or batch of raw material on the premises of the fabricator; or

    b. subject to subsection (2), before receipt of each lot or batch of raw material on the premises of the fabricator, if

        i. the fabricator:

            A. has evidence satisfactory to the Director to demonstrate that raw materials sold to him by the vendor of that lot or batch of raw material are consistently manufactured in accordance with and consistently comply with the specifications for those raw materials; and

            B. undertakes periodic complete confirmatory testing with a frequency satisfactory to the Director; and

        ii. the raw material has not been transported or stored under conditions that may affect its compliance with the specifications for that raw material.

2. After a lot or batch of raw material is received on the premises of the fabricator, the lot or batch of raw material shall be tested for identity.

Medical Gases GMPs

Rationale

Section C.02.010 outlines options as to when the testing prescribed by section C.02.009 is carried out. The purchase of raw materials is an important operation that requires a particular and thorough knowledge of the raw materials and vendor. To maintain consistency in the fabrication of drug products, raw material should originate from reliable vendors.

Interpretation

1. The testing is performed on a sample taken after the receipt on the premises of the person that fills the containers.

2. For tests other than identity tests, paragraph C.02.010 (1) (b) outlines conditions to be met, should the person choose to rely on the test results provided by the vendor.

   2.1 Evidence satisfactory to the Director should include:

   2.1.1 evidence of ongoing GMP compliance including process control and validation in accordance with these guidelines, or an audit report issued by a qualified authority demonstrating that the raw material fabricator complies with the ICH document entitled "ICH Q7 Good Manufacturing Practice Guide for Active Pharmaceutical Ingredients" or with any standard or system of equivalent quality.

   2.1.2 all lots to be accompanied by an authentic certificate of analysis exhibiting actual numerical results, and making reference to product specification and validated test methods used;

   2.1.3 complete confirmatory testing is conducted on a minimum of one lot per year of a raw material received from each vendor, with the raw material being selected on a rotational basis. Where multiple raw materials are received from the same vendor, confirmatory testing is carried out for each raw material at least once every five years.

   2.2 If any lot is rejected, the vendor must be requalified.

3. Conditions of transportation and storage should be such that they prevent alterations to the potency and purity of the raw material. In order to demonstrate that these conditions have been met, standard operating procedures and records for shipping and receiving are available and contain:

   3.1 the type of packaging to be employed;

   3.2 labelling requirements;

   3.3 mode of transportation;

   3.4 seal of package;

   3.5 verification required to ensure that each package has not been tampered with and that there are no damaged containers;

3.6 evidence that special shipping requirements have been met.

Manufacturing Control

C.02.011

Every fabricator, packager/labeller, distributor referred to in paragraph C.01A.003 (b) and importer of a drug shall have written procedures, prepared by qualified personnel, in respect of the drug to ensure that the drug meets the specifications for use of that drug.

Every person required to have written procedures referred to in subsection (1) shall ensure that each lot or batch of the drug is fabricated, packaged/labelled and tested in compliance with those procedures.

Rationale

This section requires that a number of measures be taken to maintain the integrity of a medical gas from the moment the various raw materials or bulk gases enter the plant to the time the finished product is released for sale. These measures seek to ensure that all manufacturing processes are clearly defined, systematically reviewed in light of experience, and shown to be capable of consistently manufacturing medical gas products of the required quality that comply with their established specifications.

Interpretation

1. Written procedures are available to ensure that raw materials and bulk gases are stored in appropriately labelled containers.

2. All critical production processes are validated in accordance with predefined protocols. Detailed information is provided in the Health Canada document entitled "Validation Guidelines for Pharmaceutical Dosage Forms (GUI-0029)".

3. Bulk gases are stored under conditions and handled in distribution systems that preclude product mixup, deterioration or contamination.

4. Written procedures are available to ensure that raw materials and bulk gases are:

   4.1 identified by lot number, receiving number, or laboratory control number;

   4.2 released for production or filling operations according to written procedures approved by the quality control department; and

   4.3 stored under conditions that will preserve their quality and avoid their inadvertent use.

5. Written procedures approved by the quality control department are available to ensure that containers are not filled until they are checked or tested to ensure that they meet their specifications.

Medical Gases GMPs

6. Processing operations are covered by master formula, which are prepared by, and subject to independent checks by persons having the qualifications described under section C.02.006.

7. Master formula, master production documents, or master filling documents are written to provide 100% of label claim and include:

   7.1 the name of the product;

   7.2 the name and concentration of components, including acceptable tolerances;

   7.3 the filling sequence of components;

   7.4 the fill pressure or weight of components (compressed gases);

   7.5 in-process and final quality control requirements.

8. Before any processing operation is started, all necessary steps are taken and documented to ensure that the work area and equipment are clean and free from any raw materials, products, product residues, labels or documents not required for the current operation.

9. Manufacturing and filling records contain all information pertinent to the manufacturing and filling of each batch of medical gas including:

   9.1 in-process quality control requirements;

   9.2 equipment used (if multiple systems are used for same product);

   9.3 a mark that is unique to an individual or the initials of personnel; and

   9.4 name and references to the specification for each raw material in a mixture.

10. Completed manufacturing orders include:

    10.1 appropriate check to ensure the containers have been filled;

    10.2 actual results of the quality checks performed;

    10.3 batch or lot number, receiving number, or laboratory control number of each raw material in a mixture; and

    10.4 a mark that is unique to an individual or the initials of personnel involved in the preparation of the mixture.

11. Deliveries of bulk gas may be added to the bulk storage tanks containing the same gas from previous deliveries. In this case:

    11.1 a sample of the delivered bulk gas is tested before it is added to the storage tank, and found to be satisfactory; or

11.2   when the bulk gas is a single gas accompanied by a Certificate of Analysis, the sample may be taken after allowing for sufficient mixing of the delivery in the bulk storage tank. The sample may be taken from a sampling line or from the first container filled, provided that the sampling, distribution, and filling lines have been adequately purged prior to sampling;

11.3   when the bulk gas is a mixture, the testing verifies each component.

12. Residual batches or lots in cryogenic containers or trailers may be combined or product from the bulk storage tank may be added to the containers or trailers if purity testing is performed after mixing.

13. Written instructions ensure that:

13.1 the initials of quality control personnel or qualified designate are recorded in the filling logs;

13.2 the lot number of the medical gas is assigned and appears on each container. The lot number may not appear on each bulk transport container, each storage tank filled, and each container filled at curbside, provided that traceability is documented;

13.3 filling of high pressure cylinders is controlled either by monitoring the temperature of the wall of cylinders and the pressure or by mass. Correct fill may be verified by reference to a temperature/pressure chart or a target mass chart, as applicable;

13.4 during manifold filling sequences a heat of compression check is performed, where necessary, on the exterior surface of each cylinder to demonstrate proper filling;

13.5 filled containers are effectively quarantined until released by the quality control department;

13.6 each container undergoes a leak test during filling using an appropriate method such as leak detection solution applied to the valve to detect valve packing leaks, safety plug leaks, and other valve leaks. Each filled container undergoes a second leak test after filling to detect valve outlet leaks. Leak test solutions, such as soap, that can cause corrosion or leave films should not be used.

Note: This does not apply to refrigerated or cryogenic liquids.

14. Filling is followed as quickly as possible by labelling. If labelling is delayed, appropriate procedures are applied to ensure that no mix-ups or mislabeling can occur.

14.1   Labels withdrawal is documented and reconciled.

14.2   Labelling operations are controlled by 100% verification. Verifications are documented.

14.3   Labelling operations are documented.

Medical Gases GMPs

15. All containers are appropriately labelled and identified in such a way as to be readily distinguishable as to their content. Container identification is performed according to predetermined and well-recorded procedures under the supervision of qualified personnel.

16. Materials and labels used to identify containers are stored in a limited access area and restricted to designated personnel.

17. Outdated or obsolete materials and labels are destroyed and their disposal recorded.

18. Medical gases are not released without the approval of the quality control department.

19. Water used for cooling during compression of air is monitored for microbial quality when in contact with the medical gas.

C.02.012.

1. Every fabricator, packager/labeller, distributor referred to in section C.01A.003, importer and wholesaler of a drug shall maintain:

   a. a system of control that permits complete and rapid recall of any lot or batch of the drug that is on the market; and

   b. a program of self-inspection;

2. Every fabricator and packager/labeller and, subject to subsections (3) and (4), every distributor referred to in section C.01A.003(b) and importer of a drug shall maintain a system designed to ensure that any lot or batch of the drug fabricated and packaged/labelled on premises other than their own is fabricated and packaged/labelled in accordance with the requirements of this Division.

3. The distributor referred to in paragraph C.01A.003(b) of a drug that is fabricated, packaged/labelled, and tested in Canada by a person who holds an establishment licence that authorizes those activities is not required to comply with the requirements of subsection (2) in respect of that drug.

4. If a drug is fabricated or packaged/labelled in an MRA country at a recognized building, the distributor referred to in paragraph C.01A.003(b) or importer of the drug is not required to comply with the requirements of subsection (2) in respect of that activity for that drug if

   1. the address of the building is set out in that person's establishment licence; and

   2. that person retains a copy of the batch certificate for each lot or batch of the drug received by that person.

Rationale

The purpose of a recall is to remove from the market a medical gas that represents an undue health risk. Medical gases that have left the premises of a fabricator, packager/labeller, distributor, or importer can be found in a variety of locations. Depending on the severity of the health risk, it may be necessary to recall a product to one level or another. Fabricators, packagers/labellers, distributors, and importers are expected to be able to recall to the consumer level if necessary. Additional guidance on recalls may be found in the document entitled "Product Recall Procedures".

This regulation also requires fabricators, packagers/labellers, distributors, and importers to maintain a program of self-inspection. The purpose of self-inspection is to evaluate the compliance with GMPs in all aspects of production and quality control. The self-inspection program is designed to detect any shortcomings in the implementation of GMPs and to recommend the necessary corrective actions.

Medical gases offered for sale in Canada, regardless of whether they are domestically produced or are imported, must meet the requirement of the Part C, Division 2 of the Regulations. Contract production and analysis must be correctly defined, agreed, and controlled in order to avoid misunderstanding that could result in a product, work or analysis of unsatisfactory quality. Normally, a contract or other written agreement exists between the parties involved which clearly established the duties of each party.

Interpretation

1. A written recall system is in place that ensures that:

   1.1 the Health Products and Food Branch Inspectorate is notified of the recall;

   1.2 any action taken to recall a medical gas suspected or known to be defective is prompt and in accordance with a pre-determined plan. The procedures to be followed are in writing and known to all persons that may be concerned;

   1.3 the person or persons responsible to initiate and co-ordinate all recall activities are identified;

   1.4 the recall procedures is capable of being put into operation at any time, during and outside normal working hours;

   1.5 the recall procedure outlines the means of notifying and implementing a recall and of deciding its extent;

   1.6 account is taken of any products in transit when the recall is initiated;

   1.7 the progress and efficacy of a recall is assessed at intervals;

   1.8 provisions are made for the handling and disposition of recalled medical gases.

2. A self-inspection program appropriate to the type of operations of the establishment, with respect to medical gases, ensures compliance with Part C, Division 2 of the Food and Drug Regulations in that:

   2.1 a comprehensive written procedure is available and describes the functions of the self-inspection program;

Medical Gases GMPs

2.2 periodic self-inspections are carried out;

2.3 written reports of the findings of the inspections and corrective actions are prepared.

3. The fabricator, packager/labeller, distributor or importer is responsible for assessing the continuing competence of the contractor to successfully carry out the work or tests required in accordance with the principles of GMP described in these guidelines.

3.1 Distributors of medical gases fabricated, packaged/labelled or tested at Canadian sites are required only to have a copy of the relevant valid Canadian establishment licence held by the Canadian fabricator, packager/labeller or tester.

3.2 Importers of bulk gases and finished products fabricated, packaged/labelled, or tested at a foreign site must meet the requirements described in the policy document entitled Guidance on Evidence to Demonstrate Drug GMP Compliance of Foreign sites (GUI-0080). The foreign site must be listed on the establishment licence of the importer.

Quality Control Department

C.02.013

1. Every fabricator, packager/labeller, distributor referred to in paragraph C.01A.003(b) and importer shall have on their premises in Canada a quality control department that is supervised by personnel described in section C.02.006.

2. The quality control department referred to in subsection (1) shall be a distinct organizational unit that functions and reports to management independently of any other functional unit, including the manufacturing, processing, packaging or sales unit.

Rationale

Quality control is the part of GMP concerned with sampling, specifications, and testing, and with the organization, documentation, and release procedures which ensure that the necessary and relevant tests are actually carried out and that raw materials and packaging materials are not released for use, nor products released for sale or supply, until their quality has been judged to be satisfactory. Quality control is not confined to laboratory operations but must be involved in all decisions concerning the quality of the product.

Although manufacturing and quality control personnel share the common goal of assuring the high-quality medical gases are fabricated, their interest may sometimes conflict in the short run as decisions are made that will affect a company's output. In the medical gas industry, quality control is performed by personnel in various departments using a matrix organization. For quality control issues, these personnel are responsible to the individual in charge of quality control. The independence of quality control from fabricating and packaging is considered fundamental. The rationale for the requirement that the quality control department be supervised by qualified personnel is outlined under the section C.02.006.

Interpretation

1. A person responsible for making decisions concerning quality control requirements is on-site at the manufacturer and importer. At locations with two or fewer operations staff available, the manufacturing and quality control person may be the same, provided that due consideration is given to situations where:

   1.1 it is impossible to have distinct organizational units on site;

   1.2 chances of error are eliminated;

   1.3 reporting relationship is different while the employee performs quality control functions and fabrication or packaging/labelling activities;

   1.4 the employee is fully aware of his/her dual role, understands clearly responsibilities and line authority and acts accordingly.

2. The quality control department has true and effective access to equipment and facilities for inspecting and testing, having regard to the nature of the products produced.

C.02.014

1. No lot or batch of drug shall be made available for sale unless the sale of that lot or batch is approved by the person in charge of the quality control department.

2. A drug that is returned to the fabricator, packager/labeller, distributor referred to in paragraph C.C1A.003(b) or importer thereof shall not be made available for further sale unless the sale of that drug is approved by the person in charge of the quality control department.

3. No lot or batch of raw material or of packaging/labelling material shall be used in the fabrication or packaging/labelling of a drug, unless that material is approved for that use by the person in charge of the quality control department.

4. No lot or batch of a drug shall be reprocessed without the approval of the person in charge of the quality control department.

Rationale

The responsibility for the approval of all raw materials, packaging, materials and finished products is vested in the quality control department. It is very important that adequate controls be exercised by this department in order to guarantee the quality of the end product. To maintain this level of quality, it is also important to examine all returned medical gases and to give special attention to reprocessed medical gases.

Interpretation

1. All decisions made by the quality control department pursuant to section C.02.014 are attested to by the signature of the head of the quality control department, or an authorized alternate, and are dated.

Medical Gases GMPs

2. The quality control department ensures that raw materials, bulk gases, and packaging materials are effectively quarantined, sampled, tested, and released prior to their use in fabrication or packaging/labelling of a medical gas.

3. Finished products returned from the market are destroyed unless it has been ascertained that their quality is satisfactory. Returned goods may be considered for resale only after they have been assessed in accordance with a written procedure. The reason for the return, the nature of the product, the storage conditions, the product's condition and history, and the time elapsed since it was originally sold are to be taken into consideration in this assessment. Records of any action taken are maintained.

C.02.015

1. All fabrication, packaging/labelling, testing, storage and transportation methods and procedures that may affect the quality of a drug shall be examined and approved by the person in charge of the quality control department before their implementation.

2. The person in charge of the quality control department shall cause to be investigated every complaint on quality that is received and cause corrective action to be taken if necessary.

3. The person in charge of the quality control department shall cause all tests or examinations required pursuant to this Division to be performed by a competent laboratory.

Rationale

Medical gases are designed and developed in a way that takes into account the requirements of GMP. Production procedures and other control operations are independently examined by the quality control department. Proper storage, transportation, and distribution of materials and products minimize any risk to their quality. Complaints are an indicator of problems related to quality. By tracing their causes one can determine which corrective measures should be taken to prevent recurrence. Testing carried out by a competent laboratory provides assurance that test results are genuine and accurate. Written contracts for consultants and contract laboratories describe the education, training, experience, and the types of services provided and are available for examination and inspection. Records of their activities are maintained.

Interpretation

1. All decisions made by the quality control department pursuant to section C.02.015 are attested to by the signature of the head of the quality control department, or an authorized alternate, and are dated.

2. The tests are performed by a competent laboratory in that:

   2.1 facilities are designed, equipped, and maintained to suit the testing and approval (or rejection) of raw materials, medical gases, and containers;

   2.2 the individual in charge of the laboratory is qualified in accordance with C.02.006 or functionally reports to a person having these qualifications; and

2.3 laboratory staff are sufficient in number and are qualified to carry out the work they undertake.

3. All complaints and other information concerning potentially defective products are reviewed according to written procedures. The complaint is recorded with all the original details and thoroughly investigated. Appropriate follow-up action is taken after investigation and evaluation of the complaint. All decisions and measures taken as a result of a complaint are recorded and referenced to the corresponding batch records. Complaint records are regularly reviewed for any indication of specific or recurring problems that require attention. The same procedures are applied to recalls.

4. A change control system is established to provide the mechanisms for ongoing process optimization and for assuring a continuing state of control. All changes are properly documented, evaluated, and approved by the quality control department, and are identified with the appropriate effective date. Any significant change may necessitate re-validation.

Packaging Material Testing

C.02.016

1. Each lot or batch of packaging material shall, prior to its use in the packaging of a drug, be examined or tested against the specifications for that packaging material.

2. No lot or batch of packaging material shall be used in the packaging of a drug unless the lot or batch of packaging material complies with the specifications for that packaging material.

3. The specifications referred to in subsection (1) and (2) shall

   a. be in writing;

   b. be acceptable to the Director who shall take into account the specifications contained in any publication mentioned in Schedule B to the Act; and

   c. be approved by the person in charge of the quality control department.

Rationale

Where a medical gas is presented in an inadequate container, the entire effort put into the initial research, product development and manufacturing control is wasted. Medical gas quality is directly dependent on the packaging quality. Packaging materials are required to be tested or examined prior to their use to ensure that materials of acceptable quality are used in the packaging of medical gases. Inspection and testing of medical gas containers becomes even more important since they are returned and reused.

Interpretation

1. Containers are carefully examined against their specifications before filling.

Medical Gases GMPs

2. For high pressure containers returned for filling, checks and tests are performed on each and every container. These checks and tests should include:

2.1 an external examination of valves and containers for dents, arc burns, dings, oil, grease, and other signs of external damage that might cause a container to be unacceptable or unsafe for use;

2.2 check to determine that old batch labels with lot numbers and identification, and other damaged labels have been removed;

Note: Old labels on shoulder need not be removed if they are identical to the labels currently used, in good condition, and applicable to the product being filled.

2.3 venting or blowing down to atmospheric pressure if any gas is present; or inverted and drained;

2.4 an odour or sniff test may be performed during the venting of a cylinder to detect the presence of foreign gas or odour;

2.5 check to determine that the container re-qualification has been conducted as required. Each container is required to be coded (cylinder marking) to show the date of the last hydrostatic test:

2.5.1 Steel cylinders are re-qualified every five (5) years unless a "*" follows the testing date which means the cylinder may be re-qualified every ten (10) years.

2.5.2 Aluminum cylinders are re-qualified every five (5) years.

2.5.3 Water used for hydrostatic testing is at least of drinking water quality.

2.5.4 The interior of cylinders are visually examined at appropriate intervals (usually when re-qualification is performed).

2.6 a dead ring test or hammer test is performed to determine the absence of internal corrosion;

Note: This does not apply to aluminum cylinders. Cylinders producing a dull sound are quarantined for possible internal corrosion.

2.7 evacuation of each cylinder (at least to a remaining pressure of 150 millibar) or purging by a suitable method is performed before any medical gas is introduced into the cylinder. As an alternative, full analysis of the remaining gas is carried out for each cylinder. Data should be available demonstrating the suitability of the evacuation or purge.

3. Cryogenic vessels undergo certain checks prior to filling. The required pre fill checks are usually contained in the manufacturer's manual supplied with each cryogenic vessel. At a minimum there is:

3.1 an external vessel check;

3.2 all inlet and outlet connection check;

3.3 a label check.

4. In addition to examinations as identified above, large cryogenic vessels need to be examined for Transport Canada markings and the packager must ensure that the pressure relief device on the unit is appropriate for its intended use.

5. The specifications prescribe that each container be reserved for a particular type of medical gas and be identified as such (e.g., by means of a specific colour).

6. Gauges on containers indicating volume or quantity are checked to ensure proper operation.

7. Containers failing above examinations and testing are quarantined to prevent their use.

8. Examination and testing is documented.

Note: Specific testing information can be found in CAN/CSA B-340, "Selection and Use of Cylinders, Spheres, Tubes and Other Containers for the Transportation of Dangerous Goods, Class 2".

C.02.017

1. The examination or testing referred to in section C.02.016 shall be performed on a sample taken:

   a. after receipt of each lot or batch of packaging material on the premises of the person who packages a drug; or

   b. subject to subsection (2), before receipt of each lot or batch of packaging material on the premises of the person who packages a drug:

      i. if that person

         A. has evidence satisfactory to the Director to demonstrate that packaging materials sold to him by the vendor of that lot or batch of packaging material are consistently manufactured in accordance with and consistently comply with the specifications for those packaging materials; and

         B. undertakes periodic complete confirmatory examination or testing with a frequency satisfactory to the Director; and

      ii. the packaging material has not been transported or stored under conditions that may affect its compliance with the specifications for that packaging material.

2. After a lot or batch of packaging material is received on the premises of the person who packages a drug:

   a. the lot or batch of the packaging material shall be examined or tested for identity; and

Medical Gases GMPs

b. the labels shall be examined or tested in order to ensure that they comply with the specifications for those labels.

Rationale

Section C.02.017 outlines options as to when the testing or examination prescribed by section C.02.016 is carried out. As with raw materials, the purchase of packaging materials is an important operation that involves staff who have a particular and thorough knowledge of the packaging materials and vendor.

Packaging materials originate only from vendors named in the relevant specification. It is of benefit that all aspects of the production and control of packaging materials are discussed between the manufacturer and vendor. Particular attention is paid to printed packaging materials; labels are examined or tested after receipt on the premises of the person who packages a medical gas.

Interpretation

1. This section would apply in the unlikely event that the containers would be tested on premises other than those where the filling takes place.

2. Conditions of transportation and storage should be such that they prevent alteration of the characteristics of the packaging material. In order to demonstrate that these conditions have been met, standard operating procedures and records are available and contain:

   2.1 the type of packaging to be employed;

   2.2 labelling requirements;

   2.3 mode of transportation;

   2.4 seal of package; and

   2.5 verification required to ensure the package has not been tampered with and that there are no damaged containers.

Finished Product Testing

C.02.018

1. Each lot or batch of a drug shall, prior to its availability for sale, be tested against the specification for that drug.

2. No lot or batch of a drug shall be available for sale unless it complies with the specifications for that drug.

3. The specifications referred to in subsection (1) and (2) shall:

   a. be in writing;

   b. be approved by the person in charge of the quality control department; and

c. comply with the Act and these Regulations.

Rationale

Finished product tests complement the controls employed during the manufacturing process It is at this stage that medical gases are either accepted or rejected. For these reasons, it is the responsibility of each fabricator, packager/labeller, distributor and importer to use adequate specifications and test methods that will ensure that medical gases sold are safe, and meet the standard under which they are represented.

Interpretation

1. The written specifications contain a description of the medical gas, which includes all properties and qualities, including identity, purity, and potency, that are relevant to the fabrication and use of the medical gas, together with tolerances and a description of all tests or analyses used to determine those properties and qualities, in sufficient detail to permit performance by qualified personnel. The written specifications also contain the name or identification mark that will be employed for each medical gas throughout the processing operation.

2. Specifications are in compliance with the marketing authorization. When a monograph exists in a pharmacopeia listed in Schedule B to the Food and Drugs Act, specifications meet the monograph.

3. Test methods used to test a medical gas for which there is a pharmacopeial standard are equivalent to compendial methods. Non-pharmacopeial test methods are fully validated. Guidance on analytical method validation can be obtained in publications such as the ICH document entitled "ICH Q2(R1): Validation of Analytical Procedures: Text and Methodology" or any standard listed in Schedule B to the Food and Drugs Act.

4. Each medical gas is tested to ensure that it meets its specifications. The test results are recorded in an appropriate document in a clear and concise manner. For a given filling operation of a single gas, a representative number of containers are tested to specification (usually one filled container from each manifold filling sequence). For high pressure containers filled individually manually, one filled container is tested per uninterrupted filling sequence. If the filling sequence is interrupted, then additional testing is required. For mixtures of two gases, every cylinder is tested to specifications of one of the gases, usually the active ingredient. In addition, an identity test for the other gas is performed on one cylinder from the manifold filling sequence. For mixtures containing more than two gases, every cylinder should be tested to specification of all but one of the gases, and one cylinder from each manifold filling sequence should be tested for the identity of the remaining gas.

5. Vessels filled at curbside do not have to be analyzed provided a certificate of analysis is available for the tank used to make the delivery.

C.02.019

1. Subject to subsections (3) and (4), in the case of a packager/labeller, distributor referred to in paragraph C.01A.003(b) or importer, the testing referred to in section C.02.018 shall be performed on a sample taken

       a.   after receipt of each lot or batch of the drug on the premises in Canada of the packager/labeller, distributor referred to in paragraph C.01A.003(b) or importer of the drug; or

       b.   subject to subsection (2), before receipt of each lot or batch of the drug on the premises described in paragraph (a), if;

           i.   the packager/labeller, distributor referred to in paragraph C.01A.003(b) or importer

               A.   has evidence satisfactory to the Director to demonstrate that drugs sold to him by the vendor of that lot or batch of the drug are consistently manufactured in accordance with and consistently comply with the specifications for those drugs; and

               B.   undertakes periodic complete confirmatory testing with a frequency satisfactory to the Director; and

           ii.   the drug has not been transported or stored under conditions that may affect its compliance with the specifications for that drug.

2.   Where the packager/labeller, distributor referred to in paragraph C.01A.003(b) or importer of a drug receives a lot or batch of a drug on the premises in Canada, and the useful life of the drug is more than 30 days, the lot or batch of the drug shall be tested for identity, and the packager/labeller shall confirm the identity after the lot or batch is packaged/labelled.

3.   The distributor referred to in paragraph C.01A.003(b) of a drug that is fabricated, packaged/labelled, and tested in Canada by a person who holds an establishment licence that authorizes those activities is not required to comply with the requirements of subsections (1) and (2) in respect of that drug.

4.   If a drug is fabricated, packaged/labelled, and tested in an MRA country at a recognized building, the distributor referred to in paragraph C.01A.003(b) or importer of that drug is not required to comply with the requirements of subsections (1) and (2) in respect of that drug if

       a.   the address of the building is set out in that person's establishment licence; and

       b.   that person retains a copy of the batch certificate for each lot or batch of the drug received by that person.

Rationale

Paragraph C.02.019(1)(b) outlines requirements that must be met if the testing is done before receipt on the premises of the packager/labeller, distributor or importer of the medical gas.

Interpretation

1.   Testing is performed on a sample taken after receipt on the premises of the distributor (C.01A.003 (b)) or importer of the medical gas unless the

distributor or importer chooses to rely on test results provided by the supplier.

2. Standard operating procedures and records for conditions of transportation and storage should specify:

   2.1 the type of packaging to be employed;

   2.2 labelling requirements;

   2.3 mode of transportation;

   2.4 sealing precautions;

   2.5 verifications required to ensure that the package has not been tampered with and that there are no damaged containers; and

   2.6 evidence that shipping requirements have been met.

Sites Holding a Canadian Establishment Licence

3. To demonstrate compliance with specifications, distributors of finished products that are fabricated, packaged/labelled, and tested at Canadian sites are required only to have a copy of the authentic certificate of analysis from the licensed Canadian establishment. This certificate shows actual numerical results and refers to the product specifications and test methods used. Retesting, including identity testing, is not required.

Buildings Recognized by a Regulatory Authority in a MRA Country

4. To demonstrate compliance with specifications, importers of finished products fabricated, packaged/labelled, and tested at recognized buildings authorized by a Regulatory Authority as listed by virtue of Regulation C.01A.019 are required only to have a fabricator's batch certificate from the foreign establishment in the format agreed on by the MRA partners. Re-testing, including identity testing, is not required when the drug is fabricated, packaged/labelled, and tested in an MRA country.

Sites in Non-MRA Countries

5. For testing other than identity testing, the following conditions are to be met if the importer chooses to rely on the test results provided by an establishment located in a non-MRA country:

   5.1 evidence of ongoing GMP compliance is provided according to a system described in interpretation 3 of regulation C.02.012;

   5.2 each lot is accompanied by an authentic certificate of analysis or by a copy thereof (an electronic copy with an electronic signature is acceptable). The certificate of analysis exhibits actual numerical results and makes reference to the product specifications and test methods used;

   5.3 periodic complete confirmatory testing is performed on at least one lot per year per fabricator. Products are selected on a rotational basis. Re-

Medical Gases GMPs

testing by the original laboratory is acceptable; however, it is recommended that re-testing be performed by an alternate laboratory;

5.4 provided that a specific identity test is performed, a lot or batch of a finished product selected for periodic confirmatory testing may, with the approval of the quality control department, be released for sale prior to completion of all tests.

6. Should any failure to conform to finished product testing requirements be identified, an investigation of the extent of the non-compliance is to be conducted. This procedure may include:

6.1 re-evaluation of GMP compliance; and

6.2 additional complete confirmatory testing, based on the risk associated with the non- compliance.

7. Positive identification of each lot or batch in a shipment of a finished product is carried out on a sample taken after receipt on the premises of the importer.

Records

C.02.020

1. Every fabricator, packager/labeller, distributor referred to in paragraph C.01A.003(b) and importer shall maintain on their premises in Canada for each drug sold:

    a. master production documents for the drug;

    b. evidence that each lot or batch of the drug has been fabricated, packaged/labelled, tested and stored in accordance with the procedures described in the master production documents;

    c. evidence that the conditions under which the drug was fabricated, packaged/labelled, tested and stored are in compliance with the requirements of this division;

    d. evidence establishing the period of time during which the drug in the container in which it is sold will meet the specifications for that drug; and

    e. adequate evidence of the testing referred to in section C.02.018.

2. Every distributor referred to in paragraph C.01A.003(b) and importer shall make available on request the results of testing performed on raw materials and packaging/labelling materials for each lot or batch of a drug sold.

3. Every fabricator shall maintain on his premises:

    a. the written specifications for the raw material; and

    b. adequate evidence of the raw materials testing referred to in section C.02.009.

4. Every person who packages a drug shall maintain on his premises:

   a. the written specifications for the packaging materials; and

   b. adequate evidence of the packaging material examination or testing referred to in section C.02.016.

5. Every fabricator shall maintain on their premises in Canada:

   a. detailed plans and specifications of each building in Canada at which they fabricate package/label or test; and

   b. a description of the design and construction of those buildings.

6. Every fabricator, packager/labeller, and tester shall maintain on their premises in Canada details of the personnel employed to supervise the fabrication, packaging/labelling, and testing including each person's title, responsibilities, qualifications, experience, and training.

C.02.021

1. Subject to subsection (2), all records and evidence on the fabrication, packaging/labelling, testing, and storage of a drug that are required to be maintained under this Division shall be retained for a period of at least one year after the expiration date on the label of the drug, unless otherwise specified in the person's establishment licence.

2. All records and evidence on the testing of raw materials, and packaging/labelling materials that are required to be maintained under this Division shall be retained for a period of at least five years after the materials were last used in the fabrication or packaging/labelling of a drug unless otherwise specified in the person's establishment licence.

C.02.022

Every distributor referred to in section C.01A.003, wholesaler and importer of a drug shall retain records of the sale or each lot or batch of the drug, which enable them to recall the lot or batch from the market for a period of at least one year after the expiration date of the lot or batch unless otherwise specified in their establishment licence.

C.02.023

1. On receipt of a complaint respecting the quality of a drug, every distributor referred to in paragraph C.01A.003(b) and importer of the drug shall make a record of the complaint and of its investigation and retain the record for a period of at least one year after the expiration date of the lot or batch of that drug, unless otherwise specified in their establishment licence.

2. On receipt of any information respecting the quality or hazards of a drug, every distributor referred to in paragraph C.01A.003(b) and importer of the drug shall make a record of the information and retain it for a period of at least one year after the expiration date of the lot or batch of that drug, unless otherwise specified in their establishment licence.

Medical Gases GMPs

C.02.024

1. Every fabricator, packager/labeller, distributor referred to in section C.01A.003 importer and wholesaler shall

   a. maintain records of the results of the self-inspection programme required by section C.02.012 and of any action taken in connection with that programme; and

   b. retain those records for a period of at least three years.

2. Every person who fabricates or packages/labels a drug shall

   a. maintain records on the operation of the sanitation programme required to be implemented under section C.02.007; and

   b. retain those records for a period of at least three years.

Rationale

Good documentation is an essential part of the quality assurance system and, as such, should be related to all aspects of GMP. Its aims are to define the specifications for all materials and methods of fabrication, packaging/labelling and control, to ensure that authorized persons have all the information necessary to decide whether or not to release a lot of a medical gas for sale, and to provide an audit trail that will permit investigation of the history of any suspected defective lot or batch.

Evidence that medical gases have been fabricated and packaged/labelled under prescribed conditions can be maintained only after developing adequate record systems. The information and evidence should provide assurance that imported medical gases are fabricated and packaged/labelled in a like manner to those produced in Canada.

Interpretation

C.02.020 to C.02.024

For all sections of the GMP guidelines, standard operating procedures (SOPs) are retained for reference and inspection. These SOPs are regularly reviewed and kept up to date by qualified personnel. The reasons for any revisions are documented. A system is in place to ensure that only current SOPs are in use. Records of SOPs for all computer and automated systems are retained where appropriate.

All relevant GMP documents (such as associated records of actions taken or conclusions reached) and SOPs are approved, signed, and dated by the quality control department. Documents are not altered without the approval of the quality control department. Any alteration made to a document is signed and dated; the alteration permits the reading of the original information. Where appropriate, the reason for the change is recorded.

Records may be maintained in electronic format provided that backup copies are also maintained. Electronic data must be readily retrievable in a printed format. During the retention period, such records must be secured and accessible within 48 hours to the fabricator, packager/labeller, distributor, or importer.

An electronic signature is an acceptable alternative to a handwritten signature When used, such a system must be evaluated and tested for security, validity, and reliability, and records of those evaluations and tests must be maintained. The validation of electronic signature identification systems is documented.

Any documentation requested for evaluation by Health Canada is provided in one of the official languages.

1. Records must include a copy of master filling and/or master production documents duly verified, dated and signed. Each step of the process is documented. However, rather than repeating in detail each operation in the manufacturing orders, one may refer to the master filling documents that contain all these details.

2. Section C 02.020 applies only to fabricators, packagers/labellers, distributors referred to in paragraph C.01A.003(b) and importers to the extent that they perform operations on the medical gas.

3. Documentation must be available to support the expiry date of the medical gas. In the case of very stable gases that have been used for a long time and packaged in containers that have also been used for a long time, bibliographic data is sufficient. For gas mixtures, the expiry date should be based on validation studies pertaining to the physical aspects such as the rate of stratification.

4. The following documents must be maintained by the fabricator, packager/labeller, distributor (C.01A.003), and importer of a medical gas as they relate to operations in Canada:

    4.1 distribution records of all sales of medical gas including those of professional samples are retained or readily accessible in a manner that will permit a complete and rapid recall of any lot or batch of a drug. This does not necessary imply tracking by lot number;

    4.2 records of complaints or other information that is received relating to quality, deficiencies or hazards of a medical gas. Records of any subsequent investigations, including corrective actions taken.

    4.3 Records of the results of the self-inspection program and action taken

5. The following documents must be maintained by the fabricator of medical gas mixtures:

    5.1 the written specifications for the raw materials;

    5.2 the results of the raw material testing;

    5.3 the sources of the raw materials supplied.

6. The following documents must be maintained by the packager/labeller:

    6.1 the written specifications for the packaging materials;

    6.2 the results of the packaging material examinations or testing;

    6.3 the sources of the packaging materials supplied.

Medical Gases GMPs

7. Records on the operation of the sanitation program required under section C.02.007 must be maintained by the fabricator and the packager of medical gases.

8. Records required under Regulations C.02.021(1), C.02.022, and C.02.023 are ordinarily retained for a period of at least one year past the expiration date of the drug to which the records apply. However, for medical gases which do not require an expiration date, records required under regulations C.02.021(1), C.02.022, and C.02.023 are retained for a period of at least five years from the date of fabrication or packaging/labelling.

9. Records are maintained detailing the qualifications/experience of any consultant employed for GMP purposes, along with the services that each consultant provides.

Medical Gases

C.02.030

The provisions of sections C.02.025, C.02.027 and C.02.028 do not apply to medical gases.

Appendix A

Internationally Harmonized Requirements for Batch Certification

Content of the Fabricator's/Manufacturer's Batch Certificate for Drug/Medicinal Products Exported to Countries under the Scope of a Mutual Recognition Agreement (MRA)

Explanatory Note

In the framework of Mutual Recognition Agreements, the Sectoral Annex on Good Manufacturing Practices (GMP) requires a batch certification scheme for drug/medicinal products covered by the pharmaceutical Annex. The internationally harmonized requirements for the content of the batch certificate of a drug/medicinal product are attached. The importer of the batch is to receive and maintain the batch certificate issued by the fabricator/manufacturer. Upon request, the batch certificate has to be readily available to the regulatory authority of the importing country. This certification by the manufacturer regarding the conformity of each batch is essential to exempt the importer from re-control (re-analysis).

Each batch shipped between countries having an MRA in force must be accompanied by a batch certificate issued by the fabricator/manufacturer in the exporting country. This certificate will be issued after a full qualitative and quantitative analysis of all active and other relevant constituents to ensure that the quality of the products complies with the requirements of the marketing authorization of the importing country. The certificate will attest that the batch meets the specifications and has been manufactured in accordance with the marketing authorization of the importing country; will detail the specifications of the product, the analytical methods referenced, and the analytical results obtained; and will contain a statement that the batch processing and packaging quality control records were reviewed and found in conformity with GMP. The batch certificate will be signed by the person responsible for releasing the batch for sale or supply/export at the fabrication/manufacturing recognized building.

Listed designated regulatory authorities are identified within section C.01A.019 of the Food and Drug Regulations. The most recent listing is available on the Health Canada Website at the following address:

http://www.hc-sc.gc.ca/dhp-mps/compli-conform/int/mra-arm/update-miseajour_tc-tm-eng.php

Appendix A1

Content Of The Fabricator's/manufacturer's Batch Certificate

Content of the Fabricator's/Manufacturer's Batch Certificate for Drug/Medicinal Products

Exported to Countries under the Scope of a Mutual Recognition Agreement (MRA)

[Letterhead of Exporting Manufacturer]

1. Name of product.

   Proprietary, brand, or trade name in the importing country.

2. Importing country.

3. Marketing authorization number.

   The marketing authorization number of the product in the importing country should be provided.

4. Strength/Potency.

   Identity (name) and amount per unit dose are required for all active ingredients/constituents.

5. Dosage form (pharmaceutical form).

6. Package size (contents of container) and type (e.g., vials, bottles, blisters).

7. Lot/batch number.

   As related to the product.

8. Date of fabrication/manufacture.

   In accordance with national (local) requirements.

9. Expiry date.

10. Name(s) of fabricator(s)/manufacturer(s) and address(es) of- manufacturing recognized building(s).

    All recognized buildings involved in the manufacture of the batch including packaging and quality control of the batch, should be listed. The name(s) and

Medical Gases GMPs

address(es) given must correspond to the information provided on the manufacturing authorization/establishment licence.

11. Number(s) of manufacturing authorization(s)/licence(s) or certificate(s) of GMP compliance held by fabricator(s)/manufacturer(s).

    A number should be given for each recognized building listed under Item 10.

12. Results of analysis.

    Should include the approved specifications, describe all results obtained, and refer to the analytical methods used (May refer to a separate certificate of analysis, which must be dated, signed, and attached).

13. Comments/remarks.

    Any additional information that might be of value to the importer and/or inspector who must verify the compliance of the batch certificate (e.g., specific storage or transportation conditions).

14. Certification statement.

    Should cover the fabrication/manufacturing, including packaging and quality control. The following text should be used: "I hereby certify that the above information is authentic and accurate. This batch of product has been fabricated/manufactured, including packaging and quality control, at the above-mentioned recognized building(s) in full compliance with the GMP requirements of the local regulatory authority and with the specifications in the marketing authorization of the importing country. The batch processing, packaging, and analysis records were reviewed and found to be in compliance with GMP".

15. Name and position/title of person approving the batch release.

    Must include the person's company/recognized building name and address, if more than one company is mentioned under Item 10.

16. Signature of person approving the batch release.

17. Date of signature.

Appendix B

Acronyms

DIN:	Drug Identification Number
GMP:	Good Manufacturing Practices
ICH:	International Conference on Harmonization
HPFB:	Health Products and Food Branch
NOC:	Notice of Compliance
MPD:	Master Production Documents

MRA: Mutual Recognition Agreement

PIC/S: Pharmaceutical Inspection Cooperation/Scheme

SOP: Standard Operating Procedure

Glossary of Terms

The definitions given below apply to the terms used in these guidelines. They may have different meanings in other contexts.

Batch (lot de fabrication)

A quantity of any medical gas, homogeneous within specified limits, and identified by a distinctive batch number.

Batch Certificate (certificat de lot)

"A certificate issued by the fabricator of a lot or batch of a drug that is exported within the framework of a mutual recognition agreement and in which the fabricator

a. identifies the master production document for the drug and certifies that the lot or batch has been fabricated, packaged/labelled and tested in accordance with the procedures described in that document;

b. provides a detailed description of the drug, including

i a statement of all properties and qualities of the drug, including the identity, potency and purity of the drug, and

ii. a statement of tolerances for the properties and qualities of the drug;

c. identifies the analytical methods used in testing the lot or batch and provides details of the analytical results obtained;

d. sets out the addresses of the buildings at which the lot or batch was fabricated, packaged/labelled and tested; and

e. certifies that the lot or batch was fabricated, packaged/labelled and tested in accordance with the good manufacturing practices of the regulatory authority that has recognized those buildings as meeting its good manufacturing practices standard." (C.01A.001)

(The certificate's content is also described in Appendix A).

Bulk Gas (gaz en vrac)

A medical gas (either a single gas or a mixture of gases) that requires no further processing in order to be administered, but is not in its final package (e.g., liquefied oxygen).

Change Control (contrôle des changements)

A written procedure that describes the action to be taken if a change is proposed (a) to facilities, materials, equipment, and/or processes used in the fabrication, packaging, and testing of drugs, or (b) that may affect the operation of the quality or support system.

Medical Gases GMPs

Container (contenant)

see Packaging Material.

Critical Process (procédé critique)

A process that if not properly controlled may cause significant variation in the quality of the finished product.

Cryogenic Vessel (récipient cryogénique)

A static or mobile vacuum insulated container designed to contain liquefied gas at extremely low temperatures. Mobile vessels could also be known as "Dewars".

Curbside Delivery (livraison au point de remplissage)

The filling of cryogenic vessels with cryogenic liquefied gas at the point of use.

Dead Ring Test (Hammer Test) (essai de martelage)

A test used to determine the sound of a cylinder by striking its side. If a clear bell-like sound results, the cylinder is considered to be satisfactory. If a dull sound results, the cylinder is not considered to be suitable for filling with a medical gas (not applicable to aluminum cylinders).

Distributor (distributeur)

"A person, including an association or partnership, who under their own name, or under a trade, design or word mark, trade name or other name, word, or mark controlled by them, sells a food or drug." (A.01.010)

Divisions 1A and 2 to 4 apply to the following distributors (C.01A.003):

a. a distributor of a drug listed in Schedule C or D to the Act or in Schedule F to these Regulations, a controlled drug as defined in subsection G.01.001 (1) or a narcotic as defined in the Narcotic Control Regulations who does not hold the drug identification number for the drug or narcotic; and

b. a distributor of a drug for which that distributor holds the drug identification number.

Dosage Form (forme posologique)

A drug product that has been processed to the point where it is now in the form in which it may be administered in individual doses.

Fabricate (manufacturer)

"To prepare and preserve a drug for the purposes of sale." (C.01A.001)

Finished Product (produit fini)

A product that has undergone all stages of production, including packaging in its final container and labelling.

Gas (gaz)

Products in gaseous phase and products in liquid phase at cryogenic temperatures.

Immediate Container (récipient immédiat)

The receptacle that is in direct contact with a drug.

Importer (importateur)

A person that imports into Canada a drug for the purpose of sale.

Liquefied Gas (gaz liquéfié)

A gas which has a critical temperature above 200C, which remains as a liquid in the container when under pressure.

Lot (lot)

A quantity of any drug, raw material, or packaging material, homogenous within specified limits, constituting all or part of a single batch and identified by a distinctive lot number which appears on the label of the finished product.

Manifold (rampe)

Equipment or apparatus designed to enable one or more medical gas containers to be filled at a time.

Manifold Filling Sequence (cycle de remplissage sur rampe)

A filling sequence of many containers at one time using multiple outlet manifold or rack.

Marketing Authorization (autorisation de mise en marché)

A legal document issued by Health Canada, authorizing the sale of a drug or a device based on the health and safety requirements of the Food and Drug Act and its associated Regulations. The marketing authorization may be in the form of a Drug Identification Number (DIN), a device licence for classes II, III and IV medical devices, or a natural health product licence (NPN or DIN-HM).

Master Filling Documents (documents-types de remplissage)

A set of instructions for the filling of containers with a medical gas in dosage form containing a description of the filling operation, controls, procedures, specifications, and methods of quality control of the medical gas.

Medical Gases GMPs

Master Formula (formule-type)

> A document or set of documents specifying the raw materials with their quantities and the packaging materials, together with a detailed description of the procedures and precautions required to produce a specified quantity of a finished product as well as the processing instructions, including the in-process controls.

Master Production Documents (MPD) (document-type de production)

> Documents that include specifications for raw material, for packaging material, for bulk gases, and for packaged dosage form; master formula (including composition and instructions as described in the definition above), sampling procedures, and critical processing related SOPs, whether or not these SOPs are specifically referenced in the master formula.

Medical Gas (gaz médical)

> "Any gas or mixture of gases manufactured, sold or represented for use as a drug" C.02.002)

Medical Tag (étiquette médicale)

> Refers also to the term "label" and includes any legend, word or mark attached to, belonging to or accompanying any medical gas for compliance to the Food and Drug Regulations.

MRA Country (pays participant à un ARM)

> "A country that is a participant in a mutual recognition agreement (MRA) with Canada." (C.01A.001)

Mutual Recognition Agreement (MRA) (accord de reconnaissance mutuelle (ARM))

> An international agreement that provides for the mutual recognition of compliance certification for Good Manufacturing Practices for drugs. (C.01A.001)

Package (emballer-étiqueter)

> As described in package/label, the action of packaging refers to putting a drug in its immediate container. (C.01A.001)

Packaging Material (matériel d'emballage)

> Labels, printed packaging materials and those components in direct contact with the dosage form. (refer to C.02.002)

Qualified Authority (autorité qualifiée)

> A member of the Pharmaceutical Inspection Cooperation/Scheme (PIC/S) or the United States Food and Drug Administration (USFDA).

Quality Control Department (service du contrôle de la qualité)

> A function maintained by a fabricator, packager/labeller, distributor, or importer, that is responsible only to management, and that monitors the quality of production operations and exercises control over the quality of materials required for and resulting from those operations.

Quarantine (quarantaine)

> Effective restriction of the availability of material or product for use (physically or by system), until released by a designated authority.

Raw Material (matière première)

> The individual cases that are used in the production of medical gas mixtures.

Reconciliation (bilan comparatif)

> A comparison, making due allowance for normal variation, between the amount of product or materials theoretically produced or used and the amount actually produced or used.

Regulatory Authority (autorité réglementaire)

> A government agency or other entity in an MRA country that has a legal right to control the use or sale of drugs within that country and that may take enforcement action to ensure that drugs marketed within its jurisdiction comply with legal requirements.

Standard Operating Procedure (SOP) (procédure opératoire normalisée (PON))

> A written procedure giving instructions for performing operations not necessarily specific to a given product or material but of a more general nature (e.g., equipment operation, maintenance and cleaning; validation; clearing of premises and environmental control; sampling and inspection). Certain SOPs may be used to supplement product-specific master and batch production documents.

Uninterrupted Filling Sequence (cycle de remplissage ininterrompu)

> Single, continuous filling sequence with no breaks or shutdowns occurring during the filling and no change of personnel, equipment, or lots of raw materials. This procedure applies to the individual filling of high pressure cylinders (i.e, one cylinder at time).

Validation (validation)

> The documented act of demonstrating that any procedure, process, or activity will consistently lead to the expected results. Includes the qualification of systems and equipment.

Vendor (vendeur)

> For the purpose of these guidelines, vendor means the fabricator of the item.

Medical Gases GMPs

Wholesale (vendre en gros)

"To sell any of the following drugs, other than at retail sale, where the seller's name does not appear on the label of the drugs:

a. a drug listed in Schedule C or D to the Act or in Schedule F to these Regulations or a controlled drug as defined in subsection G.01.001 (1); or

b. a narcotic as defined in the Narcotic Control Regulations." (C.01A.001

Appendix C - References

1. Food and Drugs Act

2. Food and Drug Regulations

3. Guidance on Evidence to Demonstrate Drug GMP Compliance of Foreign sites (GUI-0080)

4. GMP Questions and Answers

5. Risk classification of GMP observations (GUI-0023)

6. Product Recall Procedures

7. Cleaning Validation Guidelines (GUI-0028)

8. Validation Guidelines for Pharmaceutical Dosage Forms (GUI-0029)

9. Validation Documentation Requirements and Responsibilities for Drug Fabricators, Packagers/Labellers, Testers, Distributors and Importers (GUI-0042)

10. Process Validation Guidelines:
    Moist Heat Sterilization for Pharmaceuticals (GUI-0010)
    Irradiation Sterilization for Pharmaceuticals (GUI-0009)
    Gaseous Sterilization for Pharmaceuticals (GUI-0007)
    Form-Fill-Seal for Drugs (GUI-0008)
    Aseptic Processes for Pharmaceuticals (GUI-0006)

11. ICH Q2(R1): Validation of Analytical Procedures: Text and Methodology

12. ICH Q7: Good Manufacturing Practice Guide for Active Pharmaceutical Ingredients

13. GMP Interpretation Decision Records for Medical Gas - 2004 edition (GUI-0062)

Modification to Good Manufacturing Practices (GMP) Guidelines for Medical Gases[20]

Health Products and Food Branch

Inspectorate

Holland Cross, Tower "A"

---

[20] Available on the Health Canada website at http://www.hc-sc.gc.ca/dhp-mps/compli-conform/gmp-bpf/docs/med_gases-gaz_med_a-eng.php

2nd Floor, 11 Holland Avenue

Address Locator: 3002C

OTTAWA, Ontario

K1A 0K9

November 22, 2002

02-114075-173

To: Associations

Following the implementation of the 2002 Good Manufacturing Practices (GMP) Guidelines, the Guidelines for Medical Gases published on June 1st 2000, have been harmonized for the interpretation relating to recall systems.

Effective immediately, interpretation 4 of Regulations C.02.020 to C.02.024 related to records, reads as follow:

4. The following documents are maintained by the fabricator, the packager/labeller, the distributor, wholesaler and importer of a medical gas as they relate to the operations in Canada:

4.1 Distribution records of all sales of medical gas including those of professional samples are retained or readily accessible in a manner that will permit a complete and rapid recall of any lot or batch of a drug. This does not necessarily imply tracking by lot number.

The Guidelines for Medical Gases will be revised to include this new interpretation at a later date.

Good Manufacturing Practices Guidance Document (Natural Health Products)

Natural Health Products Directorate Guidance Document

August 2006 - Version 2.0

Good Manufacturing Practices Guidance Document[21]

About this Guidance Document

This guidance document is intended for manufacturers, packagers and labellers of natural health products (NHPs) in Canada and elsewhere, including Canadian importers and distributors of these products. It is meant to help them meet the good manufacturing practice (GMP) requirements of the Natural Health Products Regulations (the Regulations). In addition, the guidance document is a tool for the Quality Assurance Person (QAP) to implement and maintain GMP and to fulfill their role in assuring the quality of a NHP before it is made available for sale. It is the responsibility of the manufacturer, packager, labeller or importer to ensure that the QAP has the relevant training, experience and technical knowledge and the QAP is capable of carrying out all the necessary quality-related functions.

GMPs are ongoing measures designed to ensure an effective overall approach to product quality control and risk management. They do so by setting appropriate standards and practices for product testing, manufacturing, storage, handling and distribution.

The Natural Health Products Directorate (NHPD) recognizes that there are various ways of meeting the GMP and producing safe and effective NHPs. For example, specific methods to achieve GMP compliance in sanitation may vary with the particular operation. Although this guidance document sets out GMP requirements, they are not regarded as the only interpretation of the Regulations. Alternative means of complying with these Regulations will be considered by the NHPD given that the appropriate rationale or justification is provided.

Manufacturers, packagers, labellers and importers must demonstrate that they adhere to these practices before the NHPD will issue them a site licence. Distributors must follow the relevant GMPs, but are not required to hold a site licence.

Chapter 1 of the guidance document covers all of Part 3 (sections 43 to 62) of the Regulations, dividing GMP into the following categories:

---

[21] Available on the Health Canada website at http://www.hc-sc.gc.ca/dhp-mps/prodnatur/legislation/docs/gmp-bpf-eng.php

- Places (premises and equipment);
- People (personnel and quality assurance);
- Processes (sanitation program and operations); and
- Products (specifications, stability, samples, records, recall reporting and sterile products).

Each section under places, people, processes and productsbegins with a brief explanation of what the Regulations say, followed by a box with the actual Regulations. Following that is the section To Meet the Requirements, which explains in more detail how to comply with the Regulations.

Chapter 2 provides the supplementary GMP requirements for homeopathic medicines.

The definitions of terms used in this guidance document are provided in the Glossary.

A complete version of the Regulations is available on the Internet.

The first draft of this guidance document was developed in the spring of 2002 with input from the NHP industry, academics, researchers, consumers, health practitioners and representatives from other government programs. The experts represented four areas of specialty: herbal medicines and botanicals, homeopathic medicines, traditional herbal medicines, and vitamins and minerals. Shortly afterwards, NHPD held workshops for the public and industry about the GMP requirements of the Regulations. These helped provide additional information and guidance for preparing the final Good Manufacturing Practices Guidance Document. NHPD's GMPs working group compiled, analyzed and incorporated the information received at these workshops to produce the final document.

1.0 Good Manufacturing Practices

Part 3 (sections 43 to 62) of the Natural Health Products Regulations (the Regulations) sets out the good manufacturing practices (GMPs) that manufacturers, packagers, labellers and importers must meet before the Natural Health Products Directorate (NHPD) will issue a site licence for each location they intend to manufacture, package, label or import natural health products (NHPs) for sale in Canada. Distributors must follow the GMPs, as defined in the Regulations, however they are not required to hold a site licence. Distributors' responsibilities are identified in the guidance document with respect to the GMPs related to storage, distribution and transportation. For more information on site licensing, refer to the Site Licensing Guidance Document.

Prior to the sale of a NHP in Canada, the product licence holder is responsible to provide the NHPD with information, as defined in section 22 of the Regulations, concerning the manufacturer, packager, labeler or importer in Canada and their corresponding site licence numbers. They are also responsible to provide evidence that imported NHPs will be manufactured, packaged, labeled, imported, distributed and stored according to GMPs as set out in part 3 of the Regulations or their equivalent. For more information on product licences, see the Product Licensing Guidance Document.

The site licence holder is responsible to carry out each activity in which they are authorized to conduct in accordance with the GMPs. In addition, the site licence holder must ensure that all activities or services contracted out are conducted in accordance with Part 3 of the Regulations.

Part 3 begins with section 43, which states that any NHP sold must be manufactured, packaged, labelled, imported, distributed and stored according to the requirements of this part of the Regulations. NHPs that are imported into Canada must also be manufactured, packaged, labelled, imported, distributed and stored in accordance with requirements set out in Part 3 or its equivalent. It is the importer's responsibility to ensure that imported NHPs come from sites that meet the Canadian GMPs. For information related to evidence required from importers with respect to the foreign sites, refer to the Site Licensing Guidance Document.

Part 3: Good Manufacturing Practices

Premises

Section 43

1. Subject to subsection (2), no person shall sell a natural health product unless it is manufactured, packaged, labelled, imported, distributed and stored, as the case may be, in accordance with this Part.

2. A person may sell a natural health product that is manufactured, packaged, labelled, imported, distributed and stored, as the case may be, in accordance with requirements that are equivalent to those set out in this Part if the natural health product is imported.

Each section under Places, People, Processes and Products, below, begins with a brief explanation of what the Regulations say, followed by a box with the text of the relevant Regulations. Following that is the section To Meet the Requirements, which explains in more detail how to comply with the Regulations. Readers are recommended to follow GMPs described in this document to get a complete understanding of their responsibilities. However, NHPD will consider alternative means of complying with the Regulations, when additional rationale is provided.

Please note in the text that follows that the GMPs are divided into four categories (Places, People, Processes and Products). As a result, the sections of the Regulations do not run n numerical order.

1.1 Places

1.1.1 Premises

Section 45 sets out the requirements for the physical premises in which NHPs are manufactured, packaged, labeled and stored.

Part 3: Good Manufacturing Practices

Premises

Section 45

1. Every natural health product shall be manufactured, packaged, labelled and stored in premises that are designed, constructed and maintained in a manner that permits the activity to be conducted under sanitary conditions, and in particular that:

    a. permits the premises to be kept clean and orderly;

b. permits the effective cleaning of all surfaces in the premises;

c. permits the natural health product to be stored or processed appropriately;

d. prevents the contamination of the natural health product; and

e. prevents the addition of an extraneous substance to the natural health product.

2. Every natural health product shall be stored under conditions that will maintain the quality and safety of the natural health product.

To Meet the Requirements

Manufacturers, packagers, labellers, importers and distributors should ensure the following, where applicable. Alternatively, justification with rationale for the exemption of the requirements should be provided.

- Ensure that the buildings are of adequate size and are designed and built to facilitate maintenance, cleaning and sanitary operations, prevent entry of insects and other animals, facilitate waste treatment and disposal, and prevent mix-ups and cross-contamination of raw, packaging and product materials. Every site shall:

  o ensure that effective controls are in place to minimize the potential for mix-ups or the adulteration of raw, packaging and in-process materials;

  o provide separate production and non-production areas, as necessary, to prevent cross-contamination. When required, clearly identify and segregate individual manufacturing, packaging and testing areas;

  o restrict, during production, the use of doors giving direct access from manufacturing and packaging areas to the outdoors (these doors must be adequately sealed to prevent pests from entering);

  o ensure that doors, windows, walls, ceilings and floors contain no holes or gaps, except those that are part of the design;

  o ensure that floors, walls and ceilings permit cleaning, and that all surfaces are made of materials that do not shed particles;

  o seal surfaces and joints to prevent contamination from extraneous materials and to permit effective cleaning;

  o provide adequate ventilation, filtration and lighting;

  o control humidity and temperature, where required, to protect materials and products;

  o take appropriate measures to prevent pests from entering the premises.

  o provide explosion proof bulbs and fixtures to avoid glass contamination.

- Separate the rest, change, wash-up and toilet facilities from production areas, and ensure that they are sufficiently spacious and well ventilated, and permit good sanitary practices.

- Provide plumbing of an appropriate scale and design to avoid adulteration of products or contamination of water supplies or equipment, and identify outlets for liquids and gases used in production.

- Ensure supply water is of potable quality for processing and cleaning and shall meet the Guidelines for Canadian Drinking Water Quality, World Health Organization (WHO) guidelines for Drinking Water Quality or other standards specified by the regulatory agency governing the manufacturer. When purified water is required, water purification, storage and distribution equipment must be operated to ensure a reliable source of water of appropriate chemical and biological purity as defined in any standard listed in Schedule B to the Food and Drugs Act.

- Ensure that floor drains are screened and trapped.

- Maintain the grounds around the manufacturing buildings to protect against the contamination of products.

- Install refuse receptacles and follow waste disposal practices that protect against contamination or harborage of pests.

- Protect raw materials, packaging materials, in-process and finished products against physical, chemical and microbial contamination, as well as deterioration of the products and the container during storage and temporary storage while in transit (e.g. between the importer and the distributor, or between the manufacturer and the labeller).

- Clearly mark physical quarantine areas when used.

1.1.2 Equipment

Section 46 sets out the requirements for the equipment used to manufacture, package, labe and store natural health products.

Part 3: Good Manufacturing Practices

Equipment

Section 46

Every natura health product shall be manufactured, packaged, labelled and stored using equipment that is designed, constructed, maintained, operated and arranged in a manner that

a. permits the effective cleaning of its surfaces;

b. permits it to function in accordance with its intended use;

c. prevents it from contaminating the NHP; and

d. prevents it from adding an extraneous substance to the NHP.

To Meet the Requirements

Manufacturers, packagers, labellers, importers and distributors must ensure the following, where applicable. Alternatively, justifications with rationale for the exemption of the requirements should be provided.

- Production equipment is designed, constructed, installed and maintained to facilitate cleaning, sanitizing (where appropriate), and inspection of the equipment and the surrounding areas. Specifically, this means the following:

  o establishing and following procedures for cleaning and maintaining equipment and utensils used to manufacture products;

- o avoiding temporary repairs (e.g. with tape); and

- o clearly labelling defective equipment as such.

- Protect analytical instruments and associated control systems from vibration, electrical interference and contact with excessive moisture or other external factors.

- Ensure that production equipment and utensils having direct contact with materials and products are constructed of smooth, non-reactive and non-toxic materials, and are designed to withstand repeated cleaning.

- Avoid the possibility of lubricants or other maintenance materials contaminating the products by ensuring proper equipment design (e.g. tanks, chain drives and transmission gears must be enclosed or properly covered).

- Control and monitor temperature-sensitive compartments, and keep records.

- Properly maintain instruments and controls, including laboratory equipment, to ensure that they remain accurate, and retain records.

- Develop a calibration program for critical manufacturing, packaging and testing equipment, and maintain records.

- Maintain records of equipment and facility cleaning.

- Maintain equipment usage logs.

1.2 People

1.2.1 Personnel

Section 47 covers the education, training and/or experience requirements of personnel involved in manufacturing, packaging, labelling and storing NHPs.

Part 3: Good Manufacturing Practices

Personnel

Section 47

Every natural health product shall be manufactured, packaged, labelled and stored by personnel who are qualified by education, training or experience to perform their respective tasks.

To Meet the Requirements

Manufacturers, packagers, labellers, importers and distributors must ensure the following:

- ensure that individuals in charge of manufacturing and quality assurance have adequate education, training and/or practical experience to control and supervise the activities; and

- ensure that all personnel have appropriate education (including ongoing GMPs or other continuing training) and/or have the practical experience necessary to perform their assigned duties. Maintain records of education and training and update when needed.

1.2.2 Quality Assurance

Section 51 sets out the requirements and responsibilities of the quality assurance person.

Part 3: Good Manufacturing Practices

Quality Assurance

Section 51

1. Every manufacturer, packager, labeller, importer and distributor shall

    a. have a quality assurance person who

        i. is responsible for assuring the quality of the natural health product before it is made available for sale, and

        ii. has the training, experience and technical knowledge relating to the activity conducted and the requirements of this Part; and

    b. investigate and record every complaint received in respect of the quality of the natural health product and, if necessary, take corrective action.

2. Every natural health product shall be manufactured, packaged and labelled using only material that, prior to its use in the activity, has been approved for that use by a quality assurance person.

3. Every natural health product shall be manufactured, packaged, labelled and stored using methods and procedures that, prior to their implementation, have been approved by a quality assurance person.

4. Every lot or batch of a natural health product shall be approved by a quality assurance person before it is made available for sale.

5. Every natural health product that is sold and subsequently returned to its manufacturer, packager, labeller, importer or distributor, as the case may be, shall be approved by a quality assurance person before that natural health product may be made available for resale.

To Meet the Requirements

Manufacturers, packagers, labellers, importers and distributors must have a quality assurance person who is responsible to do the following:

- Establish and follow written procedures to ensure that products conform to specifications and regulatory requirements.

- Establish and follow written procedures for sampling, inspecting and testing raw and/or packaging materials, in-process and finished products.

- Approve or reject all formulations, procedures, specifications, test methods, controls and results that affect the purity, quality and composition of each ingredient and product. Written procedures shall be established and implemented.

- Approve or reject all raw materials, packaging materials and finished products, including products manufactured by contractors, based upon conformance/nonconformance to respective specifications. Written procedures shall be established and implemented.

- Review and maintain completed batch records.

- Approve or reject the product for distribution against the completed batch record.

- Approve or reject product quality deviations and product reprocessing in the manufacture of a product. Written procedure shall be established and implemented.

- Destroy returned products unless he or she determines, by assessment or other investigation, that they may be released for resale. Written procedure shall be established and implemented.

- Maintain records with respect to returned, reprocessed and redistributed products and include the name and description of the product, lot number, reason for return, quantity returned and date and means of final disposition.

- Ensure that laboratories (in-house and contract) are capable of performing all of the tasks and responsibilities assigned to them.

- Maintain laboratory records of tests and investigations.

- Set up and follow written procedures for handling product complaints. These procedures must include determining whether further investigation and corrective action are required.

- Document all complaints with the following information: the name and description of the product, the lot number, the source and nature of the complaint, and any response. When an investigation is conducted, include in the written record the findings and any follow-up action taken.

Note: It is good practice for manufacturers, packagers, labellers, importers and distributors to provide a written job description to their quality assurance person to help protect him or her from a conflict of interest that may arise when duties conflict with those outlined in section 51.

1.3 Processes

1.3.1 Sanitation Program

Section 48 sets out the sanitation requirements for the premises and the health and hygiene of personnel.

Part 3: Good Manufacturing Practices

Sanitation Program

Section 48

Every natural health product shall be manufactured, packaged, labelled and stored in accordance with a sanitation program that sets out

a. procedures for effectively cleaning the premises in which the activity is conducted;

b. procedures for effectively cleaning the equipment used in the activity;

c. procedures for handling any substance used in the activity; and

d. all requirements, in respect of the health, the hygienic behaviour and the clothing of the personnel who are involved in the activity, that are necessary to ensure that the activity is conducted in sanitary conditions.

To Meet the Requirements

Manufacturers, packagers and labellers shall have a facility sanitation program and a health and hygiene program in place as detailed below. Importers and distributors shall meet the appropriate requirements with respect to storage.

Facility Sanitation Program

- Develop a written sanitation program that includes the following elements:
    - cleaning procedures for facilities and processing equipment;
    - a list of cleaning /sanitizing agents and pesticide chemicals that shall be identified, used and stored in such a manner to prevent the contamination of raw materials and packaging and process equipment;
    - identification, use and storage of pesticide chemicals in such a manner to prevent the contamination of raw and packaging materials, and process equipment;
    - procedures for cleaning frequencies and cleaning lines between the production of different products;
    - provisions for storing cleaned equipment to avoid recontamination; and
    - procedures for the destruction and disposal of waste materials and debris.
    - Contain or ventilate dusty operations to prevent contamination of other areas.
- Develop a written pest control program outlining effective measures for preventing pest infestations of the building.

Health and Hygiene Program

- Ensure that all personnel having direct contact with raw and/or packaging materials, in-process materials and any unpackaged products, as well as personnel who use processing equipment, must follow appropriate practices to protect products against contamination. This health and hygiene program must be in writing and should include the following requirements:
    - wearing outer garments, including shoe coverings, that protect against contamination of products and equipment, when applicable;
    - removing all unsecured jewellery and hand jewellery, or covering hand jewellery that cannot be removed, when applicable;
    - using intact, clean and sanitary gloves;
    - wearing hairnets, caps, beard covers or other effective hair restraints;
    - maintaining personal cleanliness;
    - washing hands thoroughly before starting work and at any other time when hands may have become soiled or contaminated;
    - storing clothing or other personal effects outside of processing areas;

o refraining from consuming food and drink, as well as chewing products or smoking in manufacturing, packaging and testing areas;

o periodically conducting eye examinations of personnel responsible for visual inspection;

o reporting to supervisors any health conditions of personnel that could adversely affect products;

o respecting quarantine times imposed by public health authorities; and

o removing from the manufacturing facility any person who has, or appears to have, an illness that could be a possible source of product contamination, until the disease or hygienic condition is no longer a risk for possible product contamination.

1.3.2 Operations

Sections 49 and 50 set out the requirements for standard operating procedures for the manufacturing, packaging, labelling and storing of NHPs and a system for product recall.

Part 3: Good Manufacturing Practices

Operations

Section 49

Every natural health product shall be manufactured, packaged, labelled and stored in accordance with standard operating procedures that are designed to ensure that the activity is conducted in accordance with the requirements of this Part.

Part 3: Good Manufacturing Practices

Operations

Section 50

Every manufacturer, packager, labeller, importer and distributor shall establish and maintain a system of control that permits the rapid and complete recall of every lot or batch of the natural health product that has been made available for sale.

To Meet the Requirements

Manufacturers, packagers, labellers, importers and distributors shall ensure that practices and procedures in place for material control, process control, the inspection program for contractors, and product recall, where applicable. Alternately, justifications with rationale for the exemption of the requirements should be provided.

Material Control

- Set up and follow written procedures for the transportation, receipt, identification, examination, handling, sampling, testing and approval or rejection of raw and/or packaging materials. Update the procedures as required.

- Identify each lot of raw and/or packaging materials with a distinctive lot number.

- Inspect containers of raw and/or packaging materials upon receipt for closure

- and physical integrity.

- Assess each lot of raw and/or packaging materials against specifications, such as plant identity, detectable foreign matter and the integrity (appropriate characteristics) and quality of plant material or extracts.

- Retest raw and/or packaging materials after any exposure to conditions likely to adversely affect their purity, quality or composition.

- Identify and control each lot of raw and/or packaging materials according to its quality status (e.g. quarantined, approved or rejected).

- Store raw materials, in-process materials and reprocessed materials in appropriate conditions, including temperature and humidity, to protect against quality deterioration and contamination.

- Set a time limit beyond which raw materials that are subject to deterioration may not be used in production without additional testing. When appropriate, use the oldest approved stock of raw and/or packaging materials first. (Follow First In First Out system, FIFO.)

- Ensure that the quality assurance person approves and releases materials prior to their use.

- Establish appropriate systems and controls to ensure water used to fabrication products is of potable quality and meets the Guidelines for Canadian Drinking Water Quality, WHO guidelines for Drinking Water Quality or other standards specified by the regulatory agency governing the manufacturer.

- Destroy outdated or obsolete printed packaging materials and record the disposal.

Process Control

- Formulate the product to ensure that it adheres to regulatory requirements and claims stated on the label.

- Prepare a master production document for the manufacture of each product, and have the quality assurance person review and approve the document.

- Prepare and follow batch records for each batch of product. These records must be an accurate representation of the master production document and include documentation that each significant step in the manufacturing process was completed.

- Allocate and track each batch of manufactured product by an individual control number.

- Record and evaluate any deviations from written and approved manufacturing processes, standards and test methods, with final approval by the person in charge of production as well as the quality assurance person.

- Conduct manufacturing, packaging and storage operations according to written procedures and appropriate sanitation principles, in a manner that protects against adulteration and in conditions that minimize the potential for contamination.

- Identify all materials, products, samples, containers, processing lines and major equipment at all times to indicate their contents and/or status.

- Ensure procedures are in place to prevent extraneous materials from being included in the products and finished package.

- Ensure procedures are in place to identify, store and dispose of rejected or contaminated/adulterated products.

- Establish written procedures for reprocessing batches that do not conform to finished product specifications.

- Securely store labels to prevent mix-ups (e.g. stored and withdrawn against a packaging order). Specifically, this means the following:

    o preventing mix-ups by not returning samples taken away from the processing areas;

    o labelling the product as quickly as possible after filling and sealing (when labelling is delayed, follow procedures to ensure that no mix-ups or mislabelling occurs); and

    o investigating and accounting for, before release, any significant or unusual discrepancies observed during reconciliation of the amount of bulk product, printed packaging materials and/or labels.

- Prevent cross-contamination and mislabeling by establishing procedures for removing all raw and/or packaging materials and finished products from previous runs (i.e. written line clearance procedures).

- Set up and follow written procedures to ensure the correct labels and packaging materials are issued and used.

- Identify each package with a lot number and expiry date that permits determination of the history of the manufacture and control of the lot.

- Restrict access to production premises to authorized personnel.

Inspection Program for Contractors

Manufacturers, packagers, labellers or importers must ensure that activities contracted out to other sites meet the GMPs requirements, which can be demonstrated by an inspection and/or an evaluation of the contractor. This inspection program allows quality assurance of the portions of production that are contracted out (e.g. when a manufacturer contracts out labelling) and ensures compliance to NHP GMPs by all parties at all times. It is essential to clearly establish and document the roles and responsibilities of each party involved in the contracted operations (manufacturing, packaging, labeling and importing). See the records section for information related to contractors and required documentation.

Recall

Establish written procedures that define controls to ensure the effective recall of a product, including notification of Health Canada . Specifically, this means the following:

- identifying any individuals be responsible for initiating and coordinating recall activities;

- ensuring the recall procedure can be put into operation at any time, during and outside normal working hours;

- ensuring the recall procedure outlines the steps for implementing a recall
- (e.g. determining extent of the recall, and means of notifying affected parties);
- maintaining distribution records so each lot can be traced;
- identifying and storing recalled products separately in a secure area until further action is determined;
- assessing and recording at intervals the progress and efficacy of the recall, and issuing a final report, including a final reconciliation; and
- notifying all Canadian and foreign sites involved in the manufacture, distribution and import of the recalled product.

1.4 Products

1.4.1 Specifications

Section 44 sets out the specifications that NHPs must meet.

Part 3: Good Manufacturing Practices

Specifications

Section 44

1. Every natural health product available for sale shall comply with the specifications submitted in respect of that natural health product under paragraph 5(i) and with every change to those specifications made by the product licence holder.

2. The specifications shall contain the following information:

   a. detailed information respecting the purity of the natural health product, including statements indicating its purity tolerances;

   b. for each medicinal ingredient of the natural health product, detailed information respecting its quantity per dosage unit and its identity, including statements indicating its quantity and identity tolerances;

   c. if a representation relating to the potency of a medicinal ingredient is to be shown on a label of the natural health product, detailed information respecting the potency of the medicinal ingredient, including statements indicating its potency tolerances; and

   d. a description of the methods used for testing or examining the natural health product.

3. The specifications and every change to those specifications shall be approved by a quality assurance person.

To Meet the Requirements

The manufacturer, importer and, if applicable, packager and distributor must ensure the following, where applicable. Alternately, justifications with rationale for the exemption of the requirements should be provided.

Finished Products

- Develop and implement written specifications for all finished products.

- Note: Product specifications are assessed by NHPD as part of the product's licence application and verified at the site licence submission review. For guidance related to finished product specifications pertaining to identity, purity, quantity, potency and tolerances, see the Evidence for Quality of Finished Natural Health Products Guidance Document.

- Ensure specifications are maintained and every change is approved by the quality assurance person prior to use.

- Note: Changes to specifications as per section 11(i) of the Natural Health Products Regulations requires an amendment to the product licence.

- Set up and follow written procedures that describe tests to be conducted to ensure the identity, purity and quantity of finished products. When applicable, these procedures should include potency testing.

- Confirm that all test methods provide accurate and consistent results.

- Assess each lot for compliance with specifications prior to release.

  Note: Importers may apply a reduced testing program that relies on test results from their manufacturer (supplier) provided that a certificate of analysis is submitted with each lot received. The following outlines the parameters of a reduced testing program:

  o Fully test against specifications, the first lot of product received for each product and each supplier;

  o Each subsequent lot received thereafter must:

    ▪ undergo a review of the Certificate of Analysis showing actual test results;

    ▪ positively identify and verify upon receipt each lot or ensure its identification and verification by qualified personnel at another site to which the imported product is shipped;

    ▪ take precautions to ensure that transportation and storage conditions do not adversely affect product potency, purity or physical characteristics;

  o Conduct complete confirmatory testing against specifications on at least one lot per dosage form per supplier per year.

1.4.2 Stability

Section 52 sets out the requirements for product stability.

Part 3: Good Manufacturing Practices

Stability

Section 52

Every manufacturer and every importer shall determine the period of time that, after being packaged for sale, the NHP will continue to comply with its specifications when

a. it is stored under its recommended storage conditions; or

b. if it does not have recommended storage conditions, it is stored at room temperature.

To Meet the Requirements

Manufacturers and importers must ensure the following:

- Use data from accelerated or real-time stability studies or from similar product formulations to make an initial determination of the expiry date.

- Provide data and rationale to reasonably ensure that each finished product meets its label claims at the expiry date.

- Confirm and adjust the expiry date, when required, on the basis of real-time studies on product stored in the conditions noted on the label, for the period of time indicated by the expiry date.

- Display the lot expiry date on the label of each finished product.

- Ensure all packaging and labelling requirements are met, and keep the product free from contamination until the expiry date (e.g. deterioration of packaging material and labelling).

- Establish the shelf life from the date of original fabrication.

- Re-evaluate the product shelf life when significant changes are made to the formulation, process or package that may affect the product's stability.

- Carry out testing appropriate to each product.

1.4.3 Samples

Section 61 explains that the NHPD may ask a manufacturer, importer or distributor to submit samples of a lot or batch of a product if NHPD has concerns about the safety of that product.

Part 3: Good Manufacturing Practices

Lot or Batch Samples

Section 61

1. Subject to subsection (3), if the Minister has reasonable grounds to believe that a lot or batch of a natural health product made available for sale may result in injury to the health of a purchaser or consumer, the Minister may require the manufacturer, importer or distributor to provide a sample of that lot or batch.

2. The sample shall be of sufficient quantity to enable a determination of whether the lot or batch of the natural health product complies with the specifications for that natural health product.

3. The Minister shall not require a sample of a lot or batch referred to in subsection (1) to be provided if more than one year has elapsed since the expiry date of that natural health product.

To Meet the Requirements

Manufacturers, importers and distributors must ensure the following:

- retain an adequate number of samples of each lot of a finished product. Importers and distributors may have the manufacturer or a designated third party keep samples for them, provided the samples are readily available upon request;

- retain samples in their final trade packages or in containers of the same material and construction;

- store samples in the environmental conditions listed on the label;

- ensure that samples are of sufficient size to permit complete testing according to specifications; and

- maintain samples for at least one year after the expiry date. Shorter retention times may be approved by applying in writing to NHPD.

- Note: Importers are responsible to notify NHPD when making alternate arrangements for retaining samples. The applicant must commit to retaining the samples in the same containers as those marketed in Canada and conform to the conditions set out in the Application for Alternate Sample Retention form.

1.4.4 Records

Sections 53-58 set out the record-keeping requirements for manufacturers, packagers, labellers, importers and distributors.

Part 3: Good Manufacturing Practices

Records (Manufacturers)

Section 53

Every manufacturer who sells a natural health product shall maintain the following records at the site at which the natural health product is manufactured:

a. the master production document for the natural health product;

b. a list of all ingredients contained in each lot or batch of the natural health product;

c. records of any testing conducted in respect of a lot or batch of raw material used in the manufacture of the natural health product;

d. records of any testing conducted in respect of a lot or batch of the natural health product;

e. a copy of the specifications for each natural health product that is being manufactured at the site;

f. records demonstrating that each lot or batch of the natural health product was manufactured in accordance with the requirements of this Part;

g. a record of each determination made by the manufacturer in accordance with section 52 and the information that supports that determination;

h. records containing sufficient information to enable the recall of every lot or batch of the natural health product that has been made available for sale;

i. a list of all natural health products that are being manufactured at the site;

and

j. a copy of the sanitation program in use at the site.

Part 3: Good Manufacturing Practices

Records (Packagers)

Section 54

Every packager who sells a natural health product shall maintain the following records at the site at which the natural health product is packaged:

a. records of any testing conducted in respect of the material used to package the natural health product;

b. records demonstrating that each lot or batch of the natural health product was packaged in accordance with the requirements of this Part;

c. records containing sufficient information to enable the recall of every lot or batch of the natural health product that has been made available for sale;

d. a list of all natural health products that are being packaged at the site; anc

e. a copy of the sanitation program in use at the site.

Part 3: Good Manufacturing Practices

Records (Labellers)

Section 55

Every labeller who sells a natural health product shall maintain the following records at the site at which the natural health product is labelled:

a. records demonstrating that each lot or batch of the natural health product was labelled in accordance with the requirements of this Part;

b. records containing sufficient information to enable the recall of every lot or batch of the natural health product that has been made available for sale;

c. a list of all natural health products that are being labelled at the site; and

d. a copy of the sanitation program in use at the site.

Part 3: Good Manufacturing Practices

Records (Importers)

Section 56

Every importer who sells a natural health product shall maintain the following records:

a. the master production document for the natural health product;

b. a list of all ingredients contained in each lot or batch of the natural health product;

c. records of any testing conducted in respect of a lot or batch of the natural health product;

d. a copy of the specifications for the natural health product;

e. a record of each determination made by the importer in accordance with section 52 and the information that supports that determination;

f. records containing sufficient information to enable the recall of every lot or batch of the natural health product that has been made available for sale; and

g. a copy of the sanitation program in use by the importer.

Part 3: Good Manufacturing Practices

Records (Distributors)

Section 57

Every distributor shall maintain the following records at the site at which the natural health product is stored:

a. records containing sufficient information to enable the recall of every lot or batch of the natural health product that has been made available for sale;

b. a list of all natural health products that are being stored at the site; and

c. a copy of the sanitation program in use at the site.

Part 3: Good Manufacturing Practices

Record Maintenance

Section 58

Every person required under this Part to maintain a record that relates to a lot or batch of a natural health product shall maintain that record for a period of one year following the expiry date of the natural health product to which that record relates.

To Meet the Requirements

- Manufacturers, packagers, labellers, importers and distributors shall meet the minimum record-keeping requirements set out in Appendix 2.

- Records must demonstrate that each batch has been manufactured, packaged and labelled according to the procedures described in the master production document. For importers, a Certificate of Manufacture is an acceptable alternative to lot or batch documents. However, complete batch documentation must be made available upon request.

  Note : When the manufacturer is located outside Canada , specific parts of the master production document considered to be a trade secret or confidential may be held on behalf of the importer by an independent party in Canada ; however, the importer or independent party must ensure that the NHPD can access the data in a timely manner. The master production document must describe in general terms what has been deleted.

- Records must demonstrate that each lot has been manufactured, packaged, labelled and imported according to the requirements of Part 3 of the Regulations:

  - When a product is manufactured, packaged, labelled and/or imported by a contractor in Canada , it is recommended that the site licence holder:

    - maintain a copy of the contractor's site licence, when applicable; and

    - document and maintain records of all tasks carried out by the contractor;

    - establish and maintain a written document or technical agreement covering the arranged manufacturing, packaging, labelling, importing, storage or distribution in accordance with Part 3 of the Regulations. All arrangements for contracting including any proposed changes in technical arrangements should be in accordance with the GMPs as well as the marketing authorization for the product concerned.

      Note: The technical agreement or relevant parts thereof should be made available to the NHPD upon request in the event that further assessment and clarification is needed.

  - When the product is manufactured, packaged and/or labelled outside of Canada, importers must ensure that records can be accessed in a timely manner.

- Manufacturers and importers must maintain evidence establishing the expiry date of each product.

- Manufacturers must maintain evidence or records of raw material testing conducted with respect to a lot or batch of raw material used in the manufacture of the NHP.

- Packagers must maintain evidence or records of packaging material testing conducted with respect to the material used to package the NHP.

- Maintain evidence showing compliance of each finished product with specifications.

- Other record-keeping practices may include the following:

o   Retain authorized written procedures for all sections of these requirements for reference and inspection. Review written procedures regularly and ensure authorized employees keep them up-to-date. Document the reasons for revising the procedures, and establish a system to ensure that only current procedures are in use.

o   Have authorized employees approve, sign and date all relevant documents related to GMPs, such as records of actions taken or conclusions reached, and procedures. Ensure that any alteration of a document is signed and dated and that the alteration permits reading of the original information. Do not alter documents without authorization.

o   Records may be maintained by authorized person(s) in electronic format provided that there is adequate back-up. Such electronic data must be printable. Manufacturers, packagers, labellers, importers and distributors must be able to access their electronic records and documents at least one year after the product's expiry date.

o   Electronic signatures are acceptable as an alternative to handwritten signatures. The electronic signature identification system must be tested and evaluated for security, validity and reliability. The electronic signature identification system must be secured from abuse, and include electronic protection against willful or accidental damage. All stages of development of electronic signature identification systems must be documented.

o   Manufacturers, packagers, labellers, importers and distributors must maintain at their premises in Canada distribution records that contain sufficient information to enable the recall of every lot that has been made available for sale. Please refer to the recall reporting section of this guidance document (chapter 1.4.5) for further information.

o   Manufacturing, testing and distribution records must be retained for at least one year after the lot expiry date.

1.4.5 Recall Reporting

Section 62 explains what information manufacturers, importers and distributors must send to Health Canada when they recall a product.

Part 3: Good Manufacturing Practices

Recall Reporting

Section 62

Every manufacturer, importer or distributor who commences a recall of a natural health product shall provide the Minister with the following information in respect of that natural health product within three days after the day on which the recall is commenced:

a.   the proper name and the common name of each medicinal ingredient that it contains;

b.   each brand name under which it is sold;

c.   its product number;

d.   the number of each lot or batch recalled;

e. the name and address of each manufacturer, importer and distributor of the natural health product;

f. the reasons for commencing the recall;

g. the quantity manufactured or imported into Canada;

h. the quantity that was distributed in Canada;

i. the quantity remaining in the possession of each manufacturer, importer and distributor of the natural health product; and

j. a description of any other action that the manufacturer, importer or distributor, as the case may be, is taking in respect of the recall.

To Meet the Requirements

Manufacturers, importers and distributors who recall a NHP must submit product recall information to their Regional Operational Centre within three days of initiating the recall. For more information regarding recall requirements and responsibilities see the Health Products and Food Branch Inspectorate Recall Policy (POL-0016), available on the Compliance and Enforcement section of Health Canada's Web site.

1.4.6 Sterile Products

Sections 59 and 60 set out the requirements for manufacturing and packaging of sterile products.

Part 3: Good Manufacturing Practices

Sterile Natural Health Products

Section 59

Every natural health product that is intended to be sterile shall be manufactured and packaged

a. in a separate and enclosed area;

b. under the supervision of a person trained in microbiology; and

c. using a method scientifically proven to ensure its sterility.

Part 3: Good Manufacturing Practices

Ophthalmic Use

Section 60

1. Section C.01.064 of the Food and Drug Regulations applies in respect of natural health products except that it shall be read without reference to the words "or parenteral".

2. Section C.01.065 of the Food and Drug Regulations applies in respect of natural

Natural Health Products

health products except that it shall be read without reference to

a. the words "or parenteral"; and

b. the words "or to its common name if there is no proper name".

To Meet the Requirements

Manufacturers, packagers, labellers, importers and distributors must treat all sterile NHPs in the same manner as any other sterile health product. Follow the guidance for sterile products provided in the Health Canada's Health Products and Food Branch Inspectorate's Good Manufacturing Practices Guidelines, 2002 Edition, Version 2. The current version of this document is available at http://www.hc-sc.gc.ca/dhp-mps/compli-conform/gmp-bpf/guide-ld-2002/index-eng.php. The guidelines for sterile products apply in addition to the other requirements outlined in this document.

2.0 Supplementary Good Manufacturing Practices for Homeopathic Medicines

Homeopathic medicines are made from a wide range of materials such as plants, animals, chemicals and minerals, many of which are highly toxic in the raw material form. Nosodes are another type of homeopathic medicines, which are preparations derived from pathological tissues, excretions or secretions. Due to these factors, manufacturers must ensure the critical steps to process raw materials are carried out under controlled conditions.

Manufacturers, packagers and labellers of NHPs used in homeopathy, in addition to meeting the requirements in chapter 1, must meet the supplementary requirements of this chapter. The sections in chapter 1 on equipment, quality assurance, samples, records, recall reporting and sterile products fully address the requirements for homeopathic medicines, and therefore are not repeated here.

Also note, in this chapter, potency refers to the degree of dilution of a homeopathic medicine.

2.1 Places

2.1.1 Premises

To Meet the Requirements

- Manufacturers, packagers and labellers must design their premises to accommodate hazardous raw material storage and homeopathic processing requirements. These requirements include, but are not limited to, the following:

  o isolating toxic raw materials from other materials;

  o handling raw materials of biological origin in segregated areas with appropriate environmental controls suitable for each material;

  o restricting the entry of unnecessary personnel in processing areas designated for attenuation and trituration;

  o performing successive attenuations in a laminar airflow workstation; and

- o designating an area separate from the processing and storage areas to quarantine and dispose unused intermediate homeopathic potencies.
- Supporting documentation would include a floor plan showing the location of segregated areas, ventilation and flow of materials through the site.

2.2 People

2.2.1 Personnel

To Meet the Requirements

Manufacturers, packagers and labellers must provide training specific to the attenuation and/or trituration of homeopathic medicines. Supporting documents would provide details of training content and completion dates. Attire, appropriate to designated working areas, must be provided for personnel.

2.3 Processes

2.3.1 Sanitation Program

To Meet the Requirements

- Manufacturers, packagers and labellers must ensure that the sanitation program contains standard operating procedures (SOPs) appropriate for the production of homeopathic medicines. The SOPs must specify the following:
  - o cleaning requirements for raw material storage areas, including toxic and biological materials;
  - o cleaning, microbial and environmental monitoring requirements for all processing areas, with emphasis on areas designated for attenuation and trituration;
  - o methods that ensure cleaning products do not contaminate product; and
  - o cleaning production equipment and utensils using heat methods (e.g. autoclave), if applicable

2.3.2 Operations

To Meet the Requirements

Manufacturers, packagers and labellers must do the following:

- Maintain written procedures for the following:
  - o handling raw materials that are potentially toxic or pathogenic;
  - o preparing samples of raw materials, in-process materials and finished products to retain, including the conditions for their storage and the duration of such storage;
  - o retaining samples of raw materials of vegetable origin until testing of the mother tincture is completed (Note: Vegetable matter refers to plants, algae, and fungi);
  - o storing mother tincture and potencies; and
  - o disposing collections of unused intermediate homeopathic potencie

Critical Production Processes

- Control critical production processes for vegetable matter by recording the duration and efficiency of maceration and/or percolation. For trituration record the duration and intensity for each type and size of apparatus, through particle size analysis of the raw materials in the triturate matrix, when these procedures are available. Include the following information:

  o efficiency of impregnation, through the use of distribution monitors such as dyes; and

  o adequacy of the parameters established for the heat processing of the first attenuation in the preparation of nosodes, through checks for sterility.

- Label raw materials with their human safety status (e.g. allergenic, toxic) or Material Safety Data Sheet equivalent.

- On completion of each stage of processing, label the equipment and containers used during critical in-process stages.

  o For in-process attenuations or triturations, the information on the labels and/or manufacturing documentation must include the following:

    - a reference number unique to a particular series, different from the batch number assigned to the product (for combination preparations in which ingredients are potentised separately, each series is assigned a unique reference number);

    - the attenuation or trituration number at the particular stage of preparation (e.g. this could be designated by potency);

    - the name, dosage form, batch number and batch size of the preparation for which it is intended;

    - the composition or reference to the master formula;

    - the internal code and analytical control number of each raw material or mother tincture used;

    - the storage conditions, when applicable;

    - the precautions to be adopted during handling, when applicable; and

    - the date of preparation and identification of the person(s) responsible for its compounding.

  o For bulk preparations, the labels and/or manufacturing documentation must include at least the following:

    - the name, batch number and batch size of the preparation;

    - its composition or reference to the master formula;

    - the reference number(s) of attenuation or trituration series with which the dosage form is impregnated, or if the mother tincture(s) is impregnated, its internal code and analytical control number;

    - the date(s) of impregnation; and

    - the storage conditions, when applicable.

- Include the following information in the master formula:

- the system for the particular attenuation series (e.g. Hahnemannian, Korsakovian);

- the standard operating procedures, or reference to procedures, for the cleaning of vessels and containers employed in successive attenuations or triturations; and

- Standard Operating Procedures (SOPs), or reference to SOPs, to be followed at each processing stage including the following, when applicable:

  - comminution and/or size separation of raw materials, when applicable;

  - maceration and/or percolation, when applicable;

  - quarantine and/or packaging of mother tincture, when applicable;

  - number of succussions during each attenuation;

  - duration of trituration;

  - disposal of unused intermediate homeopathic potencies;

  - quarantine of target homeopathic potencies;

  - technique for impregnation;

  - manufacture and quarantine of the dosage form; and

  - in-process controls with specifications.

- the SOPs, or reference to SOPs, for washing, drying and, when applicable, sterilizing packaging materials; and

- special precautions that may be relevant to the particular classification of preparation (e.g. nosode).

- Process fresh raw materials from vegetable origin promptly.

  - When processing cannot be initiated within a few hours, do not harvest in damp weather conditions. Take adequate precautions to ensure that plants are not wet or are covered in dew when gathered.

  - When processing cannot be initiated prior to eight hours after harvesting, store raw materials under conditions that are appropriate for the conservation of the medicinal plant. Ideally refrigerate and use raw materials within 48 hours.

- Schedule manufacturing to ensure continuity within the attenuation or trituration series. Avoid prolonged storage of intermediate homeopathic potencies.

- Transport target homeopathic potencies from the processing area in hermetically sealed containers with appropriate environmental controls (e.g. for temperature and humidity).

- Transport the first attenuation in the preparation of nosodes from the processing area in a container that can be sterilized directly.

- Dispose unused intermediate homeopathic potencies according to instructions outlined in the standard operating procedures for the attenuation or trituration series.

Natural Health Products GMPs

- Record in the manufacturing order the volume or weight of tailings of destroyed finished product.

2.4 Products

2.4.1 Specifications

To Meet the Requirements

Specifications must be of pharmacopoeial (e.g. The Homeopathic Pharmacopoeia of the United States, the Pharmacopée Française, the Homöopathische Arzneimittel or the European Pharmacopoeia) or equivalent status.

Raw Materials

Manufacturers include the following in specifications for raw materials:

- Raw materials of vegetable origin:
    - identity (as Latin binomial), including genus, specific epithet and authority (e.g. Linnaeus);
    - test method to verify identity, absence of foreign materials and adulterants;
    - geographical source;
    - cultivation and collection techniques;
    - time of harvest; and
    - growth stage (e.g. of bark).
- Raw materials of animal origin:
    - identity (as Latin binomial), genus and specific epithet;
    - test method to verify identity, absence of foreign materials and adulterants;
    - part and/or constituent of the animal;
    - location and hygienic conditions of the animal's housing prior to slaughter;
    - slaughter or removal time;
    - pre-treatment, processing (e.g. freeze drying) and storage, when applicable; and
    - potentially toxic contaminants
- Include genus, specific epithet and strain, if any, in specifications for raw material of bacterial origin.
- Include identity and purity tests in specifications for raw materials of mineral origin. Identity and purity testing for homeopathic medicines is outlined in the Evidence for Homeopathic Medicines Guidance Document and the Evidence for Quality of Finished Natural Health Products Guidance Document.
- Include appropriate specifications and tests used in the manufacturing of potencies of biological origin.

- Verify the identity and potency of the raw materials. A Certificate of Identity or voucher specimen from the supplier can be used and documented.

Finished Products

Manufacturers must do the following:

- Maintain written specifications that describe the homeopathic medicine and the required test methods. For specifications pertaining to identity, purity, quantity, potency and tolerances, see the *Evidence for Homeopathic Medicines Guidance Document.*

- Follow conventional testing protocols for the dosage form (e.g. for tablets, uniformity of weight, hardness and disintegration; for liquid, alcohol type and percentage; for ointments, viscosity or rheology).

2.4.2 Stability

To Meet the Requirements

- Manufacturers should:
  - develop and maintain standard operating procedures that ensure the stability of the homeopathic medicines; and
  - maintain records of ongoing purity testing as outlined in the *Evidence for Homeopathic Medicines Guidance Document.*

    Note: Because of the unique quality of homeopathic medicines, the evidence of stability would focus on the non-medicinal ingredients.

- Additional evidence to support stability includes, but is not limited to, the following:
  - confirmation that the expiry date of an attenuation does not exceed that of the raw materials from which it is prepared.
  - dosage form testing demonstrating that the homeopathic medicine continues to meet specifications (e.g. concentration of alcohol remains consistent, granules/tablets hardness and disintegration are consistent);
  - packaging materials testing, such as bottles and caps, demonstrating that they do not contaminate product; and
  - confirmation that the labels do not fade or come away from the packaging.

References

Australian Department of Health and Ageing, Australian Code of Good Manufacturing Practice for Medicinal Products (December 11, 2002).

HACCP for Excellence (December 11, 2002).

Health Canada, Proposed Good Manufacturing Practices for Natural Health Products Workbook, used at information workshops in June-July 2002, 2002.

Health Canada, Food and Drugs Act and Regulations.

Health Canada, Good Manufacturing Practices Guidelines 2002 Edition, Version 2.

Natural Health Products GMPs

Health Canada, Natural Health Products Regulations of June 18, 2003.

Health Canada, Statement of Qualifications: Compliance Officer, Ontario Operations Centre, October 1, 2002.

Natural Nutritional Foods Association, NNFA GMP Certification Program Overview, 2001 (December 11, 2002).

NSF International Strategic Registrations, Ltd., Glossary (December 11, 2002).

NSF International, Dietary Supplements and Functional Foods & Beverages Auditor Position Description, November 15, 2002.

United States Food and Drug Administration, Good Manufacturing Practices (GMP)/Quality System (QS) Regulation, June 2002 (December 11, 2002).

United States Food and Drug Administration, Quality System Audits (December 11, 2002).

Dates in brackets are accession dates.

Glossary

The definitions given below apply to the terms used in this guidance document. Certain terms may have different meanings in other contexts.

Assess

> Steps taken by the site licence holder to ensure that the requirements in the Food and Drugs Act, the Natural Health Products Regulations and in-house standards are met. The steps could include, among others, monitoring and testing of raw and/or packaging materials, tracking of production, maintenance of records and testing of finished products.

Attenuation

> Attenuations are prepared by dissolving one part of the soluble basic substance in a sufficient quantity of purified water or other appropriate menstruum, specified in the recognized monograph, to produce (x) parts by volume of liquid attenuation (e.g. 1X, 1CH).

Batch

> A quantity of product in the processing stage, homogeneous within specified limits, produced according to a single manufacturing order and as attested by the signatories to the order. In the case of continuous manufacture, the batch corresponds to a defined fraction of the production, characterized by its intended homogeneity. It may sometimes be necessary to divide a batch into a number of sub-batches, which are later brought together to form a final homogeneous batch.

Batch number

> A distinctive combination of digits and/or letters that specifically identifies a batch, and appears on documents such as the batch record or certificate of analysis.

Batch record

> A production document that captures the quantity and lot number of all materials used, as well as production steps in the manufacturing of a single batch of a NHP in dosage form.

Bulk natural health product

> Unpackaged dosage form, usually in quantities larger than the largest commercially available package size.

Bulk preparation

> Unpackaged homeopathic preparation, usually in quantities larger than the largest commercially available package size.

Certificate

> A legally authenticated written declaration issued by a recognized institution to a person completing a course of study.

Certificate of Analysis

> A document signed by a qualified analyst that includes the product name, ingredient listing, lot number of the product, test conducted, test method and results, conclusion of the test (satisfactory or unsatisfactory), name and position of the analyst, and date of issuance.

Certificate of Manufacture

> A document issued by a vendor to a distributor or importer that attests that a specific lot of product has been produced according to its master production document. Such certificates include a summary of the current batch documentation, with reference to respective dates of revision, manufacture and packaging, and are signed and dated by the vendor's authorized quality assurance person.

Comminution

> The act of reducing to a fine powder or to small particles.

Critical process

> A process that may cause significant variation in the quality of the finished product.

Diploma

> A document issued by an educational institution, such as a university, college, or technical institute, vouching that the recipient has earned a degree or successfully completed a particular course of study.

Distributor

> A person who sells a NHP to another person for the purpose of further sale by that other person.

Dosage form

> The final physical form of the NHP which may be used by the consumer without requiring any further manufacturing.

Education

> The act or process of imparting or acquiring knowledge or skills. The learning of information by instruction, training, or study can be testified to by a degree, certificate or diploma.

Experience

> Active participation in events or activities leading to the acquisition of knowledge or skills. Also the knowledge or skills retained from personally observing, encountering, or undergoing something.

Filling

> Transferring and enclosing a bulk product into its final container.

Finished product

> A product that has undergone all stages of production, including packaging in its final container and labelling.

Formulate

> To prepare components and combine raw materials into a bulk NHP.

Hazard Analysis and Critical Control Points (HACCP)

> An internationally recognized system of food safety methods. It is a systematic approach to the identification, evaluation, and control of food safety hazards.

Homeopathic Medicines

> Medicines that are manufactured from or contain as medicinal ingredients only those substances or sources referenced in the Homeopathic Pharmacopoeia of the United States (HPUS), the Homöopathische Arzneibuch (HAB), the Pharmacopée Française (PhF), the European Pharmacopoeia or the Encyclopedia of Homeopathic Pharmacopoeia, as amended from time to time, and that are prepared in accordance with these pharmacopoeias.

Importer

> A person who imports a NHP into Canada for the purpose of sale. This includes bulk NHPs.

In-process control

> Checks performed during production to monitor and, if necessary, adjust the process to ensure that the finished product conforms to its specifications. The control of the production environment or equipment can be regarded as a part of in-process control.

In-process product

> Any materials or mixture of materials that must, to become a product in dosage form, undergo further processing.

In-process testing

> The examination or testing of any materials or mixture of materials during the manufacturing process.

ISO (International Organization for Standardization)

> A worldwide organization of national standards bodies. The ISO is a non-governmental organization that maintains a group of global standards.

Label (n)

> Includes any legend, word or mark attached to, included in, belonging to or accompanying any food, drug, cosmetic, NHP, device or package.

Label (v)

> To affix the inner or outer label of the NHP.

Lot

> A quantity of any NHP in dosage form, a raw material or a packaging material, homogeneous within specified limits, constituting all or part of a single batch and identified by a distinctive lot number which appears on the label of the finished product.

Lot number

> Any combination of letters, digits or both, by which any NHP can be traced in manufacture and identified in distribution.

Maceration

> Processing method using unheated solvent (cold or room temperature water, alcohol, or other organic solvent) to extract medicinal ingredients from a raw material.

Manufacture

> To fabricate or process a product for the purpose of sale.

Manufacturer

> A person who fabricates or processes a NHP for the purpose of sale, but does not include a pharmacist or other health care practitioner who, at the request of the patient, compounds a NHP for the purpose of sale to that patient.

Natural Health Products GMPs

Manufacturing order

> Instructions that outline in detail the materials and procedures required to manufacture, prepare and preserve a single batch of a NHP in dosage form.

Marketing authorization

> A legal document issued by the NHPD authorizing the sale of a NHP in Canada.

Master formula

> A document or set of documents specifying the raw materials with their quantities and the packaging materials, together with a detailed description of the procedures and precautions required to produce a specified quantity of a finished product.

Master production document

> A document that includes specifications (raw material, packaging material, packaged dosage form), master formula, sampling procedures and critical processing related standard operating procedures, whether these procedures are specifically referenced in the master formula. It also includes:
>
> - a complete list of raw materials used in the manufacture of the product, designated by names or codes;
> - the amount of each raw material required for the theoretical product formulation;
> - manufacturing and process control instructions and in-process testing requirements (e.g. checks on materials, pre-treatments, sequence of adding materials, mixing time and temperatures);
> - a statement of the principal equipment to be used;
> - a statement of the theoretical weight or measure of the manufactured product and the acceptable limits beyond which an investigation is required;
> - a description of the finished product containers, closures and packaging labels;
> - any special precautions to be observed; and
> - dates and times (if applicable) of commencement and completion of significant intermediate stages, such as blending or heating, and of completion of production.

Menstruum

> A combination of water and alcohol used in the extraction of herbal constituents.

Mother tincture

> A relatively concentrated aqueous alcoholic extract from which subsequent attenuations are prepared. Synonyms: mother liquor, stock solution, starting solution.

Natural health product (NHP)

> A substance set out in Schedule 1 of the Natural Health Products Regulations or a combination of substances in which all the medicinal ingredients are substances set out in Schedule 1, a homeopathic medicine or a traditional medicine that is manufactured, sold or represented for use in:
>
> - diagnosing, treating, mitigating or preventing a disease, disorder or abnormal physical state or its symptoms in humans;
> - restoring or correcting organic functions in humans; or
> - modifying organic functions in humans, such as modifying those functions in a manner that maintains or promotes health.
>
> However, a NHP does not include a substance set out in Schedule 2 of the Natural Health Products Regulations or any combination of substances that includes a substance set out in Schedule 2. See Appendix 1 for Schedules 1 and 2.

Nosodes

> These can be:
>
> - attenuations of pathological organs or tissues;
> - causative agents such as bacteria, fungi, ova, parasites, virus particles, and yeast
> - disease products; or
> - excretions or secretions.

Observation

> A deviation or deficiency of good manufacturing practice noted by an inspector or assessor.

Package (n)

> Includes any material in which any food, drug, cosmetic or device is wholly or partly contained, placed or packed.

Package (v)

> To put a product in its immediate container.

Packaging material

> Labels, printed packaging materials and those components in direct contact with the dosage form.

Packaging order

> Instructions that outline in detail the materials and special procedures required to package and label a single lot of a product in dosage form.

Percolation

> A method used for the extraction of dried substances that have been reduced to the proper degree of fineness.

Potency

> The amount per dosage unit of the standardized component(s) which further characterizes the quantity of the ingredient. It is required only when a claim on the potency is to be on the label, or it is required for a specific product (i.e. when literature supports the product with that standardized component). In the Supplementary Good Manufacturing Practices for Homeopathic Medicines, potency refers to the degree of dilution of a homeopathic medicine.

Potentization

> The process of preparing a homeopathic medicine by repeated dilution and succussion to reach a prescribed homeopathic potency.

Production

> All operations involved in the preparation of a finished product, from receipt of materials, through processing and packaging, to completion of the finished product, including storage.

Purity

> The extent to which a raw material or a product in dosage form is free from undesirable or adulterating chemical, biological or physical entities as defined by specification.

Qualification

> Requirement to be eligible for an office, position, or task by having the proper or necessary skills, knowledge, credentials, accomplishments or qualities.

Quality assurance

> All the planned and systematic activities applied within the quality system to provide adequate confidence that the predetermined standards for quality and safety will be met.

Quality assurance person

> The person who is responsible for assuring the quality of the NHP before it is made available for sale. This person should be qualified by education, training and/or experience relating to the specific activity (i.e. manufacturing, packaging, labelling and importing).

Quality Assurance Report (QAR)

> A report prepared by either a quality assurance person or a third party auditor who meets the requirements with respect to education, training, and experience according to section 51(a) (ii) of the Natural Health Products Regulations. This report is based on the assessment

against the good manufacturing practices regulations and requirements set out in the good manufacturing practices guidance document. It is considered a self-assessment document and evidence of good manufacturing practices compliance.

Quantity

The amount of medicinal ingredient(s) per dosage unit. It is always required for a product, as it is the amount of medicinal ingredient in the product.

Quarantine

Effective restriction of the availability of material or product for use (physically or by system), until released by the quality assurance person.

Raw material

Any substance, other than in-process product or packaging material, intended to be used in the manufacture of products, including those that appear in the master formula but that do not appear in the product such as solvents and processing aids.

Recognized institution

A Canadian or foreign educational facility (e.g. a university, college or professional or post-secondary institute), generally government-approved or having a secure reputation and is credible, reputable, and authoritative.

Reconciliation

A comparison, making due allowance for normal variation, between the amount of product or materials theoretically produced or used and the amount actually produced or used.

Reprocessing

Subjecting all or part of a batch or lot of an in-process product or finished product to a previous step or alternate manufacturing process due to failure to meet predetermined specifications.

Returned product

Bulk or finished product sent back to the manufacturer, distributor or importer.

Sampling

Collection of a number of units that comprises representative sample(s) from a designated lot or batch of product.

Natural Health Products GMPs

Sell (section 2 of the Food and Drugs Act)

> Sell includes offer for sale, expose for sale and have in possession for sale and distribute, regardless of whether the distribution is made for consideration.

Standard operating procedures

> An authorized written procedure giving instructions for performing operations not necessarily specific to a given product or material but of a more general nature (e.g. equipment operation, maintenance and cleaning, cleaning of premises and environmental control, sampling and inspection). Certain standard operating procedures may be used to supplement product-specific master production documents.

Succussions

> The act of vigorously shaking an attenuation, usually performed by striking against an elastic body. The combination of dilution and succussion are used to reach a prescribed potency.

Technical agreement

> A formal written document between two or more parties outlining the technical portions of a contract and the specific duties of each party involved with respect to Part 3 of the Natural Health Products Regulations. A technical agreement is mutually understood and signed by each party.

Third-party auditor

> An auditor who is independent of the company he or she is auditing and who is qualified by education, training, and experience to conduct a NHP good manufacturing practices site audit.

Training

> To make proficient with specialized instruction and practice.

Trituration

> The process of preparing a homeopathic medicine when the starting material is insoluble. This technique consists of grinding the starting material together with a powdered inactive ingredient such as lactose. This prepares the substance for potentisation.

Voucher Specimen

> A representative specimen preserved to permit independent verification of identity and to allow further examination (e.g. pressed plants or non-human animal material in preserving fluids).

Appendix 1: Schedules 1 and 2 of The Natural Health Products Regulations

Schedule 1 - Included NHP Substances

Item	Substances
1.	A plant or a plant material, an alga, a bacterium, a fungus or a non-human animal material
2.	An extract or isolate of a substance described in item 1, the primary molecular structure of which is identical to that which it had prior to its extraction or isolation
3.	Any of the following vitamins: biotin folate niacin pantothenic acid riboflavin thiamine vitamin A vitamin B 6 vitamin B 12 vitamin C vitamin D vitamin E
4.	An amino acid
5.	An essential fatty acid
6.	A synthetic duplicate of a substance described in any of items 2 to 5
7.	A mineral
8.	A probiotic

Schedule 2 - Excluded NHP Substances

Item	Substances
1.	A substance set out in Schedule C of the *Food and Drugs Act*
2.	A substance set out in Schedule D of the Act, except for the following: a drug that is prepared from any of the following micro-organisms, namely, an alga, a bacterium or a fungus; and any substance set out in Schedule D when it is prepared in accordance with the practices of homeopathic pharmacy
3.	A substance regulated under the *Tobacco Act*
4.	A substance set out in any of Schedules I to V of the *Controlled Drugs and Substances Act*
5.	A substance that is administered by puncturing the dermis
6.	An antibiotic prepared from an alga, a bacterium or a fungus or a synthetic duplicate of that antibiotic

Appendix 2: Records

In this chart, site indicates that records must be retained on the premises, while access means that records need not be kept on the premises, but rather must be readily available.

Appendix 2 - Good Manufacturing Practices Guidance Document					
Record	**Manufacturer**	**Packager**	**Labeller**	**Importer**	**Distributor**
Master production document	site			access	
Manufacturing order	site			access	
Packaging order	site	site		access	
Labelling order	site		site	access	
Test results: raw material	site			access	
Test results: packaging material	site	site		access	
Test results: finished product	site			access	
Specifications: raw material	site			access	
Specifications: packaging material	site	site		access	
Specifications: finished product	site			access	
Stability summary	site			access	
Ingredients list	site			access	
Products list	site	site	site	access	site
Distribution list	site	site	site	access	site
Complaints	site	site	site	site	site
Sanitation program	site	site	site	site	site

Risk Classification of GMP Observations (GUI-0023)

Health Products and Food Branch Inspectorate

Drugs GMP Inspection Unit

Supersedes: June 1st, 2000 edition
Date issued: April 4th , 2003
Date of implementation   June 1st, 2003

Guide-0023: Risk Classification of GMP Observations, 2003 edition[22]

1.0 Purpose

To classify the observations noted during establishment inspections according to their risk.

To ensure uniformity among the inspectors of the Health Products and Food Branch Inspectorate (the Inspectorate) in the attribution of the rating following establishment inspections.

To inform the industry of the situations that the Inspectorate considers unacceptable and that will generate a Non Compliant (NC) rating following an inspection.

2.0 Background

During an establishment inspection, deviations from the Food and Drug Regulations and the current edition of the Good Manufacturing Practices (GMP) guidelines are noted by the inspector and these deviations appear as observations in the inspection exit notice. A judgement based on these observations is then made by the inspector and an overall recommendation for the continuation or issuance of the establishment licence (rating of Compliance) or not to continue or issue the licence (rating of Non-Compliance) is given. Attribution of a NC rating may have serious consequences for a company, ranging from the implementation of important corrective measures to the temporary suspension or termination of the Establishment Licence (EL). Therefore, these situations of non-conformity have to be well defined, unambiguous and directly supported by the applicable regulations.

---

[22] Available on the Health Canada website at http://www.hc-sc.gc.ca/dhp-mps/compli-conform/gmp-bpf/docs/gui_23-eng.php

3.0 Scope

The definition of a drug in Canada covers a wide variety of products ranging from pharmaceuticals and biologics to natural health products such as homeopathics and herbal preparations. This guidance document covers all such products to which Division 2 of Part C of the Food and Drug Regulations applies and is based on the current edition of the GMP Guidelines. It is recognised that the evaluation of the conformity to the GMP should be commensurate with the risk involved taking into account the nature and extent of the deviation in relation with the category of products evaluated. Nonetheless, most of the situations involving fraud, misrepresentation or falsification of products or data will generate a NC rating, irrespective of the category of products involved.

The appendices attached to the present document describe the observations related to each category of risk. Please note that the list of observations in each appendix is not exhaustive and that additional observations may be added where appropriate.

The numbering system assigned to each section in the appendices is a reference to the applicable regulations in the current edition of the GMP guidelines.

4.0 Definitions:

The following definitions are provided to complement those already available under the glossary of terms in the current edition of the GMP Guidelines or other related documents referenced in the GMP Guidelines.

Observation

A deviation or deficiency to GMP noted by an inspector during the inspection of a drug establishment that is confirmed in writing to the company in the exit notice. The observations are classified as "Critical", "Major" and "Other" and are assigned a risk classification, ranging from 1 for "critical" to 2 for "major" to 3 for "other".

Critical Observation

Observation describing a situation that is likely to result in a non-compliant product or a situation that may result in an immediate or latent health risk and any observation that involves fraud, misrepresentation or falsification of products or data.

Appendix I lists observations that the Inspectorate considers critical which will be assigned a Risk 1.

Major Observation

Observation that may result in the production of a drug not consistently meeting its marketing authorization.

Observation that may result in the production of a drug not consistently meeting its marketing authorization. Appendix 2 lists observations that are considered major and which will be assigned a Risk 2 Certain Risk 2 observations may be upgraded to Risk 1. They are indicated with an arrow (↑)

Other Observation

> Observation that is neither critical nor major but is a departure from the GMP.
>
> "Other" observations are not listed as such (Observations that are neither critical nor major are considered as "other" and will be assigned a Risk 3). Appendix 3 lists Risk 3 observations that may be upgraded to Risk 2.

Critical Product

> A critical product is one for which one or more of the following criteria apply:
>
> - narrow therapeutic window
> - high toxicity
> - sterile product
> - biological drug

Complex Manufacturing Process

> process for which slight deviations in the control of parameters could result in a non-uniform product or a product not meeting its specifications. As example, powder mixing or granulation for low dosage solid forms, long acting / delayed action products, sterile products.
>
> Note: OTC low dosage vitamins and minerals preparations and Category 4 products (as listed in Interpretation 2.3 under section C.02.028) should not be considered as critical products even when the manufacturing processes involved are complex.

High Risk Product

> Any product that may trigger a health risk even at low levels, following cross-contamination. Those include but are not limited to penicillins, certain cytotoxic and biological products.

Low Risk Products

> Products such as Category 4 product (as listed in Interpretation 2.3 under section C.02.028), natural health products including vitamins and minerals preparations that are not a schedule drug or a sterile drug, and certain topical non prescription veterinary formulations registered as "old drugs".

Acronyms:

C:	Compliant
CIP:	Clean-In-Place
COA:	Certificate of Analysis
EL:	Establishment Licence

GMP:	Good Manufacturing Practices
HVAC:	Heat, Ventilation, Air Conditioning
IRS:	Inspection Reporting System
MRA:	Mutual Recognition Agreement
NC:	Non-compliant
OTC:	Over-The-Counter
PM:	Packaging Material
PW:	Purified Water
QC:	Quality Control
RM:	Raw Material
WFI:	Water For Injection.

5.0 Guide

5.1 Assignment of the risk to an observation

Whereas it is recognized that it is impossible to encompass every situation that may generate a risk, the following principles should be considered:

- The risk assigned will be in relation to the nature of the deviation as well as the number of occurrences.

- Generally, when only low risk products are involved, a risk 1 will not be assigned to observations described in Appendix 1, except for extreme situations such as fraud or widespread cross-contamination, infestation or unsanitary conditions.

- Where a risk 2 observation is re-evaluated as a risk 1 (risk 2 observation with an arrow), this situation is immediately brought to the attention of the company's officials, proper explanation will be provided to the establishment and this explanation should be captured in the "Inspector's Comments" field of the "Inspection Summary" in the IRS.

5.2 Assignment of the inspection rating

The overall inspection rating assigned is based on the risk involved taking into account the nature and extent of the deviations with the category of products evaluated.

5.2.1 Risk 1 observation:

Generally, a NC rating is assigned when a Risk 1observation is noted during an inspection.

Such situation is immediately brought to the attention of the company's officials. The Inspectorate management is to be notified in a timely manner.

Where in the opinion of the inspector the resulting products present a significant health hazard, appropriate enforcement actions may be initiated.

5.2.2 Risk 2 observation:

Generally, a C rating is assigned when Risk 2 observations are noted during an inspection. However, a NC rating may be assigned in the following situations:

- When numerous Risk 2 observations are noted during an inspection indicating that the company does not control its processes and operations sufficiently.

- Repetition of many Risk 2 observations noted during previous inspections indicating that the company did not:

    - implement the corrective actions submitted following the previous inspection or

    - did not put in place adequate preventive actions in a timely manner to avoid recurrence of such deviations.

5.2.3 Risk 3 observations:

A C rating will be assigned in all situations where only Risk 3 observations are noted.

5.3 Additional guidance

When a NC rating is assigned, the inspector will issue a draft Inspection Exit Notice during the exit meeting. The draft inspection exit notice will be reviewed for quality assurance purposes before the final report is issued to an establishment

When observation(s) leading to a NC rating are made, the Inspection Exit Notice could be issued with a C rating if, during the inspection:

- the establishment immediately implements all necessary actions to resolve the cause(s) of the observation(s) leading to the NC rating and,

- sufficient assurance can be provided to prevent a recurrence.

In such instances, the risk assigned to the observation will remain the same.

If the management of the company wishes to dispute the results of the inspection report, the "Dispute resolution and appeals" mechanism described in the GMP and EL Enforcement Policy POL-0004 should be followed.

Appendix 1: Risk 1 (Critical) Observations

Premises C.02.004

- No air filtration system to eliminate airborne contaminants that are likely to be generated during fabrication or packaging.

- Generalized malfunctioning of the ventilation system(s) with evidence of widespread cross-contamination.

- Inadequate segregation of manufacturing or testing areas from other manufacturing areas for high risk products.

Equipment C.02.005

◆ Equipment used for complex manufacturing operations of critical products not qualified and with evidence of malfunctioning.

Personnel C.02.006

◆ Individual in charge of Quality Control (QC) or production for a fabricator of critical / high risk products does not hold a university degree in a science related to the work being conducted and does not have sufficient practical experience in their responsibility area.

Sanitation C.02.007 C.02.008

◆ Evidence of widespread accumulation of residues / extraneous matter indicative of inadequate cleaning.

◆ Evidence of gross infestation.

Raw Material Testing C.02.009 C.02.010

◆ Evidence of falsification or misrepresentation of analytical results.

◆ No evidence of testing (COA) available from the supplier / synthetizer and no testing done by the Canadian fabricator.

Manufacturing Control C.02.011 C.02.012

◆ No written Master Formula.

◆ Master Formula or manufacturing batch document showing gross deviations or significant calculation errors.

◆ Evidence of falsification or misrepresentation of manufacturing and packaging orders.

Quality Control Department C.02.013 C.02.014 C.02.015

◆ No person in charge of QC available on premises in Canada.

◆ QC department not a distinct and independent unit, lacking real decisional power, with evidence that QC decisions are often overruled by production department or management.

Finished Products Testing C.02.018 C.02.019

◆ Finished product not tested for compliance with applicable specifications by the importer / distributor before release for sale and no evidence is available that the products have been tested by the fabricator.

◆ Evidence of falsification or misrepresentation of testing results / forgery of COA.

Records C.02.020 to C.02.024

◆ Evidence of falsification or misrepresentation of records.

Stability C.02.027 C.02.028

- No data available to establish the shelf-life of products.
- Evidence of falsification or misrepresentation of stability data / forgery of COA.

Sterile Products C.02.029

- Critical sterilization cycles based on Probability of Survival not validated.
- Water for Injection (WFI) systems not validated with evidence of problems such as microbial / endotoxin counts not within specifications.
- No media fills performed to demonstrate the validity of aseptic filling operations.
- No environmental controls / No monitoring for viable microorganisms during filling for aseptically filled products.
- Aseptic filling operations maintained following unsatisfactory results obtained for media fills.
- Batches failing initial sterility test released for sale on the basis of a second test without proper investigation.

Appendix 2: Risk 2 (Major) Observations

Premises C.02.004

- Malfunctioning of the ventilation system that could result in possible localized or occasional cross-contamination.
- Maintenance / periodic verification such as air filter replacement, monitoring of pressure differentials not performed. (↑)
- Accessory supplies (steam, air, nitrogen, dust collection, etc...) not qualified.
- Heat Ventilation Air Conditioning (HVAC) and purified water (PW) system not qualified.
- Temperature and humidity not controlled or monitored when necessary (e. g. storage not in accordance with labelling requirements).
- Damages (holes, cracks or peeling paint) to walls / ceilings immediately adjacent or above manufacturing areas or equipment where the product is exposed.
- Un-cleanable surfaces created by pipes, fixtures or ducts directly above products or manufacturing equipment.
- Surfaces finish (floors, walls and ceilings) that do not permit effective cleaning.
- Unsealed porous finish in manufacturing areas with evidence of contamination (mildew, mould, powder from previous productions, etc..) (↑)
- Insufficient manufacturing space that could lead to mix-ups. (↑)

- Physical and electronic quarantine accessible to unauthorized personnel / Physical quarantine area not well marked and /or not respected when used. (↑)

- No separate area / Insufficient precautions to prevent contamination or cross-contamination during RM sampling.

Equipment C.02.005

- Equipment does not operate within its specifications.(↑)

- Equipment used for complex manufacturing operations not qualified. (↑)

- Clean in Place (CIP) equipment not validated.

- Tanks for manufacturing of liquids and ointments not equipped with sanitary clamps.

- Stored equipment not protected from contamination.(↑)

- Inappropriate equipment for production: surfaces porous and non-cleanable / material to shed particles.(↑)

- Evidence of contamination of products by foreign materials such as grease, oil, rust and particles from the equipment.(↑)

- No covers for tanks, hoppers or similar manufacturing equipment.

- No / inadequate precautions taken when equipment such as oven or autoclave contains more than one product (possibility of cross-contamination or mix-ups).(↑)

- Equipment location does not prevent cross-contamination or possible mix-ups for operations performed in common area.(↑)

- PW system not maintained or operated to provide water of adequate quality. (↑)

- Leaking gaskets.

- No calibration program for automatic, mechanical, electronic or measuring equipment / no records maintained.

- No equipment usage logs.

Personnel C.02.006

- Individual in charge of QC or Production for a fabricator, packager/labeller or tester does not hold a university degree in a science related to the work being conducted or does not have sufficient practical experience in their responsibility area.

- Individual in charge of QC for a distributor, importer or wholesaler is not qualified by academic training and experience.

- Delegation of responsibilities for QC or Production to insufficiently qualified persons.

- Insufficient personnel for QC or Production operations resulting in a high probability of error.

- Insufficient training for personnel involved in production and QC resulting in related GMP deviations.

Sanitation C.02.007 C.02.008

- Sanitation program not in writing but premises in acceptable state of cleanliness.

- No Standard Operating Procedure (SOP) for microbial / environmental monitoring, no action limits for areas where susceptible non-sterile products are manufactured. - Cleaning procedure for production equipment not validated (including analytical methods).

- Cleaning procedure for production equipment not validated when non-dedicated equipment is used for high risk products (↑).

- Incomplete health requirements.

Raw Material Testing C.02.009 C.02.010

- Reduce testing program in place without adequate certification of the vendors / suppliers.

- Water used in the formulation is not of acceptable quality.

- No identity test performed by the manufacturer after receipt on it's premises / Testing for identity not done on each containers for APIs or after manipulation or repackaging by third party.

- COA showing incomplete testing.

- Incomplete specifications.

- Specifications not approved by QC.

- Test methods not validated.

- Use of API after the retest date without proper retesting.

- Use of inactive RM after the expiration date without proper retesting.

- Multiple lots comprising one reception not considered as separate for sampling, testing and release.

- No SOP for conditions of transportation and storage.

- Certification of brokers or wholesalers allowed without proper documentation.

Manufacturing Controls C.02.011 C.02.012

- Master Formulae prepared / verified by unqualified personnel.

- Complex production processes not validated. (↑)

- Incomplete validation studies / reports for complex manufacturing process (lack of evaluation / approval).

- Changeover procedures for manufacturing of medicinal / non-medicinal products are not validated or not available.

- Unapproved / undocumented major changes compared to Master Production Documents. (↑)

- Deviations from instructions during production not documented and not approved by QC.

- Discrepancies in yield or reconciliation following production not investigated.

- Line clearance between production of different products not covered by SOP and not documented.

- No regular checks for measuring devices / no records.

- Lack of proper identification of in-process materials and production rooms resulting in a high probability of mix-ups.

- Inadequate labelling / storage of rejected materials and products that could generate mix-ups.

- Upon receipt, bulk and in-process drugs, RM and PM not held in quarantine until released by QC.

- Production personnel using bulk and in-process drugs, RM and PM without prior authorization by QC. (↑)

- Inadequate / inaccurate labelling of bulk / in-process drugs, RM and PM.

- RM dispensing not done by qualified persons, according to an SOP.

- Master Formulae incomplete or showing inaccuracies in the processing operations.

- Changes in batch size not prepared / verified by qualified personnel.

- Inaccurate / incomplete information in manufacturing / packaging batch documents.

- Although documented, combination of batches done without QC approval / not covered by SOP.

- No written procedures for packaging operations.

- Non-standard occurrences during packaging not investigated by qualified personnel.

- Inadequate control of coded and non-coded printed PM (including storage, dispensing, printing, disposal).

- No or inadequate self-inspection program / Program does not address all applicable sections of GMPs / Records incomplete or not maintained.

- Products imported from foreign sites that are not listed on the Foreign Site Annex of the Establishment Licence (↑)

- Recall:

  - Absence of recall procedure combined with distribution practices that would not permit an adequate recall (distribution records unavailable or not kept).

  - Improper quarantine and disposal practices that would allow recalled / rejected units to be returned for sale.

Quality Control Department C.02.013 C.02.014 C.02.015

- Inadequate facilities, personnel and testing equipment. - No authority to enter production areas.(↑)

- No SOPs approved and available for sampling, inspection and testing of materials. - Products made available for sale without approval of QC department. (↑)

- Products released for sale by QC without proper verification of manufacturing and packaging documentation.

- Deviations and borderline conformances not properly investigated and documented, according to a SOP.

- RM / PM used in production without prior approval of QC.

- Reprocessing / Reworking done without prior approval of QC department. (↑)

- No system for complaint handling and returned goods.

- SOPs covering operations that can affect the quality of a product such as transportation, storage, etc...not approved by QC department / not implemented.

- Absence of change control system.

- For testing laboratories, (in house or contract) the systems and controls in place for the proper qualification, operation, calibration and maintenance of equipment, standards, solutions, and records keeping do not assure that the results and conclusions generated are accurate, precise and reliable. (↑)

Packaging Material Testing C.02.016 C.02.017

- Reduce testing program in place without adequate certification of vendors / suppliers.

- Absence of testing of PM.

- Specifications not approved by QC.

- No identity test done by the packager / labeller after receipt on its premises.

- Certificat on of brokers or wholesalers done without proper documentation.

Finished Product Testing C.02.018 C.02.019

- Noncompliant products made available for sale without proper justification.(↑)

- Incomplete / inadequate specifications.

- Finished product specifications not approved by QC.

- Incomplete testing.

- No identity testing upon receipt in Canada from non-MRA country and no periodic complete confirmatory testing.

- ◆ Test methods not validated.
- ◆ No SOP for conditions of transportation and storage.
- ◆ Use of unique identifier principles not meeting the acceptable options.

Records C.02.020 to C.02.024

- ◆ Absence of Master Production Documents.
- ◆ Unavailability of documentation from suppliers in a timely manner.

Samples C.02.025 C.02.026

- ◆ Retained samples not kept for finished products.
- ◆ Failure to submit retained samples when alternative sample retention granted.

Stability C.02.027 C.02.028

- ◆ Insufficient number of lots / insufficient data to establish shelf-life.
- ◆ No action taken when data shows that the products do not meet their specifications prior to the expiry date.
- ◆ No continuing stability program.
- ◆ No stability studies pertaining to changes in manufacturing (formulation) / packaging materials.
- ◆ Testing methods not validated.

Sterile products C.02.029

- ◆ Aqueous-based products not subject to terminal steam sterilisation without proper justification or approval through the marketing authorization.
- ◆ Inadequate room classification for processing / filling operations. (↑)
- ◆ Aseptic manufacturing suites under negative pressure compared to clean ©-D) areas. Clean ©-D) areas under negative pressure to unclassified areas. (↑)
- ◆ Insufficient number of samples for room classification / inadequate sampling methods. (↑)
- ◆ Insufficient environmental controls / Insufficient monitoring for viable microorganisms during filling for aseptically filled products. (↑)
- ◆ Premises and equipment not designed or maintained to minimize contamination / generation of particles. (↑)
- ◆ Inadequate maintenance of PW and WFI systems.
- ◆ Inadequate re-validation of PW and WFI systems after maintenance, upgrading, out-of-specs trends.
- ◆ Inadequate training of personnel.
- ◆ Inadequate gowning practices for clean and aseptic areas.

- Inadequate sanitation /disinfection program.
- Inadequate practices / precautions to minimize contamination or prevent mix-ups.
- Non-validated time lapse between cleaning, sterilization, use of components, containers and equipment.
- No consideration given to bioburden prior to sterilization.
- Non-validated time lapse between start of manufacturing and sterilization or filtration.
- Inadequate procedures for media-fills.
- Insufficient number of units filled during media-fills
- Medial fils do not simulate actual operations.
- Capability of med a to grow a wide spectrum of microorganisms not demonstrated.
- Misinterpretation of results for media-fills.
- Absence of leak test for ampules.
- Samples for sterility testing insufficient in number or not representative of the entire production run.
- Each sterilizer load not considered as a separate lot for sterility testing.
- PW is not used as the feed water for the WFI system and the clean steam generator.
- The WFI used in the preparation of parenterals is not tested for endotoxins.
- The WFI used for the final rinsing of containers and components used for parenteral drugs is not tested for endotoxins when those containers and components are not depyrogenated subsequently.

Appendix 3: Risk 3 (Other) Observations

Premises C.02.004

- Doors giving direct access to exterior from manufacturing and packaging areas used by personnel.
- Un-screened / Un-trapped floor drains.
- Outlets for liquids and gases not identified.
- Damages to surfaces not directly adjacent or above exposed products.
- Non-production activities performed in production areas.
- Inadequate rest, change, wash-up and toilet facilities.

Equipment C.02.005

- Insufficient distance between equipments and walls to permit cleaning.

- Base of immovable equipment not adequately sealed at points of contact.
- Use of temporary means or devices for repair.
- Defective or unused equipment not removed or appropriately labelled.
- Minor equipment used for non critical products not qualified.

Sanitation C.02.007 C.02.008

- Incomplete written sanitation program but premises in acceptable state of cleanliness.
- Sanitation or Health and hygiene programs not properly implemented or followed by employees.

Raw Material Testing C.02.009 C.02.010

- Lots identified for confirmatory testing used in production without QC approval.
- Incomplete validation of test methods.

Manufacturing Control C.02.011 C.02.012

- Incomplete SOPs for handling of materials and products.
- Access to production areas not restricted to authorized personnel.
- Inadequate checks for incoming materials.
- Written procedures incomplete for packaging operations.
- Incomplete recall procedure.

Packaging Material Testing C.02.016 C.02.017

- Inadequate procedures of transportation and storage.
- Inadequate handling of outdated / obsolete PM.
- Incomplete testing.
- Inadequate specifications.
- Multiple lots comprising one reception not considered as separate for sampling, testing and release.

Finished Product Testing C.02.018 - C.02.019

- Incomplete testing of physical parameters.

Records C.02.020 to C.02.024

- Incomplete records / documentation for a product.
- Incomplete plans and specifications for the manufacturing buildings.
- Incomplete documentation pertaining to supervisory personnel.
- Insufficient retention time for evidence and records to be maintained.

- No organization charts.
- Incomplete records for the sanitation program.

Samples C.02.025 C.02.026

- Samples of RM not available.
- Insufficient quantity for finished products or active pharmaceutical ingredient.
- Improper storage conditions.

Stability C.02.027 C.02.028

- Insufficient number of lots in continuing stability program.
- Incomplete testing of parameters.
- Insufficient quantities for complete testing.

Sterile Products C.02.029

- Steam used for sterilization not monitored to assure suitable quality and absence of additives.
- Inadequate control on the maximum number of personnel present in clean and aseptic areas.
- Gases used to purge solutions or blanket products not passed through a sterilizing filter.
- Inadequate inspection for particles and defects.

Cleaning Validation Guidelines (GUIDE-0028)

Health Products and Food Branch Inspectorate

Guidance Document

Supersedes: May 1, 2000

Date issued: January 1, 2008

Date of implementation: January 1, 2008

Cleaning Validation Guidelines

GUIDE-0028[23]

1.0 Scope

Disclaimer: This document does not constitute part of the Food and Drugs Act (Act) or the Food and Drugs Regulations (Regulations) and in the event of any inconsistency or conflict between that Act or Regulations and this document, the Act or the Regulations take precedence. This document is an administrative document that is intended to facilitate compliance by the regulated party with the Act, the Regulations and the applicable administrative policies. This document is not intended to provide legal advice regarding the interpretation of the Act or Regulations. If a regulated party has questions about their legal obligations or responsibilities under the Act or Regulations, they should seek the advice of legal counsel.

This document on Cleaning Validation is intended to address special considerations and issues pertaining to validation of cleaning procedures for equipment used in the manufacture of pharmaceutical products, radiopharmaceuticals, and biological drugs. The document is also intended to establish inspection consistency and uniformity with respect to equipment cleaning procedures.

Principles incorporated in international guidance have been taken into account in the preparation of this document.

The document is intended to cover validation of equipment cleaning for the removal of contaminants associated with previous products, residues of cleaning agents as well as the control of potential microbial contaminants.

---

[23] Available on the Health Canada website at http://www.hc-sc.gc.ca/dhp-mps/compli-conform/gmp-bpf/validation/gui-0028_cleaning-nettoyage_ltr-doc-eng.php

2.0 Introduction

This document provides some guidance on issues and topics related to cleaning validation. This topic reflects an area in pharmaceutical, biological and radiopharmaceutical manufacturing that is noted as being important by both the Inspectorate and the pharmaceutical industry. This guideline has been prepared to provide guidance to inspectors, evaluators and industry in reviewing the issues covered. Utilization of this information should facilitate compliance with Division 2 Part C of the Food and Drugs Regulations.

It is not intended that the recommendations made in these guidelines become requirements under all circumstances. Information provided in the document for limits to be applied in defined circumstances as well as the number of batches to be utilized for cleaning validation studies is for guidance purposes only. Inspectors, evaluators and industry may consider other limits if proposed and documented in accordance with appropriate scientific justification.

3.0 Principles

3.1   The objective of the cleaning validation is to verify the effectiveness of the cleaning procedure for removal of product residues, degradation products, preservatives, excipients, and/or cleaning agents as well as the control of potential microbial contaminants. In addition one needs to ensure there is no risk associated with cross-contamination of active ingredients.

3.2   Cleaning procedures must strictly follow carefully established and validated methods.

3.3   Appropriate cleaning procedures must be developed for all product-contact equipment used in the production process. Consideration should also be given to non-contact parts into which product may migrate (e.g., seals, flanges, mixing shaft, fans of ovens, heating elements, etc.).

3.4   Relevant process equipment cleaning validation methods are required for biological drugs because of their inherent characteristics (proteins are sticky by nature), parenteral product purity requirements, the complexity of equipment, and the broad spectrum of materials which need to be cleaned.

3.5   Cleaning procedures for products and processes which are very similar do not need to be individually validated. This could be dependent on what is common, equipment and surface area, or an environment involving all product-contact equipment.

It is considered acceptable to select a representative range of similar products and processes. The physical similarities of the products, the formulation, the manner and quantity of use by the consumer, the nature of other product previously manufactured, the size of batch in comparison to previously manufactured product are critical issues that justify a validation program.

A single validation study under consideration of the worst case can then be carried out which takes account of the relevant criteria.

For biological drugs, including vaccines, bracketing may be considered acceptable for similar products and/or equipment provided appropriate justification, based on sound and scientific rationale, is given. Some examples are cleaning of fermenters of the same design but with different vessel capacity used for the same type of recombinant proteins expressed in the same rodent cell line and cultivated in closely related growth media; a multi-antigen vaccine used to represent the individual antigen or other combinations of them when validating the same or similar equipment that is used at stages of formulation (adsorption) and/or holding. Validation of cleaning of fermenters should be done upon individual pathogen basis.

4.0 Validation of Cleaning Processes

4.1　As a general concept, until the validation of the cleaning procedure has been completed, the product contact equipment should be dedicated.

4.2　In a multi-product facility, the effort of validating the cleaning of a specific piece of equipment which has been exposed to a product and the cost of permanently dedicating the equipment to a single product should be considered.

4.3　Equipment cleaning validation may be performed concurrently with actual production steps during process development and clinical manufacturing. Validation programs should be continued through full scale commercial production.

4.4　It is usually not considered acceptable to test-until-clean. This concept involves cleaning, sampling, and testing with repetition of this sequence until an acceptable residue limit is attained.

4.5　Products which simulate the physicochemical properties of the substance to be removed may be considered for use instead of the substances themselves, when such substances are either toxic or hazardous.

4.6　Raw materials sourced from different suppliers may have different physical properties and impurity profiles. When applicable such differences should be considered when designing cleaning procedures, as the materials may behave differently.

4.7　All pertinent parameters should be checked to ensure the process as it will ultimately be run is validated. Therefore, if critical temperatures are needed to effect cleaning, then these should be verified. Any chemical agents added should be verified for type as well as quantity. Volumes of wash and rinse fluids, and velocity measurements for cleaning fluids should be measured as appropriate.

4.8　If automated procedures are utilized (Clean-In-Place: CIP), consideration should be given to monitoring the critical control points and the parameters with appropriate sensors and alarm points to ensure the process is highly controlled.

4.9　During a campaign (production of several batches of the same product), cleaning between batches may be reduced. The number of lots of the same product which could be manufactured before a complete/ full cleaning is done should be determined.

4.10　Validation of cleaning processes should be based on a worst-case scenario including:

Cleaning Validation
GUI-0028

i.   challenge of the cleaning process to show that the challenge soil can be recovered in sufficient quantity or demonstrate log removal to ensure that the cleaning process is indeed removing the soil to the required level, and

ii. the use of reduced cleaning parameters such as overloading of contaminants, over drying of equipment surfaces, minimal concentration of cleaning agents, and/or minimum contact time of detergents.

4.11 At least three (3) consecutive applications of the cleaning procedure should be performed and shown to be successful in order to prove that the method is validated. Equipment which is similar in design and function may be grouped and a worst case established for validation.

5.0 Equipment and Personnel

Equipment:

5.1 All processing equipment should be specifically designed to facilitate cleanability and permit visual inspection and whenever possible, the equipment should be made of smooth surfaces of non-reactive materials.

5.2 Critical areas (i.e., those hardest to clean) should be identified, particularly in large systems that employ semi-automatic or fully automatic CIP systems.

5.3 Dedicated product-contact equipment should be used for products which are difficult to remove (e.g., tarry or gummy residues in the bulk manufacturing), for equipment which is difficult to clean (e.g., bags for fluid bed dryers), or for products with a high safety risk (e.g., biologicals or products of high potency which may be difficult to detect below an acceptable limit).

5.4 In a bulk process, particularly for very potent chemicals such as some steroids, the issue of by-products needs to be considered if equipment is not dedicated.

Personnel:

5.5 It is difficult to validate a manual cleaning procedure (i.e. an inherently variable/cleaning procedure). Therefore, operators carrying out manual cleaning procedures should be adequately trained, monitored, and periodically assessed.

6.0 Microbiological Considerations

6.1 Whether or not CIP systems are used for cleaning of processing equipment, microbiological aspects of equipment cleaning should be considered. This consists largely of preventive measures rather than removal of contamination once it has occurred.

6.2 There should be some documented evidence that routine cleaning and storage of equipment do not allow microbial proliferation. For example, equipment shou d be dried before storage, and under no circumstances should stagnant water be allowed to remain in equipment subsequent to cleaning operatics. Time-frames for the storage of unclean equipment, prior to commencement of cleaning, as well as time frames and conditions for the storage of cleaned equipment should be established.

6.3 The control of the bio-burden through adequate cleaning and storage of equipment is important to ensure that subsequent sterilization or sanitization procedures achieve the necessary assurance of sterility. This is also particularly important from the standpoint of the control of pyrogens in sterile process ng since equipment sterilization processes may not be adequate to ach eve significant inactivation or removal of pyrogens.

7.0 Documentation

7.1 Detailed cleaning procedure(s) are to be documented in SOPs

7.2 A Cleaning Valication Protocol is required to define how the cleaning process will be validated. It should include the following:

- The objective of the validation process;
- Responsibil ties for performing and approving the validation study;
- Description of the equipment to be used;
- The interval between the end of production and the beginning of the cleaning procedure;
- The number of lots of the same product, which could be manufactured during a campaign before a full cleaning is done
- Detailed cleaning procedures to be used for each product, each manufacturing system or each piece of equipment;
- The number of cleaning cycles to be performed consecutively;
- Any routine monitoring requirement;
- Sampling procedures, including the rationale for why a certain sampling method is used;
- Clearly defined sampling locations;
- Data on reccvery studies where appropriate;
- Validated analytical methods including the limit of detection and the limit of quantitation of those methods;
- The acceptance criteria, including the rationale for setting the specific limits;
- Other products, processes, and equipment for which the planned validation is valid according to a "bracketing" concept;
- Change Control/ Re-validation.

7.3 Depending upon the complexity of the system and cleaning processes, the amount of documentation necessary for executing various cleaning steps or procedures may vary.

7.4 When more complex cleaning procedures are required, it is important to document the critical cleaning steps. In this regard, specific documentation on the equipment itself which includes information about who cleaned it, when the cleaning was carried out, the product which was previously processed on the equipment being cleaned should be available. However, for relatively simple cleaning operations, the mere documentation that the overall cleaning process was performed might be sufficient.

7.5 Other factors such as history of cleaning, residue levels found after cleaning, and variability of test results may also dictate the amount of documentation required. For example, when variable residue levels are detected following cleaning, particularly for a process that is believed to be acceptable, one must establish the effectiveness of the process and of the operator performance. Appropriate evaluations must be made, and when operator performance is deemed a problem, more extensive documentation (guidance) and training may be required.

7.6 A Final Validation Report should be prepared. The conclusions of this report should state if the cleaning process has been validated successfully. Limitations that apply to the use of the validated method should be defined (for example, the analytical limit at which cleanliness can be determined). The report should be approved by management.

8.0 Analytical Methods

8.1 The analytical methods used to detect residuals or contaminants should be specific for the substance or the class of substances to be assayed (e.g., product residue, detergent residue, and/or endotoxin) and be validated before the cleaning validation study is carried out.

8.2 If levels of contamination or residual are not detected, it does not mean that there is no residual contaminant present after cleaning. It only means that the levels of contaminant greater than the sensitivity or detection limit of the analytical method are not present in the sample.

8.3 In the case of biological drugs, the use of product-specific assay(s) such as immunoassay(s) to monitor the presence of biological carry-over may not be adequate, a negative test may be the result of denaturation of protein epitope(s). Product-specific assay(s) can be used in addition to total organic carbon (TOC) for the detection of protein residue.

8.4 The analytical method and the percent recovery of contaminants should be challenged in combination with the sampling method(s) used (see below). This is to show that contaminants can be recovered from the equipment surface and to show the level of recovery as well as the consistency of recovery. This is necessary before any conclusions can be made based on the sample results. A negative test may also be the result of poor sampling technique.

9.0 Sampling, Rinsing, Rinse Samples and Detergents

Sampling:

9.1 There are two general types of sampling that are considered to be acceptable, direct surface sampling (swab method) and indirect sampling (use of rinse solutions). A combination of the two methods is generally the most desirable, particularly in circumstances where accessibility of equipment parts can mitigate against direct surface sampling.

9.2   Direct Surface Sampling

i.   Areas hardest to clean and which are reasonably accessible can be evaluated by direct sampling method, leading to establishing a level of contamination or residue per given surface area. Additionally, residues that are "dried out" or are insoluble can be sampled by physical removal.

ii.   The suitability of the material to be used for sampling and of the sampling medium should be determined. The ability to recover a sample accurately may be affected by the choice of sampling material. It is important to assure that the sampling medium and solvent (used for extraction from the medium) are satisfactory and can be readily used.

9.3   Rinse Samples

    i.   Rinse samples allow sampling of a large surface area and of inaccessible systems or ones that cannot be routinely disassembled. However consideration should be given to the fact that the residue or contaminant may be insoluble or may be physically occluded in the equipment.

    ii.   A direct measurement of the residue or contaminant in the relevant solvent should be made when rinse samples are used to validate the cleaning process.

9.4   Indirect testing such as conductivity and TOC testing may be of some value for routine monitoring once a cleaning process has been validated. This could be applicable to reactors or centrifuge and piping between such large equipment can be sampled only using rinse solution samples.

9.5   If the placebo method is used to validate the cleaning process then it should be used in conjunction with rinse and/or swab samples. It is difficult to provide assurance that the contaminate will be uniformly dispersed throughout the system or that it would be worn off the equipment surface uniformly. Additionally, if the contaminant or residue is of large enough particle size, it may not be uniformly dispersed in the placebo. Finally, the analytical power of the assay may be greatly reduced by dilution of the contaminant.

9.6   It is important to use visual inspection in addition to analytical methodology to ensure the process is acceptable.

Detergents:

9.7   When detergents are used in the cleaning process, their composition should be known to the user and their removal should be demonstrated. The manufacturer should ensure that they are notified by the detergent supplier of any changes in the formulation of the detergent.

9.8   Detergents should be easily removable, being used to facilitate the cleaning during the cleaning process. Acceptable limits should be defined for detergent residues after cleaning. The possibility of detergent

Cleaning Validation
GUI-0028

breakdown should also be considered when validating cleaning procedures.

Last Rinse:

9.9 Water for injection should be used as the last rinse for product-contact equipment to be utilized in the fabrication of sterile products.

9.10 Purified water is considered acceptable as the last rinse for product-contact equipment used in the fabrication of non-sterile products or sterile products for ophthalmic use.

Note: Because of the presence of varying levels of organic and inorganic residues as well as of chlorine, tap water should not be used in the last rinse of any cleaning procedure for product-contact equipment.

10.0 Establishment of Limits

10.1 The fabricator's rationale for selecting limits for product residues should be logical and based on the materials involved and their therapeutic dose. The limits should be practical, achievable, and verifiable.

10.2 In establishing product residual limits, it may not be adequate to focus only on the main reactant since by-products/chemical variations (active decomposition material) may be more difficult to remove. In addition to chemical testing, Thin Layer chromatography screening may be needed in certain circumstances.

10.3 The approach for setting limits can be:

1. product specific cleaning validation for all products;

2. grouping into product families and choosing a worst case product;

3. grouping by properties (e.g., solubility, potency, toxicity or formulation ingredients known to be difficult to clean);

4. setting limits on not allowing more than a certain fraction of carryover;

5. different safety factors for different dosage forms.

10.4 Carry-over of product residues should meet defined criteria for example the most stringent of the following criteria (i, ii, iii):

i. NMT 0.1% of the normal therapeutic dose of any product to appear in the maximum daily dose of the following product;

ii. NMT 10 ppm of any product to appear in another product;

iii. No quantity of residue to be visible on the equipment after cleaning procedures are performed. Spiking studies should determine the concentration at which most active ingredients are visible.

iv. For certain highly sensitizing or highly potent ingredients (such as penicillins, cephalosporins or potent steroids and cytotoxics), the limits should be below the limit of detection by best available analytical methods. In practice this may mean that dedicated plants are used for these products.

11.0 Change Control/Revalidation

11.1 A change control system is in place to ensure that all changes that might impact the cleaning process are assessed and documented. Significant changes should follow satisfactory review and authorization of the documented change proposal through the change control procedure. Minor changes or changes having no direct impact on final or in-process product quality should be handled through the documentation system. The review should include consideration of re-validation of the cleaning procedure.

11.2 Changes which should require evaluation and likely re-validation include but not limited to:

- Changes in the cleaning procedure;
- Changes in the raw material sources;
- Changes in the formulation and/or process of products;
- New products;
- Changes in the formulation of detergents;
- New detergents;
- Modifications of equipment.

11.3 The cleaning process should be reassessed at defined intervals, and re-validated as necessary. Manual methods should be reassessed at more frequent intervals than clean-in-place (CIP) systems.

12.0 References

FDA, Guide to Inspections of Validation of Cleaning Processes, 1993.

Pharmaceutical Inspection Convention, Recommendations on Validation Master Plan, Installation and Operational Qualification, Non-Sterile Process Validation and Cleaning Validation, 2004.

Cleaning Validation
GUI-0028

Validation Guidelines for Pharmaceutical Dosage Forms (GUI-0029)

Health Products and Food Branch Inspectorate

Supersedes: October 1, 2004

Date issued: August 7, 2009

Date of implementation: December 1, 2009

Validation Guidelines for Pharmaceutical Dosage Forms (GUI-0029)[24]

1.0 Scope

This Guidance document has been prepared to provide guidance to the pharmaceutical industry in dealing with validation issues for sterile and non-sterile dosage forms, biologicals, and radiopharmaceuticals. It should be noted that additional guidance related to sterile products and not contained in this document should also be considered. These requirements may be found in supplemental process validation guidelines available on the Inspectorate's website.

It is expected that importers and distributors of drug products have documented evidence that their vendors meet validation requirements.

2.0 Introduction

This document provides guidance on issues and topics related to systems, equipment qualification, product and process validation for sterile and non-sterile dosage forms. These topics reflect an area in pharmaceutical, biological, and, radiopharmaceuticals manufacture that is noted as being important by both the Inspectorate and the pharmaceutical industry. These guidelines have been prepared to provide guidance to inspectors, evaluators and the industry in dealing with issues related to validation. Utilization of this information should facilitate compliance with Division 2, Part C of the Regulations to the Food and Drugs Act.

It is not intended that the recommendations made in these guidelines become requirements under all circumstances. Information provided in the Interpretation section for limits to be applied in defined circumstances, as well as the number of batches to be utilized for validation studies are for guidance purposes only.

---

[24] Available on the Health Canada website at http://www.hc-sc.gc.ca/dhp-mps/compli-conform/gmp-bpf/validation/gu_29-eng.php

Inspectors, evaluators and the industry may consider other alternate means if proposed and documented with appropriate scientific justification.

3.0 Purpose

These guidelines outline the general principles that the Inspectorate considers to be acceptable elements of validation which may be used by fabricators, packagers/labellers for drug products. The Guidelines on Good Manufacturing Practices (GMP), Division 2, Part C of the Food and Drug Regulations require that:

- all critical production processes be validated

- validation studies are conducted in accordance with pre-defined protocols. Written reports summarizing recorded results and conclusions are prepared, evaluated, approved and maintained

- changes to production processes, operating parameters, equipment or materials that may affect product quality and/or the reproducibility of the process are also to be validated prior to implementation.

- These guidelines are not intended to specify how validation is to be conducted, but are indicators of what is expected to be covered by fabricators, packagers/labellers.

The elements of validation presented in these guidelines are not intended to be all-encompassing. The particular requirements of validation may vary according to factors such as the nature of drug products e.g. sterile, non-sterile, biologicals, and the complexity of the process. The concepts provided in these guidelines have general applicability and provide an acceptable framework for establishing a comprehensive approach to validation.

4.0 Definitions

Change Control

> A written procedure that describes the action to be taken if a change is proposed (a) to facilities, materials, equipment, and/or processes used in the fabrication, packaging, and testing of drugs, or (b) that may affect the operation of the quality or support system.

Cleaning Validation

> The documented act of demonstrating that cleaning procedures for the equipment used in fabricating/packaging will reduce to an acceptable level all residues (products/cleaning agents) and to demonstrate that routine cleaning and storage of equipment does not allow microbial proliferation.

Concurrent Validation

> A process where current production batches are used to monitor processing parameters. It gives assurance of the present batch being studied, and offers limited assurance regarding consistency of quality from batch to batch.

Critical Process Parameter

> A parameter which if not controlled will contribute to the variability of the end product.

Equipment Qualification

> Studies which establish with confidence that the process equipment and ancillary systems are capable of consistently operating within established limits and tolerances. The studies must include equipment specifications, installation qualification (IQ), and operational qualification (OQ) of all major equipment to be used in the manufacture of commercial scale batches. Equipment qualification should simulate actual production conditions, including "worst case"/ stressed conditions.

Installation Qualification

> The documented act of demonstrating that process equipment and ancillary systems are appropriately selected and correctly installed.

Major Equipment

> A piece of equipment which performs significant processing steps in the sequence of operations required for fabrication/packaging of drug products. Some examples of major equipment include tablet compression machines, mills, blenders, fluid bed dryers, heaters, drying ovens, tablet coaters, encapsulators, fermentors, centrifuges, etc.

Master Production Document

> A document that includes specifications for raw material, for packaging material and for packaged dosage form, master formula, sampling procedures, and critical processing related standard operating procedures (SOPs), whether or not these SOPs are specifically referenced in the master formula.

Measuring Devices

> A device used in monitoring or measuring process parameters.

Operational Qualification

> The documented action of demonstrating that process equipment and ancillary systems work correctly and operate consistently in accordance with established specifications.

Process Capability

> Studies conducted to identify the critical process parameters that yield a resultant quality, and their acceptable specification ranges, based on the established +/- 3 sigma deviations of the process, under stressed conditions but when free of any assignable causes.

Process Qualification

The phase of validation dealing with sampling and testing at various stages of the manufacturing process to ensure that product specifications are met.

Process Re-validation

Required when there is a change in any of the critical process parameters, formulation, primary packaging components, raw material fabricators, major equipment or premises. Failure to meet product and process specifications in sequential batches would also require process re-validation.

Process Validation

Establishing documented evidence with a high degree of assurance, that a specific process will consistently produce a product meeting its predetermined specifications and quality characteristics. Process validation may take the form of prospective, concurrent or retrospective validation and process qualification or re-validation.

Prospective Validation

Conducted prior to the distribution of either a new product or a product made under a modified production process, where the modifications are significant and may affect the product's characteristics. It is a pre-planned scientific approach and includes the initial stages of formulation development, process development, setting of process specifications, developing in-process tests, sampling plans, designing of batch records, defining raw material specifications, completion of pilot runs, transfer of technology from scale-up batches to commercial size batches, listing major process equipment and environmental controls.

Retrospective Validation

Conducted for a product already being marketed, and is based on extensive data accumulated over several lots and over time. Retrospective Validation may be used for older products which were not validated by the fabricator at the time that they were first marketed, and which are now to be validated to conform to the requirements of Division 2, Part C of the Regulations to the Food and Drugs Act.

Validation

The documented act of demonstrating that any procedure, process, and activity will consistently lead to the expected results. Includes the qualification of systems and equipment.

Validation Master Plan

An approved written plan of objectives and actions stating how and when a company will achieve compliance with the GMP requirements regarding validation.

Validation Protocol

A written plan of actions stating how process validation will be conducted; it will specify who will conduct the various tasks and define testing parameters; sampling plans, testing methods and specifications; will specify product characteristics, and equipment to be used. It must specify the minimum number of batches to be used for validation studies; it must specify the acceptance criteria and who will sign/approve/ disapprove the conclusions derived from such a scientific study.

Validation Team

A multi-disciplinary team of personnel primarily responsible for conducting and/or supervising validation studies. Such studies may be conducted by person(s) qualified by training and experience in a relevant discipline.

Worst Case Condition

The highest and /or lowest value of a given parameter actually evaluated in the validation exercise.

5.0 Phases of Validation

The activities relating to validation studies may be classified into three phases:

Phase 1: Pre-validation phase or the qualification phase, which covers all activities relating to product research and development, formulation, pilot batch studies, scale-up studies, transfer of technology to commercial scale batches, establishing stability conditions, storage and handling of n-process and finished dosage forms, equipment qualification, installation qualification, master production documents, operational qualification, process capability.

Phase 2: Process validation phase (process qualification phase) designed to verify that all established limits of the critical process parameters are valid and that satisfactory products can be produced even under the "worst case" conditions.

Phase 3: Validation maintenance phase requiring frequent review of all process related documents, including validation audit reports to assure that there have been no changes, deviations, failures, modifications to the production process, and that all SOPs have been followed, including change control procedures.

At this stage the validation team also assures that there have been no changes/ deviations that should have resulted in requalification and revalidation.

Validation Guidelines
GUI-0029

6.0 Interpretation

General Concepts:

Quality, safety and effectiveness must be built into the product. This requires careful attention to a number of factors such as the selection of quality materials/components, product and process design, control of processes, in-process control, and end-product testing.

Due to the complexity of the drug products, routine end-product testing alone is not sufficient due to several reasons. Furthermore, quality cannot be tested into the finished drug product but rather be built in the manufacturing processes and these processes should be controlled in order that the finished product meets all quality specifications. A careful design and validation of systems and process controls can establish a high degree of confidence that all lots or batches produced will meet their intended specifications.

Validation protocol:

A written plan stating how validation will be conducted, including test parameters, product characteristics, production and packaging equipment, and decision points on what constitutes acceptable test results. This document should give details of critical steps of the manufacturing process that should be measured, the allowable range of variability and the manner in which the system will be tested.

The validation protocol provides a synopsis of what is hoped to be accomplished. The protocol should list the selected process and control parameters, state the number of batches to be included in the study, and specify how the data, once assembled, will be treated for relevance. The date of approval by the validation team should also be noted.

In the case where a protocol is altered or modified after its approval, appropriate reasoning for such a change must be documented.

The validation protocol should be numbered, signed and dated, and should contain as a minimum the following information:

- objectives, scope of coverage of the validation study
- validation team membership, their qualifications and responsibilities
- type of validation: prospective, concurrent, retrospective, re-validation
- number and selection of batches to be on the validation study
- a list of all equipment to be used; their normal and worst case operating parameters
- outcome of IQ, OQ for critical equipment
- requirements for calibration of all measuring devices
- critical process parameters and their respective tolerances
- description of the processing steps: copy of the master documents for the product
- sampling points, stages of sampling, methods of sampling, sampling plans

- statistical tools to be used in the analysis of data

- training requirements for the processing operators

- validated test methods to be used in in-process testing and for the finished product

- specifications for raw and packaging materials and test methods

- forms and charts to be used for documenting results

- format for presentation of results, documenting conclusions and for approval of study results.

Validation Master Plan:

A validation master plan is a document that summarises the company's overall philosophy, intentions and approaches to be used for establishing performance adequacy. The validation master plan should be agreed upon by management.

Validation in general requires meticulous preparation and careful planning of the various steps n the process. In addition, all work should be carried out in a structured way according to formally authorised standard operating procedures. All observations must be documented and where possible must be recorded as actual numerical results.

The validation master plan should provide an overview of the entire validation operation, its organizational structure, its content and planning. The main elements of it being the list/inventory of the items to be validated and the planning schedule. All validation activities relating to critical technical operations, relevant to product and process controls within a firm should be included in the validation master plan. It should comprise all prospective, concurrent and retrospective validations as well as re-validation.

The validation master plan should be a summary document and should therefore be brief, concise and clear. It should not repeat information documented elsewhere but should refer to existing documents such as policy documents, SOP's and validation protocols and reports.

The format and content should include:

- introduction: validation policy, scope, location and schedule

- organizational structure: personnel responsibilities

- plant/ process /product description: rational for inclusions or exclusions and extent of validation

- specific process considerations that are critical and those requiring extra attention

- list of products/ processes/ systems to be validated, summarised in a matrix format, validation approach

- re-validation activities, actual status and future planning

- key acceptance criteria

- documentation format

- reference to the required SOP's

- time plans of each validation project and sub-project.

Validation Guidelines GUI-0029

Installation and Operational Qualification:

The detail and scope of a qualification exercise is in many respects related to the complexity of the equipment involved and the critical nature of that equipment with respect to the quality of the final product. Installation and operational qualification exercises assure through appropriate performance tests and related documentation that equipment, ancillary systems and sub-systems have been commissioned correctly. The end results are that all future operations will be reliable and within prescribed operating limits.

The basic principles are:

- equipment be correctly installed in accordance with an installation plan

- requirements for calibration, maintenance and cleaning be covered in approved SOP's

- tests be conducted to assure that equipment is operating correctly, under normal and "worst case" conditions

- operator training requirements pertaining to new equipment be conducted and documented.

At various stages in a validation exercise there is need for protocols, documentation, procedures, equipment, specifications and acceptance criteria for test results. All these need to be reviewed, checked and authorised. It would be expected that representatives from the appropriate professional disciplines, e.g. engineering, research and development, manufacturing, quality control and quality assurance be actively involved in these undertakings with the final authorisation given by a validation team or the quality assurance representative.

Installation Qualification (IQ):

IQ is the method of establishing with confidence that all major processing, packaging equipment and ancillary systems are in conformance with installation specifications, equipment manuals, schematics and engineering drawings. This stage of validation includes examination of equipment design, determination of calibration, maintenance and adjustment requirements.

For complicated or large pieces of equipment, a pharmaceutical manufacturer may elect to undertake a pre-delivery check of the equipment at the supplier's assembly facility. This pre-delivery check cannot substitute for the installation qualification. However, it is acknowledged that the checks conducted and documented at this stage may duplicate a number of the checks conducted at the IQ stage, thus leading to a reduction in the scope of the IQ checks.

All equipment, gauges and services should be adequately identified and should be given a serial number or other reference number. This number should appear in the reports for the equipment validation studies conducted.

Installation qualification requires a formal and systematic check of all installed equipment against the equipment supplier's specifications and additional criteria identified by the user as part of the purchase specifications. These checks, tests and challenges should be repeated a significant number of times to assure reliable and meaningful results.

At the IQ stage the company should document preventive maintenance requirements for installed equipment. The preventive maintenance schedule should be incorporated into the routine maintenance schedule.

Note: There will be cases where installation of the equipment had not been qualified at the time of installation, and the engineering drawings and manuals for the equipment are no longer available at the manufacturing site. However, the equipment in place operates for a lengthy period of time without any problem or modifications of its design since it was first installed. In such situations, the Inspectorate considers that it may be appropriate for those specific cases to verify a limited number of the most critical parameters demonstrating that the equipment had been adequately installed. Thereafter, the company could pass directly to the operational qualification (OQ) stage if there is sufficient documented evidence that these units have always been well maintained and calibrated according to an adequate pre-established schedule.

Operational Qualification (OQ):

The conduct of an operational qualification should follow an authorised protocol. The critical operating parameters for the equipment and systems should be identified at the OQ stage. The plans for the OQ should identify the studies to be undertaken on the critical variables, the sequence of those studies and the measuring equipment to be used and the acceptance criteria to be met.

Studies on the critical variables should include a condition or a set of conditions encompassing upper and lower processing and operating limits referred to as "worst-case" conditions. The completion of a successful OQ should allow the finalisation of operating procedures and operator instructions documentation for the equipment. This information should be used as the basis for training of operators in the requirements for satisfactory operation of the equipment.

The completion of satisfactory IQ and OQ exercises should permit a formal "release" of the equipment for the next stage in the process validation exercise as long as calibration, cleaning, preventive maintenance and operator training requirements have been finalised and documented.

Re-Qualification:

Modifications to, or relocation of equipment should follow satisfactory review and authorization of the documented change proposal through the change control procedure. This formal review should include consideration of re-qualification of the equipment. Minor changes or changes having no direct impact on final or in-process product quality should be handled through the documentation system of the preventative maintenance program.

Process Validation:

It would normally be expected that process validation be completed prior to the distribution of a finished product that is intended for sale (prospective validation). Where this is not possible, it may be necessary to validate processes during routine production (concurrent validation). Processes which have been in use for some time without any significant changes may also be validated according to an approved protocol (retrospective validation).

a) Prospective Validation:

In prospective validation, the validation protocol is executed before the process is put into commercial use During the product development phase the production process should be broken down into individual steps. Each step should be evaluated on the basis of experience or theoretical considerations to determine the critical parameters that may affect the quality of the finished product. A series of experiments should be designed to determine the criticality of these factors. Each experiment should be planned and documented fully in an authorised protocol.

All equipment, production environment and the analytical testing methods to be used should have been fully validated. Master batch documents can be prepared only after the critical parameters of the process have been identified and machine settings, component specifications and environmental conditions have been determined.

Using this defined process a series of batches should be produced. In theory, the number of process runs carried out and observations made should be sufficient to allow the normal extent of variation and trends to be established to provide sufficient data for evaluation. It is generally considered acceptable that three consecutive batches/runs within the finally agreed parameters, giving product of the desired quality would constitute a proper validation of the process. In practice, it may take some considerable time to accumulate these data.

Some considerations should be exercised when selecting the process validation strategy. Amongst these should be the use of different lots of active raw materials and major excipients, batches produced on different shifts, the use of different equipment and facilities dedicated for commercial production, operating range of the critical processes, and a thorough analysis of the process data in case of requalification and revalidation.

During the processing of the validation batches, extensive sampling and testing should be performed on the product at various stages, and should be documented comprehensively. Detailed testing should also be done on the final product in its package.

Upon completion of the review, recommendations should be made on the extent of monitoring and the in-process controls necessary for routine production. These should be incorporated into the batch manufacturing and packaging record or into appropriate standard operating procedures. Limits, frequencies and actions to be taken in the event of the limits being exceeded should be specified.

Matrix or "Family" approaches to prospective process validation:

It may be possible and acceptable in particular circumstances for a manufacturer that uses the same process for several related products to develop a scientifically sound validation plan for that process rather than different plans for each product manufactured by that process.

The matrix approach generally means a plan to conduct process validation on different strengths of the same product. However, discrete manufacturing steps such as compression, and coating that involve different tools, equipment, and process conditions for the different dosage strengths can not be generally validated using the matrix approach. It should be recognized that the matrix approach has limitations when there are concerns with respect to physical characteristics such as flow properties, particle size distribution, homogeneity.

The "family" approach means a plan to conduct process validation on different products manufactured with the same processes using the same equipment.

The validation process using these approaches must include batches of different strengths or products which should be selected to represent the worst case conditions or scenarios to demonstrate that the process is consistent for all strengths or products involved.

b) Concurrent Validation:

Unconditional use of this approach is not encouraged by the Inspectorate and is not acceptable as being the "norm". In using this approach there is always the risk of having to modify process parameters or specifications over a period of time. This situation often leads to questions regarding disposition of the batches that had already been released for sale, subsequently known to have undesired quality characteristics.

Concurrent validation may be the practical approach under certain circumstances. Examples of these may be:

- when a previously validated process is being transferred to a third party contract manufacturer or to another manufacturing site
- where the product is a different strength of a previously validated product with the same ratio of active / inactive ingredients
- when the number of lots evaluated under the retrospective validation were not sufficient to obtain a high degree of assurance demonstrating that the process is fully under control
- when the number of batches produced are limited (e.g. orphan drugs).

It is important in these cases however, that the systems and equipment to be used have been fully validated previously. The justification for conducting concurrent validation must be documented and the protocol must be approved by the validation team. A report should be prepared and approved prior to the sale of each batch and a final report should be prepared and approved after the completion of all concurrent batches. It is generally considered acceptable that a minimum of three consecutive batches within the finally agreed parameters, giving the product the desired quality would constitute a proper validation of the process.

c) Retrospective Validation:

In many establishments, processes that are stable and in routine use have not undergone a formally documented validation process. Historical data may be utilized to provide necessary documentary evidence that the processes are validated.

The steps involved in this type of validation still require the preparation of a protocol, the reporting of the results of the data review, leading to a conclusion and recommendation.

Retrospective validation is only acceptable for well established detailed processes that include operational limits for each critical step of the process and will be inappropriate where there have been recent changes in the formulation of the product, operating procedures, equipment and facility.

The source of data for retrospective validation should include amongst others, batch documents, process control charts, annual product quality review reports, maintenance log books, process capability studies, finished product test results, including trend analyses, and stability results.

For the purpose of retrospective validation studies, it is considered acceptable that data from a minimum of ten consecutive batches produced be utilized. When less than ten batches are available, it is considered that the data are not sufficient to demonstrate retrospectively that the process is fully under control. In such cases the study should be supplemented with data generated with concurrent or prospective validation.

Some of the essential elements for retrospective validation are:

- Batches manufactured for a defined period (minimum of 10 last consecutive batches)
- Number of lots released per year
- Batch size/strength/manufacturer/year/period
- Master manufacturing/packaging documents
- Current specifications for active materials/finished products
- List of process deviations, corrective actions and changes to manufacturing documents
- Data for stability testing for several batches
- Trend analyses including those for quality related complaints

Process Re-Validation:

Re-validation provides the evidence that changes in a process and /or the process environment that are introduced do not adversely affect process characteristics and product quality. Documentation requirements will be the same as for the initial validation of the process.

Periodic review and trend analysis should be carried out at scheduled intervals. Re-validation becomes necessary in certain situations. The following are examples of some of the planned or unplanned changes that may require re-validation:

- Changes in raw materials (physical properties such as density, viscosity, particle size distribution, and moisture, etc., that may affect the process or product).
- Changes in the source of active raw material manufacturer
- Changes in packaging material (primary container/closure system).
- Changes in the process (e.g., mixing time, drying temperatures and batch size)
- Changes in the equipment (e.g. addition of automatic detection system). Changes of equipment which involve the replacement of equipment on a "like for like" basis would not normally require a re-validation except that this new equipment must be qualified.
- Changes in the plant/facility.
- Variations revealed by trend analysis (e.g. process drifts)

A decision not to perform re-validation studies must be fully justified and documented.

Change Control:

Written procedures should be in place to describe the actions to be taken if a change is proposed to a product component, process equipment, process environment, processing site, method of production or testing or any other change that may affect product quality or support system operations.

All changes must be formally requested, documented and accepted by the validation team. The likely impact / risk of the change on the product must be assessed and the need for the extent of re-validation should be determined.

Commitment of the company to control all changes to premises, supporting utilities, systems, materials, equipment and processes used in the fabrication/packaging of pharmaceutical dosage forms is essential to ensure a continued validation status of the systems concerned.

The change control system should ensure that all notified or requested changes are satisfactorily investigated, documented and authorised. Products made by processes subjected to changes should not be released for sale without full awareness and consideration of the change by the validation team. The team should decide if a re-validation must be conducted prior to implementing the proposed change.

7.0 References

1. Guidelines on General Principles of Process Validation, CDER, US-FDA 1987

2. Pharmaceutical Process Validation; 2nd edition, Editors: I. R. Berry and R.A. Nash, 1993

3. Recommendations on Validation Master Plan, Installation and Operational Qualification, Non-Sterile Process Validation, Cleaning Validation, PIC/S September, 2007.

Validation Guidelines
GUI-0029

Guidance Document on the Commercial Importation and Exportation of Drugs in Dosage Forms Under the Food and Drugs Act (GUIDE-0057)

Health Products and Food Branch Inspectorate

Supersedes: July 1st, 2003

Date issued: January 31, 2008

Date of implementation: January 31, 2008

GUIDE-0057
Guidance Document on the Commercial Importation and Exportation of Drugs in Dosage Forms Under the Food and Drugs Act[25]

1.0 Purpose

Disclaimer

This document does not constitute part of the Food and Drugs Act (Act) or the Food and Drugs Regulations (Regulations) and in the event of any inconsistency or conflict between that Act or Regulations and this document, the Act or the Regulations take precedence. This document is an administrative document that is intended to facilitate compliance by the regulated party with the Act, the Regulations and the applicable administrative policies. This document is not intended to provide legal advice regarding the interpretation of the Act or Regulations. If a regulated party has questions about their legal obligations or responsibilities under the Act or Regulations, they should seek the advice of legal counsel.

The purpose of this guidance is to explain the current responsibilities of establishments which import into or export drug products out of Canada under the Food and Drugs Act (FDA) or (the Act), including establishments which fabricate and package drugs for export and choose to avail themselves of the provisions of Section 37 of the said Act.

---

[25] Available on the Health Canada website at http://www.hc-sc.gc.ca/dhp-mps/compli-conform/gmp-bpf/docs/fda-lad-eng.php

Guidance Document on the Commercial Importation and Exportation of Drugs in Dosage Forms
Under the Food and Drugs Act
(GUIDE-0057)

2.0 Background

Pursuant to the Act and its Regulations (FDR),drugs imported into or fabricated in Canada for commercial use must comply with the Act and the FDR, which includes Good Manufacturing Practices (GMP) and Establishment Licence (EL) requirements. Section A.01.040 of the FDR specifies that: ".no person shall import into Canada for sale a food or drug the sale of which in Canada would constitute a violation of the Act or these Regulations".

Section 37 exempts certain drugs from the application of the FDA:

> 37. (1) "This Act does not apply to any packaged food, drug, cosmetic or device, not manufactured for consumption in Canada and not sold for consumption in Canada, if the package is marked in distinct overprinting with the word "Export" or "Exportation" and a certificate that the package and its contents do not contravene any known requirement of the law of the country to which it is or is about to be consigned has been issued in respect of the package and its contents in prescribed form and manner.

Thus, pursuant to Section 37, an establishment in Canada that fabricates a drug in Canada for export is not subject to the requirements of the Act in relation to that product, provided the product:

i.   has been manufactured in Canada solely for export;

ii. complies with the labelling requirements of Section 37; and

iii. is the subject of an Export Certificate, in the form prescribed in Appendix III of the FDR, that has been attested to under oath by the exporter of the drug.

This exemption applies only to drugs fabricated in Canada.

If a Canadian fabricator chooses to invoke Section 37 for a drug, the Health Products and Food Branch (HPFB) Inspectorate will not verify GMP compliance for the activities related to that specific drug, and therefore the HPFB Inspectorate cannot attest to the quality of the fabricator's products.

On an annual basis, when renewing establishment licences, the HPFB Inspectorate asks Canadian establishments to supply a list of drugs for which the establishments intend to invoke the exemption in Section 37. This list is provided to foreign regulatory authorities requesting a Certificate of Compliance from the HPFB Inspectorate.

3.0 Scope

This guidance document applies to drugs as defined in C.01A.001(2) that are:

*   imported into Canada for commercial purposes;

*   fabricated in Canada and sold for consumption outside of Canada when the package is clearly marked "Export" or "Exportation" and an Export Certificate has been issued in the prescribed form and manner, stating that the package and its contents do not contravene any known requirements of the law of the country to which it is or is about to be consigned.

This guidance document does not apply to:

- importation of drugs for personal use;

- medical devices;

- natural health products;

- drugs for clinical trials.

Further guidance is available in the document entitled "Conditions for Provision of Packaging/Labelling Services for Drugs under Foreign Ownership (GUI-0067)".

4.0 Definitions

Certificate Of A Pharmaceutical Product (CPP) (Certificat de produit pharmaceutique)

A certificate issued by the Inspectorate establishing the regulatory status of the pharmaceutical, biological or radiopharmaceutical product listed and the GMP status of the applicant. This certificate is in the format recommended by the World Health Organization (WHO).

Drug (drogue)

"Any substance or mixture of substances manufactured, sold, or represented for use in (a) the diagnosis, treatment, mitigation, or prevention of a disease, a disorder, an abnormal physical state, or the symptoms thereof, in humans or animals, (b) restoring, correcting, or modifying organic functions in humans or animals, or (c) "disinfection" in premises in which food is manufactured, prepared, or kept." (Section 2 of the Food and Drugs Act)

In Division 1A and Division 2 of the Food and Drug Regulations, "drug" means a drug in dosage form, or a drug that is a bulk process intermediate that can be used in the preparation of a drug listed in Schedule C to the Act or in Schedule D to the Act that is of biological origin. It does not include a dilute drug premix, a medicated feed as defined in Section 2 of the Feeds Regulations, 1983, a drug that is used only for the purposes of an experimental study in accordance with a certificate issued under Section C.08.015 or a drug listed in Schedule H to the Act. (C.01A.001(2))

Export Certificate Under Section 37 of the Food And Drugs Act (Certificat d'exportation en vertu de l'article 37 de la Loi sur les aliments et drogues)

A certificate signed by the fabricator and a Commissioner for Taking Oaths to attest that the drug for which the certificate is prepared is not manufactured or sold for consumption in Canada and that its package and the contents do not contravene any known requirement of the law of the country to which it is or is about to be consigned.

Certificate Of Compliance (CoC) (Certificat de conformité (CC))

A certificate issued by a Regulatory Authority attesting to the GMP compliance of a recognized building in that country. In Canada, the CoC is issued by the HPFB Inspectorate.

Import and Export
GUI-0057

Guidance Document on the Commercial Importation and Exportation of Drugs in Dosage Forms
Under the Food and Drugs Act
(GUIDE-0057)

Mutual Recognition Agreement (MRA) (accord de reconnaissance mutuelle (ARM))

"An international agreement that provides for the mutual recognition of compliance certification for Good Manufacturing Practices for drugs." (C.01A.001)

Package (emballage)

In this guidance document, package refers to the packaging boxes used for storage and shipping.

Regulatory Authority (autorité réglementaire)

A government agency or other entity in an MRA country that has a legal right to control the use or sale of drugs within that country and that may take enforcement action to ensure that drugs marketed within its jurisdiction comply with legal requirements. (C.01A.001)

5.0 Statement

Considering that Section 37 of the FDA applies only to drugs fabricated in Canada, the HPFB Inspectorate's position is as follows:

1. All drugs fabricated in Canada must meet all applicable requirements of the Act and the FDR, including labelling and Drug Identification Number (DIN) requirements, EL requirements and GMP requirements.

2. All drugs commercially imported into Canada must meet all applicable requirements of the Act and the FDR, including labelling and Drug Identification Number (DIN) requirements, EL requirements and GMP requirements.

3. Drugs with respect to which the fabricator in Canada has not notified the HPFB Inspectorate of its intention to invoke Section 37 are subject to compliance and enforcement activities against the requirements of the Act and Regulations, even those destined for export.

4. Drugs with respect to which the fabricator in Canada has notified the HPFB Inspectorate of its intention to invoke Section 37 but which are not properly packaged in accordance with Section 37 (i.e., marked "Export" or "Exportation" on the package), are subject to inspection under Division 2 of the FDR. Lots of in-process drugs, that are for export only and for which the packaging is not yet complete should be clearly identified as such during the fabrication process, by written indication on the manufacturing order, packaging order, and on the bulk containers.

5. Drugs with respect to which the fabricator in Canada has notified the HPFB Inspectorate of its intention to invoke Section 37 but in respect of which the Export Certificate prescribed in Section 37 is not available are subject to inspection under Division 2 of the FDR.

6. Exemptions under Section 37 do not apply to drugs imported into Canada for commercial purposes, but are limited to drugs fabricated in Canada.

7. The HPFB Inspectorate will not issue a Certificate of a Pharmaceutical Product (CPP) for a drug exempted under Section 37, or with respect to which the firm notified the HPFB Inspectorate of its intention to invoke Section 37.

8. Evidence of GMP compliance will be required if a firm decides to rescind their request for exemption with respect to Section 37.

6.0 Responsibilities

The HPFB Inspectorate is responsible for applying this guidance.

It is the establishment's responsibility to notify the HPFB Inspectorate of its intention to invoke and to rescind a request for exemption with respect to Section 37 of the Act with respect to drugs fabricated for export.

If an establishment invokes Section 37, it is its responsibility to ensure that the package be marked in distinct overprinting with the word "Export" or "Exportation" and to have in its possession a completed Export Certificate stating that the package and its contents do not contravene any known requirement of the law of the country to which it is or is about to be consigned.

7.0 Procedures

The HPFB Inspectorate will verify that the drugs for which Section 37 has been invoked are fabricated in Canada and packaged in accordance with the requirements of Section 37, and that the Export Certificate prescribed in Appendix III of the FDR is available.

Where non-conformity with the Act and/or with the FDR is identified, the firm will have the opportunity to correct deficiencies. The HPFB Inspectorate will consider actions where necessary in accordance with its Compliance and Enforcement Policy (POL-0001).

Import and Export
GUI-0057

Risk Classification of Post-Market Reporting Compliance Observations (GUI-0063)

Health Products and Food Branch Inspectorate

Supersedes: June 2004

Date issued: October 21, 2005

Date of implementation: November 21, 2005

Risk Classification of Post-Market Reporting Compliance Observations (GUI-0063)[26]

1.0 Purpose

To classify the observations noted during Post-Market Reporting Compliance drug inspections to their risk.

To ensure uniformity among the inspectors of the Health Products and Food Branch Inspectorate (Inspectorate) in the attribution of the rating following Post-Market Reporting Compliance drug inspections.

To inform the industry of the situations that the Inspectorate considers unacceptable and that will generate a NC rating (defined below) following a Post-Market Reporting Compliance drug inspection.

2.0 Background

During Post-Market Reporting Compliance drug inspections, deviations from the Food and Drug Regulations are noted by the inspector and are then recorded as observations in the Inspection Exit Notice. With the aid of this guide, a judgement is made of the observations and each observation is risk rated. Subsequently, an overall compliance rating is attributed to the inspected site. The possible compliance ratings are defined below:

C - No objectionable conditions or practices were observed with regards to regulatory requirements pertaining to reporting of adverse drug reactions and/or reporting of unusual failure in efficacy of new drugs

NC - Objectionable conditions or practices were observed with regards to regulatory requirements pertaining to reporting of adverse drug reactions and/or reporting of unusual failure in efficacy of new drugs

---

[26] Available on the Health Canada website at http://www.hc-sc.gc.ca/dhp-mps/compli-conform/gmp-bpf/docs/gui-0063_pmrc-cdac_class_risk-eng.php

It is recognized that the evaluation of the conformity of manufacturers with their regulatory responsibilities should commensurate with the risk involved taking into account the nature and extent of the deviation. Nonetheless, generally, situations involving fraud, misrepresentation or falsification of drug safety data will generate a NC rating.

The assignment of a NC rating may have serious consequences for an establishment. These consequences may include the implementation of immediate corrective measures. Therefore, these situations of non-conformity have to be well defined, unambiguous and directly supported by the applicable Regulations.

The appendices attached to the present document describe the observations related to each category of risk. Please note that the list of observations in each appendix is not exhaustive and that additional observations may be added where appropriate.

3.0 Scope

The Food and Drug Regulations set forth regulatory requirements for manufacturers to report adverse drug reactions and to report unusual failure in efficacy of new drugs to Health Canada. This guide covers the following drugs which are subject to the above requirements of the Food and Drug Regulations: pharmaceutical and biological drugs. Blood products and therapeutic and diagnostic vaccines are included in the scope of this guide. However, radiopharmaceuticals, veterinary drugs, natural health products and preventative vaccines, including immunization schedule vaccines, influenza vaccines and vaccines for travel, whole blood and blood components are excluded. In addition, this guide does not apply to adverse reaction reports resulting from drugs studied in a clinical trial where a Clinical Trial Application has been submitted to Health Canada; this includes applications to conduct clinical trials involving marketed products where the proposed use of the product is outside the parameters of the approved Notice of Compliance (NOC) or Drug Identification Number (DIN) application.

4.0 Definitions

The following definitions are provided to complement those already available under the glossary of terms in the current edition of the Guidelines for Reporting Adverse Drug Reactions to Marketed Drugs, Guidelines for the Canadian Pharmaceutical Industry on Reporting Adverse Reactions to Marketed Drugs (Vaccines Excluded), revised July 2001 and the Inspection Strategy for Post-Market Surveillance or other related documents referenced in these documents.

Annual Summary Report[27]:

An annual summary report consists of three sections: a summary line listing of ADRs received during the review period, a critical analysis of the ADR reports, and recommended actions. These sections are to be prepared according to the guideline. The summary line listing of the report must include at minimum the following types of reactions:

---

[27] For additional details, please refer to the Therapeutic Products Directorate Guidelines for Reporting Adverse Drug Reactions to Marketed Drugs. Guidelines for the Canadian Pharmaceutical Industry on Reporting Adverse Reactions to Marketed Drugs (Vaccines Excluded), revised July 2001.

- all (domestic and foreign) individual case reports sent spontaneously to the manufacturer and all published reports of ADRs known to the manufacturer that are serious, irrespective of expectedness, or non-serious unexpected,

- all domestic lack of efficacy reports for new drugs, and

- individual case reports from studies (published and unpublished) of reactions that are considered to be attributable to the drug by either the manufacturer or the investigator, and that are serious unexpected.

Annual summary reports may be submitted in the form of a Periodic Safety Update Report (PSUR) as defined by ICH Guideline E2C.

Observation:

A deviation or deficiency to the Food and Drug Regulations pertaining to reporting of adverse drug reactions and unusual failure in efficacy of new drugs noted by an inspector during the inspection of a drug establishment that is confirmed in writing to the company in the Exit Notice. The observations are classified as "Critical", "Major" and "Other" and are assigned a risk classification, ranging from Risk 1 (critical) to Risk 2 (major) to Risk 3 (other).

Critical observation:

Observation of a critical deviation from the Food and Drug Regulations that describes a situation that may produce an immediate or latent health risk as a result of the absence of drug safety information. Observations that involve fraud, misrepresentation or falsification under the Food and Drugs Act and Regulations of data are also considered critical.

Appendix 1 lists observations that the Inspectorate considers critical. These observations will be assigned a Risk 1.

Major observation:

Observation of a major deviation from the Food and Drug Regulations that describes a situation of incomplete drug safety information that may result in a latent health risk.

Appendix 2 lists observations that are considered major and which will be assigned a Risk 2. Certain Risk 2 observations may be upgraded to Risk 1, for example, if they are related to a new drug. These are indicated with an arrow (↑).

Other observation:

Observation that describes a deviation from the Food and Drug Regulations that is neither critical or major.

Appendix 3 lists "Other" observations that will be assigned a Risk 3. Certain Risk 3 observations may be upgraded to Risk 2. These are indicated with an arrow (↑).

Manufacturer: "manufacturer" or "distributor" means a person, including an association or partnership, who under their own name, or under a trade, design or word mark, trade name or other name, word or mark controlled by them, sells a food or drug (fabricant or distributeur) (A.01.010)

New Drug: "(a) a drug that contains or consists of a substance, whether as an active or inactive ingredient, carrier, coating, excipient, menstruum or other component, that has not been sold as a drug in Canada for sufficient time and in sufficient quantity to establish in Canada the safety and effectiveness of that substance for use as a drug..." (drogue nouvelle) (C.08.001)

. The Therapeutic Products Directorate, HPFB policy issue, New Drug - Sufficient Time (August 21, 1991), interprets the phrase "sufficient time" as a minimum of seven years from the initial date of marketing in Canada.

Acronyms:

ADR: Adverse Drug Reaction

CECD: Compliance and Enforcement Coordination Division

CTA: Clinical Trial Application

EL: Establishment License

GMP: Good Manufacturing Practices

HPFB: Health Products and Food Branch

IRS: Inspection Reporting System

MHPD: Marketed Health Products Directorate, Health Products and Food Branch

5.0 Guide

5.1 Assignment of the risk to an observation

Whereas it is recognized that it is impossible to encompass every situation that may generate a risk, the following principles should be considered:

- The risk assigned will be in relation to the nature of the deviation as well as the number of occurrences.

- Where a Risk 2 observation is re-evaluated as a Risk 1 (Risk 2 observation with an arrow), this situation is immediately brought to the attention of the company's officials; proper explanation will be provided to the establishment and this explanation should be captured in the "Inspector's Comments" field of the "Inspection Summary" in the Inspection Reporting System (IRS).

5.2 Assignment of the inspection rating

5.2.1 Assignment of a C rating:

A C rating is assigned in all situations where only Risk 3 observations are noted. Furthermore, a C rating is generally assigned when Risk 2 observations are noted during an inspection. However, a NC rating may be assigned in the following situations:

- When numerous Risk 2 observations are noted during an inspection indicating that the company does not sufficiently control its Post-Market Reporting Compliance activities.

- Repetition of many Risk 2 observations noted during previous inspections indicating that the company did not:
  - implement the corrective actions submitted following the previous inspection or
  - did not put in place adequate preventive actions in a timely manner to avoid recurrence of such deviation

5.2.2 Assignment of a NC rating:

Generally, a NC rating is assigned when at least one Risk 1 observation is noted during an inspection.

Such a situation is immediately brought to the attention of the company's officials. The Inspectorate management is notified in a timely manner.

Where in the opinion of the inspector the resulting products present a significant health hazard, the company is expected to address the issue immediately. Appropriate compliance and enforcement actions may be initiated according to the HPFB Compliance and Enforcement Policy (POL-0001).

5.3 Additional guidance

When a NC rating is assigned, the inspector will issue a draft Inspection Exit Notice during the exit meeting. The final Exit Notice will be issued only after a review of the draft, in accordance with the usual practices of the Inspectorate.

When observations leading to a NC rating are made, the Inspection Exit Notice could be issued with a C rating if, during the inspection:

- the establishment immediately implements all necessary actions to resolve the cause(s) of the observation(s) leading to the NC rating and,
- sufficient assurance can be provided to prevent a recurrence.

In such instances, the risk assigned to the observation will remain the same.

If the management of the company wishes to dispute the results of the inspection report, the "Dispute resolution and appeals" mechanism described in the Good Manufacturing Practices (GMP) and Establishment Licensing (EL) Enforcement Policy POL-0004 should be followed.

6.0 References

1. Health Products and Food Branch Inspectorate, Inspection Strategy for Post-Market Surveillance

2. Health Canada, Guidelines for Reporting Adverse Reactions to Marketed Drugs, Guidelines for the Canadian Pharmaceutical Industry on Reporting Adverse Reactions to Marketed Drugs (Vaccines Excluded), Revised July 2001

3. Health Canada, Health Products and Food Branch Inspectorate, Good Manufacturing Practices (GMP) and Establishment Licensing (EL) Enforcement Directive, No. POL-0004

4. Health Products and Food Branch, Therapeutic Products Directorate, New Drug - Sufficient Time, August 21, 1991

Post-Market Reporting
GUI-0063

5. Health Products and Food Branch Compliance and Enforcement Policy, No. POL-0001

6. Health Products and Food Branch, Guidance for Clinical Trial Sponsors: Clinical Trial Applications, June 25, 2003

7. International Harmonised Tripartite Guideline, Clinical Safety Data Management: Periodic Safety Update Reports for Marketed Drugs E2C, November 6, 1996

Appendix 1

Risk 1 (Critical) Observations

Adverse Drug Reaction Reporting C.01.016

- None of the domestic serious unexpected adverse drug reactions including those that occurred during studies not under a CTA (i.e. Phase IV clinical trials) received are reported to Health Canada by the manufacturer

- None of the foreign serious unexpected adverse drug reactions including those that occurred during studies not under a CTA (i.e. Phase IV clinical trials) received are reported to Health Canada by the manufacturer

Adverse Drug Reaction Reporting C.01.017

- No records of serious adverse drug reaction reports were accessible within 72 hours from the manufacturer for auditing purposes

New Drugs C.08.007

- No records of domestic unusual failure in efficacy of new drugs including those that occurred during studies not under a CTA (i.e. Phase IV clinical trials) were accessible within 72 hours from the manufacturer for auditing purposes

New Drugs C.08.008

- None of the domestic unusual failure in efficacy of new drugs including those that occurred during studies not under a CTA (i.e. Phase IV clinical trials) received are reported to Health Canada by the manufacturer

Appendix 2

Risk 2 (Major) Observations

Adverse Drug Reaction Reporting C.01.016

- None of the domestic serious expected adverse drug reactions including those that occurred during studies not under a CTA (i.e. Phase IV clinical trials) received are reported to Health Canada by the manufacturer (↑)

- ◆ Less than the tota number of reports received by the manufacturer fo domestic serious expected and unexpected adverse drug reactions including those that occurred during studies not under a CTA (i.e. Phase IV clinical trials) are reported to Health Canada

- ◆ Less than the tota number of reports received by the manufacturer of foreign serious unexpected adverse drug reactions including those that occurred during studies not under a CTA (i.e. Phase IV clinical trials) are reported to Health Canada

- ◆ Domestic serious adverse drug reactions including those that occurred during studies not under a CTA (i.e. Phase IV clinical trials) are not reported within 15 calendar days of the receipt of the reports by the manufacturer[28]

- ◆ Foreign serious unexpected adverse drug reactions including those that occurred during studies not under a CTA (i.e. Phase IV clinical trials) are not reported withir 15 calendar days of the receipt of the reports by the manufacturer

- ◆ Annual summary reports of domestic serious adverse drug reactions and foreign serious unexpected adverse drug reactions are not prepared by the manufacturer. (Refer to Section 4.0 Definitions for minimum requirements)

- ◆ Case reports and summary reports have not been submitted within 30 days after receiving the request from Health Canada

Adverse Drug Reaction Reporting C.01.017

- ◆ Not all records of serious adverse drug reaction reports were accessible within 72 hours from the manufacturer for auditing purposes

- ◆ Annual summary reports of domestic serious adverse drug reactions and foreign serious unexpected adverse drug reactions are not maintained by the manufacturer for auditing purposes.(Refer to Section 4.0 Definitiors for minimum requirements)

New Drugs C.08.007

- ◆ Not all records of domestic unusual failure in efficacy of new drugs including those that occurred during studies not under a CTA (i.e. Phase IV clinical trials) were accessible within 72 hours from the manufacturer for auditing purposes

New Drugs C.08.008

- ◆ Less than the total number of reports received by the manufacturer of reports of domestic unusual failure in efficacy of new drugs including those that occurred during studies not under a CTA (i.e. Phase IV clinical trials) are reported to Health Canada

---

[28] Exception, at the inspectors discretion, in situations where the manufacturer has upgraded the seriousness of a case and consequently, the requirement to report within 15 calendar days of the receipt of the reports by the manufacturer is not met. The manufacturer should document situations in which a case is upgraded in seriousness.

Post-Market Reporting
GUI-0063

- Domestic unusual failure in efficacy of new drugs including those that occurred during studies not under a CTA (i.e. Phase IV clinical trials) are not reported within 15 calendar days of the receipt of the reports by the manufacturer

Appendix 3

Risk 3 (Other) Observations

Adverse Drug Reaction Reporting C.01.016

- The manufacturer has not included in the annual summary reports all domestic and foreign serious adverse drug reactions, domestic and foreign non-serious unexpected adverse drug reactions and domestic unusual failure in efficacy reports that were received

- Follow-up reports to initial case reports were not sought and submitted as information became available

- The manufacturer could not demonstrate that its systems and procedures for the receipt, evaluation and reporting of adverse drug reactions are adequate to effectively sustain adverse drug reaction reporting (↑)

Conditions for Provision of Packaging/Labelling Services for Drugs under Foreign Ownership (GUIDE-0067)

Health Products and Food Branch Inspectorate

Supersedes: New document

Date issued: May 1st, 2004

Date of implementation: July 1st, 2004

Guide-0067
Conditions for Provision of Packaging/Labelling Services for Drugs under Foreign Ownership[29]

1.0 Purpose

This document clarifies the specific requirements to be met by a Canadian packager / labeller in possession of an Establishment Licence that brings a drug into Canada solely to provide contract packaging/labelling services for that drug, which is then returned to the same fabricator from whom the product was received and who retains ownership of the drug throughout the transaction.

Such drugs:

- are not sold in Canada.

- do not have a DIN

- are not represented as Canadian products

- are not sold by the Canadian establishment providing the packaging/labelling service.

If the conditions set forth are met, the Inspectorate will have a degree of confidence to the effect that the drugs received are not imported for sale in Canada in contravention of the Food and Drug Regulations (FDR) but rather are being packaged and returned to the fabricator. The Inspectorate may ask for further evidence that the drugs to be packaged are returned to the fabricator.

---

[29] Available on the Health Canada website at http://www.hc-sc.gc.ca/dhp-mps/compli-conform/gmp-bpf/docs/gui_67-eng.php

2.0 Background

Under section A.01.040 of the FDR, all drugs in dosage form that are imported into Canada for the purpose of sale must comply with the requirements of the Food and Drugs Act (FDA) and Regulations, regardless of whether the drug is to be sold to Canadian or to foreign customers. However, it has been recognized that an establishment may wish to import a commercial shipment of a drug that has not been authorized for sale in Canada solely for the purpose of providing a contract packaging/labelling service to a foreign establishment that retains ownership of the drug. Therefore certain conditions must be met in order to ensure that such drugs are not sold by the Canadian establishment and are returned to the foreign fabricator that owns the drug. It should be understood that no Certificate of Pharmaceutical Product (CPP) will be issued for these drugs.

In response to questions from industry pertaining to the requirements that must be met in order for drugs to enter into Canada, the Inspectorate developed a "Guidance document on the commercial importation and exportation of drugs in dosage forms under the Food and Drugs Act". Further information is available in this guidance document.

3.0 Scope

This document applies to commercial shipments of unapproved drugs in dosage form that are brought into Canada solely for the purpose of providing a packaging/labelling service to the foreign fabricator that owns the drug.

Drugs imported outside the scope of this document should meet all applicable requirements under the FDA and Regulations.

This document does not apply to the following:

- drugs imported for personal use

- active pharmaceutical ingredients

- samples of drugs to be tested by a Canadian laboratory

- drugs to be sold in Canada

- drugs represented as Canadian products, such as those bearing a Canadian name, logo, address, or any other Canadian symbol.

4.0 Requirements

Drugs may be brought into Canada by a licenced Packager / Labeller for the purpose of providing packaging/labelling services to a foreign fabricator that retains ownership of the drug under the following conditions:

4.1 Ten (10) days prior to each shipment to Canada a notice (see attached annex) is sent by the Canadian contract packager/labeller to Health Canada specifying the following:

- the name of the drug and the quantity that is to be received by the contract packager/labeller

- the lot number of the drug to be received

- the name and address of the foreign owner of the drug

- the name and address of Canadian contract packager/labeller

- the date and port of entry into Canada
- the anticipated date of return of the drug to the foreign owner in the same country of origin.

4.2 Ten (10) days following completion of each packaging/labelling order and the return of the drug to the foreign owner a notice (see attached annex) is sent to Health Canada specifying the following:

- confirmation of the return of the packaged/labelled drug and any bulk unpackaged drug to the same fabricator in the same country from whom it was received
- the quantity returned
- brief description of packaging format(s) returned to owner and copies of labels and any other printed packaging components used to package/label the drug.

4.3 The following information is maintained on the premises of the Canadian contract packager/labeller and will be subject to review at the time of inspection:

- a written and signed contract that specifies the services to be provided and states that the drug remains under the ownership of the foreign establishment and that it is to be returned to the same owner from which it is received
- evidence that the foreign regulatory authority has authorized the packaging/labelling activity in Canada
- copies of labels and any other printed packaging components used to package/label the drug
- packaging/labelling batch documents for all services provided
- evidence that all quantities of the drug received have been returned to the foreign owner.

4.3.1 The following information must be sent to the Health Products and Food Branch Inspectorate, Drug GMP Inspection Unit, in Ottawa:

- evidence that the foreign establishment that owns the drug is in compliance with applicable GMP requirements. Evidence acceptable is described in the document "Conditions for acceptance of foreign inspection reports for listing foreign sites on Canadian Establishment licence".

4.4 The information required under 4.1 and 4.2 must be sent to the operational centre of the Health Products and Food Branch Inspectorate located in the region of the contract packager/labeller. Please consult the attached list of Operational Centres. Acknowledgement of receipt of the notification will not be issued by the Operational Centre but this information may be verified at any time by an inspector.

4.5 A copy of the information required under 4.1 must also be included with the shipment when it is brought into Canada.

5.0 Period of Retention of Records

Records required by Section 4.0 of this document must be kept for a period of 1 year after the expiration date on the label of the drug or 4 years after the finished packaged product is returned to its owner if no such date is indicated on the label.

Health Products and Food Branch Inspectorate

Operational Centres

Atlantic Operational Centre

1505 Barrington Street, Suite 1625
Halifax, Nova Scotia, B2J 3Y6

Manager:
T 902 426 5350
F 902-426-6676

Quebec Operational Centre

1001 West St-Laurent Blvd.
Longueuil, Québec, J4K 1C7

Manager:
T 450-646-1353
F 450-928-4455

Ontario and Nunavut Operational Centre

2301 Midland Avenue
Scarborough, Ontario, M1P 4R7

Manager:
T 416-973-1600
F 416-973-1954

Manitoba and Saskatchewan Operational Centre

510 Lagimodière Blvd.
Winnipeg, Manitoba, R2J 3Y1

Manager:
T 204-984-1341
F 204-984-2155

Western Operational Centre

4595 Canada Way, 4th Floor
Burnaby, British Columbia, V5G 1J9

Manager:
T 604-666-3704
F 604-666-3149

Drug GMP Inspection Unit

Graham Spry Building, 2nd Floor
250 Lanark Avenue, P.L. 2002B
Ottawa, Ontario, K1A CK9

Manager:
T 613-957-1492
F 613-952-9805

Annex / Annexe : Notification Form / Formulaire de notification

Part 1/ Partie 1
Notification to Health Canada prior to shipment to Canada / Notification à Santé Canada avant l'envoi au Canada

Contract packager-labeller - Emballeur/étiqueteur contractuel

Name / Nom :
Address / Adresse :
City / Ville, Province :
Postal Code / Code postal :
Telephone / Téléphone :
Fax :

Drug to be packaged/labelled - Drogue à être emballée/étiquetée

Name (active ingredient) / Nom (ingrédient actif) :
Brand name / Nom de marque :
Quantity / Quantité :
Manufacture date / Date de fabrication

Foreign fabricator - Manufacturier étranger

Name / Nom :
Address / Adresse :
City / Ville :
Country / Pays :

Expected date of entry into Canada - Date prévue d'entrée au Canada

Port of entry in Canada - Port d'entrée au Canada

Expected date of return to the fabricator - Date prévue de retour au manufacturier étranger

Part 2/ Partie 2
Notification to Health Canada after the return of the drug to the foreign owner / Notification à Santé Canada après l'expédition de la drogue au propriétaire étranger

Quantity packaged - Quantité emballée

Type and format of packaging material - Type et format du matériel d'emballage

Quantity of drug per packaging unit - Quantité de drogue / unité d'emballage

Number of units packaged - Nombre d'unités emballées

Quantity of packaged units returned to the fabricator - Nombre d'unités emballées retournées au manufacturier

Date of return - Date de retour

Transport Mode - Moyen de transport

If discrepancies, please explain: - Si différence, svp expliquez

Signature :

Guidelines for Temperature Control of Drug Products during Storage and Transportation (GUIDE-0069)

Health Products and Food Branch Inspectorate

Supersedes: Draft for comments

Date issued: October 17, 2005

Date of implementation: November 17, 2005

GUIDE-0069
Guidelines for Temperature Control of Drug Products during Storage and Transportation[30]

Introduction

Distribution and wholesaling form part of the supply chain of drug products. Drug products must be shipped and stored in a manner that does not risk exposure to temperatures outside of their recommended storage conditions[31]; potentially impacting the safety and effectiveness of the drug product. Section 11 of the Food and Drugs Act, read together with the definition "unsanitary conditions" in Section 2 of the Food and Drugs Act, prohibits any person from:

> "...packag[ing] or stor[ing] for sale any drug under ...such conditions or circumstances as might ....render [a drug] injurious to health".

Fabricators, packagers/labellers, distributors, importers and wholesalers are additionally responsible for the appropriate handling, storage and distribution of drugs according to C.02.015 of the Food and Drug Regulations. These requirements are in place to maintain the quality of the drugs. Every activity in the distribution of drugs should be carried out according to requirements of the Food and Drugs Act, the principles of Good Manufacturing Practices (GMP), good storage and good distribution practices.

Environmental controls play a key role in maintaining drug quality. Temperature is one of the most important parameters to control. Drugs must be stored, handled and transported according to predetermined conditions (e.g.

---

[30] Available on the Health Canada website at http://www.hc-sc.gc.ca/dhp-mps/compli-conform/gmp-bpf/docs/gui-0069_temp_control_dproducts_storage_transportation_ltr-doc-eng.php

[31] Predetermined temperature conditions as supported by stability data.

temperature, etc.) as supported by stability data[32]. Drugs that are particularly sensitive, such as drugs that must be kept refrigerated or frozen, must be handled with appropriate care.

This guidance is not intended to cover every conceivable case. Alternative means of complying with the intent will be considered with appropriate scientific justification. Different approaches may be called for as new technologies emerge. This document is based on other pre-existing international guidance (see List of References).

Scope

These guidelines are intended to be applicable to all persons and companies involved in the storage and transportation of drug products. All persons and companies including fabricators, packagers/labellers, distributors, importers, and wholesalers share responsibility for ensuring that appropriate storage and transportation conditions are maintained from the point of manufacturing up to the delivery of the drug products to the final distribution point[33]. The maintenance of the chain of storage and transportation conditions should be supported by written contractual agreements between the distributor, the importer, the wholesaler, and the transportation provider. The responsibility of each party, is to ensure that the required storage and transportation conditions are met through their respective GMP activities.

These guidelines not only apply to drugs for human and veterinary use but also to clinical trial drugs for human use as required under C.05.010(j) and to samples that are distributed to professionals as per Section 14 of the Food and Drug Act.

Interpretation

1. Warehousing And Storage

1.1 All drugs should be stored according to conditions described on the label. When specified on the label, controls for humidity, light, etc. should be in place.

1.2 Temperatures should be controlled and monitored using calibrated monitoring devices and records of temperature and alarms, were applicable, should be maintained. Monitoring is conducted at points representing the extremes of the temperature range based on temperature mapping.

1.3 Refrigerators and freezers used to store drugs should:

♦ be well maintained,

♦ be equipped with alarms,

♦ be free from frost buildup,

---

[32] Data from the accelerated storage condition and, if appropriate, from the intermediate storage condition can be used to evaluate the effect of short term excursions outside the label storage conditions (such as might occur during shipping).

[33] The final destination where the drug will be used or sold (e.g. pharmacy, hospitals, clinics, retail stores, etc).

- when combined, be a two door unit with separate freezer compartment and door,

- allow for adequate air distribution and orderly storage within the chamber. Storage practices and loading configurations should not lead to the obstruction of air distribution,

- have sensors for continuous monitoring and alarms located at the points representing the temperature extremes.

1.4 Written procedures should be available describing the actions to be taken in the event of temperature excursions outside the labeled storage conditions. All excursions outside the labeled storage conditions must be appropriately investigated and the disposition of the stock in question must be evidence-based.

2. Product Transportation And Products In Transit

2.1 The transport process and containers should prevent damage and maintain the integrity and quality of the drug products. For example, ampoules exposed to physical stress could develop hairline cracks.

2.2 Written procedures for the shipping of drug products should be established. Such procedures should take into account the nature of the drug products, local conditions and any seasonal variations experienced, and describe any special handling precautions. These procedures should be verified to ensure that appropriate conditions are maintained under worst case scenarios.

Where controlled storage conditions[34] (e.g. temperature, relative humidity, light, etc.) are required during transit, the necessary controls[35] must be in place.

2.4 Within a transportation container, the packaging configuration, which provides the primary means of environmental control for the drug product, should ensure that the drug product remains within the acceptable temperature range.

2.5 Refrigerated vehicles/transportation containers should be mapped and monitored, if they provide the primary means for environmental control. However, this is not necessary if a qualified insulated container is used as the primary means of environmental control.

2.6 Temperature and humidity monitoring devices should be calibrated at predetermined intervals. Single use monitoring devices should be qualified.

2.7 Transportation practices by carriers[36], including any storage and/or transportation activities performed by sub-contractors, should be periodically

---

[34] Conditions that need to be maintained (e.g. humidity, temperature, light) during the time the drug is transported and stored as per the manufacturer's labelled instructions for the drug product.

[35] Procedures are followed and criteria are met.

[36] A person who is engaged in the transport of goods or passengers by any means of transport under the legislative authority of Parliament. (Uniform Classification of Accounts and Related Railway Records, April 1998, Canadian Transportation Agency)

verified by reviewing documentation. A record of the review should be kept
and any discrepancies should have a follow up.

3. Containers And Container Labelling

3.1 Any controlled transport and/or storage conditions as well as warning
statements (e.g. "Perishable Drug Product", "Do Not Freeze") should be
clearly stated on the label applied to shipping containers. This label should
be securely affixed and indelible. The shipping documents should clearly
state that these products must be transferred to the specified storage
temperature immediately upon receipt.

3.2 Selection of a shipping container and/ or box should be based on:

- the storage and transportation requirements of the drugs,

- the space required for the amount of drugs to be transported,

- the anticipated external temperature extremes,

- the estimated maximum length of time required for transportation of
the drugs, including any in transit storage.

3.3 When warm/cold packs are placed in containers used to transport
temperature sensitive drugs[37]:

- the type, size and number of packs should correspond to the
shipping duration and temperature needed,

- the location of the packs should ensure the product is maintained
within the recommended storage conditions,

- frozen packs should be conditioned prior to final packing by allowing
them to "sweat",

- adequate barrier materials should be used to avoid direct contact of
the packs with the products.

3.4 When dry ice is placed in containers used to transport temperature sensitive
drugs, in addition to safety issues, it must be ensured that the dry ice or its
vapours does not have an adverse effect on the drug product or its primary
package.

3.5 Cold-chain monitors (CCM) or temperature indicators should be used when
appropriate. If temperature excursions outside the labeled storage conditions
occur, product disposition must be evaluated and documented. Corrective
action should be implemented where necessary and documented. Clear
directions should be provided to the recipient for the evaluation or disposition
of CCM/indicators and products.

4. Receiving

4.1 Where controlled storage conditions (e.g. temperature, relative humidity,
light, etc.) are required during transit, the recipient should examine the
shipment upon reception following written procedures.

---

[37] A drug that can be altered with the exposure to temperatures that are not within the
limits that have been demonstrated to be acceptable for the drug.

4.2 Products should be promptly transferred to the appropriate environmentally controlled storage area.

5. Documentation

5.1 When commercial carriers are used, all pertinent conditions should be specified in a written contract between the distributor, importer or wholesaler, and the third-party. All contract acceptors should comply with the requirements in this guideline as applicable.

5.2 Distributors, importers and wholesalers should maintain transportation records of inbound and outbound shipments, including monitoring records where applicable, for a period of one year after expiry date.

5.3 Records of investigations and actions taken in the event of excursions outside the labeled storage conditions are kept for a minimum of one year after the expiration date of the product.

List Of References

Good Distribution Practices (GDP) For Pharmaceutical Products, WHO- 2004, # QAS/04.068

Canada Communicable Disease Report, Vol.21-11, dated 15 June 1995

"Keep it Cool: the Vaccine Cold Chain; Guidelines for Immunization Providers on Maintaining the Cold Chain", 2nd. Edition, Commonwealth of Australia 2001

EU Guidelines on Good Distribution Practice of Medicinal Products for Human Use (94/ C 63/ 03)

ICH Q7A (18). Chapter 10, "storage and dispatch"

"Medicinal Co d Chain Guideline", PDA Draft document

"Good Storage and Shipping practices: Distribution and Shipment of Pharmacopoeial Articles" USP Draft <1079>

Guidance for Pre-manufacturing and Pre-exportation Notifications (C.07.011) under Canada's Access to Medicines Regime (GUIDE-0072)

Health Products and Food Branch Inspectorate

Supersedes: New Document

Date issued: August 2007

Date of implementation: September 2007

GUIDE-0072
Guidance for Pre-manufacturing and Pre-exportation Notifications (C.07.011) under Canada's Access to Medicines Regime[38]

1.0 Purpose

The purpose of this document is to provide guidance to manufacturers on how to comply with section C.07.011 of the Food and Drug Regulations.

2.0 Background

Health Canada will conduct pre-export inspections of manufacturers exporting to developing or least-developed countries under Canada's Access to Medicines Regime. Pre-export inspections, as part of anti-diversion measures, will confirm the existence of distinguishing characteristics on the products, their immediate containers, if applicable, and their labels.

Inspections will be conducted by Health Canada under the authority of sections 23 and 24 of the Food and Drugs Act. These activities will be conducted by the Health Products and Food Branch Inspectorate. Collaboration with all stakeholders taking part in Canada's Access to Medicines Regime will be essential to ensure compliance with the new regulations.

Refer to the Health Products and Food Branch Inspectorate's Inspection Strategy for Canada's Access to Medicines Regime (POL-0055) for additional information.

---

[38] Available on the Health Canada website at http://www.hc-sc.gc.ca/dhp-mps/compli-conform/gmp-bpf/docs/gui_0072-eng.php

3.0 Scope

This document applies to manufacturers of drug products intended for export under Canada's Access to Medicines Regime. All manufacturers participating in the program must notify Health Canada as indicated in section C.07.011 of the Food and Drug Regulations and will be subject to pre-export inspections.

4.0 Definitions

HPFB Inspectorate

The Health Products and Food Branch (HPFB) directorate whose primary role is to deliver a national compliance and enforcement program for all products under the mandate of the HPFB, with the exception of products regulated as foods. (Inspectorat de la DGPSA)

Inspection

On-site monitoring and assessment against the applicable requirements of the Food and Drugs Act and its associated regulations. Inspections are routinely conducted on a predetermined cycle or as required to assess compliance. (Inspection)

Manufacturer

"manufacturer" or "distributor" means a person, including an association or partnership, who under their own name, or under a trade-, design or word mark, trade name or other name, word or mark controlled by them, sells a food or drug (section A.01.010 of the Food and Drug Regulations). (Fabricant)

For additional definitions, consult the documents listed as references at the end of this document.

5.0 Interpretation

Section C.07.011 (Notice to Minister) of the Food and Drug Regulations states:

"The manufacturer shall notify the Minister in writing not less than 15 days before commencing the manufacture of the first lot of a drug authorized to be sold under this Division and not less than 15 days before the exportation of each subsequent lot of the drug."

In order to comply with this regulatory requirement, the manufacturer must complete and sign the Division 7 Notification Form (see Attachment A) and send it to the Health Product and Food Branch Inspectorate no less than 15 calendar days prior to the start of manufacturing of the first lot of drug product authorized for sale under Part C Division 7 of the Food and Drug Regulations, and no less than 15 calendar days prior to the exportation of each subsequent lot of the drug product.

6.0 Attachments

Attachment A - "Division 7 Notification Form"

7.0 Effective date

The effective date of this document is May 29, 2007.

8.0 References

Food and Drugs Act

Food and Drug Regulations

Act to amend The Patent Act and the Food and Drugs Act (The Jean Chrétien Pledge to Africa) - Bill C-9

Regulations Amending the Food and Drug Regulations (1402 - Drugs for Developing Countries)

Health Products and Food Branch Inspectorate's Inspection Strategy for Canada's Access to Medicines Regime (POL-0055)

CAMR Notifications
GUI-0072

Attachment A

<table>
<tr>
<td>🍁</td>
<td>Health Canada
Health Products and Food Branch
HPFB Inspectorate</td>
<td></td>
</tr>
<tr>
<td colspan="3" align="center">DIVISION 7 NOTIFICATION FORM</td>
</tr>
<tr>
<td>1.</td>
<td colspan="2">This serves to notify Health Canada as required by section C.07.011 of the Food and Drug Regulations.</td>
</tr>
<tr>
<td>2.</td>
<td colspan="2">The drug product which is the subject of this notification is

    (brand name of the drug product, name of the drug product as set out in Schedule 1 of the Patent Act and, if applicable, the strength, dosage form and route of administration of the drug product),

with Export Tracking Number   .</td>
</tr>
<tr>
<td>3.</td>
<td colspan="2">This notification pertains to (check one only):

☐ the manufacturing of the first lot of the above named drug product.
The lot number is   .

OR

☐ the exportation of a subsequent lot of the above named drug product.
The lot number is   .</td>
</tr>
<tr>
<td>4.</td>
<td colspan="2">The quantity of the above named drug product to be exported for the lot in question is
    .</td>
</tr>
<tr>
<td>5.</td>
<td colspan="2">The name and address of the manufacturer are as follows:</td>
</tr>
<tr>
<td>6.</td>
<td colspan="2">The name, title, address and phone number of the undersigned authorized representative of the manufacturer are:</td>
</tr>
<tr>
<td colspan="2">Dated at   the   day of   ,   .</td>
<td></td>
</tr>
<tr>
<td colspan="2">_____
Authorized representative of the manufacturer</td>
<td></td>
</tr>
</table>

Send the completed, signed and dated form by fax or by e-mail to:

Manager, Drug GMP Inspection Unit
HPFB Inspectorate
Health Product and Food Branch
Health Canada
Fax #: 613-957-6709
E-mail Address: ATM_questions_AAM@hc-sc.gc.ca

Division 7 Notification Form

1. This serves to notify Health Canada as required by section C.07.011 of the Food and Drug Regulations.

2. The drug product which is the subject of this notification is_____

   (brand name of the drug product, name of the drug product as set out in Schedule 1 of the Patent Act and, if applicable, the strength, dosage form and route of administration of the drug product),

   with Export Tracking Number_____.

3. This notification pertains to (check one only):

   ☐ the manufacturing of the first lot of the above named drug product.

   The lot number is_____.

   OR

   ☐ the exportation of a subsequent lot of the above named drug product.

   The lot number is_____.

4. The quantity of the above named drug product to be exported for the lot in question is_____.

5. The name and address of the manufacturer are as follows:_____

6. The name, title, address and phone number of the undersigned authorized representative of the manufacturer are:_____

Dated at_____ the_____ day of_____,_____.

_____

Authorized representative of the manufacturer

Send the completed, signed and dated form by fax or by e-mail to:

Manager, Drug GMP Inspection Unit
HPFB Inspectorate
Health Product and Food Branch
Health Canada
Fax #: 613-957-6709
E-mail Address: ATM_questions_AAM@hc-sc.gc.ca

CAMR Notifications
GUI-0072

Guidance on Evidence to Demonstrate Drug GMP Compliance of Foreign Sites (GUI-0080)

Health Products and Food Branch Inspectorate

Supersedes: POL-0013 (August 27, 2003)

This document replaces POL-0013 "Conditions for Acceptance of Foreign Inspection Reports for Listing Foreign Sites on Canadian Establishment Licences"

Date issued: August 1, 2009

Date of implementation: August 1, 2009

Related Forms (FRM-0211, FRM-0212, FRM-0213, FRM 0214)

Guidance on Evidence to Demonstrate Drug GMP Compliance of Foreign Sites (GUI-0080)[39]

1.0 Purpose

The purpose of this document is to provide guidance with respect to the type of information that should be submitted in order for the Health Product and Food Branch Inspectorate (Inspectorate) to assess the compliance of foreign sites with the Canadian Good Manufacturing Practices (GMP) regulations.

This guidance refers to compliance with Division 2 (Good Manufacturing Practices) of the Food and Drug Regulations for foreign sites. The outcome of the assessment by the Inspectorate will be a Compliant (C) or Non Compliant (NC) rating for the foreign site, or a request to submit additional information.

The forms referenced in this document are only intended to facilitate the submission of GMP evidence to the Drug GMP Inspection Unit for review. Alternate means of filing may be employed, however, the information captured in these forms should be submitted.

Canadian importers may wish to seek a compliance rating for a foreign site for the purpose of adding it to their Drug Establishment License. In order for a Drug Establishment Licence (DEL) applicant/holder to add a foreign site to their establishment licence, they should submit the DEL application form (Section V) to the Establishment Licensing Unit. Additional guidance is available on the Health Canada website at: Establishment Licences.

---

[39] Available on the Health Canada website at http://www.hc-sc.gc.ca/dhp-mps/compli-conform/gmp-bpf/docs/gui-0080-eng.php

It should be noted that the establishment licence form (Section V) and "Good Manufacturing Practices - Foreign Site Submission Form (FRM-0212)" are not both required, for any given site. Information provided to either the Establishment Licensing Unit or the Drug GMP Inspection Unit will be shared as required.

Sponsors may wish to seek a compliance rating for a foreign site in support of a drug submission, for a product which will be manufactured, packaged, labelled or tested at the foreign site. It is recommended that sponsors consult with the relevant review Directorate in order to determine the GMP requirements for a drug submission (for screening and/or review).

2.0 Scope

This guidance covers certain types of evidence:

◆ Evidence to demonstrate GMP compliance for a site in a Mutual Recognition Agreement (MRA) country, for products and activities covered under the MRA.

◆ Evidence to demonstrate GMP compliance for a site not located in a MRA country, or for sites located in a MRA country for products and/or activities not covered under the MRA.

3.0 Guidance

The Inspectorate recommends that the following information be submitted in order to demonstrate GMP compliance for foreign sites. Where the original information is available in a language other than English or French, the copy of the original information must be provided with an attestation on the accuracy of the translation by the translator.

3.1 For sites located in a MRA country, for products and activities (fabrication, packaging, labelling, testing) covered under the MRA

3.1.1 Type of evidence

In accordance with section C.01A.005 (m)(i)(ii) of the Food and Drug Regulations (FDR), an importer who wishes to list a site located in a MRA country which fabricates, packages/labels or conducts tests (including, but not limited to raw material testing, packaging material testing, and/or finished product testing) under Division 2 on its establishment licence must:

A. provide the name of each fabricator, packager/labeller and tester of the drug

B. provide the address of each building at which the drug is fabricated, packaged/labelled or tested

C. specify for each building the activities and the category of drug and

(a) the dosage form class and whether the drug is in a sterile dosage form, and

(b) whether the drug is a bulk process intermediate,

D. provide the name of the regulatory authority that is designated under subsection C.01A.019(1) in respect of that activity conducted in the MRA country

3.1.2. Request of a Certificate of Compliance (CoC) by the Inspectorate

Upon receipt of the above information, the Inspectorate will contact the regulatory authority identified to request a CoC to support GMP compliance of the requested building, activities, and dosage forms. CoCs are exchanged between regulatory authorities only. Submission of a copy of a CoC to the Inspectorate by an importer, sponsor, or DEL holder is not sufficient to demonstrate GMP compliance for the foreign site.

3.1.3 Submission of information to the Inspectorate

The above information should normally be submitted to the Inspectorate in the Establishment Licence Renewal package. However, should the importer, sponsor, or DEL holder wish the Inspectorate to request a CoC at any other time, the request should be made on form entitled "Good Manufacturing Practices - Foreign Site Submission Form (FRM-0212)", available on the Inspectorate website, and faxed to 6ˊ3-957-6709 or emailed to mra-arm@hc-sc.gc.ca

3.2 For sites not located in a MRA country, or for sites located in a MRA country for products or activities not covered under the MRA

3.2.1 Type of Evidence

In accordance with sections C.01A.005 (m)(iii) and (n)(o) of the Food and Drug Regulations, an importer who wishes to list a site not located in a MRA country which fabricates, packages/labels or conducts tests (including, but not limited to raw material testing, packaging material testing, and/or finished product testing) under Division 2; or sites located in a MRA country for activities other than fabrication, packaging/labelling or testing under Division 2, or for products not covered under the MRA must:

A.

I. provide a certificate from a Canadian inspector indicating that the fabricator's, packager/labeller's or tester's buildings, equipment, practices and procedures meet the applicable requirements of Divisions 2

II. specify for each building the activities and the category of drug and

   (a) the dosage form class and whether any drugs will be in a sterile dosage form, and

   (b) whether the drugs will be a bulk process intermediate, or

B.

I. other evidence establishing that the fabricator's, packager/labeller's or tester's buildings, equipment, practices and procedures meet the applicable requirements of Divisions 2 to 4, and

II. specify for each building the activities and the category of drug and

   (a) the dosage form class and whether any drugs will be in a sterile dosage form, and

   (b) whether the drugs will be a bulk process intermediate.

3.2.1.1 The certificate from a Canadian inspector referred to above (in A.I.) is a GMP Inspection Exit Notice with a C rating from the Inspectorate. The

Foreign GMP Evidence
GUI-0080

Inspectorate suggests that other available evidence be considered before requesting an inspection by the Inspectorate (see 3.2.1.2). However, should an importer wish to request an inspection by the Inspectorate, they may do so by completing the form entitled "Good Manufacturing Practices - Request for an Inspection of a Foreign Site Form (FRM-0213)" and fax or email it to 613-957-6709 or foreign_site_etranger@hc-sc.gc.ca respectively.

The decision to proceed with the request for a foreign inspection is made by the Inspectorate. Should the Inspectorate decide to proceed with the inspection, the requester will be asked to enter into an agreement with Health Canada and sign the form "Good Manufacturing Practices - Foreign Site Inspection Services Agreement Form (FRM-0214)", once the specifics of the foreign inspection have been agreed upon, and are fax or email it to 613-957-6709 or foreign_site_etranger@hc-sc.gc.ca respectively.

Please note that an On-Site Evaluation (OSE) alone, conducted by the Biologics and Genetic Therapeutics Directorate is not considered sufficient to demonstrate the GMP compliance of a site as it does not cover all applicable sections of the GMP (Division 2 of the Food and Drug Regulations)

3.2.1.2   With reference to 'other evidence', as stated above, the Inspectorate suggests the following information be submitted in order to assess GMP compliance. The list of documentation below is provided as a guide only, however, they should all be provided in order to ensure a more efficient and timely review by the Inspectorate. It is recognized that the relationship between a Canadian site and a foreign site may be complex and in some cases particular documentation may not exist. In such cases, a written justification explaining why the required document type cannot be submitted should be provided with the submission, and the Inspectorate may consider alternate means of obtaining the information.

The act of submission alone does not guarantee that a compliant rating will be assigned to the foreign site and additional information may be requested depending on the nature of the submission.

A.   the most recent (within the last 3 years) signed inspection report issued by:

I.   a Regulatory Authority for a site outside of its jurisdiction, or

e.g.: -an Medicines and Healthcare Regulatory Agency (MHRA) (UK) inspection report for a site in India

II.   a Qualified Authority for a site within its jurisdiction, or

e.g.: -an Food Drug Administration (FDA) (US) Establishment Inspection Report for a site located inside the US

-a Medicine Control Council (MCC) (South Africa) inspection report for a site in South Africa

III.   a Qualified Authority for a site outside of its jurisdiction

e.g.: -an FDA (US) Establishment Inspection Report (EIR) for a site located outside the US

-a Health Science Authority (HSA) (Singapore) inspection report for a site in China

B. the corrective actions taken, signed by a responsible official of the foreign site

C. a copy of the Site Master File (for additional guidance, refer to the document entitled "Explanatory Notes for Industry on the Preparation of a Site Master File")

D. a copy of the site's procedures for handling deviations and out of specification test results

E. a copy of the site's procedure for finished product release

F. a copy of the quality agreement between the foreign site and the Canadian site including a list of the specific products for supply in Canada

G. if authorization has been given by another country, proof that the authorization is still valid and has not been cancelled

3.2.1.3   Should an inspection report referred to in section 3.2.1.2 not be available and depending on the nature and risk profile of the products, the Inspectorate recommends submission of a corporate or consultant audit report for sites dealing with ethical drugs (on a case by case basis based on the risk profile of the drug), over the counter Nonprescription Drugs, medical gases, and sites performing sterilization of packaging materials for products which will be aseptically filled without undergoing terminal sterilization. The information in section 3.2.1.2, subsections C to G should also be provided, and the audit report should meet the following conditions:

A. an explanation why a consultant or corporate audit report is submitted

B. the qualifications and experience of the individual(s) performing the inspection must be provided. As a minimum, the individual(s) must have sufficient experience and knowledge of GMP. Further guidance is available in the interpretation of section C.02.006 of the "Good Manufacturing Practices (GMP) Guidelines (GUI-0001)"

C. the audit is conducted, section by section, against the Canadian GMP Guidelines and all applicable sections are assessed.

D. any deficiencies noted during the audit must be classified using the document entitled "Risk Classification of GMP Observations (GUI-0023)"

Note: Any Risk 1 or Risk 2 deficiencies that would lead to a non-compliant rating according to this guide would render the site unacceptable. The classification of deficiencies will be reviewed by the Inspectorate.

E. the audit report must be signed and dated by the auditor or audit team, and must be accompanied by a copy of the corrective actions taken, which has been signed by a responsible official of the foreign site

Foreign GMP Evidence GUI-0080

F.   the adequacy of the corrective actions are assessed by the auditor or
audit team.

Note: The corrective actions will also be reviewed by the Inspectorate to
determine if they are adequate.

G.   If an inspection report more than 3 years old from a Regulatory
Authority or a Qualified Authority is available, the report should
accompany the consultant or corporate report.

A form entitled "Good Manufacturing Practices - Audit Report Form
(FRM-0211)" has been developed and may be used to ensure that all of
the criteria outlined above are met. This form is available on the
Inspectorate website. The use of this template does not guarantee that
a compliant rating will be assigned to a foreign site, however it will
ensure a more efficient and timely review by the Inspectorate. Additional
documentation may be requested depending on the nature of the
submission.

3.2.2 Submission of information to the Inspectorate

The information in sections 3.2.1.2 and/or 3.2.1.3 should be normally submitted
to the Inspectorate in the DEL Renewal package. However, should the DEL
holder, or sponsor wish to submit the information at any other time, the request
should be made on form entitled "Good Manufacturing Practices - Foreign Site
Submission Form (FRM-0212)" available on the Inspectorate website, and faxed
to 613-957-6709 or emailed to foreign_site_etranger@hc-sc.gc.ca

3.2.3 Request for additional information by the Inspectorate

At any time during the assessment of the documentation submitted, additional
information and/or clarification may be requested in order to fully assess the
compliance of the foreign site with Division 2 of the FDR. For instance, where a
site has a poor compliance history, repeat observations are noted, and/or the
information is not sufficient to fully assess compliance with Division 2. The refusal
to submit additional information and/or the submission of incomplete information
may result in the Inspectorate being unable to assess the compliance of the
foreign site, and as such, no compliance rating will be issued.

3.3 Period of validity for Drug GMP compliance evidence of foreign sites

3.3.1   For sites in a MRA country, for products and activities (fabrication,
packaging, labelling, testing) covered under the MRA, for which a CoC has
been received by the Inspectorate

The period of validity or expiry date of these CoC is assigned by the
Regulatory Authority.

To match the end of the period of validity with the expiry date of the EL, the
expiry date of the CoC will always be reassigned to December 31 using the
criteria described in 3.4.2 below

3.3.2   For sites not located in a MRA country, or for sites located in a MRA
country for products and activities not covered under the MRA.

To match the end of the period of validity of the information submitted with the expiry date of the DEL (which is December 31st of each year), the expiry date is set as December 31st and will be assigned as follows:

- generally, for reports dated June 30th or before in a given year, the expiry date will be set as 2 years plus the remaining period of the year from the date of inspection, and;

- for reports dated July 1st or after in a given year, the expiry date will be set as 3 years plus the remaining period of the year from the date of inspection.

  e.g.:

  - if a report is dated March 1st, 2008, the expiry date will be set as December 31st, 2010

  - if a report is dated August 1st, 2008, the expiry date will be set as December 31st, 2011

In most cases, the information will be considered valid for a period not exceeding 42 months from the date of the inspection but not less than 30 months.

If a site has a questionable compliance history, repeat observations are noted, and/or the Inspectorate requires additional information in order to fully assess compliance with Division 2, a shortened expiry date may be issued, until that additional information is received and assessed.

3.4 Terms and Conditions

Pursuant to sections C.01A.008 of the FDR, the Minister may set out in an establishment license terms and conditions respecting:

(a) the tests to be performed in respect of a drug, and the equipment to be used, to ensure that the drug is not unsafe for use; and

(b) any other matters necessary to prevent injury to the health of consumers, including conditions under which drugs are fabricated, packaged/labelled or tested.

And, pursuant to section C.01A.012 of the FDR, the Minister may amend the terms and conditions of an Establishment Licence if the Minister believes on reasonable grounds that an amendment is necessary to prevent injury to the health of the consumer. In such cases, the Minister shall give at least 15 days notice in writing to the holder of the Establishment Licence of the proposed amendment, the reasons for the amendment and its effective date.

Should, in the opinion of the Inspectorate, Terms and Conditions be required for a foreign site, these Terms and Conditions will be listed on the Canadian DEL.

3.5 Ownership of information

Any of the above documentation submitted to Health Canada is owned by the Crown, as duly represented by the Inspectorate and under its control, and is subject to the dispositions of any applicable Act including the Access to Information Act.

Foreign GMP Evidence GUI-0080

Appendix A

Acronyms

CoC: Certificate of Compliance

DEL: Drug Establishment Licence

FDR: Food and Drug Regulations

GMP: Good Manufacturing Practices

HPFB: Health Products and Food Branch

Inspectorate: Health Products and Food Branch Inspectorate

MRA: Mutual Recognition Agreement

PIC/S: Pharmaceutical Inspection Cooperation Scheme

Glossary of Terms

Certificate of Compliance (CoC) (certificat de conformité (CC)) - A certificate issued by a Regulatory Authority attesting to the GMP compliance of a recognized building in that country. In Canada, the CoC is issued by the HPFB Inspectorate.

Compliant (C) (conforme (C)) - At the time of the inspection, the regulated party has demonstrated that the activities it conducts are in compliance with the Food and Drugs Act and its associated Regulations. A C rating does not mean that there are no observations or corrective actions required.

Drug (drogue) - In Division 1A and Division 2 of the Food and Drug Regulations, "drug" "means a drug in dosage form, or a drug that is a bulk process intermediate that can be used in the preparation of a drug listed in Schedule C to the Act or in Schedule D to the Act that is of biological origin. It does not include a dilute drug premix, a medicated feed as defined in Section 2 of the Feeds Regulations, 1983, a drug that is used only for the purposes of an experimental study in accordance with a certificate issued under Section C.08.015 or a drug listed in Schedule H to the Act." (C.01A.001(2))

Ethical Drug (spécialité médicale) - A drug that in accordance with Federal Legislation does not require a prescription, but that is generally prescribed by a medical practitioner.

Foreign Site (site étranger) - An establishment (building) that is outside of Canada that performs fabrication, packaging/labelling, or testing for drugs that are sold in Canada.

Mutual Recognition Agreement (MRA) (accord de reconnaissance mutuelle (ARM)) - "An international agreement that provides for the mutual recognition of compliance certification for Good Manufacturing Practices for drugs." (C.01A.001)

MRA Country (pays participant à un ARM) - A country that is a participant to a mutual recogn tion agreement with Canada. (C.01A.001).

Non-Compliant (NC) (on-conforme (NC)) - At the time of the inspection, the regulated party has not demonstrated that the activities it conducts are in compliance w th the Food and Drugs Act and its associated Regulations.

On-Site Evaluation (évaluation sur place) - An On-Site Evaluation is a produc: specific evaluation conducted by the Biologics and Genetic Therapies Directorate (BGTD) at the site of manufacture of a Schedule D drug (intermediate or finished product) to assess the premises in which the drug is manufactured, the process, conditions and control of manufacture and conformity with the information submitted in support of that drug

Qualified Authority (autorité qualifiée) - A member of the Pharmaceutical Inspection Cooperation/Scheme (PIC/S) or the United States Food and Drug Administration (USFDA).

Recognized Building (bâtiment reconnu) - "In respect of the fabrication, packaging/labell ng or testing of a drug, a building that a regulatory authority that is designated under subsection C.01A.019(1) in respect of that activity has recognized as meeting its Good Manufacturing Practices standards in respect of that activity for that drug." (C.01A.001)

Regulatory Authority (autorité réglementaire) - "A government agency or other entity in a MRA country that has a legal right to control the use or sale of drugs within that country and that may take enforcement action to ensure that drugs marketed within its jurisdiction comply with legal requirements." (C.01A.001)

Part III

Annexes
to the Current Edition of the
Good Manufacturing Practices (GMP)
Guidelines

Annexes Overview

Annexes to the Current Edition of the Good Manufacturing Practices (GMP) Guidelines[40]

The list of references in this Appendix has been updated. Annex numbers and document titles have been changed to correspond to those used by the European Union (EU) and PIC/S. This is done in order to work towards the global harmonization of technical standards and procedures related to GMP, and in preparation for Health Canada's revisions on these documents, which is anticipated to start in the near future. URLs to the documents, active at the time of this GUI-0001 posting, have been provided.

Annexes are available on Health Canada's Web site in the Compliance and Enforcement section.

Annex 1 to the Current Edition of the Good Manufacturing Practices Guidelines - Selected Category IV Monograph Drugs (GUI-0066)

Annex 2 to the Current Edition of the Good Manufacturing Practices Guidelines - Schedule D Drugs, Biological Drugs Including Fractionated Blood Products (GUI-0027)

Annex 3 to the Current Edition of the Good Manufacturing Practices Guidelines - Schedule C Drugs (GUI-0026)

Annex 4 to the Current Edition of the Good Manufacturing Practices Guidelines - Veterinary Drugs (GUI-0012)

Annex 5 to the Current Edition of the Good Manufacturing Practices Guidelines - Positron Emitting Radiopharmaceuticals (PER's) (GUI-0071)

Annex 11 to the Current Edition of the Good Manufacturing Practices Guidelines - Computerised Systems (GUI-0050)

Annex 13 to the Current Edition of the Good Manufacturing Practices Guidelines - Drugs Used in Clinical Trials (GUI-0036)

Annex 14 to the Current Edition of the Good Manufacturing Practices Guidelines - Schedule D Drugs, Human Blood and Blood Components (GUI-0032)

Annex 17 to the Current Edition of the Good Manufacturing Practices Guidelines - Guidance on Parametric Release (GUI-0046)

---

[40] From Appendix C of Good Manufacturing Practices (GMP) Guidelines - 2009 Edition (GUI-0001) available on the Health Canada website at: http://www.hc-sc.gc.ca/dhp-mps/compli-conform/gmp-bpf/docs/gui-0001-eng.php#appc

Annex 1 - Selected Category IV Monograph Drugs (GUI-0066)

Health Products and Food Branch Inspectorate

Supersedes: April 1st, 2004

Date Issued: December 1st, 2004

Date of Implementation   January 1st, 2005

Ce document est aussi disponible en français.

Annex 1 to the Current Edition of the Good Manufacturing Practices Guidelines - Selected Category IV Monograph Drugs (GUI-0066)[41]

Introduction

Although the Regulations and their rationale as well as the quality management principles outlined in the GMP Guidelines apply to all drugs, it is recognized that some of the interpretations provided in the GMP Guidelines may not always be applicable or appropriate in certain situations (e.g. for some personal care products). Therefore, this Annex to the current edition of the Good Manufacturing Practices (GMP) Guidelines was developed by HC in consultation with their stakeholders. It is intended to clarify certain aspects that have relevance to the manufacture of selected Category IV monograph drugs.

Scope

1. The guidance included in this Annex, when placed in context with the GMP Guidelines, should facilitate compliance with Division 2 of the Food and Drug Regulations. In order to avoid repetition, only those interpretations that are different from the ones included in the GMP Guidelines are contained in this Annex. The numbering of each interpretation used in this Annex corresponds to that of the interpretation being modified from the GMP Guidelines. **Therefore, unless otherwise stated in this Annex, all interpretations included in the GMP Guidelines are applicable to selected Category IV monograph drugs.**

---

[41] Available on the Health Canada website at http://www.hc-sc.gc.ca/dhp-mps/compli-conform/gmp-bpf/docs/annex_3_categ_IV-eng.php

2. The modified interpretations from the GMP Guidelines contained in this Annex apply to the following non-sterile, OTC drugs for which a DIN is issued based on compliance with Category IV monograph:

- Acne Therapies (topical)
- Anticaries Products Containing Fluoride
- Antidandruff Products
- Antiperspirants
- Antiseptic Skin Cleansers
- Athletes Foot Treatments
- Medicated Skin Care Products
- Sunburn Protectants
- Throat lozenges

3. For more details regarding category IV monographs, please consult the Therapeutic Products Directorate's guidance documents. For each monograph, the following are specified: ingredients, strengths, indications, directions for use and warnings.

4. Products falling under the NHP Regulation are excluded from the scope of this document. Any sterile product is excluded from the scope of this document.

5. The content of this Annex should not be regarded as the only interpretation of the GMP Regulations nor does it intend to cover every conceivable case. Alternative means of complying with these Regulations can be considered with the appropriate scientific justification. Different approaches may be called for as new technologies emerge.

Modified Interpretations from GMP Guidelines

Sanitation

C.02.007

3.1 Cleaning procedures for all primary contact surfaces for manufacturing and filling equipment should consistently result in the absence of any visible product or cleaning agent residues. The equipment should be kept clean and dry and protected from contamination. For throat lozenges, the level of microbial contamination should be controlled and there should be no objectionable micro-organisms.

3.4 If analytical methods are used to detect residues or contaminants, they have been shown to provide accurate and consistent results.

C.02.008

1.1 Personnel who have access to any area where a drug is exposed during its fabrication or packaging / labelling must undergo health examinations prior to employment.

Raw Material Testing

C.02.009

2. Specifications of APIs are of pharmacopeial or other equivalent standards and are in compliance with the marketing authorization. Specifications of other raw materials may be based on a house standard provided that they are in compliance with the current marketing authorization of the drug.

4. Water used in the formulation of any drug product for which there is a pharmacopeial (Schedule B of the Food and Drugs Act) monograph meets the requirements of the applicable monograph.

   For drugs not appearing in a pharmacopeial (Schedule B of the Food and Drugs Act) monograph, water used in the formulation must meet appropriate specifications based on sound physical and chemical principles. In addition, specifications should include requirements for total microbial count, which should not exceed 100 cfu/ml, and for absence of Escherichia coli and Salmonella for oral preparations and Staphylococcus aureus and Pseudomonas aeruginosa for topical preparations.

5. Test methods provide accurate and consistent results.

6. A sample of each lot of raw material is fully tested against specifications. Sampling is conducted according to a statistically valid plan.

   6.1 In addition, for active pharmaceutical ingredient (API), each sample taken as part of the sampling plan is tested for identity using a specifically discriminating identity test.

   6.1.1 This interpretation does not apply.

   6.1.2 This interpretation does not apply.

8. If any API is held in storage after the established re-test date, that API is quarantined, evaluated, and tested prior to use. A batch of raw material can be re-tested and used immediately (i.e., within 30 days) after the re-test as long as it continues to comply with the specifications.

Manufacturing Control

C.02.011

2. All critical production processes have been shown to produce consistent results and are approved by the person in charge of the quality control department.

3. A written report recording results and conclusions of the evaluation of critical production processes is prepared, evaluated, approved, and maintained.

4. Changes to production processes, equipment, or materials that may affect product quality and/or process reproducibility are evaluated for suitability prior to implementation.

9. Provided that changeover procedures are evaluated and approved prior to implementation, similar non-medicinal products may be fabricated or

packaged/labelled in areas or with equipment that is also used for the production of pharmaceutical products.

Finished Product Testing

C.02.018

4. All test methods have been shown to provide accurate and consistent results.

Stability Testing

C.02.027

1.1 Accelerated stability data and/or data from similar product formulations are considered to be preliminary information only. The assignment of the expiry date may be initially based on accelerated data and data from similar formulations, and is supported by long term testing.

1.3 For new chemical entities, at least two lots of each strength are sampled for the development of shelf life data, unless such data are submitted as a part of the application for marketing approval. For existing chemical entities (e.g., generic drugs), one lot of each strength is sampled. The principle of bracketing and matrixing designs may be applied if justified.

1.7 Analytical test procedures used in stability evaluation have been shown to provide accurate and consistent results. Assays are to be stability-indicating (i.e., sufficiently specific to detect breakdown products and to distinguish between degraded and non-degraded materials). Limits for individual unidentified, individual identified and total degradation products are included.

C.02.028

1.1 A minimum of one batch of every strength of the drug, including the first batch, is enrolled in the continuing stability program at all times. The principle of bracketing and matrixing designs may be applied if justified in accordance with the TPD document entitled "Stability Testing of Existing Drug Substances and Products".

Annex 2 - Schedule D Drugs, Biological Drugs Including Fractionated Blood Products (GUI-0027)

Health Products and Food Branch Inspectorate

Good Manufacturing Practices for Schedule D Drugs
Part 1
Biological Drugs
including fractionated blood products

Supersedes: First Draft, March 24, 1998

Date issued: June 30th, 1999

Date of implementation: June 30th, 1999

*Revisions were made to this document on 2002-02-25 to reflect changes to the Health Products and Food Branch organizational structure. There were no other changes made to the content of the document.

Ce document est aussi disponible en français.

Annex 2 to the Current Edition of the Good Manufacturing Practices Guidelines - Schedule D Drugs, Biological Drugs Including Fractionated Blood Products (GUI-0027)[42]

Preface

Biological Drugs are listed in Schedule D to the Food and Drugs Act and are regulated under the Food and Drugs Regulations. The Regulations which pertain to biological drugs are, for the most part, found within Divisions 1, 1A, 2, 4 and 8. With the advent of Establishment Licensing, the requirements of Division 1A and Division 2, apply to biological drugs, both as bulk process intermediates and in dosage form. Section 12 of The Food and Drugs Act prohibits the sale of Schedule D drugs unless the premises in which the drug was manufactured and the process and conditions of manufacture therein are suitable to ensure that the drug will not be unsafe for use.

The approach to the regulatory control of biological drugs is largely determined by the source of biological starting materials and the method of manufacture. Since the biological processes employed are inherently variable, there is a consequential effect on the end products and by-products. These processes also

---

[42] Available on the Health Canada website at

have great potential for the introduction and/or proliferation of microbial contaminants.

This Annex to the GMP guidelines is intended to address special considerations and issues pertinent to the manufacture and control of biological drugs and is divided into 2 distinct parts. Part 1 addresses GMP requirements for biological drugs including fractionated blood products (animal and human) and Part 2, published separately, addresses the GMP requirements for human blood and blood components. The emerging issue of multi-product facilities (including a suite within a facility and a multi-suite complex) has also been given general consideration in developing this document.

Biological drugs include but are not limited to: vaccines; human blood and blood components; fractionated blood products (human, animal); antigens; allergens; hormones; cytokines; enzymes and products of fermentation (including monoclonal antibodies and products derived from rDNA technology).

Biological drugs whose manufacture involves the following methods fall within the scope of the Annex **Part 1:**

a. Growth of microbial agents and eukaryotic cells,

b. Extraction and/or use of biological tissues, fluids or organs from human, animal or plant,

c. Recombinant DNA (rDNA) technology,

d. Hybridoma technology,

Other regulations including the Transportation of Dangerous Goods Act and Regulations, and Regulations governing the Importation of Pathogens or Semen, should be consulted for references to specific controls required for microorganisms. The Health Canada Laboratory Biosafety Guidelines should also be consulted for classification of facilities involved in the large-scale production of microorganisms.

This Annex Part 1 should be used, in context, with the Inspectorate Guidelines for Good Manufacturing Practices (GMP) to facilitate compliance with Division 2 of the Food and Drugs Regulations by fabricators, importers, testers and distributors of biological drugs. Fabricators are invited to refer to Division 4 of the Regulations for specific product requirements. Alternate means of complying with regulatory requirements must be justified and be consistent with the market authorization for the product.

Principles incorporated in international guidance (e.g., WHO, USA, and EU guidance documents for GMP for biological medicinal products) have been taken into account in the preparation of this Annex Part 1.

Glossary Of Terms

As used in Part 1, the following additional definitions supplement the definitions provided under the Glossary of Terms in the main GMP Guidelines and should be useful to fabricators, importers, testers and distributors of biological drugs.

Adventitious Virus (virus fortuit)

Unintentionally introduced contaminant virus.

Annex 2: GUI-0027

Bio-Hazard (risque biologique)

> Biological material considered to be hazardous to personnel and/or environment.

Biological Auxiliary Material (matériel biologique accessoire)

> Raw material from a biological source which is intended to be used as a processing aid in the fabrication of the drug. It may be absent from the drug or may remain as an impurity in the drug at the end of the manufacturing process (e.g., biological additives used to supplement cell culture medium in production fermenter; human antithrombin III used to complex and remove human thrombin).

Biological Starting Material (matériel biologique de départ)

> Raw material from a biological source which is intended to be used in the fabrication of a drug and from which the active ingredient is derived either directly (eg., plasma derivatives, ascitic fluid, bovine lung, etc.) or indirectly (eg., cell substrates, host/vector production cells, eggs, viral strains etc.).

By-Product (sous-produit)

> A product arising incidentally in the fabrication of a specific biological drug.

Bulk Process Intermediate (produit intermédiaire en vrac)

> Any intermediate form of a Schedule D drug (e.g., final bulk intermediate, bulk material, bulk concentrate, drug substance) which must undergo further processing before it becomes a final product. They are usually characterized by a holding time, storage conditions and the application of in-process tests.

Campaign Production (production consécutive)

> Sequential processing of material, either more than one product in a multi-product facility or more than one lot of the same product in a dedicated facility, over a defined period of time. Campaign production could occur at any point in a production process where common rooms/suites and/or equipment are reused for multiple products/lots.

Cell Bank (banque de cellules)

> Collection of appropriate containers, whose contents are of uniform composition, stored under defined conditions. Each container represents an aliquot of a single pool of cells.

Cell Culture (culture cellulaire)

> Maintenance or propagation of cells in vitro. Cell culture is performed according to good aseptic/sterile techniques to ensure the absence of microbial contamination.

Changeover Procedures (procédures de conversion)

Logical series of validated steps ensuring a proper cleaning of suites and equipment before processing of a different product.

Cleaning Procedures Validation (validation des procédures de nettoyage)

Testing of methods used to clean equipment/surfaces in a processing suite/facility with assays to validate the effectiveness of the cleaning. The use of "worst-case" cleaning challenges and the addition of a safety factor in the standard operating procedure, can provide further assurance of acceptability. Such challenge might be created by artificially soiling a piece of equipment or by using reduced cleaning parameters (rinse time or volume).

Closed System (système fermé)

Process equipment (fermenter, transfer lines, harvest apparatus etc.) or process step in which the product is not exposed to the external environment. A closed system requires that the quality of materials entering or leaving the system and the manner in which these materials are added/removed from the system is carefully controlled.

Cold Chain (chaîne du froid)

Maintenance of a designated temperature throughout the manufacturing process and during storage, until the product is used.

Concurrent Production (confinement)

Total isolation of one or more steps of a manufacturing process to prevent cross-contamination of the product, or staff, from all other steps of the process.

Containment (médecin)

A person registered and licensed under the laws of a province to practice the profession of medicine.

Continuous Culture (culture en continu)

Process by which growth of cells is maintained by periodically replacing a portion of the cells and medium such that there is no lag or saturation phase.

Cross-Contamination (contamination croisée)

Contamination of a drug or biological starting material or in-process intermediate with another drug or biological starting material or in-process intermediate. In multi-products facilities, cross-contamination can occur throughout the manufacturing process, from generation of the MCB and WCB through finishing.

Dedicated (dédié)

Facility of piece of equipment used only in the fabrication of a particular product.

Detoxification (détoxification)

> Conversion of bacterial toxins to toxoids (non-toxic but immunogenic derivatives of toxins) by chemical treatment.

Drug Product (produit médicamenteux) (dosage form, finished product, final container product)

> A pharmaceutical product type that contains a biological drug substance, generally in association with excipients. It corresponds to the dosage form in the immediate packaging intended for marketing.

Drug Substance (substance médicamenteuse)

> A defined process intermediate containing the active ingredient, which is subsequently formulated with excipients to produce the drug product.

Fermentation (fermentation)

> A process in which cells or microorganisms are cultured in a container (bioreactor or fermenter), in liquid or solid medium, for experimental or commercial processes.

Harvesting (récolte)

> Procedure by which the cells, inclusion bodies or crude supernatants containing the unpurified active ingredient are recovered.

Inactivation (inactivation)

> Removal of infectivity of microorganisms by chemical or physical modification.

In Vitro Cell Age (for production) (âge cellulaire In vitro)

> Measure of time between thaw of the MCB or WCB vial(s) to harvest of the production vessel measured by elapsed chronological time, by population doubling level of the cells, or by passage level of the cells when subcultivated, by a defined procedure for dilution of the culture.

Master Cell Bank (MCB) (banque de cellules primaires)

> An aliquot of a single pool of cells which generally has been prepared from the selected cell clone under defined conditions, dispensed into multiple containers and stored under defined conditions. The MCB is used to derive all working cell bank (WCB). The testing performed on a new MCB (from a previous initial clone, MCB or WCB) should be the same as for the MCB unless justified.

Multi-Suite Complex (complexe multi-suites)

> Facility where each suite is dedicated to the fabrication of a biological drug. Suites are located within the same building and are independent from one another.

Annex 2: GUI-0027

Multi-Product Facility (établissement multi-produits)

> Facility where more than one product of the same type or products from different classes are fabricated (e.g., pharmaceutical and biological drugs).

Multi-Use Area (aire polyvalente)

> Area where more than one biological drug substance or drug product is manufactured. Manufacturing is either concurrent or on a campaign basis.

Product-Specific Cleaning (nettoyage adapté au produit)

> Cleaning procedure performed to ensure removal of product residuals from non-dedicated product-contact equipment/ containers which includes appropriate assays to validate the effectiveness of the cleaning.

Production Cells (cellules de production)

> Cell substrate used to fabricate the product.

Pure Culture (culture pure)

> A culture broth/ medium containing a single type of microorganism.

Reprocessing (retraitement)

> Subjecting of an in-process or a bulk process intermediate (final biological bulk intermediate) or final product of a single batch/lot to a previous step in the validated manufacturing process due to a failure to meet pre-determined specifications. Reprocessing procedures are foreseen as occasionally necessary for biological drugs and are validated and pre-approved as part of the market authorization.

Reworking (reprise)

> Subjecting of an in-process or bulk process intermediate (final biological bulk intermediate) or final product of a single batch/lot to an alternate manufacturing process due to a failure to meet predetermined specifications. Reworking is an unexpected occurrence and is not pre-approved as part of the market authorization.

Scale Up (1) (mise à l'échelle(1))

> Steps in the fermentation process whereby the production cell line/seed line is expanded until it reaches a sufficient concentration for seeding the seed and/or production bioreactors.

Scale Up (2) (mise à l'échelle(2))

> Increase in the production scale, for example, from pilot plant to production plant.

Seed Lot (lot de semences)

> Collection of appropriate containers, whose contents are of uniform composition, stored under defined conditions. In contrast to cell bank, seed lot may describe collections of plasmids, viruses etc. For master and working seed lots, refer to definitions provided for MCB and WCB.

Separated Facility (établissement séparé)

> Facility which is physically separated from one another.

Subculture (repiquage)

> Splitting of a cell population by a defined procedure to reduce the cell concentration or density and make possible cell expansion.

Suite (suite)

> Functional manufacturing area consisting of one or more rooms with shared air handling and personnel access and which is segregated from the rest of the facility. It contains a separate air supply and exhaust, separate personnel access/egress and separate process equipment. It does not necessarily include a separate supply of water, compressed air/gas or steam, provided that suitable engineering controls are in place to prevent product contamination of these systems. A suite is referred to as a facility within a facility.

Working Cell Bank (WCB) (banque de cellules de travail)

> Cell bank prepared from aliquots of a homogenous suspension of cells obtained from culturing the fully characterized MB under defined culture conditions.

Regulation

Premises

C.02.004

1. Air filtration units are dedicated to specific processing areas and air from areas handling pathogens is not recirculated but exhausted through H.E.P.A. filters which have regular, documented performance checks. Air from live areas may not be recirculated into non-live areas or into other live areas with different organisms.

   1.1 Air filtration units that supply, but are not dedicated to, specific areas handling risk group 1 or 2 pathogens may not be recirculated but must be exhausted whereby the use of H.E.P.A. filters for exhaust air is optional.

   1.2 Air filtration units are dedicated to specific processing areas and air from areas handling risk group 3 or 4 pathogens is not recirculated but exhausted through H.E.P.A. filters. In all instances where H.E.P.A. filters are used, they must have regular, documented performance checks.

Annex 2: GUI-0027

2. Positive pressure areas are used to process sterile products but negative pressure used in specific areas at point of exposure of pathogens. This is necessary for containment purposes.

3. Where negative pressure areas or safety cabinets are used for aseptic processing of pathogens, the areas are surrounded by a positive pressure zone.

   3.1 Where negative pressure areas are used for the aseptic processing of risk group 1 or 2 pathogens, the adjoining rooms surrounding the negative pressure area must be at a higher (less negative or positive) differential pressure. Where negative pressure areas are used for the aseptic processing of risk group 3 pathogens, the adjoining rooms, ceiling space, service spaces, and floor space (if hollow or the negative pressure area is not on the lowest level of a multi-level building), surrounding the negative pressure area must be at a higher controlled (less negative or positive) differential pressure.

   3.2 Where negative pressure areas are used for the aseptic processing of risk group 4 pathogens, the negative pressure area must be completely surrounded by a controlled positive pressure zone on all faces, including adjoining rooms, service spaces, the ceiling space, and floor space (if hollow).

4. Pipework systems, including valves, pumps, vent filters and housings, that come into contact with final product, or with material used in final product, or with material that contacts surfaces which contact final product, must be designed to facilitate cleaning and sterilization, where other means to ensure sterility or monitoring of contact surfaces are not used. Where possible, 'clean-in-place' (CIP) and 'sterilize-in-place' (SIP) systems should be used. Other systems are also acceptable if validation is performed and approved.

5. Facilities are designed to be effectively decontaminated and prevent cross-contamination during movement of personnel and materials between different areas. The layout and design of production areas and equipment permits effective cleaning and decontamination.

6. If different biological products are fabricated, packaged and tested, or diagnostic work done in the same premises, precautions are taken to prevent the risk of cross-contamination (e.g., location of inlet/exhaust, separation of air supply). This is dictated by the products and equipment used.

7. Spore-forming microorganisms such as Bacillus anthracis, Clostridium botulinum, Clostridium tetani, as well as BCG vaccine (attenuated Mycobacterium tuberculosis Bacillus Calmette-Guerin strain) and live organisms used in the production of tuberculin products, are handled in dedicated facilities with dedicated equipment. Procedures describing plans for entry of personnel into restricted storage and handling areas are strictly enforced.

8. Once inactivated, certain spore forming microorganisms such as Clostridium tetani may be handled in non-dedicated facilities.

9. Concurrent production in the same area using closed systems or fermenters, may be acceptable for products which pose lower safety risks such as monoclonal antibodies and products prepared by rDNA technologies.

10. Separate, specially designed rooms with appropriate environmental and physical containment controls are provided for preparing, handling and storing microorganisms. Reference should be made to the Health Canada Laboratory Biosafety Guidelines, in designing facilities involved in the large-scale production of microorganisms.

11. Animal Facilities

11.1 Animals are used for the manufacture of a number of biological drugs, for example polio vaccine (monkeys), snake antivenom (horses), rabies vaccine (rabbits, mice and hamsters) and serum gonadotropin (horses). In addition, animals may also be used in the quality control of most sera and vaccines, e.g. pertussis vaccine (mice), BCG vaccine (guinea-pigs), as well as for pyrogenicity (rabbits). Special considerations are required when animal facilities are present at a fabrication site.

11.2 Procedures for animal quarantine and husbandry are required and must conform to GLP regulations (WHO) or to the Canadian Committee on Animal Care Guidelines.

11.3 International guidelines (e.g., EC Directive 86/609/EEC) are consulted for general requirements for animal quarters, care and quarantine.

11.4 Quarters for animals used in production and control of biological products are separate from all other manufacturing areas. The health status of animals from which some biological starting materials are derived and of those used for quality control and safety testing are monitored, recorded and reported as appropriate (e.g., certification of origin and certification of fitness for use).

11.5 Separate staff are on site for animal care. Staff employed for work in animal facilities are provided with special clothing and separate changing facilities within the animal facility.

11.6 Where monkeys are used for the production or quality control of biologicals, special consideration is required. International guidance documents should be consulted (e.g., current WHO requirements for Biological Substances No. 7).

Equipment

C.02.005

1. Equipment used for handling live organisms is designed, operated and maintained in a state to ensure that pure cultures are uncontaminated by external sources during all processing and storage operations.

2. Air vent filters on fermenters have hydrophobic media, are tested for integrity prior to use and have a validated scheduled life span.

3. Facilities are designed to be effectively decontaminated and prevent cross-contamination during movement of personnel and materials between different areas. The layout and design of production areas and equipment permits effective cleaning and decontamination.

Personnel

C.02.006

1. All personnel engaged in the fabrication of biologicals receive training, specific to their duties and to the products being manufactured. Training in hygiene and microbiology is particularly relevant to biological production, owing to the susceptibility to microbial contamination.

2. Persons responsible for fabrication and quality control have an adequate background in relevant scientific disciplines such as bacteriology, biology, biometry, chemistry, medicine, pharmacy, pharmacology, virology, immunology and veterinary medicine, together with sufficient practical experience to enable them to perform their duties.

3. For fabrication involving pathogenic microorganisms (as defined by the Transportation of Dangerous Goods Act and Regulations), it may be appropriate to have a designated Biosafety Officer who is experienced and knowledgeable in handling pathogenic microorganisms and eukaryotic cells, with expertise in large scale manufacturing.

4. In the course of a working day, personnel working with live organisms or animals do not pass from one area to another area where other products or different organisms are handled.

5. Adequate numbers of qualified/ trained personnel are available to preclude having the same personnel working in different areas on the same day. Where this is unavoidable, clearly defined decontamination measures, including change of clothing and shoes and, where necessary, showering is followed by staff involved in any such fabrication.

6. Since many of the vaccine product intermediates are infectious, the hazard to employees must be considered in these types of operations and reflected in the environmental and personal protective controls.

7. The health status of personnel should be considered for their own as well as for product safety. All personnel engaged in fabrication, maintenance, testing and animal care (including any outside persons entering the areas) are vaccinated with appropriate specific vaccines and have regular health checks. Apart from the obvious problem of exposure of staff to infectious agents, potent toxins or allergens, adverse health conditions of staff may present microbiological hazards to products and may compromise product safety or quality. Persons whose presence could adversely affect the safety and quality of the product (such as a person with known infectious diseases, serious infections or exposed skin lesions) are excluded from the fabrication area.

Sanitation

C.02.007 and C.02.008

1. The disposition of unsatisfactory biological products or infectious materials not used in fabrication follow approved procedures, designed to eliminate risks to products and personnel.

2. Effluent which may contain pathogenic microorganisms is effectively decontaminated. Appropriate decontamination procedures must also be used when handling animal tissue or cultures of microorganisms, particularly when these pose a potential risk for cross-contamination.

3. Pipework systems, valves and vent filters are designed to facilitate cleaning and sterilization. Where possible CIP and SIP systems are used. Valves on fermentation vessels are of sanitary design and steam sterilizable.

4. Equipment cleaning processes are designed to remove endotoxins, bacteria, toxic elements and residual contaminating proteins and/or other identified contaminants.

5. Cleaning validation of equipment is critical for a multi-product facility involved in campaign or concurrent production of biological drugs. Validated product-specific cleaning procedures are available for non-dedicated equipment.

6. Killed vaccines (including rDNA-derived vaccines), toxoids and bacterial extracts filled in the same premises as other sterile products, following inactivation or detoxification, require validated product-specific facility and equipment cleaning and/or decontamination procedures.

Raw Material Testing

C.02.009 and C.02.010

1. Specifications for biological materials (e.g., starting material, auxiliary material or excipient) includes details of their source, origin, method of fabrication and the (biological and microbiological) controls applied to ensure their suitability for use. All bovine materials are sourced from a country that is considered at low risk of bovine spongiform encephalomyelitis (BSE) as designated by Agriculture and Agri-food Canada. Human derived products such as albumin are sourced from donors known to be free of adventitious agents as outlined in accepted criteria for blood donors and are approvable when used as an excipient. Clinical evidence of safety may also be required. If such product is used as an auxiliary material, the requirements may be less stringent, to be assessed on case by case basis.

2. Biological starting materials are evaluated against appropriate specifications prior to use in the fabrication of the drug.

3. Where the time required to perform a test is lengthy, it may be permissible to process biological starting materials before the result of the test is available. In such cases, release of a finished product is conditional on satisfactory results being obtained for those tests. This requirement is usually a part of the premarket authorization.

4. Provisions for reduced testing in the GMP Guidelines may not be applicable to some biological products because of the inherent variability in range and nature of biological starting materials and their by-products.

5. Seed lot and Cell Bank System In addition to the principles stated in other Guidelines, the following should be noted:

5.1 To prevent a drift of properties which might ensue from repeated subcultures and to ensure consistency of the biological starting material, the fabrication of biological drugs obtained by microbial culture, cell culture or propagation in embryos and animals is based on a system of master and working seed lots and cell banks.

5.2 Scale up of the process do not result in a maximum in vitro cell age for production which is greater than that provided in the market authorization.

5.3 Establishment of the seed lot and cell bank is performed in a suitably controlled environment to protect the seed lot and the cell bank and, if applicable, the personnel handling it. During the establishment of the seed lot and cell bank, no other living or infectious material (e.g., cell lines or microbial strains) is handled simultaneously in the same area or by the same persons.

5.4 Seed lots and cell banks are adequately characterized and tested for the absence of contaminants. Their suitability for use is further demonstrated by the consistency of the characteristics and quality of the successive batches of product. Seed lots and cell banks are established, stored and used in such a way as to minimize the risks of contamination or alteration.

5.5 Evidence of the stability and recovery of the seed lot and cell bank are documented. Storage containers are hermetically sealed, clearly labelled and kept at a suitable temperature. An inventory is meticulously kept. Storage temperatures are continuously recorded for freezers and properly monitored for liquid nitrogen. Any deviation from set limits and any corrective action taken are evaluated and documented.

5.6 Any material is handled by authorized personnel only, under the supervision of a responsible person. A system is in place to ensure security of inventory of seed lots or cell banks and retrievability of seed lots or cell banks vials. Different seed lots or cell banks are stored to avoid confusion or cross-contamination between them. It is desirable to split the seed lots and cell banks and to store the parts at different locations so as to minimize the risks of total loss.

5.7 All vials of master or working cell banks and seed lots are treated identically during storage. Once removed from storage, the vials are not returned to stock.

Manufacturing Control

C.02.011 and C.02.012

1. Campaign operations for different products require validated changeover procedures which include product-specific cleaning procedures for non-dedicated equipment.

2. Concurrent production of different products requires validated closed systems with effective barriers which preclude cross-contamination from other processes (e.g., adventitious agents from different host/ vector production cells). Concurrent purification not performed in closed systems requires dedicated areas.

3. Addition of media, materials or cultures to fermenters and other vessels and sampling is carried out using validated procedures to ensure that contamination and/or cross-contamination is avoided. Care is taken to avoid incorrect connections to ports during sampling and addition.

4. Additives or ingredients that must be measured or weighed during the production process (e.g., buffers) may be stored in small quantities in the production area.

5. Centrifugation and blending of products can lead to aerosol formation. Such operations must be contained to prevent transfer of live microorganisms.

6. Where possible, in-line sterilizing filters are used for routine addition of gases, media, acids, alkalis or defoaming agents to fermenters, and their usage is validated.

7. Virus removal and/or viral inactivation methods are validated using specific viruses or appropriate model viruses, and do not adversely affect the product.

8. Pure cultures are handled using appropriate controls to prevent adventitious contamination during production.

9. The storage and processing of inactivated and non-inactivated products is done in segregated areas, to avoid the potential for cross-contamination.

10. Chromatography equipment is dedicated to the purification of a single drug and the use of the same equipment at different processing steps is not recommended. The life span of columns and the acceptance criteria are defined in the sanitization / regeneration methods.

11. Batch records must document all biological starting materials and in-process materials used, in addition to all relevant test results.

12. Packaging of some biological drugs require strict control, monitoring and documenting of conditions such as temperature (e.g. maintenance of the cold-chain), humidity or light exposure.

13. If filling and sealing is not carried out immediately following fabrication of the drug, due to the need for specific assay results, a validated holding and/or shipping period in accordance with the market authorization may be allowed.

14. Special, appropriately documented precautions must be exercised in the storage and handling of microorganisms, in particular spore forming organisms.

15. The handling and destruction of rejected biological materials takes into consideration designation of the material (e.g., infectious, bio-hazard), and environmental protection requirements for their disposal.

Quality Control Department

C.02.013 to C.02.015

1. Biological analytical techniques are essential for control of most biologicals. Because of the inherent variability of biological processes, and the inability to fully characterise most biologicals, in-process controls during fabrication, packaging and labelling take on great importance in ensuring consistency in quality, safety and efficacy of the end product. Those controls which are crucial for quality (e.g., virus removal) but which cannot be carried out on the finished product, are performed at an appropriate stage of production.

2. Storage, transportation methods and procedures used (including distribution) may have major impacts on biological drugs. In some cases, transit time, transit method, temperature, humidity, light and/or vibration may be critical factors that could adversely affect the quality and effectiveness of the product. Biological drugs are stored, transported and handled in strict compliance with the market authorization.

3. Production methods utilizing continuous culture have specific requirements for in-process quality control. For example, continuous monitoring of critical parameters is required during fermentation. Such data should form part of the batch record.

4. For imported biological drugs that have been subjected to reprocessing, the quality control department is responsible for ensuring that the (documented) reprocessing carried out by the fabricator complies with the marketing authorization.

5. Reworking of an in-process or bulk process intermediate (final biological bulk intermediate) or final product of a single batch/lot is an unexpected occurrence and as such, the release of the final product is subjected to approval of both the procedure and the results by the marketing authorization review bureau within Biologics and Genetic Therapies Directorate.

Packaging Material Testing

C.02.016 and C.02.017

1. Many biological drugs are extremely susceptible to deleterious effects from container/ closure systems, and it is imperative to maintain strict control on the identity and quality of the immediate container and components in contact with the drug, in accordance with approved specifications.

2. For imported biological drugs, the quality control department is responsible for ensuring that the (documented) packaging materials used, comply with approved specifications.

Finished Product Testing

C.02.018 and C.02.019

1. The release of some finished biological drugs may be conditional on the satisfactory results of tests on biological starting materials or in-process materials.

2. For imported biological drugs, the quality control department is responsible for ensuring that finished product specifications and the testing done, comply with the marketing authorization.

Records

C.02.020 to C.02.024

1. For imported biological drugs, detailed summaries (e.g., Certified Product Information Document) of the current fabrication, packaging, labelling and testing procedures are maintained by the legal agent in Canada and master production documents are available on site at the fabricator.

2. Records are retained indefinitely on site at the fabricator, for biological drugs containing human blood-derived excipients (e.g., human albumin).

Samples

C.02.025 and C.02.026

See main GMP Guidelines

Stability

C.02.027 and C.02.028

1. For biological drugs, stability assessment is also linked to retaining biologic activity within the label claim and is subjected to premarket authorization.

2. The stability assessment includes analysis of both the lyophilized and reconstituted single and multi-dose dosage forms of the drug product.

Sterile Products

C.02.029

1. Due to their labile nature, most sterile biological drugs are produced by sterile filtration / aseptic compounding, followed by aseptic filling rather than by terminal sterilization. Direct-contact packaging materials (i.e., vials, syringes, stoppers etc.) are subjected to processing which ensures and maintains sterility prior to filling.

2. In addition to environmental standards for particulates and viable microorganisms, biological drugs are produced in an environment where temperature and humidity are controlled within specified limits, since these can have a deleterious effect on the product.

GMP Committee Members

Name	Title / Office / Bureau	Location
Jack Basarke	MRA Topic Leader, BCE*	Scarborough, Ont.
Benoit Binette, Secretary	Drug Inspector, Quebec Region, BCE	Longueuil, Que.
Francois Chevalier	GMP Specialist, Office of Compliance, Planning and Coordination, BCE	Ottawa, Ont.
France Dansereau, Chair	A/Head, Office of Compliance, Planning and Coordination, BCE	Ottawa, Ont.
Rachel Dansereau	Compliance Officer, Office of Compliance, Planning and Coordination, BCE	Ottawa, Ont.
Sandra Decoste	Drug Inspector, Atlantic Region, BCE	Darthmouth, N.S.
Sultan Ghani	A/Manager, Division of Pharmaceutical Quality, BPA**	Ottawa, Ont.
Raymond Giroux	Drug Inspector, Quebec Region, BCE	Longueuil, Que.
Daryl Krepps	Senior Regulatory Advisor, BBR***	Ottawa, Ont.
Darryl Melnyck	Drug Inspector, Central Region, BCE	Winnipeg, Man.
Cara Murray	Drug Inspector, Ontario Region, BCE	Scarborough, Ont.
Jean Saint-Pierre	Compliance Officer, Office of Compliance, Planning and Coordination, BCE	Ottawa, Ont.
Larry Young	Drug Inspector, Western Region, BCE	Burnaby, B.C.

* Bureau of Compliance and Enforcement changed to Health Products and Food Branch Inspectorate (HPFBI).
** Bureau of Pharmaceutical Assessment now part of Therapeutic Products Directorate (TPD).
*** Bureau of Biologics and Radiopharmaceuticals changed to Biologics and Genetic Therapies Directorate (BGTD).

Annex 3 - Schedule C Drugs (GUI-0026)

Health Products and Food Branch Inspectorate

Annex to the GMP Guidelines
Good Manufacturing Practices for Schedule C Drugs

Supersedes: First Draft, March 24, 1998

Date issued: June 30th, 1999

Date of implementation: June 30th, 1999

*Revisions were made to this document on 2002-03-01 to reflect changes to the Health Products and Food Branch organizational structure. There were no other changes made to the content of the document.

Ce document est aussi disponible en français.

Annex 3 to the Current Edition of the Good Manufacturing Practices Guidelines - Schedule C Drugs (GUI-0026)[43]

Preface

Radiopharmaceuticals, kits, and generators are listed in Schedule C to the Food and Drugs Act and are regulated under the Food and Drug Regulations. The Regulations which pertain to Schedule C drugs are found within Divisions 1A, 2, 3 and 8. Section 12 to the Food and Drugs Act does not permit the sale of drugs unless the premises in which the drug is manufactured and the process and conditions of manufacture therein are suitable to ensure that the drug will not be unsafe for use.

The application of Division 2 to Schedule C drugs may be different from its application to pharmaceuticals due to the unique production and handling characteristics of the former. This Annex is intended to highlight the aspects of Good Manufacturing Practices (GMP) that have a bearing on this class of drug. All sections of the main GMP Guidelines are applicable unless otherwise stated in this Annex.

Radiation safety requirements are not covered in this Annex. The Atomic Energy Control Board (AECB) provides Regulations and guidance documents which are applicable to this type of activity. More specifically, the AECB Design Guide for Basic and Intermediate Level Radioisotope Laboratories is applicable to the following sections of the GMP: PREMISES, EQUIPMENT (Fume Hood,

---

[43] Available on the Health Canada website at http://www.hc-sc.gc.ca/dhp-mps/compli-conform/gmp-bpf/docs/sched_c-annexe_c-eng.php

Plumbing, Storage and Security), SANITATION (handling and storage of radioactive wastes and personnel behavior) and MANUFACTURING CONTROL (procedure writing related to management of rejected materials). Standard Operating Procedures concerning conditions of transportation are defined under the RAW MATERIAL TESTING section of the main GMP Guidelines and should follow recommendations from the AECB Radioisotope and Transportation Division. Radioactive contamination of the environment in which a drug is prepared can directly affect its quality. Thus, in addition to AECB requirements, it is essential to follow Good Manufacturing Practices for Schedule C drugs.

Most radiopharmaceuticals are used as diagnostic agents and contain minute quantities, on a weight basis, of the drug product. In addition to chemical impurities, radiopharmaceuticals may contain radioactive (radionuclidic and radiochemical) impurities. Such impurities may have a detrimental effect on both the utility and reliability of the drug as a diagnostic agent, and possibly on the radiation dose to the patient. Radiopharmaceuticals used as therapeutic agents require additional consideration as they present greater radiation doses to the patient.

Since most radiopharmaceuticals have a short shelf-life, they are often administered to patients within a short time after fabrication (reconstitution). Release of the product before completion of certain quality control tests might be necessary in this case. For these reasons, the continuous assessment of the effectiveness of the quality assurance program becomes very important.

The guidance included in this Annex, when placed in context with the general Guidelines for Good Manufacturing Practices (GMP), should facilitate compliance with Division 2 of the Food and Drug Regulations by fabricators, packagers/labellers, distributors and importers of Schedule C drugs. Interpretations are written in general terms to allow establishments to adopt and justify procedures appropriate for their products and operations. The use of alternative approaches must be justified and be consistent with the market authorization for the product.

Principles incorporated in international documents (eg. Australian, European, and United States GMP guidance documents for radiopharmaceuticals) have been taken into account when writing this Annex.

Glossary of Terms

The following additions to supplement the definitions provided under the Glossary of Terms in the general Guidelines for Good Manufacturing Practices may be useful to fabricators, packagers/labellers, distributors and importers of Schedule C Drugs. The definitions given below apply to the terms used in this Annex. They may have different meanings in other contexts. Excerpts from the sections of the Food and Drugs Act and Regulations are shown in brackets.

Campaign Production (production consécutive)

Sequential processing of material, either different products in a multi-product facility or different lots of the same product in a dedicated facility, over a defined period of time. Campaign production could occur at any point in a production process where common rooms/suites and/or equipment are reused for multiple products/lots.

Carrier (entraîneur)

Blood collected from an individual and placed in the general blood supply for the purpose of transfusion to another person.

Component (constituant)

> A unit of a drug, other than a radionuclide, separately packaged in a kit for use in the preparation of a radiopharmaceutical, or an empty vial or other accessory item in a kit. [C.03.205]

Cross-Contamination (contamination croisée)

> Contamination of a drug or raw material or in-process intermediate with another drug, raw material or in-process intermediate. In multi-product facilities, potential cross-contamination can occur throughout the manufacturing process.

Dedicated (réservé)

> Facility or piece of equipment used only in the fabrication of a particular product or a closely related group of products.

Drug (drogue)

> A drug listed in Schedule C to the Act that is in dosage form, or a drug that is a bulk process intermediate, that can be used in the preparation of a drug listed in Schedule C to the Act that is of biological origin. [C.03.001]

Half-Life (demie-vie)

> Time during which an initial radioactivity of a radionuclide is reduced to one half.

Hot Cell (cellule chaude)

> A total containment cabinet shielded with lead.

Kit (trousse)

> A package that contains one or more separately packaged units of a drug, other than a radionuclide, and that may contain empty vials or other accessory items, for use in the preparation of radiopharmaceuticals. [C.03.205]

Master Formula (formule-type)

> A document or set of documents specifying the raw materials with their quantities, their radioactivity and the packaging materials, together with a detailed description of the procedures and precautions required to fabricate a specified quantity of a finished product as well as the processing instructions, including in-process controls.

Multiple-Dose Container (récipient multi-doses)

> Container that permits withdrawal of successive portions of the contents without changing the strength, quality or purity of the remaining portion for articles intended for parenteral use only.

Annex 3: GUI-0026

No-Carrier-Added (sans entraîneur ajouté)

Indicates the status of a radionuclide sample where no stable atom of the same element has been added purposely.

Pharmaceutical (produit pharmaceutique)

A drug other than a drug listed in Schedule C or D to the Act. [C.01A.001]

Radioactive Concentration (concentration radioactive)

Amount of radioactivity per unit volume such as mCi/mL or MBq/mL.

Radioactivity (radioactivité)

The number of disintegrations per unit of time given in Becquerel (Bq) or Curie (Ci) units.

Radiochemical Purity (pureté radiochimique)

The extent to which a drug is free from undesirable or adulterating radiochemicals as defined by specifications.

Radionuclide (radionucléide)

A nuclide with an unstable or excited nucleus (imbalance of protons and neutrons) which will undergo spontaneous transformation with emissions of subatomic particles and/or photons of energy.

Radionuclide Dose Calibrator (étalonneur de doses)

Device measuring the radioactivity in Becquerels (Bq) or Curies (Ci), of a radioactive sample.

Radionuclide Generator (générateur de radionucléides)

A radioactive parent and daughter contained in an ion exchange column or dissolved in a suitable solvent in a liquid-liquid extraction system where the radioactive daughter is separated from its parent by elution from the ion exchange column, or a solvent extraction procedure. [C.03.001]

Radionuclidic Purity (pureté radionucléidique)

The extent to which a drug is free from undesirable or adulterating radionuclides as defined by specification expressed as a percentage of the radioactivity of the specified radionuclide to the total radioactivity of the source.

Radiopharmaceutical (produit radiopharmaceutique)

A drug that exhibits spontaneous disintegration of unstable nuclei with the emission of nuclear particles or photons. [C.03.201]

Specific Activity (activité spécifique)

> Amount of radioactivity per unit mass or per mole such as mCi/mg, MBq/mg or mCi/mole, MBq/mole.

Total Containment Glove Box (boîte à gants de confinement total)

> An aseptic suite of totally enclosed environment at negative pressure, whose primary purpose is to maintain a sterile environment with the additional purpose of radioactivity workspace localization.

Total Radioactivity (radioactivité totale)

> Amount of radioactivity present in the total volume of a reconstituted preparation or total volume of an eluate or solution used for reconstitution/labelling purposes, expressed as mCi/total volume (mL) or MBq/total volume (mL).

Regulation

Premises

C.02.004

1. Radiopharmaceuticals and radionuclide generators are fabricated, packaged/labelled, stored and tested in facilities which prevent the contamination of drugs with unwanted sources of radioactivity such as radionuclidic and radiochemical contamination.

2. Facilities used for the handling of radioactivity are identified and access is restricted to people involved in the process taking place.

3. Airflow patterns do not present a contamination risk while providing the necessary protection for the product during critical operations.

4. Positive pressure areas are used to process sterile products which are not radiolabeled but negative pressure is used in specific areas at points of exposure of radioactivity.

5. Air handling filtration units are dedicated to specific processing areas.

6. Where negative pressure areas or safety cabinets are used (e.g. Hot cell, total containment glove box, etc.), the area(s) is surrounded by a positive pressure zone.

Equipment

C.02.005

1. Radiopharmaceuticals and radionuclide generators are fabricated, packaged/labelled, stored and tested with equipment which prevents the contamination of drugs with unwanted sources of radioactivity such as radionuclidic and radiochemical contamination. Dedicated equipment is recommended for campaign production to minimize the risk of cross-contamination.

Annex 3: GUI-0026

2. Radioactivity measuring equipment, such as radionuclide dose calibrators and gamma counters, is available for fabrication and control operations.

2.1 Such equipment is shielded or located to avoid any source of background radiation

2.2 The equipment is regularly calibrated for accuracy and precision. Corresponding records are kept.

2.3 This equipment is subject to installation and operational qualification. Equipment qualification is documented.

Personnel

C.02.006

1. For the fabricator, packager/labeller and tester, qualified individuals in respect of the drug and GMPs should be in charge of and retained in the manufacturing department and the quality control department.

2. Personnel working in areas where radioactive materials are handled are given specific safety training in accordance with other applicable Federal jurisdictions. Atomic Energy Control Board regulations and guidelines on radiation safety should be consulted.

Sanitation

C.02.007 and C.02.008

1. The sanitation program also includes procedures and practices in accordance with other applicable Federal jurisdictions. Atomic Energy Control Board regulations and guidelines on radiation safety should be consulted.

Raw Material Testing

C.02.009 and C.02.010

1. On arrival, packages containing radioactive raw materials are initially processed in accordance with other applicable Federal jurisdictions. Atomic Energy Control Board regulations and guidelines on radiation safety should be consulted.

2. Notwithstanding subsection C.02.009 (1), each lot or batch of raw materials containing a radionuclide where the physical half-life does not permit the completion of its tests under that subsection, may be used in the fabrication of a drug prior to the completion of its tests provided such testing is completed as soon as possible. Confirming the identity of the raw materials prior to their use is the primary objective of this section. This requirement is usually a part of the premarket authorization review.

Manufacturing Control

C.02.011 and C.02.012

1. Checks on yields and reconciliation of quantities are carried out at appropriate stages of the process to ensure that yields are within acceptable

limits for kits. Checks on yields and reconciliation of quantities do not apply to radiopharmaceuticals and radionuclide generators.

2. At all times during processing, all shielded containers are identified with the name of the contents and the batch or lot number.

3. In the case of a packaged drug, the master formula also includes for each product, package size, and type, the specific activity in the final container, and the type of shielding.

Quality Control Department

C.02.013 to C.02.015

1. The individual or authorized alternate making decisions concerning the release of a particular lot of raw material, packaging material or packaged Schedule C drug, shall be a distinct person from the ones that fabricate, package/label or sell the same lot.

2. All finished products are held in quarantine and are so identified until released by the quality control department. Where sterility and/or endotoxin testing is conducted on specific lots of short-lived radiopharmaceuticals, such lots may be released prior to completion of sterility and/or endotoxin testing, provided such testing is completed as soon as possible.

3. Radiopharmaceuticals are stored, transported and handled in strict compliance with the market authorization and other applicable Federal jurisdictions.

Packaging Material Testing

C.02.016 and C.02.017

1. The reuse of lead shielding is permitted only after a full evaluation of the risks involved, including any possible deleterious effects on product integrity. Specific provision is made for such in the premarket authorization.

2. Compatibility studies are conducted on all materials in direct contact with the drug (e.g. vials for drugs with no carrier added).

Finished Product Testing

C.02.018 and C.02.019

1. The written specifications contain a description of the drug in dosage form, which includes all properties and attributes including total radioactivity, specific activity or radioactive concentration, together with tolerances and a description of all tests or analyses used to determine those properties and attributes, in sufficient detail to permit performance by qualified personnel. Such analyses include the monitoring of generator eluate.

2. Sterility and/or endotoxin tests are conducted on batches of short-lived radiopharmaceuticals according to finished product specifications. Such batches may be released prior to completion of sterility and/or endotoxin testing, provided this overall process has been validated in advance and such testing is completed as soon as possible.

Records

C.02.020 to C.02.024

1. For imported Schedule C drugs, detailed summaries of marketing authorization of the current fabrication, packaging, labelling and testing procedures are maintained by the legal agent in Canada.

Samples

C.02.025

1. A sample of each lot or batch of radioactive raw material used in the fabrication of a drug shall be retained by the fabricator of the drug for a period of three months after this lot or batch is last used in the fabrication of the drug unless otherwise specified in the fabricator's establishment licence. Conditions for specifying raw material sample retention in the fabricator's establishment licence, may be due to, but is not limited to a short physical half-life, excessively small amounts of the raw material and high radiation exposure pursuant to the retention process. These considerations would normally be addressed at the time of the premarket authorization specific to a given product upon written request and based on appropriate justification.

2. Every distributor referred to in paragraph C.01A.003(b) and importer of a kit shall retain in Canada a sample of each lot or batch of the packaged/labelled kit for a period of at least one year after the expiration date on the label of the kit unless otherwise specified in the distributor's or importer's establishment licence.

Stability

C.02.027 and C.02.028

1. The aspects of the stability program of the drug are determined prior to marketing and prior to adoption of significant changes in formulation, fabrication procedures, or packaging materials that may affect the shelf-life of the drug. Any significant change in the source of radionuclide or any packaging components will necessitate repeat assessment of the stability.

   1.1 The shelf-life is established from the date/time of fabrication of the drug.

   1.2. The shelf-life of reconstituted kits is established from the time of radiolabeling.

   1.3 The stability schedule is designed such that data cover at least the highest specific activity, total radioactivity or radioactive concentration to be used for the preparation of the radiopharmaceutical. This design assumes that the stability of the intermediate condition samples is represented.

   1.4 The stability of reconstituted kits is demonstrated. Reconstitution is performed using the extremes of the reconstitution conditions. Tests are performed both at the time of reconstitution and at the time of expiry of the reconstituted drug. If the reconstituted product is to be transferred to a secondary container for storage or distribution, stability in that container is validated.

2. Where a drug is transferred to a second container, the stability for the storage time in that container is demonstrated. The stability is determined for the final packaged dosage form.

3. Stability data are available for the shelf-life of the product in its final container.

4. These stability requirements are subject to premarket authorization.

Sterile Products

C.02.029

1. The preparation of radiopharmaceuticals can be undertaken in any of the following qualified aseptic systems: laminar flow hood, total containment glove box.

2. Activities performed in aseptic systems/areas may include, but are not limited to:

    2.1. Aseptic addition of a sterile diluent to a sterile vial using a syringe.

    2.2. Aseptic attachments of sterile components and devices such as connecting a sterile syringe or a sterile filter device to a sterile needle; inserting a sterile needle through a sanitized stopper into a vial; and any penetration of, or creation of an open pathway into a sealed container-closure system after filling, as might occur with some postfilling sampling techniques.

3. Air velocity in aseptic areas (e.g. laminar flow hoods) is sufficient to sweep particulate matter away from the filling and closing area. Whenever possible, equipment configuration does not disrupt the laminar flow. Different areas in the fabricating process are separated by physical barriers whenever possible and may be supplemented by partial physical barriers (e.g., air curtains) where needed.

4. In cases where terminal steam sterilization is not possible or practical, due to the short physical half-life of the radionuclide involved or the thermal instability of the product, additional measures are taken to minimize contamination. Such measures may include, but are not limited to, the use of closed systems of fabrication and sterile filtration. Such equivalence must be validated and subsequent filling operations or any further operations involving the entry or opening of sterile closed containers are performed under aseptic conditions.

Annex 3: GUI-0026

Annex 4 -
Veterinary Drugs (GUI-0012)

Health Products and Food Branch Inspectorate

Veterinary Drugs Annex to Current Edition of the Good Manufacturing Practices Guidelines

Supersedes: New document

Date issued: May 1st , 2003

Date of implementation: July 1st , 2003

Ce document est aussi disponible en français.

Annex 4 to the Current Edition of the Good Manufacturing Practices Guidelines - Veterinary Drugs (GUI-0012)[44]

Introduction

This Annex to the current edition of the Good Manufacturing Practices (GMP) Guidelines is intended to clarify certain aspects that have relevance to the manufacture of veterinary drugs and were developed by Health Canada in consultation with their stakeholders. For the purpose of this Annex, GMP Guidelines means the current edition of GMP Guidelines. Although the Regulations and their rationale as well as the quality management principles outlined in the GMP Guidelines apply to all veterinary drugs, it is recognized that some of the interpretations provided in the GMP Guidelines may not always be applicable or appropriate in certain situations (e.g. premises for fabrication of veterinary drugs containing penicillin) or to the manufacture of drug premixes. For this particular type of veterinary drugs, feed ingredients are used in large quantities and invariably contain some light, powdery, flour like material, which may lead to extremely dusty conditions. This problem can be controlled with sophisticated dust extraction equipment. However, the main concern in the production of drug premixes is the potential for cross-contamination. Also, the production methods and handling characteristics of drug premixes do not necessarily call for the same complex techniques requiring highly skilled production and control staff as those required for other veterinary drugs. For that reason this Annex is separated in two sections. Section 1 addresses veterinary drugs with the exception of drug premixes and Section 2 addresses drug premixes only.

---

[44] Available on the Health Canada website at http://www.hc-sc.gc.ca/dhp-mps/compli-conform/gmp-bpf/docs/gmp-bpf-eng.php

Scope

1. The guidance included in Sections 1 and 2, when placed in context with the GMP Guidelines, should facilitate compliance with Division 2 of the Food and Drug Regulations. In order to avoid repetition, only those interpretations that are different from the ones included in the GMP Guidelines are contained in this Annex. The numbering of each interpretation used in this Annex corresponds to that of the interpretation being modified from the GMP Guidelines. Therefore, unless otherwise stated in this Annex, all interpretations included in the GMP Guidelines are applicable to veterinary drugs.

2. The modified interpretations from GMP Guidelines contained in Section 1 of this Annex apply specifically to all veterinary drugs with the following exceptions:

   2.1 Dilute Premix and Medicated Feed as per C.01A.001 (2).

   2.2 Veterinary biologics regulated under the Animal Disease and Protection Act and Regulations or other legislation.

   2.3 Drug Premixes (See Section 2)

3.1 The modified interpretations from GMP Guidelines contained in Section 2 of this Annex apply specifically to Drug Premixes. They do not apply to:

   3.1 Premixes containing only vitamin and mineral ingredients as these preparations are not considered to be drugs and are regulated by the Feeds Act (Agriculture Canada).

   3.2 Any other veterinary drugs.

The content of this Annex should not be regarded as the only interpretation of the GMP Regulations nor does it intend to cover every conceivable case. Alternative means of complying with these Regulations can be considered with the appropriate scientific justification. Different approaches may be called for as new technologies emerge.

Glossary of Terms

The following definitions are provided to complement those already available under the Glossary of Terms of the GMP Guidelines.

Drug Premix (or Medicated Premix) (prémelange médicamenteux)

> A drug for veterinary use to which a drug identification number has been assigned, where the directions on its label specify that it is to be mixed with feed as defined in section 2 of the Feeds Act. (C.01A.001 of the Food and Drugs Regulations). It is a veterinary drug product prepared in advance with a view to the subsequent manufacture of medicated feeds.

Dilute Drug Premix (prémelange médicamenteux dilué)

> A drug for veterinary use that results from mixing a drug premix with a feed as defined in section 2 of the Feeds Act, to such a level that at least 10 kg of the resulting mixture is required to medicate one tonne

of complete feed, as defined in section 2 of the Feeds Regulations, 1983, with the lowest approved dosage level of the drug.

Medicated Feed (aliment médicamenteux)

A mixed feed that contains a medicating ingredient [2.(1) of the Feeds Regulations, 1983].

Feed Ingredient (ingrédient pour aliment)

Any substance or mixture of substance that is assessed or evaluated as being acceptable for use in feeds.

Section 1: Veterinary Drugs Except Drug Premixes

Modified Interpretations from GMP Guidelines

Premises

C.02.004

11.2   Campaign production can be accepted on a product by product basis where proper justification is provided, rigorous validation is conducted, and validated controls and monitoring are in place to minimize any risk of cross-contamination.

In the case of facilities producing other veterinary drugs, campaign production of veterinary drugs containing penicillin is considered acceptable provided that the following conditions are met:

- non-penicillin drug products for human use are not fabricated, packaged/labeled or stored in the same facility.

- validated decontamination and cleaning procedures are in place to minimize any risk of cross-contamination.

Raw Material Testing

C.02.009

6.3 It is permissible to sample only a proportion of the containers for identity testing where a validated procedure has been established to ensure that no single container of API has been incorrectly labelled.

This validation should take account of at least the following aspects:

- the nature and status of the manufacturer and of the supplier and their understanding of the GMP requirements of the Pharmaceutical Industry;

- the Quality Assurance system of the manufacturer of the API;

- the manufacturing conditions under which the API is produced and controlled;

- the nature of the API and the medicinal products in which it will be used.

Annex 4: GUI-0012

Finished Product Testing

C.02.018

Note: For certain topical non-Schedule and cosmetic type products (e.g., hoof ointment) that contain only ingredients such as oils, tars and other emollients, it may be acceptable to perform identity tests based on the physical characteristics of the products such as specific gravity or viscosity. In these circumstances, there must be an attestation from the fabricator certifying that the addition of the ingredients in question was witnessed in the manufacturing process.

Section 2: Drug Premixes

Modified Interpretations from GMP Guidelines

Premises

C.02.004

2. The premises are designed, constructed and maintained such that they minimize entry of insects and other animals and the migration of extraneous material from the outside into the building and from one area to another.

    2.1 Doors, windows, walls, ceilings and floors are free of undue openings or cracks.

    2.2 Doors giving direct access to the exterior from manufacturing and packaging areas are used for emergency purposes only. Receiving and shipping area(s) do not allow direct access to production areas.

3. In all areas where raw materials, in-process drug premixes, or drug premixes are exposed, the following considerations apply to the extent necessary to prevent contamination.

    3.1 Floors, walls, and ceilings permit cleaning. Surface materials which shed particles are avoided.

    3.2 Floors, walls, ceilings, and other surfaces are made of hard and smooth materials.

    3.3 Joints between walls, ceilings, and floors do not permit the accumulation of extraneous materials.

    3.5 Floor drains are screened and trapped, as necessary, or sealed when not in use.

    3.6 Air quality is maintained through dust control, and periodic verification and replacement of air filters. Air handling systems provide adequate control of airborne dust and are subject to periodic verification to ensure compliance with their design specifications. Records are kept.

    Specific attention is given to the need to avoid cross-contamination and facilitate cleaning.

5. Rest, change, wash-up and toilet facilities are well ventilated and of a type that permits good sanitary practices.

11.2   Campaign production can be accepted on a product by product basis where proper justification is provided, rigorous validation is conducted, and validated controls and monitoring are in place to minimize any risk of cross-contamination.

In the case of facilities producing other veterinary drugs, campaign production of drug premixes containing penicillin is considered acceptable provided that the following conditions are met:

- non-penicillin drug products for human use are not fabricated, packaged/labeled or stored in the same facility.

- validated decontamination and cleaning procedures are in place to minimize any risk of cross-contamination.

Sanitation

C.02.007

3.1 Cleaning procedures for manufacturing equipment are effective.

Cleaning procedures for equipment used in the campaign production of drug premixes containing penicillin are validated.

3.4 Analytical methods used to detect penicillin residues are validated.

5.   The manufacture of drug premixes is conducted in segregated areas. Whenever possible, such segregated areas do not form part of a main manufacturing plant. Segregated areas surrounded by a buffer zone in order to minimize the risk of contamination of other manufacturing areas are considered an acceptable alternative.

Use of unit or portable dust collectors are avoided in fabrication areas, especially in dispensing, unless the effectiveness of their exhaust filtration is demonstrated and the units are regularly maintained as per written approved procedures.

Raw Material Testing

C.02.009

3.   This interpretation does not apply.

6.   A sample of each lot of raw material is fully tested against its specifications. Sampling is conducted according to a statistically valid plan.

6.1 In addition, for API, each sample taken as part of the sampling plan is tested for the identity of its content using a specifically discriminating identity test.

In lieu of testing each sample referred to in section 6.1, a composite sample is acceptable as long as the following conditions are met:

6.1.1 each composite sample should be made of no more than 10 samples; and

6.1.2 a potency test is performed on each composite sample to establish the mass balance of the composite sample.

Annex 4: GUI-0012

6.2 APIs originating from a dedicated facility that fabricates only one ingredient are exempted from the requirements outlined under Interpretation 6.1, provided that no re-packaging or re-labelling has taken place.

6.3 It is permissible to sample only a proportion of the containers for identity testing where a validated procedure has been established to ensure that no single container of API has been incorrectly labelled.

This validation should take account of at least the following aspects:

- the nature and status of the manufacturer and of the supplier and their understanding of the GMP requirements of the Pharmaceutical Industry;

- the Quality Assurance system of the manufacturer of the API;

- the manufacturing conditions under which the API is produced and controlled;

- the nature of the API and the medicinal products in which it will be used.

C.02.010

2. Identity testing is conducted on all lots of any raw material received on the premises of the person that formulates the raw material into drug premixes. This test is specific except for feed ingredients where only non specific identity tests may exist.

This identity testing is performed in accordance with C.02.009, interpretation 6.

8. Except for feed ingredients, if the same batch of raw material is subsequently received, this batch is also considered as separate for sampling, testing and release. However, full testing to specifications may not be necessary provided that all the following conditions are met:

8.1 a specifically discriminating identity test is conducted;

8.2 the raw material has not been repackaged or relabelled;

8.3 the raw material is within the re-test date assigned by the vendor;

8.4 evidence is available to demonstrate that all pre-established transportation and storage conditions have been maintained.

Manufacturing Control

C.02.011

2. All processes that affect content uniformity and potency are validated.

Packaging Material Testing

C.02.016

2. Specifications are in compliance with the marketing authorization.

3. The adequacy of test or examination methods is established and documented.

Samples

C.02.025

2. A sample of each lot or batch of API is retained by the fabricator of the drug premix.

Stability

C.02.028

1.1 At least one lot of each drug premix is enrolled in the continuing stability program at all times.

Annex 5 - Positron Emitting Radiopharmaceuticals (PER's) (GUI-0071)

Health Products and Food Branch Inspectorate

Annex to the Good Manufacturing Practices Guidelines

Good Manufacturing Practices (GMP) for Positron Emitting Radiopharmaceuticals (PERs)

(GUIDE-0071)

Annex 5 to the Current Edition of the Good Manufacturing Practices Guidelines - Positron Emitting Radiopharmaceuticals (PER's) (GUI-0071)[45]

Introduction

Positron Emitting Radiopharmaceuticals (PERs) used in Positron Emission Tomography (PET) are Schedule C drugs to the Food and Drugs Act and are regulated under the Food and Drug Regulations. The Regulations addressing the sale of Schedule C drugs are found within Part C, Divisions 1A, 2, 3, 5 and 8. In addition, Section 12 to the Food and Drugs Act does not permit the sale of drugs unless the premises in which the drug is manufactured, the process, conditions and controls of manufacture therein are suitable to ensure that the drug will meet the required quality and will not be unsafe for use.

The application of Division 2 of the Food and Drugs Regulations and the Annex to Good Manufacturing Practices (GMP) for Schedule C drugs may be different from its application to PERs due to the unique production, quality control and handling characteristics of the latter. Hence this Annex is dedicated to all the aspects of GMP that have a bearing on this class of radiopharmaceutical drugs.

PERs are used in PET as diagnostic agents as well as tools in research. In addition to the impurities of chemical source, the finished product (PER drugs) may contain other impurities of radioactive origin such as radionuclidic and/or radiochemical. Such impurities may have a detrimental effect on the utility, quality, safety and reliability of the drug as a diagnostic agent, and possibly on the radiation dose to the patient.

Due to the relatively short half-life of most positron emitting radionuclides a majority of PERs have a short shelf-life, and they are often administered to patients within a short time after fabrication (production). Release of the product

---

[45] Available on the Health Canada website at http://www.hc-sc.gc.ca/dhp-mps/compli-conform/gmp-bpf/docs/gui-0071_annex_gmp-bpf_positron_radiopharm_ltr-doc-eng.php

before completion of certain quality control tests might be necessary in order to maintain the appropriate radioactive dose regimen. For these reasons, the continuous assessment of the effectiveness of the quality assurance program is essential.

The guidance in this Annex, when placed in context with the general Guidelines for GMP, should facilitate compliance with Division 2 of the Food and Drug Regulations by fabricators, packagers/labellers, distributors and importers of PERs.

The principles and concepts adopted internationally for radiopharmaceuticals and PERs (eg. Australian Therapeutic Goods Administration (TGA), World Health Organization (WHO), and United States Food and Drug Administration (FDA)) were taken into account in the development of this Annex.

Scope

This Annex will be known as "ANNEX TO THE GMP GUIDELINES: Good Manufacturing Practices for Positron Emitting Radiopharmaceuticals (PERs)". The guidelines covered herein are applicable for all PERs. In addition, all sections of the main GMP Guidelines[46] are applicable unless otherwise stated in this Annex. Interpretations in this Annex take precedence and/or supersede those in the main GMP Guidelines. Interpretations in the main GMP Guidelines that are not applicable are indicated in this Annex.

Like the GMP Annex for Schedule C drugs, radiation safety requirements are not covered in this Annex. The Canadian Nuclear Safety Commission (CNSC) provides Regulations and guidance documents which are applicable to this type of activity. More specifically, the CNSC Design Guide for Basic and Intermediate Level Radioisotope Laboratories is applicable to the following sections of the Annex to the GMP: PREMISES, EQUIPMENT, SANITATION (handling and storage of radioactive wastes and personnel behaviour) and MANUFACTURING CONTROL (procedure writing related to management of rejected radioactive materials).

Standard Operating Procedures (SOPs) concerning conditions of transportation are defined under the RAW MATERIAL TESTING section of the main GMP Guidelines and should follow recommendations from the CNSC. Radioactive contamination of the environment in which a drug is prepared can directly affect its quality. Thus, in addition to CNSC requirements, it is essential to follow the GMP Guidelines given in this Annex for PERs.

In this guideline, "shall" is used to express a requirement, i.e., a provision that the user is obliged to satisfy in order to comply with the regulatory requirements; "should" is used to express a recommendation or that which is advised but not required; and "may" is used to express an option or that which is permissible within the limits of the guidance document.

The content of this Annex should not be regarded as the only interpretation of the GMP Regulations nor does it intend to cover every conceivable case. Alternative means of complying with these Regulations may be considered with the appropriate scientific justification. Different approaches may be called for as new technologies emerge.

The numbering of the Interpretations in this Annex is not intended to correspond to that of the GMP Guidelines.

---

[46] Good Manufacturing Practices (GMP) Guidelines 2002 Edition

Glossary of Terms

BGTD	Biologics and Genetic Therapies Directorate
Bq	Becquerel
Ci	Curie
CNSC	Canadian Nuclear Safety Commission
FDA	Food and Drug Administration
GBq	GigaBecquerel
GC	Gas Chromatography
GMP	Good Manufacturing Practices
PET	Positron Emission Tomography
PER	Positron Emitting Radiopharmaceutical
QC	Quality Control
RSU	Radiosynthesizer Unit
SOP	Standard Operating Procedure
TGA	Therapeutic Goods Administration
WHO	World Health Organization

Definitions

The following definitions which supplement the definitions provided under the Glossary of Terms in the general Guidelines for GMP may be useful to fabricators, packagers/labellers, distributors and importers of PERs. The definitions given below apply to the terms used in this Annex. They may have different meanings in other contexts. Excerpts from the sections of the Food and Drugs Act and Regulations are shown in brackets.

Accelerator (accélérateur)

A device to accelerate energetic charged particles linearly or in circular paths by means of a radiofrequency field and an electromagnetic field in case of cyclotrons. The accelerated particles cause nuclear reactions in the atoms of targets placed in their path.

Batch (lot de fabrication)

A defined quantity of final product produced in one production run often expressed either in mass (mg or g) or volume (mL or L) or total radioactivity (Ci or GBq), total number of vials or doses.

Calibration (étalonnage)

Set of tests that confirms under desired conditions, the relationship between values indicated by a measuring instrument or measuring system, or values represented by a material measure, and the corresponding values of a reference standard.

Campaign Production (production consécutive)

Sequential processing of material, either different products in a multi-product facility or different lots of the same product in a dedicated facility, over a defined period of time. Campaign production could occur at any point in a production process where common rooms/suites and/or equipment are reused for multiple products/lots.

Carrier (entraîneur)

A stable element present with a radionuclide of the same element.

Catalyst (catalyseur)

A substance usually used in small amounts relative to the reactants that modifies and increases the rate of a reaction without being consumed in the process.

Cross-Contamination (contamination croisée)

Contamination of a drug or a radionuclide or a raw material or in-process intermediate with another drug, radionuclide, raw material or in-process intermediate. In multiproduct facilities, potential cross-contamination can occur throughout the manufacturing process.

Dedicated (réservé)

Facility or piece of equipment used only in the fabrication of a particular product or a closely related group of products.

Drug (drogue)

A drug listed in Schedule C to the Act that is in dosage form, or a drug that is a bulk process intermediate, that can be used in the preparation of a drug listed in Schedule C to the Act. [C.03.001]

Half-Life (demie-vie)

Time during which an initial radioactivity of a radionuclide decays to one half.

Hot Cell (cellule chaude)

An aseptic total containment cabinet providing a Class A (with Laminar flow), or Class B (with Turbulent flow) environment, and is shielded with lead of various thickness.

Manifold (manifold)

A unit for connecting a cylindrical pipe fitting, having a number of lateral outlets, for connecting one pipe with several others used in the Radiosynthesizer Unit.

Manufacture (fabrication)

> all operations including purchase of materials and products, production, quality control, release, storage, distribution and related controls.

Master Formula (formule-type)

> A document or set of documents specifying the raw materials with their quantities, their radioactivity and the packaging materials, together with a detailed description of the procedures and precautions required to fabricate a specified quantity of a finished product as well as the processing instructions, including in-process controls.

Multiple-Dose Container (récipient multi-doses)

> Container that permits withdrawal of successive portions of the contents without changing the concentration, quality or purity of the remaining portion.

No-Carrier-Added (sans entraîneur ajouté)

> Indicates the status of a radionuclide sample where no stable atom of the same element has been added purposely.

Parametric Release (libération en fonction de paramètre)

> A validated system of release that gives the assurance that the product is of the intended quality based on information collected during the manufacturing process and on the compliance with specific GMP requirements related to Parametric Release.

Positron Emitting Radiopharmaceuticals (PERs) (produits radiopharmaceutiques émetteurs de positrons)

> Drugs labelled with positron emitting radionuclides or containing positron emitting radionuclides that exhibit spontaneous transformation of unstable nuclei through positron decay.

Precursor (précurseur)

> A chemical substance or molecule which exists as an ingredient, reactant, or intermediate that is used for the chemical or radiochemical synthesis of a particular desired end product.

Radioactive Concentration (concentration radioactive)

> Amount of radioactivity per unit volume such as mCi/mL or MBq/mL.

Radioactivity (radioactivité)

> Spontaneous decay of unstable nuclei and is quantified as the number of disintegrations per unit of time as given in Becquerel (Bq) or Curie (Ci) units.

Radiochemical Purity (pureté radiochimique)

> The extent to which a drug is free from undesirable or adulterating radiochemicals as defined by specifications.

Radionuclide (radionucléide)

> An unstable atom that undergoes spontaneous transformation with emissions of subatomic particles and/or photons of energy.

Radionuclide Dose Calibrator (étalonneur de doses)

> Device measuring the radioactivity in Becquerels (Bq) or Curies (Ci), of a radioactive sample.

Radionuclide Generator (générateur de radionucléides)

> a radioactive parent and daughter contained in an ion exchange column or dissolved in a suitable solvent in a liquid-liquid extraction system where the radioactive daughter is separated from its parent by elution from the ion exchange column, or a solvent extraction procedure. [C.03.001]

Radionuclidic Purity (pureté radionucléidique)

> The extent to which a drug is free from undesirable or adulterating radionuclides as defined by a specification expressed as a percentage of the radioactivity of the specified radionuclide to the total radioactivity of the source.

Radiosynthesizer Unit (RSU) (unité de radiosynthèse)

> A closed-system device for the synthesis of radioactive drug substances used in the manufacturing of PERs. The system may be controlled by graphical computer software programs.

Radiopharmaceutical (produit radiopharmaceutique)

> a drug that exhibits spontaneous disintegration of unstable nuclei with the emission of nuclear particles or photons.

[C.03.201]

Specific Activity (activité spécifique)

> Amount of radioactivity per unit mass or per mole such as mCi/mg, MBq/mg or mCi/mole, MBq/mole.

Starting Material (produit de depart)

> Any substance entering a production facility for use in the production of a drug product.

Target Material (cible)

> A chemical substance which is bombarded with nuclear particles to produce a desired radionuclide.

Total Containment Glove Box (boîte à gants de confinement total)

> A totally enclosed environment at negative pressure, whose primary purpose is radioactivity workspace localization.

Total Radioactivity (radioactivité totale)

> Amount of radioactivity present in the total volume of a reconstituted preparation or total volume of an eluate or solution, expressed as mCi or MBq.

Premises

Regulation

C.02.004

Interpretation

Note: Interpretation #10 of Regulation C.02.004 in the main GMP Guidelines is not applicable.

1. PERs and positron emitting radionuclide generators shall be fabricated, packaged/labelled, stored and quality tested in a manner which prevents cross-contamination and mix-up of drugs and/or radioactivity with unwanted sources of radioactivity and/or drugs such as chemical, radionuclidic, radiochemical or radiopharmaceutical contamination.

2. Facilities used for the handling of radioactivity shall be clearly identified and access should be restricted to people involved in the process taking place. Although the same room or area may be designated for various purposes such as radiochemical synthesis, quality control, packaging and storage, whenever possible each area should be separated by a physical barrier.

3. Airflow patterns and ventilation should not present a contamination risk for the products while providing the necessary protection from radioactive airborne exposure to the personnel during critical operations.

4. Aseptic work areas shall be ensured and maintained for the processing of sterile PER drug product by:

   4.1 using positive pressure areas to process sterile products which are not radiolabeled;

   4.2 using negative pressure in specifically designed areas for containment of radioactivity.

   4.3 carrying out the production in negative pressure areas or safety cabinets (e.g. Hot cell, total containment glove box, etc.) surrounded by a positive pressure zone ensuring appropriate air quality requirements.

   4.4 dedicating air handling filtration units to specific processing areas such as radioactive or non-radioactive. Air from the operations containing radioactivity shall be exhausted through appropriate filters and the filters routinely checked for efficiency. It shall be ensured that the air is not re-circulated and air outlets are designed to avoid environmental contamination of radioactive particles or gases. It shall also be ensured that a system is in place in order to prevent air from entering aseptic areas in the event the air exhaust is not functioning; alarms and systems need to be in place to alert of changes in air flow patterns in the event of exhaust failure.

4.5 cleaning transfer lines such that no contaminant is introduced into the final radiopharmaceutical product.

4.6 raw materials are stored and sampled in a separate area or containment vessel. If sampling is performed in the storage area, it is conducted in such a way as to prevent contamination or cross contamination. All materials are clearly marked and a log sheet is maintained for each material.

Equipment

Regulation

C.02.005

Interpretation

1. Radionuclide Production Target: when a positron emitting radionuclide is produced in an in-house accelerator, the following shall be ensured:

    1.1 Reusable targets are operated in a manner to ensure that the product is free of any residual radionuclidic, radiochemical or chemical contaminants.

    1.2 SOPs are available which describe the responsibility and frequency of cleaning and maintenance of the target;

    Note: Refer to the Raw Material Testing section for information.

2. Radiosynthesis apparatus (including dedicated Radiosynthesis Units): SOPs shall be required for the operation, maintenance and cleaning of all radiosynthesis apparatus, including dedicated Radiosynthesis Units. Prior to their initial use in manufacturing and production, the manufacturing process shall be validated against the specifications for the PERs being manufactured. In particular, it shall be demonstrated that a sterile and pyrogen free PER can be produced repeatedly.

    The following shall be ensured with respect to the RSU:

    2.1 cleaning/flushing the RSU as per the user's manual; 2.2 connection of all tubing, including replacement (if needed) reaction vessels; manifold/cartridges, purification columns, and final product collection vial, as needed;

    2.3 ensuring that monitoring and/or recording devices for various important chemical synthesis parameters such as temperature, pressure, flow rate, time, and date are properly functioning;

    2.4 ensuring that controlling computer systems, if applicable, are recording correctly, and that the correct program or process parameters are used.

3. PERs and positron emitting radionuclide generators shall be fabricated, packaged, stored and tested with equipment which does not contribute to the cross-contamination of drugs with unwanted sources of radioactivity such as radionuclidic and radiochemical contamination.

4. Radioactivity measuring equipment shall be shielded or located so as to avoid any source of background radiation.

5. All equipment shall be regularly calibrated for accuracy, precision and reproducibility and corresponding records maintained.

6. Critical equipment shall be subject to installation, operational, and performance qualification. The results shall be documented.

Personnel

Regulation

C.02.006

Interpretation

1. In a PERs manufacturing establishment, regardless of whether it is a hospital, centralized radiopharmacy, nuclear centre or institution, industrial manufacturer, or contract manufacturer, the head of the establishment should be a professionally qualified person with extensive knowledge in PERs and PET in general. It is reasonable to expect that the qualifications of the individual include experience in radiopharmaceutical sciences and/or nuclear medicine.

2. For the fabricator, packager/labeller and tester, qualified individuals in respect of the PERs manufacturing and quality control with additional expertise in radiochemistry and radiopharmacy including GMPs, should be in charge of, and retained in, the manufacturing department and the quality control department, respectively.

3. A minimum of two qualified persons shall be involved in the production (fabrication) and quality control of PERs. The production of the PERs shall be supervised and authorized only by a person with adequate education in radiochemistry including specialized training in PET chemistry and experience in the manufacturing of PERs. The quality control and batch release shall be supervised and approved by a different person with specialized knowledge, education and experience/training in the quality control of PERs and radiopharmaceuticals.

4. Personne working in areas where radioactive materials are handled shall be given specific safety training in accordance with other applicable Federal jurisdictions. The Canadian Nuclear Safety Commission (CNSC) regulations and guidelines on radiation safety should be consulted.

Sanitation

Regulations

C.02.007 and C.02.008

Interpretation

1. The sanitation program shall include procedures and practices in accordance with other applicable federal regulations. The CNSC regulations and guidelines on radiation safety should be consulted.

2. Specialized disposal systems shall be adopted for radioactive effluents in accordance with other applicable federal regulations. The CNSC regulations and guidelines on radiation safety should be consulted.

Raw Material Testing

Regulations

C.02.009 and C.02.010

Interpretation

Note: Interpretations #6 and #10 of Regulation C.02.009 in the main GMP Guidelines are not applicable.

1. Detailed specifications including the source, origin and (where applicable) method of manufacture, test data, suitable storage conditions and expiry dates for all materials and components including the starting materials and/or precursor used in the production and testing of PERs shall be maintained. This is to ensure their suitability for use in the production or testing.

2. As appropriate, certificates of analysis, and/or quality testing data should be obtained from the supplier. However, if these are not available or if the material is produced in-house, the PER manufacturing facility is responsible for making all the testing and data available to the full specifications of the material.

3. Acceptance testing may be necessary for the target material if it has a potential impact on the purity of the final PER product.

4. The recycling method of O-18 water shall be documented and acceptance criteria/specifications are well defined.

5. On arrival, packages containing radioactive materials such as importation of off-site PER radionuclides (e.g., F-18, Sr-82), shall be initially processed in accordance with other applicable Federal jurisdictions. The CNSC regulations and guidelines on radiation safety should be consulted.

6. The PER manufacturing facility establishes the reliability of the supplier by performing full testing against supplier specifications for the first three lots of radionuclides received and at appropriate intervals thereafter, but at a minimum, quarterly.

7. Confirming the identity of the raw materials prior to their use is the primary objective of this section. This requirement is usually a part of the pre-approval authorization review. Notwithstanding subsection C.02.009 (1), each lot or batch of raw materials containing a radionuclide where the physical half-life does not permit the completion of its tests under that subsection, validation must be provided.

Manufacturing Control

Regulations

C.02.011 and C.02.012

Interpretation

Note: Interpretations #23, 24, and 25.1 of Regulation C.02.011 in the main GMP Guidelines are not applicable

Manufacturing Control for PERs is required to ensure proper labelling in order to prevent mix-ups and to ensure cleaning and sterility since most of the critical testing is done retrospectively; and to design the production methodology in order to prevent cross-contamination. The following are guidelines for ensuring the above criteria:

1. At all times during processing, shielded containers shall be identified with the name of the contents and the batch or lot number.

2. In the case of a packaged drug, the master formula also includes for each product, (where applicable), package size and type, the range of radioactivity, concentration in the final container, and the type of radionuclide and shielding.

3. If data are available, it may be used retrospectively for process validation. The data should indicate that the process is capable of consistently producing batches which meet predetermined specifications specifically for radionuclidic purity, radiochemical purity, sterility and endotoxins. The retrospective validation should consider all failures and changes to the process.

4. Although concurrent testing for sterility and endotoxins are not appropriate for PERs, the membrane filter used for the sterile filtration of the final product shall be tested for filter integrity. Refiltration can be considered if filter integrity does not meet specifications.

5. Computer systems used in the production of PERs should be validated with a production run to demonstrate that they function as intended. Changes to the computer system including software upgrades shall be re-validated.

6. Where the final product is created in situ, validation for cleaning and sterility is required to ensure no cross-contamination of any nature such as radionuclidic, radiochemical or chemical for the target or the transferring line.

7. Validation for sterility and cleaning is required for the RSU with reusable manifolds.

8. In general, due to the short physical half-life of most PER radionuclides, most of the products are released without completing certain tests. As noted earlier, initial validation tests should be performed, followed by periodic testing. In such situations, the effectiveness of the quality assurance system should be periodically assessed and an effective recall system shall be in place.

9.   The purpose of a recall system is to prevent the use of a deviant PER product rather than its retrieval, since the return of PERs is not practical due to the radioactive nature of the product. However, in the event a sample is returned the federal guidelines for transportation (refer to CNSC guidelines) shall be followed.

Quality Control Department

Regulations

C.02.013 to **C.02.015**

Interpretation

Note: Interpretations #4, 6, 7, 8, and 9 of Regulation C.02.014 in the main GMP Guidelines are not applicable.

Interpretations #1 and 2 of Regulation C.02.015 in the main GMP Guidelines are not applicable.

1.   The quality control unit is the final decision-making authority for release of a product; the person responsible for the release of the product is a distinct person from the person (s) who fabricate, package/label or sell the same lot.

2.   The area of responsibility of the unit includes authorized decision-making concerning the release of a particular lot of raw material, packaging material or finished PERs.

3.   All finished products are held in quarantine (on-site or in transit) and are so identified until released by the quality control department. Where sterility and/or endotoxin testing is conducted on specific lots of PERs, such lots may be released prior to completion of sterility and/or endotoxin testing, provided such testing is validated a priori and is completed as soon as possible.

4.   PERs are stored, transported and handled in strict compliance with the market authorization and CNSC regulations.

Packaging Material Testing

Regulations

C.02.016 and **C.02.017**

Interpretation

1.   The reuse of lead shielding in generators is permitted only after a full evaluation of the risks involved, including any possible deleterious effects on product integrity. Specific provision is made for such in the pre-market authorization.

2.   Compatibility studies should be conducted on all materials in direct contact with the PER drug product such as vials and stoppers, as well as sterile filters, tubing, etc. for PER generators.

Finished Product Testing

Regulations

C.02.018 and C.02.019

Interpretation

Note: Interpretations #1 and 7 of Regulation C.01.019 in the main GMP Guidelines are not applicable.

The production method for various PER products may vary in different centres, and hence, the testing for the final product may also vary among centres. In general, the following guidelines should be used:

1. Written specifications should contain a description of the drug in dosage form, which may include, but is not limited to: total radioactivity, specific activity or radioactive concentration, radiochemical purity, pH, osmolality, radionuclidic purity, catalyst, residual solvents, etc., together with tolerances and a description of all test methods or analyses used to determine those properties and attributes, in sufficient detail to permit performance by qualified personnel. Such analyses include the monitoring of generator eluate for purity, radioactivity, radioactive concentration and appearance.

2. Because of the short half-life of most radionuclides and the short shelf-life of most PERs, product release tests are based (in real time) on a limited number of tests. The remaining tests are performed on a retrospective basis. However, in order to determine which tests are done on a retrospective basis, a rationale should be prepared and documented.

3. Sterility and endotoxin tests should be conducted on all batches of PERs according to finished product specifications. Such batches may be released prior to completion of sterility and/or endotoxin testing, provided this overall process has been validated in advance and such testing is completed as soon as possible.

Records

Regulations

C.02.020 to C.02.024

Interpretation

Note: Interpretation #7.1 of Regulation C.02.024 in the main GMP Guidelines is not applicable.

1. Maintenance of batch records at the PER manufacturing facility is important for all PER products as most of them are released with retrospective testing. The batch record information shall include the following:

    1.1 list of tests that are performed before release;

    1.2 list of tests that are performed retrospectively;

    1.3 results of all the test parameters as per product specification;

    1.4 record of any deviations and additional testing (if any);

Annex 5: GUI-0071

1.5 record of total amount of radioactivity per batch at the end of synthesis and at calibration time;

1.6 total volume per batch;

1.7 specific activity and/or radioactive concentration at calibration time;

2. For PERs imported into Canada, detailed summaries of marketing authorization of the current fabrication, packaging, labelling and testing procedures shall be maintained by the legal agent in Canada.

3. For PER radionuclides, detailed information on the amount received, amount used in fabrication, and the amount disposed of are maintained by the PET facility that acquires the radionuclide either from within Canada or from a country outside of Canada.

4. Distribution records shall be maintained properly.

5. Records shall be available to support an effective recall system.

Samples

Regulations

C.02.025

Interpretation

Note: Interpretation #1 of Regulation C.02.025 in the main GMP Guidelines is not applicable.

1. Samples of radioactive raw material are not required.

2. A sample of each lot or batch of non-radioactive raw material used in the fabrication of a drug shall be retained by the fabricator of the drug for a period of three months after the lot or batch is last used in the fabrication of the drug unless otherwise specified in the fabricator's establishment licence. Acceptable rationale for retaining samples may include short shelf life or extremely small amounts of raw material. These considerations would normally be addressed prior to market authorization specific to a given product upon written request and based on appropriate justification.

3. A sample of the final product shall be retained for a minimum of three months since the product is released with retrospective testing of those parameters not tested at release due to the short half-life of the radionuclide. The sample retention is also useful for investigational purposes when a batch fails to meet certain specifications, such as sterility.

Stability

Regulations

C.02.027 and C.02.028

Interpretation

Note: Interpretation #1 (with the exception of 1.2) of Regulation C.02.027 in the main GMP Guidelines is not applicable.

1. The aspects of the stability program of the drug are determined prior to marketing and prior to adoption of significant changes in formulation, fabrication procedures, or packaging materials that may affect the shelf-life of the drug. Any significant change in the source of radionuclide or any packaging components in direct contact with the product will necessitate repeat assessment of the stability. The following guidelines for stability assessment should be followed:

    1.1. the shelf-life should be stated based on time and date of fabrication of the drug.

    1.2. the stability study should be designed such that data cover at least worst case scenario such as the highest specific activity, total radioactivity or radioactive concentration to total volume that is used for the acceptance of the PER drug product as per specification.

    1.3. stability testing should include a determination of the stopper and vial compatibility with the PER drug product when in direct contact.

    1.4. stability testing addresses the situation of shipping with exposure to extremes of temperature conditions. The stability during shipping should be validated when no testing for product quality will be performed at the user end (e.g., nuclear medicine facilities).

2. Stability studies should be performed at well defined temperature and humidity, as appropriate, and at least in triplicate samples of the same batch. Appropriate parameters should be analysed to establish the stability of the PER under the proposed conditions. The test parameters used in the stability study may include radiochemical purity, appearance, pH, sterility and endotoxin determination.

3. Where a drug is transferred to a second container, the stability for the storage time in that container is demonstrated. The stability is determined for the final packaged dosage form.

Sterile Products

Regulations

C.02.029

Interpretation

Note: Interpretation #4 of Regulation C.02.029 in the main GMP Guidelines is not applicable.

1. The radiochemical synthesis or preparation of the PERs should take place in a hot cell.

2. Activities listed below shall be performed in aseptic systems/areas:

    2.1 Aseptic addition of a sterile diluent to a sterile vial using a syringe.

Annex 5: GUI-0071

2.2. Aseptic attachment of sterile components and devices such as connecting a sterile syringe or a sterile filter device to a sterile needle; inserting a sterile needle through a sanitized stopper into a vial; and any penetration of, or creation of an open pathway into a sealed container-closure system after filling, as might occur with some post-filling sampling techniques.

2.3. Sampling for final product testing and partitioning of bulk PER into separate sterile vials prior to release shall be carried out in a Grade A area. Assembly of closed RSU manifolds and components of "open systems" shall be done in a Grade A environment.

2.4 Sterile filtration requires a minimum filter rating of 0.22 m. The integrity of the filter should be verified before use and shall be verified after use by an appropriate method such as a bubble point, diffusion or pressure hold tests.

3. Air velocity in aseptic areas (e.g. laminar flow hoods) should be sufficient to sweep particulate matter away from the filling and closing area. Whenever possible, equipment configuration should not disrupt the laminar flow. Different areas in the fabricating process should be separated by physical barriers whenever possible and may be supplemented by partial physical barriers (e.g., air curtains) where needed.

4. Since terminal steam sterilization is not possible or practical for PERs, due to the short physical half-life of the radionuclide involved and/or the thermal instability of the product, additional measures should be taken to minimize contamination. Such measures may include, but are not limited to, the use of closed systems of fabrication and sterile filtration. Such equivalence shall be validated and subsequent filling operations or any further operations involving the entry or opening of sterile closed containers are performed under aseptic conditions.

References

1. "Annex 3: Guidelines on Good Manufacturing Practices for Radiopharmaceutical Products" World Health Organization (WHO) Technical Report Series No. 908, 2003

2. "Guidance: PET Drug Products - Current Good Manufacturing Practice (cGMP)" Draft Guidance by FDA, March 2002

3. "Annex to the GMP Guidelines: Good Manufacturing Practices for Schedule C Drugs" GMP Annex for Schedule C Drugs by Health Canada, June 1999

4. "Guidelines for Good Radiopharmacy Practice" A Guidance document published by Australia New Zealand Society of Nuclear Medicine Radiopharmacy Special Interest Group (ANZSNM Radiopharmacy SIG), September 2001

5. Australian Code of Good Manufacturing Practice for Medicinal Product: Annex 3, Manufacture of Radiopharmaceuticals, August 2002.

Annex 11 - Computerised Systems (GUI-0050)

Health Products and Food Branch Inspectorate

PE 009-6 (Annexes)

5 April 2007

PIC/S Annex 11: Computerised Systems

(April 5, 2007)

Contact Name: Drugs GMP Inspection Unit

Annex 11 to the Current Edition of the Good Manufacturing Practices Guidelines - Computerised Systems (GUI-0050)[47]

PIC/S Annex 11: Computerised Systems

Guide to Good Manufacturing Practice for Medicinal Products Annexes

PE 009-6 (Annexes)

5 April 2007

Editor: Secrétariat PIC/S

14, rue du Roveray

CH-1207 Genève

E-mail: info@picsheme.org

Web site: http://www.picscheme.org

---

[47] Available on the Health Canada website at http://www.hc-sc.gc.ca/dhp-mps/compli-conform/gmp-bpf/docs/comput-inform-eng.php

Annex 13 -
Drugs Used in Clinical Trials
(GUI-0036)

Health Products and Food Branch Inspectorate

Drug Good Manufacturing Practices Unit

Our Mandate: To promote good nutrition and informed use of drugs, food, medical devices and natural health products, and to maximize the safety and efficacy of drugs, food, natural health products, medical devices, biologics and related biotechnology products in the Canadien marketplace and health system.

Supersedes: June 1, 2004

Date issued: August 7, 2009

Date of implementation: December 1, 2009

Guidance Document - Annex 13 to the Current Edition of the Good Manufacturing Practices Guidelines - Drugs Used in Clinical Trials (GUI-0036)[48]

Disclaimer: This document does not constitute part of the Food and Drugs Act (Act) or the Food and Drugs Regulations (Regulations) and in the event of any inconsistency or conflict between that Act or Regulations and this document, the Act or the Regulations take precedence. This document is an administrative document that is intended to facilitate compliance by the regulated party with the Act, the Regulations and the applicable administrative policies. This document is not intended to provide legal advice regarding the interpretation of the Act or Regulations. If a regulated party has questions about their legal obligations or responsibilities under the Act or Regulations, they should seek the advice of legal counsel.

1.0 Preface

Drugs intended for use in clinical trials in Canada are regulated under Division 5 of Part C of the Food and Drug Regulations. Section C.05.010(j) requires the sponsor to ensure that drugs for use in clinical trials are manufactured, handled and stored in accordance with the applicable Good Manufacturing Practices requirements referred to in Divisions 2 to 4, except for Sections C.02.019, C.02.025 and C.02.026. Sponsors of clinical trials shall ensure that imported drugs are fabricated and packaged/labelled in accordance with these requirements.

---

[48] Available on the Health Canada website at http://www.hc-sc.gc.ca/dhp-mps/compli-conform/clini-pract-prat/docs/cln_trials-essais_cln-eng.php

This Annex to the current edition of the Canadian "Good Manufacturing Practices (GMP) Guidelines (GUI-0001)" is intended to provide guidance relevant to the fabrication and packaging/labelling of drugs intended for use in human clinical trials, including the placebo and comparator product. If further clarification is required, reference should be made to the Canadian "GMP Guidelines (GUI-0001)".

The Health Products and Food Branch Inspectorate (the Inspectorate) has based this Annex on the current Pharmaceutical Inspection Cooperation Scheme's (PIC/S) version of their Annex 13 "Manufacture of Investigational Medicinal Products" with changes necessary to adapt the text to meet Canadian requirements.

The changes are as follows:

- The name of the Annex was changed.

- Footnotes were added to clarify areas where there are differences in Canadian requirements. When the difference is repeated, the footnote is not repeated.

- The definitions in this document have been compared to definitions listed in Section C.05.001. When these definitions were different from Regulations, we have included in this Annex definitions that appear in the Canadian Food and Drugs Regulations and indicated the reference to the Regulations (i.e., C.05.001).

- The definition of "Clinical Trial" was changed to match the definition in Section C.05.001.

- References to the applicable Canadian regulations were added (in italic) for each section of the Annex.

- Some terms that are used in this guide differ from those found in the Canadian Food and Drug Regulations and the "GMP Guidelines (GUI-0001)". Appendix 1 provides a comparison of these terms.

- Section 26 was modified and sections 27-32 and Table 1 were removed in order to be replaced with C.05.011 of the Food and Drug Regulations.

- Section 36 and the part of section 12 relevant to retention samples were removed since they do not apply in Canada.

- Section 39, the notes immediately following section 55, and Table 2 were removed since they apply to European (EU) Member States and European Economic Area (EEA) partners only, and not to Canada.

- Appendix 2 provides a comparison of the structure of this Annex with the Canadian Food and Drug Regulations.

- Appendix 3 provides the applicable Food and Drug Regulations.

The "GMP Guidelines (GUI-0001)" and a link to the Food and Drug Regulations can be found on Health Canada's Compliance and Enforcement website.

2.0 Principle

Investigational medicinal products[49] are produced in accordance with the principles and the detailed guidelines of the Good Manufacturing Practice for

---

[49] The Canadian term is "Drug" as defined in section C.05.001.

Medicinal Products[50]. Other guidelines[51] should be taken into account where relevant and as appropriate to the stage of development of the product. Procedures need to be flexible to provide for changes as knowledge of the process increases, and appropriate to the stage of development of the product.

In clinical trials there may be added risk to participating subjects compared to patients treated with marketed products. The application of GMP to the manufacture of investigational medicinal products is intended to ensure that trial subjects are not placed at risk, and that the results of clinical trials are unaffected by inadequate safety, quality or efficacy arising from unsatisfactory manufacture. Equally, it is intended to ensure that there is consistency between batches of the same investigational medicinal product used in the same or different clinical trials, and that changes during the development of an investigational medicinal product are adequately documented and justified.

The production of investigational medicinal products involves added complexity in comparison to marketed products by virtue of the lack of fixed routines, variety of clinical trial designs, consequent packaging designs, the need, often, for randomisation and blinding and increased risk of product cross-contamination and mix up. Furthermore, there may be incomplete knowledge of the potency and toxicity of the product and a lack of full process validation, or, marketed products may be used which have been re-packaged or modified in some way.

These challenges require personnel with a thorough understanding of, and training in, the application of GMP to investigational medicinal products. Co-operation is required with trial sponsors who undertake the ultimate responsibility for all aspects of the clinical trial including the quality of investigational medicinal products.

The increased complexity in manufacturing operations requires a highly effective quality system.

The Annex also includes guidance on ordering, shipping, and returning clinical supplies, which are at the interface with, and complementary to, guidelines on Good Clinical Practice.

Note: *Products other than the test product, placebo or comparator may be supplied to subjects participating in a trial. Such products may be used as support or escape medication for preventative, diagnostic or therapeutic reasons and/or needed to ensure that adequate medical care is provided for the subject. They may also be used in accordance with the protocol to induce a physiological response. These products do not fall within the definition of investigational medicinal products and may be supplied by the sponsor, or the investigator[52]. The sponsor should ensure that they are in accordance with the notification/request for authorisation to conduct the trial and that they are of appropriate quality for the purposes of the trial taking into account the source of the materials, whether or not they are the subject of a marketing authorisation and whether they have been repackaged. The advice and involvement of a Qualified Person[53] is recommended in this task.*

Annex 13: GUI-0036

---

[50] Canadian "Good Manufacturing (GMP) Guidelines (GUI-0001)"
[51] Health Canada guidelines
[52] The Canadian term is "Qualified Investigator" as defined in section C.05.001.
[53] The Canadian term is "Person in charge of the Quality Control Department", as described in section C.02.006.

3.0 Glossary

Blinding

A procedure in which one or more parties to the trial are kept unaware of the treatment assignment(s). Single-blinding usually refers to the subject(s) being unaware, and double-blinding usually refers to the subject(s), investigator(s), monitor, and, in some cases, data analyst(s) being unaware of the treatment assignment(s). In relation to an investigational medicinal product, blinding shall mean the deliberate disguising of the identity of the product in accordance with the instructions of the sponsor. Unblinding shall mean the disclosure of the identity of blinded products.

Clinical Trial[54, 55]

An investigation in respect of a drug for use in humans that involves human subjects and that is intended to discover or verify the clinical, pharmacological or pharmacodynamic effects of the drug, identify any adverse events in respect of the drug, study the absorption, distribution, metabolism and excretion of the drug, or ascertain the safety or efficacy of the drug.

Comparator Product

An investigational or marketed product (i.e., active control), or placebo, used as a reference in a clinical trial.

Investigational Medicinal Product[56, 57]

A pharmaceutical form of an active substance or placebo being tested or used as a reference in a clinical trial, including a product with a marketing authorisation when used or assembled (formulated or packaged) in a way different from the authorised form, or when used for an unauthorized indication, or when used to gain further information about the authorised form.

Investigator[58, 59]

The person responsible to the sponsor for the conduct of the clinical trial at a clinical trial site, who is entitled to provide health care under

---

[54] These terms, or their comparable terms used in Canada (see Appendix 1), are defined in section C.05.001. The term "Investigator" is comparable to "Qualified Investigator" in Canada.

[55] This definition is taken from section C.05.001.

[56] These terms, or their comparable terms used in Canada (see Appendix 1), are defined in section C.05.001. The term "Investigator" is comparable to "Qualified Investigator" in Canada.

[57] This definition is taken from section C.05.001.

[58] These terms, or their comparable terms used in Canada (see Appendix 1), are defined in section C.05.001. The term "Investigator" is comparable to "Qualified Investigator" in Canada.

[59] This definition is taken from section C.05.001.

the laws of the province where that clinical trial site is located, and who is

(a) in the case of a clinical trial respecting a drug to be used for dental purposes only, a physician or dentist and a member in good standing of a professional medical or dental association; and

(b) in any other case, a physician and a member in good standing of a professional medical association.

Lot Number

Means any combination of letters, figures, or both, by which any food or drug can be traced in manufacture and identified in distribution.

Manufacturer/importer of Investigational Medicinal Products[60]

In connection with investigational medicinal products, any holder of the authorisation to manufacture/import.

Order

Instruction to process, package and/or ship a certain number of units of investigational medicinal product(s).

Product Specification File

A reference file containing, or referring to files containing, all the information necessary to draft the detailed written instructions on processing, packaging, quality control testing, batch release and shipping of an investigational medicinal product.

Randomisation

The process of assigning trial subjects to treatment or control groups using an element of chance to determine the assignments in order to reduce bias.

Randomisation Code

A listing in which the treatment assigned to each subject from the randomisation process is identified.

Shipping

The operation of packaging for shipment and sending of ordered medicinal products for clinical trials.

Sponsor[61]

An individual, corporate body, institution or organization that conducts a clinical trial.

---

[60] This definition is not applicable in Canada. Refer to Appendix 1.

[61] These terms, or their comparable terms used in Canada (see Appendix 1), are defined in section C.05.001. The term "Investigator" is comparable to "Qualified Investigator" in Canada.

Annex 13: GUI-0036

4.0 Quality Management (C.02.013, C.02.014, C.02.015)

1. The Quality System, designed, set up and verified by the manufacturer or importer, should be described in written procedures available to the sponsor, taking into account the GMP principles and guidelines applicable to investigational medicinal products.

2. The product specifications and manufacturing instructions may be changed during development but full control and traceability of the changes should be maintained.

5.0 Personnel (C.02.006)

3. All personnel involved with investigational medicinal products should be appropriately trained in the requirements specific to these types of product.

4. The Qualified Person should in particular be responsible for ensuring that there are systems in place that meet the requirements of this Annex and should therefore have a broad knowledge of pharmaceutical development and clinical trial processes. Guidance for the Qualified Person in connection with the certification of investigational medicinal products is given in sections 38 to 41.

6.0 Premises and Equipment (C.02.004, C.02.005, C.02.007)

5. The toxicity, potency and sensitising potential may not be fully understood for investigational medicinal products and this reinforces the need to minimise all risks of cross-contamination. The design of equipment and premises, inspection/test methods and acceptance limits to be used after cleaning should reflect the nature of these risks. Consideration should be given to campaign working where appropriate. Account should be taken of the solubility of the product in decisions about the choice of cleaning solvent.

7.0 Documentation

7.1 Specifications and instructions (C.02.009, C.02.010, C.02.011, C.02.015, C.02.016, C.02.018, C.02.020)

6. Specifications (for starting materials[62], primary packaging materials, intermediate, bulk products and finished products), manufacturing formulae and processing and packaging instructions should be as comprehensive as possible given the current state of knowledge. They should be periodically re-assessed during development and updated as necessary. Each new version should take into account the latest data, current technology used, regulatory and pharmacopoeial requirements, and should allow traceability to the previous document. Any changes should be carried out according to a written procedure, which should address any implications for product quality such as stability and bioequivalence.

---

[62] The Canadian term is "Raw materials" as defined in the "GMP Guidelines (GUI-0001)".

7. Rationales for changes should be recorded and the consequences of a change on product quality and on any on-going clinical trials should be investigated and documented.

7.2 Order (C.02.011)

8. The order should request the processing and/or packaging of a certain number of units and/or their shipping and be given by or on behalf of the sponsor to the manufacturer. It should be in writing (though it may be transmitted by electronic means), and precise enough to avoid any ambiguity. It should be formally authorised and refer to the Product Specification File and the relevant clinical trial protocol as appropriate.

7.3 Product Specification File (C.02.009, C.02.014, C.02.016, C.02.018, C.02.020, C.02.027)

9. The Product Specification File (see glossary) should be continually updated as development of the product proceeds, ensuring appropriate traceability to the previous versions. It should include, or refer to, the following documents:

- Specifications and analytical methods for starting materials, packaging materials, intermediate, bulk and finished product

- Manufacturing methods

- In-process testing and methods

- Approved label copy

- Relevant clinical trial protocols and randomisation codes, as appropriate

- Relevant technical agreements with contract givers, as appropriate

- Stability data

- Storage and shipment conditions

The above listing is not intended to be exclusive or exhaustive. The contents will vary depending on the product and stage of development. The information should form the basis for assessment of the suitability for certification and release of a particular batch by the Qualified Person and should therefore be accessible to him/her. Where different manufacturing steps are carried out at different locations under the responsibility of different Qualified Persons, it is acceptable to maintain separate files limited to information of relevance to the activities at the respective locations.

7.4 Manufacturing Formulae and Processing Instructions (C.02.011, C.02.020)

10. For every manufacturing operation or supply there should be clear and adequate written instructions and written records. Where an operation is not repetitive it may not be necessary to produce Master Formulae and Processing Instructions. Records are particularly important for the preparation of the final version of the documents to be used in routine manufacture once the marketing authorisation is granted.

11. The information in the Product Specification File should be used to produce the detailed written instructions on processing, packaging, quality control testing, storage conditions and shipping.

7.5 Packaging Instructions (C.02.011)

12. Investigational medicinal products are normally packed in an individual way for each subject included in the clinical trial. The number of units to be packaged should be specified prior to the start of the packaging operations, including units necessary for carrying out quality control[63]. Sufficient reconciliations should take place to ensure the correct quantity of each product required has been accounted for at each stage of processing.

7.6 Processing, testing and packaging batch records (C.02.020, C.02.021, C.05.012(4))

13. Batch records should be kept in sufficient detail for the sequence of operations to be accurately determined. These records should contain any relevant remarks which justify the procedures used and any changes made, enhance knowledge of the product and develop the manufacturing operations.

14. Batch manufacturing records should be retained for at least twenty-five years[64] after the completion or formal discontinuation of the last clinical trial in which the batch was used.

8.0 Production

8.1 Packaging materials (C.02.011, C.02.016)

15. Specifications and quality control checks should include measures to guard against unintentional unblinding due to changes in appearance between different batches of packaging materials.

8.2 Manufacturing operations (C.02.004, C.02.005, C.02.011, C.02.029)

16. During development critical parameters should be identified and in-process controls primarily used to control the process. Provisional production parameters and in-process controls may be deduced from prior experience, including that gained from earlier development work. Careful consideration by key personnel is called for in order to formulate the necessary instructions and to adapt them continually to the experience gained in production. Parameters identified and controlled should be justifiable based on knowledge available at the time.

17. Production processes for investigational medicinal products are not expected to be validated to the extent necessary for routine production but premises and equipment are expected to be validated. For sterile products, the validation of sterilising processes should be of the same standard as for products authorised for marketing. Likewise, when required, virus

---

[63] As per Regulation C.05.010(j), the requirement to maintain samples does not apply in Canada.

[64] The applicable regulation is Section C.05.012 (4).

inactivation/removal and that of other impurities of biological origin should be demonstrated, to assure the safety of biotechnologically derived products, by following the scientific principles and techniques defined in the available guidance in this area.

18. Validation of aseptic processes presents special problems when the batch size is small; in these cases the number of units filled may be the maximum number filled in production. If practicable, and otherwise consistent with simulating the process, a larger number of units should be filled with media to provide greater confidence in the results obtained. Filling and sealing is often a manual or semi-automated operation presenting great challenges to sterility so enhanced attention should be given to operator training, and validating the aseptic technique of individual operators.

8.3 Principles applicable to comparator product (C.02.011, C.02.018, C.02.027)

19. If the product is modified, data should be available (e.g,. stability, comparative dissolution, bioavailability) to demonstrate that these changes do not significantly alter the original quality characteristics of the product.

20. The expiry date stated for the comparator product in its original packaging might not be applicable to the product where it has been repackaged in a different container that may not offer equivalent protection, or be compatible with the product. A suitable use-by date, taking into account the nature of the product, the characteristics of the container and the storage conditions to which the article may be subjected, should be determined by or on behalf of the sponsor. Such a date should be justified and must not be later than the expiry date of the original package. There should be compatibility of expiry dating and clinical trial duration.

8.4 Blinding operations (C.02.011, C.02.014)

21. Where products are blinded, systems should be in place to ensure that the blind is achieved and maintained while allowing for identification of "blinded" products when necessary, including the batch numbers of the products before the blinding operation. Rapid identification of product should also be possible in an emergency.

8.5 Randomisation code (C.02.011, C.02.014, C.02.020)

22. Procedures should describe the generation, security, distribution, handling and retention of any randomisation code used for packaging investigational products, and code-break mechanisms. Appropriate records should be maintained.

8.6 Packaging (C.02.006, C.02.011, C.02.015)

23. During packaging of investigational medicinal products, it may be necessary to handle different products on the same packaging line at the same time. The risk of product mix up must be minimised by using appropriate procedures and/or, specialised equipment as appropriate and relevant staff training.

24. Packaging and labelling of investigational medicinal products are likely to be more complex and more liable to errors (which are also harder to detect)

than for marketed products, particularly when "blinded" products with similar appearance are used. Precautions against mis-labelling such as label reconciliation, line clearance, in-process control checks by appropriately trained staff should accordingly be intensified.

25. The packaging must ensure that the investigational medicinal product remains in good condition during transport and storage at intermediate destinations. Any opening or tampering of the outer packaging during transport should be readily discernible.

8.7 Labelling[65] (C.02.011, C.02.016, C.05.011)

26. The requirements for drug product labelling should comply with the Regulations of the country where the clinical trial will be conducted and in Canada, the labels on drug products to be used in clinical trials should comply with Section C.05.011 of the Food and Drug Regulations. The following information shall be included on labels in both official languages:

   (a) a statement indicating that the drug is an investigational drug to be used only by a qualified investigator; (Similar wording may be used, such as "for clinical trial use only".)

   (b) the name, number or identifying mark of the drug;

   (c) the expiration date of the drug; (See below section.)

   (d) the recommended storage conditions for the drug;

   (e) the lot number of the drug;

   (g) the name and address of the sponsor;

   (g) the protocol code or identification; and

   (h) if the drug is a radiopharmaceutical as defined in Section C.03.201, the information required by subparagraph C.03.202(1)(b)(vi).

   If stability studies to support expiry dating for a clinical trial drug are still ongoing at the time of labelling, alternate approaches to providing information regarding expiry dating can be considered. Regardless of the approach taken, data should be in place at all times to support the ongoing suitability of the clinical trial drug at the time of use.

33. If it becomes necessary to change the expiration date, an additional label should be affixed to the investigational medicinal product. This additional label should state the new expiration date and repeat the batch number. It may be superimposed on the previous expiration date, but, for quality control reasons, not on the original batch number. This operation should be performed at an appropriately authorised manufacturing site. However, when justified, it may be performed at the investigational site by or under the supervision of the clinical trial site pharmacist, or other health care professional in accordance with national regulations and with the sponsor's requirements. Where this is not possible, it may be performed by the clinical trial monitor(s) who should be appropriately trained. The operation should be performed in accordance with GMP principles, specific and standard

[65] The "Labelling" section (Paragraphs 26 to 33) was kept as a guidance, however not all elements are requirements in Canada. Reference should be made to the Canadian labelling requirements specified in section C.05.011.

operating procedures and under contract, if applicable, and should be checked by a second person. This additional labelling should be properly documented in bot⁻ the trial documentation and in the packaging records.

9.0 Quality Control (C.02.011, C.02.014)

34. As processes may not be standardised or fully validated, testing takes on more importance in ensuring that each batch meets its specification.

35. Quality control should be performed in accordance with the Product Specification File and in accordance with required information. Verification of the effectiveness of blinding should be performed and recorded.

36. [66]

37. Consideration should be given to retaining samples from each packaging run/trial period unti the clinical report has been prepared to enable confirmation of product identity in the event of, and as part of an investigation into inconsistent trial results.

10.0 Release of Batches (C.02.014)

38. Release of investigational medicinal products (see section 43) should not occur until after the Qualified Person has certified that the relevant requirements 14 have been met. The Qualified Person should take into account the elements listed in section 40 as appropriate.

39. [67]

40. Assessment of each batch for certification prior to release may include as appropriate:

   a. batch records, including control reports, in-process test reports and release reports demonstrating compliance with the product specification file, the order, protocol and randomisation code. These records should include all deviations or planned changes, and any consequent additional checks or tests, and should be completed and endorsed by the staff authorised to do so according to the quality system;

   b. production conditions;

   c. the validation status of facilities, processes and methods;

   d. examination of finished packs;

   e. where relevant, the results of any analyses or tests performed after importation;

   f. stability reports;

---

[66] As per section C.05.010(j), the requirement to maintain samples does not apply in Canada.

[67] This paragraph was removed since it is only applicable in EU and EEA countries.

g.   the source and verification of conditions of storage and shipment;

h.   audit reports concerning the quality system of the manufacturer;

i.   documents certifying that the manufacturer is authorised to manufacture investigational medicinal products or comparators for export by the appropriate authorities in the country of export;

j.   where relevant, regulatory requirements for marketing authorisation, GMP standards applicable and any official verification of GMP compliance;

k.   all other factors of which the Qualified Person is aware that are relevant to the quality of the batch.

The relevance of the above elements is affected by the country of origin of the product, the manufacturer, and the marketed status of the product (with or without a marketing authorisation, in the EU or in a third country) and its phase of development.

The sponsor should ensure that the elements taken into account by the Qualified Person when certifying the batch are consistent with the required information. See also section 44.

41.   Where investigational medicinal products are manufactured and packaged at different sites under the supervision of different Qualified Persons, other recommendations should be followed as applicable[68].

42.   Where, permitted in accordance with local regulations, packaging or labelling is carried out at the investigator site by, or under the supervision of a clinical trial pharmacist, or other health care professional as allowed in those regulations, the Qualified Person is not required to certify the activity in question. The sponsor is nevertheless responsible for ensuring that the activity is adequately documented and carried out in accordance with the principles of GMP and should seek the advice of the Qualified Person in this regard.

11.0 Shipping (C.05.006, C.02.011, C.02.012, C.02.015, C.02.022)

43.   Shipping of investigational products should be conducted according to instructions given by or on behalf of the sponsor in the shipping order.

The transportation and storage conditions should be verified and documented upon arrival of the drug used in clinical trials at the investigator site. The storage conditions must be maintained in accordance with the label indications.[69]

44.   Investigational medicinal products should remain under the control of the Sponsor until after completion of a two step release procedure: certification by the Qualified Person; and release following fulfilment of the relevant

---

[68] The applicable regulation is section C.02.014.

[69] Further guidance relating to the storage and transportation are detailed in Health Canada's document entitled "Guidelines for Temperature Control of Drug Products during Storage and Transportation (GUI-0069)".

requirements. The sponsor should ensure that these are consistent with the details actually considered by the Qualified Person. Both releases should be recorded and retained in the relevant trial files held by or on behalf of the sponsor.

45. De-coding arrangements should be available to the appropriate responsible personnel before investigational medicinal products are shipped to the investigator site.

46. A detailed inventory of the shipments made by the manufacturer or importer should be maintained. It should particularly mention the addressees' identification.

47. Transfers of investigational medicinal products from one trial site to another should remain the exception. Such transfers should be covered by standard operating procedures. The product history while outside of the control of the manufacturer, through for example, trial monitoring reports and records of storage conditions at the original trial site should be reviewed as part of the assessment of the product's suitability for transfer and the advice of the Qualified Person should be sought. The product should be returned to the manufacturer, or another authorised manufacturer for re-labelling, if necessary, and certification by a Qualified Person. Records should be retained and full traceability ensured.

12.0 Complaints (C.02.015, C.02.023)

48. The conclusions of any investigation carried out in relation to a complaint which could arise from the quality of the product should be discussed between the manufacturer or importer and the sponsor (if different). This should involve the Qualified Person and those responsible for the relevant clinical trial in order to assess any potential impact on the trial, product development and on subjects.

13.0 Recalls and Returns

13.1 Recalls (C.02.012, C.02.022)

49. Procedures for retrieving investigational medicinal products and documenting this retrieval should be agreed by the sponsor, in collaboration with the manufacturer or importer where different. The investigator and monitor need to understand their obligations under the retrieval procedure.

50. The Sponsor should ensure that the supplier of any comparator or other medication to be used in a clinical trial has a system for communicating to the Sponsor the need to recall any product supplied.

13.2 Returns (C.02.014)

51. Investigational medicinal products should be returned on agreed conditions defined by the sponsor, specified in approved written procedures.

52. Returned investigational medicinal products should be clearly identified and stored in an appropriately controlled, dedicated area. Inventory records of the returned medicinal products should be kept.

14.0 Destruction (C.02.011, C.02.014, C.05.012(3)(e))

53. The Sponsor is responsible for the destruction of unused and/or returned investigational medicinal products. Investigational medicinal products should therefore not be destroyed without prior written authorisation by the Sponsor.[70]

54. The delivered, used and recovered quantities of product should be recorded, reconciled and verified by or on behalf of the sponsor for each trial site and each trial period. Destruction of unused investigational medicinal products should be carried out for a given trial site or a given trial period only after any discrepancies have been investigated and satisfactorily explained and the reconciliation has been accepted. Recording of destruction operations should be carried out in such a manner that all operations may be accounted for. The sponsor should ensure that records are kept.

55. When destruction of investigational medicinal products takes place, a dated certificate of, or receipt for destruction, should be provided to the sponsor. These documents should clearly identify, or allow traceability to, the batches and/or patient numbers involved and the actual quantities destroyed.

Appendix 1: Comparison of terms

Terms used in this Annex	Comparable terms commonly used in Canada	Where the Canadian terms are defined / described
Qualified Person	Person in charge of the quality control department	Section C.02.006, GMP Guidelines (GUI-0001)
Investigational medicinal product	Drug	Section C.05.001
Investigator	Qualified investigator	Section C.05.001
Manufacturer	Fabricator, packager / labeller	Glossary, GMP Guidelines (GUI-0001)
Starting Material	Raw material	Glossary, GMP Guidelines (GUI-0001)

Appendix 2: Comparison of the Structure of this Annex with the Canadian Food and Drug Regulations

Sections of this Annex	Corresponding Canadian GMP Sections/ Regulations
Quality Management	Quality Control Department C.02.013-15
Personnel	Personnel C.02.006
Premises and Equipment	Premises C.02.004 Equipment C.02.005

---

[70] The applicable regulation is Section C.05.012(3)(e).

Sections of this Annex		Corresponding Canadian GMP Sections/ Regulations
		Sanitation C.02.007
Documentation	Specifications and instructions	Raw Material Testing C.02.009-10 Manufacturing Control C.02.011 Quality Control Department C.02.015 Packaging Material Testing C.02.016 Finished Product Testing C.02.018 Records C.02.020
	Order	Manufacturing Control C.02.011
	Product Specification File	Raw Material Testing C.02.009 Quality Control Department C.02.014 Packaging Material Testing C.02.016 Finished Product Testing C.02.018 Records C.02.020 Stability C.02.027
	Manufacturing Formulae and Processing Instructions	Manufacturing Control C.02.011 Records C.02.020
	Packaging Instructions	Manufacturing Control C.02.011
	Processing, testing and packaging batch records	Records C.02.020-21 Records C.05.012 (4)
Production	Packaging materials	Manufacturing Control C.02.011 Packaging Material Testing C.02.016
	Manufacturing operations	Premises C.02.004 Equipment C.02.005 Manufacturing Control C.02.011 Sterile Products C.02.029
	Principles applicable to comparator product	Manufacturing Control C.02.011 Finished Product Testing C.02.018 Stability C.02.027
	Blinding operations	Manufacturing Control C.02.011 Quality Control Department C.02.014
	Randomisation code	Manufacturing Control C.02.011 Quality Control Department C.02.014 Records C.02.020
	Packaging	Personnel C.02.006 Manufacturing Control C.02.011 Quality Control Department C.02.015

Annex 13: GUI-0036

Sections of this Annex		Corresponding Canadian GMP Sections/ Regulations
	Labelling	Manufacturing Control C.02.011 Packaging Material Testing C.02.016 Labelling C.05.011
Quality Control		Manufacturing Control C.02.011 Quality Control Department C.02.014
Release of Batches		Quality Control Department C.02.014
Shipping		Personnel C.02.006 Manufacturing Control C.02.011-12 Quality Control Department C.02.015 Records C.02.022
Complaints		Quality Control Department C.02.015 Records C.02.023
Recalls and Returns	Recalls	Manufacturing Control C.02.012 Records C.02.022
	Returns	Quality Control Department C.02.014
Destruction		Manufacturing Control C.02.011 Quality Control Department C.02.014 Records C.05.012 (3) *(e)*

Appendix 3: Canadian Food and Drug Regulations Referenced in this Document

Division 2 - Good Manufacturing Practices

Premises

C.02.004

The premises in which a lot or batch of a drug is fabricated or packaged/labelled shall be designed, constructed and maintained in a manner that;

(a) permits the operations therein to be performed under clean, sanitary and orderly conditions;

(b) permits the effective cleaning of all surfaces therein; and

(c) prevents the contamination of the drug and the addition of extraneous material to the drug

Equipment

C.02.005

The equipment with which a lot or batch of a drug is fabricated, packaged/labelled, or tested shall be designed, constructed, maintained, operated, and arranged in a manner that:

(a) permits the effective cleaning of its surfaces;

(b) prevents the contamination of the drug and the addition of extraneous material to the drug and

(c) permits it to function in accordance with its intended use.

Personnel

C.02.006

Every lot or batch of a drug shall be fabricated, packaged/labelled, tested and stored under the supervision of personnel who, having regard to the duties and responsibilities involved, have had such technical, academic and other training as the Director considers satisfactory in the interests of the health of the consumer or purchaser.

Sanitation

C.02.007

(1) Every person who fabricates or packages/labels a drug shall have a written sanitation program that shall be implemented under the supervision of qualified personnel.

(2) The sanitation program referred to in subsection (1) shall include:

    (a) cleaning procedures for the premises where the drug is fabricated or packaged/labelled and for the equipment used in the fabrication or packaging/labelling of the drug; and

    (b) instructions on the sanitary fabrication and packaging/labelling of drugs and the handling of materials used in the fabrication and packaging/labelling of drugs.

Raw Materiel Testing

C.02.009

(1) Each lot or batch of raw material shall be tested against the specifications for the raw material prior to its use in the production of a drug.

Annex 13: GUI-0036

(2) No lot or batch of raw material shall be used in the production of a drug unless that lot or batch of raw material complies with the specifications for that raw material.

(3) Notwithstanding subsection (1), water may, prior to the completion of its tests under that subsection, be used in the production of a drug.

(4) Where any property of a raw material is subject to change on storage, no lot or batch of that raw material shall be used in the production of a drug after its storage unless the raw material is retested after an appropriate interval and complies with its specifications for that property.

(5) Where the specifications referred to in subsections (1), (2) and (4) are not prescribed, they shall

    (a) be in writing;

    (b) be acceptable to the Director, who shall take into account the specifications contained in any publication mentioned in Schedule B to the Act; and

    (c) be approved by the person in charge of the quality control department.

C.02.010

(1) The testing referred to in section C.02.009 shall be performed on a sample taken

    (a) after receipt of each lot or batch of raw material on the premises of the fabricator; or

    (b) subject to subsection (2), before receipt of each lot or batch of raw material on the premises of the fabricator, if

        (i) the fabricator

            (A) has evidence satisfactory to the Director to demonstrate that raw materials sold to him by the vendor of that lot or batch of raw material are consistently manufactured in accordance with and consistently comply with the specifications for those raw materials, and

            (B) undertakes periodic complete confirmatory testing with a frequency satisfactory to the Director and

        (ii) the raw material has not been transported or stored under conditions that may affect its compliance with the specifications for that raw material.

(2) After a lot or batch of raw material is received on the premises of the fabricator, the lot or batch of raw material shall be tested for identity.

Manufacturing Control

C.02.011

(1) Every fabricator, packager/labeller, distributor referred to in paragraph C.01A.003(b) and importer of a drug shall have written procedures, prepared

by qualified personnel, in respect of the drug to ensure that the drug meets the specifications for use of that drug.

(2) Every person required to have written procedures referred to in subsection (1) shall ensure that each lot or batch of the drug is fabricated, packaged/labelled and tested in compliance with those procedures.

C.02.012

(1) Every fabricator, packager/labeller or distributor referred to in section C.01A.003, importer, and wholesaler of a drug shall maintain

    (a) a system of control that permits complete and rapid recall of any lot or batch of the drug that is on the market; and

    (b) a program of self-inspection.

(2) Every fabricator and packager/labeller and subject to subsections (3) and (4), every distributor referred to in section C.01A.003(b) and importer of a drug shall maintain a system designed to ensure that any lot or batch of the drug fabricated and packaged/labelled on premises other than their own is fabricated and packaged/labelled in accordance with the requirements of this Division.

(3) The distributor referred to in paragraph C.01A.003(b) of a drug that is fabricated, packaged/labelled, and tested in Canada by a person who holds an establishment licence that authorizes those activities is not required to comply with the requirements of subsection (2) in respect of that drug.

(4) If a drug is fabricated or packaged/labelled in an MRA country at a recognized building, the distributor referred to in paragraph C.01A.003(b) or importer of the drug is not required to comply with the requirements of subsection (2) in respect of that activity for that drug if

    (a) the address of the building is set out in that person's establishment licence; and

    (b) that person retains a copy of the batch certificate for each lot or batch of the drug received by that person.

Quality Control Department

C.02.013

(1) Every fabricator, packager/labeller, distributor referred to in paragraph C.01A.003(b) and importer shall have on their premises in Canada a quality control department that is supervised by personnel described in section C.02.006.

(2) The quality control department referred to in subsection (1) shall be a distinct organizational unit that functions and reports to management independently of any other functional units including the manufacturing, processing, packaging or sales unit.

Annex 13: GUI-0036

C.02.014

(1) No lot or batch of drug shall be made available for sale unless the sale of that lot or batch is approved by the person in charge of the quality control department.

(2) A drug that is returned to the fabricator, packager/labeller, distributor referred to in paragraph C.01A.003(b) or importer thereof shall not be made available for further sale unless the sale of that drug is approved by the person in charge of the quality control department.

(3) No lot or batch of raw material or of packaging/labelling material shall be used in the fabrication or packaging/labelling of a drug, unless that material is approved for that use by the person in charge of the quality control department.

(4) No lot or batch of a drug shall be reprocessed without the approval of the person in charge of the quality control department.

C.02.015

(1) All fabrication, packaging/labelling, testing, storage, and transportation methods and procedures that may affect the quality of a drug shall be examined and approved by the person in charge of the quality control department before their implementation.

(2) The person in charge of the quality control department shall cause to be investigated every complaint on quality that is received and cause corrective action to be taken where necessary.

(3) The person in charge of the quality control department shall cause all tests or examinations required pursuant to this Division to be performed by a competent laboratory.

Packaging Material Testing

C.02.016

(1) Each lot or batch of packaging material shall, prior to its use in the packaging of a drug, be examined or tested against the specifications for that packaging material.

(2) No lot or batch of packaging material shall be used in the packaging of a drug unless the lot or batch of packaging material complies with the specifications for that packaging material.

(3) The specifications referred to in subsections (1) and (2) shall

(a) be in writing;

(b) be acceptable to the Director who shall take into account the specifications contained in any publication mentioned in Schedule B to the Act; and

(c) be approved by the person in charge of the quality control department.

Finished Product Testing

C.02.018

(1) Each lot or batch of a drug shall, prior to its availability for sale, be tested against the specifications for that drug.

(2) No lot or batch of a drug shall be available for sale unless it complies with the specifications for that drug.

(3) The specifications referred to in subsections (1) and (2) shall

    (a) be in writing;

    (b) be approved by the person in charge of the quality control department; and

    (c) comply with the Act and these Regulations.

Records

C.02.020

(1) Every fabricator, packager/labeller, distributor referred to in paragraph C.01A.003(b) and importer shall maintain on their premises in Canada for each drug sold

    (a) master production documents for the drug;

    (b) evidence that each lot or batch of the drug has been fabricated, packaged/labelled, tested and stored in accordance with the procedures described in the master production documents;

    (c) evidence that the conditions under which the drug was fabricated, packaged/labelled, tested and stored are in compliance with the requirements of this Division;

    (d) evidence establishing the period of time during which the drug in the container in which it is sold will meet the specifications for that drug; and

    (e) adequate evidence of the testing referred to in section C.02.018.

(2) Every distributor referred to in paragraph C.01A.003(b) and importer shall make available on request the results of testing performed on raw materials and packaging/labelling materials for each lot or batch of a drug sold.

(3) Every fabricator shall maintain on his premises

    (a) the written specifications for the raw material; and

    (b) adequate evidence of the raw materials testing referred to in section C.02.009.

(4) Every person who packages a drug shall maintain on his premises

    (a) the written specifications for the packaging materials; and

        (b) adequate evidence of the packaging material examination or testing referred to in section C.02.016.

    (5) Every fabricator shall maintain on their premises in Canada:

        (a) detailed plans and specifications of each building in Canada at which they fabricate, package/label or test; and

        (b) a description of the design and construction of those buildings.

    (6) Every fabricator, packager/labeller and tester shall maintain on their premises in Canada details of the personnel employed to supervise the fabrication, packaging/labelling and testing, including each person's title, responsibilities, qualifications, experience and training.

C.02.021

    (1) Subject to subsection (2), all records and evidence on the fabrication, packaging/labelling, testing and storage of a drug that are required to be maintained under this Division shall be retained for a period of at least one year after the expiration date on the label of the drug, unless otherwise specified in the person's establishment licence.

    (2) All records and evidence on the testing of raw materials and packaging/labelling materials that are required to be maintained under this Division shall be retained for a period of at least five years after the materials were last used in the fabrication or packaging/labelling of a drug unless otherwise specified in the person's establishment licence.

C.02.022

Every distributor referred to in section C.01A.003, wholesaler and importer of a drug shall retain records of the sale of each lot or batch of the drug, which enable them to recall the lot or batch from the market for a period of at least one year after the expiration date of the lot or batch unless otherwise specified in their establishment licence.

C.02.023

    (1) On receipt of a complaint respecting the quality of a drug, every distributor referred to in paragraph C.01A.003(b), and importer of the drug shall make a record of the complaint and of its investigation and retain the record for a period of at least one year after the expiration date of the lot or batch of the drug, unless otherwise specified in their establishment licence.

    (2) On receipt of any information respecting the quality or hazards of a drug, every distributor referred to in paragraph C.01A.003(b), and importer of the drug shall make a record of the information and retain it for a period of at least one year after the expiration date of the lot or batch of the drug unless otherwise specified in their establishment licence.

Stability

C.02.027

Every distributor referred to in paragraph C.01A.003(b) and importer shall establish the period of time during which each drug in the package in which it is sold comply with the specifications.

Sterile Products

C.02.029

In addition to the other requirements of this Division, a drug that is intended to be sterile shall be fabricated and packaged/labelled;

(a) in separate and enclosed areas;

(b) under the supervision of personnel trained in microbiology; and

(c) by a method scientifically proven to ensure sterility.

Division 3 - Schedule C Drugs

C.03.202

(1) Every package containing a radiopharmaceutical, other than a radionuclide generator, shall carry,

    (b) on the outer label

        (vi) the radiation warning symbol required by the Atomic Energy Control Regulations and the statement "Caution-Radioactive Material" "Attention-Produit radioactif",

        (vii) the names and a statement of the amounts of any preservatives or stabilizing agents contained in the drug,

Division 5 - Drugs for clinical trials involving human subjects

C.05.001

The definitions in this section apply to this Division.

"clinical trial" means an investigation in respect of a drug for use in humans that involves human subjects and that is intended to discover or verify the clinical, pharmacological or pharmacodynamic effects of the drug, identify any adverse events in respect of the drug, study the absorption, distribution, metabolism and excretion of the drug, or ascertain the safety or efficacy of the drug.

"drug" means a drug for human use that is to be tested in a clinical trial.

"qualified investigator" means the person responsible to the sponsor for the conduct of the clinical trial at a clinical trial site, who is entitled to provide health care under the laws of the province where that clinical trial site is located, and who is;

(a) in the case of a clinical trial respecting a drug to be used for dental purposes only, a physician or dentist and a member in good standing of a professional medical or dental association; and

(b) in any other case, a physician and a member in good standing of a professional medical association.

"sponsor" means an individual, corporate body, institution or organization that conducts a clinical trial.

C.05.010

Every sponsor shall ensure that a clinical trial is conducted in accordance with good clinical practices and, without limiting the generality of the foregoing, shall ensure that ... (j) the drug is manufactured, handled and stored in accordance with the applicable good manufacturing practices referred to in Divisions 2 to 4 except sections C.02.019, C.02.025 and C.02.026.

C.05.011

Despite any other provision of these Regulations respecting labelling, the sponsor shall ensure that the drug bears a label that sets out the following information in both official languages:

(a) a statement indicating that the drug is an investigational drug to be used only by a qualified investigator;

(b) the name, number or identifying mark of the drug;

(c) the expiration date of the drug;

(d) the recommended storage conditions for the drug;

(e) the lot number of the drug;

(f) the name and address of the sponsor;

(g) the protocol code or identification; and

(h) if the drug is a radiopharmaceutical as defined in section C.03.201, the information required by subparagraph C.03.202(1)(b)(vi).

C.05.012

(3) The sponsor shall maintain complete and accurate records in respect of the use of a drug in a clinical trial, including

(e) records respecting the shipment, receipt, disposition, return and destruction of the drug.

(4) The sponsor shall maintain all records referred to in this Division for a period of 25 years.

Annex 14 - Schedule D Drugs, Human Blood and Blood Components (GUI-0032)

Health Products and Food Branch Inspectorate

Annex to the GMP Guidelines

Good Manufacturing Practices for Schedule D Drugs
Part 2
Human Blood and Blood Components

Supersedes: First draft, March 24, 1998

Date issued: December 1, 1999

Date of implementation: December 1, 1999

*Revisions were made to this document on 2002-02-25 to reflect changes to the Health Products and Food Branch organizational structure. There were no other changes made to the content of the document.

Ce document est aussi disponible en français.

Annex 14 to the Current Edition of the Good Manufacturing Practices Guidelines - Schedule D Drugs, Human Blood and Blood Components (GUI-0032)[71]

Preface

The purpose to this document is to provide specific guidance for the application of good manufacturing practices to blood establishments.

Glossary of Terms

Autologous Donation (don autologue)

> Blood collected from an individual for the purpose of transfusion back to the same individual.

---

[71] Available on the Health Canada website at http://www.hc-sc.gc.ca/dhp-mps/compli-conform/info-prod/don/sched_d_part2-annexe_d_part2-eng.php

Allogeneic Donation (don allogénique)

> Blood collected from an individual and placed in the general blood
> supply for the purpose of transfusion to another person.

Antibody Screen (dépistage des anticorps)

> Serological test by which donor serum/plasma is tested with reagent
> red cells of known antigenic profile to determine if unexpected
> clinically significant antibodies are present. "Clinically significant"
> refers to antibodies that may cause adverse reactions in the recipient
> due to incompatibility.

Blood (sang)

> Whole blood collected from a single donor and processed either for
> transfusion or further manufacturing. The term is often used to
> describe blood components in general.

Blood Component (composant du sang)

> A therapeutic agent produced by physical or mechanical separation of
> the constituents of whole blood. Components include, but are not
> limited to, red blood cells, platelets, plasma and cryoprecipitated Anti-
> Haemophiliac Factor (AHF).

Closed System (circuit fermé)

> A system for collecting and/or processing blood in containers that
> have been connected together before sterilization, so that there is no
> possibility of microbial contamination from outside after collection of
> blood from the donor.

Confidential Unit Exclusion (CUE) (demande d'exclusion confidentielle)

> A system that allows the donor, in private, to indicate that his/her
> collected blood should, or should not, be used for transfusion to
> another individual.

Contract Facility (établissement externe)

> Organisation performing work associated with the manufacturing
> process for the manufacturer.

Critical Labelling (étiquetage critique)

> Labelling which identifies a product or status, such as a quarantine
> label or blood group label, if it is used to control release for inventory.

Directed Donation (don dirigé)

> Blood collected from an individual for the purpose of transfusion to a
> different individual, named by the donor, who has been identified in
> advance to be compatible.

Facilities (installations)

> Any area, including mobile clinic sites, used for the collection, testing, component production, storage (including records) or distribution of blood and blood components.

Leukapheresis (leucophérèse)

> Separation of leukocytes by removing whole blood from the donor, separating the leukocytes, and returning the formed elements and plasma back to the donor.

Leuko Reduced Components (composants à teneur réduite en leucocytes)

> Component units that have been treated by centrifugation, filtration or other methods to reduce the amount of leukocytes per unit to a level below a standard acceptable value.

Lookback (étude des dons antérieurs)

> The process of identifying current or previous donations from a donor subsequently confirmed positive for a transfusion-transmitted agent in order to identify and notify consignees and recipients of suspect blood components from that donor, and retrieve available components. A lookback may be initiated through a traceback investigation or by a report of seroconversion or infection in a donor.

Medical Officer (médecin)

> A person registered and licensed under the laws of a province to practice the profession of medicine.

Mobile Clinic Site (centre de collecte itinérant)

> Blood collection location, not under the control of the fabricator, to which equipment and supplies must be brought prior to the donor clinic and from which they are removed at the conclusion of the clinic.

Open System (système ouvert)

> A blood collection and/or processing system which has been breached but where every effort is made to prevent external contamination by using sterilised materials and aseptic handling techniques in a clean environment.

Plasma

> The fluid portion of whole blood collected, stabilized against clotting and separated from the red blood cells.

Plasmapheresis (plasmaphérèse)

> Separation of plasma from whole blood and the continuous or intermittent return of red blood cells and formed elements to the donor. Plasma collected by plasmapheresis may be used either as source plasma for further manufacturing or fresh frozen plasma for transfusion.

Annex 14: GUI-0032

Plateletpheresis (thrombocytaphérèse)

> Separation of platelets from whole blood and the continuous or intermittent return of red blood cells, with or without platelet-reduced plasma, to the donor. If plasma is collected as a final product during plateletpheresis, the regulations for plasmapheresis apply.

Post Donation Information (PDI) (renseignements obtenus après le don)

> Information related to a donor or a donation made available to the collection facility following a donation. The information can be provided by the donor or other source. It may adversely affect the safety and/or quality of the donated blood/component. PDI does not include errors, accidents or anomalies that occur during screening or later during collection, processing or testing but are discovered at some point after the donation is made.

Processing (traitement)

> Any fabricating step performed between the collection of blood and the issuing of a component.

Quality Assurance (QA) (assurance de la qualité)

> The actions, planned and performed, to provide confidence that all systems and elements that influence the quality of the product are working as expected individually and collectively.

Quality Assurance Program (programme d'assurance qualité)

> Comprehensive system of an establishment for manufacturing safe, effective, and quality products according to regulatory requirements. This program includes preventing, detecting, and correcting deficiencies that may compromise product quality.

Quality Control (QC) (contrôle de la qualité)

> A component of a QA program that includes the activities and controls used to determine the accuracy and reliability of the establishment's personnel, equipment, reagents, and operations in the fabricating of blood components including testing and product release.

Quality Control/Assurance Unit (unité de contrôle/d'assurance de la qualité)

> One or more individuals designated by, and reporting directly to, management with defined authority and responsibility to assure that all quality assurance policies are carried out in the organization.

Recovered Plasma (plasma récupéré)

> The liquid portion of a single donation of whole blood separated from cellular components and intended for further manufacture.

Serum (sérum)

> The liquid portion of clotted blood.

Source Plasma (plasma par aphérèse)

Plasma collected by plasmapheresis and used for further manufacture.

Sub-Centre (centre secondaire)

Permanent site under the control of a Blood Centre, which is licensed for limited fabrication activities.

Traceback (enquête sur les produits sanguins transfusés)

The process of investigating a report of a suspected transfusion-associated infection in order to identify a potential implicated donor. The purpose of the investigation is to determine whether any donor who contributed to the transfusion is infected with, or positive for, serologic markers of the same infectious agent, and to retrieve available blood components from that donor, and to notify consignees and recipients of components collected from the same donor.

Unit (unité)

A specific volume of blood or one of its components obtained from a single collection of blood from one donor.

Regulation

Premises

C.02.004

1. See section C.02.007 (Sanitation) for additional explanation on premises.

2. Premises must be located, designed, constructed and adapted to suit the operations to be carried out. Their design and furnishing must be chosen to minimise the risk of errors. Premises should, if possible, be designed so that operations can proceed in an orderly manner. Buildings should be maintained so as to protect against the effects of weather or ground seepage and the entry of vermin, pests and birds.

3. The facility should be designed to align with the process flow but shall include:

   3.1 An area set aside for donor screening which maintains confidentiality for questioning and examination of individuals to determine their suitability as blood donors. If the Confidential Unit Exclusion (CUE) is used, a private area must be provided.

   3.2 An area set aside for the safe withdrawal of blood from donors and equipped with appropriate supplies for the treatment of donors experiencing adverse reactions or injuries from events associated with blood donation.

   3.3 A means of communication (e.g. telephone, cellular phone) whenever donors are being bled to ensure that emergency help is available, if required.

Annex 14: GUI-0032

3.4 A separate controlled area for the quarantine storage of blood or blood components prior to completion of processing, and for reagents and test kits prior to acceptance testing and approval at the processing facility.

3.5 A separate secure area for the quarantine storage, handling and disposition of blood components and reagents not suitable for use or recalled.

3.6 A secure area in both quarantine and released storage for units collected under special criteria (e.g., Autologous/Directed Donation)

3.7 Separate dedicated areas for component preparation and laboratory testing. Entry to these areas shall be restricted to authorized personnel.

3.8 Separate controlled storage areas for released components available for distribution.

3.9 A designated area for safe storage of waste and items used during the collection, processing and testing of blood and blood components, or rejected blood or blood components, prior to disposal.

3.10 A dedicated area for the labelling and release of components into inventory.

3.11 A designated alternate storage site for blood components in the event of equipment or power failure in the main storage facility.

3.12 Adequate storage space for the dry, clean and orderly placement of stored material under monitored temperature conditions compatible with conditions specified on label. Storage areas shall provide for suitable and effective separation of quarantined and released material.

4. When blood collection clinics are conducted by mobile teams, a realistic attitude towards environmental standards is necessary. The premises should satisfy common sense requirements for the health and safety of both the mobile teams, and the donors concerned, with due regard for relevant legislation or regulation. Points to check should include adequate heating, lighting and ventilation, general cleanliness, provision of a secure supply of water and electricity, adequate sanitation, compliance with fire regulations, satisfactory access for unloading and loading of equipment, adequate space to allow free access to the bleed and rest beds. An area shall be provided for a confidential interview with a donor.

Equipment

C.02.005

1. See section C.02.015 (Quality Control Department) for Laboratory Testing Equipment information and water purification systems.

2. Schedules and procedures for equipment validation, maintenance and calibration must be maintained and followed. This requirement applies to all instruments, equipment and measuring devices critical to ensure that the

provision of blood and blood components conform to applicable regulations, requirements and standards.

3. Manufacturing equipment used, or intended to be used, in whole blood collection, apheresis procedures, and component production should be designed and maintained to suit its intended purpose and shall not present any hazard to donors, components or operators. All equipment shall be maintained, standardized and calibrated on a regularly scheduled basis according to established procedures described in operating procedures (OPs) and/or the equipment manual. If the instrument has been disturbed or is suspected of malfunctioning, these tests shall be carried out before further use.

4. Computers, which maintain data used to identify donors, to make decisions regarding the suitability of blood components for transfusion or further manufacture, and/or to maintain data used to trace a unit of blood or a blood component from collection to its final disposition, must be validated in accordance with current Health Canada guidelines (Validation of Computerised Systems in Blood Establishments) prior to implementation and must be maintained in a validated state.

Personnel

C.02.006

1. There shall be an organization chart showing the hierarchical structure with clear delineation of lines of responsibility and the relationship of individuals responsible for key functions.

2. A blood establishment shall be under the direction of designated, qualified personnel who shall exercise control of the establishment in all matters relating to good manufacturing practices (GMP) for blood component manufacturing. Designated staff shall have an understanding of the scientific principles and techniques involved in the manufacture of blood components. Training and competency evaluations must be documented.

3. The fabricator shall ensure the employment of adequate personnel qualified by education and/or experience, as specified in their job descriptions. The tasks and responsibilities of all individuals must be clearly understood and documented. All personnel shall be trained in the principles of GMP relevant to their work. Records of the qualifications, training, and continuing competence of individuals shall be maintained.

4. Personnel shall receive initial and continued training appropriate to their duties. Training programs shall be available for this purpose; the effectiveness of the programs shall be assessed by regular competency evaluation.

5. Key personnel shall include at least a Production Manager, a Quality Assurance (QC/QA) Manager and a Medical Officer. An individual may have more than one function but the Production Manager and Quality Assurance Manager must be independent of each other.

6. The Medical Officer, who is a licensed physician and qualified by training or experience, shall have responsibility and authority for all medical and

technical procedures, including those that affect laboratory personnel and test performance, and for the consultative and support services that relate to the care and safety of donors. The acceptability of donors must be determined by trained qualified staff under the supervision of a qualified licensed physician.

7. Individuals in charge of production should hold a post secondary qualification (e.g., in management, medical laboratory science, general science or nursing) and have had practical experience under professional guidance in the manufacture and control of therapeutic products made under GMP. Individuals with equivalent combination of education, training and experience may be qualified.

8. QC/QA staff must hold a university degree in science or equivalent experience/knowledge directly related to Immunohematology or nursing.

Sanitation

C.02.007

1. Blood establishments routinely fabricate blood components in a closed system so that there is no possibility of microbial contamination from outside after collection of blood from the donor.

2. The blood establishment should be maintained in a clean and sanitary condition. A written sanitation program should be available that addresses good housekeeping issues. An accidental spill clean up procedure must be available and include instructions to dispose of blood spills as biohazardous material.

3. Blood and its components must be handled and discarded with precautions that recognize the potential for exposure to infectious agents.

4. There must be procedures for biological, chemical and radiation safety, where applicable.

5. Adequate hand washing facilities must be available for staff collecting and handling blood units. At mobile sites where hand washing facilities are not available, an alternate method to clean hands, i.e. bactericidal hand wipes, is acceptable.

C.02.008

1. Persons whose presence can adversely affect the safety or quality of the product shall be excluded from areas where the collection, processing, testing, storage or distribution of blood or blood components is conducted.

2. Personnel shall be aware that microbial contamination of themselves, the donors, the blood components and the environment must be prevented.

3. Hygiene instructions, including clothing and behaviour requirements, must be present in each department. These instructions should be understood and followed by all personnel.

Raw Material Testing

C.02.009

1. Because whole blood is the source material for blood components, special considerations are given to the procedures for donor screening and vendor audit (C.02.010).

2. Donor Screening

   2.1 All blood donors must be found acceptable each time they donate based on the approved health screening criteria. A document shall be available at each blood collection site that details the approved health screening criteria for acceptance/deferral of donors.

   2.2 Potential donors who do not meet all the applicable acceptance criteria for donating must be informed of the reason they cannot donate and the circumstances under which they have been deferred.

   2.3 A comprehensive list of donors who are temporarily or permanently deferred must be maintained. If a blood manufacturer has multiple collection and processing facilities, a composite donor deferral registry, including the names and/or unique identifiers of all donors deferred at each facility, must be made available to each site and updated on a regular basis.

3. The collection bags, which are approved Medical Devices, do not require further testing. The certificate of analysis for each lot of collection bags must be reviewed and approved prior releasing for clinic use. Each collection bag must be visually examined prior to its use for blood collection, again at the time of product release into available inventory, and finally before the released product is distributed.

C.02.010

1. Vendor Audits

   1.1 All vendors which supply critical materials that are used in blood collection (eg blood collection bags, apheresis harness sets and apheresis collection bags) should be audited periodically by the manufacturer of blood/components to ensure that the vendor operates in compliance with GMPs and that the products they supply consistently meet pre established specifications.

   1.2 There must be a system in place to ensure the timely reporting of complaints or product defects to the vendor and prompt effective remedial action by the vendor.

Manufacturing Control

C.02.011

1. Written Operating Procedures (OPs)

   1.1 Every manufacturer shall maintain and control all documents (policies, processes, procedures and forms) relating to the requirements for each activity in the manufacturing process.

   1.2 OPs must be clear, concise, current and approved, and be available in the area where the activity is performed.

   1.3 The issue of OPs and any changes made shall be controlled by a documented system which ensures that all OPs in use are current and authorised, and that obsolete documents are archived and protected.

   1.4 The OPs must describe the significant steps of the operation:

      1.4.1 The determination of donor acceptability and deferral status, including the process for donor identification.

      1.4.2 Method of accurately and uniquely relating the blood components or product(s) to the donor, donor samples, and all associated records, for each donation.

      1.4.3 The procedure(s) used for blood collection, including methods used to prepare the site of phlebotomy, and to link critical materials (e.g., the collection pack lot number) to the clinic and donor.

      1.4.4 Specific manufacturing procedure(s) for the preparation of all components, including labelling steps (i.e., type of labels and method of labelling).

      1.4.5 All tests and repeat tests performed on blood and blood components including testing for infectious disease markers. Procedure(s) shall address the shipment of samples to off-site and contract facilities, as required.

      1.4.6 Procedure(s) for the capturing, assessing, investigating and monitoring of adverse donor and recipient reactions.

      1.4.7 Procedure(s) for determining the suitability of blood components for transfer to available inventory, i.e., formally approving the blood component for release. There must be a suitable means of identification to ensure that blood components which cannot be released for issue can be distinguished from those which conform to specification and are ready for release.

      1.4.8 Procedure(s) for the voluntary return of issued blood and blood components, specifying the conditions under which the returned blood may be suitable for re issue.

      1.4.9 Procedure(s) used for tracking a unit of blood or any blood component from the donor to its final disposition.

1.4.10 Procedure(s) for the quality control of blood components, processing methods and laboratory testing.

1.4.11 Procedure(s) for plasmapheresis, plateletpheresis and leukapheresis, including precautions to be taken to ensure reinfusion of a donor's own cells, if applicable.

1.4.12 Procedure(s) for the operation, maintenance and validation of all computerized systems that contribute to decisions regarding the suitability and/or traceability of blood and blood components.

1.4.13 Procedure(s) for capturing, assessing, investigating, and monitoring errors and accidents (i.e., manufacturing discrepancies). Defined methods for identification, data collection, analysis, and follow-up of corrective and preventive action shall be used for process improvement.

1.4.14 Procedure(s) and criteria for performance of lookback and traceback investigations.

1.4.15 Procedure(s) which detail the requirements for units collected under special criteria (such as Autologous and Directed Donations).

1.4.16 Procedure(s) which details recall procedures including the identification of the person or persons responsible for initiating and co-ordinating the recall activities as well as the process for notifying the regulatory authorities.

1.4.17 Procedure(s) to detail the receipt, inspection, and storage of material and products within the premises.

1.4.18 Procedure(s) to describe the calibration of equipment. It shall include the method to be used, frequency of calibration and act on to be taken when results deviate from defined acceptance limits. Parameters being tested should approximate operating conditions for that equipment.

1.4.19 Procedure(s) for the packaging and transport of blood components, to ensure they remain within specifications.

2. A system shall be established and maintained to identify, document, review, approve and contro all process and product changes.

3. Supplies and Reagents

3.1 Each blood collecting container and its satellite container(s), if present, must be examined visually for damage or evidence of contamination prior to its use (before blood collection) and before the product is distributed. Where any defect, improper labelling or abnormal appearance is observed, the container shall not be used, or, if detected after filling, the component shall be properly discarded.

3.2 Representative samples of each lot of reagents or solutions shall be inspected and/or tested on each day of use as described in the Operating Procedure(s) to determine their suitability for use.

Annex 14: GUI-0032

4. Labelling of blood components

4.1 See labelling requirements described in Division 4 of the Regulations.

4.2 Blood component labelling occurs at various stages in the manufacturing process. Each critical labelling procedure must include effective in process controls, appropriate to the system and equipment, to ensure correct labels have been applied. Component labelling must be reviewed prior to final product release

4.3 Each donation shall be identified in a unique manner and shall allow for the traceability of each blood component back to the donor and forward to final disposition.

4.4 If coloured labels are used to identify products for transfusion, the colours must follow the conventions outlined in the Guidelines for Blood Collection and Component Manufacturing (Part IV section 2.4.2) .

4.5 Each successful donation must be classified as to ABO and Rh group. Whole blood (WB), red cell concentrate (RCC), platelets (PLT), and granulocytes (GRAN) must be labelled with both ABO and Rh (D) groups, based on test of record. The label shall specify: "Rh positive" if D or weak D positive, or "Rh negative" if D and weak D negative.

4.6 The label shall state the composition and volume of anticoagulant/additive, the Establishment Licence Number and address of the component fabricator, and date of expiry. Expiry labels for products with a shelf-life of 72 hours or less must include the time of expiry.

4.7 Information and cautionary statements specific to blood component fabricating are outlined in the Guidelines for Blood Collection and Component manufacturing (Part IV).

5. Circular of Information

5.1 An information circular (package insert) is an extension of the blood component labelling and shall be available for distribution if the component or blood product is intended for transfusion. The information circular shall provide adequate directions for storage and use, including information on the composition and properties of the product, the indications for use, contraindications, and possible adverse events.

5.2 Packaging differs from pharmaceutical manufacturing, in that, the initial whole blood container with satellites is also the final packaging material.

C.02.012

1. Whole Blood and Blood Component Recall

    1.1 All complaints and other information that may suggest that defective blood components have been issued must be carefully investigated. Written procedures must exist for recalling defective blood components or blood components suspected of being defective. All complaints about delivered blood components shall be dealt with and investigated as quickly as possible.

1.2 Blood establishments shall maintain a system of control that permits complete and rapid recall of any component to the consignee level (e.g., hospitals or fractionator). Distribution records shall be readily available and easy to follow so as to expedite the recall of any blood component or material whenever necessary.

1.3 Post Donation Information reports may lead to recall of all in date components.

1.4 The guidance on recalls in the document entitled "Product Recall Procedures" published by the Health Protection Branch does not apply in its entirety to Blood Components.

2. Internal audit

2.1 Internal audits are required to ensure that all procedures and the associated quality control are performed according to GMP, and applicable regulations and legislation. Internal audits should be comprehensive and performed according to an established program. The findings shall be documented.

2.2 The internal audit personnel shall be knowledgeable in the subject matter and process being audited, and shall have defined responsibilities and authority.

Quality Control Department

C.02.013

1. Quality Control/Quality Assurance department shall be a distinct organizational unit that is not linked to fabricating of blood components.

2. For sub-centres and mobile clinic sites, which are technically multiple sites of a single licence, it must be demonstrated that the overall supervision of quality and production is adequately controlled by the blood centre.

C.02.014

1. Sections C.02.014 (1), (3), and (4) do not apply to blood fabricators due to their nature, the fact that each component is a separate lot and that they are not reprocessed (as per definition of reprocessing for pharmaceuticals).

2. Within a blood component fabricating operation, the requirements of this section may be fulfilled by positions or departments other than the Quality Control Department as specified in the operating procedures.

3. Because of their intended use, good quality is crucial to blood components. Therefore the collection of blood and the processing, storage and distribution of blood components must be organised in a way to ensure a high component quality. This can only be achieved if the fabricator has a system of quality management. Quality management is an integrated system of quality assurance covering all matters which individually or collectively influence the components in order to guarantee their quality.

4. The person or group of persons who coordinate, monitor and facilitate all QA activities is the QC/QA unit.

5. The quality requirements involve the following topics:

- premises, equipment and materials

- personnel and organisation

- donor screening and blood collection

- blood processing

- documentation

- quality control and proficiency testing

- complaints and component recall

- internal and external audits

6. In the case of C.02.014 (2), if blood components are returned to the manufacturer they are only acceptable for re-issue if the manufacturer can document that the product, while out of their hands, was continuously stored under the appropriate storage conditions.

C.02.015

1. The donor screening criteria (see Raw Material Testing) and donor sample testing (Quality Control Department) are factors in determining the acceptable quality and safety of blood and blood components. In process controls, as specified in approved OPs, provide specific GMP for Blood Component fabrication.

2. A quality control program for assessing the quality and performance of all reagents and test kits used in the processing of blood components, must be in place.

3. Test kit procedures, acceptable to Health Canada, must follow the strict protocol of their applicable package inserts.

4. Detailed specifications for purchase of critical reagents and materials are required. Only reagents and materials that meet the documented requirements shall be used. Manufacturers shall provide a certificate of compliance for these reagents and materials.

5. Serological and Transmissible Disease Testing

5.1 Testing is performed on blood samples (pilot samples) collected at the time of donation. The samples are marked with an identifier which links the sample to the donor and the corresponding unit of blood. Pilot samples must be collected by a technique that prevents external contamination of the blood product.

5.2 Responsibilities between contract laboratories and the blood establishment shall be defined by written agreement.

5.3 All donors of whole blood must be tested for the following serological tests at the time of each donation:

- ABO group, including forward and reverse grouping

- Rh group (D and weak D testing)

- Antibody screen

5.4 All donors must be screened for the following transmissible disease markers at the time of each donation:

- Syphilis

- Hepatitis B surface antigen (HBsAg)

- Antibody to Hepatitis C virus (HCV)

- Antibody to HIV type 1 and 2

- Antibody to HTLV-I/II (except plasma for further manufacturing use only)

- HIV-1 p24 Ag

- Any disease marker(s) specifically required by the Minister

5.5 Units that are repeat reactive for a transmissible disease marker listed above must not be issued for allogeneic transfusion.

5.6 All donors that are found repeat reactive for a transmissible disease marker listed above must be deferred.

6. A quality control program which assesses the quality of all manufactured blood components must be followed by every fabricator. The frequency of quality control testing, expressed as a percent of overall production, as well as the minimum number specified over a period of time, and the acceptable criteria for quality control testing of each type of component must be established by each fabricator.

7. The results of quality control testing must be analysed on an ongoing basis and appropriate corrective action taken when values fall outside the acceptable limits.

8. Although blood is not a sterile drug, sterility testing should be performed as part of Quality Control testing. Sterility testing must be done with a methodology specific to aerobic and anaerobic pathogens in blood. Sterility testing serves as a monitor of the effectiveness of the protocol for phlebotomy site preparation.

9. Blood establishments must participate in a proficiency testing program. Proficiency testing is an aspect of Quality Assurance which monitors the ability to perform laboratory procedures within acceptable limits of accuracy through the analysis of unknown specimens.

Packaging Material Testing

C.02.016 and C.02.017

1. Packaging Material testing does not apply to blood component manufacturing as original collection bags and satellite bags must be approved Medical Devices. Additional routine testing is not required for use of approved collection bags. However, testing may be required during the investigation of a complaint or an adverse reaction.

Finished Product Testing

C.02.018 and C.02.019

1. The requirements for finished product testing cannot be applied to the manufacture of blood components since each unit of blood collected represents a separate lot. The safety of each component depends on the selection of donors, blood collection, and serological and transmissible disease testing. The quality of components is established by quality control testing as a method of the fabricating process eg. Factor VIII level in cryoprecipitate.

Records

C.02.020

1. Records shall be maintained concurrently with the performance of each significant step in the collection, processing, testing, storage and distribution of each unit of blood and blood components so that all steps can be clearly traced.

2. All records shall be legible and indelible, and shall identify the person performing the work, include dates of the various entries, show test results, the interpretation of the results, any retests or invalidation of test results.

3. All manual transcription of test results shall be independently verified.

C.02.021

1. Section C.02.021 does not apply to blood establishments as blood component records must be kept indefinitely. Blood establishments may decide to use microfiche, microfilm or other means of retaining permanent records. Records must be accessible at all times.

2. Records that substantiate the safety of blood and blood components and the traceability of the components from donor to final disposition shall be retained indefinitely. The records must enable the fabricator to trace blood or blood components to donors in the case of a traceback investigation, and to the point of end use in case of lookbacks.

C.02.022

1. Section C.02.022 applies directly to blood establishments in that procedures must clearly determine the distribution of all whole blood and blood components which will ensure an effective recall, if necessary. Records shall demonstrate that a blood component can be readily located during transportation to another site.

C.02.023

1. Records of complaints regarding blood components issued to consignees must be completely investigated.

2. Records of adverse transfusion reaction reports must be maintained.

3. Section C.02.023 (2) does not apply in that records are maintained indefinitely.

C.02.024

1. Records of self audits performed within the blood establishment must be available for review C.02.024 (1)(b) does not apply as records are maintained indefinitely.

2. Records of sanitation need not to be retained.

Samples

C.02.025 and C.02.026

1. The provisions of this section do not apply to blood component manufacturing due to the fact that each unit is a lot. When a transfused blood component is associated with a post transfusion infection or serious adverse reaction, a thorough investigation is undertaken.

2. Blood components intended for transfusion which are stored long term in a frozen state (eg. frozen red cell units) must have a serum or plasma sample kept for future testing purposes.

Stability

C.02.027 and C.02.028

1. Blood components must be stored at all times under appropriate monitored storage conditions.

2. During shipment, blood components must be placed in appropriate shipping containers that ensure the maintenance of appropriate storage temperature during shipment as well as the security of the contents.

3. Shipment documentation must specify the shipping conditions of the blood components.

Sterile Products

C.02.029

1. Blood components are injectable but are generally not considered to be sterile products.

2. Using an appropriate sampling plan, blood components should periodically have sterility testing performed as part of routine quality control testing to evaluate the overall effectiveness of the arm scrub.

3. If a sterile connecting device is used to produce sterile welds (i.e. maintaining closed system) it must be an approved medical device. The weld made must be inspected for completeness.

4. A sample taken from every final product processed in an open system (e.g., red blood cells, deglycerolized) shall be tested retrospectively for sterility.

GMP requirements for blood manufacturing activities

Section	Regulation	Applies Directly	*Applies in part	**Does Not Apply
Premises	C.02.004		X	
Equipment	C.02.005		X	
Personnel	C.02.006		X	
Sanitation	C.02.007			X
	C.02.008			X
Raw Material Testing	C.02.009			X
	C.02.010			X
Manufacturing Control	C.02.011		X	
	C.02.012	X		
Quality Control	C.02.013		X	
	C.02.014			X
	C.02.015		X	
Packaging Material Testing	C.02.016			X
	C.02.017			X
Finished Product Testing	C.02.018			X
	C.02.019			X
Records	C.02.020		X	
	C.02.021			X
	C.02.022	X		
	C.02.023		X	
	C.02.024		X	
Samples	C.02.025			X
	C.02.026			X
Stability	C.02.027			X
	C.02.028			X
Sterile Products	C.02.029			X

*applies in part = applies as described in annex
**does not apply = does not apply as described in the guidelines, only applies as described in the annex

Annex 17 - Guidance on Parametric Release (GUI-0046)

Health Products and Food Branch Inspectorate

Guidance on Parametric Release - Pharmaceutical Inspection Co-Operation Scheme (PIC/S)

PI 005-1

3 August 2001

Annex 17 to the Current Edition of the Good Manufacturing Practices Guidelines - Guidance on Parametric Release (GUI-0046)[72]

PIC/S Annex 17: Recommendation on the Guidance on Parametric Release

Pharmaceutical Inspection Convention

Pharmaceutical Inspection Co-Operation Scheme

PI 005-1

3 August 2001

Recommendation on the Guidance on Parametric Release

Editor: PIC/S Secretariat
9 - 11 rue de Varembé
CH-1211 Geneva 20

Tel. + 41 22 749 13 24
Fax + 41 22 740 14 37
E-mail: pics@efta.int
Web site: http //www.picscheme.org

---

[72] Available on the Health Canada website at http://www.hc-sc.gc.ca/dhp-mps/compli-conform/int/part/parame-eng.php

Part IV

Questions
and Answers

Questions and Answers Overview

Enquiries may be submitted by industry as questions directed to Operational Centres during an inspection, to Inspectorate Ottawa or through trade associations. In most instances the responses to such enquiries will have already been established and will have been addressed in the main Good Manufacturing Practices (GMP) Guideline or its Annexes, or through the compilation of existing GMP questions and answers (Q&As), based on previous responses to industry and trade associations.[73]

However, when an exceptional situation arises, and for which there is no established interpretation already available in writing, the response to the situation may warrant it's inclusion in this list of Q&As. Alternate approaches to the situations described in these Q&As may be acceptable provided they are supported by adequate scientific justification.

Enquiries may be submitted by stakeholders or associations either by writing to the regional Operational Centres of the Inspectorate or to Inspectorate Ottawa. The enquiries should be sent to the respective Managers of the Drug GMP Inspection Unit of the Operational Centre or the Manager of the Drug GMP Inspection Unit within Inspectorate Ottawa. The addresses of the Operational Centres and Inspectorate Ottawa are available on Health Canada's Web site. Enquiries may be submitted by mail (regular or electronic) or by Fax.

- Good Manufacturing Practices (GMP) Questions and Answers

- Medical Gas - Good Manufacturing Practices (GMP) Questions and Answers

- Importation and Exportation Questions and Answers

---

[73] Available on the Health Canada website at http://www.hc-sc.gc.ca/dhp-mps/compli-conform/gmp-bpf/question/index-eng.php

Good Manufacturing Practices - Questions and Answers

Health Canada

Unit Name: Drug GMP Inspection Unit

Telephone: 613-957-1492
Fax: 613-957-6709
Email: GMP_questions_BPF@hc-sc.gc.ca

The GMP questions and answers (Q&A) presented below were previously found in the document entitled "GMP Interpretation Decision Records - 2003 Edition". This Q&A list will be updated on a regular basis. Note that the date at the end of each Q&A represents the date on which the Q&A was added to the list.

Good Manufacturing Practices (GMP) Questions and Answers[74]

Premises - C.02.004

Q. 1 Are firms required to use HEPA filters in the manufacture of non-sterile dosage forms?

A.1   The GMP regulations do not specifically require manufacturing facilities for non-sterile drugs to maintain high-efficiency particulate air (HEPA) filtered air.

The Regulations do require the use of equipment for adequate control over air pressure, microorganisms, dust, humidity and temperature, when appropriate. In addition, this section calls for use of air filtration systems, including prefilters and particulate matter air filters on air supplies to production areas, as appropriate. These provisions speak to measures to prevent cross contamination, and the key phrase is "when appropriate".

Despite the lack of an explicit GMP requirement, some firms may elect to use HEPA filtered air systems as part of their dust control procedures. For example, firms may perform dust containment assessments and decide that such filters are warranted to prevent cross contamination of highly potent drugs that, even in small quantities, could pose a significant health hazard when carried over into other products. (September 9, 2003)

---

[74] Available on the Health Canada website at http://www.hc-sc.gc.ca/dhp-mps/compli-conform/gmp-bpf/question/gmp-bpf-eng.php

Q.2 Is there an acceptable substitute for dioctyl phtalate (DOP) to integrity testing of HEPA filters?

A.2   Yes. Dioctyl phthalate aerosols also called Di (2-ethylhexyl) phthalate, di-sec octyl phthalate, DOP, or DEHP, have long been used to test the integrity of high efficiency particulate air (HEPA) filters but concern about the potential health effects to people working with DOP test aerosols has led to a search for a safer equivalent replacement.

The product of choice from US Army testing with assistance from various private companies was a Henkel Corporation (Emery Group) product called Emery 3004 PAO. This product is a polyalphaolefin (POA) in the 4 centistoke (4 cSt) viscosity grade, used primarily as a lubricant base stock for oils, lubricants, and electrical/hydraulic fluids.

Emery 3004 (POA) can replace DOP in HEPA integrity testing. (September 9, 2003)

Q.3 A firm uses a dedicated suite for the manufacturing of antineoplastics which is under negative pressure to the rest of the facility and has the air vented to the outside; the equipment, however is not dedicated. Is this arrangement acceptable?

A.3   According to the 2002 edition of the GMP Guidelines, under Premises C.02.004, interpretation 11, self-contained facilities should be used for the production of certain biological and cytotoxic drugs. Under this interpretation, a self-contained facility is a facility which provides total separation of all aspects of the operation, including equipment movement. Although not an absolute requirement, dedicated equipment for the manufacture of certain cytotoxic drugs is highly recommended. However, use of non-dedicated equipment may be acceptable under certain circumstances, depending on the nature of the antineoplastics produced, but it must be supported by properly validated cleaning and decontamination procedures. (September 9, 2003)

Q.4 What is the acceptable limit for dew point of the compressed air used in pneumatic equipment and to dry the manufacturing tanks after cleaning?

A.4   Under the GMP guidelines, there is no limit for the relative humidity % of the air used for pneumatic equipment and to dry manufacturing tanks. From a general perspective, based on interpretation 4 under "Premises", the humidity must be controlled where required to safeguard sensitive materials. Consequently, it is the fabricator, packager/labeller's responsibility to establish the pertinence of such control. If the humidity % of the compressed air used at the last step of drying of a reservoir is too high, micro-droplets of water could be generated on the internal surfaces by condensation, hence contributing to the possibility of microbial growth following storage. Similarly, it is important to make sure that residual water has been completely eliminated from hard to reach surfaces of the equipment after cleaning operations. (September 9, 2003)

Q.5 What are the requirements applicable to QC and engineering personnel who travel many times daily between self-contained facilities and the regular facilities?

A.5 Movement of personnel between self-contained and other facilities must be subject to procedures that will prevent cross-contamination. This may include but is not limited to decontamination procedures such as showering and change of clothes. (September 9, 2003)

Q.6 In Interpretation 11.2 under Premises, a reference is made to "campaign production". However, this term is not defined in the glossary of the GMPs. Could you elaborate more on this approach of manufacturing.

A.6 The following definition is included in the Annex for Schedule D Drugs - Part 1 and should be used: "Sequential processing of material, either more than one product in a multi-product facility or more than one lot of the same product in a dedicated facility, over a defined period of time. Campaign production could occur at any point in a production process where common rooms/suites and/or equipment are reused for multiple products/lots."

This definition will be included in the subsequent revision of the GMP Guidelines. (September 9 2003)

Q.7 What should be the standard of compressed air used in the manufacture of a drug?

A.7 Air that comes into direct contact with primary contact surfaces and/or the product should be monitored to control the level of particulates, microbial contamination, and the absence of hydrocarbons. Limits used should take into consideration the stage of manufacture, product, etc. Additional tests might be required due to the nature of the product. Gas used in aseptic processes must be sterile and filters checked for integrity. (January 3, 2008)

Q.8 Does the concept of self-contained facilities apply equally to research and development laboratories (susceptible to contain highly sensitizing, highly potent or potentially pathogenic material in the analytical scale) that may be in the same building as the manufacturing facilities, or is this concept limited to actual manufacturing operations?

A.8 It is the responsibility of the manufacturer to ensure that their premises and operations have been designed in such a manner that the risk of contamination between products is minimized. This would include research and development areas within facilities where marketed drug products are fabricated and packaged. Further guidance can be found under interpretation 11, Premises of the main GMP guide. (January 3, 2008)

Equipment - C.02.005

Q. 1 Should equipment be labelled with calibration dates?

A.1 Major equipment should be identified with a distinctive number or code that is recorded in batch records. This identification requirement is intended to help document which pieces of equipment were used to make which batches of drug product.

The GMP regulations do not require that each piece of equipment bear status labelling as to its state of calibration or maintenance. However, equipment must be calibrated and/or maintained according to an established schedule, and records must be kept documenting such activities.

The regulations do not distinguish critical from non-critical equipment for calibration and maintenance purposes. However, the need for calibrating a given piece of equipment depends on its function. In general, equipment that measure materials warrant calibration. Equipment not requiring calibration/maintenance need not be tracked or included in the firm's calibration/maintenance program, but the firm must be able to support its decision to exclude a particular piece of equipment from the calibration/maintenance program.

During an inspection a firm should be able to document when a specific piece of equipment was last calibrated/maintained, the results or action, and when its next calibration/maintenance is scheduled. The absence of such documentation is considered a GMP deviation. While the absence of a calibration/maintenance tag is not objectionable, the presence of a calibration/maintenance tag alone should not be assumed to satisfy regulatory demands, and the supporting documentation should be audited. The firm should also be able to support its decision to not include a particular piece of equipment in the calibration/maintenance program. (September 9, 2003)

Personnel - C.02.006

Q.1 Can you expand on the delegation of authority for the person in charge of QC and manufacturing departments for a fabricator, packager/labeller or tester of drugs?

A.1   According to Interpretation 1.1 under C.02.006, the only two persons that are required to hold a university degree for a drug fabricator, packager/labeller or tester are the person in charge of the manufacturing department and of the QC department. Specific tasks are required by the GMP regulations to be performed by one of these two persons. However, the Inspectorate acknowledges the fact that this may represent a workload that is impossible to carry for one person. In line with interpretation 1.4, those tasks can be delegated to a person in possession of a diploma, certificate or other evidence of formal qualifications awarded on completion of a course of study at a university, college or technical institute in a science related to the work being carried out combined with at least two years relevant practical experience. The person in charge remains, however, accountable for the tasks delegated and retains the necessary authority. (September 9, 2003)

Q. 2 Is a company required to notify the Inspectorate of a change in key personnel, such as the person in charge of QC or manufacturing department?

A.2   No. However, it is the company's responsibility to make sure that the new person meets the requirements of interpretation 1 or 3 under C.02.006, depending on the activities performed. (September 9, 2003)

Q.3 With respect to Interpretation 1.1 of Section C.02.006 what is meant by a university degree or equivalent?

A.3   Under this interpretation, the individuals in charge of the manufacturing department and the quality control department for a fabricator, packager/labeller and tester must hold a Canadian university degree or recognized as equivalent by a Canadian university or Canadian accreditation body in a science related to the work being carried out. (May 12, 2006)

Sanitation - C.02.007 & C.02.008

Q.1 Is fumigation a requirement under sanitation?

A.1   The written sanitation program should include procedures for pest control as well as precautions required to prevent contamination of a drug when fumigating agents are used.

Fumigation is not a requirement per se. Infestation should be monitored and controlled. Where fumigation is used, appropriate precautions should be taken.

Methods of sanitary control that satisfy the requirements of Sections 8 and 11 of the Food and Drugs Act would be considered to be acceptable. (September 9, 2003)

Q.2 What limits are acceptable on product residues regarding sanitation?

A.2   Guidance for the establishment of limits can be obtained from the Cleaning Validation Guidelines available on the Health Canada's Compliance and Enforcement website. (September 9, 2003)

Q.3 Should individuals who are known carriers of communicable disease be allowed to work in production areas?

A.3   Under Section C.02.008 of the GMP regulations a person who is a carrier of a disease in a communicable form should not have access to any area where a drug is exposed. The likelihood of disease transmission by means of a drug product would depend on the nature of the disease and the type of work the employee carries out. It may be advisable to consult with a physician. Certain diseases could be transmitted through a drug product if proper hygiene procedures are not followed by an infected employee handling the product. However, an employee may also be a carrier of a communicable disease and not be aware of it. Therefore, in addition to strict personal hygiene procedures, systems should be in place to provide an effective barrier that would preclude contamination of the product. These procedures must be followed at all times by all employees. (September 9, 2003)

Q.4 Are gowning rooms required even in pilot plant operations?

A.4   Even in a pilot plant consisting of a small laminar flow area where the apparatus for filter sterilization of solutions are set up, it is an unacceptable practice to gown in there. A change room should be available besides their sterile pilot plant production area.

Based on the assumption that the pilot plant will produce drugs for sale - including clinical studies - then the same principles and considerations that apply to full scale production operations must also be utilized in pilot plant facilities. (September 9, 2003)

Q.5 What are considered as being acceptable limits for cross-contamination when performing cleaning validation?

A.5   Contamination may include not only carry over from a previous product or residual cleaning solvents, but also detergents and surfactants.

No established standard acceptance limits for cleaning validation exist. Due to the wide variation in both equipment and products produced, it would be unrealistic for a regulatory body to determine a specific limit.

However, firms need to establish limits that reflect the practical capability of their cleaning processes, as well as the specificity of the analytical test method.

When determining the acceptance limit, relevant factors generally include: (1) Evaluation of the therapeutic dose carryover; (2) toxicity of the potential contaminant; (3) concentration of the contaminant in rinse and swab samples; (4) limit of detection of the analytical test method; and, (5) visual examination.

Guidance for the establishment of limits can be obtained from the Cleaning Validation Guideline available on the Health Canada's Compliance and Enforcement website. (September 9, 2003)

Q.6 In terms of cleaning, what would be the frequency and type of cleaning for equipment and premises for successive manufacturing of batches of the same product? And for different strengths of the same product?

A.6   Interpretation 3.5 under C.02.007 specifies that "a cleaning procedure requiring complete product removal may not be necessary between batches of the same drug". The frequency and type of cleaning for equipment and premises must address the length of time between consecutive lots with the ultimate goal that a particular lot won't be contaminated by the previous lot or the environment. It must also ensure that residual quantities of the previous lot won't impact on the quality of the following lot. Thus, a partial cleaning would be required between two lots of the same product, especially for forms such as liquids or suspensions, in order to prevent a few units at the beginning of a new lot from being filled with residual quantifies from the previous lot that may be located in packaging equipment such as hoses or pistons. It would be required to establish a procedure for the adequate removal of residual quantities from the previous lot and to validate a maximum period of time between two successive productions in order to avoid problems such as microbial contamination or residue drying for certain forms such as creams or ointments. (September 9, 2003)

Q.7 Clothing: Is it acceptable to have two levels of clothing in the non-sterile manufacturing areas, i.e. one level for operators with full gowning and coveralls and another level for QA auditors and visitors? What environmental monitoring data is required?

A.7   Yes. There are basic clothing requirements for any person entering the manufacturing areas, such as hair, mustache and beard covering, as well as protective garments. However, a firm may decide to apply more stringent requirements for operators, such as dedicated shoes and garments providing a higher level of protection. There are no specific environmental monitoring requirements for clothing worn in the non- sterile manufacturing areas. (September 9 2003)

Q.8 Can the sampling for the microbial monitoring of air in non-sterile areas where susceptible products are produced be conducted when there are no manufacturing packaging activities?

A.8   The sampling should occur during actual manufacturing or packaging in order to reflect the conditions to which the products being produced are really exposed. Monitoring between production runs is also advisable in order to detect potential problems before they arise. (September 9, 2003)

Q.9 Must written procedures be available to prevent objectionable microorganisms in drug products not required to be sterile?

A.9   Yes. Appropriate written procedures, designed to prevent objectionable microorganisms in drug products not required to be sterile, should be established and followed. This means that even though a drug product is not sterile, a firm must follow written procedures that pro-actively prevent contamination and proliferation of microorganisms that are objectionable. (September 9, 2003)

Raw Material Testing - C.02.009 & C.02.010

Q.1 What are the acceptable microbial limits for Purified Water. When Purified Water is used as a raw material in drug product formulations, what tests should be performed in terms of monitoring of its microbial quality ? Should tests be performed for E. Coli, Salmonella, Staphylococcus aureus and Pseudomonas aeruginosa?

A.1   According to interpretation 4, under Section C.02.009 of the current Good Manufacturing Practices Guidelines: "Purified Water that meets any standard listed in Schedule B of the Food and Drugs Act, is used in the formulation of a drug product".

Unless otherwise stated in a monograph or in the marketing authorisation, the recommended microbial limit for purified water is less than 100 cfu/ ml . Furthermore, the limit should be more stringent than the microbial limits set for the end drug product.

In addition purified water used for the formulation of oral solutions and suspensions should be tested for Escherichia coli and Salmonella and when used for the formulation of topical preparations tested for Pseudomonas aeruginosa and Staphylococcus aureus. (January 3, 2008)

Q.2 What are requirements of maintaining an impurity profile?

A.2   The USP defines an impurity profile as "a description of the impurities present in a typical lot of drug substance produced by a given manufacturing process." (ref. USP <1086>). Each commercial lot should be comparable in purity to this standard release profile which is developed early on and maintained for each pharmaceutical chemical. We can also call this profile a "Reference Profile" because the quality control unit refers to it (1) when assessing the purity of each batch of active pharmaceutical ingredient (API), and (2) when evaluating the viability of proposed process changes.

For further information regarding the control of impurities, refer to the following documents available on the International Conference on Harmonization Website (http://www.ich.org):

- Impurities in New Drug Substances - ICH Topic Q3A®);

- Impurities in New Drug Products - ICH Topic Q3B®).

(September 9, 2003)

Q.3 Does every individual container of an active pharmaceutical ingredient (API) need to be sampled for identification (ID) purposes regardless of the number of containers of the same lot available or are composite samples acceptable provided they are obtained from a maximum of 10 containers?

A.3   For human drugs, according to interpretation 6.1 under C.02.009, each container of an API must be tested for identity. Therefore, each container must be opened and sampled. Then, 2 options are available:

1)   To test every sample for ID using a discriminating method (it is not mandatory to perform all ID tests in the specifications, for example USP, but the test must be specific).

2)   The other option is to mix and pool individual samples taken from each containers in a composite sample but without exceeding 10 individual samples in a composite. A specific ID test is then performed on each composite AND, in addition, a potency test is performed to assure the mass balance of the composite. (In such cases, an equal quantity of each individual sample in the composite must be weighed to ensure that the mass balance is representative.)

As an example, say 72 containers of the same lot of an API are received. Each and all containers must be opened and a sample taken from each container. After that, the first option is to test each sample for ID (which implies 72 ID tests). The second option is to combine equal quantities of those individual samples in a way that the number of samples in any composite does not exceed 10 and test those composites for ID and potency. In this case, the easiest way to combine those samples would be 8 composites of 9 individual samples. For a given composite, a potency result of 88.8 % or so would indicate that one of the containers does not contain the right material as each individual sample contributes 1/9 or 11.11% of the total mass of the composite (similarly a result of 77,7 % would indicate 2 containers with the wrong material). In such case, each container selected for this particular composite would have to be tested for ID to pinpoint the one (or more) containers with the wrong material.

However, the use of a composite sample to establish the ID of an API cannot be used when the potency limits are too wide or, similarly, when the precision of the assay method is not sufficient to properly establish the mass balance. (September 9, 2003)

Q.4 Some of our finished products contain active pharmaceutical ingredients (APIs) such as sodium chloride, calcium chloride, magnesium chloride, dextrose...which are generally used as inactive ingredients in

pharmaceutical products. This type of API is received in shipments comprising a large number of containers. Is it acceptable to test a reduced number of containers for ID purposes in relation with interpretation 6.1 of Section C.02.009?

A.4　　For that type of API, it would be acceptable to perform the ID testing on a reduced number of containers provided that sampling is conducted according to a statistically valid plan. Although ($\sqrt{n}+1$) is not recognized as a statistically valid plan, it would nevertheless be considered acceptable for the ID testing of such APIs. This approach would only apply in cases where the raw material is sourced directly from the original vendor or from the broker or wholesaler that supplies materials received from the original vendor without changing the existing labels, packaging, certificate of analysis, and general information. The certification program of the raw material vendor is another issue that is covered under the interpretations of C.02.010. (May 12, 2006)

Q.5 An API can be used after the retest date assigned by the API fabricator if a re-analysis done immediately before use shows that it still meets its specifications. Can the new data generated be used by the drug fabricator to assign a longer retest date to future lots of this API obtained from the same fabricator?

A.5　　No. The extension of the retest date originally assigned to the API should be supported by data generated through a formal stability protocol. This may require the filing of a notifiable change submission. Please refer to the appropriate review Directorate. (September 9, 2003)

Q.6 What about inactive ingredients?

A.6　　Normally, any inactive raw material should bear an expiry date. When an inactive raw material is received without an expiry date, it is not mandatory for the finished product fabricator to assign one if it can be demonstrated based on stability data or other documented evidence that this raw material is not subject to chemical / physical modifications or is not susceptible to microbial contamination. (September 9, 2003)

Q.7 We are a subsidiary of a US corporation. This US corporation supplies us with APIs that are fully tested after receipt on its premises. Can the US site be certified for the purpose of testing exemptions for the Canadian site?

A.7　　The US parent company cannot be considered the vendor. To be certified, the vendor must be the original source of the API (the manufacturer - synthetizer). In this instance, the US company would have to certify the manufacturer - synthetizer as per interpretation 1 under C.02.010 and provide this information to the Canadian site. When received by the Canadian site, a specific ID test must be performed and if for an API, the testing must be as per interpretation 6.1 under C.02.009 (i.e. each container sampled and tested). The above mentioned would be acceptable based on the fact that no repackaging is done by the US site, i.e. the materials must be supplied in their original containers with the original labels and Certificate of Analysis (C of A) as received from the vendor (manufacturer - synthetizer). (September 9, 2003)

Q.8 (Question regarding interpretation 6 of Section C.02.009 of Annex 3 to the Current Edition of the Good Manufacturing Practices Guidelines for Selected Category IV Monograph Drugs) One would assume that 'sample' in interpretation 6.0 is meant to be understood as the composite sample, comprised of the sub-samples from a statistically significant number of containers of the lot of raw material. Then in interpretation 6.1 respecting identity testing of the active we find the wording "Each sample taken as part of the sampling plan is tested..." What is the requirement? If there are 12 containers of the Active Pharmaceutical Ingredient (API) and we decide that sampling X containers would be sufficient, then would we do one analysis on the composite sample or X number of analyses from X containers?

A.8   For APIs, a statistically valid sampling plan should designate the number of containers to be sampled. Each sample taken from each of the selected containers must be tested for identity. (December 16, 2005)

Q.9 Does Health Canada recommend method transfer/lab qualification as described in USP <1226> methods for drug substances? For excipients?

A.9   Yes. Please refer to interpretation 5 of section C.02.009 of the main GMP Guidelines. Additionally, a similar interpretation is made in the GMP Q&A #10 under Finished Product Testing (C.02.018 and C.02.019). (December 16, 2005)

Q.10 What documentation does a laboratory have to have in place to be considered qualified to run a test method for raw materials (drug substances and excipients) in order to satisfy Health Canada Regulations?

A.10   As recommended in the proposed USP <1226>, documentation should include a summary of the analytical data, an assessment of the results and comparison to the acceptance criteria, and a conclusion as to the acceptability of the data as they relate to the ability of the laboratory analysts to successfully perform the compendial procedure in the particular laboratory. (December 16, 2005)

Q.11 Is the sampling plan based on the (/n+1) acceptable for identifying the number of containers of raw material to be sampled?

A.11   Sampling plans and procedures must be statistically valid and should be based on scientifically sound sampling practices taking into account the risk associated with the acceptance of the defective product based on predetermined classification of defects, criticality of the material, and past quality history of the vendor. In some circumstances, such as for large number of containers, a sampling plan based on (/n+1) may be acceptable. However, a sampling plan based on (/n+1) may present a significant risk of accepting defective goods in certain circumstances, such as the sampling of a small number of containers. As with all sampling plans, documented justification must be available. (January 3, 2008)

Q.12 With respect to the re-test date of the drug substances, we have the stability data of a drug substance for up to 24 months at real time stability

condition. The re-test period is assigned up to 24 months. According to the ICH guidelines Q1E, 2.4.1.1(the proposed retest period or shelf life can be up to twice, but should not be more than 12 months beyond, the period covered by long-term data), the retest period can be assigned up to 36 months. Can we assign the retest period up 36 months? If yes, does it require retesting of the active pharmaceutical ingredient (API) at 24 months?

A.12   Retest period and expiry date for active pharmaceutical ingredient (API) should be based on stability data. If an expiry date has been assigned to an API then its batches cannot be used after the expiry period. However, if a retest period has been assigned to the API, then after the retest period is over the API batch can be tested and used immediately (e.g., within one month of the testing). In the scenario presented above extrapolation of expiry date beyond 24 months should be based on stability data both at long-term and accelerated storage conditions. If the test results are satisfactory the retest period can be extended to a period not exceeding 36 months. Once the retest period of the API has been extended to 36 months, testing batches at the 24 months time point would be part of the ongoing stability protocol (it will not be considered retest). For further guidance on retest period and expiry period please consult ICH Q1 A (R2) & Q 1 E, which are available on Health Canada's website at the following address: http://www.hc-sc.gc.ca/dhp-mps/prodpharma/applic-demande/guide-ld/ich/index-eng.php (January 3, 2008)

Manufacturing Control - C.02.011 & C.02.012

Q.1 Can a single lot number be assigned to two or more co-mingled lots of bulk finished drug products packaged during the same run?

A.1   GMP guidelines require each batch must be identified by an individually numbered manufacturing batch document, each lot or batch of the finished product shall be fully tested against the specification and retained samples for each lot or batch shall be kept. If these requirements are met, a company can decide to package under one lot number from 2 or more manufacturing batches of bulk finished drug products. The shortest expiry date of all the lots packaged must be indicated on the label.

However, in case of a product recall, the company must recall the entire lot comprising all the sub-lots. (September 9, 2003)

Q.2 What is the acceptable deviation in physical counts of finished product stock?

A.2   The allowable deviation between physical counts versus counts as per records (including computer records) should be zero. All finished product stock must be fully accounted for and records of distribution and disposition must be maintained. Any deviations from physical counts versus expected counts as per the records, should be investigated and the results of such investigations should be documented. (September 9, 2003)

Q.3 What is the Inspectorate's position on software verification?

A.3   Software is regarded as an adjunct to procedures, manufacturing controls and records keeping and subject to the GMP Regulations. Software validation is the responsibility of the user.

The Pharmaceutical Inspection Cooperation Scheme (PIC/S) Annex 11: Computerized Systems was adopted by Health Canada in 2003.

Inspectors will review a company's procedures and systems, including computer systems, to determine that the requirements of the GMP Regulations are being met. It is possible that the company will be asked how they know a computer system in place is functioning as it should. (December 16, 2005)

Q.4 When are independent checks by another operator necessary?

A.4   The Guidelines indicate that a number of measures be taken to maintain the integrity of a drug product from the moment the various relevant raw materials enter the plant to the time the finished dosage form is released for sale. These measures seek to eliminate as many sources of error as possible so that only those drugs which have met established specifications are distributed.

One of the approaches proposed to achieve this goal is to have written procedures that ensure that each ingredient added to a batch is subjected to one or more checks for identity and quantity by qualified personnel.

If by its design, construction, operations and security features the procedure is such that the company assures that it is impossible to make an error, an independent check by another operator may not be considered necessary.

Checks for identity and quantity of dispensed materials also require independent checks by a second individual.

However, independent checks that materials have been added to the batch have traditionally been assumed to take place at the time of actual addition of the materials.

Other means of verifying the addition of materials may be considered. One alternative involves checking staged materials in the immediate compounding area prior to starting processing and then afterwards, verifying the empty containers before clearing the compounding area. This would be in conjunction with the use of individual processing rooms, otherwise we would need to be satisfied that there was very good separation of compounding operations. (September 9, 2003)

Q.5 What are the expectations on label accountability?

A.5   It is expected that sufficient controls are in place to ensure that correct labels are applied during a labelling operation and that printed packaging materials are accounted for.

One acceptable means of meeting this requirement is to issue an accurately counted number of labels. That number should be reconciled with the number of labels used, damaged and returned to stock.

In theory, the target set in your procedure should be "0" deviation for labels and other printed packaging materials. However, a certain tolerance can be allowed for a few "not accounted for" labels after reconciliation. The limits should take into account the size of the lot especially if they are set in %, as a 0.1% limit for a

1000 unit lot is quite different than for a 50,000 unit lot. The limits could also depend of the type of labels as some types are easier to manipulate than others. (September 9, 2003)

Q.6 Is verification of empty containers an acceptable check for addition of ingredients?

A.6   Yes. It is acceptable to check staged materials prior to and after processing as a method of checks for addition through verification of empty containers.

The preferred method for conducting addition checks is by direct observation by the verifier. The verification of empty containers is an acceptable alternative, but only where stringent controls exist regarding the handling of dispensed raw materials.

Such controls include:

*   assurance that a dispensed raw material does not end up in the wrong batch; locked portable cages are being used by some firms and only pertinent cages are permitted in the room at the same time.

*   adequate operator awareness, training and motivation; the operator has to assure that additions are performed in the proper sequence; any spillage of raw materials must be promptly reported.

*   pre and post checking should be performed by qualified personnel and whenever possible should be the same person.

*   the post processing check must be performed prior to removal of any material from the area.

(September 9, 2003)

Q.7 Are there guidelines for in-house computer systems?

A.7   Computer systems should be validated for their intended purpose and will be reviewed by inspectors to determine that the requirements of the GMP regulations are being met.

The Pharmaceutical Inspection Cooperation Scheme (PIC/S) Annex 11: Computerized Systems was adopted by Health Canada in September 2003 and was implemented in October 2003.

A company is expected to know the efficiency, capability, functionality and reliability of their computer system.

When fully computerized systems are used, backup systems must be available in case of system failure. (December 16, 2005)

Q.8 What are the expectations of software validation pertaining to product release systems?

A.8   Manufacturers are expected to develop and maintain evidence demonstrating that software and equipment are operating as designed. (September 9, 2003)

Q.9 Are quarantine and release stickers required on all containers of raw materials and packaging materials?

A.9   Quarantine and release stickers are required on all containers of raw materials and packaging components to identify status when a physical quarantine/release system is used.

However, such stickers are not required when a validated electronic quarantine system which effectively prevents the possibility of inadvertent use of unreleased material is in place.

When fully computerized storage systems are used, backup systems should be available in case of system failure. (September 9, 2003)

Q.10 Is an answering machine acceptable for recall activation outside normal working hours?

A.10   A telephone answering machine may be used as part of the provisions for off-hours product recall activation. It should provide information on who to contact; their phone numbers etc. Its use, functions and monitoring requirements should be included in the written procedures. (September 9, 2003)

Q.11 Is it necessary to document quantities by lot numbers of finished stock destroyed?

A.11   For products returned to the distributor's facility for destruction due to reasons such as damaged or expired product, it may not be mandatory to document the quantities destroyed by lot number.

For products returned following a recall, it is mandatory to document the returns by lot number as it is a requirement to perform a final reconciliation.

If an establishment recall procedures depend on dates of first and last sale of a given lot, records of destruction by lot numbers may provide necessary information pertaining to accountability per lot. (September 9, 2003)

Q.12 Is there a standard on what should be stated in a recall procedure?

A.12   Regulations C.02.012(1)(a) requires that every fabricator, packager/labeller, distributor, importer, and wholesaler of a drug maintains a system of control that permits complete and rapid recall of any lot of batch of the drug that is on the market. Such a system must be tailored to an individual organization and operation.

A written recall system should be in place to ensure compliance with Section C.01.051 of the Food and Drug Regulations and should include the requirements outlined in interpretations 1.1 to 1.9 under the Manufacturing Control Section C.02.012 of the current GMP Guidelines. (September 9, 2003)

Q.13 Under what circumstances must one initiate a recall?

A.13   The decision to recall a drug product rests with the distributor/importer of the drug.

In most instances, recalls are carried out voluntarily when a company discovers that one or more of its drugs is defective. When a Class 1 or 2 health hazard has been identified, the company is expected to initiate a recall.

In other instances Health Canada may inform a company of findings that one of its drugs is defective and recommends that a recall be initiated. (September 9, 2003)

Q.14 May firms omit second person component weight check if scales are connected to a computer system?

A.14   No, for an automated system that do not include checks on component quality control release status and proper identification of containers.

Yes, for a validated automated system with bar code reader that registers the raw materials identification, lot number and expiry date and that is integrated with the recorded accurate weight data. (September 9, 2003)

Q.15 For a contract fabricator, is it a requirement to test the raw materials offered by customers?

A.15   Testing of raw materials (RM) is a responsibility of the fabricator. Therefore, an observation will be made to a fabricator for not testing a particular RM (even when this RM is provided by the client) if he is not excluded by his client according to a contract. Interpretation 3.2 under Section C.02.012 covers the written agreements with regard to the fabrication, packaging/labelling or testing among the parties involved. If no such agreement is in place, the observation will be made against the party responsible according to the GMP. (September 9, 2003)

Q.16 If the customer asks a contract fabricator not to test a finished product, is it necessary for the contract fabricator to test the product?

A.16   Interpretation 3.2 under Section C.02.012 covers the written agreements with regard to the fabrication, packaging/labelling or testing among the parties involved. If no such agreement is in place, the observation will be made against the party responsible according to the GMP. (September 9, 2003)

Q.17 Is a contract fabricator or packager responsible for qualification of utilities and systems and cleaning validation or is it the responsibility of the distributor? And what about the validation of the manufacturing/packaging process and test methods?

A.17   The contract fabricator is responsible for the qualification of utilities and systems and cleaning validation as those requirements are not product specific.

For process validation and test method validation, the main responsibility rests with the distributor, according to Section C.02.003 of the GMP regulations. The contract fabricator, packager or tester retains responsibility in terms of process or test methods validation unless a written agreement is signed by both parties that excludes the responsibility of the contract fabricator, packager or tester to perform validation activities. (September 9, 2003)

Q.18 How long in advance can the raw materials be weighed?

A.18   It is acceptable to weigh the raw material (RM) a few days prior to the scheduled date of production. However, the firm should be able to demonstrate that the materials and design of the containers in which the RM are weighed and kept will not alter their quality, the characteristics of the RM must also be taken into consideration. Interpretation 2 of Section C.02.026 may provide guidance to this effect. (September 9, 2003)

Q.19 Should virus protection be part of computerised systems (CS) validation?

A.19   Yes. Where a computerised system is exposed to external data-sources, security measures should be part of the system design and maintenance. Where security updates from the vendor, or third-party suppliers are required, their installation should be appropriately evaluated and recorded. (December 16, 2005)

Q.20 Is a written agreement required when an establishment has used an external consultant for computerised systems (CS) validation?

A.20   Yes. Where an external consultant is used to provide a computerized system validation, a formal agreement should be available including a statement of responsibilities, as per the Pharmaceutical Inspection Cooperation Scheme (PIC/S) Annex 11: Computerised Systems adopted by Health Canada in 2003. In general, these agreements are covered in the GMP guidelines under C.02.020 and C.02.012. (December 16, 2005)

Q. 21 (Question regarding interpretation 2 of section C.02.011 of Annex 3 to the Current Edition of the Good Manufacturing Practices Guidelines for Selected Category IV Monograph Drugs) For importers and distributors of Category IV monograph drugs, what is deemed sufficient to meet the requirements to demonstrate that critical production processes have been shown to produce consistent results?

A.21   Importers and distributors of Category IV monograph drugs must have finished product test results that are satisfactory and evidence that each batch was manufactured in accordance with the master production document, for at least 3 batches. (December 16, 2005)

Q.22 If a licensed packager/labeller is packaging a drug for a foreign establishment which is not intended to be sold in Canada as described under Section 1.0 of "GUIDE-0067 Conditions for Provision of Packaging/Labelling Services for Drugs under Foreign Ownership", should this foreign site be listed on the licence of the packager/labeller?

A.22   No. Since this drug would not be sold by the packager/labeller, this establishment would not be considered as an importer under Division 1A and thus, this site would not have to be listed on the licence of the packager/labeller. However, the packager/labeller would still need to fulfil all the requirements outlined under Section 4.0 of GUIDE-0067 that is: obtaining evidence of GMP compliance of the foreign site and supplying the proper information to Health Canada within the prescribed time frame. (January 3, 2008)

Quality Control Department - C.02.013, C.02.014 & C.02.015

Q.1 If a product fails its particulate matter specifications, can it be released for sale?

A.1   No. The particulate matter requirement is treated in the same way as any other specification: failure would constitute non-compliance with the labelled standard. (September 9, 2003)

Q.2 Are the USP general notices enforceable?

A.2   Yes. The USP General Notices provide in summary form the basic guidelines for interpreting and applying the standards, tests, assays, and other specifications of the USP so that these general statements do not need to be repeated in the various monographs and chapters throughout the book. Where exceptions to the General Notices exist, the wording in an individual monograph or general test chapter takes precedence.

This concept is further emphasized in the introduction to the General Information chapters which states, "The official requirements for Pharmacopeial articles are set forth in the General Notices, the individual monographs, and the General Tests and Assays chapters of this Pharmacopeia." The General Tests and Assays chapters are those numbered lower than 1000. (September 9, 2003)

Q.3 If a lot meets USP specifications but fails the firm's internal specifications, can it be released?

A.3   If a lot does not meet its declared release specifications, then the lot should not be released Where more stringent internal specifications act as an alert limit and not as the basis for release, then the lot may be released after investigation and justification provided it meets its release specifications. (September 9, 2003)

Q.4 Is it acceptable for firms to export expired drugs for charity?

A.4   No. While it is recognized the dire need for drugs in distressed parts of the world, once the expiration date has passed there is no assurance that the drugs have the safety, identity, strength, quality and purity characteristics they purport or represent to possess. As such, expired drugs are considered adulterated and their introduction or delivery for introduction into commerce is prohibited. (September 9, 2003)

Q.5 Explain the USP measurement uncertainty (MU) requirement for balances.

A.5   USP General Chapter <41> Weights and Balance states a weighing device providing accurate weighing for assay and test is to have MU of less than

0.1% of the reading and gives an example of 50 mg ± 50 µg as acceptable. To qualify MU of a balance, an appropriate NIST traceable weight within the weighing range of the balance is weighed 10 times or more. The resulting weights are calculated so that three times the calculated standard deviation divided by the amount weighed should be less than 0.001.

For different balance class designations and detailed information on weights and balance, the USP General Chapter <41> is to be consulted. (September 9, 2003)

Q.6 Can an older version of an official method be used or must the most updated version always be used?

A.6　　In resolving issues of conformance to an "official standard", the most up to date version of the analytical method is the method that must be used to determine compliance. (September 9, 2003)

Q.7 What is the Inspectorate's position on the use of secondary reference standards and what are the conditions for the use of secondary reference standards?

A.7　　While the Inspectorate recommends the use of the official standards for the analysis of compendia articles, the use of a secondary RS is acceptable if each lot's suitability is determined prior to use by comparison against the current official reference standard and each lot is requalified periodically in accordance with a written protocol. The protocol should clearly address the receipt, storage, handling and use of primary reference standards, the purification of secondary standards, and their qualification against official reference standards. (September 9, 2003)

Q.8 Is it acceptable to use a third party lab's available pharmacopeial reference standard to qualify an establishment's secondary standard?

A.8　　This practice is acceptable providing the contract testing lab has an Establishment Licence (EL) and has been audited by the client to demonstrate its capability to qualify the secondary standard (ie. the official standard and the proper equipment is available on the tester's premises, the method used has been validated, etc.). Transfer of the standard between the sites should be under controlled conditions. (September 9, 2003)

Q.9 What is the Inspectorate's position on the use of loose work sheets as opposed to bound notebooks for the purpose of recording laboratory data?

A.9　　The recommended method of recording laboratory data is a bound book but the use of loose work sheets would be acceptable as long as it is controlled by a system or a procedure to ensure that all raw data are true and accurate, properly recorded and captured, adequately maintained and easily retrievable. The system should also provide accountability and traceability of work sheets. (September 9, 2003)

Q.10 It is generally accepted in the industry to perform process validation on three consecutive lots. How does the Inspectorate view validation when reworking is required (i.e. three consecutive incidents will never happen)?

A.10   Reworking of a batch should be a very rare occurrence. As such, validation of reworking is not considered mandatory as it is not generally feasible. The reworking should be carried out in accordance with a defined procedure approved by QC and with the conditions described in interpretation 6 of C.02.014. This procedure should include supplementary measures and testing during the reworking operations to ensure that the quality of the final product is not compromised.

It is mandatory that rework proposals and reworked product also be fully investigated with respect to impact on release characteristics and potential impact on bio-availability. Changes in formulation due to reworks including the incorporation of additional lubricant or dissolution aid or additional critical processes may require comparative bio-availability studies. Furthermore concomitant stability studies must be undertaken on reworked batches to ensure that critical characteristics are not compromised with time due to the rework. (September 9 2003)

Q.11 Is it mandatory for the approval of a procedure to sign each page or is it acceptable to only sign the first page?

A.11   It is not mandatory for the approvers to sign each page of the procedure. It would also be acceptable to only sign the last page. (September 9, 2003)

Packaging Material Testing - C.02.016 & C.02.017

Q.1 What is the Inspectorate's position on 2-mercaptobenzothiazole (MBT) in rubber closures?

A.1   MBT is sometimes used in the manufacture of rubber stoppers used as closures for vials or as components of syringes. Due to the concerns about the potential toxicity of MBT, its use in the manufacture of packaging materials that are in direct contact with injectable drugs is not permitted. (September 9, 2003)

Q.2 Is it necessary to include a chemical identification test in a specification for a packaging component (such as a plastic bottle)? Must this chemical ID be conducted for each lot received? Would vendor certification be considered an acceptable substitution for testing upon receipt?

A.2   If the type of material is described on the Certificate of Analysis (C of A) and if a specific test has been performed by the fabricator of the packaging materials confirming the identity of the starting polymer used to manufacture a specific lot, it is not necessary to repeat the chemical ID (such as IR). But each lot of packaging materials should be visually examined to confirm the identity. (September 9. 2003)

Q.3 Can industrial grade nitrogen be used as a blanketing agent during the manufacture of a drug product?

A.3   No. Any gas used as a blanketing agent should be of compendial standard. (September 9, 2003)

Finished Product Testing - C.02.018 & C.02.019

Q.1 Do bacteriostasis and fungistasis testing have to be performed for each lot of product in reference to the USP sterility test?

A.1   No. This needs to be established only once for a specific formulation to determine the suitable level of inoculate for that product. If the formulation has not changed for a number of years, periodic verification can be done as microorganisms become resistant to preservatives in a formulation. (September 9, 2003)

Q.2 Does the Inspectorate encourage the use of environmental isolates for preservative effectiveness testing?

A.2   While the use of environmental isolates in addition to the specified compendia cultures is acceptable, the use of environmental isolates alone is not acceptable. (September 9, 2003)

Q.3 What are the Inspectorate's expectations for process parametric release for foreign and Canadian manufacturers?

A.3   The Inspectorate published on its website, in October 2001, the PIC/S document entitled Guidance on Parametric Release. Please note that requests will be considered only for terminally sterilized drugs in their immediate containers and following submission and approval of evidence acceptable according to this guidance. (September 9, 2003)

Q.4 Does the Inspectorate accept ATP bioluminescence technology as an alternate for traditional microbiology; if so, to what extent of validation is required?

A.4   The ATP bioluminescence technology has been studied as an alternate for the traditional standard plate count analysis in certain products. So far, the procedures described are only tentative and useful only under tightly defined circumstances.

If used, each method should be validated because of the possibility of false positive as a result of non-microbial ATP or false negative produced by degradation of ATP or interference by the material itself. (September 9, 2003)

Q.5 Should an inspector observe and question a technician's analytical work?

A.5   An inspector may verify if the laboratory staff is qualified to carry out the work they undertake. This could occasionally include the observation of what the laboratory technicians are performing and question their actual analytical work in conjunction with SOP's, methods or equipment used.

Also, inspectors will frequently examine testing data from the laboratory for format, accuracy, completeness, and adherence to written procedures. These matters would usually be regarded as Quality Control Dept. C.02.015. The general requirements are outlined in Interpretation para 6, in particular 6.3 laboratory supervisors must sign off subordinates work as per 6.3. (September 9, 2003)

Q.6 Does the official method DO-25 apply to tablets labelled as being professed or as manufacturer's standard?

A.6   Section C.01.015 of the Food and Drug Regulations specifies requirements relating to tablet disintegration times. These regulations require that all drugs in tablet form, ntended to be swallowed whole, disintegrate in not more than 60 minutes when tested by the official method.

The regulations also prescribe a specific disintegration requirement and test for tablets which are enteric coated. Subsection (2) specifies conditions where subsection (1) requirements for DO-25 are not required, i.e. (e) drug demonstrated by an acceptable method to be available to the body, and (f) tablets which are for example extended release. Refer to C.01.011 and C.01.012.

The Inspectorate has no objection to the use of an alternate disintegration or dissolution method to demonstrate compliance with the prescribed release requirements provided that the method had been properly validated. It is understood the DO-25 is not generally used for new drugs. (September 9, 2003)

Q.7 Do tests for impurities have to be repeated for finished products if they have been done on the raw materials?

A.7   The sponsor may have evidence that a related impurity present in the drug product is a previously identified/qualified synthetic impurity. In this case, no further qualification for that impurity is required at the drug product stage. The concentration reported for the established synthetic impurity may be excluded from the calculation of the total degradation products in the drug product, and should be clearly indicated as such in the drug product specifications. Evidence should be provided in the submission demonstrating the related impurity is indeed a synthetic impurity (e.g., by showing constant levels during accelerated and/or shelf-life stability studies and confirmation by providing chromatograms of spiked samples). In cases where the methodology applied to the drug substance and drug product differs, the claim should be confirmed by appropriate studies and the results submitted (e.g., using actual reference standards for that compound).

For further information regarding the control of impurities, refer to the following documents available on the International Conference on Harmonization Website (http://www.ich.org):

- Impurities in New Drug Substances - ICH Topic Q3A®);

- Impurities in New Drug Products - ICH Topic Q3B®).

(September 9, 2003)

Q.8 What is the minimum testing requirements for solid dosage drugs?

A.8   The testing requirements for solid dosage form products include description, identification, purity, and potency and other applicable quality tests depending on the dosage form (e.g., dissolution/disintegration/drug release, uniformity of dosage units, etc.).

For new drugs, the minimum testing requirements have to be approved by the review Directorates. (September 9, 2003)

Q.9 What are the standards other than the USP that have official status in Canada?

A.9   The acceptable standards are described in Schedule B of the Food and Drugs Act. Trade standards are also acceptable under certain conditions. (September 9, 2003)

Q.10 Should compendial test methods be validated?

A.10   Since compendial methods cannot encompass all possible formulations of a drug product, the applicability of a compendia method to a company's particular formulation of a drug product must be demonstrated. It must be determined that there is nothing in the product that causes an interference with the compendia method or affects the performance of the method. It must also be established that the impurities that would be expected from the route of synthesis or formulation are controlled by the compendia method.

The main objective of validation of an analytical procedure is to demonstrate that the procedure is suitable for its intended purpose.

For guidance on validation of analytical procedures, please refer to ICH guides Q2A and Q2B. (September 9, 2003)

Q.11 Must all identification tests stated in a compendial monograph be performed?

A.11   Yes, all tests stated in the monograph must be performed. (September 9, 2003)

Q.12 Are solid dosage drugs exempted from dissolution testing if sold under a manufacturer's standard?

A.12   No, solid dosage drugs should include a routine test for monitoring release characteristics (e.g., dissolution). (September 9, 2003)

Q.13 Does a product labelled as BP have to meet USP specifications?

A.13   No, drugs must meet the standard under which they are labelled and for new drugs, their marketing authorization. (September 9, 2003)

Q.14 Do products labelled as USP have to be tested as per the USP test methods?

A.14　　No. An alternate method can be used, but the distributor must demonstrate that USP drugs comply with USP specifications when tested by USP methods. If an alternate method is used, it must be fully validated and results from a correlation study should be available. (September 9, 2003)

Q.15 What should be the calibration frequency for a dissolution apparatus used with both baskets & paddles?

A.15　　The GMP regulations call for equipment calibration at suitable intervals. Although specific time periods are not given, equipment should be calibrated at a frequency necessary to ensure reliable and reproducible results and covered in the firm's SOP. The firm may consult the apparatus manufacturer's manual for guidance. Historical or validation data may also be used by the firm to support an appropriate calibration frequency.

In case of any event that might change operating characteristics of equipment, such as maintenance or moving it, it should be calibrated as required. (September 9, 2003)

Q.16 In performing system suitability as per USP <621>, do all replicate injections have to be completed before any analyte sample injections are made?

A.16　　No. (September 9, 2003)

Q.17 Is routine product pH testing required for endotoxin (LAL) testing?

A.17　　No, provided that the method is validated and the firm has not committed to such testing in a new drug submission. (September 9, 2003)

Q.18 Is the use of recycled solvents for HPLC columns acceptable?

A.18　　Yes, provided that appropriate validation studies have been performed. (September 9, 2003)

Q.19 Can the lot chosen for the periodic confirmatory testing be released for sale before the re-testing is complete?

A.19　　Yes, provided all product release specifications are met. (September 9, 2003)

Q.20 If one lot of a product made in an MRA country is split into two separate shipments, is it mandatory for the importer to obtain separate manufacturer's batch certificate for each shipment?

A.20　　No. However, the importer should demonstrate that the conditions of transportation and storage applicable to this product have been met for each shipment. (September 9, 2003)

Q.21 Is it acceptable to perform the testing, including the potency, before packaging or is it mandatory to perform this testing after packaging?

A.21   Other than the Identity testing which must be performed after packaging, as per Interpretation 1 under C.02.019 of the Food and Drug Regulations, there is no specific requirement to perform the other tests after packaging including potency. In such cases, the manufacturing process must be validated to demonstrate that the packaging / filling operation does not alter the quality of the product (including potency). These validation data must also demonstrate that the homogeneity of a product is maintained by appropriate means throughout the entire filling process for dosage forms such as lotion, creams or other suspensions. For parenteral, ophthalmic, and other sterile products, at least identity and sterility testing must be performed on the product in the immediate final container.

For the requirement to perform the identity testing after packaging, the unique identifier principle can be used as long as the chemical / biological identity test has been performed after the unique identifier is applied to the product.

Q.22 A product is manufactured in a non-MRA country, then shipped in bulk in a MRA country where it is packaged and tested before being released and exported to Canada. Would the testing exemption provided by Interpretation 4 under C.02.019 apply?

A.22   No. (September 9, 2003)

Records - C.02.020, C.02.021, C.02.022, C.02.023 & C.02.024

Q.1 Must SOP's referenced in master production documents be available at the importer's premises?

A.1   Procedures related to critical processes must be available, whether or not they are referenced in the MPD. (September 9, 2003)

Q.2 Are electronic documents acceptable where it is stated "written" in the GMP regulations?

A.2   It is acceptable that procedures, policies, data and records be stored electronically and that signatures be generated electronically, provided that there are appropriate controls to ensure that such entries, revisions and signatures can only be made by authorized individuals and that paper copies can be generated upon request. (September 9, 2003)

Q.3 Can chromatograms be stored on disc instead of retaining the hard copy?

A.3   Yes, refer to the interpretation under the Records section and question Q.2. (September 9, 2003)

Q.4 Does the person in charge of quality control have to sign QC data and documents?

A.4   QC data and documents must be signed by the person in charge of QC or by a designated alternate as per interpretation 1.4 of section C.02.006. The person in charge remains accountable for the tasks delegated and retains the necessary authority. (September 9, 2003)

Q.5 According to section C.02.020, documents to be kept by the fabricator, packager/labeller, distributor and importer must be stored on their premises in Canada. In the case of a distributor or importer particularly, these documents are sometimes kept only on the premises of a consultant hired to provide QC services, therefore they are not available on the premises of the distributor or importer at the time of the inspection. Is this practice acceptable?

A.5   No. All documents required under Division 2 of the Food and Drug Regulations must be available on the premises of the distributor or importer. Exceptionally, the consultant may bring a file home for a short time to review it but if at the time of the inspection, required documentation are not available on the premises of the distributor or importer, an observation to this effect will be made in the report. In some cases, this could also lead to a NC rating. (December 16, 2005)

Q.6 If electronic signature is not validated, must the signed paper copy be available?

A.6   Yes. The signed paper copy should be available if the electronic signature system has not been validated. (December 16, 2005)

Samples - C.02.025 & C.02.026

Q.1 What is considered an adequate sample when tank loads of a raw material is received?

A.1   As per Interpretation 3 under the Samples section, the retained sample should represent at least twice the amount necessary to complete all required tests. For bulk materials received in tankers, the retained sample should be taken before being mixed-up with the unused quantities still present in the storage tank. (September 9, 2003)

Q.2 A pressurized tanker of hydrocarbon raw materials (isobutan, propane, etc.) is normally sampled and approved before pumping. What is the current Inspectorate policy for sample retention given the inherent risks generated by these flammable gases under pressure?

A.2   The intent of regulation C.02.030 is applied to these cases. Samples of pressurized raw materials are not expected to be retained by manufacturers. (September 9, 2003)

Q.3 If a product is fabricated in Canada and exported outside of Canada (the product is not sold on the Canadian market), are samples of this finished product to be retained in Canada?

A.3   No. This Canadian site is a contract fabricator and not a distributor. Subsection C.02.025 (1) of the Food and Drug Regulations (FDR) requires that a sample of each lot of the packaged/labelled drug be kept by the distributor and the importer (not the fabricator). This is also applicable if the Canadian fabricator manufactures a product for a Canadian distributor (DIN owner). While subsection C.02.025(2) of the FDR for retained samples of raw materials, the requirement applies to the fabricator (the person that transforms the raw material into a finished product), not the distributor. (December 16, 2005)

Q.4 If a product is fabricated in Canada, and contract packaged by another company in Canada and then exported outside of Canada (the product is not sold on the Canadian market), who is responsible for retaining samples of the finished products?

A.4   The Canadian fabricator and the Canadian packager/labeller are not responsible for retaining samples of the finished product. Subsection C.02.025(1) of the Food and Drug Regulations (FDR) requires that a sample of each lot of the packaged/labelled drug be kept by the distributor and the importer (not the fabricator). This is also applicable if the Canadian fabricator manufactures a product for a Canadian distributor (DIN owner). This could vary according to the requirement of each health authority. On the other hand, both parties (Canadian fabricator or packager/labeller) could negotiate a written contract or agreement with the foreign client (the distributor/owner of the product) in order to clearly mention who will be responsible to keep the retained samples of the finished product, as long as this is acceptable to the health authority of that country. Each country could have their own regulatory requirement. (December 16, 2005)

Stability - C.02.027 & C.02.028

Q.1 What is considered to be adequate stability testing for each type of packaging materials?

A.1   In addition to the current GMP guidelines, for guidance regarding the stability testing of finished products packaged in different container / closure materials, refer to:

- ICH/TPP guideline Stability Testing in New Drug Substances and Products

- ICH/TPP guideline Stability Testing: Photostability Testing of New Drug Substances and Products

- ICH/TPP guideline Stability Testing: Requirements for New Dosage Forms

- TPP guidance Stability Testing of Existing Drug Substances and Products

(September 9, 2003)

Q.2 Do batches have to be tested for preservatives at initial release and then in the continuing stability program?

A.2   Yes. Finished products have to be tested against their specifications for release and this should include testing for preservative content when such ingredients are part of the formulation.

An antimicrobial preservative effectiveness testing is performed during the development phase of the product to establish the minimal effective level of preservatives that will be available up to the stated expiry date, and for which a single regular production batch of the drug is to be tested for antimicrobial preservative effectiveness at the end of the proposed shelf life. Once the minimal effective preservative level has been determined, all lots of any preservative containing dosage form included in the stability program must be tested at least once at the expiry date for preservative content. For sterile drugs, the declaration of preservatives on the label is mandatory and those should be treated as for active ingredients, i.e. tested for preservative content at every pre-established control points of the continuing stability program. (September 9, 2003)

Q.3 Can it be assumed that USP chromatographic assay methods are stability indicating?

A.3   No. (September 9, 2003)

Q.4 Is it acceptable to place an expiry date on a bottle cap instead of on the bottle label?

A.4   No. Please refer to section C.01.004(c)(v). The expiration date must appear on any panel of the inner and outer label. (September 9, 2003)

Q.5 When the labelled expiration date states only the month and year does it mean the end of the month?

A.5   Yes. The product should meet approved specifications up to the last day of the specified month. (September 9, 2003)

Q.6 Can accelerated stability data of less than three months be used?

A.6   Accelerated stability studies of any length are considered as preliminary information only and should be supported by long term testing.

The assigning of expiry dates should be based on long term testing. (September 9, 2003)

Q.7 Should drugs packaged into kits and subsequently sterilized, be tested for stability?

A.7   Yes. These operations are part of manufacturing. For drugs that are packaged into trays or kits and the resulting package is sterilized prior to being marketed, data should be available to demonstrate that the sterilization process does not adversely affect the physical and chemical properties of the drug. The testing should be sensitive enough to detect any potential chemical reactions and/or degradation, and the test results should be compared with test values obtained prior to sterilization. (September 9, 2003)

Sterile Products - C.02.029

Q.1 Does the supervisor of a sterile product manufacturing facility need to have a degree in microbiology?

A.1   Section C.02.029(b) of Division 2 of the Food and Drug Regulations requires that "...a drug that is intended to be sterile shall be produced under the supervision of personnel trained in microbiology...". The expression "trained in microbiology" does not mean that this person must have a University degree in microbiology. However, the person must have taken university courses in microbiology. (September 9, 2003)

Q.2 If water that has already been used in compounding is later found to contain endotoxins, what actions need to be taken?

A.2   Water can be used for production prior to obtaining microbiological testing results but the results of these tests must be available prior to final release of the product. GMP's require release only after testing is completed and demonstrates compliance of the product with its specifications.

Since sterilization would not remove endotoxins, an injectable sold with a potential for the presence of endotoxins would be a violation of the Food and Drug Regulations and the hazard to health associated with its use must be determined. A recall would usually be required.

The appropriate action would include an investigation into:

(i)   the potential sources of endotoxins;

(ii) the sanitation and maintenance of the water system.

If there was a GMP deficiency that allowed injectable products to be released prior to receiving test results, procedures should be revised to prevent further occurrences. (September 9, 2003)

Q.3 Are sterile products in amber glass and plastic ampoules exempt from 100% visual inspection?

A.3   No. Each final container of injections must be subjected to a visual inspection. The 100% visual inspection test does not limit itself to particulate matter but includes sealing defects, charring, glass defects, underfills and overfills, missing print, etc. Please refer to interpretation 20 in the Manufacturing Control section of C.02.029. (September 9, 2003)

Q.4 What are the room classification requirements for the capping (crimping) operation of aseptically filled vials (without terminal sterilization)?

A.4   It is important to distinguish between filling / stoppering and crimping which are 2 different operations requiring different environmental conditions. For aseptically filled vials, the filling / stoppering must be performed under Grade A conditions with a Grade B background. When this filling / stoppering is finished, the product is usually taken to a lower grade environment by means of a conveyor belt where the crimping is performed. Because complete integrity may not yet be achieved at this point, it is considered that a Grade C environment, when in operation, is the minimal grade to be used for the crimping operation. The following must also be considered:

- The crimping should be done as soon as possible after the stoppering.

- The distance between the exit of the Grade A/B to the actual point of crimping in the lower environment should be kept as short as possible.

- The conveyor belts for aseptically filled products must not re-enter Grade A or B from an area of lower cleanliness unless they are continuously sterilized (as per Interpretation 5 in the Equipment sub-section of C.02.029).

- Procedures are in place to ensure that the stoppers are properly seated prior to the crimping operation.

- Equipment utilization logs should indicate line stoppages and time lapses.

- Stoppered vials which do not get crimped within the established time lapse should be segregated and disposed off in accordance with SCP.

Another important point to consider is the validation of the entire aseptic process including periodic verifications by media-fills. (September 9, 2003)

Q.5 What are the requirements in terms of monitoring/testing for the release of sterile gowns to be used in a controlled environment (grade A or B) when those are obtained from a supplier?

A.5   There is no specific requirements in the GMP for the sterility testing of the protective garments to be worn in grade A and B areas. However, the sterility cycle used by an outside supplier to sterilize these garments should have been validated according to scientifically sound procedures. Among other aspects, validation should address penetration/distribution studies of the sterilizing medium (gas, radiation, heat, etc.), load patterns of the sterilizers, determination of the Sterility Assurance Level with Bio indicators, etc. Also, the integrity of the outside wrapping in order to maintain sterility should be demonstrated. (September 9, 2003)

Q.6 What are the room classification requirements for the preparation of containers and other packaging materials to be used in the fabrication of sterile products?

A.6   The preparation (cleaning, washing, etc.) of containers and packaging materials is normally performed in a "clean" room (grade C or D). After these operations, the containers and materials used for drugs sterilized by filtration (and not further subjected to terminal sterilization in their final containers) must be depyrogenated and sterilized before being introduced in the aseptic rooms by the use of double-ended sterilizers or any other validated method. The depyrogenation step can be done using pyrogen-free WFI for the last rinse prior sterilization or by performing the depyrogenation and sterilization in one operation using a dry heat oven. Filling of these products normally takes place in a class A with a B background.

For products submitted to terminal sterilization, it is not mandatory to use containers and packaging materials that are sterile but those that are in direct contact with the product should be free of pyrogen. This is usually achieved by using pyrogen-free WFI for the last rinse of these materials unless they are subsequently depyrogenated by another method (e.g., dry heat oven).

In addition, the initial bioburden of these materials should meet pre-established limits (that are based on sound science) and the risk of contamination during their introduction in the filling areas should be kept to a minimum. (September 9, 2003)

Q.7 For the validation of moist heat sterilization cycles, will the new standards include the use of prions as the organism of choice instead of Bacillus stearothermophilus?

A.7   At the present time, it is recognized in the scientific and pharmaceutical community that the spores of Bacillus stearothermophilus are the organisms of choice for the validation of moist heat sterilization cycles. Validation of such cycles is based on biological indicators containing a known count of organisms in order to determine a lethality factor for a given cycle. Those studies are based on parameters such as the "D" value of certain organisms and also imply a microbiological testing of these indicators at the end of the cycle in order to establish a survival rate. The use of prions (infectious proteins) could be inadequate in that their detection and quantification, which is based on animal models, is very difficult. Moreover, those organisms are very difficult to destroy and could present a danger should they accidentally be spread in a plant. (September 9, 2003)

Q.8 Is it acceptable to use purified water in the formulation of ophthalmic preparations instead of WFI?

A.8   There is a distinction between Intra-Ocular and Ophthalmic use: Intra-ocular implies a use when the eye surface is compromised (such as irrigation solutions used to rinse the operating site during cataract removal), whereas Ophthalmic implies use on the intact surface of the eyeball, such as artificial tears.

The requirement to use WFI as referenced in interpretation 4 under "Water Treatment Systems" in Section C.02.029 of the GMP's should not apply to Ophthalmic products. The latest edition of the BP, in the general monographs for "Eye Preparations", defines Eye Drops as a solution or suspension in Purified Water. The individual monograph for "Atropine Eye Drops", for example, is defined as "a sterile solution of Atropine sulfate in Purified Water" in the BP.

In the current edition of the USP, it is specifically indicated in chapter <1231> Water for Pharmaceutical Purposes, figure 3 "selection of water for pharmaceutical purposes" that WFI is used for dosage forms for parenteral use. As well, the individual monographs for WFI and PW emphasize this fact: in the WFI monograph, it is mentioned that WFI is intended for use in the preparation of parenteral solutions and in the PW monograph, that PW is intended to be used, among others, for sterile preparations other than parenterals.

Based on the above, it is acceptable to use PW in the formulation of an ophthalmic preparation, unless specified otherwise by the review Directorates for particular products. (September 9, 2003)

Q.9 What conditions (incubation time and temperature) should be used for the incubation of media filled units?

A.9   Following the aseptic processing of the medium, the filled containers are incubated at 22.5 °C ± 2.5 °C or at 32.5 °C ± 2.5 °C. All media filled containers should be incubated for a minimum of 14 consecutive days. If two temperatures are used for incubation of media filled samples, than these filled containers should be incubated for at least 7 consecutive days at each temperature starting with the lower temperature. (December 16, 2005)

Q.10 For aseptic filtration should integrity of the sterilized filter be verified before or after use?

A.10   For an aseptic process the integrity of the sterilized 0.22 micron filter should be verified before use and should be confirmed immediately after use by an appropriate method such as bubble point, pressure hold or diffusion.

If more than one 0.22 micron filters are used in series the above mentioned test for filter integrity should be performed on both the filters after being connected in series.

Please refer to the Inspectorate guideline Process Validation: Aseptic Processes for Pharmaceuticals. (September 9, 2003)

Q. 11 What are the requirements for the environment to be used to perform the sterility test?

A.11   The facility for sterility testing should be such as to comply with the microbial limits of an aseptic production facility which should conform to a Grade A within a Grade B background or in an isolator of a Grade A within a Grade D background. (December 16, 2005)

Q.12 According to the monograph on parenteral products (0520) of the 4th edition (2002) of the European Pharmacopeia (EP), injections for veterinary use with a volume dose of less than 15 mL are exempted from bacterial endotoxins/pyrogen testing by the European Union (EU). Is this interpretation correct? If so, would this EU exemption be applicable in Canada?

A.12   Yes, this interpretation is correct but this exemption is not applicable in Canada.

As per section C.01.067(1) of the Food and Drug Regulations, it is required that each lot of a drug for parenteral use be tested for the presence of pyrogens using an acceptable method and be found to be non-pyrogenic. The Bacterial Endotoxins and Pyrogen test methods described in the USP and EP are considered acceptable methods for that purpose. For all parenteral drug products, the Bacterial Endotoxins test should be preferred over the Pyrogen test unless the latter is demonstrated to be justified (more appropriate) or has been approved by a review Directorate. Therefore, the specification of all drug products for parenteral use intended for the Canadian market should include a test for Bacterial Endotoxins or Pyrogens and the EU current "15 mL exemption" is not applicable in Canada.

The only acceptable exemptions are those provided by section C.01.067(2), i.e., for parenteral drug products inherently pyrogenic or those which cannot be tested for the presence of pyrogens by either test methods. In other words, not testing a parenteral drug product for the presence of pyrogens would be considered acceptable only if documentation is available demonstrating that the parenteral drug product is inherently pyrogenic or that it cannot be tested by any of the methods. (September 9, 2003)

Q.13 For radiopharmaceuticals, can it be acceptable to verify the integrity of the sterilizing filter only after use and to not perform the pre-filtration integrity testing?

A.13   As per interpretation 4.7 under the "General" interpretations of Section C.02.029 of the current GMP guidelines, the integrity of the sterilizing filter must be verified before and after use. However, the pre-filtration integrity testing for that type of products could lead to radioactive contamination as a result of the venting process of the filter assembly that must be performed before the start of product filtration. This would pose an unacceptable health risk for the operators and could result in disruption of production until the facility is decontaminated. It is therefore acceptable to use two filters of a minimum filter rating of 0.22 micron and to verify the integrity of the sterilizing filters after use only for these products. However, data should be available from the filter manufacturer that the filters are supplied pre-assembled and individually integrity tested by the filter manufacturer. (December 16, 2005)

Q.14 What is the Inspectorate's position on pooling of samples within the same batch (e.g., 7 samples in one pool) for testing for sterility? The Ph. Eur. does not mention explicitly a pooling of samples for testing for sterility.

A.14   It is acceptable if companies pool samples for sterility testing with the membrane filtration method. However, it is not acceptable to pool samples when the direct inoculation method is used. Exceptions can be tolerated, when the volume of the sample-pool does not exceed 10% of the culture medium volume. (January 3, 2008)

Good Manufacturing Practices for Medical Gases - Questions and Answers

Health Canada

The Medical Gas GMP questions and answers (Q&A) presented below were previously found in the document entitled "GMP Interpretation Decision Records for Medical Gas - 2004 Edition". This Q&A list will be updated on a regular basis. Note that the date at the end of each Q&A represents the date on which the Q&A was added to the list.

Medical Gas - Good Manufacturing Practices (GMP) Questions and Answers[75]

Premises - C.02.004

Equipment - C.02.005

Q.1 Is the use of a hoke bomb acceptable for sampling gases from a storage tank?

A.1   Yes, provided the firm has validated the process. A hoke bomb is a stainless steel cylinder with a valve on each end which allows a gaseous product to flow through. The most significant step in the validation process is the time required to fully purge the cylinder which provides assurance that complete evacuation of the cylinder has been accomplished. (April 1, 2004)

Q.2 What is the extent of calibration required for vacuum gauges?

A.2   Vacuum gauges are used during the essential evacuation of residual gas from high pressure cylinders, and therefore, need adequate calibration.

At periodic intervals, vacuum gauges should be calibrated to standards established by the National Institute of Standards and Technology or another recognized standard. The frequency of calibration should be based on manufacturer's recommendations. A firm could also establish its own frequency based on usage and experience. Vacuum gauges should be checked prior to use with no vacuum present to ensure that the needle on the gauge returns to the "zero." Records should be maintained. (April 1, 2004)

---

[75] Available on the Health Canada website at http://www.hc-sc.gc.ca/dhp-mps/compli-conform/gmp-bpf/question/med_gas-gaz_med-eng.php

Personnel - C.02.006

Sanitation - C.02.007 & C.02.008

Raw Material Testing - C.02.009 & C.02.010

Manufacturing Control - C.02.011 & C.02.012

Q.1 A firm receives liquid nitrogen from a supplier with a valid certificate of analysis for each delivery. Firm's operation involves the filling of high pressure cylinders via a heat exchanger or a vaporizer. Should a test for identity and assay be performed on one filled container from each manifold filling sequence or can we rely on the test results provided by the supplier with no further testing?

A.1   The liquid nitrogen received from a supplier should be tested as per the GMP requirements under Manufacturing Control. In addition, one filled cylinder from each manifold should be tested in accordance with the GMP requirements under Finished Product Testing. (October 13, 2006)

Q.2 Is cylinder colour an acceptable mean of segregation between different products?

A.2   Product segregation by cylinder colour can be an acceptable method if there is evidence that the personnel involved are adequately trained. Additional measures are necessary to segregate quarantined and released cylinders. (April 1, 2004)

Q.3 Is transfilling of medical gases considered a "package" activity or a "distribute" activity?

A.3   Transfilling of medical gases either at the facility or curbside is considered a "package" activity, pursuant to Section C.01A.001(1) of the Food and Drug Regulations, which defines the term "package" as "to put a drug in its immediate container", and section C.01.001, which defines the term "immediate container" as "the receptacle that is in direct contact with a drug". (October 13, 2006)

Q.4 Can you provide examples of which operations at a medical gas facility is considered a "fabricate" activity and what is considered a "package" activity?

A.4   The following operations are considered a "fabricate" activity:

- medical gases produced via air liquefaction (i.e., air separation plants) and/or

- medical gas mixtures made by filling into cylinders

Transfilling of gases either at the facility or curbside is considered a "package" activity. If the company transfilling hold the DIN, the activity would be classified as both as distribution and packaging/labelling, and must meet the requirements of Divisions 1A and 2 of the Food and Drug Regulations.

Medical gas facilities should have establishment licences that reflect what activity they are doing. (October 13, 2006)

Quality Control Department - C.02.013, C.02.014 & C.02.015

Packaging Material Testing - C.02.016 & C.02.017

Finished Product Testing - C.02.018 & C.02.019

Q.1 Should medical air USP be exempt from the analysis for water/oil, carbon dioxide, nitric oxide/nitrogen dioxide and sulphur dioxide when produced synthetically from raw materials meeting oxygen USP and nitrogen NF specifications?

A.1   If compendial specifications require impurity tests, then they must be performed. (April 1, 2004)

Q.2 When is oxygen exempt from being tested for carbon dioxide?

A.2   The USP exempts oxygen with purity of no less than 99% from the requirements of the tests for carbon dioxide and carbon monoxide when the oxygen has been produced by the air liquefaction method. Other Schedule B (compendial) monographs may have similar exemptions.

Documentation should be available indicating that the specific lot of oxygen has been produced by the air liquefaction process. (April 1, 2004)

Q.3 Can mixtures of medical gases be labelled only as being a USP mixture?

A.3   Only mixtures of medical gases which meet USP monographs as mixtures may be labelled as USP. (April 1, 2004)

Q4. A mixture of two gases is first filled into a series of storage buffer tanks. From the storage buffer tanks the mixture is then transfilled into finished product cylinders (cylinders labelled and ready for sale to clients). Can we only test each buffer tanks for one of the two gases (usually the active ingredient) and test only one cylinder after filling a series of cylinders or is it mandatory to test each cylinder after filling (usually for the active ingredient) as per C.02.018, interpretation 4?

A.4   When a mixture of two different gases is made in a tank, stratification may occur and each cylinder of the gas mixture must be tested as per interpretation 4 of C.02.018 (i.e., every cylinder is tested to specifications of one of the gases, usually the active ingredient and an identity test for the other gas is performed on one cylinder from the manifold filling sequence). But if the mixing process of the gases in the buffer tanks can be validated to demonstrate that the mixture remains homogenous within the buffer tanks and during the filling process, then full testing of one cylinder per filling sequence or manifold could be acceptable. (April 1, 2004)

Q.5 In terms of testing, what is expected when filling homecare units with liquid oxygen USP on company's premises?

A.5   If the source container is accompanied by a certificate of analysis, the filler for homecare units can perform identity testing only. (April 1, 2004)

Q.6 Is an importer required to perform and identity test for mixtures of ethylene oxide/carbon dioxide?

A.6   Due to the carcinogenic nature of ethylene oxide, an identity test is not required to be performed on mixtures of ethylene oxide/carbon dioxide by the importer if the importer sells the gas mixture "as is in the same container" and does not perform any additional fabricating and/or packaging operations for this gas mixture. A certificate of analysis will be required from the fabricator of the gas mixture. (October 13, 2006)

Q.7 In terms of testing, what is expected when a fabricator/distributor supplies liquid nitrogen NF in an open-top dewar?

A.7   When a fabricator/distributor supplies small quantities of liquid nitrogen NF in an unpressurized open-top dewar for professional use, no additional testing is required provided that the source container has been tested, met appropriate specifications and has been released. (October 13, 2006)

Records - C.02.020, C.02.021, C.02.022, C.02.023 & C.02.024

Q.1 What is the extent of documentation required to be maintained by a medical gas distributor for new cylinders and valves?

A.1   Certification issued by Transport Canada may be acceptable as a means of compliance for new cylinders. Records may be maintained in a central location provided that the data is accessible or retrievable. It is expected that written specifications are available which outline the checks which are to be performed on empty cylinders prior to filling and that a record of those checks is maintained.

Valves on cylinders should be checked for functionality and records maintained. (April 1, 2004)

Q.2 What is the retention time for GC charts by a medical gas distributor?

A.2   GC charts are considered to be records/evidence of testing and must be maintained for 5 years from the date of filling. (April 1, 2004)

Importation and Exportation
Questions and Answers

Health Canada

Unit Name: Drug GMP Inspection Unit

Telephone: 613-957-1492

Fax: 613-957-6709

Email: GMP_questions_BPF@hc-sc.gc.ca

The Importation and Exportation questions and answers (Q&A) was previously found under the document entitled "Q&A on the commercial importation and exportation of drugs in dosage forms". The Q&As have been updated and are moving to the Q&A page of the website. This Q&A list will be updated on a regular basis. Note that the date at the end of each Q&A represents the date on which the Q&A was added to the list.

This Importation and Exportation questions and answers (Q&A) list will be updated on a regular basis. Note that the date at the end of each Q&A represents the date on which the Q&A was added to the list.

Importation and Exportation Questions and Answers[76]

Importation

Q.1 What type of information should I submit to demonstrate the GMP compliance of a foreign drug establishment?

A.1   Please consult the Health Products and Food Branch Inspectorate policy document entitled "Guidance on Evidence to Demonstrate Drug Compliance of Foreign Sites (GUI-0080)".

Q.2 An On-Site Evaluation was performed for a specific product. Is the On-Site Evaluation Report sufficient to demonstrate GMP compliance of the foreign drug establishment?

A.2   No. An On-Site Evaluation (OSE) is a product-specific evaluation of the manufacture of a drug conducted on-site by a Qualified Authority to assess the conformity with the drug submission. An OSE does not cover all the sections of GMP requirements and when submitted alone is not considered sufficient to demonstrate GMP compliance of the foreign drug establishment. For further

---

[76] Available on the Health Canada website at http://www.hc-sc.gc.ca/dhp-mps/compli-conform/gmp-bpf/question/imp-exp_q&a_tc-tm-eng.php

information, please consult the Health Products and Food Branch Inspectorate policy document "Guidance on Evidence to Demonstrate Drug Compliance of Foreign Sites (GUI-0080)".

Q.3 If I want to import a drug, for additional packaging steps in Canada and, then re-export it, what do I have to do?

A.3　　A drug importer is required to hold an Establishment Licence and meet the GMP requirements. The foreign site must be GMP compliant and be listed on the importer's Establishment Licence.

If the drug product is being imported from a foreign site and exported back to the same foreign site, which retains ownership of the drug product throughout the process, the establishment is required to hold an Establishment Licence for packaging. The document entitled "Conditions for Provision of Packaging/Labelling Services for Drugs under Foreign Ownership (GUI-0067)" should be consulted for further guidance and additional requirements.

If the drug product is being imported from a foreign site and exported to another foreign site, you cannot be exempted from the requirements of the Food and Drugs Act & Regulations, and you cannot use the exemption provided under Section 37 . This is considered a commercial importation. All commercial importation of drugs in dosage form must meet all the requirements of the Food and Drug Regulations, including Division 1 "Drugs", Division 1A "Establishment Licensing", Division 2 "Good Manufacturing Practices", and any other applicable requirements depending on the drug product. The site where the imported drug is fabricated must be listed on the importer's Establishment Licence and its compliance to the GMP requirements must be demonstrated. See Q&A #1 above. (July 1, 2003)

Exportation

Q.1 What is the difference between an Export Certificate issued under Section 37 of the Food and Drugs Act and a CPP?

A.1　　An Export Certificate issued under Section 37 of the Food and Drugs Act is a certificate signed by the fabricator and a Commissioner for Taking Oaths to attest that the drug for which the certificate is prepared is not manufactured, or sold, for consumption in Canada and that its package and the contents do not contravene any known requirement of the law of the country to which it is or is about to be consigned.

A Certificate of a Pharmaceutical Product (CPP) is a certificate issued by the Health Products and Food Branch Inspectorate establishing the regulatory status of the pharmaceutical, biological or radiopharmaceutical product listed and the GMP status of the applicant. This certificate is in the format recommended by the World Health Organization (WHO). (July 1, 2003)

Q.2 If I'm exporting products, do I need to invoke Section 37?

A.2　　No, it is the establishment's choice whether or not to invoke Section 37.

Section 37(1) of the Food and Drugs Act states: "This Act does not apply to any packaged food, drug, cosmetic or device, not manufactured for consumption in Canada and not sold for consumption in Canada, if the package is marked in distinct overprinting with the word "Export" or "Exportation" and a certificate that the package and its contents do not contravene any known requirement of the law of the country to which it is or is about to be consigned has been issued in respect of the package and its contents in prescribed form and manner."

Guidance is available in the document entitled "Guidance Document on the Commercial Importation and Exportation of Drugs in Dosage Forms Under the Food and Drugs Act (GUI-0057)". (July 1, 2003)

Q.3 If I have invoked Section 37 for a product, is it still possible to receive a Certificate of Pharmaceutical Product (CPP) for this product?

A.3   No. If a Canadian fabricator chooses to invoke Section 37, the Health Products and Food Branch Inspectorate will not issue a CPP for these drugs. If a Certificate of Compliance is requested for an establishment, a list of drugs for which the fabricator has invoked Section 37 will also be provided to the foreign Regulatory Authority. (July 1, 2003)

Q.4 When and how do I notify the Health Products and Food Branch Inspectorate of my intention to invoke Section 37?

A.4   Establishments should notify the Health Products and Food Branch Inspectorate of their intention to invoke Section 37 of the Food and Drugs Act upon renewal of the Establishment Licence each year. The Establishment Licence renewal package includes a form entitled "Intention to invoke Section 37 of the Canada Food and Drugs Act for products being exported". This form requires establishments to declare the list of drug products for which they intend to invoke the exemption under Section 37. You must fill out this form and return it along with your Establishment Licence renewal to the Health Products and Food Branch Inspectorate. If a decision is made at another time during the year to invoke Section 37, the same form should be used and the information sent to the Health Products and Food Branch Inspectorate. Copies of Export Certificates must be provided.

Import and Export Q&A

Part V

International Conference on Harmonisation (ICH) Guidance Documents

ICH Q1A(R2):
Stability Testing of New Drug Substances and Products

Health Products and Food Branch Guidance Document

September 25, 2003

Notice
Our file number: 03-118437-914

Date Adopted 2003/09/25

Effective Date 2004/01/01

Effective Date for the intermediate storage condition of 30 C ± 2 C/65% RH ± 5% RH, if applicable 2007/01/01

Guidance for Industry: Stability Testing of New Drug Substances and Products: ICH Topic Q1A(R2)[77]

Adoption of ICH[78] Guidance: Stability Testing of New Drug Substances and Products - ICH Topic Q1A(R2)

This guidance document is a revised version of the ICH Q1A(R) guidance document and defines the stability data package for a new drug substance or drug product. This revised Q1A(R2) guidance document was necessary as a result of the adoption of ICH guidance document Q1F - Stability Data Package for Registration Applications in Climatic Zones III and IV. The changes made to the Q1A(R) guidance document are outlined in the accompanying covering note to this guidance document.

This guidance has been developed by the appropriate ICH Expert Working Group and has been subject to consultation by the regulatory parties, in accordance with the ICH Process. The ICH Steering Committee has endorsed the final draft and recommended its adoption by the regulatory bodies of the European Union, Japan and USA.

In adopting this ICH guidance, Health Canada endorses the principles and practices described therein. This document should be read in conjunction with

---

[77] Available on the Health Canada website at http://www.hc-sc.gc.ca/dhp-mps/prodpharma/applic-demande/guide-ld/ich/qual/q1a(r2)-eng.php
[78] International Conference on Harmonisation of Technical Requirements for the Registration of Pharmaceuticals for Human Use

this accompanying notice and with the relevant sections of other applicable Health Canada guidances.

It is recognized that the scope and subject matter of current Health Canada guidances may not be entirely consistent with those of the ICH guidances that are being introduced as part of our commitment to international harmonization and the ICH Process. In such circumstances, Health Canada adopted ICH guidances take precedence.

Health Canada is committed to eliminating such discrepancies through the implementation of a phased-in work plan that will examine the impact associated with the adoption of ICH guidances. This will result in the amendment or, depending on the extent of revisions required, withdrawal of some Health Canada guidances.

This and other Guidance documents are available on the Therapeutic Products Directorate / Biologics and Genetic Therapies Directorate / Marketed Health Products Directorate Website (s) (http://www.hc-sc.gc.ca/dhp-mps/index-eng.php). The availability of printed copies of guidance documents may be confirmed by consulting the Guidelines and Publications Order Forms (available on the TPD/BGTD/MHPD Website) or by contacting the Publications Coordinator[79].

Should you have any questions regarding the content of the guidance, please contact:

Bureau of Pharmaceutical Sciences
Therapeutic Products Directorate
Health Canada
Finance Building (A/L 0202A2)
Ottawa, Ontario
K1A 1B9

Internet: bps_enquiries@hc-sc.gc.ca
Phone: (613) 941-3184
Fax: (613) 957-3989

Foreword

This guidance has been developed by the appropriate ICH Expert Working Group and has been subject to consultation by the regulatory parties, in accordance with the ICH Process. The ICH Steering Committee has endorsed the final draft and recommended its adoption by the regulatory bodies of the European Union, Japan and USA.

In adopting this ICH guidance, Health Canada endorses the principles and practices described therein. This document should be read in conjunction with the accompanying notice and the relevant sections of other applicable guidances.

Guidance documents are meant to provide assistance to industry and health care professionals on how to comply with the policies and governing statutes and regulations. They also serve to provide review and compliance guidance to staff, thereby ensuring that mandates are implemented in a fair, consistent and effective manner.

Guidance documents are administrative instruments not having force of law and, as such, allow for flexibility in approach. Alternate approaches to the principles

---

[79] Tel: (613) 954-6466; E-mail: publications_coordinator@hc-sc.gc.ca

and practices described in this document may be acceptable provided they are supported by adequate scientific justification. Alternate approaches should be discussed in advance with the relevant program area to avoid the possible finding that applicable statutory or regulatory requirements have not been met.

As a corollary to the above, it is equally important to note that Health Canada reserves the right to request information or material, or define conditions not specifically described in this guidance, in order to allow the Department to adequately assess the safety, efficacy or quality of a therapeutic product. Health Canada is committed to ensuring that such requests are justifiable and that decisions are clearly documented.

Cover Note for Revision of Q1A(R)

The purpose of this note is to outline the changes made in Q1A(R) that result from adoption of ICH Q F "Stability Data Package for Registration Applications in Climatic Zones III and IV". These changes are:

1. The intermediate storage condition has been changed from 30°C ± 2°C/60% RH ± 5% RH to 30°C ± 2°C/65% RH ± 5% RH in the following sections:

    *   2.1.7.1 Drug Substance - Storage Conditions - General Case

    *   2.2.7.1 Drug Product - Storage Conditions - General Case

    *   2.2.7.3 Drug products packaged in semi-permeable containers

    *   3 Glossary - "Intermediate testing"

2. 30°C ± 2°C/65% RH ± 5% RH can be a suitable alternative long-term storage condition to 25°C ± 2°C/60% RH ± 5% in the following sections:

    *   2.1.7.1 Drug Substance - Storage Conditions - General Case

    *   2.2.7.1 Drug Product - Storage Conditions - General Case

3. 30°C ± 2°C/35% RH ± 5% RH has been added as a suitable alternative long-term storage condition to 25°C ± 2°C/40% RH ± 5% and the corresponding example for the ratio of water-loss rates has been included in the following section:

    *   2.2.7.3 Drug products packaged in semi-permeable containers

Mid-stream switch of the intermediate storage condition from 30°C ± 2°C/60% RH ± 5% RH to 30°C ± 2°C/65% RH ± 5% RH can be appropriate provided that the respective storage conditions and the date of the switch are clearly documented and stated in the registration application.

It is recommended that registration applications contain data from complete studies at the intermediate storage condition 30°C ± 2°C/65% RH ± 5% RH, if applicable, by three years after the date of publication of this revised guideline in the respective ICH tripartite region.

1. Introduction

1.1. Objectives of this Guidance Document

The following guidance document is a revised version of the ICH Q1A guidance document and defines the stability data package for a new drug substance or drug product that is sufficient for a registration application within the three regions

---

of the EC, Japan, and the United States. It does not seek necessarily to cover the testing for registration in or export to other areas of the world.

The guidance document seeks to exemplify the core stability data package for new drug substances and products, but leaves sufficient flexibility to encompass the variety of different practical situations that may be encountered due to specific scientific considerations and characteristics of the materials being evaluated. Alternative approaches can be used when there are scientifically justifiable reasons.

1.2. Scope of this Guidance Document

The guidance document addresses the information to be submitted in registration applications for new molecular entities and associated drug products. This guidance document does not currently seek to cover the information to be submitted for abbreviated or abridged applications, variations, clinical trial applications, etc.

Specific details of the sampling and testing for particular dosage forms in their proposed container closures are not covered in this guidance document.

Further guidance on new dosage forms and on biotechnological/biological products can be found in ICH guidances Q1C and Q5C, respectively.

1.3. General Principles

The purpose of stability testing is to provide evidence on how the quality of a drug substance or drug product varies with time under the influence of a variety of environmental factors such as temperature, humidity, and light, and to establish a re-test period for the drug substance or a shelf life for the drug product and recommended storage conditions.

The choice of test conditions defined in this guidance is based on an analysis of the effects of climatic conditions in the three regions of the EC, Japan and the United States. The mean kinetic temperature in any part of the world can be derived from climatic data, and the world can be divided into four climatic zones, I-IV. This guidance document addresses climatic zones I and II. The principle has been established that stability information generated in any one of the three regions of the EC, Japan and the United States would be mutually acceptable to the other two regions, provided the information is consistent with this guidance document and the labeling is in accord with national/regional requirements.

2. Guidelines

2.1. Drug Substance

2.1.1. General

Information on the stability of the drug substance is an integral part of the systematic approach to stability evaluation.

2.1.2. Stress Testing

Stress testing of the drug substance can help identify the likely degradation products, which can in turn help establish the degradation pathways and the intrinsic stability of the molecule and validate the stability indicating power of the analytical procedures used. The nature of the stress testing will depend on the individual drug substance and the type of drug product involved.

Stress testing is likely to be carried out on a single batch of the drug substance. It should include the effect of temperatures (in 10°C increments (e.g., 50°C, 60°C, etc.) above that for accelerated testing), humidity (e.g., 75% RH or greater) where appropriate, oxidation, and photolysis on the drug substance. The testing should also evaluate the susceptibility of the drug substance to hydrolysis across a wide range of pH values when in solution or suspension. Photostability testing should be an integral part of stress testing. The standard conditions for photostability testing are described in ICH Q1B.

Examining degradation products under stress conditions is useful in establishing degradation pathways and developing and validating suitable analytical procedures. However, it may not be necessary to examine specifically for certain degradation products if t has been demonstrated that they are not formed under accelerated or long term storage conditions.

Results from these studies will form an integral part of the information provided to regulatory authorities.

2.1.3. Selection of Batches

Data from formal stability studies should be provided on at least three primary batches of the drug substance. The batches should be manufactured to a minimum of pilot scale by the same synthetic route as, and using a method of manufacture and procedure that simulates the final process to be used for, production batches. The overall quality of the batches of drug substance placed on formal stability studies should be representative of the quality of the material to be made on a production scale.

Other supporting data can be provided.

2.1.4. Container Closure System

The stability studies should be conducted on the drug substance packaged in a container closure system that is the same as or simulates the packaging proposed for storage and distribution.

2.1.5. Specification

Specification, which is a list of tests, reference to analytical procedures, and proposed acceptance criteria, is addressed in ICH Q6A and Q6B. In addition, specification for degradation products in a drug substance is discussed in Q3A.

Stability studies should include testing of those attributes of the drug substance that are susceptible to change during storage and are likely to influence quality, safety, and/or efficacy. The testing should cover, as appropriate, the physical, chemical, biological, and microbiological attributes. Validated stability-indicating analytical procedures should be applied. Whether and to what extent replication should be performed will depend on the results from validation studies.

2.1.6. Testing Frequency

For long term studies, frequency of testing should be sufficient to establish the stability profile of the drug substance. For drug substances with a proposed re-test period of at least 12 months, the frequency of testing at the long term storage condition should normally be every 3 months over the first year, every 6 months over the second year, and annually thereafter through the proposed re-test period.

At the accelerated storage condition, a minimum of three time points, including the initial and final time points (e.g., 0, 3, and 6 months), from a 6-month study is recommended. Where an expectation (based on development experience) exists that results from accelerated studies are likely to approach significant change criteria, increased testing should be conducted either by adding samples at the final time point or by including a fourth time point in the study design.

When testing at the intermediate storage condition is called for as a result of significant change at the accelerated storage condition, a minimum of four time points, including the initial and final time points (e.g., 0, 6, 9, 12 months), from a 12-month study is recommended.

2.1.7. Storage Conditions

In general, a drug substance should be evaluated under storage conditions (with appropriate tolerances) that test its thermal stability and, if applicable, its sensitivity to moisture. The storage conditions and the lengths of studies chosen should be sufficient to cover storage, shipment, and subsequent use.

The long term testing should cover a minimum of 12 months' duration on at least three primary batches at the time of submission and should be continued for a period of time sufficient to cover the proposed re-test period. Additional data accumulated during the assessment period of the registration application should be submitted to the authorities if requested. Data from the accelerated storage condition and, if appropriate, from the intermediate storage condition can be used to evaluate the effect of short term excursions outside the label storage conditions (such as might occur during shipping).

Long term, accelerated, and, where appropriate, intermediate storage conditions for drug substances are detailed in the sections below. The general case applies if the drug substance is not specifically covered by a subsequent section. Alternative storage conditions can be used if justified.

2.1.7.1. General case

Study	Storage condition	Minimum time period covered by data at submission
Long term*	25°C ± 2°C/60% RH ± 5% RH or 30°C ± 2°C/65% RH ± 5% RH	12 months
Intermediate**	30°C ± 2°C/65% RH ± 5% RH	6 months
Accelerated	40°C ± 2°C/75% RH ± 5% RH	6 months

* It is up to the applicant to decide whether long term stability studies are performed at 25 ± 2°C/60% RH ± 5% RH or 30°C ± 2°C/65% RH ± 5% RH.

** If 30°C ± 2°C/65% RH ± 5% RH is the long-term condition, there is no intermediate condition.

If long-term studies are conducted at 25°C ± 2°C/60% RH ± 5% RH and "significant change" occurs at any time during 6 months' testing at the accelerated storage condition, additional testing at the intermediate storage condition should be conducted and evaluated against significant change criteria.

Testing at the intermediate storage condition should include all tests, unless otherwise justified. The initial application should include a minimum of 6 months' data from a 12-month study at the intermediate storage condition.

"Significant change" for a drug substance is defined as failure to meet its specification.

2.1.7.2. Drug substances intended for storage in a refrigerator

Study	Storage condition	Minimum time period covered by data at submission
Long term	5°C ± 3°C	12 months
Accelerated	25°C ± 2°C/60% RH ± 5% RH	6 months

Data from refrigerated storage should be assessed according to the evaluation section of this guidance document, except where explicitly noted below.

If significant change occurs between 3 and 6 months' testing at the accelerated storage condition, the proposed re-test period should be based on the real time data available at the long term storage condition.

If significant change occurs within the first 3 months' testing at the accelerated storage condition, a discussion should be provided to address the effect of short term excursions outside the label storage condition, e.g., during shipping or handling. This discussion can be supported, if appropriate, by further testing on a single batch of the drug substance for a period shorter than 3 months but with more frequent testing than usual. It is considered unnecessary to continue to test a drug substance through 6 months when a significant change has occurred within the first 3 months.

2.1.7.3. Drug substances intended for storage in a freezer

Study	Storage condition	Minimum time period covered by data at submission
Long term	- 20°C ± 5°C	12 months

For drug substances intended for storage in a freezer, the re-test period should be based on the real time data obtained at the long term storage condition. In the absence of an accelerated storage condition for drug substances intended to be stored in a freezer, testing on a single batch at an elevated temperature (e.g., 5°C ± 3°C or 25°C ± 2°C) for an appropriate time period should be conducted to address the effect of short term excursions outside the proposed label storage condition, e.g., during shipping or handling.

2.1.7.4. Drug substances intended for storage below -20°C

Drug substances intended for storage below -20°C should be treated on a case-by-case basis.

2.1.8. Stability Commitment

When available long term stability data on primary batches do not cover the proposed re-test period granted at the time of approval, a commitment should be made to continue the stability studies post approval in order to firmly establish the re-test period.

Where the submission includes long term stability data on three production batches covering the proposed re-test period, a post approval commitment is considered unnecessary. Otherwise, one of the following commitments should be made:

1. If the submission includes data from stability studies on at least three production batches, a commitment should be made to continue these studies through the proposed re-test period.

2. If the submission includes data from stability studies on fewer than three production batches, a commitment should be made to continue these studies through the proposed re-test period and to place additional production batches, to a total of at least three, on long term stability studies through the proposed re-test period.

3. If the submission does not include stability data on production batches, a commitment should be made to place the first three production batches on long term stability studies through the proposed re-test period.

The stability protocol used for long term studies for the stability commitment should be the same as that for the primary batches, unless otherwise scientifically justified.

2.1.9. Evaluation

The purpose of the stability study is to establish, based on testing a minimum of three batches of the drug substance and evaluating the stability information (including, as appropriate, results of the physical, chemical, biological, and microbiological tests), a re-test period applicable to all future batches of the drug substance manufactured under similar circumstances. The degree of variability of individual batches affects the confidence that a future production batch will remain within specification throughout the assigned re-test period.

The data may show so little degradation and so little variability that it is apparent from looking at the data that the requested re-test period will be granted. Under these circumstances, it is normally unnecessary to go through the formal statistical analysis; providing a justification for the omission should be sufficient.

An approach for analyzing the data on a quantitative attribute that is expected to change with time is to determine the time at which the 95% one-sided confidence limit for the mean curve intersects the acceptance criterion. If analysis shows that the batch-to-batch variability is small, it is advantageous to combine the data into one overall estimate. This can be done by first applying appropriate statistical tests (e.g., p values for level of significance of rejection of more than 0.25) to the slopes of the regression lines and zero time intercepts for the individual batches. If it is inappropriate to combine data from several batches, the overall re-test period should be based on the minimum time a batch can be expected to remain within acceptance criteria.

The nature of any degradation relationship will determine whether the data should be transformed for linear regression analysis. Usually the relationship can be represented by a linear, quadratic, or cubic function on an arithmetic or logarithmic scale. Statistical methods should be employed to test the goodness of fit of the data on all batches and combined batches (where appropriate) to the assumed degradation line or curve.

Limited extrapolation of the real time data from the long term storage condition beyond the observed range to extend the re-test period can be undertaken at approval time, if justified. This justification should be based on what is known about the mechanism of degradation, the results of testing under accelerated conditions, the goodness of fit of any mathematical model, batch size, existence of supporting stability data, etc. However, this extrapolation assumes that the same degradation relationship will continue to apply beyond the observed data.

Any evaluation should cover not only the assay, but also the levels of degradation products and other appropriate attributes.

2.1.10. Statements/Labeling

A storage statement should be established for the labeling in accordance with relevant national/regional requirements. The statement should be based on the stability evaluation of the drug substance. Where applicable, specific instructions should be provided, particularly for drug substances that cannot tolerate freezing. Terms such as "ambient conditions" or "room temperature" should be avoided.

A re-test period should be derived from the stability information, and a retest date should be displayed on the container label if appropriate.

2.2. Drug Product

2.2.1. General

The design of the formal stability studies for the drug product should be based on knowledge of the behavior and properties of the drug substance and from stability studies on the drug substance and on experience gained from clinical formulation studies. The likely changes on storage and the rationale for the selection of attributes to be tested in the formal stability studies should be stated.

2.2.2. Photostability Testing

Photostability testing should be conducted on at least one primary batch of the drug product if appropriate. The standard conditions for photostability testing are described in ICH Q1B.

2.2.3. Selection of Batches

Data from stability studies should be provided on at least three primary batches of the drug product. The primary batches should be of the same formulation and packaged in the same container closure system as proposed for marketing. The manufacturing process used for primary batches should simulate that to be applied to production batches and should provide product of the same quality and meeting the same specification as that intended for marketing. Two of the three batches should be at least pilot scale batches and the third one can be smaller, if justified. Where possible, batches of the drug product should be manufactured by using different batches of the drug substance.

Stability studies should be performed on each individual strength and container size of the drug product unless bracketing or matrixing is applied.

Other supporting data can be provided.

2.2.4. Container Closure System

Stability testing should be conducted on the dosage form packaged in the container closure system proposed for marketing (including, as appropriate, any secondary packaging and container label). Any available studies carried out on the drug product outside its immediate container or in other packaging materials can form a useful part of the stress testing of the dosage form or can be considered as supporting information, respectively.

2.2.5. Specification

Specification, which is a list of tests, reference to analytical procedures, and proposed acceptance criteria, including the concept of different acceptance criteria for release and shelf life specifications, is addressed in ICH Q6A and

Q6B. In addition, specification for degradation products in a drug product is addressed in Q3B.

Stability studies should include testing of those attributes of the drug product that are susceptible to change during storage and are likely to influence quality, safety, and/or efficacy. The testing should cover, as appropriate, the physical, chemical, biological, and microbiological attributes, preservative content (e.g., antioxidant, antimicrobial preservative), and functionality tests (e.g., for a dose delivery system). Analytical procedures should be fully validated and stability indicating. Whether and to what extent replication should be performed will depend on the results of validation studies.

Shelf life acceptance criteria should be derived from consideration of all available stability information. It may be appropriate to have justifiable differences between the shelf life and release acceptance criteria based on the stability evaluation and the changes observed on storage. Any differences between the release and shelf life acceptance criteria for antimicrobial preservative content should be supported by a validated correlation of chemical content and preservative effectiveness demonstrated during drug development on the product in its final formulation (except for preservative concentration) intended for marketing. A single primary stability batch of the drug product should be tested for antimicrobial preservative effectiveness (in addition to preservative content) at the proposed shelf life for verification purposes, regardless of whether there is a difference between the release and shelf life acceptance criteria for preservative content.

2.2.6. Testing Frequency

For long term studies, frequency of testing should be sufficient to establish the stability profile of the drug product. For products with a proposed shelf life of at least 12 months, the frequency of testing at the long term storage condition should normally be every 3 months over the first year, every 6 months over the second year, and annually thereafter through the proposed shelf life.

At the accelerated storage condition, a minimum of three time points, including the initial and final time points (e.g., 0, 3, and 6 months), from a 6-month study is recommended. Where an expectation (based on development experience) exists that results from accelerated testing are likely to approach significant change criteria, increased testing should be conducted either by adding samples at the final time point or by including a fourth time point in the study design.

When testing at the intermediate storage condition is called for as a result of significant change at the accelerated storage condition, a minimum of four time points, including the initial and final time points (e.g., 0, 6, 9, 12 months), from a 12-month study is recommended.

Reduced designs, i.e., matrixing or bracketing, where the testing frequency is reduced or certain factor combinations are not tested at all, can be applied, if justified.

2.2.7. Storage Conditions

In general, a drug product should be evaluated under storage conditions (with appropriate tolerances) that test its thermal stability and, if applicable, its sensitivity to moisture or potential for solvent loss. The storage conditions and the lengths of studies chosen should be sufficient to cover storage, shipment, and subsequent use.

Stability testing of the drug product after constitution or dilution, if applicable, should be conducted to provide information for the labeling on the preparation, storage condition, and in-use period of the constituted or diluted product. This testing should be performed on the constituted or diluted product through the proposed in-use period on primary batches as part of the formal stability studies at initial and final time points and, if full shelf life long term data will not be available before submission, at 12 months or the last time point for which data will be available. In general, this testing need not be repeated on commitment batches.

The long term testing should cover a minimum of 12 months' duration on at least three primary batches at the time of submission and should be continued for a period of time sufficient to cover the proposed shelf life. Additional data accumulated during the assessment period of the registration application should be submitted to the authorities if requested. Data from the accelerated storage condition and, if appropriate, from the intermediate storage condition can be used to evaluate the effect of short term excursions outside the label storage conditions (such as might occur during shipping).

Long term, accelerated, and, where appropriate, intermediate storage conditions for drug products are detailed in the sections below. The general case applies if the drug product is not specifically covered by a subsequent section. Alternative storage conditions can be used, if justified.

2.2.7.1. General case

Study	Storage condition	Minimum time period covered by data at submission
Long term*	25°C ± 2°C/60% RH ± 5% RH or 30°C ± 2°C/65% RH ± 5% RH	12 months
Intermediate**	30°C ± 2°C/65% RH ± 5% RH	6 months
Accelerated	40°C ± 2°C/75% RH ± 5% RH	6 months

* It is up to the applicant to decide whether long term stability studies are performed at 25 ± 2°C/60% RH ± 5% RH or 30°C ± 2°C/65% RH ± 5% RH.

** If 30°C ± 2°C/65% RH ± 5% RH is the long-term condition, there is no intermediate condition.

If long-term studies are conducted at 25°C ± 2°C/60% RH ± 5% RH and "significant change" occurs at any time during 6 months' testing at the accelerated storage condition, additional testing at the intermediate storage condition should be conducted and evaluated against significant change criteria. The initial application should include a minimum of 6 months' data from a 12-month study at the intermediate storage condition.

In general, "significant change" for a drug product is defined as:

1. A 5% change in assay from its initial value; or failure to meet the acceptance criteria for potency when using biological or immunological procedures;

2. Any degradation product's exceeding its acceptance criterion;

3. Failure to meet the acceptance criteria for appearance, physical attributes, and functionality test (e.g., color, phase separation, resuspendibility, caking, hardness, dose delivery per actuation); however, some changes in physical attributes (e.g., softening of suppositories, melting of creams) may be expected under accelerated conditions;

and, as appropriate for the dosage form:

4. Failure to meet the acceptance criterion for pH; or

5. Failure to meet the acceptance criteria for dissolution for 12 dosage units.

2.2.7.2. Drug products packaged in impermeable containers

Sensitivity to moisture or potential for solvent loss is not a concern for drug products packaged in impermeable containers that provide a permanent barrier to passage of moisture or solvent. Thus, stability studies for products stored in impermeable containers can be conducted under any controlled or ambient humidity condition.

2.2.7.3. Drug products packaged in semi-permeable containers

Aqueous-based products packaged in semi-permeable containers should be evaluated for potential water loss in addition to physical, chemical, biological, and microbiological stability. This evaluation can be carried out under conditions of low relative humidity, as discussed below. Ultimately, it should be demonstrated that aqueous-based drug products stored in semi-permeable containers can withstand low relative humidity environments. Other comparable approaches can be developed and reported for non-aqueous, solvent-based products.

Study	Storage condition	Minimum time period covered by data at submission
Long term*	25°C ± 2°C/40% RH ± 5% RH or 30°C ± 2°C/35% RH ± 5% RH	12 months
Intermediate**	30°C ± 2°C/65% RH ± 5% RH	6 months
Accelerated	40°C ± 2°C/not more than (NMT) 25% RH	6 months

* It is up to the applicant to decide whether long term stability studies are performed at 25 ± 2°C/40% RH ± 5% RH or 30°C ± 2°C/35% RH ± 5% RH.

** If 30°C ± 2°C/35% RH ± 5% RH is the long-term condition, there is no intermediate condition.

For long-term studies conducted at 25°C ± 2°C/40% RH ± 5% RH, additional testing at the intermediate storage condition should be performed as described under the general case to evaluate the temperature effect at 30 °C if significant change other than water loss occurs during the 6 months' testing at the accelerated storage condition. A significant change in water loss alone at the accelerated storage condition does not necessitate testing at the intermediate storage condition. However, data should be provided to demonstrate that the drug product will not have significant water loss throughout the proposed shelf life if stored at 25°C and the reference relative humidity of 40% RH.

A 5% loss in water from its initial value is considered a significant change for a product packaged in a semi-permeable container after an equivalent of 3 months' storage at 40°C/NMT 25% RH. However, for small containers (1 mL or less) or unit-dose products, a water loss of 5% or more after an equivalent of 3 months' storage at 40°C/NMT 25% RH may be appropriate, if justified.

An alternative approach to studying at the reference relative humidity as recommended in the table above (for either long term or accelerated testing) is performing the stability studies under higher relative humidity and deriving the water loss at the reference relative humidity through calculation. This can be achieved by experimentally determining the permeation coefficient for the container closure system or, as shown in the example below, using the calculated ratio of water loss rates between the two humidity conditions at the same temperature. The permeation coefficient for a container closure system can be experimentally determined by using the worst case scenario (e.g., the most diluted of a series of concentrations) for the proposed drug product.

Example of an approach for determining water loss:

For a product in a given container closure system, container size, and fill, an appropriate approach for deriving the water loss rate at the reference relative humidity is to multiply the water loss rate measured at an alternative relative humidity at the same temperature by a water loss rate ratio shown in the table below. A linear water loss rate at the alternative relative humidity over the storage period should be demonstrated.

For example, at a given temperature, e.g., 40°C, the calculated water loss rate during storage at NMT 25% RH is the water loss rate measured at 75% RH multiplied by 3.0, the corresponding water loss rate ratio.

Alternative relative humidity	Reference relative humidity	Ratio of water loss rates at a given temperature
60% RH	25% RH	1.9
60% RH	40% RH	1.5
65% RH	35% RH	1.9
75% RH	25% RH	3

Valid water loss rate ratios at relative humidity conditions other than those shown in the table above can also be used.

2.2.7.4. Drug products intended for storage in a refrigerator

Study	Storage condition	Minimum time period covered by data at submission
Long term	5°C ± 3°C	12 months
Accelerated	25°C ± 2°C/60% RH ± 5% RH	6 months

If the drug product is packaged in a semi-permeable container, appropriate information should be provided to assess the extent of water loss.

Data from refrigerated storage should be assessed according to the evaluation section of this guidance document, except where explicitly noted below.

If significant change occurs between 3 and 6 months' testing at the accelerated storage condition, the proposed shelf life should be based on the real time data available from the long term storage condition.

If significant change occurs within the first 3 months' testing at the accelerated storage condition, a discussion should be provided to address the effect of short term excursions outside the label storage condition, e.g., during shipment and handling. This discussion can be supported, if appropriate, by further testing on a single batch of the drug product for a period shorter than 3 months but with more frequent testing than usual. It is considered unnecessary to continue to test a product through 6 months when a significant change has occurred within the first 3 months.

2.2.7.5. Drug products intended for storage in a freezer

Study	Storage condition	Minimum time period covered by data at submission
Long term	-20°C ± 5°C	12 months

For drug products intended for storage in a freezer, the shelf life should be based on the real time data obtained at the long term storage condition. In the absence of an accelerated storage condition for drug products intended to be stored in a freezer, testing on a single batch at an elevated temperature (e.g., 5°C ± 3°C or 25°C ± 2°C) for an appropriate time period should be conducted to address the effect of short term excursions outside the proposed label storage condition.

2.2.7.6. Drug products intended for storage below -20°C

Drug products intended for storage below -20°C should be treated on a case-by-case basis.

2.2.8. Stability Commitment

When available long term stability data on primary batches do not cover the proposed shelf life granted at the time of approval, a commitment should be made to continue the stability studies post approval in order to firmly establish the shelf life.

Where the submission includes long term stability data from three production batches covering the proposed shelf life, a post approval commitment is considered unnecessary. Otherwise, one of the following commitments should be made:

1. If the submission includes data from stability studies on at least three production batches, a commitment should be made to continue the long term studies through the proposed shelf life and the accelerated studies for 6 months.

2. If the submission includes data from stability studies on fewer than three production batches, a commitment should be made to continue the long term studies through the proposed shelf life and the accelerated studies for 6 months, and to place additional production batches, to a total of at least three, on long term stability studies through the proposed shelf life and on accelerated studies for 6 months.

3. If the submission does not include stability data on production batches, a commitment should be made to place the first three production batches on long term stability studies through the proposed shelf life and on accelerated studies for 6 months.

The stability protocol used for studies on commitment batches should be the same as that for the primary batches, unless otherwise scientifically justified.

Where intermediate testing is called for by a significant change at the accelerated storage condition for the primary batches, testing on the commitment batches can be conducted at either the intermediate or the accelerated storage condition.

However, if significant change occurs at the accelerated storage condition on the commitment batches, testing at the intermediate storage condition should also be conducted.

2.2.9. Evaluation

A systematic approach should be adopted in the presentation and evaluation of the stability information, which should include, as appropriate, results from the physical, chemical, biological, and microbiological tests, including particular attributes of the dosage form (for example, dissolution rate for solid oral dosage forms).

The purpose of the stability study is to establish, based on testing a minimum of three batches of the drug product, a shelf life and label storage instructions applicable to all future batches of the drug product manufactured and packaged under similar circumstances. The degree of variability of individual batches affects the confidence that a future production batch will remain within specification throughout its shelf life.

Where the data show so little degradation and so little variability that it is apparent from looking at the data that the requested shelf life will be granted, it is normally unnecessary to go through the formal statistical analysis; providing a justification for the omission should be sufficient.

An approach for analyzing data of a quantitative attribute that is expected to change with time is to determine the time at which the 95 one-sided confidence limit for the mean curve intersects the acceptance criterion. If analysis shows that the batch-to-batch variability is small, it is advantageous to combine the data into one overall estimate. This can be done by first applying appropriate statistical tests (e.g., p values for level of significance of rejection of more than 0.25) to the slopes of the regression lines and zero time intercepts for the individual batches. If it is inappropriate to combine data from several batches, the overall shelf life should be based on the minimum time a batch can be expected to remain within acceptance criteria.

The nature of the degradation relationship will determine whether the data should be transformed for linear regression analysis. Usually the relationship can be represented by a linear, quadratic, or cubic function on an arithmetic or logarithmic scale. Statistical methods should be employed to test the goodness of fit on all batches and combined batches (where appropriate) to the assumed degradation line or curve.

Limited extrapolation of the real time data from the long term storage condition beyond the observed range to extend the shelf life can be undertaken at approval time, if justified. This justification should be based on what is known about the mechanisms of degradation, the results of testing under accelerated conditions, the goodness of fit of any mathematical model, batch size, existence of supporting stability data, etc. However, this extrapolation assumes that the same degradation relationship will continue to apply beyond the observed data.

Any evaluation should consider not only the assay but also the degradation products and other appropriate attributes. Where appropriate, attention should be paid to reviewing the adequacy of the mass balance and different stability and degradation performance.

2.2.10. Statements/Labeling

A storage statement should be established for the labeling in accordance with relevant national/regional requirements. The statement should be based on the stability evaluation of the drug product. Where applicable, specific instruction should be provided, particularly for drug products that cannot tolerate freezing. Terms such as "ambient conditions" or "room temperature" should be avoided.

There should be a direct link between the label storage statement and the demonstrated stability of the drug product. An expiration date should be displayed on the container label.

3. Glossary

The following definitions are provided to facilitate interpretation of the guidance document.

Accelerated Testing

Studies designed to increase the rate of chemical degradation or physical change of a drug substance or drug product by using exaggerated storage conditions as part of the formal stability studies. Data from these studies, in addition to long term stability studies, can be used to assess longer term chemical effects at non-accelerated conditions and to evaluate the effect of short term excursions outside the label storage conditions such as might occur during shipping. Results from accelerated testing studies are not always predictive of physical changes.

Bracketing

The design of a stability schedule such that only samples on the extremes of certain design factors, e.g., strength, package size, are tested at all time points as in a full design. The design assumes that the stability of any intermediate levels is represented by the stability of the extremes tested. Where a range of strengths is to be tested, bracketing is applicable if the strengths are identical or very closely related in composition (e.g., for a tablet range made with different compression weights of a similar basic granulation, or a capsule range made by filling different plug fill weights of the same basic composition into different size capsule shells). Bracketing can be applied to different container sizes or different fills in the same container closure system.

Climatic Zones

The four zones in the world that are distinguished by their characteristic prevalent annual climatic conditions. This is based on the concept described by W. Grimm (Drugs Made in Germany, 28:196-202, 1985 and 29:39-47, 1986).

Commitment batches

Production batches of a drug substance or drug product for which the stability studies are initiated or completed post approval through a commitment made in the registration application.

Container closure system

The sum of packaging components that together contain and protect the dosage form. This includes primary packaging components and secondary packaging components, if the latter are intended to provide additional protection to the drug product. A packaging system is equivalent to a container closure system.

Dosage form

> A pharmaceutical product type (e.g., tablet, capsule, solution, cream) that contains a drug substance generally, but not necessarily, in association with excipients.

Drug product

> The dosage form in the final immediate packaging intended for marketing.

Drug Substance

> The unformulated drug substance that may subsequently be formulated with excipients to produce the dosage form.

Excipient

> Anything other than the drug substance in the dosage form.

Expiration Date

> The date placed on the container label of a drug product designating the time prior to which a batch of the product is expected to remain within the approved shelf life specification if stored under defined conditions, and after which it must not be used.

Formal Stability Studies

> Long term and accelerated (and intermediate) studies undertaken on primary and/or commitment batches according to a prescribed stability protocol to establish or confirm the re-test period of a drug substance or the shelf life of a drug product.

Impermeable Containers

> Containers that provide a permanent barrier to the passage of gases or solvents, e.g., sealed aluminum tubes for semi-solids, sealed glass ampoules for solutions.

Intermediate Testing

> Studies conducted at 30°C/65% RH and designed to moderately increase the rate of chemical degradation or physical changes for a drug substance or drug product intended to be stored long term at 25°C.

Long Term Testing

> Stability studies under the recommended storage condition for the re-test period or shelf life proposed (or approved) for labeling.

Mass Balance

> The process of adding together the assay value and levels of degradation products to see how closely these add up to 100% of the initial value, with due consideration of the margin of analytical error.

ICH Q1A(R2)

Matrixing

The design of a stability schedule such that a selected subset of the total number of possible samples for all factor combinations is tested at a specified time point. At a subsequent time point, another subset of samples for all factor combinations is tested. The design assumes that the stability of each subset of samples tested represents the stability of all samples at a given time point. The differences in the samples for the same drug product should be identified as, for example, covering different batches, different strengths, different sizes of the same container closure system, and, possibly in some cases, different container closure systems.

Mean Kinetic Temperature

A single derived temperature that, if maintained over a defined period of time, affords the same thermal challenge to a drug substance or drug product as would be experienced over a range of both higher and lower temperatures for an equivalent defined period. The mean kinetic temperature is higher than the arithmetic mean temperature and takes into account the Arrhenius equation.

When establishing the mean kinetic temperature for a defined period, the formula of J. D. Haynes (J. Pharm. Sci., 60:927-929, 1971) can be used.

New Molecular Entity

An active pharmaceutical substance not previously contained in any drug product registered with the national or regional authority concerned. A new salt, ester, or non-covalent-bond derivative of an approved drug substance is considered a new molecular entity for the purpose of stability testing under this guidance.

Pilot Scale Batch

A batch of a drug substance or drug product manufactured by a procedure fully representative of and simulating that to be applied to a full production scale batch. For solid oral dosage forms, a pilot scale is generally, at a minimum, one-tenth that of a full production scale or 100,000 tablets or capsules, whichever is the larger.

Primary Batch

A batch of a drug substance or drug product used in a formal stability study, from which stability data are submitted in a registration application for the purpose of establishing a re-test period or shelf life, respectively. A primary batch of a drug substance should be at least a pilot scale batch. For a drug product, two of the three batches should be at least pilot scale batch, and the third batch can be smaller if it is representative with regard to the critical manufacturing steps. However, a primary batch may be a production batch.

Production Batch

> A batch of a drug substance or drug product manufactured at production scale by using production equipment in a production facility as specified in the application.

Re-Test Date

> The date after which samples of the drug substance should be examined to ensure that the material is still in compliance with the specification and thus suitable for use in the manufacture of a given drug product.

Re-Test Period

> The period of time during which the drug substance is expected to remain within its specification and, therefore, can be used in the manufacture of a given drug product, provided that the drug substance has been stored under the defined conditions. After this period, a batch of drug substance destined for use in the manufacture of a drug product should be re-tested for compliance with the specification and then used immediately. A batch of drug substance can be re-tested multiple times and a different portion of the batch used after each re-test, as long as it continues to comply with the specification. For most biotechnological/biological substances known to be labile, it is more appropriate to establish a shelf life than a re-test period. The same may be true for certain antibiotics.

Semi-Permeable Containers

> Containers that allow the passage of solvent, usually water, while preventing solute loss. The mechanism for solvent transport occurs by absorption into one container surface, diffusion through the bulk of the container material, and desorption from the other surface. Transport is driven by a partial-pressure gradient. Examples of semi-permeable containers include plastic bags and semi-rigid, low-density polyethylene (LDPE) pouches for large volume parenterals (LVPs), and LDPE ampoules, bottles, and vials.

Shelf Life (also referred to as expiration dating period)

> The time period during which a drug product is expected to remain within the approved shelf life specification, provided that it is stored under the conditions defined on the container label.

Specification

> See Q6A and Q6B.

Specification - Release

> The combination of physical, chemical, biological, and microbiological tests and acceptance criteria that determine the suitability of a drug product at the time of its release.

Specification - Shelf Life

> The combination of physical, chemical, biological, and microbiological tests and acceptance criteria that determine the suitability of a drug substance throughout its re-test period, or that a drug product should meet throughout its shelf life.

Storage Condition Tolerances

> The acceptable variations in temperature and relative humidity of storage facilities for formal stability studies. The equipment should be capable of controlling the storage condition within the ranges defined in this guidance document. The actual temperature and humidity (when controlled) should be monitored during stability storage. Short term spikes due to opening of doors of the storage facility are accepted as unavoidable. The effect of excursions due to equipment failure should be addressed, and reported if judged to affect stability results. Excursions that exceed the defined tolerances for more than 24 hours should be described in the study report and their effect assessed.

Stress Testing (Drug Substance)

> Studies undertaken to elucidate the intrinsic stability of the drug substance. Such testing is part of the development strategy and is normally carried out under more severe conditions than those used for accelerated testing.

Stress Testing (Drug Product)

> Studies undertaken to assess the effect of severe conditions on the drug product. Such studies include photostability testing (see ICH Q1B) and specific testing on certain products, (e.g., metered dose inhalers, creams, emulsions, refrigerated aqueous liquid products).

Supporting Data

> Data, other than those from formal stability studies, that support the analytical procedures, the proposed re-test period or shelf life, and the label storage statements. Such data include (1) stability data on early synthetic route batches of drug substance, small scale batches of materials, investigational formulations not proposed for marketing, related formulations, and product presented in containers and closures other than those proposed for marketing; (2) information regarding test results on containers; and (3) other scientific rationales.

4. References

ICH Q1B: "Photostability Testing of New Drug Substances and Products"

ICH Q1C: "Stability Testing of New Dosage Forms"

ICH Q3A: "Impurities in New Drug Substances"

ICH Q3B: "Impurities in New Drug Products"

ICH Q5C: "Stability Testing of Biotechnological/Biological Products"

ICH Q6A: "Specifications: Test Procedures and Acceptance Criteria for New Drug Substances and New Drug Products: Chemical Substances"

ICH Q6B: "Specifications: Test Procedures and Acceptance Criteria for Biotechnological/Biological Products"

ICH Q1A(R2)

ICH Q1B:
Stability Testing: Photostability Testing of New Drug Substances and Products

Therapeutic Products Programme Guideline

Health Canada

International Conference on Harmonisation of Technical Requirements for the Registration of Pharmaceuticals for Human Use

ICH Harmonised Tripartite Guideline

1999-02-12

ICH Q1B: Stability Testing: Photostability Testing of New Drug Substances and Products[80]

Foreword

This guideline has been developed by the appropriate ICH Expert Working Group and has been subject to consultation by the regulatory parties, in accordance with the ICH Process. The ICH Steering Committee has endorsed the final draft and recommended its adoption by the regulatory bodies of the European Union, Japan and USA.

The Therapeutic Products Programme (TPP) has adopted this guideline and reproduced it in this document. This guideline represents an approach that will be considered acceptable for the review of new drug substances and products. This document should be read in conjunction with the relevant sections of other applicable Directorate guidelines.

Alternate approaches to the principles and practices described in this document may be acceptable provided they are supported by adequate scientific justification. Submission sponsors may discuss, in advance, alternate approaches with the Directorate to avoid the withdrawal/ rejection of a submission.

1. General

The ICH Harmonized Tripartite Guideline on Stability Testing of New Drug Substances and Products (hereafter referred to as the parent guideline) notes

---

[80] Available on the Health Canada website at http://www.hc-sc.gc.ca/dhp-mps/prodpharma/applic-demande/guide-ld/ich/qual/q1b-eng.php

that light testing should be an integral part of stress testing. This document is an annex to the parent guideline and addresses the recommendations for photostability testing.

A. Preamble

The intrinsic photostability characteristics of new drug substances and products should be evaluated to demonstrate that, as appropriate, light exposure does not result in unacceptable change. Normally, photostability testing is carried out on a single batch of material selected as described under "Selection of Batches" in the parent guideline. Under some circumstances these studies should be repeated if certain variations and changes are made to the product (e.g., formulation, packaging). Whether these studies should be repeated depends on the photostability characteristics determined at the time of initial filing and the type of variation and/or change made.

The guideline primarily addresses the generation of photostability information for submission in registration applications for new molecular entities and associated drug products. The guideline does not cover the photostability of drugs after administration (i.e., under conditions of use) and those applications not covered by the parent guideline. Alternative approaches may be used if they are scientifically sound and justification is provided.

A systematic approach to photostability testing is recommended covering, as appropriate, studies such as:

i.   Tests on the drug substance;

ii.   Tests on the exposed drug product outside of the immediate pack; and if necessary;

iii. Tests on the drug product in the immediate pack; and if necessary;

iv.   Tests on the drug product in the marketing pack.

The extent of drug product testing should be established by assessing whether or not acceptable change has occurred at the end of the light exposure testing as described in the Decision Flow Chart for Photostability Testing of Drug Products. Acceptable change is change within limits justified by the applicant.

The formal labeling requirements for photolabile drug substances and drug products are established by national/regional requirements.

B. Light Sources

The light sources described below may be used for photostability testing. The applicant should either maintain an appropriate control of temperature to minimize the effect of localized temperature changes or include a dark control in the same environment unless otherwise justified. For both options 1 and 2, a pharmaceutical manufacturer/applicant may rely on the spectral distribution specification of the light source manufacturer.

Option 1

Any light source that is designed to produce an output similar to the D65/ID65 emission standard such as an artificial daylight fluorescent lamp combining visible and ultraviolet (UV) outputs, xenon, or metal halide lamp. D65 is the internationally recognized standard for outdoor daylight as defined in ISO 10977

(1993). ID65 is the equ valent indoor indirect daylight standard. For a light source emitting significant radiation below 320 nanometers (nm), an appropriate filter(s) may be fitted to eliminate such radiation.

Option 2

For option 2 the same sample should be exposed to both the cool white fluorescent and near ultraviolet lamp.

1. A cool wh te fluorescent lamp designed to produce an output similar to that specified in ISO 10977 (1993); and

2. A near UV fluorescent lamp having a spectral distribution from 320 nm to 400 nm with a maximum energy emission between 350 nm and 370 nm; a significant proportion of UV should be in both bands of 320 to 360 nm and 360 to 400 nm.

C. Procedure

For confirmatory studies, samples should be exposed to light providing an overall illumination of not less than 1.2 million lux hours and an integrated near ultraviolet energy of not less than 200 watt hours/square meter to allow direct comparisons to be made between the drug substance and drug product.

Samples may be exposed side-by-side with a validated chemical actinometric system to ensure the specified light exposure is obtained, or for the appropriate duration of time when conditions have been monitored using calibrated radiometers/lux meters. An example of an actinometric procedure is provided in the Annex.

If protected samples (e.g., wrapped in aluminum foil) are used as dark controls to evaluate the contribution of thermally induced change to the total observed change, these should be placed alongside the authentic sample.

Decision Flow Chart for Photostability Testing of Drug Products

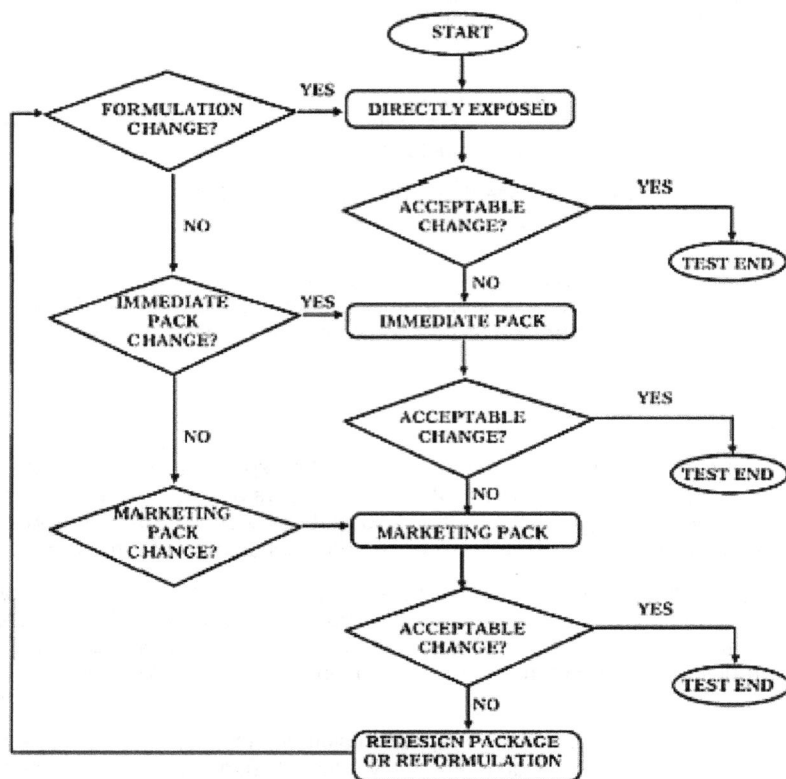

2. Drug Substance

For drug substances, photostability testing should consist of two parts: Forced degradation testing and confirmatory testing.

The purpose of forced degradation testing studies is to evaluate the overall photosensitivity of the material for method development purposes and/or degradation pathway elucidation. This testing may involve the drug substance alone and/or in simple solutions/suspensions to validate the analytical procedures. In these studies, the samples should be in chemically inert and transparent containers. In these forced degradation studies, a variety of exposure conditions may be used, depending on the photosensitivity of the drug substance involved and the intensity of the light sources used. For development and validation purposes, it is appropriate to limit exposure and end the studies if extensive decomposition occurs. For photostable materials, studies may be terminated after an appropriate exposure level has been used. The design of these experiments is left to the applicant's discretion although the exposure levels used should be justified.

Under forcing conditions, decomposition products may be observed that are unlikely to be formed under the conditions used for confirmatory studies. This information may be useful in developing and validating suitable analytical methods. If in practice it has been demonstrated they are not formed in the confirmatory studies, these degradation products need not be further examined.

Confirmatory studies should then be undertaken to provide the information necessary for handling packaging, and labeling (see section I.C., Procedure, and II.A., Presentation of Samples, for information on the design of these studies).

Normally, only one batch of drug substance is tested during the development phase, and then the photostability characteristics should be confirmed on a single batch selected as described in the parent guideline if the drug is clearly photostable or photolab le. If the results of the confirmatory study are equivocal, testing of up to two adcitional batches should be conducted. Samples should be selected as described in the parent guideline.

A. Presentation of Samples

Care should be taken to ensure that the physical characteristics of the samples under test are taken into account and efforts should be made, such as cooling and/or placing the samples in sealed containers, to ensure that the effects of the changes in physical states such as sublimation, evaporation, or melting are minimized. All such precautions should be chosen to provide minimal interference with the exposure of samples under test. Possible interactions between the samples and any material used for containers or for general protection of the sample should also be considered and eliminated wherever not relevant to the test being carried out.

As a direct challenge for samples of solid drug substances, an appropriate amount of sample should be taken and placed in a suitable glass or plastic dish and protected with a suitable transparent cover if considered necessary. Solid drug substances should be spread across the container to give a thickness of typically not more than 3 millimeters. Drug substances that are liquids should be exposed in chemically inert and transparent containers.

B. Analysis of Samples

At the end of the exposure period, the samples should be examined for any changes in physical properties (e.g., appearance, clarity, or color of solution) and for assay and degradants by a method suitably validated for products likely to arise from photochemical degradation processes.

Where solid drug substance samples are involved, sampling should ensure that a representative portion is used in individual tests. Similar sampling considerations, such as homogenization of the entire sample, apply to other materials that may not be homogeneous after exposure. The analysis of the exposed sample should be performed concomitantly with that of any protected samples used as dark control if these are used in the test.

C. Judgment of Results

The forced degradation studies should be designed to provide suitable information to develop and validate test methods for the confirmatory studies. These test methods should be capable of resolving and detecting photolytic degradants that appear during the confirmatory studies. When evaluating the results of these studies, it is important to recognize that they form part of the stress testing and are not therefore designed to establish qualitative or quantitative limits for change.

The confirmatory studies should identify precautionary measures needed in manufacturing or in formulation of the drug product, and if light resistant packaging is needed. When evaluating the results of confirmatory studies to determine whether change due to exposure to light is acceptable, it is important to consider the results from other formal stability studies in order to assure that the drug will be within justified limits at time of use (see the relevant ICH Stability and Impurity Guidelines).

3. Drug Product

Normally, the studies on drug products should be carried out in a sequential manner starting with testing the fully exposed product then progressing as necessary to the product in the immediate pack and then in the marketing pack. Testing should progress until the results demonstrate that the drug product is adequately protected from exposure to light. The drug product should be exposed to the light conditions described under the procedure in section I.C.

Normally, only one batch of drug product is tested during the development phase, and then the photostability characteristics should be confirmed on a single batch selected as described in the parent guideline if the product is clearly photostable or photolabile. If the results of the confirmatory study are equivocal, testing of up to two additional batches should be conducted.

For some products where it has been demonstrated that the immediate pack is completely impenetrable to light, such as aluminum tubes or cans, testing should normally only be conducted on directly exposed drug product.

It may be appropriate to test certain products, such as infusion liquids or dermal creams, to support their photostability in-use. The extent of this testing should depend on and relate to the directions for use, and is left to the applicant's discretion.
The analytical procedures used should be suitably validated.

A. Presentation of Samples

Care should be taken to ensure that the physical characteristics of the samples under test are taken into account and efforts, such as cooling and/or placing the samples in sealed containers, should be made to ensure that the effects of the changes in physical states are minimized, such as sublimation, evaporation, or melting. All such precautions should be chosen to provide minimal interference with the irradiation of samples under test. Possible interactions between the samples and any material used for containers or for general protection of the sample should also be considered and eliminated wherever not relevant to the test being carried out.

Where practicable when testing samples of the drug product outside of the primary pack, these should be presented in a way similar to the conditions mentioned for the drug substance. The samples should be positioned to provide maximum area of exposure to the light source. For example, tablets, capsules, should be spread in a single layer.

If direct exposure is not practical (e.g., due to oxidation of a product), the sample should be placed in a suitable protective inert transparent container (e.g., quartz).

If testing of the drug product in the immediate container or as marketed is needed, the samples should be placed horizontally or transversely with respect to the light source, whichever provides for the most uniform exposure of the samples. Some adjustment of testing conditions may have to be made when testing large volume containers (e.g., dispensing packs).

B. Analysis of Samples

At the end of the exposure period, the samples should be examined for any changes in physical properties (e.g., appearance, clarity, or color of solution, dissolution/disintegration for dosage forms such as capsules) and for assay and degradants by a method suitably validated for products likely to arise from photochemical degradation processes.

When powder samples are involved, sampling should ensure that a representative portion is used in individual tests. For solid oral dosage form products, testing should be conducted on an appropriately sized composite of, for example, 20 tablets or capsules. Similar sampling considerations, such as homogenization or solubilization of the entire sample, apply to other materials that may not be homogeneous after exposure (e.g., creams, ointments, suspensions, etc.). The analysis of the exposed sample should be performed concomitantly with that of any protected samples used as dark controls if these are used in the test.

C. Judgment of Results

Depending on the extent of change, special labeling or packaging may be needed to mitigate exposure to light. When evaluating the results of photostability studies to determine whether change due to exposure to light is acceptable, it is important to consider the results obtained from other formal stability studies in order to assure that the product will be within proposed specifications during the shelf life (see the relevant ICH Stability and Impurity Guidelines).

4. Annex

A. Quinine Chemical Actinometry

The following provides details of an actinometric procedure for monitoring exposure to a near UV fourescent lamp (based on FDA/National Institute of Standards and Technology study). For other light sources/actinometric systems, the same approach may be used, but each actinometric system should be calibrated for the light source used.

Prepare a sufficient quantity of a 2 percent weight/volume aqueous solution of quinine monohydrochloride dihydrate (if necessary, dissolve by heating).

Option 1

Put 10 milliliters (mL) of the solution into a 20 mL colorless ampoule, seal it hermetically, and use this as the sample. Separately, put 10 mL of the solution into a 20 mL colorless ampoule (see note 1), seal it hermetically, wrap in aluminum foil to protect completely from light, and use this as the control. Expose the sample and control to the light source for an appropriate number of hours. After exposure determine the absorbances of the sample (AT) and the control (AO) at 400 nm using a 1 centimeter (cm) pathlength. Calculate the change in absorbance, $A = AT - AO$. The length of exposure should be sufficient to ensure a change in absorbance of at least 0.9.

Option 2

Fill a 1 cm quartz cell and use this as the sample. Separately fill a 1 cm quartz cell, wrap in aluminum foil to protect completely from light, and use this as the control. Expose the sample and control to the light source for an appropriate number of hours. After exposure determine the absorbances of the sample (AT)

ICH Q1B

and the control (AO) at 400 nm. Calculate the change in absorbance, A = AT - AO. The length of exposure should be sufficient to ensure a change in absorbance of at least 0.5.

Alternative packaging configurations may be used if appropriately validated. Alternative validated chemical actinometers may be used.

Note 1: Shape and Dimensions (See Japanese Industry Standard (JIS) R3512 (1974) for ampoule specifications)

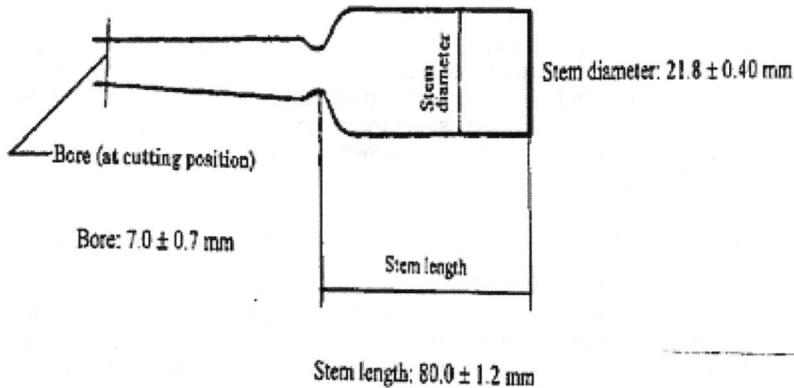

Stem diameter: 21.8 ± 0.40 mm

Bore (at cutting position)

Bore: 7.0 ± 0.7 mm

Stem length

Stem length: 80.0 ± 1.2 mm

5. Glossary

Immediate (Primary) Pack

is that constituent of the packaging that is in direct contact with the drug substance or drug product, and includes any appropriate label.

Marketing Pack

is the combination of immediate pack and other secondary packaging such as a carton.

Forced Degradation Testing Studies

are those undertaken to degrade the sample deliberately. These studies, which may be undertaken in the development phase normally on the drug substances, are used to evaluate the overall photosensitivity of the material for method development purposes and/or degradation pathway elucidation.

Confirmatory Studies

are those undertaken to establish photostability characteristics under standardized conditions. These studies are used to identify precautionary measures needed in manufacturing or formulation and whether light-resistant packaging and/or special labeling is needed to mitigate exposure to light. For the confirmatory studies, the batch(es) should be selected according to batch selection for long-term and accelerated testing which is described in the parent guideline.

6. *References*

Yoshioka, S., et al., "Quinine Actinometry as a Method for Calibrating Ultraviolet Radiation Intensity in Light-Stability Testing of Pharmaceuticals", Drug Development and Industrial Pharmacy, 20(13):2049-2062, 1994.

ICH Q1B

ICH Q1C:
Stability Testing for New Dosage Forms

Therapeutic Products Programme Guideline

Health Canada

International Conference on Harmonisation of Technical Requirements for the Registration of Pharmaceuticals for Human Use

ICH Harmonised Tripartite Guideline

Q1C - Stability Testing: Requirements for New Dosage Forms

1999-01-18

ICH Q1C: Stability Testing for New Dosage Forms[81]

Foreword

This guideline has been developed by the appropriate ICH Expert Working Group and has been subject to consultation by the regulatory parties, in accordance with the ICH Process. The ICH Steering Committee has endorsed the final draft and recommended its adoption by the regulatory bodies of the European Union, Japan and USA.

The Therapeutic Products Programme (TPP) has adopted this guideline and reproduced it in this document. This guideline represents an approach that will be considered acceptable for the review of new drug substances and products. This document should be read in conjunction with the relevant sections of other applicable Directorate guidelines.

Alternate approaches to the principles and practices described in this document may be acceptable provided they are supported by adequate scientific justification. Submission sponsors may discuss, in advance, alternate approaches with the Directorate to avoid the withdrawal/ rejection of a submission.

1. General

The ICH harmonised Tripartite Guideline on Stability Testing of New Drug Substances and Products was issued on October 27, 1993. This document is an annex to the ICH parent stability guideline and addresses the recommendations on what should be submitted regarding stability of new dosage forms by the

---

[81] Available on the Health Canada website at http://www.hc-sc.gc.ca/dhp-mps/prodpharma/applic-demande/guide-ld/ich/qual/q1c-eng.php

owner of the original application, after the original submission for new drug substances and products.

2. New Dosage Forms

A new dosage form is defined as a drug product which is a different pharmaceutical product type, but contains the same active substance as included in the existing drug product approved by the pertinent regulatory authority.

Such pharmaceutical product types include products of different administration route (e.g., oral to parenteral), new specific functionality/delivery systems (e.g., immediate release tablet to modified release tablet) and different dosage forms of the same administration route (e.g., capsule to tablet, solution to suspension).

Stability protocols for new dosage forms should follow the guidance in the parent stability guideline in principle. However, a reduced stability database at submission time (e.g., 6 months accelerated and 6 months long-term data from ongoing studies) may be acceptable in certain justified cases.

ICH Q2(R1): Validation of Analytical Procedures: Text and Methodology

ICH Harmonised Tripartite Guideline

International Conference on Harmonisation of Technical Requirements for the Registration of Pharmaceuticals for Human Use

Current Step 4 version
Parent Guideline dated 27 October 1994
(Complementary Guideline on Methodology dated 6 November 1996 incorporated in November 2005)

Validation of Analytical Procedures: Text and Methodology Q2(R1)[82]

This Guideline has been developed by the appropriate ICH Expert Working Group and has been subject to consultation by the regulatory parties, in accordance with the ICH Process. At Step 4 of the Process the final draft is recommended for adoption to the regulatory bodies of the European Union, Japan and USA.

Part I:
Text on Validation of Analytical Procedures

Having reached Step 4 of the ICH Process at the ICH Steering Committee meeting on 27 October 1994, this guideline is recommended for adoption to the three regulatory parties to ICH.

---

[82] Available on the Health Canada website at
http://www.ich.org/LOB/media/MEDIA417.pdf

Q2(R1)
Document History

First Codification	History	Date	New Codification November 2005

Parent Guideline: Text on Validation of Analytical Procedures

Q2	Approval by the Steering Committee under *Step 2* and release for public consultation.	26 October 1993	Q2
Q2A	Approval by the Steering Committee under *Step 4* and recommendation for adoption to the three ICH regulatory bodies.	27 October 1994	Q2

Guideline on Validation of Analytical Procedures: Methodology developed to complement the Parent Guideline

Q2B	Approval by the Steering Committee under *Step 2* and release for public consultation.	29 November 1995	in Q2(R1)
Q2B	Approval by the Steering Committee under *Step 4* and recommendation for adoption to the three ICH regulatory bodies.	6 November 1996	in Q2(R1)

Current *Step 4* version

Q2A and Q2B	The parent guideline is now renamed Q2(R1) as the guideline Q2B on methology has been incorporated to the parent guideline. The new title is "Validation of Analytical Procedures: Text and Methodology".	November 2005	Q2(R1)

1. Introduction

This document presents a discussion of the characteristics for consideration during the validation of the analytical procedures included as part of registration applications submitted within the EC, Japan and USA. This document does not necessarily seek to cover the testing that may be required for registration in, or export to, other areas of the world. Furthermore, this text presentation serves as a collection of terms, and their definitions, and is not intended to provide direction on how to accomplish validation. These terms and definitions are meant to bridge the differences that often exist between various compendia and regulators of the EC, Japan and USA.

The objective of validation of an analytical procedure is to demonstrate that it is suitable for its intended purpose. A tabular summation of the characteristics applicable to identification, control of impurities and assay procedures is included. Other analytical procedures may be considered in future additions to this document.

2. Types of Analytical Procedures to be Validated

The discussion of the validation of analytical procedures is directed to the four most common types of analytical procedures:

- Identification tests;
- Quantitative tests for impurities' content;
- Limit tests for the control of impurities;

- Quantitative tests of the active moiety in samples of drug substance or drug product or other selected component(s) in the drug product.

Although there are many other analytical procedures, such as dissolution testing for drug products or particle size determination for drug substance, these have not been addressed in the initial text on validation of analytical procedures. Validation of these additional analytical procedures is equally important to those listed herein and may be addressed in subsequent documents.

A brief description of the types of tests considered in this document is provided below.

- Identification tests are intended to ensure the identity of an analyte in a sample. This is normally achieved by comparison of a property of the sample (e.g., spectrum, chromatographic behavior, chemical reactivity, etc) to that of a reference standard;

- Testing for impurities can be either a quantitative test or a limit test for the impurity in a sample. Either test is intended to accurately reflect the purity characteristics of the sample. Different validation characteristics are required for a quantitative test than for a limit test;

- Assay procedures are intended to measure the analyte present in a given sample. In the context of this document, the assay represents a quantitative measurement of the major component(s) in the drug substance. For the drug product, similar validation characteristics also apply when assaying for the active or other selected component(s). The same validation characteristics may also apply to assays associated with other analytical procedures (e.g., dissolution).

The objective of the analytical procedure should be clearly understood since this will govern the validation characteristics which need to be evaluated. Typical validation characteristics which should be considered are listed below:

- Accuracy
  - Precision
  - Repeatability
- Intermediate Precision
- Specificity
- Detection Limit
- Quantitation Limit
- Linearity
- Range

Each of these validation characteristics is defined in the attached Glossary. The table lists those validation characteristics regarded as the most important for the validation of different types of analytical procedures. This list should be considered typical for the analytical procedures cited but occasional exceptions should be dealt with on a case-by-case basis. It should be noted that robustness is not listed in the table but should be considered at an appropriate stage in the development of the analytical procedure.

Furthermore revalidation may be necessary in the following circumstances:

- changes in the synthesis of the drug substance;
- changes in the composition of the finished product;

ICH Q2(R1)

- changes in the analytical procedure.

The degree of revalidation required depends on the nature of the changes. Certain other changes may require validation as well.

TABLE

Type of analytical procedure characteristics	IDENTIFICATION	TESTING FOR IMPURITIES		ASSAY - dissolution (measurement only) - content/potency
		quantitat.	limit	
Accuracy	-	+	-	+
Precision				
Repeatability	-	+	-	+
Interm.Precision	-	+ (1)	-	+ (1)
Specificity (2)	+	+	+	+
Detection Limit	-	- (3)	+	-
Quantitation Limit	-	+	-	-
Linearity	-	+	-	+
Range	-	+	-	+

- signifies that this characteristic is not normally evaluated

+ signifies that this characteristic is normally evaluated

(1) in cases where reproducibility (see glossary) has been performed, intermediate precision is not needed

(2) lack of specificity of one analytical procedure could be compensated by other supporting analytical procedure(s)

(3) may be needed in some cases

Glossary

1. Analytical Procedure

The analytical procedure refers to the way of performing the analysis. It should describe in detail the steps necessary to perform each analytical test. This may include but is not limited to: the sample, the reference standard and the reagents preparations, use of the apparatus, generation of the calibration curve, use of the formulae for the calculation, etc.

2. Specificity

Specificity is the ability to assess unequivocally the analyte in the presence of components which may be expected to be present. Typically these might include impurities, degradants, matrix, etc.

Lack of specificity of an individual analytical procedure may be compensated by other supporting analytical procedure(s).

This definition has the following implications:

Identification

> to ensure the identity of an analyte.

Purity Tests

> to ensure that all the analytical procedures performed allow an accurate statement of the content of impurities of an analyte, i.e. related substances test, heavy metals, residual solvents content, etc.

Assay (content or potency)

> to provide an exact result which allows an accurate statement on the content or potency of the analyte in a sample.

3. Accuracy

The accuracy of an analytical procedure expresses the closeness of agreement between the value which is accepted either as a conventional true value or an accepted reference value and the value found.

This is sometimes termed trueness.

4. Precision

The precision of an analytical procedure expresses the closeness of agreement (degree of scatter) between a series of measurements obtained from multiple sampling of the same homogeneous sample under the prescribed conditions. Precision may be considered at three levels: repeatability, intermediate precision and reproducibility.

Precision should be investigated using homogeneous, authentic samples. However, if it s not possible to obtain a homogeneous sample it may be investigated using artificially prepared samples or a sample solution.

The precision of an analytical procedure is usually expressed as the variance, standard deviation or coefficient of variation of a series of measurements.

4.1. Repeatability

Repeatability expresses the precision under the same operating conditions over a short interval of time. Repeatability is also termed intra-assay precision .

4.2. Intermediate precision

Intermediate precision expresses within-laboratories variations: different days, different analysts, different equipment, etc.

4.3. Reproducibility

Reproducibility expresses the precision between laboratories (collaborative studies, usually applied to standardization of methodology).

ICH Q2(R1)

5. Detection Limit

The detection limit of an individual analytical procedure is the lowest amount of analyte in a sample which can be detected but not necessarily quantitated as an exact value.

6. Quantitation Limit

The quantitation limit of an individual analytical procedure is the lowest amount of analyte in a sample which can be quantitatively determined with suitable precision and accuracy. The quantitation limit is a parameter of quantitative assays for low levels of compounds in sample matrices, and is used particularly for the determination of impurities and/or degradation products.

7. Linearity

The linearity of an analytical procedure is its ability (within a given range) to obtain test results which are directly proportional to the concentration (amount) of analyte in the sample.

8. Range

The range of an analytical procedure is the interval between the upper and lower concentration (amounts) of analyte in the sample (including these concentrations) for which it has been demonstrated that the analytical procedure has a suitable level of precision, accuracy and linearity.

9. Robustness

The robustness of an analytical procedure is a measure of its capacity to remain unaffected by small, but deliberate variations in method parameters and provides an indication of its reliability during normal usage.

Part II:
Validation of Analytical Procedures: Methodology

ICH Harmonised Tripartite Guideline

Having reached Step 4 of the ICH Process at the ICH Steering Committee meeting on 6 November 1996, and incorporated into the core guideline in November 2005, this guideline is recommended for adoption to the three regulatory parties to ICH

Introduction

This document is complementary to the parent document which presents a discussion of the characteristics that should be considered during the validation of analytical procedures. Its purpose is to provide some guidance and recommendations on how to consider the various validation characteristics for each analytical procedure. In some cases (for example, demonstration of specificity), the overall capabilities of a number of analytical procedures in combination may be investigated in order to ensure the quality of the drug substance or drug product. In addition, the document provides an indication of the data which should be presented in a registration application .

All relevant data collected during validation and formulae used for calculating validation characteristics should be submitted and discussed as appropriate.

Approaches other than those set forth in this guideline may be applicable and acceptable. It s the responsibility of the applicant to choose the validation procedure and protocol most suitable for their product. However it is important to remember that the main objective of validation of an analytical procedure is to demonstrate that the procedure is suitable for its intended purpose. Due to their complex nature, analytical procedures for biological and biotechnological products in some cases may be approached differently than in this document.

Well-characterized reference materials, with documented purity, should be used throughout the validation study. The degree of purity necessary depends on the intended use.

In accordance with the parent document, and for the sake of clarity, this document considers the various validation characteristics in distinct sections. The arrangement of these sections reflects the process by which an analytical procedure may be developed and evaluated.

In practice, it is usually possible to design the experimental work such that the appropriate validation characteristics can be considered simultaneously to provide a sound, overall knowledge of the capabilities of the analytical procedure, for instance: specificity, linearity, range, accuracy and precision.

1. Specificity

An investigation of specificity should be conducted during the validation of identification tests, the determination of impurities and the assay. The procedures used to demonstrate specificity will depend on the intended objective of the analytical procedure.

It is not always possible to demonstrate that an analytical procedure is specific for a particular analyte (complete discrimination). In this case a combination of two or more analytical procedures is recommended to achieve the necessary level of discrimination.

1.1. Identification

Suitable identification tests should be able to discriminate between compounds of closely related structures which are likely to be present. The discrimination of a procedure may be confirmed by obtaining positive results (perhaps by comparison with a known reference material) from samples containing the analyte, coupled with negative results from samples which do not contain the analyte. In addition, the identification test may be applied to materials structurally similar to or closely related to the analyte to confirm that a positive response is not obtained. The choice of such potentially interfering materials should be based on sound scientific judgement with a consideration of the interferences that could occur.

1.2. Assay and Impurity Test(s)

For chromatographic procedures, representative chromatograms should be used to demonstrate specificity and individual components should be appropriately labelled. Similar considerations should be given to other separation techniques.

Critical separations in chromatography should be investigated at an appropriate level. For critical separations, specificity can be demonstrated by the resolution of the two components which elute closest to each other.

In cases where a non-specific assay is used, other supporting analytical procedures should be used to demonstrate overall specificity. For example,

ICH Q2(R1)

where a titration is adopted to assay the drug substance for release, the combination of the assay and a suitable test for impurities can be used.

The approach is similar for both assay and impurity tests:

1.2.1 Impurities are available

For the assay , this should involve demonstration of the discrimination of the analyte in the presence of impurities and/or excipients; practically, this can be done by spiking pure substances (drug substance or drug product) with appropriate levels of impurities and/or excipients and demonstrating that the assay result is unaffected by the presence of these materials (by comparison with the assay result obtained on unspiked samples).

For the impurity test, the discrimination may be established by spiking drug substance or drug product with appropriate levels of impurities and demonstrating the separation of these impurities individually and/or from other components in the sample matrix.

1.2.2 Impurities are not available

If impurity or degradation product standards are unavailable, specificity may be demonstrated by comparing the test results of samples containing impurities or degradation products to a second well-characterized procedure e.g.: pharmacopoeial method or other validated analytical procedure (independent procedure). As appropriate, this should include samples stored under relevant stress conditions: light, heat, humidity, acid/base hydrolysis and oxidation.

- for the assay, the two results should be compared;
- for the impurity tests, the impurity profiles should be compared.

Peak purity tests may be useful to show that the analyte chromatographic peak is not attributable to more than one component (e.g., diode array, mass spectrometry).

2. Linearity

A linear relationship should be evaluated across the range (see section 3) of the analytical procedure. It may be demonstrated directly on the drug substance (by dilution of a standard stock solution) and/or separate weighings of synthetic mixtures of the drug product components, using the proposed procedure. The latter aspect can be studied during investigation of the range.

Linearity should be evaluated by visual inspection of a plot of signals as a function of analyte concentration or content. If there is a linear relationship, test results should be evaluated by appropriate statistical methods, for example, by calculation of a regression line by the method of least squares. In some cases, to obtain linearity between assays and sample concentrations, the test data may need to be subjected to a mathematical transformation prior to the regression analysis. Data from the regression line itself may be helpful to provide mathematical estimates of the degree of linearity.

The correlation coefficient, y-intercept, slope of the regression line and residual sum of squares should be submitted. A plot of the data should be included. In addition, an analysis of the deviation of the actual data points from the regression line may also be helpful for evaluating linearity.

Some analytical procedures, such as immunoassays, do not demonstrate linearity after any transformation. In this case, the analytical response should be described by an appropriate function of the concentration (amount) of an analyte in a sample.

For the establishment of linearity, a minimum of 5 concentrations is recommended. Other approaches should be justified.

3. Range

The specified range is normally derived from linearity studies and depends on the intended application of the procedure. It is established by confirming that the analytical procedure provides an acceptable degree of linearity, accuracy and precision when applied to samples containing amounts of analyte within or at the extremes of the specified range of the analytical procedure.

The following minimum specified ranges should be considered:

- for the assay of a drug substance or a finished (drug) product: normally from 80 to 120 percent of the test concentration;

- for content uniformity, covering a minimum of 70 to 130 percent of the test concentration, unless a wider more appropriate range, based on the nature of the dosage form (e.g., metered dose inhalers), is justified;

- for dissolution testing: +/-20 % over the specified range;

e.g., if the specifications for a controlled released product cover a region from 20%, after 1 hour, up to 90%, after 24 hours, the validated range would be 0-110% of the label claim

- for the determination of an impurity: from the reporting level of an impurity1 to 120% of the specification;

- for impurities known to be unusually potent or to produce toxic or unexpected pharmacological effects, the detection/quantitation limit should be commensurate with the level at which the impurities must be controlled;

   Note: for validation of impurity test procedures carried out during development, it may be necessary to consider the range around a suggested (probable) limit.

- if assay and purity are performed together as one test and only a 100% standard is used linearity should cover the range from the reporting level of the impurities[33] to 120% of the assay specification.

4. Accuracy

Accuracy should be established across the specified range of the analytical procedure.

4.1. Assay

4.1.1 Drug Substance

Several methods of determining accuracy are available:

ICH Q2(R1)

---

[33] see chapters "Reporting Impurity Content of Batches" of the corresponding ICH-Guidelines: "Impurities in New Drug Substances" and "Impurities in New Drug Products"

a) application of an analytical procedure to an analyte of known purity (e.g. reference material);

b) comparison of the results of the proposed analytical procedure with those of a second well-characterized procedure, the accuracy of which is stated and/or defined (independent procedure, see 1.2.);

c) accuracy may be inferred once precision, linearity and specificity have been established.

4.1.2 Drug Product

Several methods for determining accuracy are available:

a) application of the analytical procedure to synthetic mixtures of the drug product components to which known quantities of the drug substance to be analysed have been added;

b) in cases where it is impossible to obtain samples of all drug product components , it may be acceptable either to add known quantities of the analyte to the drug product or to compare the results obtained from a second, well characterized procedure, the accuracy of which is stated and/or defined (independent procedure, see 1.2.);

c) accuracy may be inferred once precision, linearity and specificity have been established.

4.2. Impurities (Quantitation)

Accuracy should be assessed on samples (drug substance/drug product) spiked with known amounts of impurities.

In cases where it is impossible to obtain samples of certain impurities and/or degradation products, it is considered acceptable to compare results obtained by an independent procedure (see 1.2.). The response factor of the drug substance can be used.

It should be clear how the individual or total impurities are to be determined e.g., weight/weight or area percent, in all cases with respect to the major analyte.

4.3. Recommended Data

Accuracy should be assessed using a minimum of 9 determinations over a minimum of 3 concentration levels covering the specified range (e.g., 3 concentrations/3 replicates each of the total analytical procedure).

Accuracy should be reported as percent recovery by the assay of known added amount of analyte in the sample or as the difference between the mean and the accepted true value together with the confidence intervals.

5. Precision

Validation of tests for assay and for quantitative determination of impurities includes an investigation of precision.

5.1. Repeatability

Repeatability should be assessed using:

a) a minimum of 9 determinations covering the specified range for the procedure (e.g., 3 concentrations/3 replicates each);

or

b) a minimum of 6 determinations at 100% of the test concentration.

5.2. Intermediate Precision

The extent to which intermediate precision should be established depends on the circumstances under which the procedure is intended to be used. The applicant should establish the effects of random events on the precision of the analytical procedure. Typical variations to be studied include days, analysts, equipment, etc. It is not considered necessary to study these effects individually. The use of an experimental design (matrix) is encouraged.

5.3. Reproducibility

Reproducibility is assessed by means of an inter-laboratory trial. Reproducibility should be considered in case of the standardization of an analytical procedure, for instance, for inclusion of procedures in pharmacopoeias. These data are not part of the marketing authorization dossier.

5.4. Recommended Data

The standard deviation, relative standard deviation (coefficient of variation) and confidence interval should be reported for each type of precision investigated.

6. Detection Limit

Several approaches for determining the detection limit are possible, depending on whether the procedure is a non-instrumental or instrumental. Approaches other than those listed below may be acceptable.

6.1. Based on Visual Evaluation

Visual evaluation may be used for non-instrumental methods but may also be used with instrumental methods.

The detection limit is determined by the analysis of samples with known concentrations of analyte and by establishing the minimum level at which the analyte can be reliably detected.

6.2. Based on Signal-to-Noise

This approach can only be applied to analytical procedures which exhibit baseline noise.

Determination of the signal-to-noise ratio is performed by comparing measured signals from samples with known low concentrations of analyte with those of blank samples and establishing the minimum concentration at which the analyte can be reliably detected. A signal-to-noise ratio between 3 or 2:1 is generally considered acceptable for estimating the detection limit.

6.3 Based on the Standard Deviation of the Response and the Slope

The detection limit (DL) may be expressed as:

ICH Q2(R1)

$$DL = \frac{3.3\ \sigma}{S}$$

where σ = the standard deviation of the response

           S = the slope of the calibration curve

The slope S may be estimated from the calibration curve of the analyte. The estimate of σ may be carried out in a variety of ways, for example:

6.3.1 Based on the Standard Deviation of the Blank

Measurement of the magnitude of analytical background response is performed by analyzing an appropriate number of blank samples and calculating the standard deviation of these responses.

6.3.2 Based on the Calibration Curve

A specific calibration curve should be studied using samples containing an analyte in the range of DL. The residual standard deviation of a regression line or the standard deviation of y-intercepts of regression lines may be used as the standard deviation.

6.4 Recommended Data

The detection limit and the method used for determining the detection limit should be presented. If DL is determined based on visual evaluation or based on signal to noise ratio, the presentation of the relevant chromatograms is considered acceptable for justification.

extrapolation, this estimate may subsequently be validated by the independent analysis of a suitable number of samples known to be near or prepared at the detection limit.

7. Quantitation Limit

Several approaches for determining the quantitation limit are possible, depending on whether the procedure is a non-instrumental or instrumental. Approaches other than those listed below may be acceptable.

7.1. Based on Visual Evaluation

Visual evaluation may be used for non-instrumental methods but may also be used with instrumental methods.

The quantitation limit is generally determined by the analysis of samples with known concentrations of analyte and by establishing the minimum level at which the analyte can be quantified with acceptable accuracy and precision.

7.2. Based on Signal-to-Noise Approach

This approach can only be applied to analytical procedures that exhibit baseline noise.

Determination of the signal-to-noise ratio is performed by comparing measured signals from samples with known low concentrations of analyte with those of blank samples and by establishing the minimum concentration at which the analyte can be reliably quantified. A typical signal-to-noise ratio is 10:1.

7.3. Based on the Standard Deviation of the Response and the Slope

The quantitation limit (QL) may be expressed as:

$$QL = \frac{10\,\sigma}{S}$$

where σ = the standard deviation of the response

S = the slope of the calibration curve

The slope S may be estimated from the calibration curve of the analyte. The estimate of σ may be carried out in a variety of ways for example:

7.3.1 Based on Standard Deviation of the Blank

Measurement of the magnitude of analytical background response is performed by analyzing an appropriate number of blank samples and calculating the standard deviation of these responses.

7.3.2 Based on the Calibration Curve

A specific calibration curve should be studied using samples, containing an analyte in the range of QL. The residual standard deviation of a regression line or the standard deviation of y-intercepts of regression lines may be used as the standard deviation.

7.4 Recommended Data

The quantitation limit and the method used for determining the quantitation limit should be presented.

The limit should be subsequently validated by the analysis of a suitable number of samples known to be near or prepared at the quantitation limit.

8. Robustness

The evaluation of robustness should be considered during the development phase and depends on the type of procedure under study. It should show the reliability of an analysis with respect to deliberate variations in method parameters.

If measurements are susceptible to variations in analytical conditions, the analytical conditions should be suitably controlled or a precautionary statement should be included in the procedure. One consequence of the evaluation of robustness should be that a series of system suitability parameters (e.g., resolution test) is established to ensure that the validity of the analytical procedure is maintained whenever used.

Examples of typical variations are:

- stability of analytical solutions;
- extraction time.

In the case of liquid chromatography, examples of typical variations are:

- influence of variations of pH in a mobile phase;
- influence of variations in mobile phase composition;

ICH Q2(R1)

- different columns (different lots and/or suppliers);
- temperature;
- flow rate.

In the case of gas-chromatography, examples of typical variations are:

- different columns (different lots and/or suppliers);
- temperature;
- flow rate.

9. System Suitability Testing

System suitability testing is an integral part of many analytical procedures. The tests are based on the concept that the equipment, electronics, analytical operations and samples to be analyzed constitute an integral system that can be evaluated as such. System suitability test parameters to be established for a particular procedure depend on the type of procedure being validated. See Pharmacopoeias for additional information.

ICH Q7A: Good Manufacturing Practice Guide for Active Pharmaceutical Ingredients

Health Products and Food Branch Guidance Document

Date Adopted - 2002/10/03

Effective Date - The Effective Date will be the date the regulations associated with this guidance come into force.

Notice of Intent Published in Canada Gazette Part I, December 7, 2002 and Good Manufacturing Practices Guide for Active Pharmaceutical Ingredients (ICH Topic Q7A)

Date Modified 2003-01-17

ICH Q7A: Good Manufacturing Practice Guide for Active Pharmaceutical Ingredients[84]

Food and Drug Regulations - Amendment

This notice is to advise the public of Health Canada's intention to proceed with the development of a regulatory framework for Active Pharmaceutical Ingredients (APIs).

Health Canada has a commitment to establish an open and transparent process for the development of regulatory frameworks and through this Notice of Intent, we would like to invite all interested parties to comment on the Health Canada Health Products and Food Branch's (HPFB) proposal.

APIs destined for human use:

Over the past decade, the extension of Good Manufacturing Practices (GMP) to Active Pharmaceutical Ingredients (APIs) has been internationally recognized as a necessary element in ensuring the overall quality and consistency of marketed drug products For this reason, the International Conference on Harmonization (ICH) formed a working group in 1997 to develop a GMP Guidance for APIs. A draft of this Guidance was published for comment by Health Canada in July 1999, followed by discussions with the pharmaceutical industry and associations as part of a workshop on selected ICH topics held in November of that year. The final consensus document entitled Good Manufacturing Practice Guide for Active Pharmaceutical Ingredients (Q7A) was adopted by the ICH Steering Committee on November 10th, 2000, and is currently being implemented by the three ICH regions (USA, Japan and European Union).

---

[84] Available on the Health Canada website at http://www.hc-sc.gc.ca/dhp-mps/compli-conform/legislation/gazette1-q7a-eng.php

Thus, Health Canada is adopting the ICH Q7A Guidance for APIs. A proposed regulatory framework will be developed in order to ensure the implementation of the ICH Q7A Guidance for APIs destined for human use.

You may view the Good Manufacturing Practice Guide for Active Pharmaceutical Ingredients on the following website:

http://www.hc-sc.gc.ca/dhp-mps/compli-conform/index-eng.php

APIs destined for veterinary use:

While the scope of the ICH Q7A Guidance is limited, by virtue of the mandate of ICH, to APIs that will be used in the manufacture of pharmaceuticals for human use, the principles and practices described are internationally recognized as having relevance to APIs for veterinary use.

Thus, it is the intent that the proposed regulatory framework will be designed to allow future implementation of GMP requirements for APIs destined for veterinary use.

Proposed approach:

Until such time as the regulatory framework is in place, Health Canada encourages industry to familiarize themselves and apply the principles outlined in the ICH Q7A Guidance. However, whenever there is cause for safety concerns, Health Canada will follow the HPFB Inspectorate's Compliance and Enforcement Policy (POL-0001).

In addition, a step staged approach will be used in order to facilitate a transition towards confidence building and a fully implemented framework.

Consultations:

Once proposed regulations are developed, they will be published within Canada Gazette Part I for a period of at least 75 days. We anticipate that the proposed regulations would be published for comment in the Spring of 2004.

This Notice of Intent is posted on the Health Products and Food Branch Inspectorate website at the following address:

http://www.hc-sc.gc.ca/dhp-mps/compli-conform/index-eng.php

Comments on this notice may be sent to the Policy and Regulations Division, National Coordination Centre, Health Products and Food Branch Inspectorate, 11 Holland Avenue, Tower A, 2nd Floor, Address Locator: 3002C, Ottawa, Ontario, K1A 0K9 by January 24, 2003 or by Email to Insp_pol@hc-sc.gc.ca or by fax at 613-952-9805.

Persons submitting comments should stipulate any parts of the comments that should not be disclosed pursuant to the Access to Information Act (in particular, pursuant to sections 19 and 20 of that Act), the reason why those parts should not be disclosed and the period during which they should remain undisclosed. Representations should also stipulate those parts of the comments for which there is consent to disclosure pursuant to the Access to Information Act.

1. Introduction

1.1 Objective

This guidance document is intended to provide guidance regarding good manufacturing practice (GMP) for the manufacturing of active pharmaceutical ingredients (APIs) under an appropriate system for managing quality. It is also intended to help ensure that APIs meet the requirements for quality and purity that they purport or are represented to possess.

In this guidance document "manufacturing" is defined to include all operations of receipt of materials, production, packaging, repackaging, labelling, relabelling, quality control, release, storage and distribution of APIs and the related controls. In this guidance document the term "should" indicates recommendations that are expected to apply unless shown to be inapplicable or replaced by an alternative demonstrated to provide at least an equivalent level of quality assurance. For the purposes of this guidance document, the terms "current good manufacturing practices" and "good manufacturing practices" are equivalent.

The guidance document as a whole does not cover safety aspects for the personnel engaged in the manufacture, nor aspects of protection of the environment. These controls are inherent responsibilities of the manufacturer and are governed by national laws.

This guidance document is not intended to define registration/filing requirements or modify pharmacopoeial requirements. This guidance document does not affect the ability of the responsible regulatory agency to establish specific registration/filing requirements regarding APIs within the context of marketing/manufacturing authorizations or drug applications. All commitments in registration/filing documents must be met.

1.2 Regulatory Applicability

Within the world community, materials may vary as to the legal classification as an API. When a material is classified as an API in the region or country in which it is manufactured or used in a drug product, it should be manufactured according to this guidance document.

1.3 Scope

This guidance document applies to the manufacture of APIs for use in human drug (medicinal) products. It applies to the manufacture of sterile APIs only up to the point immediately prior to the APIs being rendered sterile. The sterilization and aseptic processing of sterile APIs are not covered by this guidance, but should be performed in accordance with GMP guidances for drug (medicinal) products as defined by local authorities.

This guidance document covers APIs that are manufactured by chemical synthesis, extraction, cell culture/fermentation, by recovery from natural sources, or by any combination of these processes. Specific guidance for APIs manufactured by cell culture/fermentation is described in Section 18.

This guidance document excludes all vaccines, whole cells, whole blood and plasma, blood and plasma derivatives (plasma fractionation), and gene therapy APIs. However, it does include APIs that are produced using blood or plasma as raw materials. Note that cell substrates (mammalian, plant, insect or microbial cells, tissue or animal sources including transgenic animals) and early process steps may be subject to GMP but are not covered by this guidance document. In addition, the guidance document does not apply to medical gases, bulk-

ICH Q7A

packaged drug (medicinal) products, and manufacturing/control aspects specific to radiopharmaceuticals. Section 19 contains guidance that only applies to the manufacture of APIs used in the production of drug (medicinal) products specifically for clinical trials (investigational medicinal products).

An "API Starting Material" is a raw material, intermediate, or an API that is used in the production of an API and that is incorporated as a significant structural fragment into the structure of the API. An API Starting Material can be an article of commerce, a material purchased from one or more suppliers under contract or commercial agreement, or produced in-house. API Starting Materials normally have defined chemical properties and structure.

The company should designate and document the rationale for the point at which production of the API begins. For synthetic processes, this is known as the point at which "API Starting Materials" are entered into the process. For other processes (e.g. fermentation, extraction, purification, etc), this rationale should be established on a case-by-case basis. Table 1 gives guidance on the point at which the API Starting Material is normally introduced into the process.

From this point on, appropriate GMP as defined in this guidance document should be applied to these intermediate and/or API manufacturing steps. This would include the validation of critical process steps determined to impact the quality of the API. However, it should be noted that the fact that a company chooses to validate a process step does not necessarily define that step as critical.

The guidance in this document would normally be applied to the steps shown in gray in Table 1. It does not imply that all steps shown should be completed. The stringency of GMP in API manufacturing should increase as the process proceeds from early API steps to final steps, purification, and packaging. Physical processing of APIs, such as granulation, coating or physical manipulation of particle size (e.g. milling, micronizing), should be conducted at least to the standards of this guidance document.

This GMP guidance document does not apply to steps prior to the introduction of the defined "API Starting Material".

Table 1: Application of this Guidance to API Manufacturing

Type of Manufacturing	Application of this Guidance to steps (shown in grey) used in this type of manufacturing				
Chemical Manufacturing	Production of the API Starting Material	Introduction of the API Starting Material into process	Production of Intermediate(s)	Isolation and purification	Physical processing, and packaging
API derived from animal sources	Collection of organ, fluid, or tissue	Cutting, mixing, and/or initial processing	Introduction of the API Starting Material into process	Isolation and purification	Physical processing, and packaging
API extracted from plant sources	Collection of plants	Cutting and initial extraction(s)	Introduction of the API Starting Material into process	Isolation and purification	Physical processing, and packaging

Type of Manufacturing	Application of this Guidance to steps (shown in grey) used in this type of manufacturing				
Herbal extracts used as API	Collection of plants	Cutting and initial extraction		Further extraction	Physical processing, and packaging
API consisting of comminuted or powdered herbs	Collection of plants and/or cultivation and harvesting	Cutting/ comminuting			Physical processing, and packaging
Biotechnology: fermentation/ cell culture	Establishment of master cell bank and working cell bank	Maintenance of working cell bank	Cell culture and/or fermentation	Isolation and purification	Physical processing, and packaging
"Classical" Fermentation to produce an API	Establishment of cell bank	Maintenance of the cell bank	Introduction of the cells into fermentation	Isolation and purification	Physical processing, and packaging

Increasing GMP requirements ————————→

2. Quality management

2.1 Principles

2.10   Quality should be the responsibility of all persons involved in manufacturing.

2.11   Each manufacturer should establish, document, and implement an effective system for managing quality that involves the active participation of management and appropriate manufacturing personnel.

2.12   The system for managing quality should encompass the organisational structure, procedures, processes and resources, as well as activities necessary to ensure confidence that the API will meet its intended specifications for quality and purity. All quality related activities should be defined and documented.

2.13   There should be a quality unit(s) that is independent of production and that fulfills both quality assurance (QA) and quality control (QC) responsibilities. This can be in the form of separate QA and QC units or a single individual or group, depending upon the size and structure of the organization.

2.14   The persons authorised to release intermediates and APIs should be specified.

2.15   All quality related activities should be recorded at the time they are performed.

ICH Q7A

2.16   Any deviation from established procedures should be documented and explained. Critical deviations should be investigated, and the investigation and its conclusions should be documented.

2.17   No materials should be released or used before the satisfactory completion of evaluation by the quality unit(s) unless there are appropriate systems in place to allow for such use (e.g. release under quarantine as described in Section 10.20 or the use of raw materials or intermediates pending completion of evaluation).

2.18   Procedures should exist for notifying responsible management in a timely manner of regulatory inspections, serious GMP deficiencies, product defects and related actions (e.g. quality related complaints, recalls, regulatory actions, etc.).

2.2 Responsibilities of the Quality Unit(s)

2.20   The quality unit(s) should be involved in all quality-related matters.

2.21   The quality unit(s) should review and approve all appropriate quality-related documents.

2.22   The main responsibilities of the independent quality unit(s) should not be delegated. These responsibilities should be described in writing and should include but not necessarily be limited to:

1. Releasing or rejecting all APIs. Releasing or rejecting intermediates for use outside the control of the manufacturing company;

2. Establishing a system to release or reject raw materials, intermediates, packaging and labelling materials;

3. Reviewing completed batch production and laboratory control records of critical process steps before release of the API for distribution;

4. Making sure that critical deviations are investigated and resolved;

5. Approving all specifications and master production instructions;

6. Approving all procedures impacting the quality of intermediates or APIs;

7. Making sure that internal audits (self-inspections) are performed;

8. Approving intermediate and API contract manufacturers;

9. Approving changes that potentially impact intermediate or API quality;

10. Reviewing and approving validation protocols and reports;

11. Making sure that quality related complaints are investigated and resolved;

12. Making sure that effective systems are used for maintaining and calibrating critical equipment;

13. Making sure that materials are appropriately tested and the results are reported;

14. Making sure that there is stability data to support retest or expiry dates and storage conditions on APIs and/or intermediates where appropriate; and

15. Performing product quality reviews (as defined in Section 2.5).

2.3 Responsibility for Production Activities

The responsibility for production activities should be described in writing, and should include but not necessarily be limited to:

1. Preparing, reviewing, approving and distributing the instructions for the production of intermediates or APIs according to written procedures;

2. Producing APIs and, when appropriate, intermediates according to pre-approved instructions;

3. Reviewing all production batch records and ensuring that these are completed and signed;

4. Making sure that all production deviations are reported and evaluated and that critical deviations are investigated and the conclusions are recorded;

5. Making sure that production facilities are clean and when appropriate disinfected;

6. Making sure that the necessary calibrations are performed and records kept;

7. Making sure that the premises and equipment are maintained and records kept;

8. Making sure that validation protocols and reports are reviewed and approved;

9. Evaluating proposed changes in product, process or equipment; and

10. Making sure that new and, when appropriate, modified facilities and equipment are qualified.

2.4 Internal Audits (Self Inspection)

2.40   In order to verify compliance with the principles of GMP for APIs, regular internal audits should be performed in accordance with an approved schedule.

2.41   Audit findings and corrective actions should be documented and brought to the attention of responsible management of the firm. Agreed corrective actions should be completed in a timely and effective manner.

ICH Q7A

2.5 Product Quality Review

2.50   Regular quality reviews of APIs should be conducted with the objective of verifying the consistency of the process. Such reviews should normally be conducted and documented annually and should include at least:

- A review of critical in-process control and critical API test results;

- A review of all batches that failed to meet established specification(s);

- A review of all critical deviations or non-conformances and related investigations;

- A review of any changes carried out to the processes or analytical methods;

- A review of results of the stability monitoring program;

- A review of all quality-related returns, complaints and recalls; and

- A review of adequacy of corrective actions.

2.51   The results of this review should be evaluated and an assessment made of whether corrective action or any revalidation should be undertaken. Reasons for such corrective action should be documented. Agreed corrective actions should be completed in a timely and effective manner.

3. Personnel

3.1 Personnel Qualifications

3.10   There should be an adequate number of personnel qualified by appropriate education, training and/or experience to perform and supervise the manufacture of intermediates and APIs.

3.11   The responsibilities of all personnel engaged in the manufacture of intermediates and APIs should be specified in writing.

3.12   Training should be regularly conducted by qualified individuals and should cover, at a minimum, the particular operations that the employee performs and GMP as it relates to the employee's functions. Records of training should be maintained. Training should be periodically assessed.

3.2 Personnel Hygiene

3.20   Personnel should practice good sanitation and health habits.

3.21   Personnel should wear clean clothing suitable for the manufacturing activity with which they are involved and this clothing should be changed when appropriate. Additional protective apparel, such as head, face, hand, and arm coverings, should be worn when necessary, to protect intermediates and APIs from contamination.

3.22   Personnel should avoid direct contact with intermediates or APIs.

3.23   Smoking, eating, drinking, chewing and the storage of food should be restricted to certain designated areas separate from the manufacturing areas.

3.24   Personnel suffering from an infectious disease or having open lesions on the exposed surface of the body should not engage in activities that could result in compromising the quality of APIs. Any person shown at any time (either by medical examination or supervisory observation) to have an apparent illness or open lesions should be excluded from activities where the health condition could adversely affect the quality of the APIs until the condition is corrected or qualified medical personnel determine that the person's inclusion would not jeopardize the safety or quality of the APIs.

3.3 Consultants

3.30   Consultants advising on the manufacture and control of intermediates or APIs should have sufficient education, training, and experience, or any combination thereof, to advise on the subject for which they are retained.

3.31   Records should be maintained stating the name, address, qualifications, and type of service provided by these consultants.

4. Buildings and facilities

4.1 Design and Construction

4.10   Buildings and facilities used in the manufacture of intermediates and APIs should be located, designed, and constructed to facilitate cleaning, maintenance, and operations as appropriate to the type and stage of manufacture. Facilities should also be designed to minimize potential contamination. Where microbiological specifications have been established for the intermediate or API, facilities should also be designed to limit exposure to objectionable microbiological contaminants as appropriate.

4.11   Buildings and facilities should have adequate space for the orderly placement of equipment and materials to prevent mix-ups and contamination.

4.12   Where the equipment itself (e.g., closed or contained systems) provides adequate protection of the material, such equipment can be located outdoors.

4.13   The flow of materials and personnel through the building or facilities should be designed to prevent mix-ups or contamination.

4.14   There should be defined areas or other control systems for the following activities:

- Receipt, identification, sampling, and quarantine of incoming materials, pending release or rejection;
- Quarantine before release or rejection of intermediates and APIs;
- Sampling of intermediates and APIs;
- Holding rejected materials before further disposition (e.g., return, reprocessing or destruction);
- Storage of released materials;
- Production operations;

ICH Q7A

- Packaging and labelling operations; and

- Laboratory operations.

4.15   Adequate, clean washing and toilet facilities should be provided for personnel. These washing facilities should be equipped with hot and cold water as appropriate, soap or detergent, air driers or single service towels. The washing and toilet facilities should be separate from, but easily accessible to, manufacturing areas. Adequate facilities for showering and/or changing clothes should be provided, when appropriate.

4.16   Laboratory areas/operations should normally be separated from production areas. Some laboratory areas, in particular those used for in-process controls, can be located in production areas, provided the operations of the production process do not adversely affect the accuracy of the laboratory measurements, and the laboratory and its operations do not adversely affect the production process or intermediate or API.

4.2 Utilities

4.20   All utilities that could impact on product quality (e.g. steam, gases, compressed air, and heating, ventilation and air conditioning) should be qualified and appropriately monitored and action should be taken when limits are exceeded. Drawings for these utility systems should be available.

4.21   Adequate ventilation, air filtration and exhaust systems should be provided, where appropriate. These systems should be designed and constructed to minimise risks of contamination and cross-contamination and should include equipment for control of air pressure, microorganisms (if appropriate), dust, humidity, and temperature, as appropriate to the stage of manufacture. Particular attention should be given to areas where APIs are exposed to the environment.

4.22   If air is recirculated to production areas, appropriate measures should be taken to control risks of contamination and cross-contamination.

4.23   Permanently installed pipework should be appropriately identified. This can be accomplished by identifying individual lines, documentation, computer control systems, or alternative means. Pipework should be located to avoid risks of contamination of the intermediate or API.

4.24   Drains should be of adequate size and should be provided with an air break or a suitable device to prevent back-siphonage, when appropriate.

4.3 Water

4.30   Water used in the manufacture of APIs should be demonstrated to be suitable for its intended use.

4.31   Unless otherwise justified, process water should, at a minimum, meet World Health Organization (WHO) guidelines for drinking (potable) water quality.

4.32   If drinking (potable) water is insufficient to assure API quality, and tighter chemical and/or microbiological water quality specifications are called for, appropriate specifications for physical/chemical attributes, total microbial counts, objectionable organisms and/or endotoxins should be established.

4.33   Where water used in the process is treated by the manufacturer to achieve a defined quality, the treatment process should be validated and monitored with appropriate action limits.

4.34   Where the manufacturer of a non-sterile API either intends or claims that it is suitable for use in further processing to produce a sterile drug (medicinal) product water used in the final isolation and purification steps should be monitored and controlled for total microbial counts, objectionable organisms, and endotoxins.

4.4 Containment

4.40   Dedicated production areas, which can include facilities, air handling equipment and/or process equipment, should be employed in the production of highly sensitizing materials, such as penicillins or cephalosporins.

4.41   Dedicated production areas should also be considered when material of an infectious nature or high pharmacological activity or toxicity is involved (e.g., certain steroids or cytotoxic anti-cancer agents) unless validated inactivation and/or cleaning procedures are established and maintained.

4.42   Appropriate measures should be established and implemented to prevent cross-contamination from personnel, materials, etc. moving from one dedicated area to another.

4.43   Any production activities (including weighing, milling, or packaging) of highly toxic non-pharmaceutical materials such as herbicides and pesticides should not be conducted using the buildings and/or equipment being used for the production of APIs. Handling and storage of these highly toxic non-pharmaceutical materials should be separate from APIs.

4.5 Lighting

4.50   Adequate lighting should be provided in all areas to facilitate cleaning, maintenance, and proper operations.

4.6 Sewage and Refuse

4.60   Sewage, refuse, and other waste (e.g., solids, liquids, or gaseous by-products from manufacturing) in and from buildings and the immediate surrounding area should be disposed of in a safe, timely, and sanitary manner. Containers and/or pipes for waste material should be clearly identified.

4.7 Sanitation and Maintenance

4.70   Buildings used in the manufacture of intermediates and APIs should be properly maintained and repaired and kept in a clean condition.

4.71   Written procedures should be established assigning responsibility for sanitation and describing the cleaning schedules, methods, equipment, and materials to be used in cleaning buildings and facilities.

4.72   When necessary, written procedures should also be established for the use of suitable rodenticides, insecticides, fungicides, fumigating agents, and

ICH Q7A

cleaning and sanitizing agents to prevent the contamination of equipment, raw materials, packaging/labelling materials, intermediates, and APIs.

5. Process equipment

5.1 Design and Construction

5.10   Equipment used in the manufacture of intermediates and APIs should be of appropriate design and adequate size, and suitably located for its intended use, cleaning, sanitization (where appropriate), and maintenance.

5.11   Equipment should be constructed so that surfaces that contact raw materials, intermediates, or APIs do not alter the quality of the intermediates and APIs beyond the official or other established specifications.

5.12   Production equipment should only be used within its qualified operating range.

5.13   Major equipment (e.g., reactors, storage containers) and permanently installed processing lines used during the production of an intermediate or API should be appropriately identified.

5.14   Any substances associated with the operation of equipment, such as lubricants, heating fluids or coolants, should not contact intermediates or APIs so as to alter their quality beyond the official or other established specifications. Any deviations from this should be evaluated to ensure that there are no detrimental effects upon the fitness for purpose of the material. Wherever possible, food grade lubricants and oils should be used.

5.15   Closed or contained equipment should be used whenever appropriate. Where open equipment is used, or equipment is opened, appropriate precautions should be taken to minimize the risk of contamination.

5.16   A set of current drawings should be maintained for equipment and critical installations (e.g., instrumentation and utility systems).

5.2 Equipment Maintenance and Cleaning

5.20   Schedules and procedures (including assignment of responsibility) should be established for the preventative maintenance of equipment.

5.21   Written procedures should be established for cleaning of equipment and its subsequent release for use in the manufacture of intermediates and APIs. Cleaning procedures should contain sufficient details to enable operators to clean each type of equipment in a reproducible and effective manner. These procedures should include:

- Assignment of responsibility for cleaning of equipment;
- Cleaning schedules, including, where appropriate, sanitizing schedules;
- A complete description of the methods and materials, including dilution of cleaning agents used to clean equipment;
- When appropriate, instructions for disassembling and reassembling each article of equipment to ensure proper cleaning;

- Instructions for the removal or obliteration of previous batch identification;

- Instructions for the protection of clean equipment from contamination prior to use;

- Inspection of equipment for cleanliness immediately before use, if practical; and

- Establishing the maximum time that may elapse between the completion of processing and equipment cleaning, when appropriate.

5.22   Equipment and utensils should be cleaned, stored, and, where appropriate, sanitized or sterilized to prevent contamination or carry-over of a material that would alter the quality of the intermediate or API beyond the official or other established specifications.

5.23   Where equipment is assigned to continuous production or campaign production of successive batches of the same intermediate or API, equipment should be cleaned at appropriate intervals to prevent build-up and carry-over of contaminants (e.g. degradants or objectionable levels of micro-organisms).

5.24   Non-dedicated equipment should be cleaned between production of different materials to prevent cross-contamination.

5.25   Acceptance criteria for residues and the choice of cleaning procedures and cleaning agents should be defined and justified.

5.26   Equipment should be identified as to its contents and its cleanliness status by appropriate means.

5.3 Calibration

5.30   Control, weighing, measuring, monitoring and test equipment that is critical for assuring the quality of intermediates or APIs should be calibrated according to written procedures and an established schedule.

5.31   Equipment calibrations should be performed using standards traceable to certified standards, if existing.

5.32   Records of these calibrations should be maintained.

5.33   The current calibration status of critical equipment should be known and verifiable.

5.34   Instruments that do not meet calibration criteria should not be used.

5.35   Deviations from approved standards of calibration on critical instruments should be investigated to determine if these could have had an impact on the quality of the intermediate(s) or API(s) manufactured using this equipment since the last successful calibration.

5.4 Computerized Systems

5.40   GMP related computerized systems should be validated. The depth and scope of validation depends on the diversity, complexity and criticality of the computerized application.

ICH Q7A

5.41   Appropriate installation qualification and operational qualification should demonstrate the suitability of computer hardware and software to perform assigned tasks.

5.42   Commercially available software that has been qualified does not require the same level of testing. If an existing system was not validated at time of installation, a retrospective validation could be conducted if appropriate documentation is available.

5.43   Computerized systems should have sufficient controls to prevent unauthorized access or changes to data. There should be controls to prevent omissions in data (e.g. system turned off and data not captured). There should be a record of any data change made, the previous entry, who made the change, and when the change was made.

5.44   Written procedures should be available for the operation and maintenance of computerized systems.

5.45   Where critical data are being entered manually, there should be an additional check on the accuracy of the entry. This can be done by a second operator or by the system itself.

5.46   Incidents related to computerized systems that could affect the quality of intermediates or APIs or the reliability of records or test results should be recorded and investigated.

5.47   Changes to the computerized system should be made according to a change procedure and should be formally authorized, documented and tested. Records should be kept of all changes, including modifications and enhancements made to the hardware, software and any other critical component of the system. These records should demonstrate that the system is maintained in a validated state.

5.48   If system breakdowns or failures would result in the permanent loss of records, a back-up system should be provided. A means of ensuring data protection should be established for all computerized systems.

5.49   Data can be recorded by a second means in addition to the computer system.

6. Documentation and records

6.1 Documentation System and Specifications

6.10   All documents related to the manufacture of intermediates or APIs should be prepared, reviewed, approved and distributed according to written procedures. Such documents can be in paper or electronic form.

6.11   The issuance, revision, superseding and withdrawal of all documents should be controlled with maintenance of revision histories.

6.12   A procedure should be established for retaining all appropriate documents (e.g., development history reports, scale-up reports, technical transfer reports, process validation reports, training records, production records, control records, and distribution records). The retention periods for these documents should be specified.

6.13   All production control, and distribution records should be retained for at least 1 year after the expiry date of the batch. For APIs with retest dates, records should be retained for at least 3 years after the batch is completely distributed.

6.14   When entries are made in records, these should be made indelibly in spaces provided for such entries, directly after performing the activities, and should identify the person making the entry. Corrections to entries should be dated and signed and leave the original entry still readable.

6.15   During the retention period, originals or copies of records should be readily available at the establishment where the activities described in such records occurred. Records that can be promptly retrieved from another location by electronic or other means are acceptable.

6.16   Specifications, instructions, procedures, and records can be retained either as originals or as true copies such as photocopies, microfilm, microfiche, or other accurate reproductions of the original records. Where reduction techniques such as microfilming or electronic records are used, suitable retrieval equipment and a means to produce a hard copy should be readily available.

6.17   Specifications should be established and documented for raw materials, intermediates where necessary, APIs, and labelling and packaging materials. In addition, specifications may be appropriate for certain other materials, such as process aids, gaskets, or other materials used during the production of intermediates or APIs that could critically impact on quality. Acceptance criteria should be established and documented for in-process controls.

6.18   If electronic signatures are used on documents, they should be authenticated and secure.

6.2 Equipment Cleaning and Use Record

6.20   Records of major equipment use, cleaning, sanitization and/or sterilization and maintenance should show the date, time (if appropriate), product, and batch number of each batch processed in the equipment, and the person who performed the cleaning and maintenance.

6.21   If equipment is dedicated to manufacturing one intermediate or API, then individual equipment records are not necessary if batches of the intermediate or API follow in traceable sequence. In cases where dedicated equipment is employed, the records of cleaning, maintenance, and use can be part of the batch record or maintained separately.

6.3 Records of Raw Materials, Intermediates, API Labelling and Packaging Materials

6.30   Records should be maintained including:

- The name of the manufacturer, identity and quantity of each shipment of each batch of raw materials, intermediates or labelling and packaging

ICH Q7A

materials for API's; the name of the supplier; the supplier's control number(s), if known, or other identification number; the number allocated on receipt; and the date of receipt;

- The results of any test or examination performed and the conclusions derived from this;

- Records tracing the use of materials;

- Documentation of the examination and review of API labelling and packaging materials for conformity with established specifications; and

- The final decision regarding rejected raw materials, intermediates or API labelling and packaging materials.

6.31 Master (approved) labels should be maintained for comparison to issued labels.

6.4 Master Production Instructions (Master Production and Control Records)

6.40 To ensure uniformity from batch to batch, master production instructions for each intermediate and API should be prepared, dated, and signed by one person and independently checked, dated, and signed by a person in the quality unit(s).

6.41 Master production instructions should include:

- The name of the intermediate or API being manufactured and an identifying document reference code, if applicable;

- A complete list of raw materials and intermediates designated by names or codes sufficiently specific to identify any special quality characteristics;

- An accurate statement of the quantity or ratio of each raw material or intermediate to be used, including the unit of measure. Where the quantity is not fixed, the calculation for each batch size or rate of production should be included. Variations to quantities should be included where they are justified;

- The production location and major production equipment to be used;

- Detailed production instructions, including the:

    - sequences to be followed,

    - ranges of process parameters to be used,

    - sampling instructions and in-process controls with their acceptance criteria, where appropriate,

    - time limits for completion of individual processing steps and/or the total process, where appropriate; and

    - expected yield ranges at appropriate phases of processing or time;

- Where appropriate, special notations and precautions to be followed, or cross-references to these; and

- The instructions for storage of the intermediate or API to assure its suitability for use, including the labelling and packaging materials and special storage conditions with time limits, where appropriate.

6.5 Batch Production Records (Batch Production and Control Records)

6.50   Batch production records should be prepared for each intermediate and API and should include complete information relating to the production and control of each batch. The batch production record should be checked before issuance to assure that it is the correct version and a legible accurate reproduction of the appropriate master production instruction. If the batch production record is produced from a separate part of the master document, that document should include a reference to the current master production instruction being used.

6.51   These records should be numbered with a unique batch or identification number, dated and signed when issued. In continuous production, the product code together with the date and time can serve as the unique identifier until the final number is allocated.

6.52   Documentation of completion of each significant step in the batch production records (batch production and control records) should include:

- Dates and, when appropriate, times;

- Identity of major equipment (e.g., reactors, driers, mills, etc.) used;

- Specific identification of each batch, including weights, measures, and batch numbers of raw materials, intermediates, or any reprocessed materials used during manufacturing;

- Actual results recorded for critical process parameters;

- Any sampling performed;

- Signatures of the persons performing and directly supervising or checking each critical step in the operation;

- In-process and laboratory test results;

- Actual yield at appropriate phases or times;

- Description of packaging and label for intermediate or API;

- Representative label of API or intermediate if made commercially available;

- Any deviation noted, its evaluation, investigation conducted (if appropriate) or reference to that investigation if stored separately; and

- Results of release testing.

6.53   Written procedures should be established and followed for investigating critical deviations or the failure of a batch of intermediate or API to meet specifications. The investigation should extend to other batches that may have been associated with the specific failure or deviation.

6.6 Laboratory Control Records

6.60   Laboratory control records should include complete data derived from all tests conducted to ensure compliance with established specifications and standards, including examinations and assays, as follows:

ICH Q7A

- A description of samples received for testing, including the material name or source, batch number or other distinctive code, date sample was taken, and, where appropriate, the quantity and date the sample was received for testing;

- A statement of or reference to each test method used;

- A statement of the weight or measure of sample used for each test as described by the method; data on or cross-reference to the preparation and testing of reference standards, reagents and standard solutions;

- A complete record of all raw data generated during each test, in addition to graphs, charts, and spectra from laboratory instrumentation, properly identified to show the specific material and batch tested;

- A record of all calculations performed in connection with the test, including, for example, units of measure, conversion factors, and equivalency factors;

- A statement of the test results and how they compare with established acceptance criteria;

- The signature of the person who performed each test and the date(s) the tests were performed; and

- The date and signature of a second person showing that the original records have been reviewed for accuracy, completeness, and compliance with established standards.

6.61   Complete records should also be maintained for:

- Any modifications to an established analytical method;

- Periodic calibration of laboratory instruments, apparatus, gauges, and recording devices;

- All stability testing performed on APIs; and

- Out-of-specification (OOS) investigations.

6.7 Batch Production Record Review

6.70   Written procedures should be established and followed for the review and approval of batch production and laboratory control records, including packaging and labelling, to determine compliance of the intermediate or API with established specifications before a batch is released or distributed.

6.71   Batch production and laboratory control records of critical process steps should be reviewed and approved by the quality unit(s) before an API batch is released or distributed. Production and laboratory control records of non-critical process steps can be reviewed by qualified production personnel or other units following procedures approved by the quality unit(s).

6.72   All deviation, investigation, and OOS reports should be reviewed as part of the batch record review before the batch is released.

6.73   The quality unit(s) can delegate to the production unit the responsibility and authority for release of intermediates, except for those shipped outside the control of the manufacturing company.

7. Materials management

7.1 General Controls

7.10   There should be written procedures describing the receipt, identification, quarantine, storage, handling, sampling, testing, and approval or rejection of materials.

7.11   Manufacturers of intermediates and/or APIs should have a system for evaluating the suppliers of critical materials.

7.12   Materials should be purchased against an agreed specification, from a supplier or suppliers approved by the quality unit(s).

7.13   If the supplier of a critical material is not the manufacturer of that material, the name and address of that manufacturer should be known by the intermediate and/or API manufacturer.

7.14   Changing the source of supply of critical raw materials should be treated according to Section 13, Change Control.

7.2 Receipt and Quarantine

7.20   Upon receipt and before acceptance, each container or grouping of containers of materials should be examined visually for correct labelling (including correlation between the name used by the supplier and the in-house name, if these are different), container damage, broken seals and evidence of tampering or contamination. Materials should be held under quarantine until they have been sampled, examined or tested as appropriate, and released for use.

7.21   Before incoming materials are mixed with existing stocks (e.g., solvents or stocks n silos), they should be identified as correct, tested, if appropriate, and released. Procedures should be available to prevent discharging incoming materials wrongly into the existing stock.

7.22   If bulk deliveries are made in non-dedicated tankers, there should be assurance of no cross-contamination from the tanker. Means of providing this assurance could include one or more of the following:

- certificate of cleaning
- testing for trace impurities
- audit of the supplier.

7.23   Large storage containers, and their attendant manifolds, filling and discharge lines should be appropriately identified.

7.24   Each container or grouping of containers (batches) of materials should be assigned and identified with a distinctive code, batch, or receipt number. This number should be used in recording the disposition of each batch. A system should be in place to identify the status of each batch.

ICH Q7A

7.3 Sampling and Testing of Incoming Production Materials

7.30　　At least one test to verify the identity of each batch of material should be conducted, with the exception of the materials described below in 7.32. A supplier's Certificate of Analysis can be used in place of performing other tests, provided that the manufacturer has a system in place to evaluate suppliers.

7.31　　Supplier approval should include an evaluation that provides adequate evidence (e.g., past quality history) that the manufacturer can consistently provide material meeting specifications. Full analyses should be conducted on at least three batches before reducing in-house testing. However, as a minimum, a full analysis should be performed at appropriate intervals and compared with the Certificates of Analysis. Reliability of Certificates of Analysis should be checked at regular intervals.

7.32　　Processing aids, hazardous or highly toxic raw materials, other special materials, or materials transferred to another unit within the company's control do not need to be tested if the manufacturer's Certificate of Analysis is obtained, showing that these raw materials conform to established specifications. Visual examination of containers, labels, and recording of batch numbers should help in establishing the identity of these materials. The lack of on-site testing for these materials should be justified and documented.

7.33　　Samples should be representative of the batch of material from which they are taken. Sampling methods should specify the number of containers to be sampled, which part of the container to sample, and the amount of material to be taken from each container. The number of containers to sample and the sample size should be based upon a sampling plan that takes into consideration the criticality of the material, material variability, past quality history of the supplier, and the quantity needed for analysis.

7.34　　Sampling should be conducted at defined locations and by procedures designed to prevent contamination of the material sampled and contamination of other materials.

7.35　　Containers from which samples are withdrawn should be opened carefully and subsequently reclosed. They should be marked to indicate that a sample has been taken.

7.4 Storage

7.40　　Materials should be handled and stored in a manner to prevent degradation, contamination, and cross-contamination.

7.41　　Materials stored in fiber drums, bags, or boxes should be stored off the floor and, when appropriate, suitably spaced to permit cleaning and inspection.

7.42　　Materials should be stored under conditions and for a period that have no adverse affect on their quality, and should normally be controlled so that the oldest stock is used first.

7.43 Certain materials in suitable containers can be stored outdoors, provided identifying labels remain legible and containers are appropriately cleaned before opening and use.

7.44 Rejected materials should be identified and controlled under a quarantine system designed to prevent their unauthorised use in manufacturing.

7.5 Re-evaluation

7.50 Materials should be re-evaluated as appropriate to determine their suitability for use (e.g., after prolonged storage or exposure to heat or humidity).

8. Production and in-process controls

8.1 Production Operations

8.10 Raw materials for intermediate and API manufacturing should be weighed or measured under appropriate conditions that do not affect their suitability for use. Weighing and measuring devices should be of suitable accuracy for the intended use.

8.11 If a material is subdivided for later use in production operations, the container receiving the material should be suitable and should be so identified that the following information is available:

- Material name and/or item code;

- Receiving or control number;

- Weight or measure of material in the new container; and

- Re-evaluation or retest date if appropriate.

8.12 Critical weighing, measuring, or subdividing operations should be witnessed or subjected to an equivalent control. Prior to use, production personnel should verify that the materials are those specified in the batch record for the intended intermediate or API.

8.13 Other critical activities should be witnessed or subjected to an equivalent control.

8.14 Actual yields should be compared with expected yields at designated steps in the production process. Expected yields with appropriate ranges should be established based on previous laboratory, pilot scale, or manufacturing data. Deviations in yield associated with critical process steps should be investigated to determine their impact or potential impact on the resulting quality of affected batches.

8.15 Any deviation should be documented and explained. Any critical deviation should be investigated.

8.16 The processing status of major units of equipment should be indicated either on the individual units of equipment or by appropriate documentation, computer control systems, or alternative means.

ICH Q7A

8.17   Materials to be reprocessed or reworked should be appropriately controlled to prevent unauthorized use.

8.2 Time Limits

8.20   If time limits are specified in the master production instruction (see 6.41), these time limits should be met to ensure the quality of intermediates and APIs. Deviations should be documented and evaluated. Time limits may be inappropriate when processing to a target value (e.g., pH adjustment, hydrogenation, drying to predetermined specification) because completion of reactions or processing steps are determined by in-process sampling and testing.

8.21   Intermediates held for further processing should be stored under appropriate conditions to ensure their suitability for use.

8.3 In-process Sampling and Controls

8.30   Written procedures should be established to monitor the progress and control the performance of processing steps that cause variability in the quality characteristics of intermediates and APIs. In-process controls and their acceptance criteria should be defined based on the information gained during the development stage or historical data.

8.31   The acceptance criteria and type and extent of testing can depend on the nature of the intermediate or API being manufactured, the reaction or process step being conducted, and the degree to which the process introduces variability in the product's quality. Less stringent in-process controls may be appropriate in early processing steps, whereas tighter controls may be appropriate for later processing steps (e.g., isolation and purification steps).

8.32   Critical in-process controls (and critical process monitoring), including the control points and methods, should be stated in writing and approved by the quality unit(s).

8.33   In-process controls can be performed by qualified production department personnel and the process adjusted without prior quality unit(s) approval if the adjustments are made within pre-established limits approved by the quality unit(s). All tests and results should be fully documented as part of the batch record.

8.34   Written procedures should describe the sampling methods for in-process materials, intermediates, and APIs. Sampling plans and procedures should be based on scientifically sound sampling practices.

8.35   In-process sampling should be conducted using procedures designed to prevent contamination of the sampled material and other intermediates or APIs. Procedures should be established to ensure the integrity of samples after collection.

8.36   Out-of-specification (OOS) investigations are not normally needed for in-process tests that are performed for the purpose of monitoring and/or adjusting the process.

8.4 Blending Batches of Intermediates or APIs

8.40   For the purpose of this guidance document, blending is defined as the process of combining materials within the same specification to produce a homogeneous intermediate or API. In-process mixing of fractions from single batches (e.g., collecting several centrifuge loads from a single crystallization batch) or combining fractions from several batches for further processing is considered to be part of the production process and is not considered to be blending.

8.41   Out-Of-Specification batches should not be blended with other batches for the purpose of meeting specifications. Each batch incorporated into the blend should have been manufactured using an established process and should have been individually tested and found to meet appropriate specifications prior to blending.

8.42   Acceptable blending operations include but are not limited to:

- Blending of small batches to increase batch size

- Blending of tailings (i.e., relatively small quantities of isolated material) from batches of the same intermediate or API to form a single batch.

8.43   Blending processes should be adequately controlled and documented and the blended batch should be tested for conformance to established specifications where appropriate.

8.44   The batch record of the blending process should allow traceability back to the individual batches that make up the blend.

8.45   Where physical attributes of the API are critical (e.g., APIs intended for use in solid oral dosage forms or suspensions), blending operations should be validated to show homogeneity of the combined batch. Validation should include testing of critical attributes (e.g., particle size distribution, bulk density, and tap density) that may be affected by the blending process.

8.46   If the blending could adversely affect stability, stability testing of the final blended batches should be performed.

8.47   The expiry or retest date of the blended batch should be based on the manufacturing date of the oldest tailings or batch in the blend.

8.5 Contamination Control

8.50   Residual materials can be carried over into successive batches of the same intermediate or API if there is adequate control. Examples include residue adhering to the wall of a micronizer, residual layer of damp crystals remaining in a centrifuge bowl after discharge, and incomplete discharge of fluids or crystals from a processing vessel upon transfer of the material to the next step in the process. Such carryover should not result in the carryover of degradants or microbial contamination that may adversely alter the established API impurity profile.

8.51   Production operations should be conducted in a manner that will prevent contamination of intermediates or APIs by other materials.

ICH Q7A

8.52   Precautions to avoid contamination should be taken when APIs are handled after purification.

9. Packaging and identification labelling of APIs and intermediates

9.1 General

9.10   There should be written procedures describing the receipt, identification, quarantine, sampling, examination and/or testing and release, and handling of packaging and labelling materials.

9.11   Packaging and labelling materials should conform to established specifications. Those that do not comply with such specifications should be rejected to prevent their use in operations for which they are unsuitable.

9.12   Records should be maintained for each shipment of labels and packaging materials showing receipt, examination, or testing, and whether accepted or rejected.

9.2 Packaging Materials

9.20   Containers should provide adequate protection against deterioration or contamination of the intermediate or API that may occur during transportation and recommended storage.

9.21   Containers should be clean and, where indicated by the nature of the intermediate or API, sanitized to ensure that they are suitable for their intended use. These containers should not be reactive, additive, or absorptive so as to alter the quality of the intermediate or API beyond the specified limits.

9.22   If containers are re-used, they should be cleaned in accordance with documented procedures and all previous labels should be removed or defaced.

9.3 Label Issuance and Control

9.30   Access to the label storage areas should be limited to authorised personnel.

9.31   Procedures should be used to reconcile the quantities of labels issued, used, and returned and to evaluate discrepancies found between the number of containers labelled and the number of labels issued. Such discrepancies should be investigated, and the investigation should be approved by the quality unit(s).

9.32   All excess labels bearing batch numbers or other batch-related printing should be destroyed. Returned labels should be maintained and stored in a manner that prevents mix-ups and provides proper identification.

9.33   Obsolete and out-dated labels should be destroyed.

9.34   Printing devices used to print labels for packaging operations should be controlled to ensure that all imprinting conforms to the print specified in the batch production record.

9.35   Printed labels issued for a batch should be carefully examined for proper identity and conformity to specifications in the master production record. The results of this examination should be documented.

9.36   A printed label representative of those used should be included in the batch production record.

9.4 Packaging and Labelling Operations

9.40   There should be documented procedures designed to ensure that correct packaging materials and labels are used.

9.41   Labelling operations should be designed to prevent mix-ups. There should be physical or spatial separation from operations involving other intermediates or APIs.

9.42   Labels used on containers of intermediates or APIs should indicate the name or identifying code, the batch number of the product, and storage conditions, when such information is critical to assure the quality of intermediate or API.

9.43   If the intermediate or API is intended to be transferred outside the control of the manufacturer's material management system, the name and address of the manufacturer, quantity of contents, and special transport conditions and any special legal requirements should also be included on the label. For intermediates or APIs with an expiry date, the expiry date should be indicated on the label and Certificate of Analysis. For intermediates or APIs with a retest date, the retest date should be indicated on the label and/or Certificate of Analysis.

9.44   Packaging and labelling facilities should be inspected immediately before use to ensure that all materials not needed for the next packaging operation have been removed. This examination should be documented in the batch production records, the facility log, or other documentation system.

9.45   Packaged and labelled intermediates or APIs should be examined to ensure that containers and packages in the batch have the correct label. This examination should be part of the packaging operation. Results of these examinations should be recorded in the batch production or control records.

9.46   Intermediate or API containers that are transported outside of the manufacturer's control should be sealed in a manner such that, if the seal is breached or missing, the recipient will be alerted to the possibility that the contents may have been altered.

10. Storage and distribution

10.1 Warehousing Procedures

10.10   Facilities should be available for the storage of all materials under appropriate conditions (e.g. controlled temperature and humidity when

ICH Q7A

necessary). Records should be maintained of these conditions if they are critical for the maintenance of material characteristics.

10.11   Unless there is an alternative system to prevent the unintentional or unauthorised use of quarantined, rejected, returned, or recalled materials, separate storage areas should be assigned for their temporary storage until the decision as to their future use has been taken.

10.2 Distribution Procedures

10.20   APIs and intermediates should only be released for distribution to third parties after they have been released by the quality unit(s). APIs and intermediates can be transferred under quarantine to another unit under the company's control when authorized by the quality unit(s) and if appropriate controls and documentation are in place.

10.21   APIs and intermediates should be transported in a manner that does not adversely affect their quality.

10.22   Special transport or storage conditions for an API or intermediate should be stated on the label.

10.23   The manufacturer should ensure that the contract acceptor (contractor) for transportation of the API or intermediate knows and follows the appropriate transport and storage conditions.

10.24   A system should be in place by which the distribution of each batch of intermediate and/or API can be readily determined to permit its recall.

11. Laboratory controls

11.1 General Controls

11.10   The independent quality unit(s) should have at its disposal adequate laboratory facilities.

11.11   There should be documented procedures describing sampling, testing, approval or rejection of materials, and recording and storage of laboratory data. Laboratory records should be maintained in accordance with Section 6.6.

11.12   All specifications, sampling plans, and test procedures should be scientifically sound and appropriate to ensure that raw materials, intermediates, APIs, and labels and packaging materials conform to established standards of quality and/or purity. Specifications and test procedures should be consistent with those included in the registration/filing. There can be specifications in addition to those in the registration/filing. Specifications, sampling plans, and test procedures, including changes to them, should be drafted by the appropriate organizational unit and reviewed and approved by the quality unit(s).

11.13   Appropriate specifications should be established for APIs in accordance with accepted standards and consistent with the manufacturing process. The specifications should include a control of the impurities (e.g. organic impurities, inorganic impurities, and residual solvents). If the API has a specification for microbiological purity, appropriate action limits for total microbial counts and objectionable organisms should be established and met. If the API has a specification for endotoxins, appropriate action limits should be established and met.

11.14 Laboratory controls should be followed and documented at the time of performance. Any departures from the above described procedures should be documented and explained.

11.15 Any out-of-specification result obtained should be investigated and documented according to a procedure. This procedure should require analysis of the data, assessment of whether a significant problem exists, allocation of the tasks for corrective actions, and conclusions. Any resampling and/or retesting after OOS results should be performed according to a documented procedure.

11.16 Reagents and standard solutions should be prepared and labelled following written procedures. "Use by" dates should be applied as appropriate for analytical reagents or standard solutions.

11.17 Primary reference standards should be obtained as appropriate for the manufacture of APIs. The source of each primary reference standard should be documented. Records should be maintained of each primary reference standard's storage and use in accordance with the supplier's recommendations. Primary reference standards obtained from an officially recognised source are normally used without testing if stored under conditions consistent with the supplier's recommendations.

11.18 Where a primary reference standard is not available from an officially recognized source, an "in-house primary standard" should be established. Appropriate testing should be performed to establish fully the identity and purity of the primary reference standard. Appropriate documentation of this testing should be maintained.

11.19 Secondary reference standards should be appropriately prepared, identified, tested, approved, and stored. The suitability of each batch of secondary reference standard should be determined prior to first use by comparing against a primary reference standard. Each batch of secondary reference standard should be periodically requalified in accordance with a written protocol.

11.2 Testing of Intermediates and APIs

11.20 For each batch of intermediate and API, appropriate laboratory tests should be conducted to determine conformance to specifications.

11.21 An impurity profile describing the identified and unidentified impurities present in a typical batch produced by a specific controlled production process should normally be established for each API. The impurity profile should include the identity or some qualitative analytical designation (e.g. retention time), the range of each impurity observed, and classification of each identified impurity (e.g. inorganic, organic, solvent). The impurity profile is normally dependent upon the production process and origin of the API. Impurity profiles are normally not necessary for APIs from herbal or animal tissue origin. Biotechnology considerations are covered in ICH Guidance Q6B.

ICH Q7A

11.22   The impurity profile should be compared at appropriate intervals against the impurity profile in the regulatory submission or compared against historical data in order to detect changes to the API resulting from modifications in raw materials, equipment operating parameters, or the production process.

11.23   Appropriate microbiological tests should be conducted on each batch of intermediate and API where microbial quality is specified.

11.3 Validation of Analytical Procedures - see Section 12.

11.4 Certificates of Analysis

11.40   Authentic Certificates of Analysis should be issued for each batch of intermediate or API on request.

11.41   Information on the name of the intermediate or API including where appropriate its grade, the batch number, and the date of release should be provided on the Certificate of Analysis. For intermediates or APIs with an expiry date, the expiry date should be provided on the label and Certificate of Analysis. For intermediates or APIs with a retest date, the retest date should be indicated on the label and/or Certificate of Analysis.

11.42   The Certificate should list each test performed in accordance with compendial or customer requirements, including the acceptance limits, and the numerical results obtained (if test results are numerical).

11.43   Certificates should be dated and signed by authorised personnel of the quality unit(s) and should show the name, address and telephone number of the original manufacturer. Where the analysis has been carried out by a repacker or reprocessor, the Certificate of Analysis should show the name, address and telephone number of the repacker/reprocessor and a reference to the name of the original manufacturer.

11.44   If new Certificates are issued by or on behalf of repackers/reprocessors, agents or brokers, these Certificates should show the name, address and telephone number of the laboratory that performed the analysis. They should also contain a reference to the name and address of the original manufacturer and to the original batch Certificate, a copy of which should be attached.

11.5 Stability Monitoring of APIs

11.50   A documented, on-going testing program should be designed to monitor the stability characteristics of APIs, and the results should be used to confirm appropriate storage conditions and retest or expiry dates.

11.51   The test procedures used in stability testing should be validated and be stability indicating.

11.52   Stability samples should be stored in containers that simulate the market container. For example, if the API is marketed in bags within fiber drums, stability samples can be packaged in bags of the same material and in smaller-scale drums of similar or identical material composition to the market drums.

11.53   Normally the first three commercial production batches should be placed on the stability monitoring program to confirm the retest or expiry date. However, where data from previous studies show that the API is expected to remain stable for at least two years, fewer than three batches can be used.

11.54   Thereafter, at least one batch per year of API manufactured (unless none is produced that year) should be added to the stability monitoring program and tested at least annually to confirm the stability.

11.55   For APIs with short shelf-lives, testing should be done more frequently. For example, for these biotechnological/biologic and other APIs with shelf-lives of one year or less, stability samples should be obtained and should be tested monthly for the first three months, and at three month intervals after that. When data exist that confirm that the stability of the API is not compromised, elimination of specific test intervals (e.g. 9 month testing) can be considered.

11.56   Where appropriate, the stability storage conditions should be consistent with the ICH guidances on stability.

11.6 Expiry and Retest Dating

11.60   When an intermediate is intended to be transferred outside the control of the manufacturer's material management system and an expiry or retest date is assigned, supporting stability information should be available (e.g. published data, test results).

11.61   An API expiry or retest date should be based on an evaluation of data derived from stability studies. Common practice is to use a retest date, not an expiration date.

11.62   Preliminary API expiry or retest dates can be based on pilot scale batches if (1) the pilot batches employ a method of manufacture and procedure that simulates the final process to be used on a commercial manufacturing scale; and (2) the quality of the API represents the material to be made on a commercial scale.

11.63   A representative sample should be taken for the purpose of performing a retest.

11.7 Reserve/Retention Samples

11.70   The packaging and holding of reserve samples is for the purpose of potential future evaluation of the quality of batches of API and not for future stability testing purposes.

11.71   Appropriately identified reserve samples of each API batch should be retained for one year after the expiry date of the batch assigned by the manufacturer, or for three years after distribution of the batch, whichever is the longer. For APIs with retest dates, similar reserve samples should be retained for three years after the batch is completely distributed by the manufacturer.

11.72   The reserve sample should be stored in the same packaging system in which the API is stored or in one that is equivalent to or more protective than

ICH Q7A

the marketed packaging system. Sufficient quantities should be retained to conduct at least two full compendial analyses or, when there is no pharmacopoeial monograph, two full specification analyses.

12. Validation

12.1 Validation Policy

12.10   The company's overall policy, intentions, and approach to validation, including the validation of production processes, cleaning procedures, analytical methods, in-process control test procedures, computerized systems, and persons responsible for design, review, approval and documentation of each validation phase, should be documented.

12.11   The critical parameters/attributes should normally be identified during the development stage or from historical data, and the ranges necessary for the reproducible operation should be defined. This should include:

- Defining the API in terms of its critical product attributes;

- Identifying process parameters that could affect the critical quality attributes of the API;

- Determining the range for each critical process parameter expected to be used during routine manufacturing and process control.

12.12   Validation should extend to those operations determined to be critical to the quality and purity of the API.

12.2 Validation Documentation

12.20   A written validation protocol should be established that specifies how validation of a particular process will be conducted. The protocol should be reviewed and approved by the quality unit(s) and other designated units.

12.21   The validation protocol should specify critical process steps and acceptance criteria as well as the type of validation to be conducted (e.g. retrospective, prospective, concurrent) and the number of process runs.

12.22   A validation report that cross-references the validation protocol should be prepared, summarising the results obtained, commenting on any deviations observed, and drawing the appropriate conclusions, including recommending changes to correct deficiencies.

12.23   Any variations from the validation protocol should be documented with appropriate justification.

12.3 Qualification

12.30   Before starting process validation activities, appropriate qualification of critical equipment and ancillary systems should be completed. Qualification is usually carried out by conducting the following activities, individually or combined:

- Design Qualification (DQ): documented verification that the proposed design of the facilities, equipment, or systems is suitable for the intended purpose.

- Installation Qualification (IQ): documented verification that the equipment or systems, as installed or modified, comply with the approved design, the manufacturer's recommendations and/or user requirements.

- Operational Qualification (OQ): documented verification that the equipment or systems, as installed or modified, perform as intended throughout the anticipated operating ranges.

- Performance Qualification (PQ): documented verification that the equipment and ancillary systems, as connected together, can perform effectively and reproducibly based on the approved process method and specifications.

12.4 Approaches to Process Validation

12.40   Process Validation (PV) is the documented evidence that the process, operated within established parameters, can perform effectively and reproducibly to produce an intermediate or API meeting its predetermined specifications and quality attributes.

12.41   There are three approaches to validation. Prospective validation is the preferred approach, but there are exceptions where the other approaches can be used. These approaches and their applicability are listed below.

12.42   Prospective validation should normally be performed for all API processes as defined in 12.12. Prospective validation performed on an API process should be completed before the commercial distribution of the final drug product manufactured from that API.

12.43   Concurrent validation can be conducted when data from replicate production runs are unavailable because only a limited number of API batches have been produced, API batches are produced infrequently, or API batches are produced by a validated process that has been modified. Prior to the completion of concurrent validation, batches can be released and used in final drug product for commercial distribution based on thorough monitoring and testing of the API batches.

12.44   An exception can be made for retrospective validation for well established processes that have been used without significant changes to API quality due to changes in raw materials, equipment, systems, facilities, or the production process. This validation approach may be used where:

1.   Critical quality attributes and critical process parameters have been identified;

2.   Appropriate in-process acceptance criteria and controls have been established;

3.   There have not been significant process/product failures attributable to causes other than operator error or equipment failures unrelated to equipment suitability; and

4.   Impurity profiles have been established for the existing API.

12.45   Batches selected for retrospective validation should be representative of all batches made during the review period, including any batches that failed

ICH Q7A

to meet specifications, and should be sufficient in number to demonstrate process consistency. Retained samples can be tested to obtain data to retrospectively validate the process.

12.5 Process Validation Program

12.50   The number of process runs for validation should depend on the complexity of the process or the magnitude of the process change being considered. For prospective and concurrent validation, three consecutive successful production batches should be used as a guide, but there may be situations where additional process runs are warranted to prove consistency of the process (e.g., complex API processes or API processes with prolonged completion times). For retrospective validation, generally data from ten to thirty consecutive batches should be examined to assess process consistency, but fewer batches can be examined if justified.

12.51   Critical process parameters should be controlled and monitored during process validation studies. Process parameters unrelated to quality, such as variables controlled to minimize energy consumption or equipment use, need not be included in the process validation.

12.52   Process validation should confirm that the impurity profile for each API is within the limits specified. The impurity profile should be comparable to or better than historical data and, where applicable, the profile determined during process development or for batches used for pivotal clinical and toxicological studies.

12.6 Periodic Review of Validated Systems

12.60   Systems and processes should be periodically evaluated to verify that they are still operating in a valid manner. Where no significant changes have been made to the system or process, and a quality review confirms that the system or process is consistently producing material meeting its specifications, there is normally no need for revalidation.

12.7 Cleaning Validation

12.70   Cleaning procedures should normally be validated. In general, cleaning validation should be directed to situations or process steps where contamination or carryover of materials poses the greatest risk to API quality. For example, in early production it may be unnecessary to validate equipment cleaning procedures where residues are removed by subsequent purification steps.

12.71   Validation of cleaning procedures should reflect actual equipment usage patterns. If various APIs or intermediates are manufactured in the same equipment and the equipment is cleaned by the same process, a representative intermediate or API can be selected for cleaning validation. This selection should be based on the solubility and difficulty of cleaning and the calculation of residue limits based on potency, toxicity, and stability.

12.72   The cleaning validation protocol should describe the equipment to be cleaned, procedures, materials, acceptable cleaning levels, parameters to be monitored and controlled, and analytical methods. The protocol should also indicate the type of samples to be obtained and how they are collected and labelled.

12.73   Sampling should include swabbing, rinsing, or alternative methods (e g., direct extraction), as appropriate, to detect both insoluble and soluble residues. The sampling methods used should be capable of quantitatively measuring levels of residues remaining on the equipment surfaces after cleaning. Swab sampling may be impractical when product contact surfaces are not easily accessible due to equipment design and/or process limitations (e.g., inner surfaces of hoses, transfer pipes, reactor tanks with small ports or handling toxic materials, and small intricate equipment such as micronizers and microfluidizers).

12.74   Validated analytical methods having sensitivity to detect residues or contaminants should be used. The detection limit for each analytical method should be sufficiently sensitive to detect the established acceptable level of the residue or contaminant. The method's attainable recovery level should be established. Residue limits should be practical, achievable, verifiable and based on the most deleterious residue. Limits can be established based on the minimum known pharmacological, toxicological, or physiological activity of the API or its most deleterious component.

12.75   Equipment cleaning/sanitization studies should address microbiological and endotoxin contamination for those processes where there is a need to reduce total microbiological count or endotoxins in the API, or other processes where such contamination could be of concern (e.g., non-sterile APIs used to manufacture sterile products).

12.76   Cleaning procedures should be monitored at appropriate intervals after validation to ensure that these procedures are effective when used during routine production. Equipment cleanliness can be monitored by analytical testing and visual examination, where feasible. Visual inspection can allow detection of gross contamination concentrated in small areas that could otherwise go undetected by sampling and/or analysis.

12.8 Validation of Analytical Methods

12.80   Analytical methods should be validated unless the method employed is included in the relevant pharmacopoeia or other recognised standard reference. The suitability of all testing methods used should nonetheless be verified under actual conditions of use and documented.

12.81   Methods should be validated to include consideration of characteristics included within the ICH guidances on validation of analytical methods. The degree of analytical validation performed should reflect the purpose of the analysis and the stage of the API production process.

12.82   Appropriate qualification of analytical equipment should be considered before starting validation of analytical methods.

12.83   Complete records should be maintained of any modification of a validated analytical method. Such records should include the reason for the modification and appropriate data to verify that the modification produces results that are as accurate and reliable as the established method.

ICH Q7A

13. Change control

13.10   A formal change control system should be established to evaluate all changes that may affect the production and control of the intermediate or API.

13.11   Written procedures should provide for the identification, documentation, appropriate review, and approval of changes in raw materials, specifications, analytical methods, facilities, support systems, equipment (including computer hardware), processing steps, labelling and packaging materials, and computer software.

13.12   Any proposals for GMP relevant changes should be drafted, reviewed, and approved by the appropriate organisational units, and reviewed and approved by the quality unit(s).

13.13   The potential impact of the proposed change on the quality of the intermediate or API should be evaluated. A classification procedure may help in determining the level of testing, validation, and documentation needed to justify changes to a validated process. Changes can be classified (e.g. as minor or major) depending on the nature and extent of the changes, and the effects these changes may impart on the process. Scientific judgement should determine what additional testing and validation studies are appropriate to justify a change in a validated process.

13.14   When implementing approved changes, measures should be taken to ensure that all documents affected by the changes are revised.

13.15   After the change has been implemented, there should be an evaluation of the first batches produced or tested under the change.

13.16   The potential for critical changes to affect established retest or expiry dates should be evaluated. If necessary, samples of the intermediate or API produced by the modified process can be placed on an accelerated stability program and/or can be added to the stability monitoring program.

13.17   Current dosage form manufacturers should be notified of changes from established production and process control procedures that can impact the quality of the API.

14. Rejection and re-use of materials

14.1 Rejection

14.10   Intermediates and APIs failing to meet established specifications should be identified as such and quarantined. These intermediates or APIs can be reprocessed or reworked as described below. The final disposition of rejected materials should be recorded.

14.2 Reprocessing

14.20   Introducing an intermediate or API, including one that does not conform to standards or specifications, back into the process and reprocessing by repeating a crystallization step or other appropriate chemical or physical manipulation steps (e.g., distillation, filtration, chromatography, milling) that are part of the established manufacturing process is generally considered acceptable. However, if such reprocessing is used for a majority of batches, such reprocessing should be included as part of the standard manufacturing process.

14.21   Continuation of a process step after an in-process control test has shown that the step is incomplete is considered to be part of the normal process. This is not considered to be reprocessing.

14.22   Introducing unreacted material back into a process and repeating a chemical reaction is considered to be reprocessing unless it is part of the established process. Such reprocessing should be preceded by careful evaluation to ensure that the quality of the intermediate or API is not adversely impacted due to the potential formation of by-products and over-reacted materials.

14.3 Reworking

14.30   Before a decision is taken to rework batches that do not conform to established standards or specifications, an investigation into the reason for non-conformance should be performed.

14.31   Batches that have been reworked should be subjected to appropriate evaluation, testing, stability testing if warranted, and documentation to show that the reworked product is of equivalent quality to that produced by the original process. Concurrent validation is often the appropriate validation approach for rework procedures. This allows a protocol to define the rework procedure, how it will be carried out, and the expected results. If there is only one batch to be reworked, then a report can be written and the batch released once it is found to be acceptable.

14.32   Procedures should provide for comparing the impurity profile of each reworked batch against batches manufactured by the established process. Where routine analytical methods are inadequate to characterize the reworked batch, additional methods should be used.

14.4 Recovery of Materials and Solvents

14.40   Recovery (e.g. from mother liquor or filtrates) of reactants, intermediates, or the API is considered acceptable, provided that approved procedures exist for the recovery and the recovered materials meet specifications suitable for their intended use.

14.41   Solvents can be recovered and reused in the same processes or in different processes, provided that the recovery procedures are controlled and monitored to ensure that solvents meet appropriate standards before reuse or co-mingling with other approved materials.

14.42   Fresh and recovered solvents and reagents can be combined if adequate testing has shown their suitability for all manufacturing processes in which they may be used.

14.43   The use of recovered solvents, mother liquors, and other recovered materials should be adequately documented.

ICH Q7A

14.5 Returns

14.50 Returned intermediates or APIs should be identified as such and quarantined.

14.51 If the conditions under which returned intermediates or APIs have been stored or shipped before or during their return or the condition of their containers casts doubt on their quality, the returned intermediates or APIs should be reprocessed, reworked, or destroyed, as appropriate.

14.52 Records of returned intermediates or APIs should be maintained. For each return, documentation should include:

- Name and address of the consignee

- Intermediate or API, batch number, and quantity returned

- Reason for return

- Use or disposal of the returned intermediate or API

15. Complaints and recalls

15.10 All quality related complaints, whether received orally or in writing, should be recorded and investigated according to a written procedure.

15.11 Complaint records should include:

- Name and address of complainant;

- Name (and, where appropriate, title) and phone number of person submitting the complaint;

- Complaint nature (including name and batch number of the API);

- Date complaint is received;

- Action initially taken (including dates and identity of person taking the action);

- Any follow-up action taken;

- Response provided to the originator of complaint (including date response sent); and

- Final decision on intermediate or API batch or lot.

15.12 Records of complaints should be retained in order to evaluate trends, product-related frequencies, and severity with a view to taking additional, and if appropriate, immediate corrective action.

15.13 There should be a written procedure that defines the circumstances under which a recall of an intermediate or API should be considered.

15.14 The recall procedure should designate who should be involved in evaluating the information, how a recall should be initiated, who should be informed about the recall, and how the recalled material should be treated.

15.15   In the event of a serious or potentially life-threatening situation, local, national, and/or international authorities should be informed and their advice sought.

16. Contract manufacturers (including laboratories)

16.10   All contract manufacturers (including laboratories) should comply with the GMP defined in this guidance document. Special consideration should be given to the prevention of cross-contamination and to maintaining traceability.

16.11   Contract manufacturers (including laboratories) should be evaluated by the contract giver to ensure GMP compliance of the specific operations occurring at the contract sites.

16.12   There should be a written and approved contract or formal agreement between the contract giver and the contract acceptor that defines in detail the GMP responsibilities, including the quality measures, of each party.

16.13   The contract should permit the contract giver to audit the contract acceptor's facilities for compliance with GMP.

16.14   Where subcontracting is allowed, the contract acceptor should not pass to a third party any of the work entrusted to him under the contract without the contract giver's prior evaluation and approval of the arrangements.

16.15   Manufacturing and laboratory records should be kept at the site where the activity occurs and be readily available.

16.16   Changes in the process, equipment, test methods, specifications, or other contractual requirements should not be made unless the contract giver is informed and approves the changes.

17. Agents, Brokers, Traders, Distributors, Repackers, and Relabellers

17.1 Applicability

17.10   This section applies to any party other than the original manufacturer who may trade and/or take possession, repack, relabel, manipulate, distribute or store an API or intermediate.

17.11   All agents, brokers, traders, distributors, repackers, and relabellers should comply with GMP as defined in this guidance document.

17.2 Traceability of Distributed APIs and Intermediates

17.20   Agents, brokers, traders, distributors, repackers, or relabellers should maintain complete traceability of APIs and intermediates that they distribute. Documents that should be retained and available include:

- Identity of original manufacturer
- Address of original manufacturer

ICH Q7A

- Purchase orders
- Bills of lading (transportation documentation)
- Receipt documents
- Name or designation of API or intermediate
- Manufacturer's batch number
- Transportation and distribution records
- All authentic Certificates of Analysis, including those of the original manufacturer
- Retest or expiry date

17.3 Quality Management

17.30   Agents, brokers, traders, distributors, repackers, or relabellers should establish, document and implement an effective system of managing quality, as specified in Section 2.

17.4 Repackaging, Relabelling and Holding of APIs and Intermediates

17.40   Repackaging, relabelling and holding of APIs and intermediates should be performed under appropriate GMP controls, as stipulated in this guidance document, to avoid mix-ups and loss of API or intermediate identity or purity.

17.41   Repackaging should be conducted under appropriate environmental conditions to avoid contamination and cross-contamination.

17.5 Stability

17.50   Stability studies to justify assigned expiration or retest dates should be conducted if the API or intermediate is repackaged in a different type of container than that used by the API or intermediate manufacturer.

17.6 Transfer of Information

17.60   Agents, brokers, distributors, repackers, or relabellers should transfer all quality or regulatory information received from an API or intermediate manufacturer to the customer, and from the customer to the API or intermediate manufacturer.

17.61   The agent, broker, trader, distributor, repacker, or relabeller who supplies the API or intermediate to the customer should provide the name of the original API or intermediate manufacturer and the batch number(s) supplied.

17.62   The agent should also provide the identity of the original API or intermediate manufacturer to regulatory authorities upon request. The original manufacturer can respond to the regulatory authority directly or through its authorized agents, depending on the legal relationship between the authorized agents and the original API or intermediate manufacturer. (In this context "authorized" refers to authorized by the manufacturer.)

17.63   The specific guidance for Certificates of Analysis included in Section 11.4 should be met.

17.7 Handling of Complaints and Recalls

17.70   Agents, brokers, traders, distributors, repackers, or relabellers should maintain records of complaints and recalls, as specified in Section 15, for all complaints and recalls that come to their attention.

17.71   If the situation warrants, the agents, brokers, traders, distributors, repackers, or relabellers should review the complaint with the original API or intermediate manufacturer in order to determine whether any further action, either with other customers who may have received this API or intermediate or with the regulatory authority, or both, should be initiated. The investigation into the cause for the complaint or recall should be conducted and documented by the appropriate party.

17.72   Where a complaint is referred to the original API or intermediate manufacturer, the record maintained by the agents, brokers, traders, distributors, repackers, or relabellers should include any response received from the original API or intermediate manufacturer (including date and information provided).

17.8 Handling of Returns

17.80   Returns should be handled as specified in Section 14.52. The agents, brokers, traders, distributors, repackers, or relabellers should maintain documentation of returned APIs and intermediates.

18. Specific guidance for apis manufactured by cell culture/fermentation

18.1 General

18.10   Section 18 is intended to address specific controls for APIs or intermediates manufactured by cell culture or fermentation using natural or recombinant organisms and that have not been covered adequately in the previous sections. It is not intended to be a stand-alone Section. In general, the GMP principles in the other sections of this document apply. Note that the principles of fermentation for "classical" processes for production of small molecules and for processes using recombinant and non-recombinant organisms for production of proteins and/or polypeptides are the same, although the degree of control will differ. Where practical, this section will address these differences. In general, the degree of control for biotechnological processes used to produce proteins and polypeptides is greater than that for classical fermentation processes.

18.11   The term "biotechnological process" (biotech) refers to the use of cells or organisms that have been generated or modified by recombinant DNA, hybridoma or other technology to produce APIs. The APIs produced by biotechnological processes normally consist of high molecular weight substances, such as proteins and polypeptides, for which specific guidance is given in this Section. Certain APIs of low molecular weight, such as antibiotics, amino acids, vitamins, and carbohydrates, can also be produced

ICH Q7A

by recombinant DNA technology. The level of control for these types of APIs is similar to that employed for classical fermentation.

18.12 The term "classical fermentation" refers to processes that use microorganisms existing in nature and/or modified by conventional methods (e.g. irradiation or chemical mutagenesis) to produce APIs. APIs produced by "classical fermentation" are normally low molecular weight products such as antibiotics, amino acids, vitamins, and carbohydrates.

18.13 Production of APIs or intermediates from cell culture or fermentation involves biological processes such as cultivation of cells or extraction and purification of material from living organisms. Note that there may be additional process steps, such as physicochemical modification, that are part of the manufacturing process. The raw materials used (media, buffer components) may provide the potential for growth of microbiological contaminants. Depending on the source, method of preparation, and the intended use of the API or intermediate, control of bioburden, viral contamination, and/or endotoxins during manufacturing and monitoring of the process at appropriate stages may be necessary.

18.14 Appropriate controls should be established at all stages of manufacturing to assure intermediate and/or API quality. While this guidance document starts at the cell culture/fermentation step, prior steps (e.g. cell banking) should be performed under appropriate process controls. This guidance document covers cell culture/fermentation from the point at which a vial of the cell bank is retrieved for use in manufacturing.

18.15 Appropriate equipment and environmental controls should be used to minimize the risk of contamination. The acceptance criteria for quality of the environment and the frequency of monitoring should depend on the step in production and the production conditions (open, closed, or contained systems).

18.16 In general, process controls should take into account:

- Maintenance of the Working Cell Bank (where appropriate);

- Proper inoculation and expansion of the culture;

- Control of the critical operating parameters during fermentation/cell culture;

- Monitoring of the process for cell growth, viability (for most cell culture processes) and productivity where appropriate;

- Harvest and purification procedures that remove cells, cellular debris and media components while protecting the intermediate or API from contamination (particularly of a microbiological nature) and from loss of quality;

- Monitoring of bioburden and, where needed, endotoxin levels at appropriate stages of production; and

- Viral safety concerns as described in ICH Guidance Q5A Quality of Biotechnological Products: Viral Safety Evaluation of Biotechnology Products Derived from Cell Lines of Human or Animal Origin.

18.17   Where appropriate, the removal of media components, host cell proteins, other process-related impurities, product-related impurities and contaminants should be demonstrated.

18.2 Cell Bank Maintenance and Record Keeping

18.20   Access to cell banks should be limited to authorized personnel.

18.21   Cell banks should be maintained under storage conditions designed to maintain viability and prevent contamination.

18.22   Records of the use of the vials from the cell banks and storage conditions should be maintained.

18.23   Where appropriate, cell banks should be periodically monitored to determine suitability for use.

18.24   See ICH Guidance Q5D Quality of Biotechnological Products: Derivation and Characterization of Cell Substrates Used for Production of Biotechnological/Biological Products for a more complete discussion of cell banking.

18.3 Cell Culture/Fermentation

18.30   Where aseptic addition of cell substrates, media, buffers, and gases is needed, closed or contained systems should be used where possible. If the inoculation of the initial vessel or subsequent transfers or additions (media, buffers) are performed in open vessels, there should be controls and procedures in place to minimize the risk of contamination.

18.31   Where the quality of the API can be affected by microbial contamination, manipulations using open vessels should be performed in a biosafety cabinet or similarly controlled environment.

18.32   Personnel should be appropriately gowned and take special precautions handling the cultures.

18.33   Critical operating parameters (for example temperature, pH, agitation rates, addition of gases, pressure) should be monitored to ensure consistency with the established process. Cell growth, viability (for most cell culture processes), and, where appropriate, productivity should also be monitored. Critical parameters will vary from one process to another, and for classical fermentation, certain parameters (cell viability, for example) may not need to be monitored.

18.34   Cell culture equipment should be cleaned and sterilized after use. As appropriate, fermentation equipment should be cleaned, and sanitized or sterilized.

18.35   Culture media should be sterilized before use when appropriate to protect the quality of the API.

18.36   There should be appropriate procedures in place to detect contamination and determine the course of action to be taken. This should include procedures to determine the impact of the contamination on the

ICH Q7A

product and those to decontaminate the equipment and return it to a condition to be used in subsequent batches. Foreign organisms observed during fermentation processes should be identified as appropriate and the effect of their presence on product quality should be assessed, if necessary. The results of such assessments should be taken into consideration in the disposition of the material produced.

18.37   Records of contamination events should be maintained.

18.38   Shared (multi-product) equipment may warrant additional testing after cleaning between product campaigns, as appropriate, to minimize the risk of cross-contamination.

18.4 Harvesting, Isolation and Purification

18.40   Harvesting steps, either to remove cells or cellular components or to collect cellular components after disruption, should be performed in equipment and areas designed to minimize the risk of contamination.

18.41   Harvest and purification procedures that remove or inactivate the producing organism, cellular debris and media components (while minimizing degradation, contamination, and loss of quality) should be adequate to ensure that the intermediate or API is recovered with consistent quality.

18.42   All equipment should be properly cleaned and, as appropriate, sanitized after use. Multiple successive batching without cleaning can be used if intermediate or API quality is not compromised.

18.43   If open systems are used, purification should be performed under environmental conditions appropriate for the preservation of product quality.

18.44   Additional controls, such as the use of dedicated chromatography resins or additional testing, may be appropriate if equipment is to be used for multiple products.

18.5 Viral Removal/Inactivation steps

18.50   See the ICH Guidance Q5A Quality of Biotechnological Products: Viral Safety Evaluation of Biotechnology Products Derived from Cell Lines of Human or Animal Origin for more specific information.

18.51   Viral removal and viral inactivation steps are critical processing steps for some processes and should be performed within their validated parameters.

18.52   Appropriate precautions should be taken to prevent potential viral contamination from pre-viral to post-viral removal/inactivation steps. Therefore, open processing should be performed in areas that are separate from other processing activities and have separate air handling units.

18.53   The same equipment is not normally used for different purification steps. However, if the same equipment is to be used, the equipment should be appropriately cleaned and sanitized before reuse. Appropriate precautions should be taken to prevent potential virus carry-over (e.g. through equipment or environment) from previous steps.

19. APIs For use in clinical trials

19.1 General

19.10   Not all the controls in the previous sections of this guidance document are appropriate for the manufacture of a new API for investigational use during its development. Section 19 provides specific guidance unique to these circumstances.

19.11   The controls used in the manufacture of APIs for use in clinical trials should be consistent with the stage of development of the drug product incorporating the API. Process and test procedures should be flexible to provide for changes as knowledge of the process increases and clinical testing of a drug product progresses from pre-clinical stages through clinical stages. Once drug development reaches the stage where the API is produced for use in drug products intended for clinical trials, manufacturers should ensure that APIs are manufactured in suitable facilities using appropriate production and control procedures to ensure the quality of the API.

19.2 Quality

19.20   Appropriate GMP concepts should be applied in the production of APIs for use in clinical trials with a suitable mechanism of approval of each batch.

19.21   A quality unit(s) independent from production should be established for the approval or rejection of each batch of API for use in clinical trials.

19.22   Some of the testing functions commonly performed by the quality unit(s) can be performed within other organizational units.

19.23   Quality measures should include a system for testing of raw materials, packaging materials, intermediates, and APIs.

19.24   Process and quality problems should be evaluated.

19.25   Labelling for APIs intended for use in clinical trials should be appropriately controlled and should identify the material as being for investigational use.

19.3 Equipment and Facilities

19.30   During all phases of clinical development, including the use of small-scale facilities or laboratories to manufacture batches of APIs for use in clinical trials, procedures should be in place to ensure that equipment is calibrated, clean and suitable for its intended use.

19.31   Procedures for the use of facilities should ensure that materials are handled in a manner that minimizes the risk of contamination and cross-contamination.

19.4 Control of Raw Materials

19.40   Raw materials used in production of APIs for use in clinical trials should be evaluated by testing, or received with a supplier's analysis and subjected

ICH Q7A

to identity testing. When a material is considered hazardous, a supplier's analysis should suffice.

19.41   In some instances, the suitability of a raw material can be determined before use based on acceptability in small-scale reactions (i.e., use testing) rather than on analytical testing alone.

19.5 Production

19.50   The production of APIs for use in clinical trials should be documented in laboratory notebooks, batch records, or by other appropriate means. These documents should include information on the use of production materials, equipment, processing, and scientific observations.

19.51   Expected yields can be more variable and less defined than the expected yields used in commercial processes. Investigations into yield variations are not expected.

19.6 Validation

19.60   Process validation for the production of APIs for use in clinical trials is normally inappropriate, where a single API batch is produced or where process changes during API development make batch replication difficult or inexact. The combination of controls, calibration, and, where appropriate, equipment qualification assures API quality during this development phase.

19.61   Process validation should be conducted in accordance with Section 12 when batches are produced for commercial use, even when such batches are produced on a pilot or small scale.

19.7 Changes

19.70   Changes are expected during development, as knowledge is gained and the production is scaled up. Every change in the production, specifications, or test procedures should be adequately recorded.

19.8 Laboratory Controls

19.80   While analytical methods performed to evaluate a batch of API for clinical trials may not yet be validated, they should be scientifically sound.

19.81   A system for retaining reserve samples of all batches should be in place. This system should ensure that a sufficient quantity of each reserve sample is retained for an appropriate length of time after approval, termination, or discontinuation of an application.

19.82   Expiry and retest dating as defined in Section 11.6 applies to existing APIs used in clinical trials. For new APIs, Section 11.6 does not normally apply in early stages of clinical trials.

19.9 Documentation

19.90   A system should be in place to ensure that information gained during the development and the manufacture of APIs for use in clinical trials is documented and available.

19.91   The development and implementation of the analytical methods used to support the release of a batch of API for use in clinical trials should be appropriately documented.

19.92   A system for retaining production and control records and documents should be used. This system should ensure that records and documents are retained for an appropriate length of time after the approval, termination, or discontinuation of an application.

20. Glossary

Acceptance Criteria

Numerical limits, ranges, or other suitable measures for acceptance of test results.

Active Pharmaceutical Ingredient (API) (or Drug Substance)

Any substance or mixture of substances intended to be used in the manufacture of a drug (medicinal) product and that, when used in the production of a drug, becomes an active ingredient of the drug product. Such substances are intended to furnish pharmacological activity or other direct effect in the diagnosis, cure, mitigation, treatment, or prevention of disease or to affect the structure and function of the body.

API Starting Material

A raw material, intermediate, or an API that is used in the production of an API and that is incorporated as a significant structural fragment into the structure of the API. An API Starting Material can be an article of commerce, a material purchased from one or more suppliers under contract or commercial agreement, or produced in-house. API Starting Materials are normally of defined chemical properties and structure.

Batch (or Lot)

A specific quantity of material produced in a process or series of processes so that it is expected to be homogeneous within specified limits. In the case of continuous production, a batch may correspond to a defined fraction of the production. The batch size can be defined either by a fixed quantity or by the amount produced in a fixed time interval.

Batch Number (or Lot Number)

A unique combination of numbers, letters, and/or symbols that identifies a batch (or lot) and from which the production and distribution history can be determined.

Bioburden

The level and type (e.g. objectionable or not) of micro-organisms that can be present in raw materials, API starting materials, intermediates or APIs. Bioburden should not be considered contamination unless the levels have been exceeded or defined objectionable organisms have been detected.

ICH Q7A

Calibration

> The demonstration that a particular instrument or device produces results within specified limits by comparison with those produced by a reference or traceable standard over an appropriate range of measurements.

Computer System

> A group of hardware components and associated software, designed and assembled to perform a specific function or group of functions.

Computerized System

> A process or operation integrated with a computer system.

Contamination

> The undesired introduction of impurities of a chemical or microbiological nature, or of foreign matter, into or onto a raw material, intermediate, or API during production, sampling, packaging or repackaging, storage or transport.

Contract Manufacturer

> A manufacturer performing some aspect of manufacturing on behalf of the original manufacturer.

Critical

> Describes a process step, process condition, test requirement, or other relevant parameter or item that must be controlled within predetermined criteria to ensure that the API meets its specification.

Cross-Contamination

> Contamination of a material or product with another material or product.

Deviation

> Departure from an approved instruction or established standard.

Drug (Medicinal) Product

> The dosage form in the final immediate packaging intended for marketing. (Reference Q1A)

Drug Substance

> See Active Pharmaceutical Ingredient

Expiry Date (or Expiration Date)

> The date placed on the container/labels of an API designating the time during which the API is expected to remain within established shelf life specifications if stored under defined conditions, and after which it should not be used.

Impurity

> Any component present in the intermediate or API that is not the desired entity.

Impurity Profile

> A description of the identified and unidentified impurities present in an API.

In-Process Control (or Process Control)

> Checks performed during production in order to monitor and, if appropriate, to adjust the process and/or to ensure that the intermediate or API conforms to its specifications.

Intermediate

> A material produced during steps of the processing of an API that undergoes further molecular change or purification before it becomes an API. Intermediates may or may not be isolated. (Note: this guidance document only addresses those intermediates produced after the point that the company has defined as the point at which the production of the API begins.)

Lot

> See Batch

Lot Number

> See Batch Number

Manufacture

> All operations of receipt of materials, production, packaging, repackaging, labelling, relabelling, quality control, release, storage, and distribution of APIs and related controls.

Material

> A general term used to denote raw materials (starting materials, reagents, solvents), process aids, intermediates, APIs and packaging and labelling materials.

Mother Liquor

> The residual liquid which remains after the crystallization or isolation processes. A mother liquor may contain unreacted materials, intermediates, levels of the API and/or impurities. It may be used for further processing.

Packaging Material

> Any material intended to protect an intermediate or API during storage and transport.

ICH Q7A

Procedure

A documented description of the operations to be performed, the precautions to be taken and measures to be applied directly or indirectly related to the manufacture of an intermediate or API.

Process Aids

Materials, excluding solvents, used as an aid in the manufacture of an intermediate or API that do not themselves participate in a chemical or biological reaction (e.g. filter aid, activated carbon, etc).

Process Control

See In-Process Control

Production

All operations involved in the preparation of an API from receipt of materials through processing and packaging of the API.

Qualification

Action of proving and documenting that equipment or ancillary systems are properly installed, work correctly, and actually lead to the expected results. Qualification is part of validation, but the individual qualification steps alone do not constitute process validation.

Quality Assurance (QA)

The sum total of the organised arrangements made with the object of ensuring that all APIs are of the quality required for their intended use and that quality systems are maintained.

Quality Control (QC)

Checking or testing that specifications are met.

Quality Unit(s)

An organizational unit independent of production which fulfills both Quality Assurance and Quality Control responsibilities. This can be in the form of separate QA and QC units or a single individual or group, depending upon the size and structure of the organization.

Quarantine

The status of materials isolated physically or by other effective means pending a decision on their subsequent approval or rejection.

Raw Material

A general term used to denote starting materials, reagents, and solvents intended for use in the production of intermediates or APIs.

Reference Standard, Primary

> A substance that has been shown by an extensive set of analytical tests to be authentic material that should be of high purity. This standard can be (1) obtained from an officially recognised source, or (2) prepared by independent synthesis, or (3) obtained from existing production material of high purity, or (4) prepared by further purification of existing production material.

Reference Standard, Secondary

> A substance of established quality and purity, as shown by comparison to a primary reference standard, used as a reference standard for routine laboratory analysis.

Reprocessing

> Introducing an intermediate or API, including one that does not conform to standards or specifications, back into the process and repeating a crystallization step or other appropriate chemical or physical manipulation steps (e.g., distillation, filtration, chromatography milling) that are part of the established manufacturing process. Continuation of a process step after an in-process control test has shown that the step is incomplete is considered to be part of the normal process, and not reprocessing.

Retest Date

> The date when a material should be re-examined to ensure that it is still suitable for use.

Reworking

> Subjecting an intermediate or API that does not conform to standards or specifications to one or more processing steps that are different from the established manufacturing process to obtain acceptable quality ntermediate or API (e.g., recrystallizing with a different solvent).

Signature (signed)

> See definition for signed

Signed (signature)

> The record of the individual who performed a particular action or review. This record can be initials, full handwritten signature, personal seal, or authenticated and secure electronic signature.

Solvent

> An inorganic or organic liquid used as a vehicle for the preparation of solutions or suspensions in the manufacture of an intermediate or API.

ICH Q7A

Specification

A list of tests, references to analytical procedures, and appropriate acceptance criteria that are numerical limits, ranges, or other criteria for the test described. It establishes the set of criteria to which a material should conform to be considered acceptable for its intended use. "Conformance to specification" means that the material, when tested according to the listed analytical procedures, will meet the listed acceptance criteria.

Validation

A documented program that provides a high degree of assurance that a specific process, method, or system will consistently produce a result meeting pre-determined acceptance criteria.

Validation Protocol

A written plan stating how validation will be conducted and defining acceptance criteria. For example, the protocol for a manufacturing process identifies processing equipment, critical process parameters/operating ranges, product characteristics, sampling, test data to be collected, number of validation runs, and acceptable test results.

Yield, Expected

The quantity of material or the percentage of theoretical yield anticipated at any appropriate phase of production based on previous laboratory, pilot scale, or manufacturing data.

Yield, Theoretical

The quantity that would be produced at any appropriate phase of production, based upon the quantity of material to be used, in the absence of any loss or error in actual production

ICH Q9: Quality Risk Management

ICH Harmonised Tripartite Guideline

Quality Risk Management
Q9

Current Step 4 version dated 9 November 2005

Having reached Step 4 of the ICH Process at the ICH Steering Committee meeting on 9 November 2005, this guideline is recommended for adoption to the three regulatory parties to ICH

ICH Q9: Quality Risk Management[85]

Q9
Document History

First Codification	History	Date	New Codification November 2005
Q9	Approval by the Steering Committee under *Step 2* and release for public consultation.	22 March 2005	Q9
Q9	Approval by the Steering Committee of *Post Step 2* correction	15 June 2005	Q9

Current *Step 4* version

Q9	Approval by the Steering Committee under *Step 4* and recommendation for adoption to the three ICH regulatory bodies.	9 November 2005	Q9

1. Introduction

Risk management principles are effectively utilized in many areas of business and government including finance, insurance, occupational safety, public health, pharmacovigilance, and by agencies regulating these industries. Although there are some examples of the use of quality risk management in the pharmaceutical industry today, they are limited and do not represent the full contributions that risk management has to offer. In addition, the importance of quality systems has been recognized in the pharmaceutical industry and it is becoming evident that quality risk management is a valuable component of an effective quality system.

It is commonly understood that risk is defined as the combination of the probability of occurrence of harm and the severity of that harm. However, achieving a shared understanding of the application of risk management among diverse stakeholders is difficult because each stakeholder might perceive different potential harms, place a different probability on each harm occurring and

---

[85] Available from the Health Canada website at http://www.ich.org/LOB/media/MEDIA1957.pdf

attribute different severities to each harm. In relation to pharmaceuticals, although there are a variety of stakeholders, including patients and medical practitioners as well as government and industry, the protection of the patient by managing the risk to quality should be considered of prime importance.

The manufacturing and use of a drug (medicinal) product, including its components, necessarily entail some degree of risk. The risk to its quality is just one component of the overall risk. It is important to understand that product quality should be maintained throughout the product lifecycle such that the attributes that are important to the quality of the drug (medicinal) product remain consistent with those used in the clinical studies. An effective quality risk management approach can further ensure the high quality of the drug (medicinal) product to the patient by providing a proactive means to identify and control potential quality issues during development and manufacturing. Additionally, use of quality risk management can improve the decision making if a quality problem arises. Effective quality risk management can facilitate better and more informed decisions, can provide regulators with greater assurance of a company's ability to deal with potential risks and can beneficially affect the extent and level of direct regulatory oversight.

The purpose of this document is to offer a systematic approach to quality risk management. It serves as a foundation or resource document that is independent of, yet supports, other ICH Quality documents and complements existing quality practices, requirements, standards, and guidelines within the pharmaceutical industry and regulatory environment. It specifically provides guidance on the principles and some of the tools of quality risk management that can enable more effective and consistent risk based decisions, both by regulators and industry, regarding the quality of drug substances and drug (medicinal) products across the product lifecycle. It is not intended to create any new expectations beyond the current regulatory requirements.

It is neither always appropriate nor always necessary to use a formal risk management process (using recognized tools and/ or internal procedures e.g., standard operating procedures). The use of informal risk management processes (using empirical tools and/ or internal procedures) can also be considered acceptable. Appropriate use of quality risk management can facilitate but does not obviate industry's obligation to comply with regulatory requirements and does not replace appropriate communications between industry and regulators.

2. Scope

This guideline provides principles and examples of tools for quality risk management that can be applied to different aspects of pharmaceutical quality. These aspects include development, manufacturing, distribution, and the inspection and submission/review processes throughout the lifecycle of drug substances, drug (medicinal) products, biological and biotechnological products (including the use of raw materials, solvents, excipients, packaging and labeling materials in drug (medicinal) products, biological and biotechnological products).

3. Principles of Quality Risk Management

Two primary principles of quality risk management are:

- The evaluation of the risk to quality should be based on scientific knowledge and ultimately link to the protection of the patient; and

- The level of effort, formality and documentation of the quality risk management process should be commensurate with the level of risk.

4. General Quality Risk Management Process

Quality risk management is a systematic process for the assessment, control, communication and review of risks to the quality of the drug (medicinal) product across the product lifecycle. A model for quality risk management is outlined in the diagram (Figure 1). Other models could be used. The emphasis on each component of the framework might differ from case to case but a robust process will incorporate consideration of all the elements at a level of detail that is commensurate with the specific risk.

Figure 1: Overview of a typical quality risk management process

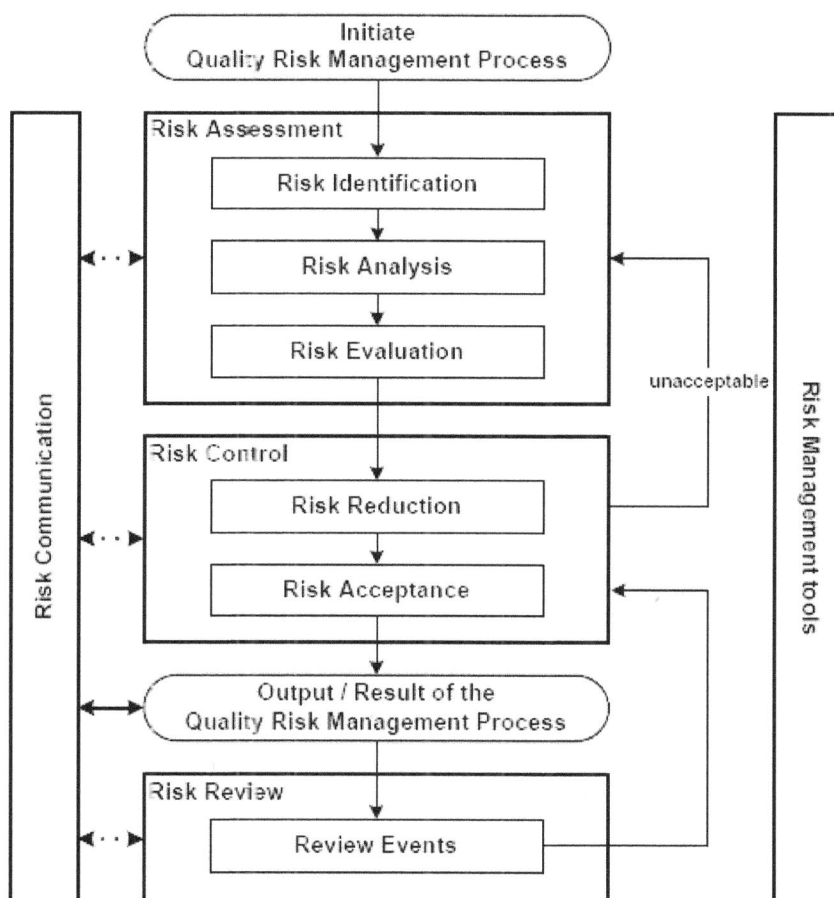

Decision nodes are not shown in the diagram above because decisions can occur at any point in the process. These decisions might be to return to the previous step and seek further information, to adjust the risk models or even to terminate the risk management process based upon information that supports such a decision. Note: "unacceptable" in the flowchart does not only refer to statutory, legislative or regulatory requirements, but also to the need to revisit the risk assessment process.

4.1 Responsibilities

Quality risk management activities are usually, but not always, undertaken by interdisciplinary teams. When teams are formed, they should include experts from the appropriate areas (e.g., quality unit, business development, engineering, regulatory affairs, production operations, sales and marketing, legal, statistics and clinical) in addition to individuals who are knowledgeable about the quality risk management process.

Decision makers should:

- take responsibility for coordinating quality risk management across various functions and departments of their organization; and
- assure that a quality risk management process is defined, deployed and reviewed and that adequate resources are available.

4.2 Initiating a Quality Risk Management Process

Quality risk management should include systematic processes designed to coordinate, facilitate and improve science-based decision making with respect to risk. Possible steps used to initiate and plan a quality risk management process might include the following:

- Define the problem and/or risk question, including pertinent assumptions identifying the potential for risk;
- Assemble background information and/ or data on the potential hazard, harm or human health impact relevant to the risk assessment;
- Identify a leader and necessary resources;
- Specify a timeline, deliverables and appropriate level of decision making for the risk management process.

4.3 Risk Assessment

Risk assessment consists of the identification of hazards and the analysis and evaluation of risks associated with exposure to those hazards (as defined below). Quality risk assessments begin with a well-defined problem description or risk question. When the risk in question is well defined, an appropriate risk management tool (see examples in section 5) and the types of information needed to address the risk question will be more readily identifiable. As an aid to clearly defining the risk(s) for risk assessment purposes, three fundamental questions are often helpful:

1. What might go wrong?

2. What is the likelihood (probability) it will go wrong?

3. What are the consequences (severity)?

Risk identification is a systematic use of information to identify hazards referring to the risk question or problem description. Information can include historical data, theoretical analysis, informed opinions, and the concerns of stakeholders. Risk identification addresses the "What might go wrong?" question, including identifying the possible consequences. This provides the basis for further steps in the quality risk management process.

Risk analysis is the estimation of the risk associated with the identified hazards. It is the qualitative or quantitative process of linking the likelihood of occurrence and severity of harms. In some risk management tools, the ability to detect the harm (detectability) also factors in the estimation of risk.

Risk evaluation compares the identified and analyzed risk against given risk criteria. Risk evaluations consider the strength of evidence for all three of the fundamental questions.

In doing an effective risk assessment, the robustness of the data set is important because it determines the quality of the output. Revealing assumptions and reasonable sources of uncertainty will enhance confidence in this output and/or help identify its limitations. Uncertainty is due to combination of incomplete knowledge about a process and its expected or unexpected variability. Typical sources of uncertainty include gaps in knowledge gaps in pharmaceutical science and process understanding, sources of harm (e.g., failure modes of a process, sources of variability), and probability of detection of problems.

The output of a risk assessment is either a quantitative estimate of risk or a qualitative description of a range of risk. When risk is expressed quantitatively, a numerical probability is used. Alternatively, risk can be expressed using qualitative descriptors, such as "high", "medium", or "low", which should be defined in as much detail as possible. Sometimes a "risk score" is used to further define descriptors in risk ranking. In quantitative risk assessments, a risk estimate provides the likelihood of a specific consequence, given a set of risk-generating circumstances. Thus, quantitative risk estimation is useful for one particular consequence at a time. Alternatively, some risk management tools use a relative risk measure to combine multiple levels of severity and probability into an overall estimate of relative risk. The intermediate steps within a scoring process can sometimes employ quantitative risk estimation.

4.4 Risk Control

Risk control includes decision making to reduce and/or accept risks. The purpose of risk control is to reduce the risk to an acceptable level. The amount of effort used for risk control should be proportional to the significance of the risk. Decision makers might use different processes, including benefit-cost analysis, for understanding the optimal level of risk control.

Risk control might focus on the following questions:

* Is the risk above an acceptable level?

* What can be done to reduce or eliminate risks?

* What is the appropriate balance among benefits, risks and resources?

* Are new risks introduced as a result of the identified risks being controlled?

it exceeds a specified (acceptable) level (see Fig. 1). Risk reduction might include actions taken to mitigate the severity and probability of harm. Processes that improve the detectability of hazards and quality risks might also be used as part of a risk control strategy. The implementation of risk reduction measures can introduce new risks into the system or increase the significance of other existing risks. Hence, it might be appropriate to revisit the risk assessment to identify and evaluate any possible change in risk after implementing a risk reduction process.

Risk acceptance is a decision to accept risk. Risk acceptance can be a formal decision to accept the residual risk or it can be a passive decision in which residual risks are not specified. For some types of harms, even the best quality risk management practices might not entirely eliminate risk. In these

---

circumstances, it might be agreed that an appropriate quality risk management strategy has been applied and that quality risk is reduced to a specified (acceptable) level. This (specified) acceptable level will depend on many parameters and should be decided on a case-by-case basis.

4.5 Risk Communication

Risk communication is the sharing of information about risk and risk management between the decision makers and others. Parties can communicate at any stage of the risk management process (see Fig. 1: dashed arrows). The output/result of the quality risk management process should be appropriately communicated and documented (see Fig. 1: solid arrows). Communications might include those among interested parties; e.g., regulators and industry, industry and the patient, within a company, industry or regulatory authority, etc. The included information might relate to the existence, nature, form, probability, severity, acceptability, control, treatment, detectability or other aspects of risks to quality. Communication need not be carried out for each and every risk acceptance. Between the industry and regulatory authorities, communication concerning quality risk management decisions might be effected through existing channels as specified in regulations and guidances.

4.6 Risk Review

Risk management should be an ongoing part of the quality management process. A mechanism to review or monitor events should be implemented.

The output/results of the risk management process should be reviewed to take into account new knowledge and experience. Once a quality risk management process has been initiated, that process should continue to be utilized for events that might impact the original quality risk management decision, whether these events are planned (e.g., results of product review, inspections, audits, change control) or unplanned (e.g., root cause from failure investigations, recall). The frequency of any review should be based upon the level of risk. Risk review might include reconsideration of risk acceptance decisions (section 4.4).

5. Risk Management Methodology

Quality risk management supports a scientific and practical approach to decision-making. It provides documented, transparent and reproducible methods to accomplish steps of the quality risk management process based on current knowledge about assessing the probability, severity and sometimes detectability of the risk.

Traditionally, risks to quality have been assessed and managed in a variety of informal ways (empirical and/ or internal procedures) based on, for example, compilation of observations, trends and other information. Such approaches continue to provide useful information that might support topics such as handling of complaints, quality defects, deviations and allocation of resources.

Additionally, the pharmaceutical industry and regulators can assess and manage risk using recognized risk management tools and/ or internal procedures (e.g., standard operating procedures). Below is a non-exhaustive list of some of these tools (further details in Annex 1 and chapter 8):

- Basic risk management facilitation methods (flowcharts, check sheets etc.);
- Failure Mode Effects Analysis (FMEA);
- Failure Mode, Effects and Criticality Analysis (FMECA);

- Fault Tree Analysis (FTA);

- Hazard Analysis and Critical Control Points (HACCP);

- Hazard Operability Analysis (HAZOP);

- Preliminary Hazard Analysis (PHA);

- Risk ranking and filtering;

- Supporting statistical tools.

It might be appropriate to adapt these tools for use in specific areas pertaining to drug substance and drug (medicinal) product quality. Quality risk management methods and the supporting statistical tools can be used in combination (e.g., Probabilistic Risk Assessment). Combined use provides flexibility that can facilitate the application of quality risk management principles.

The degree of rigor and formality of quality risk management should reflect available knowledge and be commensurate with the complexity and/ or criticality of the issue to be addressed.

6. Integration of Quality Risk Management into Industry and Regulatory Operations

Quality risk management is a process that supports science-based and practical decisions when integrated into quality systems (see Annex II). As outlined in the introduction, appropriate use of quality risk management does not obviate industry's obligation to comply with regulatory requirements. However, effective quality risk management can facilitate better and more informed decisions, can provide regulators with greater assurance of a company's ability to deal with potential risks, and might affect the extent and level of direct regulatory oversight. In addition, quality risk management can facilitate better use of resources by all parties.

Training of both industry and regulatory personnel in quality risk management processes provides for greater understanding of decision-making processes and builds confidence in quality risk management outcomes.

Quality risk management should be integrated into existing operations and documented appropriately. Annex II provides examples of situations in which the use of the quality risk management process might provide information that could then be used in a variety of pharmaceutical operations. These examples are provided for illustrative purposes only and should not be considered a definitive or exhaustive list. These examples are not intended to create any new expectations beyond the requirements laid out in the current regulations.

Examples for industry and regulatory operations (see Annex II):

- Quality management.

Examples for industry operations and activities (see Annex II):

- Development;

- Facility, equipment and utilities;

- Materials management;

- Production;

- Laboratory control and stability testing;

- Packaging and labeling.

Examples for regulatory operations (see Annex II):

- Inspection and assessment activities.

While regulatory decisions will continue to be taken on a regional basis, a common understanding and application of quality risk management principles could facilitate mutual confidence and promote more consistent decisions among regulators on the basis of the same information. This collaboration could be important in the development of policies and guidelines that integrate and support quality risk management practices.

7. Definitions

Decision Maker(s)

Person(s) with the competence and authority to make appropriate and timely quality risk management decisions.

Detectability

The ability to discover or determine the existence, presence, or fact of a hazard.

Harm

Damage to health, including the damage that can occur from loss of product quality or availability.

Hazard

The potential source of harm (ISO/IEC Guide 51).

Product Lifecycle

All phases in the life of the product from the initial development through marketing until the product's discontinuation.

Quality

The degree to which a set of inherent properties of a product, system or process fulfills requirements (see ICH Q6A definition specifically for "quality" of drug substance and drug (medicinal) products.)

Quality Risk Management

A systematic process for the assessment, control, communication and review of risks to the quality of the drug (medicinal) product across the product lifecycle.

Quality System

The sum of all aspects of a system that implements quality policy and ensures that quality objectives are met.

Requirements

The explicit or implicit needs or expectations of the patients or their surrogates (e.g., health care professionals, regulators and legislators).

In this document, "requirements" refers not only to statutory, legislative, or regulatory requirements, but also to such needs and expectations.

Risk

The combination of the probability of occurrence of harm and the severity of that harm (ISO/IEC Guide 51).

Risk Acceptance

The decision to accept risk (ISO Guide 73).

Risk Analysis

The estimation of the risk associated with the identified hazards.

Risk Assessment

A systematic process of organizing information to support a risk decision to be made within a risk management process. It consists of the identification of hazards and the analysis and evaluation of risks associated with exposure to those hazards.

Risk Communication

The sharing of information about risk and risk management between the decision maker and other stakeholders.

Risk Control

Actions implementing risk management decisions (ISO Guide 73).

Risk Evaluation

The comparison of the estimated risk to given risk criteria using a quantitative or qualitative scale to determine the significance of the risk.

Risk Identification

The systematic use of information to identify potential sources of harm (hazards) referring to the risk question or problem description.

Risk Management

The systematic application of quality management policies, procedures, and practices to the tasks of assessing, controlling, communicating and reviewing risk.

Risk Reduction

Actions taken to lessen the probability of occurrence of harm and the severity of that harm.

Risk Review

> Review or monitoring of output/results of the risk management process considering (if appropriate) new knowledge and experience about the risk.

Severity

> A measure of the possible consequences of a hazard.

Stakeholder

> Any individual, group or organization that can affect, be affected by, or perceive itself to be affected by a risk. Decision makers might also be stakeholders. For the purposes of this guideline, the primary stakeholders are the patient, healthcare professional, regulatory authority, and industry.

Trend

> A statistical term referring to the direction or rate of change of a variable(s).

8. References

ICH Q8 Pharmaceutical Development.

ISO/IEC Guide 73:2002 - Risk Management - Vocabulary - Guidelines for use in Standards.

ISO/IEC Guide 51:1999 - Safety Aspects - Guideline for their inclusion in standards.

Process Mapping by the American Productivity & Quality Center, 2002, ISBN 1928593739.

IEC 61025 - Fault Tree Analysis (FTA).

IEC 60812 Analysis Techniques for system reliability—Procedures for failure mode and effects analysis (FMEA).

Failure Mode and Effect Analysis, FMEA from Theory to Execution, 2nd Edition 2003, D. H. Stamatis, ISBN 0873895983.

Guidelines for Failure Modes and Effects Analysis (FMEA) for Medical Devices, 2003 Dyadem Press, ISBN 0849319102.

The Basics of FMEA, Robin McDermott, Raymond J. Mikulak, Michael R. Beauregard 1996, ISBN 0527763209.

WHO Technical Report Series No 908, 2003, Annex 7 Application of Hazard Analysis and Critical Control Point (HACCP) methodology to pharmaceuticals.

IEC 61882 - Hazard Operability Analysis (HAZOP).

ISO 14971:2000 - Application of Risk Management to Medical Devices.

ISO 7870:1993 - Control Charts.

ISO 7871:1997 - Cumulative Sum Charts.

ISO 7966:1993 - Acceptance Control Charts.

ISO 8258:1991 - Shewhart Control Charts.

What is Total Quality Control?; The Japanese Way, Kaoru Ishikawa (Translated by David J. Liu), 1985, ISBN 0139524339.

Annex I: Risk Management Methods and Tools

The purpose of this annex is to provide a general overview of and references for some of the primary tools that might be used in quality risk management by industry and regulators. The references are included as an aid to gain more knowledge and detail about the particular tool. This is not an exhaustive list. It is important to note that no one tool or set of tools is applicable to every situation in which a quality risk management procedure is used.

I.1 Basic Risk Management Facilitation Methods

Some of the simple techniques that are commonly used to structure risk management by organizing data and facilitating decision-making are:

- Flowcharts;

- Check Sheets;

- Process Mapping;

- Cause and Effect Diagrams (also called an Ishikawa diagram or fish bone diagram).

I.2 Failure Mode Effects Analysis (FMEA)

FMEA (see IEC 60812) provides for an evaluation of potential failure modes for processes and their likely effect on outcomes and/or product performance. Once failure modes are established, risk reduction can be used to eliminate, contain, reduce or control the potential failures. FMEA relies on product and process understanding. FMEA methodically breaks down the analysis of complex processes into manageable steps. It is a powerful tool for summarizing the important modes of failure, factors causing these failures and the likely effects of these failures.

Potential Areas of Use(s)

FMEA can be used to prioritize risks and monitor the effectiveness of risk control activities.

FMEA can be applied to equipment and facilities and might be used to analyze a manufacturing operation and its effect on product or process. It identifies elements/operations within the system that render it vulnerable. The output/ results of FMEA can be used as a basis for design or further analysis or to guide resource deployment.

I.3 Failure Mode, Effects and Criticality Analysis (FMECA)

FMEA might be extended to incorporate an investigation of the degree of severity of the consequences, their respective probabilities of occurrence, and their detectability, thereby becoming a Failure Mode Effect and Criticality Analysis (FMECA; see IEC 60812). In order for such an analysis to be performed, the product or process specifications should be established. FMECA can identify places where additional preventive actions might be appropriate to minimize risks.

Potential Areas of Use(s)

FMECA application in the pharmaceutical industry should mostly be utilized for failures and risks associated with manufacturing processes; however, it is not limited to this application. The output of an FMECA is a relative risk "score" for each failure mode, which is used to rank the modes on a relative risk basis.

I.4 Fault Tree Analysis (FTA)

The FTA tool (see IEC 61025) is an approach that assumes failure of the functionality of a product or process. This tool evaluates system (or sub-system) failures one at a time but can combine multiple causes of failure by identifying causal chains. The results are represented pictorially in the form of a tree of fault modes. At each level in the tree, combinations of fault modes are described with logical operators (AND, OR, etc.). FTA relies on the experts' process understanding to identify causal factors.

Potential Areas of Use(s)

FTA can be used to establish the pathway to the root cause of the failure. FTA can be used to investigate complaints or deviations in order to fully understand their root cause and to ensure that intended improvements will fully resolve the issue and not lead to other issues (i.e. solve one problem yet cause a different problem). Fault Tree Analysis is an effective tool for evaluating how multiple factors affect a given issue. The output of an FTA includes a visual representation of failure modes. It is useful both for risk assessment and in developing monitoring programs.

I.5 Hazard Analysis and Critical Control Points (HACCP)

HACCP is a systematic, proactive, and preventive tool for assuring product quality, reliability, and safety (see WHO Technical Report Series No 908, 2003 Annex 7). It is a structured approach that applies technical and scientific principles to analyze, evaluate, prevent, and control the risk or adverse consequence(s) of hazard(s) due to the design, development, production, and use of products.

HACCP consists of the following seven steps:

(1) conduct a hazard analysis and identify preventive measures for each step of the process;

(2) determine the critical control points;

(3) establish critical limits;

(4) establish a system to monitor the critical control points;

(5) establish the corrective action to be taken when monitoring indicates that the critical control points are not in a state of control;

(6) establish system to verify that the HACCP system is working effectively;

(7) establish a record-keeping system.

Potential Areas of Use(s)

HACCP might be used to identify and manage risks associated with physical, chemical and biological hazards (including microbiological contamination). HACCP is most useful when product and process understanding is sufficiently comprehensive to support identification of critical control points. The output of a HACCP analysis is risk management information that facilitates monitoring of critical points not only in the manufacturing process but also in other life cycle phases.

I.6 Hazard Operability Analysis (HAZOP)

HAZOP (see IEC 61882) is based on a theory that assumes that risk events are caused by deviations from the design or operating intentions. It is a systematic brainstorming technique for identifying hazards using so-called "guide-words". "Guide-words" (e.g., No More, Other Than, Part of, etc.) are applied to relevant parameters (e.g., contamination, temperature) to help identify potential deviations from normal use or design intentions. It often uses a team of people with expertise covering the design of the process or product and its application.

Potential Areas of Use(s)

HAZOP can be applied to manufacturing processes, including outsourced production and formulation as well as the upstream suppliers, equipment and facilities for drug substances and drug (medicinal) products. It has also been used primarily in the pharmaceutical industry for evaluating process safety hazards. As is the case with HACCP, the output of a HAZOP analysis is a list of critical operations for risk management. This facilitates regular monitoring of critical points in the manufacturing process.

I.7 Preliminary Hazard Analysis (PHA)

PHA is a tool of analysis based on applying prior experience or knowledge of a hazard or failure to identify future hazards, hazardous situations and events that might cause harm, as well as to estimate their probability of occurrence for a given activity, facility, product or system. The tool consists of: 1) the identification of the possibilities that the risk event happens, 2) the qualitative evaluation of the extent of possible injury or damage to health that could result and 3) a relative ranking of the hazard using a combination of severity and likelihood of occurrence, and 4) the identification of possible remedial measures.

Potential Areas of Use(s)

PHA might be useful when analyzing existing systems or prioritizing hazards where circumstances prevent a more extensive technique from being used. It can be used for product, process and facility design as well as to evaluate the types of hazards for the general product type, then the product class, and finally the specific product. PHA is most commonly used early in the development of a project when there is little information on design details or operating procedures; thus, it will often be a precursor to further studies. Typically, hazards identified in the PHA are further assessed with other risk management tools such as those in this section.

I.8 Risk Ranking and Filtering

Risk ranking and filtering is a tool for comparing and ranking risks. Risk ranking of complex systems typically requires evaluation of multiple diverse quantitative and qualitative factors for each risk. The tool involves breaking down a basic risk question into as many components as needed to capture factors involved in the risk. These factors are combined into a single relative risk score that can then be used for ranking risks. "Filters," in the form of weighting factors or cut-offs for risk scores, can be used to scale or fit the risk ranking to management or policy objectives.

Potential Areas of Use(s)

Risk ranking and filtering can be used to prioritize manufacturing sites for inspection/audit by regulators or industry. Risk ranking methods are particularly helpful in situations in which the portfolio of risks and the underlying consequences to be managed are diverse and difficult to compare using a single tool. Risk ranking is useful when management needs to evaluate both quantitatively-assessed and qualitatively-assessed risks within the same organizational framework.

I.9 Supporting Statistical Tools

Statistical tools can support and facilitate quality risk management. They can enable effective data assessment, aid in determining the significance of the data set(s), and facilitate more reliable decision making. A listing of some of the principal statistical tools commonly used in the pharmaceutical industry is provided:

- Control Charts, for example:
    - Acceptance Control Charts (see ISO 7966);
    - Control Charts with Arithmetic Average and Warning Limits (see ISO 7873);
    - Cumulative Sum Charts (see ISO 7871);
    - Shewhart Control Charts (see ISO 8258);
    - Weighted Moving Average.
- Design of Experiments (DOE);
- Histograms;
- Pareto Charts;
- Process Capability Analysis.

Annex II: Potential Applications for Quality Risk Management

This Annex is intended to identify potential uses of quality risk management principles and tools by industry and regulators. However, the selection of particular risk management tools is completely dependent upon specific facts and circumstances.

These examples are provided for illustrative purposes and only suggest potential uses of quality risk management. This Annex is not intended to create any new expectations beyond the current regulatory requirements.

II.1 Quality Risk Management as Part of Integrated Quality Management

ICH Q9

Documentation

To review current interpretations and application of regulatory expectations;

To determine the desirability of and/or develop the content for SOPs, guidelines, etc.

Training and education

To determine the appropriateness of initial and/or ongoing training sessions based on education, experience and working habits of staff, as well as on a periodic assessment of previous training (e.g., its effectiveness);

To identify the training, experience, qualifications and physical abilities that allow personnel to perform an operation reliably and with no adverse impact on the quality of the product.

Quality defects

To provide the basis for identifying, evaluating, and communicating the potential quality impact of a suspected quality defect, complaint, trend, deviation, investigation, out of specification result, etc;

To facilitate risk communications and determine appropriate action to address significant product defects, in conjunction with regulatory authorities (e.g., recall).

Auditing/Inspection

To define the frequency and scope of audits, both internal and external, taking into account factors such as:

- Existing legal requirements;
- Overall compliance status and history of the company or facility;
- Robustness of a company's quality risk management activities;
- Complexity of the site;
- Complexity of the manufacturing process;
- Complexity of the product and its therapeutic significance;
- Number and significance of quality defects (e.g., recall);
- Results of previous audits/inspections;
- Major changes of building, equipment, processes, key personnel;
- Experience with manufacturing of a product (e.g., frequency, volume, number of batches);
- Test results of official control laboratories.

Periodic review

To select, evaluate and interpret trend results of data within the product quality review;

To interpret monitoring data (e.g., to support an assessment of the appropriateness of revalidation or changes in sampling).

Change management / change control

To manage changes based on knowledge and information accumulated in pharmaceutical development and during manufacturing;

To evaluate the impact of the changes on the availability of the final product;

To evaluate the impact on product quality of changes to the facility, equipment, material, manufacturing process or technical transfers;

To determine appropriate actions preceding the implementation of a change, e.g., additional testing, (re)qualification, (re)validation or communication with regulators.

Continual improvement

To facilitate continual improvement in processes throughout the product lifecycle.

II.2 Quality Risk Management as Part of Regulatory Operations

Inspection and assessment activities

To assist with resource allocation including, for example, inspection planning and frequency, and inspection and assessment intensity (see "Auditing" section in Annex II.1);

To evaluate the significance of, for example, quality defects, potential recalls and inspectional findings;

To determine the appropriateness and type of post-inspection regulatory follow-up;

To evaluate information submitted by industry including pharmaceutical development information;

To evaluate impact of proposed variations or changes;

To identify risks which should be communicated between inspectors and assessors to facilitate better understanding of how risks can be or are controlled (e.g., parametric release, Process Analytical Technology (PAT)).

II.3 Quality Risk Management as Part of development

To design a quality product and its manufacturing process to consistently deliver the intended performance of the product (see ICH Q8);

To enhance knowledge of product performance over a wide range of material attributes (e.g., particle size distribution, moisture content, flow properties), processing options and process parameters;

To assess the critical attributes of raw materials, solvents, Active Pharmaceutical Ingredient (API) starting materials, APIs, excipients, or packaging materials;

To establish appropriate specifications, identify critical process parameters and establish manufacturing controls (e.g., using information from pharmaceutical development studies regarding the clinical significance of quality attributes and the ability to control them during processing);

To decrease variability of quality attributes:

- reduce product and material defects;

- reduce manufacturing defects.

To assess the need for additional studies (e.g., bioequivalence, stability) relating to scale up and technology transfer;

To make use of the "design space" concept (see ICH Q8).

II.4 Quality Risk Management for Facilities, Equipment and Utilities

Design of facility / equipment

To determine appropriate zones when designing buildings and facilities, e.g.,

- flow of material and personnel;
- minimize contamination;
- pest control measures;
- prevention of mix-ups;
- open versus closed equipment;
- clean rooms versus isolator technologies;
- dedicated or segregated facilities / equipment.

To determine appropriate product contact materials for equipment and containers (e.g., selection of stainless steel grade, gaskets, lubricants);

To determine appropriate utilities (e.g., steam, gases, power source, compressed air, heating, ventilation and air conditioning (HVAC), water);

To determine appropriate preventive maintenance for associated equipment (e.g., inventory of necessary spare parts).

Hygiene aspects in facilities

To protect the product from environmental hazards, including chemical, microbiological, and physical hazards (e.g., determining appropriate clothing and gowning, hygiene concerns);

To protect the environment (e.g., personnel, potential for cross-contamination) from hazards related to the product being manufactured.

Qualification of facility/equipment/utilities

To determine the scope and extent of qualification of facilities, buildings, and production equipment and/or laboratory instruments (including proper calibration methods).

Cleaning of equipment and environmental control

To differentiate efforts and decisions based on the intended use (e.g., multi-versus single-purpose, batch versus continuous production);

To determine acceptable (specified) cleaning validation limits.

Calibration/preventive maintenance

To set appropriate calibration and maintenance schedules.

Computer systems and computer controlled equipment

To select the design of computer hardware and software (e.g., modular, structured, fault tolerance);

To determine the extent of validation, e.g.,

- identification of critical performance parameters;
- selection of the requirements and design;
- code review;
- the extent of testing and test methods;
- reliability of electronic records and signatures.

II.5 Quality Risk Management as Part of Materials Management

Assessment and evaluation of suppliers and contract manufacturers

To provide a comprehensive evaluation of suppliers and contract manufacturers (e.g., auditing, supplier quality agreements).

Starting material

To assess differences and possible quality risks associated with variability in starting materials (e.g., age, route of synthesis).

Use of materials

To determine whether it is appropriate to use material under quarantine (e.g., for further internal processing);

To determine appropriateness of reprocessing, reworking, use of returned goods.

Storage, logistics and distribution conditions

To assess the adequacy of arrangements to ensure maintenance of appropriate storage and transport conditions (e.g., temperature, humidity, container design);

To determine the effect on product quality of discrepancies in storage or transport conditions (e.g., cold chain management) in conjunction with other ICH guidelines;

To maintain infrastructure (e.g., capacity to ensure proper shipping conditions, interim storage, handling of hazardous materials and controlled substances, customs clearance);

To provide information for ensuring the availability of pharmaceuticals (e.g., ranking risks to the supply chain).

II.6 Quality Risk Management as Part of Production

Validation

To identify the scope and extent of verification, qualification and validation activities (e.g., analytical methods, processes, equipment and cleaning methods;

To determine the extent for follow-up activities (e.g., sampling, monitoring and re-validation);

To distinguish between critical and non-critical process steps to facilitate design of a validation study.

In-process sampling & testing

To evaluate the frequency and extent of in-process control testing (e.g., to justify reduced testing under conditions of proven control);

To evaluate and justify the use of process analytical technologies (PAT) in conjunction with parametric and real time release.

Production planning

To determine appropriate production planning (e.g., dedicated, campaign and concurrent production process sequences).

II.7 Quality Risk Management as Part of Laboratory Control and Stability Studies

Out of specification results

To identify potential root causes and corrective actions during the investigation of out of specification results.

Retest period / expiration date

To evaluate adequacy of storage and testing of intermediates, excipients and starting materials.

II.8 Quality Risk Management as Part of Packaging and Labelling

Design of packages

To design the secondary package for the protection of primary packaged product (e.g., to ensure product authenticity, label legibility).

Selection of container closure system

To determine the critical parameters of the container closure system.

Label controls

To design label control procedures based on the potential for mix-ups involving different product labels, including different versions of the same label.

Part VI

Compliance Policies

Drug Good Manufacturing Practices (GMP) and Establishment Licencing (EL) Enforcement Directive (POL-0004)

Health Products and Food Branch Inspectorate

Supersedes: January 1st, 1998

Date issued: December 1st, 2003

Date of implementation: January 1st, 2004

Drug Good Manufacturing Practices (GMP) and Establishment Licencing (EL) Enforcement Directive (POL-0004)[86]

1. Purpose

The purpose of this document is to ensure the uniform, efficient, and effective enforcement of the requirement for all Canadian drug establishments[87], and any foreign drug establishments providing drug products to the Canadian market, to comply with Division 2 of Part C of the Food and Drug Regulations[88] (FDR) and to the requirements for Canadian drug establishments to hold an establishment licence (EL) to fabricate package, label, distribute, import, wholesale, or test a drug in Canada.

This document is also intended to increase transparency by providing the industry with a clear description of the Inspectorate's role in applying the Drug Good Manufacturing Practices (GMP) and EL regulatory scheme and the internal steps followed when a proposal to suspend an establishment licence is contested.

---

[86] Available on the Health Canada website at http://www.hc-sc.gc.ca/dhp-mps/compli-conform/licences/directives/pol_4_tc-tm-eng.php

[87] Includes establishments not subject to EL requirements as per C.01A.002 (d).

[88] C.R.C., c. 870, as amended. Also referred to as the "Good Manufacturing Practices" (GMP) Regulations".

2. Background

2.1 General

The mandate of the HPFB is to take an integrated approach to the management of the risks and benefits to health related to health products and food by: minimizing health risk factors to Canadians while maximizing the safety of the regulatory system for health products and food; and, promoting conditions that enable Canadians to make healthy choices and providing information so that they can make informed decisions about their health. To this end, the HPFB created a branch-level Inspectorate which works to ensure the compliance with and enforcement of federal legislation that sets standards for quality, health and safety, conditions for sale and the prevention of fraud and diversion from legitimate uses.

The Inspectorate is responsible for branch-wide compliance and enforcement activities, and provides an opportunity to achieve consistency of approach across the spectrum of regulated products. Using risk management principles and employing the best science available, appropriate standards are applied to regulated products and activities in order to maximize safety while balancing the availability and quality of the products.

2.2 Drug GMP Requirements

Drug GMP is that part of quality assurance which ensures that drugs are consistently produced and controlled to the quality standards appropriate to their intended use as required by the marketing authorization.

The Drug GMP requirements under Division 2 Part C of the FDR apply to all drug establishments that fabricate, package, label, distribute, import, wholesale, or test a drug and to which Division 1A (EL requirements) applies. Establishments exempted under Section C.01A.002 (d) are also required to comply with Drug GMPs. Compliance with Drug GMP requirements is assessed by conducting inspections of these establishments pursuant to the powers provided in s. 23 of the Food and Drugs Act (FDA) and complemented by corresponding with regulatees or making specific inquiries. As described in the next section, these inspections and the determination of compliance with Drug GMP requirements are the basis for the issuance of ELs to domestic sites.

2.3 EL Requirements

Important regulatory changes were introduced on January 1st, 1998 to provide for an EL framework under Division 1A of Part C of the FDR and to extend Division 2 to apply uniform GMPs for all drugs.

These EL requirements apply to all Canadian drug establishments except those exempted under FDR s. C.01A.002. Natural Health Products (NHP) establishments have been so exempted by paragraph (d) of that section. Despite this exemption to EL, FDR s. C.02.003 requires NHP manufacturers and importers to meet GMP requirements set on in Division 2 of the FDR

NHP will continue to be so exempted from EL requirements until S. C.01A.002 (d) is repealed, if the manufacturer chooses to retain its DIN during the transition period. This transition will run until the issuance of an NHP site licence or

December 31, 2005 whichever comes first; see sections 3 and 113 of the Natural Health Product Regulations.[89]

It should also be noted that an establishment which performs the tests specified in Division 2 must hold a licence as a testing facility. Although licenced fabricators, packagers/labellers, distributors (who holds a DIN), and/or importers who have their own testing laboratory, are not required to hold a licence which specifies testing laboratory, the testing is listed on the EL, thus providing more information on all the activities being carried out at a particular site. Wholesalers are not addressed in the exclusion since there are no product or material testing requirements for wholesalers.

It is Health Canada position that drugs presently subject to the drug EL framework (e.g. not exempted by C.01A.002 (d) which nonetheless fall within the scope of the new NHP Regulations) will remain subject to the drug EL requirements only until the day on which their NHP site licence is issued or December 31, 2005, whichever comes first.

In addition to the Establishment Licence under Division 1A of the FDR, fabricators, packagers/labellers, testers, distributors, importers and wholesalers of narcotics or controlled drugs, must hold a valid licence or have applied for a licence under the Narcotic Control Regulations[90] or Part G of the FDR, or under the Controlled Drugs and Substances Act. This licence is issued by the Office of Controlled Substances, Healthy Environments and Consumer Safety Branch, Health Canada.

An establishment wishing to obtain an EL must demonstrate that applicable requirements for Drug GMP have been met. To demonstrate Drug GMP compliance, the establishment will need to provide evidence that its buildings, equipment and proposed practices and procedures meet the applicable requirements of Divisions 2 to 4 of the FDR, ie. the establishment must have been inspected by the Inspectorate and have been subsequently found to comply with Drug GMP requirements and consequently been assigned a C rating[91]. For foreign sites, they must demonstrate Drug GMP compliance by submitting inspection reports as described in the policy document entitled Conditions for

---

[89] Section 3 of the NHP Regulations:-Except where otherwise indicated in these Regulations, the provisions of Food and Drug Regulations do not apply to Natural Health Products Section 113 of the NHP Regulations. -
  1. A person who, before January 1, 2004, manufactures, packages, labels or import for sale a drug to which these Regulations apply may continue to conduct these activity in respect of that drug without complying with the requirements of Parts 2 and 3, until the earlier of
    a. the day on which that person's application for a site licence to conduct that activity in respect of the drug is disposed of or withdrawn, and
    b. December 31, 2005
  2. A person who conducts an activity under subsection (1) shall conduct that activity in accordance with the requirements of the Food and Drug Regulations.
[90] C.R.C., c. 1041, as amended
[91] Ratings are classified according to the Inspectorate document entitled "GUI 0023 - Risk Classification of GMP Observations." There are two possible inspection ratings:
C = recommended for the continuation or issuance of the EL
NC = not recommended for the continuation or issuance of the LE.
Inspection ratings pertaining to establishments meeting the criteria of Section C.01A.002(d) are defined as conforming (C), or not conforming (NC) with the Drug GMP requirements.

Acceptance of Foreign Inspections Reports for listing foreign sites on Canadian Establishment Licences. These report are assessed to determine Drug GMP Compliance.

3. Scope

This policy applies to all persons subjected to the Drug GMP requirements outlined in Division 2 of Part C of the FDR including manufacturers of drugs for clinical trials and those subjected to the EL requirements outlined in Division 1A of Part C of the FDR.

4. Definitions

Terms used in this document have the same meaning as in the Food and Drugs Act[92] (FDA) and Regulations (FDR). However, the following terms are defined for the purposes of this policy:

Class Monograph

A document prepared by Health Canada that:

a. lists the types and strengths of medicinal ingredients that may be contained in drugs of a specified class; and

b. sets out labelling and other requirements that apply to those drugs.

Drug

Under the FDA, a drug includes any substance or mixture of substances manufactured, sold or represented for use in:

a. the diagnosis, treatment, mitigation or prevention of a disease, disorder or abnormal physical state, or its symptoms, in human beings or animal;

b. restoring, correcting or modifying organic functions in human beings or animals; or

c. disinfection in premises in which food is manufactured, prepared or kept.

Under Division 1A and Division 2 of Part C of the FDR, a drug means drug in dosage form (C.01A.001(2)), or a drug that is a bulk process intermediate that can be used in the preparation of a drug listed in Schedule C or D to the FDA that is of biological origin. It does not include a dilute drug premix, a medicated feed as defined section 2 of the Feeds Regulations, 1983, a drug that is used only for the purposes of an experimental study in accordance with a certificate issued under section C.08.015 or a drug listed in Schedule H to the FDA.

Establishment

Includes fabricators, packagers/labelers, distributors, importers, wholesalers and testing laboratories of biologicals, blood and blood components, pharmaceuticals, vaccines and radiopharmaceuticals.

---

[92] R.S. 1985, c. F-27, as amended.

GMP

> means Drug Good Manufacturing Practices - Part C, Division 2 of the FDR and the interpretive guidelines.

HPFB

> Health Products and Food Branch

Inspection

> General monitoring activities to assess the industry's compliance with the Food and Drug Act and Regulations in accordance with established policies and procedures.

Inspector

> A person designated as an Inspector under the FDA and authorised to conduct inspections of regulated establishments (Inspectorate Compliance Officer).

Inspectorate

> Health Products and Food Branch Inspectorate

5. Policy Statement

An establishment, whether or not it is subject to the Drugs EL requirements, may be found to be non-compliant with Drug GMP requirements. In addition to being non-compliant with Drug GMPs, an establishment whose activities are covered under the Drugs EL Regulations, may not be in possession of a valid EL for the activities it conducts or wishes to conduct, for the following reasons:

- the establishment has not applied for an EL;

- the establishment has not renewed their EL by December 31st;

- the establishment has applied for, but was refused a licence due to a non-compliant (NC) inspection rating;

- the establishment has applied for a licence but certain foreign sites have not been approved for inclusion on the EL;

- the establishment has applied for an EL amendment or gave notice of a major change, but this request was denied;

- the establishment EL's terms and conditions have been amended or new terms and conditions have been imposed; or

- the establishment's EL has been suspended.

Consistent with the Inspectorate's Compliance and Enforcement Policy (POL-0001), appropriate enforcement actions will be considered in these situations, as the Inspectorate will not permit establishments to conduct regulated drug related activities without compliance with Drug GMP and/or EL requirements. These enforcement actions will be coordinated with any other violation discovered, such as Drug Identification Number (DIN) violations. Non-compliance with any other EL regulatory requirement, such as failure to apply for amendments, and failure to notify regarding changes made or proposed, may also result in enforcement action being taken.

Although the Inspectorate will work with drug establishments to help bring their operations into Drug GMP compliance, it will not tolerate chronic non-compliance with the regulations, which are meant to ensure that the health of the consumer is protected through quality and safety standards being met. Appropriate enforcement action must be considered in such situations to prevent further distribution of potentially unsafe drug products.

5.1 Non-Compliance with Drug GMP Requirements

Whether or not a drug establishment requires an EL, all must comply with Drug GMP requirements. Establishments that are found non-compliant with these requirements must take the necessary and timely corrective action to bring their operations into compliance. These firms must provide evidence of their commitment to comply with the Drug GMP requirements and submit a written plan of corrective action. Compliance is normally achieved following a cooperative approach between the regulated party and the Inspectorate; however, when this is not possible, or when the regulated party is unable to correct non-conformities, a number of enforcement options may be used to respond to non-compliance with Drug GMP requirements.

(a) Drug Establishments not Subject to EL Requirements

Enforcement action will normally be taken following a "Stepped Approach" (see section 6.2.4 "Stepped Enforcement Approach" for more details) following an evaluation by the Inspectorate to determine the most appropriate enforcement action(s) to be taken. This determination will consider the various circumstances of each case and will take into account, along with other applicable information, a number of factors as identified in the Compliance and Enforcement Policy.

(b) Drug Establishments Subject to EL Requirements

Establishments subject to EL requirements must also comply with Drug GMP requirements, however, the EL regulations provide the Inspectorate with additional measures to deal with non-compliance such as:

- Refusal to Issue or Amend EL;
- Amendment of Terms and Conditions of EL; and
- Suspension of EL

The Inspectorate may, in addition to using these measures, use any of the other enforcement actions identified in the Compliance and Enforcement Policy.

5.2 Non-Compliance with Drugs EL Requirements

The Minister may suspend an establishment licence without giving the licensee an opportunity to be heard if it is necessary to do so to prevent injury to the health of the consumer, by giving the licensee a notice in writing that states the reason for the suspension. (C.01A.017(1)). All other situations will be handled according to the following:

(a) No application for an EL or no renewal by December 31 was submitted

Subject to paragraphs (I) and (ii), where an establishment is known to be conducting licensable drug-related activities and is required to hold an EL but has not applied for an EL, the Inspectorate will request, in writing, that the establishment suspend, within 15 calendar days of receipt of the notice, all licensable activities until they have received an EL.

a. Establishments that have not applied for an EL but have been inspected and are in compliance with the Drug GMP regulations ('C' rating), including establishments which have submitted acceptable action plans or commitments to comply, will be permitted to complete any production that is in process, any importation in transit, and sell any stock on hand, during the 15 calendar days period following receipt of the notice.

b. Establishments that have not applied for an EL and are not in compliance with the Drug GMP regulations ('NC' rating), will not be permitted to engage in any licensable activity until they meet licensing requirements and are issued an EL.

Any establishment that does not comply with licence application requirements within 15 calendar days of receipt of this notice, but continues to conduct licensable activities, is subject to immediate enforcement action.

(b) Application for an EL was received but licence was refused

Where an establishment has applied for a licence but the Minister refuses to issue the licence, in whole or in part, the Inspectorate's Director General, on behalf of the Minister, will notify the applicant, in writing, of the reason for the refusal and will give the applicant an opportunity to be heard. The applicant must suspend those activities, categories or dosage form classes for which the licence was refused, until EL requirements are met. Failure to comply with this notice within 15 calendar days of receipt of the notice will result in immediate enforcement action. This delay could be shortened based on risk evaluation.

(c) Application for an EL was received but certain foreign sites have not been approved for inclusion on the EL

Where an establishment applies for a licence as an "importer" but the Minister refuses to include a specified foreign site on that licence, the Inspectorate's Director General, on behalf of the Minister, will issue a notice advising the establishment not to import drug products from that site until that site has been approved and included on the licence and will give the applicant an opportunity to be heard. Failure to comply with this notice within 15 calendar days of receipt of the notice will result in action being taken to prevent products from being imported from unapproved foreign sites.

(d) Application for an EL amendment or notice of a major change was made, but was denied

Once licences have been issued, where an establishment has applied for a licence amendment or has given notice of a reportable change, and where this request has been denied, the Inspectorate's Director General, on behalf of the Minister, will issue a notice advising that the establishment is not to engage in the licensable or reportable change requested, and will give the establishment an opportunity to be heard with respect to refusal of amendments. Failure to comply with this notice within 15 calendar days of receipt of the notice will result in immediate enforcement action.

(e) EL's Terms and Conditions have been Imposed or Amended

Where a licence has been issued and subsequently amended by the Inspectorate's Director General, on behalf of the Minister, the establishment must comply with the new or amended terms and conditions. The Inspectorate's Director General will provide the establishment, in writing, with at least 15 calendar days notice of the reasons for the amendment and the date on which the notice becomes effective. Failure to comply with the terms and conditions will result in immediate enforcement action.

(f) EL has been suspended

Where a licence has been suspended by the Inspectorate's Director General, on behalf of the Minister, the establishment must suspend all licensable activities as of the effective suspension date until the EL in question has been reinstated pursuant to s. C.01A.018 of the FDR or another EL has been issued. Failure to comply with the final suspension notice will result in immediate enforcement action.

6. Responsibilities/Procedures

6.1 Responsibilities

The implementation of this policy is the responsibility of the staff of the Inspectorate.

In general, Inspectors are responsible for:

- inspecting domestic drug establishments for Drug GMP compliance and making EL recommendations;
- monitoring regulatory compliance; and
- recommending and taking enforcement action.

In general, Managers of the Operational Centres are responsible for:

- if required, signing the letter confirming the NC rating
- representing the Inspectorate during the meeting with the Regional Director.

In general, Regional Directors are responsible for:

- chairing meetings to resolve issues related to non-compliance with Drug GMPs; and
- gathering facts and recommending to the HPFB Assistant Deputy Minister (ADM) the rating for the establishment.

In general, the Inspectorate's National Coordination Centre is responsible for:

- evaluating Drug GMP compliance of foreign drug establishments and making EL recommendations;
- recommending enforcement action where appropriate; and
- coordinating compliance activities.

In general, the Inspectorate's Director General is responsible for:

- issuing ELs;

and

- issuing notices of refusal to issue or amend a licence, and notices to suspend a licence.

In general, the HPFB Assistant Deputy Minister is responsible for:

- taking final decisions on the rating of an establishment or the suspension of the licence in case of contestation.

6.2 Procedures

6.2.1 Assignment of NC Inspection Ratings (see Appendix A)

In case of issuance of a NC inspection report, the Inspector will provide the management of the establishment with a letter and draft Inspection Report informing the establishment that the results may lead to enforcement action(s) being taken, including the suspension of its EL. The establishment will also be informed that the report will be submitted to an internal review group for quality assurance purposes and that as a consequence, the rating will either be confirmed or changed. Confirmation of the rating will be communicated to the establishment in a maximum of 45 calendar days, from the date the draft inspection report was provided to the establishment. However, establishments are encouraged to address the NC concerns immediately. During that period, measures other than EL suspension may also be taken to mitigate the risk. The final report will identify the deficiencies observed, if any, corrective actions to be taken by the establishment and the time within which the action(s) must be taken.

If the NC rating is changed to a C rating, the establishment will be informed in writing that the rating was changed. If applicable, the letter will identify the deficiencies, any action to be taken and the time within which the corrective action(s) must be taken. If the recommendation is to maintain the NC rating, the Inspector and/or Operational Manager will communicate with the establishment to inform them of the intent to maintain the NC rating and will provide the establishment with an opportunity to meet with them.

The meeting will provide both parties an opportunity to discuss the draft Inspection Report, the corrective actions that should be taken to bring the establishment into compliance, time periods within which these should be taken, and possible terms and conditions or amendments to terms and conditions that could be imposed on the EL to prevent enforcement actions.

Following the meeting, the Operational Manager and Inspector will provide the establishment with the final Inspection Report and a letter confirming the NC rating, reiterating deficiencies and if any, the actions to be taken within 15 days. If no action can be taken within 15 days, the letter may identify possible terms and conditions or amendments to terms and conditions on the EL. The letter will also indicate that, unless the corrective actions are taken within 15 days, terms and conditions accepted, or an Intent to Contest is filed, enforcement actions will be taken[93].

6.2.2 Establishment's Response to Letter Confirming NC Rating

a) Establishment responds within 15 days that they have taken corrective actions

A re-inspection will be conducted by the Inspector to confirm that appropriate corrective actions have been taken. This re-inspection will be normally limited to one day. If the corrective actions are confirmed, the Inspector will issue a new Inspection Report with a C rating. If the inspection reveals that the corrective actions have not been taken, first notice of intent to initiate enforcement action

---

[93] In the case of an EL, a proposal to suspend the EL will be made to the Inspectorate's Director General.

will be issued, by certified mail, by the Inspector to the establishment outlining the offence and action to be taken by the firm. In the case of an establishment that possesses an EL, a proposal to suspend the EL will be forwarded to the Inspectorate's Director General.

b) Establishment responds that they will not take corrective actions and they don't intend to contest

A first notice of intent to initiate enforcement action will be made by the Inspector. In the case of an establishment that possesses an EL, a proposal to suspend the EL will be forwarded to the Inspectorate's Director General.

c) Establishment responds that they will not take corrective actions and they intend to contest

No notice of intent to initiate enforcement action will be given, unless a risk to the health of consumers exists (refer to 6.2.3). In the case of an establishment that possesses an EL, no proposal to suspend the EL will be forwarded to the Inspectorate's Director General. The establishment will be required to forward a letter of Intent to Contest to the Regional Director where the site is located. Please refer to section 5 (Policy Statement).

d) In the case of an establishment that possesses an EL, the establishment responds that they accept terms and conditions

A re-inspection will be conducted to confirm that the establishment respects the new terms and conditions imposed on the EL. These terms and conditions will be related to prevent injury to the health of the consumer. If the inspection reveals that the new terms and conditions are respected, the Inspectorate's Director General will send a letter to the establishment to confirm the issuance of a new EL with the terms and conditions.

6.2.3 Situations where an immediate risk to the health of consumers exist

It should be noted that where it is necessary to do so to prevent injury to the health of consumers, immediate enforcement action such as product seizure, request for a recall of the product or products may be taken. In the case of an EL, a proposal to suspend an EL under section C.01A.017 of the FDR may be made to the Inspectorate's Director General at any time. The Operational Manager and Inspector may also, following the meeting with the establishment, when they are faced with a situation where no satisfying corrective actions are possible (for example, when there is evidence of record falsification or concealment) immediately recommend that a proposal to suspend the Establishment Licence under section C.01A.016 of the FDR be made to the Inspectorate's Director General.

6.2.4 Stepped Enforcement Approach based on the risk to the health of consumers

Notwithstanding the content of this Section 6.2.4, should any serious health risk be identified during the course of implementing enforcement action, more severe and immediate measures may be taken to ensure that no potentially hazardous products continue to be sold. Additional measures, such as recall or injunction, may be necessary to remove violative products from the market and prevent further distribution.

The first notice of intent to initiate enforcement action will be issued, by certified mail, by an Inspector to the establishment outlining the offence, enforcement action contemplated, and action to be taken. Notices issued by the Inspectorate's Director General, relative to refusal to issue a licence or refusal to amend a licence are also considered to be first level notices.

Where an establishment does not comply with the requirements of the first notice, within 15 calendar days of receipt of that notice, a second notice will be issued by certified mail, by the Inspectorate Operational Manager, requesting the establishment to stop sale of all drug products subject to the action and to suspend all specified licensable activities, until the establishment complies with Drug GMP and EL requirements. A Notice of licence suspension, issued by the Inspectorate's Director General, is also defined as a second notice.

Where no satisfactory response is received within 15 calendar days of receipt of the second notice and where there is evidence of continuing non-conformance, Inspectors will take all measures necessary to protect the health of consumers. Where applicable, the National Coordination Centre will also issue an alert to Canada Customs and Revenue Agency to refuse further importations.

In the case of a foreign site, a first notice will be sent by the Inspector in the National Coordination Centre (NCC) and failure to respond to that notice within 45 days will result in a notice issued by the Inspectorate's Director General advising the importer that the foreign site will be removed from the EL.

Where an establishment wishes to discontinue distribution of drug products in question, forfeiture, export, or other options may be proposed by the establishment to dispose of products in question. Such requests would be evaluated according to existing policies and procedures and according to any enforcement action in progress.

Where the products are to be exported to a country with which Canada has a Mutual Recognition Agreement (MRA), a Memorandum of Understanding (MOU) or that is a member of the Pharmaceutical Inspection Co-operation Scheme (PIC/S), the foreign authority will be informed by the Inspectorate. Where no such agreements are in place, the Inspectorate will make every efforts to inform the foreign regulatory authority of the status of the exported products.

6.2.5. Steps followed when a proposal to suspend an establishment licence is contested (see Appendix B)

The management of the establishment wishing to contest a decision confirming a NC rating is required to submit a letter of Intent to Contest to the Regional Director where the establishment's site is located. See Appendix C.

Within 15 calendar days of submitting a letter of Intent to Contest, the management of the establishment must file a comprehensive document with the Regional Director explaining their position and containing full supporting information in relation to the decision being contested. Should the establishment wish to meet with the Regional Director, this should be indicated when filing the comprehensive document. The purpose of this meeting will be to provide the establishment with an opportunity to reiterate the major aspects of their contest as stated in their comprehensive document and to provide the establishment an opportunity to ensure the Regional Director is aware of the salient points of the establishment's position. There will not be a debate of the issues at this meeting. The Inspector and Operational Manager responsible for the original decision may attend this meeting.

The Regional Director's recommendation will be based only on the information and material upon which the original decision was taken. Any new information referenced or contained in the comprehensive document will result in its return to the establishment.

The Regional Director is responsible for reviewing all of the relevant documents and submissions and issuing a recommendation and report to the HPFB ADM regarding the contest. A copy of this recommendation will also be sent to the establishment. Within 20 calendar days from the filing of the comprehensive document or from the date of the meeting if one is requested, the Regional Director will make one of the following recommendations to the HPFB ADM :

- Recommendation that the NC rating be maintained;

- Recommendation that the NC rating be changed to a C rating;

- Recommendation that the NC rating be changed to a C rating with Terms and Conditions as identified in the original decision imposed on the EL.

The Regional Director's recommendation will be provided to the HPFB ADM in a package of information, that will include, in addition to the Regional Director's report, the following documents:

- Inspectorate Compliance Officer's Inspection Report;

- Internal Review Group's Report;

- Letter from Operational Manager and Inspector to establishment confirming NC rating;

- Comprehensive document filed by establishment;

- Minutes of Meetings; and

- Any other correspondence sent to or received from the establishment.

At the latest 5 days after the receipt of the Regional Director's recommendation, the establishment can submit in writing comments to the HPFB ADM. Within 15 calendar days of the receipt of the Regional Director's recommendation the HPFB ADM will consider the recommendations and inform the establishment of its final decision. The HPFB ADM's decision will be one of the following:

- Maintain the NC rating;

- Change the NC rating to a C rating;

- NC rating changed to C rating with Terms and Conditions imposed on the EL.

If the HPFB ADM's decision is to maintain the NC rating, a Notice of Suspension of the EL under section C.01A.016 of the FDR will be sent to the establishment, by the Inspectorate Director General, within 15 calendar days of the final decision. In this case, if a Certificate of Compliance was previously issued to a country with which Canada as a Mutual Recognition Agreement (MRA), the Certificate of Compliance will be cancelled by the Inspectorate and the foreign authority will be informed.

7. Approval/Effective Date

This Drug Good Manufacturing Practices and Establishment Licensing Enforcement Directive was approved on October 27, 2003 by the Inspectorate Management Committee and is effective as of January 1st, 2004.

Appendix A. Steps in the Attribution of Inspection Ratings and Suspension of an EL under s. C.01A.016

View Image 1. Steps in the Attribution of Inspection Ratings and Suspension of an EL under s. C.01A.016

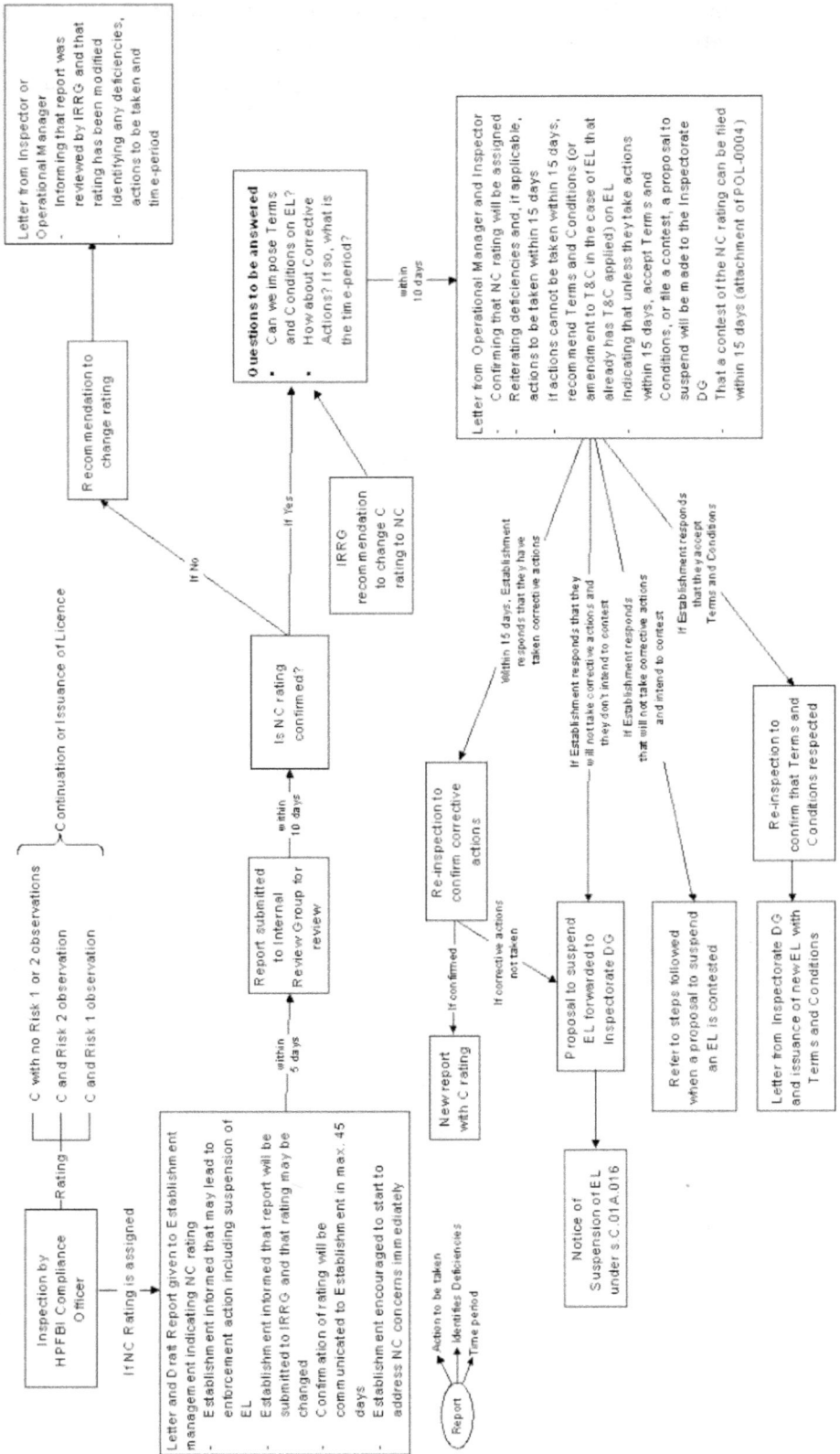

Appendix B. Steps followed when a proposal to suspend an Establishment Licence is contested

View Image 2. Steps followed when a proposal to suspend an Establishment Licence is contested

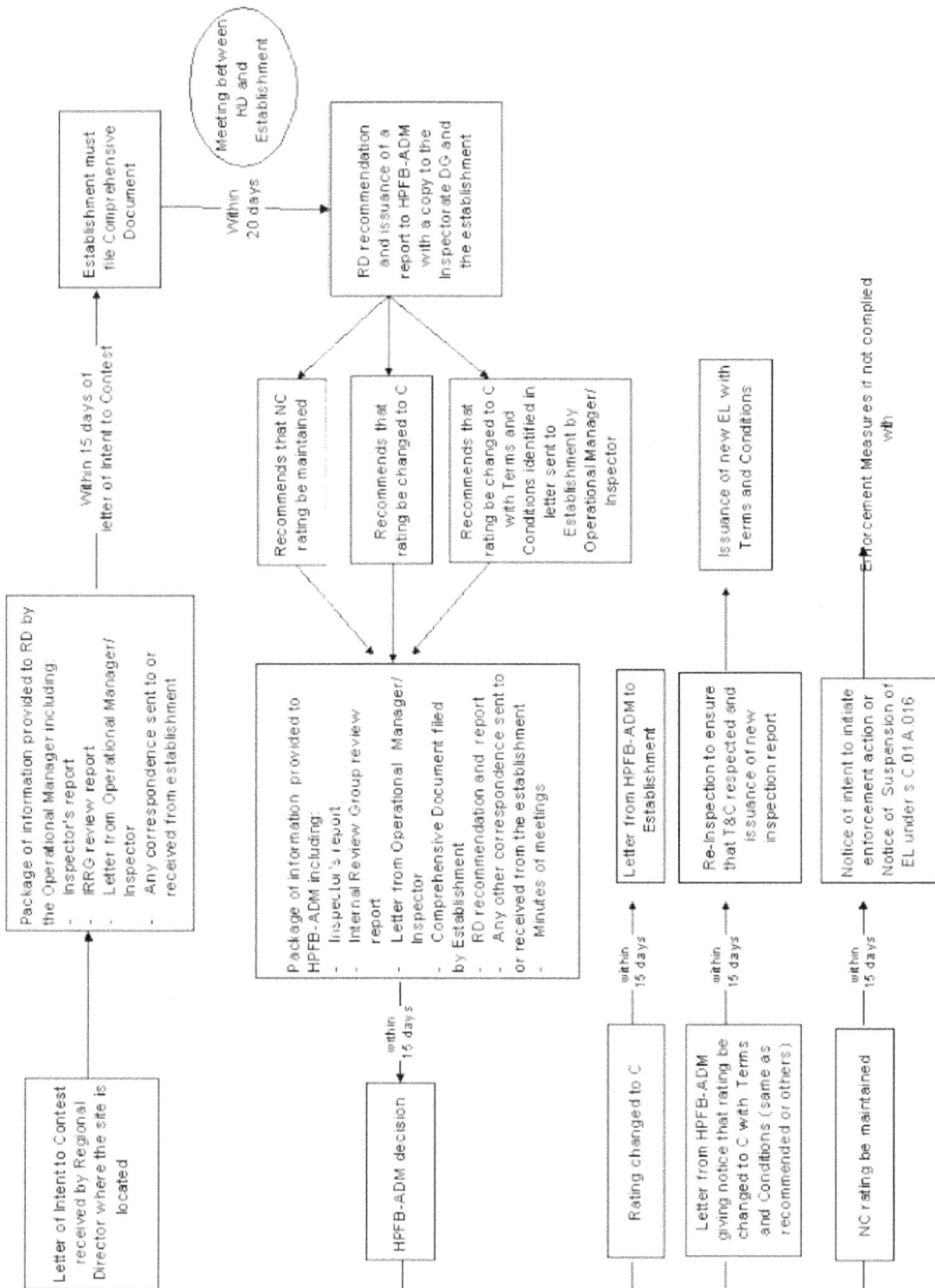

Appendix C. List of Regional Directors offices

Atlantic Region

Suite 1625
1505 Barrington Street
Halifax, Nova Scotia, B3J 3Y6

T 902-426-2161
F 902-426-7108

Quebec Region

1001 West St-Laurent Blvd
Longueuil, Québec, J4K 1C7

T 450-646-1353
F 450-928-4455

Ontario and Nunavut Region

2301 Midland Avenue
Scarborough, Ontario, M1P 4R7

T 416-973-1475
F 416-954-4582

Manitoba and Saskatchewan Region

510 Lagimodière Blvd
Winnipeg, Manitoba, R2J 3Y1

T 204-983-3004
F 204-983-2363

British-Colombia and Yukon Region

3155 Willingdon Green
Burnaby, British-Columbia, V5G 4P2

T 604-666-3704
F 604-666-1398

GMP Inspection Policy for Canadian Drug Establishments (POL-0011)

Health Products and Food Branch Inspectorate

Supersedes: January 1 2004

Date Issued: January 31st, 2008

Date of implementation: January 31st, 2008

GMP Inspection Policy for Canadian Drug Establishments (POL-0011)[94]

1.0 Purpose

Disclaimer

This document does not constitute part of the Food and Drugs Act (Act) or the Food and Drugs Regulations (Regulations) and in the event of any inconsistency or conflict between that Act or Regulations and this document, the Act or the Regulations take precedence. This document is an administrative document that is intended to facilitate compliance by the regulated party with the Act, the Regulations and the applicable administrative policies. This document is not intended to provide legal advice regarding the interpretation of the Act or Regulations. If a regulated party has questions about their legal obligations or responsibilities under the Act or Regulations, they should seek the advice of legal counsel.

This policy describes the Health Products and Food Branch Inspectorate approach to planning and cycles of GMP inspections in relation with the issuance of Establishment Licences (EL).

2.0 Background

Numerous changes related to the Good Manufacturing Practices (GMP) have occurred since 1996. These include:

- the promulgation of Division 1A - Establishment Licences (EL) Regulation of the Food and Drug Regulations applicable to fabricators, packagers/labellers, testers, distributors, importers and wholesalers of drugs;

- the acceptance of Canada as a member of the Pharmaceutical Inspection Cooperation Scheme in 1999 (PIC/S);

---

[94] Available on the Health Canada website at http://www.hc-sc.gc.ca/dhp-mps/compli-conform/gmp-bpf/pol/pol_0011_insp_drug_ltr-doc-eng.php

- the signing by Canada of Mutual Recognition Agreements (MRAs) with the European Community (EC), Switzerland, Australia and the European Free Trade Association (EFTA) which are presently in their operational phase.

The signing of these agreements involved a formal evaluation process or a confidence building phase to ensure that the GMP compliance programme of these different Regulatory Authorities are equivalent, including the frequency of inspections.

3.0 Scope

This policy is applicable to all Canadian drug establishments for which an EL is required.

The scope of this policy does not include:

- Blood Establishments
- Semen Establishments
- Inspection of foreign sites
- Inspection activities related to Clinical Trials which are covered in the document "Inspection Strategy for Clinical Trials" published on the Inspectorate website on January 15, 2002
- Inspection of Biological drugs for veterinary use that are regulated under the "Health of Animals Act and Regulations" administered by Agriculture and Agri-Food Canada or by the Canadian Food Inspection Agency (CFIA).

4.0 Definitions

Inspection

On-site monitoring and assessment against the applicable requirements of the Food and Drugs Act (FDA) and its associated Regulations. Inspections are routinely conducted on a predetermined cycle or as required to assess compliance.

Initial Inspection

The first inspection conducted at an establishment where not all applicable requirements of the FDA and its associated Regulations are assessed. This is not considered to be a regular inspection. For drug sites this is done prior to issuance of a new/first establishment licence.

Partial Inspection

An inspection during which not all of the applicable requirements of the FDA and its associated Regulations are assessed.

Regular Inspection

An inspection during which all of the applicable requirements of the FDA and its associated Regulations are assessed.

Re-inspection

> A follow-up inspection carried out when unacceptable practices have been identified which resulted in an NC rating and for which the purpose is to ensure that corrective actions have been implemented.

Re-assessment

> A follow-up inspection to an inspection which has resulted in a C rating and which is carried out for the purpose of ensuring that corrective actions have been implemented

5.0 Policy Statement

Any Canadian establishment involved in the fabrication, packaging / labelling, testing, distribution, importation or wholesaling of a category of drugs listed in Table II of Section C.01A.008 must comply with the requirements of Division 2 (GMP) of the Food and Drug Regulations. Compliance will be assessed by conducting inspections with a different cycle of these establishments based on a priority ranking scale and a risk-based approach.

5.1 Inspection cycle

Noting that similar inspection cycles of pharmaceutical regulators in other jurisdictions, and taking account of the resources and priorities of the Inspectorate, the following inspection cycle targets have been established:

- fabricator, packager / labeller and testing laboratory: 24 months;
- importer, distributor and wholesaler: 36 months

These inspections are the basis for the issuance of EL to domestic sites according to the requirements described in Division 1A of the Food and Drug Regulations.

New establishments applying for an EL, must be ready for an inspection when submitting their application since the Inspectorate expects that all proper information and systems are in place at the time of inspection. The Inspectorate is committed to perform an initial inspection within 3 months following the date of receipt of the request. Generally this initial inspection will be followed by a regular inspection within the next 12 months (from the initial inspection).

If establishments are not prepared for an initial inspection when contacted by the Inspectorate, their EL application will be withdrawn. The company will have to resubmit an EL application with all supporting information.

Notice of upcoming inspection may or may not be provided. However, inspections are generally announced as a courtesy.

Once the date of inspection has been set and the establishment informed, the inspection should take place on the date scheduled by the Inspectorate.

Changes to dates of scheduled inspections will only be done at the discretion of the Inspectorate and upon receipt of sufficient justification from the establishment.

5.2 Reporting

All GMP related inspection activities are recorded in the Inspection Reporting System (IRS).

GMP Inspection Policy POL-0011

All GMP observations are based on the current GMP guidelines and a risk is assigned to each observation according to the Guide-0023 "Risk Classification of GMP Observations". All observations are discussed with the firm during the exit meeting and confirmed to the establishment in the Inspection Exit Notice. Either a C rating (recommended for the continuation or issuance of the Establishment Licence) or NC rating (not recommended for the continuation or issuance of the Establishment Licence), is assigned at the conclusion of the inspection.

The result of these inspections is used for the issuance of EL and Certificates of Compliance (exchanged in the framework of Mutual Recognition Agreements (MRA)).

5.3 Enforcement actions

During the course of an inspection, an inspector may face situations of non compliance. These situations will be assessed according to Health Canada's risk determination principles and appropriate enforcement actions will be taken in accordance with the principles described in "Compliance and Enforcement Policy (POL-0001)" and "GMP and EL Enforcement Directive (POL-0004)".

6.0 Responsibilities

To ensure the proper implementation of this policy:

6.1 Compliance Officers in Operational Centres are responsible for:

- inspecting domestic establishments for GMP compliance and making recommendations in support of the issuance of a license;
- suggesting terms and conditions for an Establishment Licence.

6.2 Operational Centres Managers / Supervisors are responsible for:

- planning the inspections of domestic sites within the inspection cycle target;
- ensuring the quality and uniformity of the Inspection Exit Notices issued in their Operational Centre;
- submitting all NC reports and some C reports to the Inspection Rating Review Group (IRRG).

6.3 Inspectorate Ottawa is responsible for:

- recommending the issuance of establishment licences to domestic sites based on GMP status;
- verifying that the information to demonstrate GMP compliance is valid in support of the issuance of certificates of compliance requested by Regulatory Authorities;
- ensure the uniformity of the Terms and conditions for an Establishment Licence.

6.4 Director General is responsible for:

- issuing establishment licences, with terms and conditions when appropriate;
- issuing certificates of compliance requested by Regulatory Authorities.

7.0 Effective Date

This Policy will become effective January 31st, 2008.

8.0 Associated Documents

POL-0001: Compliance and Enforcement Policy

POL-0004: GMP and EL Enforcement Directive

**GMP Inspection Policy
POL-0011**

Inspection Strategy for Post-Market Surveillance (POL-0041)

Health Products and Food Branch Inspectorate

Supersedes: New document

Date issued: June 2004

Date of implementation: August 1st, 2004

Policy Document

Inspection Strategy for Post-Market Surveillance[95]

1. Purpose

The purpose of this document is to detail the strategy for the effective and uniform implementation of a national inspection programme to assess compliance of manufacturers with the Food and Drugs Act (Act) and the Food and Drug Regulations (Regulations) with regards to reporting of adverse drug reactions and reporting of unusual failure in efficacy of new drugs to Health Canada.

2. Background

The Regulations set forth requirements for manufacturers regarding reporting of adverse drug reactions and the reporting of unusual failure in efficacy of new drugs to Health Canada. Currently, there is no formal inspection programme in place to assess industry's compliance with these regulations. However, as part of its mandate to maximize the safety and efficacy of drugs, Health Canada is implementing an inspection programme for Post-Market Surveillance.

Inspections will be conducted by Health Canada under the authority of sections 23 and 24 of the Act. These activities will be conducted by the Health Products and Food Branch Inspectorate (Inspectorate).

3. Scope

This inspection programme applies to:

- Manufacturers of pharmaceutical and biological drugs

Blood products and therapeutic and diagnostic vaccines are included in the scope of this programme. However, radiopharmaceuticals, veterinary drugs, natural health products and preventative vaccines, including immunization

---

[95] Available on the Health Canada website at http://www.hc-sc.gc.ca/dhp-mps/compli-conform/gmp-bpf/docs/pol_41-eng.php

schedule vaccines, influenza vaccines and vaccines for travel, whole blood and blood components are excluded. In addition, this inspection programme does not apply to drugs for which a Clinical Trial Application has been submitted to Health Canada.

4. Definitions

Adverse drug reaction: a noxious and unintended response to a drug, which occurs at doses normally used or tested for the diagnosis, treatment or prevention of a disease or the modification of an organic function; (réaction indésirable à une drogue) (C.01.001 (1)).

HPFB

The mandate of the Health Products and Food Branch of Health Canada is to take an integrated approach to the management of the risks and benefits to health related to health products and food by minimizing health risk factors to Canadians while maximizing the safety provided by the regulatory system for health products and food; and, promoting conditions that enable Canadians to make healthy choices and providing information so that they can make informed decisions about their health. (DGPSA)

Importer

A person who imports into Canada a drug for the purpose of sale. (importateur)

Inspection

An independent evaluation, conducted by an objective, unbiased inspector, or inspection team, to assess an establishment's compliance against set standards or Regulations. Inspections are normally conducted on a multi-year cycle or as required. (inspection)

Inspector

Any person designated as an inspector for the purpose of the enforcement of the Food and Drugs Act under subsection 22(1) or the Controlled Drugs and Substances Act under section 30. (inspecteur)

Inspectorate

The Directorate of the HPFB whose primary role is to deliver a national compliance and enforcement program for all products under the mandate of the HPFB, with the exception of products regulated as foods. (Inspectorat)

Manufacturer

"Manufacturer" or "distributor" means a person, including an association or partnership, who under their own name, or under a trade-, design or word mark, trade name or other name, word or mark controlled by them, sells a food or drug (fabricant or distributeur) (A.01.010)

MHPD

The Marketed Health Products Directorate of HPFB is responsible for coordination of consistency of post-approval surveillance and assessment of signals and safety trends concerning all marketed health products. (DPSC)

New Drug

"(a) a drug that contains or consists of a substance, whether as an active or inactive ingredient, carrier, coating, excipient, menstruum or other component, that has not been sold as a drug in Canada for sufficient time and in sufficient quantity to establish in Canada the safety and effectiveness of that substance for use as a drug..." (Drogue nouvelle) (C.08.001)

The Therapeutic Products Directorate, HPFB policy issue, New Drug - Sufficient Time (August 21, 1991), interprets the phrase "sufficient time" as a minimum of seven years from the initial date of marketing in Canada.

Serious adverse drug reaction

a noxious and unintended response to a drug that occurs at any dose and that requires in-patient hospitalization or prolongation of existing hospitalization, causes congenital malformation, results in persistent or significant disability or incapacity, is life-threatening or results in death; (réaction indésirable grave à une drogue) (C.01.001 (1))

Serious unexpected adverse drug reaction

a serious adverse drug reaction that is not identified in nature, severity or frequency in the risk information set out on the label of the drug; (réaction indésirable grave et imprévue à une drogue) (C.01.001 (1))

For additional definitions, consult the documents listed as references at the end of this strategy.

5. Compliance and Monitoring Activities

The Inspectorate will provide information and encourage voluntary compliance with Canadian regulatory requirements. Compliance will be assessed through inspections conducted by the Inspectorate.

5.1 Inspections

Within the scope of the Post-Market Surveillance Drug Inspection programme, manufacturers of pharmaceutical and biological drugs will be inspected by the Inspectorate. The Inspectorate will assess the compliance of manufacturers with the Regulations pertaining to adverse drug reaction reporting, specifically, sections C.01.016, C.01.017 of the Regulations. The compliance of establishments with regards to requirements for reporting failure in efficacy of new drugs, as set forth n sections C.08.007 and C.08.008 of the Regulations will also be assessed.

The Post-Market Surveillance inspection cycles will begin in 2004. Up to twenty-five percent of the establishments under the scope of this strategy will be inspected in the first year. The inspection programme will be assessed after the first year of operation in order to determine whether modifications are required.

5.1.1 Inspection activities

The assessment for post-market surveillance will be conducted in conjunction with the assessment of establishments for compliance with Part C, Division 2, Good Manufacturing Practices (GMP) of the Regulations. Therefore, the inspection cycles for the Post-Market Surveillance Drug Inspection programme will be integrated into the inspection cycles for the GMP inspections. Additional time will be allocated for the overall visit to accommodate both types of inspections. Not all firms inspected for compliance with Division 2 will be inspected for compliance with post-market surveillance activities in a given inspection cycle.

5.1.2 Duration of inspections

The average duration of the inspection will vary depending on the type of activities and the size of the establishment, in addition to the volume of adverse drug reactions recorded by the firm, but is estimated at 1 day. The average time for an inspection will be re-assessed after the first year of operation of the inspection programme.

5.2 Inspection Rating and Reporting:

Rating:

Two ratings will be used:

- C - No objectionable conditions or practices were observed with regards to regulatory requirements pertaining to reporting of adverse drug reactions and/or reporting of unusual failure in efficacy of new drugs

- NC - Objectionable conditions or practices were observed with regards to regulatory requirements pertaining to reporting of adverse drug reactions and/or reporting of unusual failure in efficacy of new drugs

Reporting:

- An Inspection report will be issued to the inspected establishment in a timely manner. The Inspection Report will contain observations noted during the inspection. An Exit Notice will be issued to the establishment.

- Responses to observations noted in the Inspection Report (Inspection Exit Notice) will be required from the inspected establishment within a specified period of time. Responses should outline corrective actions to any deficiencies recorded.

6. *Response to Non-Compliance*

Where non-conformity to the Act and/or Regulations is identified, the inspected establishment will have the opportunity to correct identified deficiencies. Where necessary, the Inspectorate will consider enforcement actions in accordance with the HPFB Compliance and Enforcement Policy (POL-0001).

7. Responsibilities

It is the responsibility of the Inspectorate and the Marketed Health Products Directorate (MHPD) to collaborate and act in partnership in the application of this Inspection Strategy. It is the Inspectorate's responsibility to perform inspections and the responsibility of MHPD to analyze the data provided by the Inspectorate in conjunction with their objectives.

8. Procedures

Specific inspection activities will be documented and supported by detailed standard operating procedures.

9. Effective Date

The implementation date of this Inspection Strategy is August 1st, 2004.

10. References

1. Food and Drugs Act
2. Food and Drug Regulations
3. Health Products and Food Branch Compliance and Enforcement Policy, No. POL-0001
4. Health Canada, Guidelines for Reporting Adverse Reactions to Marketed Drugs, Guidelines for the Canadian Pharmaceutical Industry on Reporting Adverse Reactions to Marketed Drugs (Vaccines Excluded), Revised July 2001
5. Health Products and Food Branch, Therapeutic Products Directorate, New Drug - Sufficient Time (August 21, 1991)

Inspection Strategy POL-0041

Policy on Manufacturing and Compounding Drug Products in Canada (POL-0051)

Health Products and Food Branch Inspectorate

Supersedes: GUI-0030 (July 30, 2001)

Date issued: January 26, 2009

Date of implementation   January 26, 2009

Policy on Manufacturing and Compounding Drug Products in Canada (POL-0051)[96]

1.0 Purpose

The purpose of this document is:

1. To provide background information on the compounding and manufacturing of drugs in Canada;

2. To provide a policy framework to assist in distinguishing between compounding and manufacturing activities of drug products in Canada.

2.0 Scope

The scope of this policy framework covers drugs for human and veterinary use. This policy applies to all scheduled drugs regulated under the Food and Drugs Act (i.e., Schedule C (Radiopharmaceuticals), Schedule D (Biologics), Schedule F (Prescription drugs) and Schedule G (controlled substances) as well as Over the Counter drugs). Note, however, that this policy does not apply to natural health products (NHP) regulated under the Natural Health Products Regulations. A separate document will be provided by the Natural Health Products Directorate for compounding NHP.

3.0 Background

In Canada, compounding of drugs is practised primarily by pharmacists as an integral part of their profession and is regulated by the respective regulatory authorities in each province/territory. Other healthcare professionals such as physicians, veterinarians or dentists may also be involved in compounding activities when licensed to do so by the province/territory in which they practice. Drug manufacturing, on the other hand, is regulated by Health Canada under the

---

[96] Available on the Health Canada website at http://www.hc-sc.gc.ca/dhp-mps/compli-conform/gmp-bpf/docs/pol_0051-eng.php

federal Food and Drugs Act and Food and Drug Regulations. Since the maintenance and enhancement of health and safety is a responsibility that is shared between government (federal and provincial/territorial) and industry, consumers, healthcare professionals and their respective associations, it is important that the definitions for compounding and manufacturing be clearly understood so that the respective parties can fulfil their responsibilities in a coordinated and effective way.

In February 1997, a multidisciplinary workshop was held on the subject of the compounding and manufacturing of drugs in Canada. The need for clarity across roles and jurisdictions, as well as concerns related to particular products, processes and service providers were among the many issues highlighted. In July 2000, the policy document entitled Manufacturing and Compounding Drug Products in Canada was published by Health Canada following consultation with the National Association of Pharmacy Regulatory Authorities (NAPRA) and the Canadian Society of Hospital Pharmacists (CSHP).

Since the initial workshop, the compounding market has evolved greatly. The Health Products and Food Branch Inspectorate (HPFBI) held a facilitated focus group session in April 2004 to discuss the current issues on compounding, in an attempt to better differentiate compounding from the process of manufacturing. In addition, discussions also took place on developing a uniform approach to address issues that Federal and Provincial/Territorial regulators and healthcare professionals involved in compounding are confronted with. In essence, there is a need to develop a Canada wide consistency in approach to ensure that drug compounding and drug manufacturing are each regulated by the appropriate authorities.

4.0 Determination of Regulatory Responsibility / Jurisdiction

The following illustration (Figure 1.0) demonstrates the process to be followed by federal regulators, provincial/territorial regulators and healthcare professionals when dealing with jurisdictional issues related to compounding and manufacturing. Adopting this process will help develop a consistent Canada wide approach ensuring that all products and activities are appropriately regulated.

Figure 1.0 - Process in Addressing Manufacturing and Compounding Issues

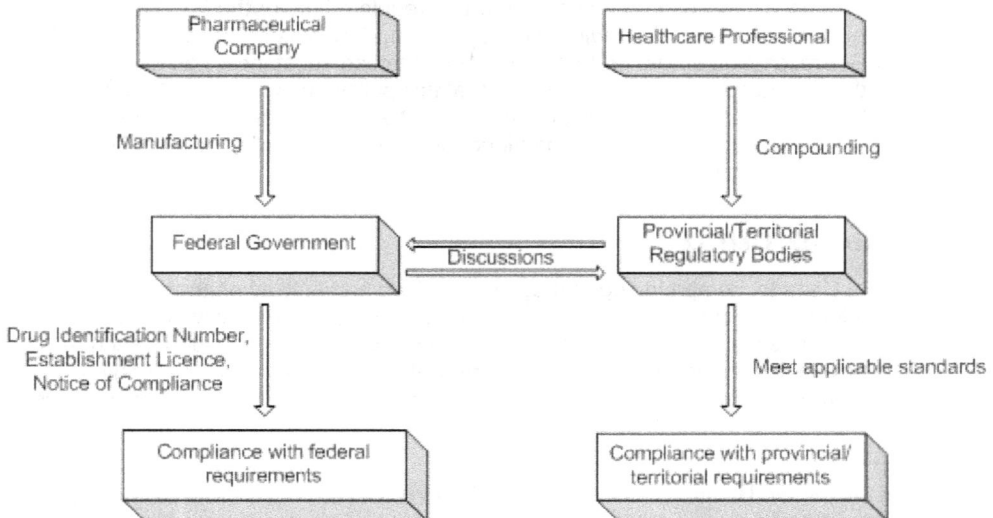

In essence, in circumstances where an individual cannot clearly determine whether a particular activity is considered to be manufacturing or compounding, they may contact either the Health Products and Food Branch Inspectorate or the respective provincial/territorial regulatory body (see Section 7.0 Associated Documents/Links - contact list). At that point, discussions may take place between the two jurisdictions for final determination of whether an activity is considered to be compounding or manufacturing.

Note that, in situations where the provincial/territorial regulatory authority decides that an activity does not fall within its jurisdiction, the activity is likely to be manufacturing and the parties involved must follow the federally regulated drug approval process for manufactured drugs.

4.1 Federal Jurisdiction

Manufacturers of drugs in dosage form must comply with the requirements of the Food and Drugs Act and Food and Drug Regulations including all associated standards and guidelines. In particular, manufactured drugs must be authorized for sale in Canada, meaning that the product authorization application received is reviewed for quality, safety and efficacy by Health Canada. In order to be sold in Canada, a drug will also require a Drug Identification Number (DIN) and/or Notice of Compliance (NOC) (Some products such as radiopharmaceuticals will not have a DIN). Furthermore all fabricators, packagers/labellers, distributors, importers, testers, and wholesalers will be required to obtain an Establishment Licence (EL) (Division 1A of Food and Drugs Act and Food and Drug Regulations), and meet the applicable sections of Division 2 relating to Good Manufacturing Practices (GMP) and comply with other relevant sections of the Food and Drug Regulations.

All healthcare professionals importing drug products must also comply with all applicable sections of the Food and Drugs Act and Food and Drug Regulations (C.01.005 (2) and C.01A.002(b) for importing drug products used in compounding).

All healthcare professionals compounding drug product must also comply with all relevant sections of the Food and Drugs Act including sections 3 - Prohibited advertising; 8 - Prohibited sales of drugs; 9 - Deception regarding drugs; and 11 - Unsanitary manufacture of drug.

4.2 Provincial/Territorial Jurisdiction

Healthcare Professionals

For the purpose of this Policy, Healthcare Professionals are those who are licensed to practise by their respective provincial/territorial regulatory authorities. Compounding is therefore a licensed or authorized act that falls within the scope of the practice of the professions such as pharmacy and medicine/dentistry/veterinary medicine or other healthcare professionals. Healthcare professionals who are engaged in compounding must comply with applicable provincial/territorial/federal regulations and their standards for these services. The responsibility for risk arising from compounding activities is assumed by licensed healthcare professionals in the treatment and servicing of their patients/clients.

The licensing of hospital pharmacies varies from province/territory to province/territory and may also depend if drug products are supplied only within the hospital or also to outpatients and third parties. The appropriate

Compounding
POL-0051

provincial/territorial regulatory authority should be consulted for additional information.

The use of compounded drugs in food animals is discouraged and the veterinarian is solely responsible for establishing an appropriate withdrawal time when using compounded drugs. Veterinarians should be aware that Canadian global Food Animal Residue Avoidance Databank (gFARAD) will not provide advice on withdrawal period for compounded drugs.

5.0 Policy Statement

This policy document is intended to embody the following guiding principles (key concepts are shown in bold):

General Guiding Principles

Compounding must be a legitimate part of the practice of regulated healthcare professionals and must not be used as a means to bypass the federal drug review and approval system.

All drug compounding and manufacturing activities performed are to be regulated and fall under either the federal or the provincial/territorial jurisdiction.

The distinguishing between compounding and manufacturing activities is made on a case-by-case basis.

5.1 Compounding

Factors to be considered when assessing whether an activity is compounding:

a. Healthcare professionals who provide compounding related services and products to patients/clients must be able to demonstrate that a patient-healthcare professional relationship exists.

b. Activity is regulated and facility may be inspected by provincial/territorial regulatory authorities.

c. It is expected that healthcare professionals who compound products will have appropriate risk management processes in place to manage risks associated with the compounded product and the workplace (facilities, safety etc.), in line with the standards set by their provincial/territorial regulatory bodies (for example but not limited to the toxicology, pharmacology, therapeutic value, stability, adverse reactions, labelling requirements etc. of the compounded product).

d. A pharmacy may prepare drugs in very limited quantities, in anticipation of a prescription. For the purpose of this Policy, preparation involves compounding or repackaging of multiple units, not for immediate use, in a single process, by the same operator in accordance with a standardized batch preparation procedure.

e. Compounding should only be done if there is a therapeutic need or lack of product availability and should not be done solely for economic reasons for the healthcare professionals.

f. The compounded product must provide a customized therapeutic solution to improve patient care without duplicating an approved drug product.

g. When there is a shortage or no supply of a commercially available product and the healthcare professional has determined a medical need for this product, the product may be compounded during the period of shortage or no supply only.

h. Drugs should not be compounded in order to be sold to third parties who will in turn sell/deliver to patients outside of their defined patient-healthcare professional relationship (see definition of "sell"). Pharmacists that do not provide specific compounding services may contract this activity to another pharmacist who provides this type of specific compounding service.

i. Compounding of clinical trial drugs is only permitted if this activity is authorized in the clinical trial application or experimental or investigational authorization.

j. Product should be produced from an authorized drug or Active Pharmaceutical Ingredient (API) used in an authorized drug for use in Canada or listed in a recognized Pharmacopoeia (USP, PhEur, PhF, PhI, BP, CF, NF, Codex - Schedule B Food and Drugs Act.)

k. Those engaged in sterile compounding should be knowledgeable and obtain specialized technical training in this area (The Canadian Society of Hospital Pharmacists as well as United States Pharmacopoeia (USP) have developed guidelines for the preparation of sterile preparations). Compounding of sterile products is only permitted in hospitals or other practice settings where carefully established standards for the operation of clean rooms and the preparation of sterile products are in place and documented, in accordance with a recognized source. The products are dispensed directly to patients or to those who administer to patients, and are operating within a demonstrated patient-healthcare professional relationship. Pharmacists may delegate some of the compounding responsibilities to pharmacy technicians if they are adequately trained in compounding sterile products or if the provincial/territorial laws authorize it.

l. Pharmacists in hospitals providing compounding services to other hospitals should be within the same province, and operate under the same hospital management board (ie. inter-hospital transfer, where the hospital may be composed of several facilities at different locations).

m. The compounded product must comply with all relevant sections of the Food and Drugs Act including sections 3 - Prohibited advertising; 8 - Prohibited sales of drugs; 9 - Deception regarding drugs; and 11 - Unsanitary manufacture of drug.

n. The expiration date of the compounded product is based on known stability data. If stability data is not available, the expiration date should be short, usually limited to the duration of the prescription or use.

5.2 Manufacturing

An activity will be considered manufacturing in the following circumstances:

a. Healthcare professionals who cannot demonstrate that a patient-healthcare professional relationship exists.

b. Producing an identical product that is already commercially available, unless there is a shortage (see section on compounding).

c. Producing or selling the product by a third party.

d. Healthcare professionals who produce products intended for distribution or sale outside the demonstrated patient-healthcare professional relationship.

e. Producing products made in such a scale, time and frequency to fall outside of a patient-healthcare professional relationship.

f. Clinical trial application, experimental or investigational authorization does not specify authorization to compound clinical trial drugs.

g. Producing a drug product that requires only minor modification prior to direct administration when such modification amounts to mere directions for use. Examples of such include the addition of liquid to a powder or adding a powder to animal drinking water. Compounding does not include mixing, reconstituting, or any other manipulation that is performed in accordance with the directions for use on an approved drug's labelling material (Aside added: "within the normal practice of pharmacy").

h. Repackaging commercially available drugs in finished dosage form outside the normal dispensing activities within the practice of pharmacy.

General guidelines on compounding and manufacturing activities is summarized in Appendix I.

For additional information, contact the appropriate provincial/territorial professional regulatory authority or Health Products and Food Branch Inspectorate in Ottawa. Refer to section 7.0 Associated Documents/Links for a complete list of College of Pharmacies and Health Canada website links.

6.0 Definitions

Active Pharmaceutical Ingredient (API)

Any substance or mixture of substances intended to be used in the manufacture of a drug (medicinal) product and that, when used in the production of a drug, becomes an active ingredient of the drug product. Such substances are intended to furnish pharmacological activity or other direct effect in the diagnosis, cure, mitigation, treatment, or prevention of disease or to affect the structure and function of the body. (ICH Q7)

Anticipation of a prescription

Pharmacies may prepare drugs in very limited quantities before receiving a valid prescription, provided they can document a history of receiving valid prescriptions that have been generated solely within an established patient-healthcare professional relationship, and provided further that they maintain the prescription on file as required by provincial law.

Compounding

> Health Canada considers compounding to be the following: The combining or mixing together of two or more ingredients (of which at least one is a drug or pharmacologically active component) to create a final product in an appropriate form for dosing. It can involve raw materials or the alteration of the form and strength of commercially available products. It can include reformulation to allow for a novel drug delivery. Compounding does not include mixing, reconstituting, or any other manipulation that is performed in accordance with the directions for use on an approved drug's labelling material (Aside added: "within the normal practice of pharmacy").

> For other definitions of compounding, see Section 7.0 Associated Documents/Links (USP, NAPRA, QCP, NSCP).

Customized Medication

> A formulation resulting from the combination of drugs or, APIs and/or non-medicinal ingredients that meets the patient's or animal's specific therapeutic needs.

Patient-Healthcare Professional Relationship

> A relationship that can be demonstrated to exist between a patient and a regulated healthcare professional in which a professional service is provided. When the relationship involves an animal, a valid veterinarian-client-patient relationship (VCPR) is required.

Healthcare Professional

> A person lawfully entitled under the laws of a province or a territory to provide health services in the place in which the services are provided by that person including a pharmacist, dentist, medical practitioner or a veterinarian.

Patient

> An individual or animal with unique requirements receiving medical treatment distinct from a group.

Pharmacist

> An individual who (a) is registered or otherwise authorized under the laws of a province or territory to practise pharmacy; and (b) is practising pharmacy in that province.

Prescription

> An order given by a practitioner directing that a stated amount of any drug or mixture of drugs specified therein be dispensed for the person named in the order (Food and Drug Regulations C.01.001).

Repackaging

Subsidizing or breaking up a manufacturer's original package of a drug for the purpose of dividing and assembling the drug in larger or smaller quantities for redistribution or sale by retail.

Sell

Includes offer for sale, expose for sale, have in possession for sale and distribute, whether or not the distribution is made for consideration. (Food and Drugs Act)

Third Party

Any individual, organization, or company outside of a patient-healthcare professional or valid veterinarian-client-patient relationship.

Valid Veterinarian-Client-Patient Relationship (VCP or VCPR)

See Patient-Healthcare Professional Relationship

A valid VCPR exists when these conditions apply:

- The client (owner or owner's agent of the animal[s]) has given the responsibility of medical care to the veterinarian and has agreed to follow the instructions of the veterinarian, and;

- the veterinarian has assumed the responsibility from the client for making clinical judgement regarding the health of the animal(s), the need for medical treatment, and for ensuring the provision of ongoing medical care for the animal(s);

- the veterinarian has sufficient knowledge of the health status of the animal(s) and the care received or to be received. The knowledge has been obtained through a recent examination of the animal(s) and the premises where they are (it is) kept or through a history of medically appropriate and timely examinations and interventions, and;

- the veterinarian is readily available, or has made the necessary arrangements with another veterinarian, for ongoing medical care of adverse reactions or therapy failure.

Withdrawal Period

The length of time between the last administration of a drug to an animal and the time when tissues or products collected from the treated animal for consumption as food contain a level of residue of the drug that would not likely cause injury to human health. (Food and Drug Regulations C.01.001)

7.0 Associated Documents/Links

Guidelines for Bulk Compounding of Products in Hospitals, Canadian Society of Hospital Pharmacists, Ottawa, Ontario 1992.

Guidelines for Preparation of Sterile Products in Pharmacies, Canadian Society of Hospital Pharmacists, Ottawa, Ontario 1996.

Guidelines for Repackaging Products in Healthcare Facilities, Canadian Society of Hospital Pharmacists, Ottawa, Ontario 1998.

Guidelines For The Legitimate Use Of Compounded Drugs in Veterinary Practice, Canadian Veterinary Medical Association, 2005

Guidelines to Pharmacy Compounding (Draft), National Association of Pharmacy Regulatory Authorities (NAPRA), Ottawa, Ontario 2005

Model Standards of Practice for Canadian Pharmacists, National Association of Pharmacy Regulatory Authorities (NAPRA), Ottawa, Ontario 2003.

National Association of Boards of Pharmacy Good Compounding Practices Applicable to State Licensed Pharmacies. National Association of Boards of Pharmacy. Park Ridge, IL, 2001; 151.

USP Chapter <795> Pharmaceutical Compounding: Nonsterile Preparations

USP Chapter <797> Pharmaceutical Compounding: Sterile Preparations

Some of the following hyperlinks are to sites of organizations or other entities that are not subject to the Official Language Act. The material found there is therefore in the language(s) used by the sites in question.

Website addresses:

College of Pharmacies

1. **British Columbia:** College of Pharmacists of British Columbia

   http://www.bcpharmacists.org/#College%20of%20Pharmacists%20of%20British%20Columbia

2. **Alberta:** Alberta college of pharmacists

   https://pharmacists.ab.ca/nCollege/default.aspx

3. **Saskatchewan:** Saskatchewan College of Pharmacists

   http://www.napra.org/docs/0/203/262/266.asp

4. **Manitoba:** Manitoba Pharmaceutical Association

   http://www.napra.org/docs/0/203/262/266.asp

5. **Ontario:** Ontario College of Pharmacists

   http://www.ocpinfo.com/

6. **Quebec:** Ordre des pharmaciens du Québec

   http://www.opq.org/fr/

7. **New Brunswick:** New Brunswick Pharmaceutical Society

   http://www.nbpharmacists.ca/

Compounding
POL-0051

8. **Nova Scotia:** Nova Scotia College of Pharmacists

   http://www.nspharmacists.ca/

9. **Newfoundland:** Newfoundland & Labrador Pharmacy Board

   http://www.nlpb.ca/

10. **Prince Edward Island:** Prince Edward Island Pharmacy Board

    http://www.napra.org/docs/0/203/260.asp

11. **Yukon:** Yukon Community Services

    http://www.napra.org/docs/0/203/264/279.asp

12. **Northwest Territories:** Northwest Territories Department of Health and Social Services

    http://www.napra.org/docs/0/203/263/278.asp

Health Canada

1. **DIN Applications:** Guideline on Preparation of DIN Submissions

   http://www.hc-sc.gc.ca/dhp-mps/prodpharma/applic-demande/guide-ld/din/pre_din_ind-eng.php

2. **Drug Establishment Licences:** Drug Establishment Licences

   http://www.hc-sc.gc.ca/dhp-mps/compli-conform/licences/drugs-drogues/index-eng.php

3. **Drug Submissions:** Guidance on Drug Establishment Licences (GUIDE-0002)

   http://www.hc-sc.gc.ca/dhp-mps/compli-conform/licences/directives/gui_0002_tc-tm-eng.php

4. **EDR:** Veterinary Drugs - Emergency Drug Release (EDR)

   http://www.hc-sc.gc.ca/dhp-mps/vet/edr-dmu/index-eng.php

5. **Good Manufacturing Practices:** Good Manufacturing Practices - Guidance documents

   http://www.hc-sc.gc.ca/dhp-mps/compli-conform/gmp-bpf/docs/index-eng.php

6. **HPFBI:** Health Products and Food Branch Inspectorate - Compliance and Enforcement

   http://www.hc-sc.gc.ca/dhp-mps/compli-conform/index-eng.php

7. **SAP:** Special Access to Drugs and Health Products

   http://www.hc-sc.gc.ca/dhp-mps/acces/index-eng.php

Associations

1. **ASHP:** American Society of Health-System Pharmacists

   http://www.ashp.org/

2. **CSHP:** Canadian Society of Hospitals Pharmacists

   http://www.cshp.ca/

3. **NAPRA:** National Association of Pharmacy Regulatory Authorities

   http://www.napra.org/pages/home/default.aspx

8.0 Authors

This Policy Framework was developed by the Health Products and Food Branch Inspectorate in collaboration with other Health Products and Food Branch directorates and members of the April 2004 focus group session.

Appendix I General Guideline on Compounding and Manufacturing Activities

1) Is there a demonstrated patient-healthcare professional relationship?

   - Compounding - Yes
   - Manufacturing - No

2) Is there third party reselling of the product outside of the patient-healthcare professional relationship?

   - Compounding - No
   - Manufacturing - Yes

3) Is the activity regulated, and facility possibly inspected, by the province/territory?

   - Compounding - Yes
   - Manufacturing - No

4) If producing product in anticipation of a prescription, is the amount produced consistent with the history of prescriptions received?

   - Compounding - Yes
   - Manufacturing - No

5) Is there an inordinate amount of product produced or on a regular basis?

   - Compounding - No
   - Manufacturing - Yes

Compounding POL-0051

6) Is an identical product (e.g. dosage form, strength, formulation) commercially available?

- Compounding - No
- Manufacturing - Yes

7) Is the product and/or compounding service promoted or advertised to the general public rather than strictly to healthcare professionals?

- Compounding - No
- Manufacturing - Yes

8) Does the drug product require only minor modification prior to direct administration when such modification amounts to mere directions for use?

- Compounding - No
- Manufacturing - Yes

Inspection Strategy for Canada's Access to Medicines Regime (CAMR) (POL-0055)

Health Products and Food Branch Inspectorate

Supersedes: New document

Date issued: August 2007

Date of implementation: September 2007

Inspection Strategy for Canada's Access to Medicines Regime (POL-0055)[97]

1. Purpose

The purpose of this document is to detail the Health Product and Food Branch Inspectorate's strategy for the effective and uniform implementation of Canada's Access to Medicines Regime (CAMR) inspection program to assess compliance with the regulatory requirements as detailed in the Act to amend the Patent Act and the Food and Drugs Act (The Jean Chrétien Pledge to Africa), formerly Bill C-9, and in the Regulations Amending the Food and Drug Regulations (1402 - Drugs for Developing Countries).

2. Background

There are two key components to the compliance and enforcement efforts with respect to Canada's Access to Medicines Regime: the pre-export inspection and the amendment to section 37 of the Food and Drugs Act that requires a drug manufacturer under this program to adhere to all applicable requirements of the Food and Drugs Act and its regulations.

Health Canada has committed to pre-export inspections of manufacturers exporting to developing or least- developed countries under Canada's Access to Medicines Regime. Pre-export inspections, as part of anti-diversion measures, will confirm the existence of distinguishing characteristics on the products, their immediate containers, if applicable, and their labels.

Inspections will be conducted by Health Canada under the authority of sections 23 and 24 of the Food and Drugs Act. These activities will be conducted by the Health Products and Food Branch Inspectorate (Inspectorate). Collaboration with all stakeholders taking part in Canada's Access to Medicines Regime will be essential to ensure compliance with the new regulations.

---

[97] Available on the Health Canada website at http://www.hc-sc.gc.ca/dhp-mps/compli-conform/gmp-bpf/docs/pol_0055-eng.php

3. Scope

This inspection strategy applies to manufacturers of drug products intended for exportation under Canada's Access to Medicines Regime.

The notification required under the Food and Drug Regulations is linked to the exportation of the manufactured product. All manufacturers participating in the program must notify Health Canada as indicated in section C.07.011 of the Food and Drug Regulations and will be subject to pre-export inspections.

4. Definitions

Authorization under section 21.04 of the Patent Act

> This is an authorization to use a patented invention granted by the Commissioner of Patents at the Canadian Intellectual Property Office (CIPO) under section 21.04 of the Patent Act. This authorization is often referred to as a "compulsory licence". (Autorisation en vertu de l'article 21.04 de la Loi sur les brevets)

Compliance verification

> Action taken to verify compliance in response to information regarding known or suspected noncompliance with the applicable requirements of the Food and Drugs Act and its associated regulations. This includes actions such as information gathering via either off-site or on-site visits. (Vérification de la conformité)

Inspection

> On-site monitoring and assessment against the applicable requirements of the Food and Drugs Act and its associated regulations. Inspections are routinely conducted on a predetermined cycle or as required to assess compliance. (Inspection)

Inspectorate

> The Health Products and Food Branch (HPFB) directorate whose primary role is to deliver a national compliance and enforcement program for all products under the mandate of the HPFB, with the exception of products regulated as foods. (Inspectorat)

Investigation

> Action taken to gather evidence to support case referral for potential judicial determination regarding specific violations of the Food and Drugs Act and its associated regulations. This includes activities carried out under the Criminal Code such as taking witness statements and executing search warrants. (Enquête)

Inspector

> Any person designated as an inspector for the purpose of the enforcement of the Food and Drugs Act under subsection 22(1). (Inspecteur)

Manufacturer

> "manufacturer" or "distributor" means a person, including an association or partnership, who under their own name, or under a trade-, design or word mark, trade name or other name, word or mark controlled by them, sells a food or drug (A.01.010). (Fabricant)

For additional definitions, consult the documents listed as references at the end of this strategy.

5. Compliance and Monitoring Activities

The Inspectorate will provide information and encourage voluntary compliance with Canadian regulatory requirements. Compliance will be assessed through inspections and compliance verifications conducted by the Inspectorate.

5.1 Pre-export inspection

The Inspectorate will assess the compliance of manufacturers with the regulatory requirements pertaining to Canada's Access to Medicines Regime, including sections C.07.008 (Marking and Labelling), C.07.009 (Export Tracking Number), C.07.010 (Records) of the Food and Drug Regulations.

Note: *All regulatory requirements that a manufacturer must meet for drug products destined for the Canadian market also apply to CAMR products, in addition to Part C Division 7 of the Food and Drug Regulations. Therefore, inspections regarding establishment licensing and good manufacturing practices (GMP) will continue to take place for manufacturers of these products.*

The pre-export inspections under Canada's Access to Medicines Regime will begin in 2006. The inspection program will be assessed after the first year of operation in order to determine whether modifications are required.

5.1.1 Inspection activities

- The Inspectorate will perform a pre-export inspection of each lot of drug product exported under the Authorization under section 21.04 of the Patent Act.

- A pre-export inspection will verify the existence of distinguishing characteristics on the products, the immediate containers if applicable, and their labels to dentify them as having been manufactured under compulsory licence (authorization under section 21.04 of the Patent Act). The distinguishing characteristics are required by section C.07.008 of the Food and Drug Regulations, as a measure to prevent diversion and re-importation.

- A pre-export inspection will verify the quantity of drug product that is authorized to be manufactured and sold for export under Canada's Access to Medicines Regime and will check the information that identifies the parties that will be handling the product while it is in transit from Canada to the country or World Trade Organization (WTO) Member to which t is to be exported.

- A pre-export inspection will be undertaken prior to export of each shipment. To facilitate these inspections, the manufacturer is required to notify the Minister in writing not less than 15 days before commencing the manufacture of the first lot of a drug product authorized to be sold under Part C Division 7 of the Food and Drug Regulations and not less than 15 days before the exportation of each subsequent lot of the drug product.

◆ In addition to the pre-export inspection, Health Canada's legislative/regulatory authority to conduct compliance and enforcement activities, including the delivery of unannounced/random inspections and sampling of finished products for analysis in Health Canada laboratories, continues to exist under Canada's Access to Medicines Regime. Regular good manufacturing practices (GMP) inspections will be performed on a scheduled basis. If a regularly scheduled GMP inspection coincides with the planned export of a shipment, then the inspections could happen simultaneously.

◆ Sampling of the finished product will be carried out at every pre-export inspection in accordance with SOP-0200 - Sampling Procedures. The subject of sampling will the be revisited to determine the frequency needed after the first year of pre-export inspections is complete.

◆ The Certificate of Pharmaceutical Product (CPP) is currently offered as an optional service to Canadian establishments desiring to export to countries which request the CPP as evidence of the status of the pharmaceutical product listed on the certificate and the GMP status of the applicant for the certificate. This option will continue to exist under Canada's Access to Medicines Regime.

5.1.2 Duration of inspections

The average duration of the inspection is estimated at one day. The average time for an inspection will be re-assessed after the first year of operation of the inspection program.

5.1.3 Inspection Rating and Reporting:

◆ Two ratings will be used:

◆ C - No objectionable conditions or practices were observed with regards to regulatory requirements

◆ NC - Objectionable conditions or practices were observed with regards to regulatory requirements

◆ An Inspection report will be issued to the inspected establishment in a timely manner. The Inspection Report will contain observations noted during the inspection. An Exit Notice will be issued to the establishment.

◆ Responses to observations noted in the Inspection Report (Inspection Exit Notice) will be required from the inspected establishment within a specified period of time. Responses should outline corrective actions to any deficiencies recorded.

5.2 Compliance Verification

When a potential non-compliance or risk has been identified by Health Canada, compliance verification will be conducted if deemed necessary. Problems or concerns related to the performance of Canada's Access to Medicines Regime may originate from:

- External sources or referrals from other jurisdictions.

- Internal Departmental and Branch sources, such as the Therapeutic Products Directorate (TPD), Biologics and Genetic Therapies Directorate (BGTD), and Marketed Health Products Directorate (MHPD).

6. Response to Non-Compliance

Where non-conformity to the Food and Drugs Act and/or the Food and Drug Regulations is identified, the inspected establishment will have the opportunity to correct identified deficiencies.

In all cases, the results will be communicated to the appropriate Directorate(s): TPD or BGTD and/or MHPD if applicable.

Where a drug authorized to be sold under Canada's Access to Medicines Regime is determined to no longer meet the requirements of the Food and Drugs Act and the Food and Drug Regulations, the Inspectorate's Director General will notify the Commissioner of Patents (CIPO) in the form of a "Notice to the Commissioner of Patents".

7. Responsibilities

It is the responsibility of the Inspectorate and all stakeholders to collaborate and act in partnership in the application of this inspection strategy.

8. Procedures

Specific inspection, compliance verification and investigation activities will be documented and supported by detailed standard operating procedures.

9. Effective Date

The effective date of this Inspection Strategy is August 29, 2007.

10. References

1. Food and Drugs Act

2. Food and Drug Regulations

3. Act to amend The Patent Act and the Food and Drugs Act (The Jean Chrétien Pledge to Africa) - Bill C-9

4. Regulations Amending the Food and Drug Regulations (1402 - Drugs for Developing Countries)

5. Health Products and Food Branch Inspectorate's Guidance for Access to Medicines Pre-manufacturing and Pre-exportation Notifications C.07.011), No. GUI-0072

CAMR
POL-0055

Part VII

Forms

Alternate Sample Retention Site

Health Products and Food Branch Inspectorate

(October 10, 2006)

Unit Name: Drug GMP Inspection Unit

Alternate Sample Retention Site Application Form [98]

---

[98] Available on the Health Canada website at

Santé Canada
Health Canada

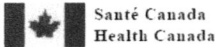

Alternate Sample Retention Site Application Form
Formulaire de demande de site alternatif pour la rétention d'échantillons

*Once completed, please fax this application form to the Health Products and Food Branch Inspectorate at (613) 952-9805 or e-mail it to <u>GMP_Questions_BPF@hc-sc.gc.ca</u> .
Une fois complété, veuillez faire parvenir ce formulaire de demande à l'Inspectorat de la Direction générale des produits de santé et des aliments par télécopieur au (613) 952-9805 ou par courriel à l'adresse suivante <u>GMP_Questions_BPF@hc-sc.gc.ca</u> .

---

1. Importer or Distributor / *Importateur ou distributeur*

Name / *Nom* :
Address / *Adresse* :
Telephone number / *Numéro de téléphone* :
Fax number / *Numéro de télécopieur* :

2. Product / *Produit*

Name / *Nom* :
DIN (if applicable) / *DIN (le cas échéant)* :

3. Fabricator / *Manufacturier*

Name / *Nom* :
Address / *Adresse* :
Telephone number / *Numéro de téléphone* :
Fax number / *Numéro de télécopieur* :

4. Site where samples are to be retained / *Établissement où les échantillons seront conservés*

Name / *Nom* :
Address / *Adresse* :
Telephone number / *Numéro de téléphone* :
Fax number / *Numéro de télécopieur* :

*Please note that if the alternate site is located outside of Canada, it must be listed as a foreign site on a Canadian establishment's Drug Establishment Licence. If the alternate site is located in Canada, the Canadian establishment must hold a Drug Establishment Licence.
Veuillez prendre note que si le site alternatif est situé à l'extérieur du Canada, il doit être inscrit en tant que site étranger sur la licence d'établissement pharmaceutique d'un établissement canadien. Si le site alternatif est situé au Canada, l'établissement canadien doit détenir une licence d'établissement pharmaceutique.

5. Criteria for assessment (complete as applicable) / *Critères d'évaluation (remplir selon le cas)*

a. The testing of this product requires specialized product-specific methodology that is not available in Canada :
L'analyse de ce produit exige une méthode spécialisée, spécifique au produit, qui n'est pas disponible au Canada :

        Yes/Oui ☐   No/Non ☐

If yes, please specify (e.g. unique bioassay involving the use of cell lines or animals) :
Dans l'affirmative, veuillez préciser (p. ex. dosage biologique particulier exigeant le recours à des lignées cellulaires ou à des animaux) :

Page 1 of / de 3

Health Canada
Santé Canada

---

b. This product is subject to Health Canada's lot release programme : *Le produit est visé par le programme d'autorisation de mise en circulation des lots de Santé Canada :* Yes/Oui ☐   No/Non ☐

c. Estimated Canadian utilization :
Consommation canadienne estimative :
     i. Approximate number of lots sold annually in Canada :
     Nombre approximatif de lots vendus annuellement au Canada :
     ii. Approximate number of units sold annually in Canada :
     Nombre approximatif d'unités vendues annuellement au Canada :

d. Average batch size imported to Canada / *Taille moyenne d'un lot de fabrication importé au Canada :*
e. Approximate unit cost/value per sample / *Coût/valeur unitaire approximatif par échantillon :*
f. Shelf life of perishable drug / *Durée de vie de la drogue périssable :*
g. Radiopharmaceuticals / *Produits radiopharmaceutiques :* Yes/Oui ☐   No/Non ☐

h. Non-prescription drug (see Category IV product monographs) :
Drogues en vente libre (voir les monographies de produit de la catégorie IV) :
Yes/Oui ☐ (Specify below/*Spécifier ci-dessous)*   No/Non ☐
 	
_____ ☐ Acne therapies / *produits contre l'acné (topique)*
          ☐ Anti dandruff products / *produits antipelliculaires*
          ☐ Antiperspirants / *produits antisudorifiques*
          ☐ Antiseptic skin cleansers / *nettoyants antiseptiques pour la peau*
          ☐ Athletes foot treatments / *traitements contre le pied d'athlète*
          ☐ Fluoride-containing anti-caries products / *produits contre la carie dentaire contenant du fluorure*
          ☐ Medicated skin care products / *produits médicamenteux pour le soin de la peau*
          ☐ Sunburn protectants / *agents de protection solaire*

i. Hard surface disinfectants / *désinfectants pour surface dure :* Yes/Oui ☐   No/Non ☐
j. The fabricator of the drug is located in Canada and is responsible for keeping the retained samples. *Le manufacturier du médicament est situé au Canada et est responsable de la rétention d'échantillons.* Yes/Oui ☐   (Complete section 4 / *Remplir la section 4)*   No/Non ☐

Page 2 of de 3

Health Canada
Santé Canada

Alternate Sample Retention Site Application Form (...continued)
Formulaire de demande de site alternatif pour la rétention d'échantillons (...suite)

6. Attestation / *Attestation*
We have formally arranged with the storage site to maintain sufficient numbers of samples of lots and retained as per storage conditions indicated on the label, with the same container-closure sold in Canada to allow access by all pertinent regulatory authorities including Health Canada.   *Nous avons pris des dispositions officielles avec l'établissement d'entreposage pour qu'il conserve, conformément aux conditions d'entreposage indiquées sur l'étiquette, des nombres suffisants d'échantillons de lots doté du même système contenant-fermeture vendus au Canada de manière à ce que toutes les autorités réglementaires concernées, y compris Santé Canada, puissent y avoir accès.*   Yes/Oui ☐   No/Non ☐

7. Commitment / *Engagement*
We have a written commitment with the responsible person at the storage site that samples will be provided within 48 hours of receiving a request from Health Canada.   *Nous avons un engagement écrit avec la personne responsable de l'établissement d'entreposage pour qu'il fournisse des échantillons dans les 48 heures qui suivent la réception d'une demande provenant de Santé Canada.*   Signature, Responsible Officer / *Signature de l'agent responsable* :   Title / *Titre* :   Emergency Telephone Number / *Numéro de téléphone en cas d'urgence* :

Please note that your Alternate Sample Retention Site Application expires with the Drug Establishment Licence (i.e. December 31 of the year of issue) or with the Terms & Conditions, if shorter.

Veuillez noter que votre demande de site alternatif pour la rétention d'échantillon vient à échéance au même moment que votre licence d'établissement de produits pharmaceutiques (soit le 31 décembre de l'année courante) ou avec les modalités et conditions, selon la plus courte échéance.

Drugs under Foreign Ownership

(May 1st, 2004)

Notification Form / Conditions for Provision of Packaging/Labelling Services for Drugs under Foreign Ownership (GUIDE-0067)[99]

---

[99] Available on the Health Canada website at http://www.hc-sc.gc.ca/dhp-mps/compli-conform/gmp-bpf/form/gui_67_form_tc-tm-eng.php

Notification Form / Formulaire de notification

Part 1/ Partie 1 **Notification to Health Canada prior to shipment to Canada /** **Notification à Santé Canada avant l'envoi au Canada**

Contract packager-labeller	Emballeur/étiqueteur contractuel
Name / Nom : Address / Adresse : City / Ville, Province : Postal Code / Code postal : Telephone / Téléphone : Fax :	
Drug to be packaged/labelled	Drogue à être emballée/étiquetée
Name (active ingredient) / Nom (ingrédient actif) : Brand name / Nom de marque : Quantity / Quantité : Manufacture date / Date de fabrication :	
Foreign fabricator	Manufacturier étranger
Name / Nom : Address / Adresse : City / Ville : Country / Pays :	
Expected date of entry into Canada	Date prévue d'entrée au Canada
Port of entry in Canada	Port d'entrée au Canada
Expected date of return to the fabricator	Date prévue de retour au manufacturier étranger

Part 2/ Partie 2 **Notification to Health Canada after the return of the drug to the foreign owner /** **Notification à Santé Canada après l'expédition de la drogue au propriétaire étranger**

Quantity packaged Type and format of packaging material	Quantité emballée Type et format du matériel d'emballage
Quantity of drug per packaging unit Number of units packaged	Quantité de drogue / unité d'emballage Nombre d'unités emballées
Quantity of packaged units returned to the fabricator Date of return Transport Mode	Nombre d'unités emballées retournées au manufacturier Date de retour Moyen de transport
If discrepancies, please explain:	Si différence, svp expliquez
Signature :	

Foreign Sites

Good Manufacturing Practices Forms

Audit Report Form (FRM-0211)

Audit Report Form (FRM-0211) – Instructions

Foreign Site Submission Form (FRM-0212)

Request for Inspection of a Foreign Site Form (FRM-0213)

Foreign Site Inspection Services Agreement Form (FRM-0214)

Audit Report Form (FRM-0211)[100]

Applicants may submit a corporate or consultant audit report, using the Audit Report Form, as evidence to establish the compliance of a foreign site with Division 2 (GMP) of the Food and Drug Regulations (FDR), so long as the criteria outlined in the guidance "Guidance on Evidence to Demonstrate Drug GMP Compliance of Foreign Sites" (GUI-0080) are met.

The audit must be conducted by an individual(s) that possesses sufficient knowledge of and experience with Good Manufacturing Practices (GMP) and is qualified according to section C.02.006 of the FDR.

Note: The Audit Report Form (FRM-0211) is a 43 page document available as both a PDF and Word document on the Health Canada website. The following two pages are examples of the first two pages of that document.

---

[100] Available on the Health Canada website at http://www.hc-sc.gc.ca/dhp-mps/alt_formats/hpfb-dgpsa/pdf/compli-conform/gui-0080-form-0211-eng.pdf

I✦I Health   Santé
Canada   Canada

GOOD MANUFACTURING PRACTICES - AUDIT REPORT FORM (FRM-0211)
Health Products and Food Branch Inspectorate

HC USE ONLY	
File Number	Date/Time of Receipt

Please refer to the Instructions on how to complete this form.

GENERAL INFORMATION

A. Submission Information

1a. Date(s) of audit	2a. Date of last inspection
1b. Purpose of audit:	**2b. Type of last inspection:**

1b. Purpose of audit:

New Establishment Licence Application ☐
Amendment to Establishment Licence ☐
Renewal of Establishment Licence ☐
In Support of a Drug Submission ☐ (please specify)

2b. Type of last inspection:

Corporate Audit ☐
Consultant Audit ☐
Regulatory Agency ☐ (please specify)
Qualified Authority ☐ (please specify)
Other ☐ (please specify)

B. Building Information

3. Building Name

4. Address, Number/Street/Suite/Land Location/Plot

5. City/Town	6. Province/State	7. Postal Code/Zip Code	8. Country
9. Telephone Number	10. Fax Number	11. Website	

C. Personnel

12a. Opening meeting attendees	12b. Closing meeting attendees

D. Scope of Audit

13. Operation(s):

14. Product(s)/Dosage Form(s):

E. Auditor Information

15. Name(s):	16. Type:
17. Qualifications and experience:	Corporate ☐ Consultant ☐

F. Background Information:

18.

FRM-0211 v1 (2008)

Canadä

Premises [C.02.004]

The premises in which a lot or batch of a drug is fabricated or packaged/labelled shall be designed, constructed and maintained in a manner that

(a) permits the operations therein to be performed under clean, sanitary and orderly conditions;	Yes ☐	No ☐
(b) permits the effective cleaning of all surfaces therein; and	Yes ☐	No ☐
(c) prevents the contamination of the drug and the addition of extraneous material to the drug.	Yes ☐	No ☐

If yes, describe.

If no, provide a rationale (e.g. Not applicable because…)

Deviations

Identify and describe any noted GMP deviation(s) and the rationale for the deviation, where applicable.

No.	Observations	Risk Classification

Corrective actions

Detail the corrective action(s) taken and/or to be taken.

Attachments

Attach supporting documentation such as SOPs, action plans with timelines for each corrective action identified above.

List of attachments:

FRM-0211 v1 (2008)

Canadä

Audit Report Form (FRM-0211) - Instructions[101]

Applicants may submit a corporate or consultant audit report, using the Audit Report Form, as evidence to establish the compliance of a foreign site with Division 2 (GMP) of the Food and Drug Regulations (FDR), so long as the criteria outlined in the guidance "Guidance on Evidence to Demonstrate Drug GMP Compliance of Foreign Sites" (GUI-0080) are met.

The audit must be conducted by an individual(s) that possesses sufficient knowledge of and experience with Good Manufacturing Practices (GMP) and is qualified according to section C.02.006 of the FDR.

General Information

Instructions:

1a) Indicate the date(s) when the audit was conducted.

1b) Define the type of submission by checking off one of the following boxes

- **New Establishment Licence Application:** First-time applications

- **Amendment to Establishment Licence:** Submission for amendment

- **Renewal of Establishment Licence:** Submission for renewal

- **In support of a Drug Submission:** If this audit report is being submitted in support of a drug submission, indicate the submission control number, along with the name of the product for which the submission has been filed.

2a) Date of the last inspection at the building identified under B.

2b) Define the type of the last inspection by checking off one of the following boxes:

- **Corporate audit:** inspection was conducted internally

- **Consultant audit:** inspection was conducted by an independent person(s) or organization

- **Regulatory Authority:** as defined in Section C.01A.001(1) of the FDR, a government agency or other entity in a Mutual Recognition Agreement (MRA) country that has a legal right to control the use or sale of drugs within that country and that may take enforcement action to ensure that drugs marketed within its jurisdiction comply with legal requirements

- **Qualified Authority:** an authority member of the Pharmaceutical Inspection Co-operation Scheme (PIC/S) or the United States Food and Drug Administration (USFDA)

- **Other:** any other type of inspection

3) The registered name of the building

---

[101] Available on the Health Canada website at http://www.hc-sc.gc.ca/dhp-mps/compli-conform/gmp-bpf/form/gui-0080-instr-dir-0211-eng.php

4-11) Indicate the street address, city/town, province/state, postal/zip code, country where the building is located.

Building refers to one location, one address. When an applicant carries out activities in more than one building at different addresses, an Audit Report must be completed for each address.

12a) The list of attendees present at the opening meeting, along with their title.

12b) The list of attendees present at the closing meeting, along with their title.

13) Indicate the activity(ies) that is(are) being performed in this building: manufacturing, packaging, labelling and/or testing.

14) Indicate the product(s) that were covered during the audit. Include the product(s)'s Drug Identification Number, if assigned, along with its dosage form(s).

15) Identify the name of the auditor(s).

16) Define the type of audit that was conducted by checking off one of the following boxes:

- **Corporate:** audit was conducted internally
- **Consultant:** audit was conducted by an independent person(s) or organization

17) Indicate how the person(s) identified in box #15 is considered to be qualified by specifying his/her education, training, technical knowledge, etc.

18) Include general information with respect to the layout of the facility. It is recommended that a site map be included for facilities with numerous buildings. In addition, include a brief history of the facility, including any changes that have occurred since the last inspection, as well as any other information that is not captured under any of the above boxes.

If the audit was product-specific, include an overview of the product's manufacturing process, as well as any other pertinent information.

Detailed Report

Division 2 of the FDR sets out the Good Manufacturing Practices (GMP) that manufacturers, packagers, labellers, testers, importers, distributors and wholesalers must meet before an Establishment Licence (EL) will be issued.

Statements/Questions: Yes/No

The statements/questions in this report are divided into sections in accordance with those outlined in Division 2 of the FDR.

Check off the response to the statement/question as either Yes that the statement/question is correct or No that the statement/question is not correct. If the statement/question is unclear, refer to the appropriate section(s) in the GMP guidance document (GUI-0001) for assistance.

If the answer to the statement/question is yes, clearly describe, in the space provided, how the site complies with the referenced section of FDR.

If the answer is no, provide a clear rationale, in the space provided, as to why the statement/question is not applicable to the activities conducted at the site.

Note: Additional pages may be attached if the space provided is not sufficient. Identify the additional pages that have been attached under the Supporting Documentation section.

Deviations

For each statement/question, list in the provided table all of the deviations from Division 2 of the FDR that were observed during the audit. Assess the risk associated with each observation, based on Health Canada's guide "Risk Classification of GMP Observations (GUI-0023)":

"Risk 1" (critical) are observations describing a situation that is likely to result in a non-compliance product or a situation that may result in an immediate or health risk and any observation that involves fraud, misrepresentation or falsification of products or data.

"Risk 2" (major) are observations that may result in the production of a drug non consistently meeting its marketing authorization.

"Risk 3" (other) are observations that are neither "Risk 1" nor "Risk 2" but are a departure from the GMP.

Corrective Actions

If deviation(s) were listed above, describe in the space provided the details of the corrective action(s) that were taken or will be taken, along with time lines, in addition to any preventive measures to avoid recurrence, as needed.

For each listed deviation(s), a corrective action plan may be attached and listed under the Supporting Documentation section.

Supporting Documentation

List all supporting documentation as described above (SOP(s), corrective action plan(s), etc.), and attach the document(s) directly behind the statement/question page.

For each statement/question, the applicant is required to list the title(s) and the number(s) of the relevant standard operating procedure(s) that are in use at the site. However, the actual SOP(s) does not need to be attached, unless the applicant feels that the SOP(s) will help in the assessment of the site's compliance with Division 2 of the FDR. In addition, a copy of any SOP may be requested at any time during the assessment of the site's compliance with Division 2 of the FDR.

Overall Rating

A judgement is required on the part of the auditor(s) as to the overall compliance, based on Health Canada's guide "Risk Classification of GMP Observations (GUI-0023)", of the site with Division 2 of the FDR.

If the answer to the statement/question is yes, clearly describe, in the space provided, how the site complies with Division 2 of the FDR.

If the answer is no, provide a clear rationale, in the space provided, as to why the site does not comply with Division 2 of the FDR.

Attestation

The person(s) that conducted the audit, as identified in box #15, is(are) required to Print and Sign his/her name and Date this part of the Audit Report form.

In addition, if deviations were observed during the audit, it is requested that an official with signing authority, from the audited foreign site, Print and Sign his/her name and Date the second attestation.

Foreign Site Submission Form (FRM-0212)[102]

Section 1: Requester Information

Company Name:

Establishment Licence and/or Drug Submission Control Number(s):

Do you wish to have this foreign site added to the above Establishment Licence? (Yes No)

(The Establishment Licence Unit will be informed of this review)

Contact:

Telephone:

Fax:

E-mail:

Section 2: Foreign Site Information

Company Name:

Street:

Suite:

Post Office Box:

City:

Province/State:

Country:

Postal Code:

Section 3: Product(s) Information

Product Name and DIN (Drug Identification Number)

Activity

F = Fabricate

P = Package/Label

---

[102] Available on the Health Canada website at http://www.hc-sc.gc.ca/dhp-mps/compli-conform/gmp-bpf/form/gui-0080-form-0212-eng.php

T = Test

Category

1 = Pharmaceutical

2 = Vaccine

3 = Blood & Blood Components

4 = Biological

5 = Radiopharmaceutical

Dosage Form Class

1 = Parenteral

2 = Tablet

3 = Capsule

4 = Solution

5 = Suspension

6 = Aerosol

7 = Powder

8 = Suppository

9 = Medical Gas

10 = Veterinary Premix

11 = Bulk Intermediates

12 = Other (Specify)

Sterile (Yes No)

Section 4: Type of Evidence

a.) Site in the Mutual Recognition Agreement (MRA) country? (Yes/No) If yes, please specify the Regulatory Authority.

b.) Site not located in the MRA or not covered under a MRA? (Yes/No) If yes, please specify the name and date of the document(s) being submitted.

c.) Site currently approved by Health Canada? (Yes/No)

Name of Authorized Signing Official

Title

Signature / Date

Good Manufacturing Practices - Foreign Site Submission Form (FRM-0212)

SECTION 1: REQUESTER INFORMATION		
Company Name:		
Establishment Licence and/or Drug Submission Control Number(s):		
Do you wish to have this foreign site added to the above Establishment Licence? (*The Establishment Licensing Unit will be informed of this review.*)	Yes ☐	No ☐
Contact:		
Telephone:	Fax:	
E-mail:		

SECTION 2: FOREIGN SITE INFORMATION		
Company Name:		
Street:	Suite:	Post Office Box:
City:	Province/State:	
Country:	Postal Code:	

SECTION 3: PRODUCT(S) INFORMATION

Product Name and DIN	Activity	Category	Dosage Form Class		Sterile (Y / N)
	F = Fabricate P = Package/Label T = Test	1 = Pharmaceutical 2 = Vaccine 3 = Blood & Blood Components 4 = Biological 5 = Radiopharmaceutical	1 = Parenteral 2 = Tablet 3 = Capsule 4 = Solution 5 = Suspension 6 = Aerosol	7 = Powder 8 = Suppository 9 = Medical Gas 10 = Veterinary Premix 11 = Bulk Intermediates 12 = Other (Specify)	

SECTION 4: TYPE OF EVIDENCE

(a) Site in MRA country? If yes, please specify the Regulatory Authority.	Yes ☐	No ☐
(b) Site not located in MRA country or not covered under a MRA? **If yes, please specify the name and date of the document(s) being submitted.**	Yes ☐	No ☐
(c) Site currently approved by Health Canada?	Yes ☐	No ☐

Name of Authorized Signing Official:	Title:
Signature:	Date:

Request for Inspection of a Foreign Site Form (FRM-0213)[103]

Section 1: Requester Information

Company Name:

Establishment Licence and/or Drug Submission Control Number(s):

Contact:

Telephone:

Fax:

E-mail:

Section 2: Foreign Site Information

Company Name:

Street:

Suite:

Post Office Box:

City:

Province/State:

Country:

Postal Code:

Section 3: Product(s) Information

Product Name and DIN (Drug Identification Number):

Activity

F = Fabricate

P = Package/Label

T = Test

Category

1 = Pharmaceutical

2 = Vaccine

3 = Blood & Blood Components

4 = Biological

5 = Radiopharmaceutical

---

[103] Available on the Health Canada website at http://www.hc-sc.gc.ca/dhp-mps/compli-conform/gmp-bpf/form/gui-0080-form-0213-eng.php

Dosage Form Class

1 = Parenteral

2 = Tablet

3 = Capsule

4 = Solution

5 = Suspension

6 = Aerosol

7 = Powder

8 = Suppository

9 = Medical Gas

10 = Veterinary Premix

11 = Bulk Intermediates

12 = Other (Specify)

Sterile (Yes No)

Section 4: Reason for request

Section 5: Site Reference File

Site Reference File available? (Yes No)

Section 6: Confirmation

Has as inspection been conducted, within the last three years, by a Qualified or Regulatory Authority, as defined in the document Guidance on Evidence to Demonstrate Drug Compliance for Foreign Sites, which covered the activity(ies) and dosage form(s) requested at the aforementioned foreign site?   (Yes No)

If so, by whom was it conducted?

Name of Authorized Signing Official

Title

Signature

Date

Health Santé
Canada Canada

Good Manufacturing Practices –
Request for Inspection of a Foreign Site Form (FRM-0213)

SECTION 1: REQUESTER INFORMATION	
Company Name:	
Establishment Licence and/or Drug Submission Control Number(s):	
Contact:	
Telephone:	Fax:
E-mail:	

SECTION 2: FOREIGN SITE INFORMATION		
Company Name:		
Street:	Suite:	Post Office Box:
City:	Province/State:	
Country:		Postal Code:

SECTION 3: PRODUCT(S) INFORMATION

Product Name and DIN	Activity	Category	Dosage Form Class		Sterile (Y/N)
	F = Fabricate P = Package/Label T = Test	1 = Pharmaceutical 2 = Vaccine 3 = Blood & Blood Components 4 = Biological 5 = Radiopharmaceutical	1 = Parenteral 2 = Tablet 3 = Capsule 4 = Solution 5 = Suspension 6 = Aerosol	7 = Powder 8 = Suppository 9 = Medical Gas 10 = Veterinary Premix 11 = Bulk Intermediates 12 = Other (Specify)	

SECTION 4: REASON FOR REQUEST

SECTION 5: SITE REFERENCE FILE		
Site Reference File available?	Yes ☐	No ☐

SECTION 6: CONFIRMATION		
Has an inspection been conducted, within the last three years, by a Qualified or Regulatory Authority, as defined in the document *Guidance on Evidence to Demonstrate Drug GMP Compliance for Foreign Sites*, which covered the activity(ies) and dosage form(s) requested at the aforementioned foreign site?	Yes ☐	No ☐
If so, by whom was it conducted?		

Name of Authorized Signing Official:	Title:
Signature:	Date:

Canada

Foreign Site Inspection Services Agreement Form (FRM-0214)[104]

Between: Health Canada

And: Name of Requester (the "Requester")

        Address

        Schedule inspection date

1.0 Definitions

In this Agreement, unless the context otherwise requires,

"Agreement" means this written Agreement between Health Canada and the Requester, these general conditions, any supplemental general conditions specified in this written Agreement and every other document specifed or referred to in any of them as forming part of this Agreement, all of which may be amended by written Agreement of the Parties, from time to time.

"Compliant (C) rating" means, at the time of providing the Inspection Services, the establishment has demonstrated that it is in control of regulated activities pertaining to the Food and Drugs Act ant its associated Regulations;

"Departmental Representative" means the person designated as such in this Agreement, or by notice to the Requester, to act as the representative of Health Canada in the management of this Agreement.

"Foreign Site" means the following site:

"Host Country" means the country in which the Inspection Services will be provided;

"Inspection Services" means assessing the Foreign Site's compliance with all relevant sections of Division 2 of the Food and Drug Regulations. The guidance document entitled "Good Manufacturing Practices (GMP) Guidelines (GUI-0001)", as well as any other document referenced therein, may be consulted for further guidance;

"Inspector" means any person designated as an inspector for the purpose of the enforcement of the Food and Drugs Act under subsection 22(1);

"Non compliant (NC) rating" means, at the time of providing the Inspection Services, the establishment has not demonstrated that it is in control of regulated activities pertaining to the Food and Drugs Act ant its associated Regulations;

---

[104] Available on the Health Canada website at http://www.hc-sc.gc.ca/dhp-mps/compli-conform/gmp-bpf/form/gui-0080-form-0214-eng.php

"Parties" means Health Canada and the Requester, both of which are signatories to this Agreement;

"Requester Representative" means the person designated as such in this Agreement, or by notice to Health Canada, to act as the representative of the Requester in the management of this Agreement;

"Site Master File" means a document that contains specific information about the quality assurance, the production and/or quality control of pharmaceutical manufacturing operations carried out at the Foreign Site and any closely integrated operations at adjacent and nearby buildings. The guidance document entitled "Explanatory Notes for Industry on the Preparation of a Site Master File" may be consulted for further guidance.

2.0 Objective

Objective: The objective of this Agreement is to conduct Inspection Services of the Foreign Site.

3.0 Time Frame of the Inspection Services

This Agreement will commence on the date of its signature by both Parties and will end once the responsibilities of both Parties have been fulfilled.

4.0 Roles and Responsibilities of Health Canada

4.1   Health Canada, through its Inspector(s), will complete the Inspection Services of the Foreign Site as requested by the Requester.

4.2   Health Canada reserves the right to cancel and/or reschedule the Inspection Services of the Foreign Site at its discretion and/or if any of the Requester's responsibilities outlined in this Agreement are not met.

4.3   Health Canada will cover any costs incurred by the Inspector(s) and/or Departmental Representative and/or any person(s) accompanying them as a result of the Inspection Services requested, in compliance with the Treasury Board of Canada Travel Directives:

4.3.1 Accommodation;

4.3.2 Transportation;

4.3.3 Additional business expenses;

4.3.4 Meals;

4.3.5 Incidental expenses; and

4.3.6 Any other expenses related to the Inspection Services requested, including, but not limited to, translation services.

For additional information, the Treasury Board Travel Directives may be consulted.

4.4   Health Canada will invoice the Requester for the costs incurred as a result of the Inspection Services, as set out in Section 4.3:

4.4.1 After the Inspection Services have been completed by the Inspector(s); or

4.4.2 After the Inspector(s) has attempted to conduct the Inspection Services, but has been unable to do so due to, but not limited to:

4.4.2.1 The actions or inactions of the Requester and/or the Foreign Site; or

4.4.2.2 Any other situation that may jeopardize the safety and/or security of the Inspector(s) and/or the Departmental Representative and/or any person(s) accompanying them.

4.5 The Inspector(s) will present his/her official Health Canada identification card upon arrival at the Foreign Site.

4.6 Health Canada will advise the Foreign Site, in writing, of all deviations from the requirements of the Food and Drug Regulations that are noted during the performance of the Inspection Services.

4.7 Health Canada will assign a rating ("C rating" or "NC rating") to the Foreign Site, in accordance with the guidance document entitled "Risk Classification of GMP Observations(GUI-0023)", and will advise the Foreign Site and the Requester, if different, in writing, of the rating that is assigned.

5.0 Roles and responsibilities of the Requester

5.1 The Requester will submit a Site Master File on the Foreign Site to Health Canada no later than 30 days prior to: (schedule inspection date)

5.2 The Requester will investigate any security and safety issues in the Host Country and/or at the Foreign Site and will communicate this information, in an expeditious manner, to the Departmental Representative and/or, if applicable, to the Inspector(s), prior to and/or during the provision of the Foreign Site Inspection Services.

5.3 The Requester will ensure that all possible steps are taken to ensure the safety and security of the Inspector(s) and/or Departmental Representative and/or any person(s) accompanying them as he/she performs the Inspection Services at the Foreign Site.

5.4 The Requester shall take all necessary steps to coordinate the visit(s) of the Inspector(s) and/or the Departmental Representative and/or any person(s) accompanying them to the Foreign Site for the provision of the Inspection Services requested.

5.5 The Requester will ensure that the Inspector(s) has access to all areas, personnel and documentation necessary to conduct the Inspection Services at the Foreign Site.

5.6 The Requester will reimburse the costs incurred as a result of the Inspection Services requested, as set out in Section 4.3, within 30 days of the invoice date

5.7 The Requester is aware of and will comply with the Treasury Board of Canada Travel Directives.

6.0 Notice

6.1 The Departmental Representative designated as primary contact for Health Canada:

6.2 The Requester Representative designated as primary contact for the Requester:

7.0 Assignment

7.1 This Agreement shall not be assigned in whole or in part by either Party without the prior written consent of the other Party, and any assignment made without such consent shall be void and of no effect.

8.0 Conflict of Interest

8.1 It is a term of this Agreement that no current or former public servant or public office holder to whom The Conflict of Interest and Post-Employment Code for the Public Service, The Values and Ethics Code for the Public Services or the Conflict of Interest Act applies, shall derive any direct benefit from this Agreement, including any employment, payments or gifts, unless the provision and receipt of such benefits is in compliance with such Codes or Act.

8.2 No member of the House of Commons shall be admitted to any share or part of this Agreement or to any benefit to arise therefrom.

9.0 Indemnification

The Requester shall indemnify and save harmless at its own cost, Health Canada from and against all claims, demands, losses, damages, costs (including solicitor and own-client costs), actions, suits or other proceedings, all in any manner based upon, arising out of, related to, occasioned by or attributable to, any acts or conduct of the Requester (whether by reason of negligence or otherwise) in the performance or breach by the Requester of the provisions of this Agreement or any activity undertaken or purported to be undertaken under the authority or pursuant to the terms of this Agreement.

10.0 Applicable Law

10.1 This Agreement shall be governed by and construed in accordance with the laws of (applicable legal jurisdiction of host country) and the applicable laws of Canada.

11.0 Entire Agreement

11.1 This Agreement constitutes the entire Agreement between the Parties with respect to the provision of the Inspection Services and supersedes all previous negotiations, communications and other agreements relating to it, unless they are incorporated by reference herein.

12.0 Amendments

12.1 The Parties agree that this Agreement shall not be altered or amended without the written mutual consent of both the Departmental Representative and the Requester Representative.

For Health Canada:

Name / Title / Date

For requester:

Name / Title / Date

Products being Exported - Section 37

Intention to Invoke Section 37 of the Canada Food and Drugs Act for Products being Exported[105]

Section 37 of the Food and Drugs Act states as follows:

> "This Act does not apply to any packaged food, drug, cosmetic or device, not manufactured for consumption in Canada and not sold for consumption in Canada, if the package is marked in distinct overprinting with the word <<Export>> or <<Exportation>> and a certificate that the package and its contents do not contravene any known requirement of the law of the country to which it is or is about to be consigned has been issued in respect of the package and its contents in prescribed form and manner."

The Export Certificate that must accompany the packaged food, drug, cosmetic or device can be found on the Health Canada website Establishment Licensing page at :

http://hc-sc.gc.ca/dhp-mps/compli-conform/licences/index-eng.php

You are asked to inform us of the packages and contents of products that are exported in compliance with Section 37 of the Food and Drug Act at the time of Drug Establishment Licence renewal. This form must be used when you intend to invoke Section 37 for any drug products fabricated in Canada that you are to export. Please complete the following and return this document to the Health Products and Food Branch Inspectorate at fax (613) 957-6709 or e-mail it to GMP_Questions_BPF@hc-sc.gc.ca.

Drug Establishment Licence Number:

Name of Establishment:

- The above establishment does not intend to invoke Section 37 for any products that they are exporting.

- As the above establishment intends to invoke Section 37 for exportation, I ensure that the Export Certificate has been duly signed by the Commissioner of Taking Oaths, that the Export Certificate is kept on the premises and covers the following products: (An attached list is acceptable.)

Please provide a copy of the duly signed Export Certificate for these packages.

- Product Name

---

[105] Available on the Health Canada website at http://www.hc-sc.gc.ca/dhp-mps/compli-conform/licences/frm-0038_sec_37_fda-art_37_export_ltr-frm-eng.php

- DIN (if any)

- Dosage Form

- Strength

- Lot number

- Expiry Date

- Sterile (Y) or (N)

If you intend to market the same products for consumption in Canada, please provide a statement of confirmation that the manufacturing of the packages for consumption in Canada meets all Good Manufacturing Practices.

Be advised that evidence of Good Manufacturing Practices compliance is required to rescind Section 37.

Name of Regulatory Person:

Signature of Regulatory Person:

Date:

INTENTION TO INVOKE SECTION 37 OF THE CANADA *FOOD AND DRUGS ACT* FOR PRODUCTS BEING EXPORTED

Section 37 of the Food and Drugs Act states as follows:

"This Act does not apply to any packaged food, drug, cosmetic or device, not manufactured for consumption in Canada and not sold for consumption in Canada if the package is marked in distinct overprinting with the word <<Export>> or <<Exportation>> and a certificate that the package and its contents do not contravene any known requirement of the law of the country to which it is or is about to be consigned has been issued in respect of the package and its contents in prescribed form and manner."

The Export Certificate that must accompany the packaged food, drug, cosmetic or device can be found on the Health Canada website Establishment Licensing page at :

http://hc-sc.gc.ca/dhp-mps/compli-conform/licences/index_e.html

You are asked to inform us of the packages and contents of products that are exported in compliance with Section 37 of the *Food and Drug Act* at the time of Drug Establishment Licence renewal. This form must be used when you intend to invoke Section 37 for any drug products <u>fabricated in Canada</u> that you are to export. Please complete the following and return this document to the Health Products and Food Branch Inspectorate at fax (613) 957-6709 or e-mail it to GVP_Questions_BPF@hc-sc.gc.ca .

Drug Establishment Licence Number: _____

Name of Establishment: _____

□   The above establishment **does not intend to invoke Section 37** for any products that they are exporting.

□   As the above establishment **intends to invoke Section 37** for exportation, I ensure that the Export Certificate has been duly signed by the Commissioner of Taking Oaths, that the Export Certificate is kept on the premises and covers the following products: (**An attached list is acceptable.**)

Please provide a copy of the duly signed Export Certificate for these packages.

Product name	DIN (if any)	Dosage form	Strength	Lot number	Expiry Date	Sterile (Y) or (N)

If you intend to market the same products for consumption in Canada, please provide a statement of confirmation that the manufacturing of the packages for consumption in Canada meets all Good Manufacturing Practices.

Be advised that evidence of Good Manufacturing Practices compliance is required to rescind Section 37.

Name of Regulatory Person: _____

Signature of Regulatory Person: _____

Date: _____

Export Certificate (FRM-0176)[106]

(Under the Food and Drugs Act* - R.S.C. 1985, c. F-27)

The undersigned exporter hereby certifies that the (description of article) packaged and labelled as follows:

and marked in distinct overprinting with the word "Export"

1. is not manufactured for consumption in Canada,

2. is not sold for consumption in Canada, and

3. Packages and contents of such packages do not contravene any known requirements of the law of (Name of country or countries) to which it is or is about to be consigned.

Dated at() , this day of ()

Canada:In the matter of an Export Certificate under the Food and Drugs Act,

Province of:

To Wit:

I, () of the () of () in the () of ()

do solemnly declare:

1. that I am the "Exporter" issuing the certificate above set out and have a knowledge of the matters and facts herein declared to by me,

    or

    I am () of ()

    the "Exporter" issuing the certificate above set out and have a knowledge of the matters and facts herein declared to by me (describe position of declarant as the agent of the "Exporter" in care of a Corporation issuing the certificate),

2. that the information set out in the said certificate is true,

3. that all information relevant to the purpose of said certificate is set out herein and no information relevant thereto has been knowingly withheld.

And I make this solemn declaration conscientiously believing it to be true, and knowing that it is of the same force and effect as it made under oath, and by virtue of The Canada Evidence Act.

Declared before me at () this () day of ().

() A commissioner for Taking Oaths

* See section 37 of the Food and Drugs Act and Appendix III of the Food and Drug Regulations.

---

[106] Available on the Health Canada website at http://www.hc-sc.gc.ca/dhp-mps/compli-conform/licences/form/frm_0176_export_cert_frm_ltr-doc-eng.php

APPENDIX III

FORMS

EXPORT CERTIFICATE

(Under the *Food and Drugs Act* – R.S.C. 1985, c. F-27)

The undersigned exporter hereby certifies that the (description of article)

_____

packaged and labelled as follows: _____

and marked in distinct overprinting with the word "Export"

    1.   is not manufactured for consumption in Canada,
    2.   is not sold for consumption in Canada, and
    3.   Packages and contents of such packages do not contravene any known requirements of the law of

_____

(*Name of country or countries*) to which it is or is about to be consigned.

Dated at _____, this _____ day of _____ 20 ___ .

Canada: In the matter of an Export Certificate under the *Food and Drugs Act*.

Province of _____

To Wit: I, _____

        of the _____ of _____

        in the _____ of _____

        do solemnly declare:

        1. that I am the "Exporter" issuing the certificate above set out and have a knowledge of the matters and facts herein declared to by me,

                or

        I am _____ of _____

_____

        the "Exporter" issuing the certificate above set out and have a knowledge of the matters and facts herein declared to by me describe position of declarant as the agent of the "Exporter" in care of a Corporation issuing the certificate),

        2. that the information set out in the said certificate is true,

        3. that all information relevant to the purpose of said certificate is set out herein and no information relevant thereto has been knowingly withheld.

        And I make this solemn declaration conscientiously believing it to be true, and knowing that it is of the same force and effect as it made under oath, and by virtue of *The Canada Evidence Act*.

Declared before me at _____ this _____ day of _____ 20 ___ .

_____   _____

    A commissioner for Taking Oaths

*See section 37 of the Food and Drugs Act and Appendix III of the *Food and Drug Regulations*.

Part VIII

Index

Index

Cell Bank, 201, 203, 205, 210, 409,
411, 413, 418, 636, 637
cell culture, 201, 210, 409, 418, 599,
601, 635 – 637
Cell Culture, 201, 409, 637
cephalosporins, 109, 340, 607
certificate, 15, 17, 73, 75, 78, 79, 91,
94, 113, 121, 122, 131, 140, 144,
145, 147, 148, 150, 154, 180 – 185,
187, 223, 228, 248, 252, 261 – 263,
268, 270, 271, 292, 307, 308, 358,
359, 391, 396, 472, 477, 491, 496,
510, 515, 529, 540, 542, 544, 545,
615, 672, 712, 741, 744
Certificate, 180 – 183, 185, 187,
247, 251, 268, 269, 271, 292, 297,
305, 307, 319, 358 – 361, 372, 391,
396, 515, 525, 544, 545, 616, 621,
624, 680, 712, 741, 744
Certificate of a Pharmaceutical
Product (CPP), 361, 544
certificate of analysis, 121, 122, 140,
144, 145, 148, 150, 182, 223, 248,
261, 263, 270, 292, 307, 491, 515,
540, 542
Certificate of Analysis, 185, 247,
251, 292, 307, 319, 515, 525, 616,
621, 624
Certificate of Analysis (COA), 185
Certificate of Compliance (CoC), 185,
391, 396
certificate of manufacture, 154
Certificate of Manufacture, 185,
297, 307
Certificate of Pharmaceutical Product
(CPP), 185, 372, 545, 712
certification, 74, 102, 121, 122, 144,
145, 180, 189, 207, 268, 274, 325,
327, 360, 396, 415, 464, 465, 469,
470, 471, 515, 525
Certification, 180, 182, 268, 270,
306, 325, 327, 542
certified, 59, 104, 121, 122, 140, 144,
145, 237, 243, 469, 515, 609, 678,
679
Certified, 213, 421
change control, 139, 257, 327, 341,
347, 351, 355, 630, 652, 662

Change Control, 185, 271, 337,
341, 344, 354, 615
changeover procedure, 124, 211, 405,
419
Changeover Procedure, 185, 202,
410
changeover procedures, 124, 211,
405, 419
Changeover Procedures, 202, 410
charts, 155, 173, 175, 331, 349, 353,
542, 614
Charts, 656, 657, 660
child resistant package, 24, 25, 50
Child Resistant Package, 48
clarity of solution, 160
class monograph, 74, 76
Class Monograph, 672
clean area, 163, 165, 170, 183
Clean Area, 185
cleaning, 88, 89, 107 – 111, 114, 115,
126, 165, 167, 169 – 172, 185, 192,
202, 204, 206, 208, 209, 211, 240 –
242, 244, 245, 275, 281 – 284, 286,
287, 301, 303, 314, 322, 323, 329,
333 – 341, 344, 350, 351, 404, 410,
412, 414, 416, 417, 419, 435 – 437,
448, 451, 464, 474, 475, 508, 512,
521, 535, 605, 607 – 609, 611, 615,
616, 626, 628, 629, 638, 663, 664
Cleaning, 115, 194, 202, 204, 209,
245, 276, 325, 333 – 335, 337, 341,
344, 355, 404, 410, 412, 417, 437,
511, 512, 608, 611, 628, 629, 663
cleaning agents, 171, 245, 333, 334,
336, 344, 608, 609
cleaning methods, 664
Cleaning Procedures Validation, 202,
410
cleaning schedules, 607
cleaning validation, 334, 335, 338,
340, 512, 521, 628, 663
Cleaning Validation, 115, 194, 245,
276, 333, 337, 341, 344, 355, 511,
512, 628
climatic zones, 552
Climatic zones, 564

Concentration, 426, 445
concurrent production, 209, 417, 665
Concurrent Production, 202, 410
concurrent validation, 351, 353, 627, 628
Concurrent Validation, 344, 353
conditions, storage, 347
Confidential Unit Exclusion (CUE), 216, 219, 484, 487
confirmation, 38, 127, 150, 305, 373, 469, 527, 742
Confirmation, 677, 733
conformance to specification, 623
conformance to specifications, 623
conformity, 16, 128, 163, 180, 268, 317, 318, 361, 364, 397, 543, 612, 621, 694, 713
conformity to specifications, 621
construction, 19, 65, 95, 110, 151, 155, 241, 242, 265, 294, 480, 518
Construction, 605, 608
consultant, 154, 268, 393, 394, 522, 531, 723, 726
Consultant, 726, 727
consultants, 138, 256, 605
Consultants, 114, 244, 605
container, 14, 18, 19, 20, 24, 33, 34, 41, 47, 52, 64 – 66, 72, 74, 75, 94, 109, 119, 120, 125, 126, 148, 150, 151, 154, 156, 159, 162, 172, 176, 181, 184, 187, 189, 190, 192, 193, 201, 203, 212, 225, 226, 242, 251, 257 – 259, 261, 264, 269, 272 – 274, 283, 303, 308, 312, 354, 379, 380, 409, 411, 420, 429 – 431, 435, 438, 451, 455, 456, 467, 479, 493, 494, 514, 515, 530, 532, 534, 540, 542, 552, 553, 557, 560, 561, 564 – 567, 575, 576, 615 – 617, 624, 634, 642, 664, 665
Container, 252, 272, 273, 380, 425, 445, 553, 557, 564
container closure system, 159, 184, 189, 553, 557, 561, 564, 566, 665
Container closure system, 564
container-closure system, 126, 431, 456
container damage, 615

containers, 50, 105, 109, 117, 119, 122, 124, 125, 128, 129, 138, 145, 150, 156, 162, 166, 171 – 175, 177, 179, 186, 192, 201, 203 – 205, 210, 216, 231, 238, 240, 241, 248 – 252, 256 – 261, 263, 267, 273, 289, 290, 294, 302, 303, 310, 325, 329, 360, 379, 380, 383, 409, 411 – 413, 418, 429, 431, 435, 438, 451, 456, 484, 499, 514 – 516, 518 – 522, 526, 535 – 537, 551, 560, 567, 568, 574 – 576, 608, 615 – 617, 620, 621, 624, 632, 663, 709, 711
Containers, 18, 19, 125, 160, 242, 257, 259, 380, 565, 567, 607, 616, 620
containment, 108, 206, 207, 414, 415, 425, 427, 431, 444, 447, 448, 507
Containment, 186, 202, 410, 427, 447, 607
contamination, 65, 88, 107, 108 – 111, 114 – 117, 124, 128, 139, 143, 161 – 169, 171, 173 – 176, 179, 185, 186, 201, 202, 205, 206, 208 – 211, 216, 217, 222, 225, 228, 240 – 242, 244 – 246, 249, 281 – 283, 287 – 290, 293, 319 – 321, 323, 324, 328, 329, 334, 336, 338, 339, 404, 409, 410, 413, 414, 416 – 419, 424, 425, 427, 431, 433, 435 – 437, 442, 444, 447 – 449, 451, 456, 461, 464, 475, 484, 485, 490, 493, 496, 507, 509, 511 – 513, 515, 536, 538, 604 – 609, 615, 616, 618 – 620, 628, 629, 633, 634, 636 – 639, 641, 659, 663
Contamination, 110, 164, 172, 202, 241, 410, 425, 444, 512, 619, 642
continual improvement, 662
continued, 221, 335, 355, 489, 554, 559
continuous culture, 212, 420
Continuous Culture, 202, 410
contract, 133, 138, 141, 224, 228, 253, 256, 286, 314, 327, 353, 371 – 373, 381, 449, 465, 469, 492, 496, 521, 524, 532, 600, 602, 622, 633, 641, 664, 701

172, 173, 189, 209, 212, 220, 223 –
225, 228, 242, 245, 249, 273, 274,
284, 300, 302, 310, 318, 319, 322,
330, 334, 335, 338, 344 – 353, 364,
365, 405, 417, 420, 427, 447, 451,
466, 488, 491, 492, 494, 496, 510,
522, 525, 530, 566, 589, 600, 602 –
604, 608 – 610, 613 – 615, 617 –
619, 621, 622, 626, 627, 630, 636,
638, 646, 658, 659, 662, 664, 665,
728
   Critical, 105, 186, 216, 237, 272,
302, 307, 308, 318, 319, 321, 323,
336, 345, 365, 368, 449, 484, 589,
602, 617, 618, 627, 628, 637, 642,
653, 656, 658
critical area, 165, 166, 172
   Critical Area, 186
critical labelling, 225, 494
   Critical Labelling, 216, 484
Critical observation, 318, 365
   Critical Observation, 318
critical process, 104, 173, 189, 274,
310, 345 – 348, 352, 525, 530, 600,
602, 613, 614, 617, 618, 626, 627,
638, 646, 662, 664
   Critical process, 307, 628
   Critical Process, 185, 272, 345
critical process parameter, 345 – 348,
613, 626, 627, 646, 662
   Critical Process Parameter, 345
critical product, 123, 249, 302, 319,
322, 330, 344, 405, 522, 626
   Critical Product, 302, 319
critical steps, 112, 242, 300, 348
cross contamination, 242, 448, 507
   cross-contamination, 109, 111,
124, 186, 202, 206, 208 – 211, 282,
290, 319, 320, 321, 323, 324, 334,
410, 414, 416 – 419, 425, 427, 433,
435 – 437, 444, 447, 449, 451, 461,
464, 509, 512, 606, 607, 609, 615,
616, 633, 634, 638, 639, 662
   Cross-Contamination, 202, 410,
425, 444, 642
cryogenic vessel, 258, 259, 272
   Cryogenic vessel, 258
   Cryogenic Vessel, 272

culture, 140, 201, 202 – 205, 210, 212,
409 – 413, 418, 420, 538, 599, 601,
635 – 637
   Culture, 201, 202, 204, 409, 410,
412, 637
Curbside Delivery, 272
cure, 15, 21, 76, 183, 641, 703
customer, 521, 624, 634
cylinder, 251, 258, 261, 272, 275, 539,
540, 541
cytotoxics, 109, 340
damage, 225, 258, 298, 379, 493, 615,
654, 659
   Damage, 125, 654
data, 24, 41, 72, 120, 125, 137, 141,
153, 154, 156 – 160, 162, 164, 172,
179, 180, 212, 221, 225, 266, 267,
293, 297, 298, 318, 323, 328, 346,
348, 349, 352, 353, 364, 365, 377,
378, 406, 420, 430, 431, 450, 451,
455, 462, 464, 465, 467, 468, 489,
493, 512, 515, 516, 517, 521, 522,
524, 527, 529, 530, 531, 533, 538,
542, 549, 551 – 557, 559 – 563,
566, 568, 582, 588, 590, 593, 603,
610, 613, 614, 617, 618, 622 – 629,
646, 650, 651, 657, 660, 661, 695,
702, 728
   Data, 258, 302, 337, 354, 368, 378,
549, 551, 553 – 555, 557, 559, 561,
564, 568, 590, 592 – 595, 610
data, test, 625
date, 24, 26, 33, 34, 37, 38, 58 – 61,
65, 78, 82, 84, 95, 96, 120, 121,
123, 125, 126, 128 – 130, 139, 140,
151 – 153, 155, 156, 158, 159, 181,
185 – 187, 191, 226, 227, 257, 258,
265 – 269, 277, 286, 290, 293, 294,
296 – 298, 302, 305, 307, 325, 328,
348, 366, 373 – 375, 381, 385, 394,
395, 405, 406, 430, 438, 448, 455,
467, 468, 480, 482, 494, 495, 507,
515 – 517, 521 – 524, 533, 539,
542, 543, 551, 557, 564, 565, 567,
597, 611 – 614, 617, 619, 621, 624,
625, 632, 634, 635, 642, 645, 665,
676, 677, 680, 687, 693, 695, 702,
713, 726, 730, 735 – 737

203, 204, 213, 248, 272, 343 – 345,
348, 357, 377 – 380, 384, 387, 405,
411, 412, 421, 424, 434, 435, 437,
446, 447, 452, 455, 468, 509 – 511,
513, 517, 518, 520, 526 – 528, 537,
538, 544, 545, 549, 551, 552, 557 –
568, 572, 573, 575, 576, 578, 582,
585, 588, 590, 592, 597, 599, 627,
639, 641, 669, 674, 675, 679, 697,
699 – 703, 708, 710 – 712, 741
Drug product, 377, 551, 560, 561,
562, 565
Drug Product, 138, 194, 195, 203,
377, 380, 411, 456, 470, 514, 527,
551, 557, 568, 569, 572, 574, 576,
591, 592, 697, 698
drug product container, 173
drug product containers, 173
drug product specifications, 527
drug product testing, 572
drug products, 114, 116, 120, 132,
248, 343 – 345, 348, 357, 377 –
379, 384, 435, 437, 468, 509, 513,
517, 537, 538, 545, 552, 559, 560,
562, 563, 572, 576, 585, 597, 639,
669, 674, 675, 679, 697, 699, 700,
710, 711, 741
Drug Products, 138, 194, 195, 377,
456, 470, 514, 527, 568, 569, 572,
574, 591, 697, 698
drug quality, 109, 377
drug safety, 364, 365
drug substance, 184, 191, 201, 203,
204, 409, 411, 412, 446, 513, 516,
527, 549, 551 – 557, 564 – 567,
568, 571 – 576, 578, 581, 582, 585,
588, 590 – 592, 648, 653, 654, 659
Drug Substance, 159, 195, 203,
406, 411, 514, 527, 532, 549, 551,
552, 565, 568, 569, 571, 574, 581,
591, 641, 642
dust, 108 – 110, 115, 165, 241, 323,
433, 436, 437, 507, 606
eating, 117, 604, 608
education, 138, 221, 222, 256, 284,
313, 314, 449, 489, 490, 604, 605,
661, 727
Education, 308

effectiveness, 36, 103, 104, 114, 116,
130, 131, 142, 159, 160, 202, 204,
212, 221, 229, 231, 236, 237, 244,
334, 338, 348, 366, 377, 410, 412,
420, 424, 437, 442, 451, 469, 489,
497, 499, 526, 533, 558, 657, 661,
693
effluents, 450
electrical interference, 109, 284
electronic record, 298, 611, 664
electronic signature, 148, 153, 263,
267, 298, 531, 611, 645
emergency, 77, 108, 219, 436, 467,
487
Emergency, 10, 707
enforcement, 4, 5, 7, 75, 191, 275,
320, 360, 367, 384, 397, 669, 670,
673 – 679, 688, 692, 694, 709, 710,
712, 726, 735
Enforcement, 6, 7, 193, 194, 236,
299, 321, 361, 366 – 368, 401, 422,
460, 511, 512, 598, 669, 673, 674,
678, 680, 688, 689, 694, 695, 707
environmental conditions, 106, 186,
238, 294, 352, 534, 634, 638
equipment, 78 – 80, 83, 88, 89, 103,
105, 108 – 112, 114, 115, 123, 124,
126 – 128, 130, 134 – 136, 139,
163 – 165, 167, 170 – 174, 176 –
179, 185, 188, 190, 192, 193, 201,
202, 204 – 206, 208, 209, 211, 217,
218, 220, 225, 226, 228, 236, 238,
240 – 242, 244 – 246, 250, 255,
271, 275, 280, 282 – 284, 286, 287,
290, 300 – 302, 309, 310, 314, 323
– 325, 327 – 330, 333 – 341, 343 –
348, 350 – 355, 391, 395, 404 –
406, 409, 410, 412 – 414, 416, 417,
419, 424, 425, 427, 428, 431, 433,
437, 444, 449, 456, 464, 466, 467,
475, 485, 486, 488, 489, 493, 494,
496, 507 – 510, 512, 519, 524, 527,
529, 567, 568, 587, 593, 596, 602,
603, 605 – 609, 611 – 613, 617,
624, 626 – 630, 633, 636, 637 –
640, 644, 646, 653, 657, 659, 661 –
664, 671

313, 314, 482, 483, 489, 599, 711, 712

Good Manufacturing Practices, 1, 5, 87, 101, 105, 112, 121, 153, 180, 182, 189, 191, 193 – 195, 199, 200, 215, 235 – 237, 268, 270, 274, 276, 277, 279 – 281, 283 – 286, 288, 291 – 296, 298 – 300, 305, 306, 312, 316, 317, 320, 344, 358, 360, 366, 367, 377, 389, 390 – 394, 396, 397, 399, 401, 403, 407, 408, 423, 424, 433, 441 – 443, 456, 457, 459, 460, 474, 483, 501, 505, 507, 513, 516, 522, 539, 544, 597, 669, 673, 680, 685, 694, 699, 707, 723, 726, 727, 735, 742, 801

graphs, 614

Group 2 Products, 188

growth promotion, 175, 179

Growth Promotion, 188

guidelines, 101, 102, 104, 123, 134, 138, 153, 157 – 159, 175, 183, 185, 200, 207, 221, 232, 235, 236, 248, 254, 266, 271, 275, 283, 289, 300, 317, 318, 334, 343, 344, 378, 408, 415, 428, 442, 449 – 453, 455, 460, 461, 464, 489, 500, 508, 517, 519, 522, 523, 532, 538, 571, 581, 606, 648, 654, 661, 664, 673, 688, 699, 701, 702

Guidelines, 1, 101, 109, 112, 115, 138, 157, 193 – 195, 199, 200, 207, 210, 213, 215, 226, 235, 242, 245, 249, 276, 277, 283, 289, 300, 306, 318, 333, 343, 344, 355, 364, 367, 377, 381, 393, 399, 401, 403, 404, 407, 408, 415, 418, 421, 423, 424, 433 – 436, 441 – 443, 447, 450 – 457, 459 – 461, 464, 470, 472, 483, 494, 501, 508, 509, 511, 513, 516, 518, 520, 522, 550, 552, 576, 577, 591, 656, 695, 705, 735

HACCP, 305, 308, 653, 656, 658, 659

half-life, 428, 430, 431, 441, 450, 451, 453, 454, 456

Half-Life, 425, 444

hammer test, 258

Hammer Test, 272

handwritten signature, 153, 267, 298, 645

hard copy, 530, 611

harm, 49, 647, 650, 651, 654, 655, 659

Harm, 654

harvesting, 303, 601

Harvesting, 203, 411, 638

hazard, 18, 19, 134, 161, 208, 212, 221, 320, 367, 416, 420, 489, 507, 521, 534, 650, 654, 656, 658, 659

Hazard, 201, 308, 409, 653, 654, 656, 658, 659

Hazard Analysis and Critical Control Points (HACCP), 308, 653, 658

head, 255, 256, 449, 604

Head, 422

health habits, 604

HEPA filters, 166, 507, 508

herbicides, 109, 607

high risk product, 321, 322, 325

High Risk Product, 319

history, 2, 84, 105, 119, 136, 152, 238, 256, 266, 290, 338, 394, 395, 471, 516, 610, 616, 641, 661, 703, 704, 708, 727

holding, 156, 184, 201, 211, 335, 409, 420, 625, 634

Holding, 148, 263, 605, 634

homeopathic drugs, 76

homeopathic medicines, 280, 300, 301, 304, 305

Homeopathic Medicines, 300, 304, 305, 308, 312

hormones, 200, 408

hospitals, 226, 235, 378, 495, 701, 702

Hospitals, 705, 707

host country, 738

Host Country, 735, 737

hot cell, 455

Hot Cell, 425, 444

HPFB, 1 – 5, 182, 185, 270, 358 – 361, 366, 367, 384, 387, 396, 597, 598, 670, 673, 676, 680, 692 – 694, 710, 723

HPFB Inspectorate, 3, 4, 185, 358 – 361, 384, 387, 396, 598

humidity, 108, 138, 141, 171, 174, 175, 211 – 213, 282, 289, 303, 323,

inactivation, 109, 171, 203, 209, 211, 337, 411, 417, 419, 467, 607, 638
Inactivation, 203, 411, 638
inactive ingredient, 156, 314, 353, 366, 514, 515, 693
incoming materials, 330, 605, 615
independent verification, 315
infected, 116, 219, 487, 511
infectious, 114, 167, 208 – 210, 212, 219, 222, 224, 244, 245, 416 – 418, 420, 487, 490, 492, 536, 605, 607
infestation, 320, 322
Infestation, 511
infusion, 576
inhalation, 160
initial inspection, 687
Initial Inspection, 686
initials, 250, 251, 645
inner label, 14, 19, 20, 34, 41, 47, 51, 60, 66 – 68, 70 – 72
in-process, 104, 108, 110, 111, 116, 117, 124 – 128, 130, 133 – 136, 139, 141, 184, 188, 189, 191, 192, 201, 202, 204, 211 – 213, 237, 250, 274, 282, 283, 285, 287, 289, 301 – 303, 309, 310, 313, 326, 341, 346, 347 – 349, 351, 352, 360, 409, 410, 412, 419 – 421, 425, 436, 444, 445, 466, 468, 469, 604, 606, 611, 612, 617, 618, 626, 627, 631, 645, 665
In-process, 124, 188, 309, 465, 613, 618, 619, 665
in-process control, 126, 128, 130, 133, 188, 189, 212, 274, 303, 309, 348, 352, 420, 425, 445, 466, 468, 604, 606, 611, 612, 617, 618, 626, 631, 645, 665
In-process control, 124, 309, 618
In-process Control, 188
In-Process Control, 643, 644
In-Process Control (or Process Control), 643
in-process controls, 126, 128, 130, 133, 189, 212, 274, 303, 352, 420, 425, 445, 466, 606, 611, 612, 617, 618

in-process drug, 108, 111, 116, 117, 125, 134, 135, 139, 141, 191, 192, 326, 360, 436
In-process Drug, 188
in-process material, 117, 125, 126, 211, 213, 282, 287, 289, 301, 326, 419, 421, 618
in-process materials, 126, 211, 213, 282, 287, 289, 301, 326, 419, 421, 618
in-process product, 313, 341, 351
In-process product, 309
in-process testing, 136, 310, 349
In-process testing, 309, 465
In-process Testing, 188
in-process tests, 184, 201, 346, 409, 618
insecticides, 115, 607
insects, 282, 436
inspected, 78, 112, 143, 179, 187, 225, 231, 363, 493, 499, 621, 671, 675, 693, 694, 700, 708, 712, 713
inspection, 4, 5, 7, 65, 78, 80, 90, 95, 104, 106, 110, 121, 129, 131 – 133, 138, 152, 153, 155, 179, 192, 225, 237, 239, 252, 253, 256, 266, 267, 275, 283, 288, 290, 298, 314, 317, 318, 320, 321, 326, 327, 331, 333, 336, 339, 360, 363, 365 – 367, 373, 392 – 397, 464, 477, 493, 505, 510, 531, 534, 590, 616, 629, 648, 660, 662, 671, 673, 677, 678, 686 – 688, 691, 692, 694, 695, 709 – 713, 726, 727, 733, 735, 737
Inspection, 4, 6, 10, 16, 102, 182, 190, 257, 271, 274, 290, 317, 320, 321, 341, 363, 364, 366, 367, 373, 375, 383 – 385, 387, 389 – 392, 396, 397, 457, 460, 501, 505, 507, 518, 519, 522, 543, 603, 609, 654, 661, 662, 671, 673, 677, 679 – 681, 685 – 688, 69 – 695, 709 – 713, 717, 723, 726, 732, 735 – 738
inspection report, 321, 367, 373, 392, 393, 394, 671, 677
Inspection report, 694, 712
Inspection Report, 320, 366, 389, 392, 677, 680, 687, 694, 712

modification, 16, 23, 203, 411, 629, 636, 692, 702, 708

monitors, 128, 229, 275, 302, 380, 497

mother liquor, 311, 631, 643
  Mother Liquor, 643

mother tincture, 301 – 303
  Mother tincture, 311

mra, 269, 391

MRA, 74, 75, 78, 83, 91, 94, 102, 131, 147 – 149, 154, 180 – 182, 185, 189, 191, 252, 262, 263, 268, 269, 271, 274, 275, 320, 327, 360, 390, 391, 394, 396, 397, 422, 477, 529, 530, 679, 680, 688, 726, 730
  MRA Country, 148, 189, 263, 274, 397

Multiple-Dose Container, 425, 445

multi-product facility, 184, 201, 209, 335, 409, 417, 424, 444, 509
  Multi-Product Facility, 204, 412

multi-suite complex, 200, 408
  Multi-Suite Complex, 203, 411

Multi-Use Area, 204, 412

mutual recognition agreement, 73, 74, 183, 189, 271, 274, 397
  Mutual Recognition Agreement, 102, 180 – 182, 189, 268, 269, 271, 274, 320, 360, 390, 396, 679, 680, 686, 688, 726, 730
  Mutual Recognition Agreement (MRA), 180, 181, 189, 268, 269, 274, 360, 390, 396, 679, 680, 726, 730

name, 14, 23 – 25, 27, 32 – 35, 37, 47, 58 – 61, 63, 65, 69, 75, 77 – 80, 83, 125 – 128, 150, 155, 175, 181, 182, 185, 186, 193, 250, 261, 269, 270, 272, 276, 286, 298, 299, 302, 307, 365, 372, 375, 384, 387, 390, 429, 451, 460, 468, 482, 605, 611, 612, 614, 615, 617, 621, 624, 632, 634, 692, 711, 726, 727, 729, 730
  Name, 27, 181, 182, 269, 270, 375, 422, 457, 507, 543, 632, 634, 717, 729, 730, 732, 733, 735, 739, 741, 742, 744

national regulations, 468

new drug, 37, 39, 61, 70, 363 – 365, 368 – 370, 527 – 529, 549, 551, 552, 571, 572, 581, 582, 691, 693, 694
  New Drug, 159, 195, 366 – 369, 514, 527, 532, 549, 568, 569, 571, 581, 591, 693, 695

new molecular entity, 566
  New Molecular Entity, 566

NF, 541, 542, 701

No-Carrier-Added, 426, 445

Non compliant (NC) rating, 735
  Non-Compliant (NC), 397

non-conformity, 317, 361, 364, 694, 713

non-penicillin drug, 435, 437

nosodes, 302, 303
  Nosodes, 300, 311

objectionable microorganisms, 118, 513

objectives, 118, 246, 346, 348, 654, 660, 695
  Objectives, 551

observation, 24, 318, 320, 321, 363, 365 – 367, 519, 521, 526, 531, 605, 688, 728
  Observation, 311, 318, 319, 365

official drug, 24

official method, 14, 18, 19, 40, 62, 524, 527

On-Site Evaluation, 392, 397, 543

open lesions, 116, 245, 605

open system, 231, 456, 500, 638
  Open System, 217, 485

operational qualification, 112, 242, 345, 347, 350, 351, 428, 610
  Operational Qualification, 190, 341, 345, 350, 351, 355, 627
  Operational Qualification (OQ), 351, 627

operations, 88, 104, 106, 107, 109 – 113, 115, 122, 125 – 129, 133 – 135, 138, 141, 145, 154, 162 – 167, 170 – 172, 175 – 177, 186, 190, 192, 207, 208, 211, 218, 219, 235, 237, 238, 240, 241, 243, 249 – 251, 253 – 256, 267, 275, 277, 280, 282, 287, 289, 290, 312, 314, 321 – 324,

product, 4, 7, 20, 23, 25, 38, 39, 45,
47, 63, 71, 102, 104, 106, 107, 109,
112, 115 – 119, 123 – 138, 141 –
144, 146 – 150, 154, 156 – 160,
162, 163, 166, 167, 169, 170, 172 –
174, 176 – 192, 200 – 206, 208 –
213, 216, 218, 222 – 226, 228, 230,
231, 235, 237 – 240, 243, 245, 246,
248, 249 – 251, 253 – 258, 261,
263, 264, 268 – 270, 272 – 275,
279 – 286, 288 – 302, 304 – 314,
316, 318, 319, 322 – 324, 327, 330,
334 – 338, 340, 341, 343 – 355,
358, 359, 364, 371, 374, 377, 379 –
381, 384, 387, 390, 391, 393, 397,
404 – 406, 408 – 414, 416 – 422,
424, 425, 427, 429 – 431, 434, 435,
437, 441, 443 – 448, 450 – 456,
460 – 473, 484, 486, 490 – 494,
496, 498, 500, 508 – 513, 515 –
523, 525 – 530, 532 – 536, 538,
539, 541, 543 – 545, 549, 551, 552,
557 – 561, 563 – 568, 572, 573,
575 – 578, 582, 585, 588 – 592,
599, 602, 603, 606, 607, 611, 613,
618, 621, 626, 627, 629, 631, 632,
637 – 639, 641, 642, 646, 648, 649,
652 – 654, 657 – 659, 661 – 665,
671, 678, 699 – 703, 707, 708, 710
– 712, 726 – 728
Product, 93, 103, 130, 131, 145,
185, 187, 195, 201, 203, 204, 213,
227, 230, 232, 253, 260, 273, 276,
280, 292, 319, 327, 330, 338, 359,
361, 372, 379, 380, 384, 387, 389,
406, 409, 411, 412, 421, 429, 436,
453, 456, 462, 463, 465, 466, 469,
473, 479, 495, 498, 500, 516, 526,
540, 541, 544, 545, 551, 557, 568,
576, 592, 604, 642, 654, 671, 701,
709, 712, 729, 732, 741
product defects, 223, 491, 602, 661
product lifecycle, 648, 649, 654, 662
Product Lifecycle, 654
product name, 307
Product Name, 729, 732, 741
product specification file, 469

Product Specification File, 463,
465, 466, 469, 473
product specifications, 136, 144, 148,
154, 213, 263, 290, 292, 327, 346,
421, 429, 453, 464, 527
production, 63, 73, 94, 103, 104, 106,
108, 109, 111, 112, 115, 117, 118,
123, 124, 127, 132, 133, 135, 136,
139, 143, 144, 150, 153, 154, 159,
161, 168, 169, 172, 175, 176, 178,
183 – 185, 187, 188, 190, 192, 200,
201, 203, 204, 206 – 213, 216, 220,
222, 227, 229, 235 – 237, 239 –
241, 243, 245, 246, 249, 250, 253,
260, 264, 267, 271, 273 – 275, 282,
284, 287, 289, 290, 294, 296, 297,
301, 302, 306 – 311, 314, 316, 318,
322, 324 – 327, 329, 330, 334, 335,
337, 344 – 348, 351, 352, 355, 405,
406, 408, 409, 411, 412, 414 – 421,
423, 424, 427, 433, 435 – 437, 441,
443 – 451, 453, 461, 466, 467, 469,
475, 476, 479, 485, 489, 490, 495,
497, 507 – 509, 511 – 513, 522,
530, 533, 534, 537, 538, 553, 555 –
557, 562, 563, 566, 567, 599 – 603,
606 – 614, 617 – 619, 621, 623 –
630, 635, 636, 639 – 646, 650, 658,
659, 663, 665, 675, 703, 728, 736
Production, 104, 108, 138, 182,
184, 185, 189, 190, 201, 202, 204,
212, 221, 237, 256, 270, 274, 283,
302, 312, 324 – 326, 328, 345, 409,
410, 412, 420, 424, 444, 448, 466,
473, 489, 564, 567, 600, 603, 605,
608, 612 – 614, 616, 617, 619, 636,
637, 640, 644, 653, 664, 665
production and process control, 630
production area, 108, 115, 117, 124,
135, 206, 208, 211, 241, 282, 327,
329, 330, 414, 416, 419, 436, 507,
511, 606, 607
production areas, 108, 115, 117,
124, 135, 206, 208, 241, 282, 327,
329, 330, 414, 416, 436, 507, 511,
606, 607

purchase, 14, 15, 120, 144, 228, 248, 260, 350, 445, 496
  Purchase, 634
pure culture, 207, 415
  Pure Culture, 204, 412
purge, 258, 331, 539
purified water, 109, 283, 306, 323, 513, 536
  Purified Water, 190, 320, 513, 536
purity, 13, 24, 36, 63, 73, 87, 105, 111, 122, 146, 173, 184, 187, 192, 239, 248, 251, 261, 271, 283, 285, 289, 291, 292, 304, 305, 334, 425, 445, 450, 451, 453, 455, 513, 523, 528, 541, 585, 589, 590, 591, 592, 599, 601, 622, 623, 626, 634, 645
  Purity, 160, 190, 312, 426, 446, 587
pyrogen testing, 157, 537
QA, 218, 221, 222, 227, 486, 489, 490, 495, 512, 601, 644, 800
qualification, 112, 121, 130, 145, 193, 222, 242, 258, 275, 327, 343, 345 – 347, 350, 351, 428, 449, 490, 516, 521, 524, 527, 610, 626, 629, 640, 644, 662, 663, 664
  Qualification, 188, 190, 312, 341, 345, 346, 350, 351, 355, 626, 627, 644, 663
qualified authority, 121, 248
  Qualified Authority, 190, 274, 392, 394, 397, 543, 726
qualified investigator, 468, 481, 482
  Qualified Investigator, 461 – 463
qualified person, 89, 90, 103, 112 – 114, 123 – 125, 127 – 129, 133, 135, 141, 144, 146, 153, 169, 177, 221, 236, 242 – 244, 249, 252, 254, 261, 266, 292, 324, 326, 429, 449, 453, 475, 477, 489, 518, 519
  Qualified Person, 461, 464, 465, 469, 470, 471, 472
quality, 4, 13, 63, 82, 87, 90 – 93, 95, 102 – 110, 112 – 114, 116 – 118, 120 – 125, 127, 130 – 140, 142, 143, 145, 146, 148, 149, 152, 153, 155, 156, 159, 163, 168, 169, 171, 172, 174, 178, 180 – 182, 185, 186, 190, 191, 202, 207, 208, 210, 212,

213, 218, 222, 224, 227 – 231, 236 – 244, 246, 248 – 258, 260, 264 – 273, 275, 279 – 281, 283 – 286, 289 – 292, 300, 305, 307, 312, 313, 321, 324, 325, 327, 331, 341, 344 – 346, 348, 350 – 355, 358, 377, 379, 393, 403, 405, 410, 415, 416, 418, 420, 421, 424, 425, 428, 429, 433, 436, 441, 442, 445, 447, 449 – 452, 455, 461, 463 – 472, 476 – 480, 486, 490, 493, 495 – 499, 511 – 514, 516, 521 – 523, 525, 528, 530, 531, 551 – 553, 557, 558, 588, 597, 599 – 612, 614 – 618, 620 – 622, 624 – 628, 630 – 634, 636 – 640, 643 – 645, 647 – 655, 657, 658, 660 – 662, 664, 670, 674, 677, 688, 699, 736
  Quality, 91, 102, 103, 105, 119, 130, 134, 135, 143, 162, 179, 190, 195, 212, 218, 220, 221, 227 – 229, 232, 236, 238, 254, 275, 279, 283, 285, 289, 292, 304, 306, 312, 313, 320, 322, 327, 348, 420, 422, 429, 435, 438, 443, 452, 461, 464, 469, 472 – 474, 477, 486, 488, 489, 495 – 497, 500, 523, 527, 541, 601, 602, 604, 634, 636 – 639, 644, 647 – 650, 652 – 654, 656, 657, 660 – 665, 800
quality assurance, 103 – 105, 152, 218, 227, 236, 237, 266, 280, 284 – 286, 289 – 292, 300, 307, 313, 321, 350, 424, 442, 451, 486, 495, 599, 601, 670, 677, 736
  Quality Assurance, 103, 119, 143, 218, 221, 227, 229, 236, 279, 285, 313, 435, 438, 486, 489, 495, 497, 644, 800
  Quality Assurance (QA), 218, 486, 644, 800
quality assurance person, 285, 286, 289, 291, 292, 307, 313
  Quality Assurance Person, 279
quality assurance program, 424, 442
  Quality Assurance Program, 218, 486

spatial separation, 621
special notations, 612
special problems, 127, 128, 467
specific activity, 313, 429, 430, 453, 454, 455
Specific Activity, 427, 446
specific duties, 113, 243, 314
specific failure, 613
specification, 118, 130, 146, 159, 168, 182, 192, 224, 246 – 248, 250, 260, 261, 312, 345, 393, 426, 446, 453, 455, 469, 492, 517, 523, 525, 537, 553, 554, 556 – 558, 563, 565, 567, 572, 591, 604, 614, 615, 618, 619, 623, 626, 642, 646, 661, 665
Specification, 140, 463, 465, 466, 469, 473, 553, 557, 567, 568, 619, 646
Specification - Release, 567
Specification - Shelf life, 568
specifications, 83, 87, 89, 90, 92 – 96, 104 – 106, 108, 111, 117 – 121, 123, 125 – 127, 130, 134, 136, 137, 142 – 148, 151, 152, 154 – 158, 172, 180, 182, 185, 188 – 192, 204, 209, 212, 213, 223, 225, 228, 237 – 239, 246, 247, 249, 254, 257, 259, 260 – 268, 270, 273, 274, 280, 285, 286, 289 – 294, 296, 297, 303 – 305, 309, 310, 313, 319, 322 – 325, 327, 328, 330, 345 – 350, 352 – 354, 405, 412, 417, 420, 421, 426, 429, 436 – 438, 446, 448, 450, 451, 453, 454, 464, 475 – 481, 491, 493, 496, 514, 515, 518, 523, 527 – 529, 533, 534, 541, 542, 557, 577, 578, 591, 601, 602, 605, 606, 608, 609, 611 – 614, 616, 619 – 623, 627, 628, 630, 631, 633, 640, 642 – 645, 657, 662
Specifications, 118, 146, 171, 192, 209, 247, 261, 291, 304, 316, 325, 327, 405, 417, 438, 464 – 466, 473, 569, 610, 611, 622
specificity, 512, 586 – 590, 592
Specificity, 585, 586, 589
spectra, 614

sponsor, 391, 394, 459, 461, 462, 464, 465, 467, 468, 470 – 472, 481, 482, 527
Sponsor, 463, 470 – 472
stability characteristics, 624
stability data, 120, 156, 158, 323, 377, 378, 406, 515 – 517, 533, 549, 551, 552, 555, 556, 562, 563, 566, 568, 582, 603, 702
Stability Data, 549, 551
stability studies, 157 – 159, 185, 293, 328, 468, 525, 527, 533, 553 – 557, 559, 560, 562, 564, 568, 576, 577, 625
Stability Studies, 565, 665
stability testing, 354, 455, 532, 552, 566, 614, 619, 624, 625, 631, 653
Stability Testing, 159, 195, 406, 532, 549, 568, 571, 579, 581
staff, 15, 186, 202, 207, 208, 221, 222, 242, 244, 255, 257, 260, 410, 415, 416, 433, 467 – 469, 489, 490, 526, 550, 661, 676
Staff, 207, 415
stakeholder, 647
Stakeholder, 656
Standard Operating Procedure (SOP), 192, 275, 325
standard operating procedures, 122, 145, 153, 170, 178, 248, 260, 266, 288, 301, 303 – 305, 310, 314, 345, 349, 352, 469, 471, 648, 652, 695, 713
Standard operating procedures, 138, 263, 314
standard solutions, 614, 623
standards, 1, 4, 13, 26, 74 – 76, 78, 102, 105, 112, 118, 140, 163, 167, 169, 172, 191, 193, 213, 220, 237, 243, 279, 283, 289, 306, 309, 312, 327, 397, 401, 405, 422, 470, 488, 489, 523, 524, 527, 528, 536, 539, 590, 600, 609, 613, 614, 622, 623, 630, 631, 645, 648, 656, 670, 674, 692, 699, 700, 701
Standards, 1, 26, 164, 539, 577, 656, 705

---

written specifications, 94, 146, 151,
155, 261, 264, 265, 267, 292, 305,
429, 479, 542

Yield, Expected, 646
Yield, Theoretical, 646
yields, 124, 126, 127, 428, 617, 640

About the author

Mindy J. Allport-Settle was born in Beckley and raised in Oak Hill, West Virginia. She moved to North Carolina to attend the N.C. School of the Arts for high school and now lives near Raleigh. Following in the footsteps of Gordon Allport, all of her books are built on a foundation of psychology and sociology with a focus on improving some aspect of industry through research and education.

Her career in healthcare began when she was a teenager working as an emergency medical technician. Since then, she has joined the U.S. Navy's advanced hospital corps, worked in organ and human tissue procurement, specialized in ophthalmology, and moved on to serve as a key executive, board member, and consultant for some of the best companies in the pharmaceutical, medical device, and biotechnology industry. She has provided guidance in regulatory compliance, corporate structuring, restructuring and turnarounds, new drug submissions, research and development and product commercialization strategies, and new business development. Her experience and dedication have resulted in international recognition as the developer of the only FDA-recognized and benchmarked quality systems training and development business methodology.

Her education includes a Bachelor's degree from the University of North Carolina, an MBA in Global Management from the University of Phoenix, and completion of the corporate governance course series in audit committees, compensation committees, and board effectiveness at Harvard Business School.

About PharmaLogika

Since 2002, PharmaLogika, Inc has established itself as one of the world's premier consulting firms for Pharmaceutical, Biotech, and Medical Device companies across the globe. In so doing, it has earned the trust of executives in Life Sciences for its integrity, accuracy, and unwavering commitment to independent thought with regard to its products and services as well as those of its customers. Through www.PharmaLogika.com, its involvement in sponsored events, and personal references it has reached millions in print and online. Its mission, to provide flawlessly designed and executed products and services to startups as well as established industry leaders to facilitate their growth from discovery and clinical trial navigation to the commercialization and marketing of their products.

PharmaLogika consults with pharmaceutical, biotech, and medical device quality units to provide third party audits, training, pre approval inspections (PAIs), compliance remediation, and a portfolio of related quality and regulatory affairs products and services. Those products include but are not limited to Quality Assurance Forms, SOP and clinical templates, and the highly successful Integrated Development Training System.

Regulatory action guidance as well as quality systems guidance are delivered as part of its standard products and services. Through the use of highly skilled resources throughout the process, each offering is designed to enact a comprehensive quality systems approach in addressing Quality Assurance (QA) issues. The results insure a close adherence to current Good Manufacturing Practice (cGMP) standards.

PharmaLogika also has a Research and Development OTC line for human consumption that targets alpha 1-antitrypsin deficiency, Fibromyalgia, Restless Legs Syndrome, and Attention Deficit Disorder. A veterinary OTC is currently available that provides canine and feline oral debriding and cleansing agents as well as a sta n remover and topical antiseptic. These products combine to provide a strong pipeline of both current and future deliverables.

Other books available

Current Good Manufacturing Practices: Pharmaceutical, Biologics, and Medical Device Regulations and Guidance Documents Concise Reference

Good Manufacturing Practice (GMP) Guidelines: The Rules Governing Medicinal Products in the Eurpean Union, EudraLex Volume 4 Concise Reference

FDA Acronyms, Abbreviations and Terminology: Human and Veterinary Regualtory Reference

Course Development 101: Developing Training Programs for Regulated Industries

Compliance Remediation for Pharmaceutical Manufacturing: A Project Management Guide for Re-establishing FDA Compliance

Investigations Operations Manual: FDA Field Inspection and Investigation Policy and Procedure Concise Reference

Please visit www.PharmaLogika.com for additional titles

Need More Copies?

Visit

www.PharmaLogika.com

for a list of resellers

* Companion products and bulk discounts are only available at
www.PharmaLogika.com

---

www.ingramcontent.com/pod-product-compliance
Lightning Source LLC
Chambersburg PA
CBHW080221270326
41926CB00020B/4106

9 780982 147641